Understanding
Environmental Law

Carolina Academic Press Understanding Series

Understanding
Environmental Law

FOURTH EDITION

Kevin Anthony Reilly
PRINCIPAL APPELLATE COURT ATTORNEY (RETIRED)
NEW YORK STATE SUPREME COURT
APPELLATE DIVISION, FIRST DEPARTMENT &
ADJUNCT PROFESSOR OF LAW
ST. JOHN'S UNIVERSITY SCHOOL OF LAW

Philip Weinberg
PROFESSOR OF LAW (RETIRED)
ST. JOHN'S UNIVERSITY SCHOOL OF LAW
ADJUNCT PROFESSOR OF LAW
COLUMBIA COLLEGE, COLUMBIA UNIVERSITY

CAROLINA ACADEMIC PRESS
Durham, North Carolina

Library of Congress Cataloging-in-Publication Data

Names: Reilly, Kevin, 1955- author. | Weinberg, Philip, author.
Title: Understanding environmental law / by Kevin A. Reilly, Philip
    Weinberg.
Description: Fourth edition. | Durham, North Carolina : Carolina Academic
    Press, LLC, [2022] | Series: Understanding series | Includes index.
Identifiers: LCCN 2022018406 (print) | LCCN 2022018407 (ebook) | ISBN
    9781531019006 (paperback) | ISBN 9781531019013 (ebook)
Subjects: LCSH: Environmental law--United States.
Classification: LCC KF3817 .W45 2022 (print) | LCC KF3817 (ebook) | DDC
    344.7304/6--dc23/eng/20220801
LC record available at https://lccn.loc.gov/2022018406
LC ebook record available at https://lccn.loc.gov/2022018407

Carolina Academic Press
700 Kent Street
Durham, North Carolina 27701
(919) 489-7486
www.cap-press.com

To my children, Kevin and Alanna, who, everyday, make everything worthwhile, and to my wife Mary.
— Kevin A. Reilly

To Mary, Bill, and Matt.
— Philip Weinberg

Contents

Preface to the Fourth Edition

This fourth edition of *Understanding Environmental Law* is being prepared a quarter century after Professor Philip Weinberg, a generous friend since my law student days, asked me to co-author this book with him. Philip Weinberg had already achieved an eminent reputation as a young lawyer in the young but growing field of Environmental Law in New York, which he had helped to shape in government service before departing to teach law. Interestingly, Phil's call to me in 1996 was about a quarter century after some of the formative federal environmental laws addressed in this book were enacted, some a bit earlier and some amendments a bit later, but I think that the early 1970s can be looked back on as a seminal period in the history of Environmental Law. So, a half century later, Environmental Law has moved from novelty to mainstream. It has invaded countless once-staid traditional legal realms, among them real estate and banking, corporate transactions and securities law, land use planning and local governance, and it has partnered with public health policies; it has grafted on a new branch of administrative law, coopted or supplemented many traditional common law remedies when pollution caused injury or crossed boundaries, and has initiated new constitutional inquiries and occasionally required a reconsideration of seemingly settled principles of constitutional law. However, beyond this, the practice of environmental law often draws upon various subfields of civil engineering, hydrology, biology, chemistry, physics, other sciences, land use, demographics, economics, and so on. Increasingly, climate science and debates over its policies, extant and proposed, have been crowding their way onto the public and the political radar screens. Moreover, federal Environmental Law, which is the focus of this book, has parented numerous and sundry laws among the fifty states with countless land use ramifications at more local levels. And, of course, environmental lawyers will often have to be in close contact with local officials and remain familiar with the nuances of local landscapes, economic as well as natural. It can be fascinating, but it can also be challenging. Environmental Law, it is safe to say, has become a very complicated and comprehensive body of statutes, regulations and policies, and by the third decade of the 21st century, it demands acknowledgment as a significant branch of American jurisprudence.

This book is intended to serve as a primer for lawyers or even law students who hope to get a handle on how the field's major statutes and agency regulations work, and how they have been reshaped over the years to be more effective and, often, to address new urgencies. The goal is to outline basic principles, avoid excessive details that are more appropriate for a treatise, yet to provide sufficient depth where necessary so that the reader can achieve an adequate understanding — the ambition is set forth in the book's title itself—of what these statutes are expected to achieve and how they operate towards that end. Hopefully, readers will find this book helpful in undertaking their introduction to the field.

Readers who have used earlier editions of this book should be aware that parts of Chapters 9, 12, 13 and 14 have been substantially revised to reflect developments in the law. Lesser portions of Chapters 5 and 6 have been updated to address recently evolving policies and jurisprudence. Chapter 7 pertains to hazardous wastes, an actively litigated area, as to which lawyers will want to pay continuing attention to some of its subtopics.

Kevin Anthony Reilly

Preface to the First Edition

As the historian Barbara Tuchman sagely observed, "the best book is a collaboration between author and reader."* We have endeavored to keep our end of the bargain by furnishing students and practitioners with a concise, direct introduction to the burgeoning field of environmental law.

Environmental law, an increasingly significant area of legal study and practice, encompasses a full range of issues from tort law through property law to constitutional considerations. This volume attempts to present this mosaic, as its title suggests, in an understandable way. We have tried to avoid either undue concentration on the individual titles or an equally inappropriate focus on generalities.

The book covers not only the traditional terrain of air and water quality, solid and hazardous waste, and pesticides, but also the environmental implications of land use, energy generation and use, and the increasingly important area of international environmental law. It also tries to connect environmental law with the political and constitutional bases for the statutes and court decisions it examines.

Environmental law does not presuppose a background in science, and the references in this book to chemistry, biology and hydrogeology are kept simple and, we hope, understandable — a task rendered easier by the authors' own lack of scientific expertise.

As the reader will see, environmental law was not born fully-grown, like Botticelli's Venus, with the advent of the modern regulatory statutes. It stems from tort law, property law and related concepts that trace their roots to the common law. This book attempts to relate those common-law principles to today's regulatory framework, from which modern environmental law directly descends.

Readers should know that Kevin Reilly wrote chapters seven and fourteen and the bulk of chapters five, six, and eight. Philip Weinberg wrote chapters one through four and nine through thirteen, as well as minor portions of chapters five, six, and eight.

We earnestly hope this book will prove useful to the reader in achieving precisely what its title proffers: understanding environmental law.

Philip Weinberg
Kevin A. Reilly

---

* BARBARA TUCHMAN, PRACTICING HISTORY 24.

Understanding
Environmental Law

Chapter 1

Administrative, Judicial, and Constitutional Aspects of Environmental Law

Synopsis

§ 1.01 Administrative Decision-Making and Judicial Review

[A] Decision-Making

Environmental law is largely decided and implemented at the administrative agency level. Entities seeking to discharge pollutants into the environment, or to build such facilities as power plants and landfills that may have a substantial impact on the environment, must obtain permits from such agencies as the United States Environmental Protection Agency (EPA) or its state counterparts. Violation of the restrictions contained in these permits will frequently result in the assessment of penalties or the issuance of abatement orders by the agencies. The courts may become involved in these cases, but generally this will only occur when a party seeks to judicially review an administrative decision, or when the agency seeks to enforce it. For these reasons, it is important to an understanding of environmental law to see how agencies arrive at their decisions and how courts review those decisions.

As discussed in Chapter 3, common law remedies such as public and private nuisance continue to be important and have generally not been preempted by statutory or administrative remedies. Nonetheless, the vast majority of environmental decisions are made by agencies enforcing regulatory statutes.

Decisions by administrative agencies fall into two major classes: (1) those in which the permit applicant or permit holder (usually referred to in environmental law as the "source" of discharges of pollutants) is entitled to a hearing, and (2) those in which it is not. The scope of judicial review, discussed in [B], *below*, differs as between these classes of agency decisions.

Practice before federal agencies is governed by the Administrative Procedure Act (APA),[1] which prescribes rules for notice of and conduct at hearings. Many states have counterparts to the APA controlling procedure before state and local government

---

1. 5 U.S.C. §§ 500 to 706.

agencies.[2] Although the details of administrative procedure law are beyond the scope of this book, it may generally be said that permit holders are entitled to an evidentiary hearing before the imposition of a penalty or loss of their permit.[3] Such hearings at the agency level are conducted more informally than trials in the courts. For example, hearsay evidence may be introduced.[4] Hearings are held before an administrative law judge (ALJ), who may be employed by the agency, but is usually insulated from the agency's enforcement and other staff, to avoid conflicts or undue influence.[5] Applicants typically have the burden of proving eligibility for a permit, while agencies bear the burden of proving violations.[6] ALJs' decisions are usually reviewable by the chief officer of the agency, and this remedy must be exhausted before a court may review the case.[7]

[B] Judicial Review

Although some agency decisions are purely discretionary, or entirely mandatory (like the issuance of a building permit), and thus not reviewable at all,[8] the vast majority of administrative decisions in the environmental area may be judicially reviewed. However, the scope of review turns on whether the agency's decision was based on an evidentiary hearing.[9] Determinations following a hearing may be overturned if the court finds there was no substantial evidence in the record at the hearing — the "substantial evidence" rule.[10] On the other hand, decisions made without an evidentiary, or trial-type hearing may be set aside if found to be arbitrary or capricious — that is, lacking a rational basis,[11] or if they are deemed an abuse of discretion or otherwise unlawful.[12] Whether or not there has been an evidentiary hearing, if the agency has acted within the scope of its authority, courts will generally show great deference to the agency's expertise and discretion.[13]

In the landmark case, *Citizens to Preserve Overton Park v. Volpe*,[14] the United States Supreme Court superimposed on the arbitrary and capricious standard the

---

2. *See, e.g.*, N.Y. STATE ADMIN. PROC. ACT.

3. *See* 5 U.S.C. § 558(c).

4. 5 U.S.C. § 556(d). *See* Richardson v. Perales, 402 U.S. 389 (1971).

5. *See* 5 U.S.C. § 3105.

6. United States Steel Corp. v. Train, 556 F.2d 822 (7th Cir. 1977).

7. *See* 5 U.S.C. § 704; Glisson v. U.S. Forest Service, 55 F.3d 1325 (7th Cir. 1995) (agency remedies must be exhausted).

8. 5 U.S.C. § 701(a) (no review available when precluded by statute, or when agency action is committed by law to agency discretion). *See* Arnow v. United States Nuclear Regulatory Comm'n, 868 F.2d 223 (7th Cir. 1989), *cert. denied*, 493 U.S. 813 (1989).

9. *See generally* 5 U.S.C. § 706.

10. *See* 5 U.S.C. § 706(2)(E).

11. *See* Olenhouse v. Commodity Credit Corp., 42 F.3d 1560 (10th Cir. 1994).

12. 5 U.S.C. § 706(2)(A).

13. *See* Arkansas v. Oklahoma, 503 U.S. 91 (1992); Lodge Tower Condominium Ass'n v. Lodge Properties, Inc., 85 F.3d 476 (10th Cir. 1996).

14. 401 U.S. 402 (1971).

requirement that reviewing courts, in cases in which significant public concerns are at stake, take a "searching and careful look" at the agency's decision. The Court held a closer examination of the administrative determination was needed when it affected the public generally, rather than a single litigant or small group. This rule has become known as the "hard look doctrine," and it is employed in many environmental cases. For example, in one case, the reviewing court took a "hard look" at EPA's decision to phase out leaded gasoline under the Clean Air Act — although it ultimately upheld that decision.[15]

A reviewing court may sustain, set aside, or modify an agency decision. It may also compel agency action that has been unlawfully withheld or unreasonably delayed.[16] Modification of the agency's decision may include the rarely exercised power of reducing a penalty imposed by an agency, which requires a showing that the penalty was so disproportionate to the offense as to shock one's sense of fairness.[17] In addition, a reviewing court may remand a proceeding to the agency for further hearings if it finds the agency failed to consider evidence it should have weighed.[18]

[C] Rule-Making

Another important role of agencies is the adoption of rules, a power delegated to administrative agencies since they have, or at least are presumed to have, greater expertise than legislative bodies over their subject-matter. Rules may be procedural, relating to the conduct of the agency's hearings, permit issuance, and the like, or they may be substantive, dealing, for example, with requirements for the operation of a power plant or incinerator. Rule-making often is preceded by a public or "legislative-type" hearing, at which the views of various interested persons are aired, but does not require an evidentiary hearing.[19]

Rules and regulations adopted by federal agencies are codified in the Code of Federal Regulations (C.F.R.), a multi-volume series keyed to the rules of each agency. The states have equivalent codifications.

Court review of agency rule-making adheres to the arbitrary and capricious test referred to in [B], *above*, as circumscribed when appropriate by the hard look doctrine.[20] The science-based nature of environmental law has led to the adoption of

---

15. Ethyl Corp. v. Environmental Prot. Agency, 541 F.2d 1 (D.C. Cir. 1976), *cert. denied*, 426 U.S. 941 (1976).

16. 5 U.S.C. § 706(1).

17. New York Site Development Corp. v. New York State Dept. of Envtl. Conservation, 630 N.Y.S.2d 335 (App. Div. 1995).

18. Scenic Hudson Preservation Conference v. Federal Power Comm'n, 354 F.2d 608 (2d Cir. 1965), *cert. denied*, 384 U.S. 941 (1966).

19. Vermont Yankee Nuclear Power Corp. v. Natural Resources Defense Council, Inc., 435 U.S. 519 (1978); *see also* 5 U.S.C. § 553(c).

20. International Fabricare Institute v. U.S. E.P.A., 972 F.2d 384 (D.C. Cir. 1992); State of Colorado v. U.S. Dep't of Interior, 880 F.2d 481 (D.C. Cir. 1989).

numerous agency rules implementing the regulatory statutes enacted by Congress and the states' legislatures, and the courts show great deference to agency discretion in this regard. In the well-known *Chevron USA, Inc. v. Natural Resources Defense Council, Inc.*[21] decision, the Supreme Court held that if Congress spoke directly to the issue, "that is the end of the matter; for the court, as well as the agency, must give effect to the unambiguously expressed intent of Congress." On the other hand, the *Chevron* Court went on to hold, if the statute is less than clear, the courts will defer to the consistent construction of its terms followed by the agency.

A reviewing court also has the power to compel an agency to adopt rules and regulations, or to take other actions that have been unlawfully withheld or unreasonably delayed.[22]

§ 1.02 Standing and Related Issues

[A] Standing

[1] Introduction

Certain ground rules have evolved as to whether, and when, a court will review an agency's decision. First (and foremost), the plaintiff must have legal standing to challenge the determination. In addition, a challenger must exhaust the administrative remedies available before seeking judicial review (see [B], *below*), and the case must be ripe for review (see [C], *below*).

[2] Economic Injury Not Required

Whether a plaintiff has standing to seek review of an agency's action is especially important in environmental litigation since economic injury, the classic form of legal standing, is often not present. Many administrative decisions threaten those subject to them with economic harm — loss of a license or employment, for example. This occurs as well in the environmental law context when an agency denies or revokes a permit. Such action would constitute economic injury, conferring standing on the applicant or permit holder. But if the agency grants a permit, do the permit holder's opponents have standing to seek judicial review of that decision?

The courts have held that economic injury is not required to confer standing upon the plaintiff in an environmental suit. However, the plaintiff must show that he or she is (1) within the zone of interests the statute aims to protect, and (2) threatened with actual injury.[23] These two requirements comprise the Administrative Procedure

---

21. 467 U.S. 837 (1984).

22. 5 U.S.C. §706(1). *See, e.g.*, Animal Legal Defense Fund, Inc. v. Glickman, 943 F. Supp. 44 (D.D.C. 1996) (11 year delay in issuance of regulations after passage of enabling legislation); Raymond Proffitt Foundation v. U.S. E.P.A., 930 F. Supp. 1088 (E.D. Pa. 1996) (19 month delay in publishing proposed water quality standards after disapproval of state standards).

23. Sierra Club v. Morton, 405 U.S. 727 (1972); Data Processing Service v. Camp, 397 U.S. 150 (1970).

Act's mandate that a plaintiff be "aggrieved."[24] State courts adhere to essentially the same rule.[25]

An organization may show standing by asserting the interests of its members.[26]

[3] Actual Injury Required

The doctrine of standing is derived from the Constitution's case or controversy requirement.[27] If the parties are not litigating an actual legal dispute in which the plaintiff has a personal stake — an "actual injury" — courts lack jurisdiction to become involved since the Constitution did not establish a judicial power to decide matters involving claims that are not legally recognized, speculative claims or merely abstract differences between the parties.[28] A plaintiff may establish standing by showing that he has changed his personal behavior, such as by abandoning previously regular activities, because of "particularized fears of serious health and environmental consequences" resulting from an environmental violation.[29] But to establish the necessary injury, the fear must be valid and the behavior must have actually been pre-existing and altered. Merely having a vague desire to visit a location that may now be prevented because of alleged pollution could be insufficiently concrete to constitute an aggrievement for standing purposes.[30] There are numerous cases challenging disposals of toxic pollutants that will likely end up in water bodies which may be a source for drinking water and fish intended for the dinner table. However, the claim was too speculative to survive dismissal in a case where the plaintiff lived a substantial distance away and in a different water district from where he claimed lead bullets had been discharged, he failed to show where the fish that he ate originated, and tests established that his local drinking water was safe.[31]

In environmental cases, individual plaintiffs must establish standing on behalf of themselves, but many environmental cases are brought by environmental or other advocacy organizations, which adds to the usual standing requirement. For organizational standing, at least one member of the organizational plaintiff must have individual standing, and the claim on which the organizational plaintiff relies must be within its zone of interests.[32] In either case, the actual injury requirement is a real one.

In *Sierra Club v. Morton*,[33] in which the plaintiff asserted organizational standing, the United States Supreme Court held that even a large and long-established environmental conservation group may lack standing to review a government decision

---

24. 5 U.S.C. §702.

25. *See, e.g.*, Garrison Corp., Inc. v. Dept. of Health & Rehabilitative Services, 662 So. 2d 1374 (Fla. App. 1st Dist. 1995); Stephens v. Gordon, 202 A.D.2d 437, 610 N.Y.S.2d 531 (2d Dept. 1994).

26. Friends of the Earth v. Laidlaw Environmental Services, 528 U.S. 167 (2000); Sierra Club v. Morton, 405 U.S. 727 (1972) (dictum).

27. U.S. Const., art III.

28. Summers v. Earth Island Institute, 555 US 488 (2009).

29. Sierra Club v. United States Environmental Protection Agency, 755 F.3d 968 (D.C. Cir. 2014).

30. Summers v. Earth Island Institute, 555 U.S. 488 (2009).

31. Pollack v. United States Department of Justice, 577 F.3d 736 (7th Cir. 2009).

32. Friends of the Earth v. Laidlaw Environmental Services, 528 U.S. 167, 189 (2000).

33. 405 U.S. 727 (1972).

to build a road across a wilderness area, in the absence of assertions that its members actually used the land in question. The Court rejected the Sierra Club's claim that its general interest in environmental protection conferred standing to challenge the government's action. In contrast, in *Friends of the Earth v. Laidlaw Environmental Services*,[34] the Supreme Court subsequently upheld the standing of an environmental group whose members asserted the pollution of a river interfered with their fishing, swimming, and boating.

However, the courts show great reluctance to review general administrative programs and policies, as opposed to determinations affecting individual locations.[35]

Even if a legal dispute might have conferred standing on a plaintiff at its inception, if that issue becomes moot, there no longer exists a case or controversy, and standing is lost as to that claim.[36]

[4] Standing Is Determined on Case-by-Case Basis

Whether standing exists can be quite fact-specific. In one case, the Supreme Court denied standing to plaintiffs seeking to challenge exclusionary zoning laws, despite their claims that they sought to live in the town but were prevented from doing so by the zoning regulations, which prevented them from building affordable homes.[37] A few years later, however, the Court found standing in a similar case in which one plaintiff actually worked in the village, but alleged that he could not reside there because of its zoning regulations, and another plaintiff, a builder, asserted that he had specific plans to build affordable housing on a tract he had acquired, but was prevented from doing so by the zoning ordinance.[38] These additional allegations were sufficient to confer standing. It is evident that the issue of standing hinges greatly on the particular facts alleged by the plaintiff.

Perhaps the broadest decision conferring standing on environmental plaintiffs lacking economic injury was reached in *United States v. SCRAP*.[39] This action was brought by students challenging the disparity in government-approved freight rates between scrap metal and newly minted metal. The students claimed that the higher

---

34. 528 U.S. 167 (2000).
35. *See* Lujan v. National Wildlife Federation, 497 U.S. 871 (1990).
36. South Carolina Coastal Commission v. United States Army Corps of Engineers, 789 F.3d 475 (4th Cir. 2015); Sierra Club v. U.S. Army Corps of Engineers, 277 Fed. Appx. 170 (3d Cir. 2008). Even if mootness occurs during rather than prior to the litigation, it can be fatal to the claim, since there will no longer be an existing case or controversy. Catawba Riverkeeper Foundation v. North Carolina Department of Transportation, 843 F.3d 583 (4th Cir. 2016). There is a caveat, though, that if the plaintiff can persuasively show that the case should be heard because the perceived mootness may be temporary and the defendant can revive the injurious activity again, a court has a basis to find that a case or controversy still exists and can decide the merits. Friends of the Earth v. Laidlaw Environmental Services, 528 U.S. 167, 189 (2000). Mootness as to one claim, though, would not itself operate to require dismissal of other claims in the case which are not moot. *See* Gunpowder Riverkeeper v. Federal Energy Regulatory Commission, 807 F.3d 267 (D.C. Cir. 2015).
37. Warth v. Seldin, 422 U.S. 490 (1975).
38. Village of Arlington Hts. v. Metropolitan Housing Dev. Corp., 429 U.S. 252 (1977).
39. 412 U.S. 669 (1973).

charges for scrap metal resulted in litter along trails in parks used for hiking by members of the plaintiffs' group. The Supreme Court ruled they had standing because the increased litter stemmed from the disincentive to recycle aluminum and steel created by the government's higher freight rates for recycled products, thus encouraging industry to use newly-minted metal. However, in a later case the Supreme Court stated that *SCRAP*'s "expansive" view of standing "has never since been emulated by this Court...."[40] In that subsequent decision the Court rejected standing by a conservation group to review a program of the Interior Department making land available for grazing. It held the injury to plaintiffs was too diffuse, and that they were seeking to overturn an entire program, not just a specific decision as to a discrete project. Yet, the Supreme Court has held that Massachusetts had standing to challenge the Environmental Protection Agency's refusal to list carbon dioxide as a pollutant under the Clean Air Act since that state would be damaged by climate change resulting from carbon dioxide emissions as a result.[41]

[B] Exhaustion of Administrative Remedies

In addition to possessing standing, a plaintiff seeking to review an agency decision must show it has exhausted its administrative remedies — any appeals obtainable within the agency itself.[42] If such review within the agency is required by statute or regulation, the aggrieved party must employ it before bringing an action in court.[43]

By contrast, when the applicable statutes and regulations do not explicitly require the exhaustion of administrative remedies before filing suit, the court may review the agency decision without first requiring administrative appeal.[44]

[C] Ripeness

A final concern expressed by the courts in reviewing agency determinations is that the case be "ripe" for adjudication. In other words, the injury to the plaintiff must be imminent. For plaintiffs challenging the action of many federal agencies, the Administrative Procedure Act requires final agency action.[45] Similar requirements exist under state laws for state agencies. Moreover, to be final, the agency action must be direct and immediate.[46] The Supreme Court has described finality as "the consummation of the agency's decision-making process" in that "rights and obligations have been determined, or from which legal consequences flow."[47]

---

40. Lujan v. National Wildlife Federation, 497 U.S. 871, 889 (1990).
41. Massachusetts v. Environmental Protection Agency, 127 S. Ct. 1438 (2007).
42. *See generally* 5 U.S.C. § 704.
43. Glisson v. U.S. Forest Service, 55 F.3d 1325 (7th Cir. 1995).
44. Oregon Natural Desert Ass'n v. Green, 953 F. Supp. 1133 (D. Or. 1997). *See* 5 U.S.C. § 704.
45. 5 U.S.C. § 704. The statute defines that as an "agency rule, order, license, sanction, relief, or the equivalent or denial thereof, or failure to act." 5 U.S.C. § 551(13).
46. Franklin v. Massachusetts, 505 U.S. 788 (1992).
47. Bennett v. Spear, 520 U.S. 154 (1997).

By way of example, plaintiff could challenge the agency's issuance of a FONSI statement (Finding of No Significant Impact) in its attempt to circumvent the NEPA requirement (see Chapter 4) that an Environmental Impact Statement might be necessary for the construction of flood control levees, since the FONSI statement would settle that as a practical matter. There was ripeness as to the claimed procedural defect. However, in the same case, the plaintiff lacked standing to challenge the flood control project itself, since Congress had not provided funding and additional steps would be necessary. There was no final decision yet about the project, because there could not be, so to that extent the claim was unripe.[48] Just because a zoning applicant is involved in a lengthy administrative process during which money and opportunities may be at stake does not itself confer finality until a decision is made on the application.[49]

Clearly, a controversy is not ripe for judicial review when the agency has not yet finalized its action. Thus, when an agency's review of a permit application is not yet complete, an action to judicially review the issuance of the permit is not ripe.[50]

§ 1.03 Citizen Suit Provisions

In many of the major environmental statutes, Congress has expressly provided for a suit by "any person" to enjoin violations, obviating the need to show standing (see § 1.02[A]) under the traditional rules. This device was intended by Congress to provide a way to enforce environmental statutes when EPA or whichever agency has jurisdiction fails to do so. The agency's dereliction of duty may result from political influence, or from an otherwise onerous workload, with the result that some enforcement matters drift to the bottom of the proverbial pile, or it may simply be that the agency has a narrow interpretation of its authority in a particular area. In any case, the statutes often allow private citizens (including organizations) to act, in effect, as private Attorneys General in commencing litigation to enforce the statute against an alleged violator. These citizen suit provisions, as they are universally (and somewhat inaccurately) known,[51] also allow the courts to award civil penalties. Citizen suit provisions, though, do not create a private right of action for the plaintiff. Hence, the plaintiff cannot use these statutory provisions to sue to recover damages. Any fines resulting from the citizen suit are delivered to the United States Treasury.[52]

---

48. Sierra Club v. United States Army Corp of Engineers, 446 F.3d 808 (8th Cir. 2006).

49. Ethan Michael, Inc. v. Union Township, 108 Fed. Appx. 43 (3d Cir. 2004). However, there is a caveat that once it becomes apparent that the process is being dragged out for the purpose of avoiding a decision, so that, in effect, a non-decision actually is a negative decision, there may be a narrow avenue to assert standing to challenge the process. Lauderbaugh v. Hopewell Township, 319 F.3d 568 (3d Cir. 2003).

50. Alabamians for a Clean Environment v. Thomas, 26 Env't Rptr. Cases (BNA) 2116 (N.D. Ala. 1987).

51. The plaintiff need not literally be a United States citizen under these statutes, which give a "person" the right to sue.

52. *See, e.g.*, penalty provisions under 42 U.S.C. §§ 6972(a), 7604(a), and 9659(c).

The Clean Air Act,[53] Resource Conservation and Recovery Act,[54] and Comprehensive Environmental Response, Compensation and Liability Act (CERCLA), also known as the Superfund law,[55] have such provisions, as do the statutes of several states.[56] The Clean Water Act contains a similar provision, but it is limited to persons with "an interest that is or may be adversely affected."[57] The courts construe that language to require a showing of actual or threatened injury similar to proof that one is aggrieved under the Administrative Procedure Act.[58] See the discussion at § 1.02[A][3].

In addition to reducing concerns over standing, the federal citizen suit statutes provide for the recovery of reasonable attorneys' fees and expert witness fees — a valuable item in terms of leveling the playing field as between individual plaintiffs or citizen groups and large corporate or governmental defendants.[59]

Although citizen suits have become a vital weapon in environmental litigation, the United States Supreme Court has ruled that the Constitution imposes some outer limits on the ability of Congress to confer citizen suit jurisdiction. Article III of the Constitution requires that there be a "case" or "controversy" to invoke the jurisdiction of a federal court. In *Lujan v. Defenders of Wildlife*,[60] the Court held the citizen suit provision of the Endangered Species Act[61] would violate Article III were it construed to permit citizens without injury to sue to require federal officials to confer with the Department of the Interior over acts that might interfere with the critical habitat of an endangered species. As to such a procedural issue, the Court held Congress may not "convert the undifferentiated public interest in executive officers' compliance with the law into an 'individual right' vindicable in the courts...."[62] The result doubtless would have been different had the plaintiffs been able to show some actual or imminent injury. For example, the Court upheld standing under a citizen suit statute in *Friends of the Earth v. Laidlaw Environmental Services* (§ 1.02[A][3]), where specific assertions of injury were made. The Court went on to reject the defendant's claim that the action was moot since it had abated its pollution, noting that "voluntary cessation of a challenged practice does not deprive a federal court of its power to determine the legality of the practice" since if it did the defendant would be "free to return to [its] old ways."[63]

The citizen suit provisions bar such a suit when the agency (or a state agency with jurisdiction) has commenced, and is diligently prosecuting, an action of its own in

---

53. *See* 42 U.S.C. § 7604.
54. *See* 42 U.S.C. § 6972.
55. *See* 42 U.S.C. § 9659.
56. *See, e.g.,* Mass. Laws Ann. 214 § 7A; Mich. Comp. Laws § 324.1701.
57. 33 U.S.C. § 1365(g).
58. Coeur d'Alene Lake v. Kiebert, 790 F. Supp. 998 (D. Idaho 1992).
59. *See, e.g.,* 33 U.S.C. § 1365(d) (Clean Water Act); 42 U.S.C. § 7604(d) (Clean Air Act); 42 U.S.C. § 6972(e) (RCRA); 42 U.S.C. § 9659(f) (CERCLA).
60. 504 U.S. 555 (1992).
61. 16 U.S.C. § 1540.
62. Lujan v. Defenders of Wildlife, 504 U.S. 555, 577 (1992).
63. 528 U.S. 167, 189 (2000).

the courts within the time periods established by each statute. This typically requires the citizen plaintiff to give specific notice of the alleged violation to the violator as well as EPA, and then wait for sixty days before commencing the action. If the government starts enforcement proceedings within the prescribed time period, the citizen suit will be dismissed. The courts have consistently construed this language to apply as well to administrative proceedings commenced by such agencies, as long as the relief obtainable at the agency level is generally equivalent to what a court may furnish.[64] Enforcement action by the government, even if it was not fast, defeats the purpose of allowing for citizen suits. The notice requirements are strict. Any claims falling outside of the notice will be dismissed.[65]

§ 1.04 Constitutional Basis for Environmental Law

[A] Commerce Power

Activities affecting the environment are regulated at both the state and federal level. Many of the comprehensive regulatory statutes in the field have been enacted by Congress, though most of these contemplate state as well as federal implementation. This issue is discussed in detail at § 2.05. In addition, every state today has its own body of statutory as well as common law dealing with environmental protection.

The Constitutional support for much of the body of federal environmental legislation is the Commerce Power of Congress. The Constitution explicitly grants Congress power to "regulate Commerce ... among the several States...."[66] This has been broadly construed to encompass the channels of interstate commerce, the instrumentalities of that commerce, including "things in interstate commerce," and "activities that substantially affect interstate commerce."[67] The Clean Air Act,[68] Clean Water Act,[69] and federal laws governing solid and hazardous waste,[70] pesticides,[71] toxic chemicals,[72] and nuclear energy[73] are all based on this power. In one salient decision the hauling of solid waste across state borders was held to be commerce, because even though waste is valueless, its transport and disposal is a lucrative industry.[74] Likewise, it has been held that air or water pollution from a source wholly

---

64. Baughman v. Bradford Coal Co., 592 F.2d 215 (3d Cir. 1979), *cert. denied*, 441 U.S. 961 (1979).
65. *See, e.g.*, for the Clean Water Act's citizen suits provisions, Friends of the Earth v. Gaston Copper Recycling Corp., 629 F.3d 387 (4th Cir. 2011).
66. U.S. CONST. art. I, § 8, cl. 3.
67. United States v. Lopez, 514 U.S. 549, 559 (1995).
68. 42 U.S.C. § 7401, *et seq.*
69. 33 U.S.C. § 1251, *et seq.*
70. 42 U.S.C. § 6901, *et seq.*
71. 7 U.S.C. § 136, *et seq.*
72. 15 U.S.C. § 2601, *et seq.*
73. 42 U.S.C. § 5801, *et seq.*
74. City of Philadelphia v. New Jersey, 437 U.S. 617 (1978).

within a state is nonetheless clearly within the regulatory power of Congress under the Commerce Clause, because of its impact on other states.[75] Thus, Congress can plainly regulate activity within the states under its Commerce Power. Whether it may regulate activities of the states themselves is a complex issue, explored at § 1.05[D]. The precise extent to which Congress may regulate discharges into wetlands and non-navigable waterways, the subject of much litigation, is discussed at § 6.07[A][2].

[B] Other Congressional Powers

Additional Constitutional support for federal environmental statutes stems from the power to spend for the general welfare,[76] under which Congress may condition financial aid to the states on their adopting certain legislation.[77] This is the basis for the Coastal Zone Management Act, under which states adopting laws to protect their coastal resources receive federal funds for that purpose.[78] See § 11.02[B][2]. Similarly, states with serious air quality problems were induced to mandate inspection of exhaust emission controls on automobiles through the threat of withholding federal funds for highways or clean air enforcement.[79] This issue is discussed at § 5.04.

The Congressional power to regulate federal property[80] forms the basis for federal legislation regarding wilderness lands, national forests, offshore oil drilling, and a variety of similar subjects.

[C] The Treaty Power

Since much environmental law has international dimensions, the United States has entered into treaties and similar international agreements respecting destruction of the ozone layer, transport of hazardous waste, protection of endangered species, and other topics. These stem from the power of the President to sign treaties with the advice and consent of the Senate,[81] and are discussed in detail in Chapter 13 as well as § 10.05.

[D] The States' Police Power

Although nowhere expressly referred to in the Constitution, the states' police power has aptly been described as "the least limitable of all the powers of government."[82] This

---

75. *See* Hodel v. Virginia Surface Mining and Reclamation Ass'n, 452 U.S. 264 (1981) (strip mining).

76. U.S. CONST. art. I, § 8, cl. 1.

77. *See, e.g.*, South Dakota v. Dole, 483 U.S. 203 (1987) (Congress may withhold highway funds from states failing to impose a minimum drinking age of 21).

78. 16 U.S.C. § 1451, *et seq.*

79. 42 U.S.C. § 7506(a).

80. U.S. CONST. art. IV, § 3, cl. 2.

81. U.S. CONST. art. II, § 2, cl. 2.

82. Engelsher v. Jacobs, 157 N.E.2d 626, 627 (N.Y. 1959), *cert. denied*, 360 U.S. 902 (1959).

power enables the states to legislate concerning the health, safety, or welfare of their citizens—language broad enough to encompass every facet of environmental law.

Within those wide areas, the police power is circumscribed only by the limits imposed by the Constitution itself, examined in § 1.05. The Constitution, as construed by the courts, limits the powers of Congress and the states to legislate in the environmental area. It is vital for practitioners and students to bear these restrictions in mind, as they have been the source of much controversy and litigation.

§ 1.05 Constitutional Restrictions

[A] Preemption

The Supremacy Clause of the Constitution makes clear that the "Constitution, and the laws of the United States which shall be made in pursuance thereof; and all treaties ... shall be the supreme law of the land...."[83] This has been construed to mean that federal statutes preempt state law when Congress has occupied the field, or when Congress is acting within its constitutional authority and the two laws conflict. However, when the state is acting with the jurisdiction allowed to it by the federal Constitution, there is a general presumption against preemption in a particular area of law unless Congress's intent to preempt has been clearly expressed.[84] Even then, there are different kinds and degrees of preemption.[85]

In environmental law, Congress has for the most part elected to provide for tandem implementation by federal agencies, such as the United States Environmental Protection Agency (EPA), and their state counterparts. For example, the Clean Air Act requires states to adopt implementation plans for each of the major regulated air pollutants.[86] See § 5.02. Under the Clean Water Act, states may obtain authority from EPA to take over the water pollutant permit program within their borders.[87] See § 6.03[D]. In those situations, state law is of course not preempted unless the state law conflicts with federal law.

However, certain federal environmental statutes do preempt state law totally. The Clean Air Act, for example, does so with regard to requirements for emission control systems for new automobiles, as well as for automotive fuels.[88] And the labeling of pesticides is likewise preempted by federal statute.[89] See § 8.01[C][2]. In

---

83. U.S. Const. art. VI, cl. 2.

84. Arizona v. United States, 567 U.S. 387, 132 S. Ct. 2492, 183 L. Ed. 2d 351 (2012); Emerson v. Kansas City Railway Co., 503 F.3d 1126 (10th Cir. 2007).

85. For a discussion of the different kinds of preemption, which range from partial to complete, see Wyeth v Levine, 555 U.S. 555 (2009); Cippollone v. Liggett Group, Inc., 505 U.S. 504 (1992); Gade v. National Solid Waste Management Association, 505 U.S. 88 (1992).

86. 42 U.S.C. § 7410.

87. 33 U.S.C. § 1342(b).

88. 42 U.S.C. § 7545(c)(4)(A).

89. 7 U.S.C. § 136v. The Supreme Court has held the federal preemption of labeling does not bar a tort action based on defective design, Bates v. Agrosciences LLC, 544 U.S. 431 (2005), but the courts

both these cases federal preemption was dictated by the perceived need for nation-wide uniformity.

Preemption may occur even when a federal agency which is empowered to regulate fails to do so. *Ray v. Atlantic Richfield Co.*[90] dealt with the Ports and Waterways Safety Act,[91] which authorizes the Coast Guard to promulgate regulations for oil tankers. Although the Coast Guard had not required tankers to have twin propellers, double bottoms (to protect their cargo from collisions), or two radar sets, a state law mandating those safeguards was found to be preempted. The Supreme Court took the view that by failing to impose those features, the Coast Guard had found them not to be necessary. The Coast Guard in fact later required many of these safeguards. *See* § 6.06.

When a statute fails to specify whether it preempts state law, the presumption runs against preemption. This is especially so when the topic, such as wildlife conservation or tort law, is traditionally controlled by the states.[92] In *Silkwood v. Kerr-McGee Corp.*,[93] the Supreme Court ruled that the Atomic Energy Act[94] did not preempt an award of punitive damages under state law for radioactive contamination. This decision is discussed at § 12.02.

State law similarly may preempt local law, and the dual requirements for preemption are the same: the state must have occupied the field entirely, or the two laws must conflict.[95]

[B] Burden on Interstate Commerce

[1] "Dormant Commerce Clause"

Although the Commerce Clause is silent as to the states' power to regulate interstate commerce, the Supreme Court has consistently ruled that the Clause nonetheless bars the states from either unduly burdening or discriminating against interstate commerce. This doctrine, known as the "dormant Commerce Clause," stems from the idea, as pithily expressed in an opinion by Justice Cardozo, that the states "must sink or swim together," and may not legislate to Balkanize the United States.[96] In the

---

differ as to whether this preemption over labeling bars state tort suits based on a failure to warn pesticide users or third party victims. *See, e.g.,* Welchert v. American Cyanamid, Inc., 59 F.3d 69 (8th Cir. 1995) (state tort action preempted); Ferebee v. Chevron Chem. Co., 736 F.2d 1529 (D.C. Cir. 1984) (not preempted).

90. 435 U.S. 151 (1978).

91. 33 U.S.C. § 1221, *et seq.*

92. A. E. Nettleton Co. v. Diamond, 264 N.E.2d 118 (N.Y. 1970), *appeal dismissed sub nom.* Reptile Products Ass'n v. Diamond, 401 U.S. 969 (1971).

93. 464 U.S. 238 (1984).

94. 42 U.S.C. § 5801, *et seq.*

95. *See, e.g.,* Oriental Boulevard Co. v. Heller, 265 N.E.2d 72 (N.Y. 1970), *appeal dismissed,* 401 U.S. 986 (1971) (state law did not preempt local law controlling incinerators).

96. Baldwin v. G.A.F. Seelig, Inc., 294 U.S. 511, 523 (1935).

environmental field, this doctrine bars a state from excluding, or charging more for, disposal of solid waste from other states.[97] The Supreme Court first so held in *City of Philadelphia v. New Jersey*,[98] in which the state, to protect its landfills from overflowing, barred waste from beyond its borders. The Court first found that the hauling of waste was "commerce," since it is a profitable activity. The Court then held that for New Jersey to exclude waste from other states violated the dormant Commerce Clause, basing its holding on earlier decisions which barred states from excluding milk and other products from beyond their borders. The Court further rejected New Jersey's claim that the transporting of waste could be excluded because it was itself dangerous.

In later decisions, the Court has likewise set aside state and local laws imposing greater fees on the disposal of waste from out-of-state.[99] Similarly, the Court has held that states (and localities) may not require all solid waste to remain within their jurisdiction in order to supply a transfer station or incinerator.[100] These issues are discussed in detail in § 7.04[B][1].

It has also been held that state or local laws imposing curfews or noise limits at airports may likewise place an undue burden on commerce.[101] These laws also raise preemption issues, examined in [A], *above*. However, state laws restricting plastic packaging have been held not to unduly burden commerce.[102]

[2] When State Is a Market Participant

An important exception to the dormant Commerce Clause occurs when a state has actually entered the marketplace and is acting as a participant rather than as a regulator. Thus, for example, local controls that limit access to a municipally operated incinerator to solid waste generated in the town do not run afoul of the dormant Commerce Clause.[103] Similarly, a municipality may require all solid waste generated within its borders to be hauled to a town-operated incinerator.[104]

In addition, Congress may finesse the dormant Commerce Clause by legislating to permit states to close their borders to a commodity such as solid waste. The Supreme Court has so ruled in decisions upholding higher state taxes on out-of-state insurance companies. These taxes would have run afoul of the dormant Commerce

---

97. Oregon Waste Systems v. Oregon Dept. of Environmental Quality, 511 U.S. 93 (1994) (higher fee); City of Philadelphia v. New Jersey, 437 U.S. 617 (1978) (exclusion).

98. 437 U.S. 617 (1978).

99. *See* Oregon Waste Systems v. Oregon Dept. of Environmental Quality, 511 U.S. 93 (1994).

100. C&A Carbone, Inc. v. Town of Clarkstown, 511 U.S. 383 (1994).

101. British Airways Bd. v. Port Authority of N.Y. and N.J., 558 F.2d 75 (2d Cir. 1977).

102. Minnesota v. Clover Leaf Creamery Co., 449 U.S. 456 (1981).

103. Swin Resources Systems, Inc. v. Lycoming County, 883 F.2d 245 (3d Cir. 1989), *cert. denied*, 493 U.S. 1077 (1990).

104. United Haulers Ass'n v. Oneida-Herkimer Solid Waste Management Auth., 127 S. Ct. 1786 (2007); SSC Corp. v. Town of Smithtown, 66 F.3d 502 (2d Cir. 1995), *cert. denied*, 516 U.S. 1112 (1996).

Clause, but were saved by Congressional legislation specifically permitting these taxes.[105]

[C] Takings of Property

[1] Excessive Regulation of Property Deemed a "Taking" Requiring Just Compensation

The Fifth Amendment of the United States Constitution provides that private property may not be taken except for public use, and on payment of just compensation. This provision, applicable to the states through the Fourteenth Amendment, originally was intended to restrict the governmental power of eminent domain. However, in a series of decisions, the United States Supreme Court has held that a regulation of property that goes too far amounts to a "de facto taking" — a taking of the property in effect — requiring government to pay the owner just compensation for the property.[106]

[2] There Are Two Categories of Takings

Modern decisions hold that a taking occurs when a land-use control (1) deprives the owner of all reasonable investment-based expectations,[107] or (2) results in a physical invasion of the property.[108] These two categories of taking (not mutually exclusive) each impose important limits on the ability of government to regulate land for environmental purposes.

[3] Factors Used in Determining Whether a Taking Has Occurred

[a] No Taking If Owner Retains Reasonable Value

In *Penn Central Transportation Co. v. City of New York*,[109] the Supreme Court sustained a historic landmark law as against taking claims. The decision by Justice Brennan, itself a landmark, ruled that a statute which restricts any development that is inconsistent with the preservation of an historic or architecturally significant building is valid, as long as it does not deny the owner its reasonable investment-based expectations. In this case the owner of New York's Grand Central Terminal was denied permission to build a 55-story office building atop the station. Although the lower courts had found the owner retained reasonable use of the structure, the company contended all the value of its air rights over the station had been taken, and

---

105. *See* Western & Southern Life Insurance Co. v. State Board of Equalization, 451 U.S. 648 (1981); Metropolitan Life Insurance Co. v. Ward, 470 U.S. 869 (1985).

106. *See* Pennsylvania Coal Co. v. Mahon, 260 U.S. 393, 415 (1922).

107. Penn Central Transportation Co. v. City of New York, 438 U.S. 104 (1978).

108. Loretto v. TelePrompTer Manhattan CATV Corp., 458 U.S. 419 (1982).

109. 438 U.S. 104 (1978).

further that the city's landmark law arbitrarily singled out certain structures for protection and thus led to a taking.

The Court rejected both these claims. It held that the air rights over a building are not severable from the owner's property interest, and that whether a taking has occurred must be measured by the reduction in the value of the entire parcel. The test is not whether the owner retains the parcel's maximum value, but whether, despite the regulation, the owner retains some reasonable value. As the Court noted, even the loss of 7/8 the value of a parcel is not a taking as long as the owner retains some reasonable value.[110] As for the owner's second claim, the Court held that landmark preservation laws are not arbitrary if, as here, the selection of property for protection is based on objective architectural and historical criteria.

Using similar reasoning, the Court has held that a statute limiting the amount of coal the owner of subsurface rights may remove from beneath an occupied structure will be sustained as against a taking claim as long as it permits the subsurface owner to remove a reasonable amount of the coal.[111] However, a statute totally denying the right to mine was held a taking in the classic *Pennsylvania Coal Co. v. Mahon* decision, written by Justice Holmes,[112] since it deprived the subsurface owner of all beneficial use of the property.

[b] Landmark Preservation Laws and the Free Exercise Clause

Historic landmark preservation laws have been sustained as applied to churches, where the courts have rejected de facto taking claims as long as the property could continue to be used for religious purposes.[113] The courts have also ruled that preservation laws do not interfere with the free exercise of religion as protected by the First Amendment since these statutes apply equally to religious and secular buildings.[114]

The free exercise issue became convoluted when the Supreme Court ruled, in *Employment Division, Department of Resources of Oregon v. Smith*,[115] that laws of general application challenged as violative of free exercise need only have a rational basis. That case upheld an Oregon statute prohibiting the use of peyote as a controlled substance even though employed in a religious service. The Court distinguished earlier decisions subjecting statutes assertedly interfering with free exercise to strict

---

110. *Id.* at 131 (citing Goldblatt v. Town of Hempstead, 369 U.S. 590 (1962)); Hadacheck v. Sebastian, 239 U.S. 394 (1915).

111. Keystone Bituminous Coal Ass'n v. DeBenedictis, 480 U.S. 470 (1987).

112. 260 U.S. 393 (1922).

113. *See* Rector of St. Bartholomew's Church v. City of New York, 914 F.2d 348 (2d Cir. 1990), *cert. denied*, 499 U.S. 905 (1991).

114. *See id.*

115. 494 U.S. 872 (1990).

scrutiny, which required them to be narrowly tailored to serve a compelling governmental interest.[116]

Congress responded by enacting the Religious Freedom Restoration Act,[117] which bars the federal and state governments from "substantially burdening" the free exercise of religion unless the law is the least restrictive means of furthering a compelling governmental interest. This Act might have jeopardized the applicability of preservation laws to religious structures if it could be proven that the law substantially burdened the free exercise of the denomination's adherents. However, in 1997, the Supreme Court, in *City of Boerne v. Flores*,[118] set aside the Act as unconstitutional, as applied to state laws, viewing it as beyond the power of Congress to so alter a rule of constitutional interpretation adopted by the Court. It rejected the contention that Congress could adopt the compelling interest test pursuant to § 5 of the Fourteenth Amendment, giving Congress power to legislate to enforce that amendment's guarantees. *Flores* involved a free exercise claim by a church in an historic preservation district. Congress reacted to *Flores* by enacting a narrower statute, the Religious Land Use and Institutionalized Persons Act (RLUIPA),[119] which directs the compelling interest test for laws regulating land use (as well as inmates of prisons and similar entities that receive federal funds) that substantially burden religious practices. The Supreme Court upheld this statute as applied to state prisoners.[120]

[c] No Taking if Regulation Tantamount to Abating a Nuisance

It is clear that if a taking is found, the government must pay just compensation.[121] But even when a land use regulation denies the owner all reasonable use, it will nevertheless be upheld if the state had the power at common law to eliminate the development as a public nuisance (discussed in § 3.01), or to prohibit the development sought by the owner through the public trust doctrine (discussed in § 3.06) or some similar remedy. The Supreme Court so held in *Lucas v. South Carolina Coastal Council*,[122] where the state totally barred beach-front construction after the owner purchased the parcel. The Court remanded the case for the state courts to decide whether South Carolina could have barred that construction at common law. If it could have, then the owner would be presumed to have bought the property with awareness of those restrictions. For example, common law could bar "a land filling operation that would have the effect of flooding others' land," the Court noted.[123] But here, on remand,

---

116. *See* Thomas v. Review Bd., 450 U.S. 707 (1981); Sherbert v. Verner, 374 U.S. 398 (1963).
117. 42 U.S.C. §§ 2000bb to 2000bb-4.
118. 521 U.S. 507 (1997).
119. 42 U.S.C. § 2000cc.
120. Cutter v. Wilkinson, 544 U.S. 709 (2005).
121. First English Evangelical Lutheran Church v. County of Los Angeles, 482 U.S. 304 (1987).
122. 505 U.S. 1003 (1992).
123. *Id.* at 1029.

the South Carolina Supreme Court held that no common law principle could have halted development of Lucas's beachfront parcel.[124]

[d] Reasonable Expectations Measured as of
Date of Purchase

As discussed in [a], *above*, a land use regulation that deprives an owner of its reasonable expectation of return on its investment will be considered a taking. The situation is quite different, however, when an owner buys after a regulation limiting use of a parcel takes effect. In this situation, the owner must be presumed to have been aware of the restriction, so his or her reasonable investment-based expectations were reduced from the start.[125] The restriction would in fact almost certainly have lowered the purchase price of the tract.

However, the Supreme Court has ruled that one who acquires land after a land-use restriction is in place is not barred from asserting a taking. It held a contrary rule would render property owners "stripped of the ability to transfer the interest which was possessed prior to the regulation."[126] But the Court failed to agree as to the extent to which a subsequent owner's reasonable investment backed expectations are reduced.

[e] Regulation Must Have Nexus with Intended Purpose

A land-use control, even if it does not deny the owner all reasonable use, must have a close nexus, or connection, with the purpose it is supposed to serve. Thus, a permit to build along a shoreline, but requiring the owners to allow public access across their property, was held to lack a sufficient nexus to the state's purpose.[127] Public access to the coast, the Court held, could surely have been accomplished through less intrusive means, such as a viewing platform.

[f] Need for "Rough Proportionality" between
Regulation and Purpose

The Supreme Court has held that in addition to the nexus between the regulation and its purpose, there must be "rough proportionality" between them as well. In *Dolan v. City of Tigard*,[128] the granting of a building permit was conditioned on the owner dedicating part of her property that lay in a flood plain as a public walkway and bicycle path. The Court held that, while these requirements served commendable public purposes, they were not sufficiently proportionate to the city's concerns over construction in the flood plain. Less intrusive restrictions, such as simply barring

---

124. 424 S.E.2d 484 (S.C. 1992).
125. Gazza v. New York State Dept. of Environmental Conservation, 679 N.E.2d 1035 (N.Y. 1997).
126. Palazzolo v. Rhode Island, 533 U.S. 606, 627 (2001).
127. Nollan v. California Coastal Comm'n, 483 U.S. 825 (1987).
128. 512 U.S. 374 (1994).

construction in that zone, would have sufficed. In both *Dolan* and *Nollan*, the land-use restriction, although denoted "regulatory," amounted to a physical invasion, depriving the owners of their right to exclude others. This factor surely influenced the Court to hold both regulations excessive, although neither denied the owner all reasonable expectations.

[g] Parcel Viewed as a Unitary Tract; Partial Restriction Not a Taking

Another issue in taking law is the nature of the parcel alleged to have been taken. Some landowners have argued that by denying the right to build in a wetland, government has taken the wetland portion of their parcel. Under traditional taking law the courts view the parcel as unitary, so that if only part has been restricted, the owner's ability to use the rest will defeat a taking claim.[129] Although some cases call this into question,[130] in all likelihood the courts will continue to apply taking rules to an entire tract and not permit the owner to separate the restricted portion from the remainder.

[h] Physical Invasion May Be a Taking

A physical invasion of property is plainly a species of taking, which need not deprive the owner of all reasonable expectations. Thus, a permit to dredge the channel to a formerly private lagoon, when conditioned on allowing access to the lagoon by the public, has been found to be a taking.[131] Similarly, a local law requiring apartment building owners to allow cable television operators to attach equipment to the building with only a nominal payment is a taking because of the element of physical invasion.[132] Note that government need not itself be the invader. A taking exists as well if government authorizes others to invade, as in the cable television decision.

[D] States' Reserved Powers

The Tenth Amendment provides that all powers not conferred on Congress are reserved to the states. Until the mid-1930s, this provision proved a great limitation on the ability of Congress to legislate in such areas as manufacturing, mining, agriculture, and the like under the Commerce Clause. See the discussion in § 1.04. The modern view is that the Tenth Amendment does not bar Congress from legislating with regard to the activities of entities, private or public, within the states,[133] but that it prevents Congress from requiring states to themselves legislate.

---

129. Andrus v. Allard, 444 U.S. 51 (1979).

130. *See, e.g.*, Loveladies Harbor, Inc. v. United States, 28 F.3d 1171 (Fed. Cir. 1994).

131. Kaiser Aetna v. United States, 444 U.S. 164 (1979).

132. Loretto v. TelePrompter Manhattan CATV Corp., 458 U.S. 419 (1982).

133. Thus, for example, federal regulations may validly apply to state-operated transportation systems. Garcia v. San Antonio Metro. Transit Auth., 469 U.S. 528 (1985).

An environmental case, *New York v. United States*,[134] furnishes a dramatic instance of the force of the Tenth Amendment. In the Low Level Radioactive Waste Policy Act,[135] discussed at § 12.02[D][2], Congress left controls over this form of hazardous waste to the states, which may establish federally approved disposal facilities or enter into compacts with other states to use such facilities. States failing to do either must take title to, and assume legal responsibility for, all such waste within their borders.[136] The Supreme Court ruled that this provision of the Act violated the Tenth Amendment, since it "requires the States to govern according to Congress' instructions," and "commandeers the legislative processes of the States by directly compelling them to enact and enforce a federal regulatory program" on pain of having to take title to privately generated waste.[137] As the Court noted, that would enable Congress to escape political responsibility for difficult decisions while thrusting those decisions onto the states.

Congress is free to encourage the states to act by withholding federal aid unless they do so. *See* § 1.04. But Congress may not compel the states to legislate or otherwise regulate others.[138]

[E] Sovereign Immunity and the Eleventh Amendment

[1] *Federal Sovereign Immunity Is Limited by Congress*

The common law doctrine of sovereign immunity from suit has taken on constitutional dimensions. In the environmental area, the Supreme Court has held that states may not impose penalties or permit requirements on federal facilities without a clear showing of Congressional intent to waive sovereign immunity.[139] However, Congress may so legislate, and has done so. Federal entities must obtain state permits under the Clean Air Act,[140] Clean Water Act,[141] and similar statutes, and in some (though not all) cases may be subject to state penalties and even criminal prosecution.[142] These statutes are discussed under enforcement of these regulatory Acts.

Federal case law immunizes the United States from tort suits by members of the Armed Forces.[143] Application of this rule, known as the "Feres Doctrine," has barred

---

134. 505 U.S. 144 (1992).

135. 42 U.S.C. §§ 2021b–2021j.

136. 42 U.S.C. § 2021e(d)(2)(C).

137. New York v. United States, 505 U.S. 144, 176 (1992).

138. For a decision beyond the environmental area so holding, see *Printz v. United States*, 521 U.S. 898 (1997) (federal gun-control law invalid to extent it requires state law enforcement officials to check backgrounds of gun purchasers until federal checking scheme in place).

139. Department of Energy v. Ohio, 503 U.S. 607 (1992); Hancock v. Train, 426 U.S. 167 (1976).

140. *See* 42 U.S.C. § 7418.

141. *See* 33 U.S.C. § 1323.

142. *See* U.S. Dept. of Energy v. Ohio, 503 U.S. 607 (1992) (United States subject to liability for civil penalties, not punitive fines, under Clean Water Act); United States v. Tennessee Air Pollution Control Bd., 967 F. Supp. 975 (M.D. Tenn. 1997) (waiver of sovereign immunity extends to civil punitive penalties under Clean Air Act).

143. Feres v. United States, 340 U.S. 135 (1950).

service members from recovering in tort against the United States for injuries assertedly caused by their exposure to Agent Orange, a defoliant used during the Vietnam War.[144]

The federal Tort Claims Act[145] was enacted in 1946 to curtail the sovereign immunity of the United States in certain instances. Although it has been used in suits to recover damages in environmental and toxic tort cases, it bars punitive damages,[146] does not provide for jury trials,[147] and exempts the discretionary acts of federal officers.[148] There has been a great deal of dispute over whether nuclear testing, placement of hazardous waste sites, and similar activities fall within the discretionary acts exception to liability.[149]

[2] States' Sovereign Immunity and the Eleventh Amendment's Limits on Suits against States in Federal Courts

Like the federal government, the states also possess sovereign immunity, and most have enacted legislation modeled on the federal Tort Claims Act, with comparable defenses and limitations.

The Eleventh Amendment to the Constitution bars suit in federal court against a state. Read literally, the amendment prohibits suit by a citizen of one state against another state in a federal court, but the Supreme Court has glossed over that distinction and has held that the Amendment bars federal action by a plaintiff against his or her own state as well.[150] However, in *Ex Parte Young*,[151] the Supreme Court held that the Eleventh Amendment does not prohibit a suit for injunctive relief against a state official or agency charged with acting in violation of the United States Constitution or a federal statute. For the *Ex Parte Young* exception to apply, the plaintiff must be suing to vindicate a federal right.

Nevertheless, melding the Eleventh Amendment together with concepts of the states' sovereign immunity, the Court has ruled that suits in federal courts for non-injunctive relief, such as damages and the like, are barred by the Amendment, even when directed at a state agency or official rather than the state itself.[152] In the 1990s, the Supreme Court ruled that an Indian tribe's suit against state officials in federal court to quiet title to a lake bed was barred by the Eleventh Amendment, even though

---

144. *In re* Agent Orange Product Liability Litigation, 506 F. Supp. 762 (E.D.N.Y. 1980), *appeal dismissed*, 745 F.2d 161 (2d Cir. 1984).

145. 28 U.S.C. §§ 2671–2680.

146. 28 U.S.C. § 2674.

147. 28 U.S.C. § 2402.

148. 28 U.S.C. § 2680(a).

149. *See* Lockett v. United States, 938 F.2d 630 (6th Cir. 1991) (waste remediation discretionary); United States Fidelity & Guaranty Co. v. United States, 837 F.2d 116 (3d Cir. 1988), *cert. denied*, 487 U.S. 1235 (1988) (same); Allen v. United States, 816 F.2d 1417 (10th Cir. 1987), *cert. denied*, 484 U.S. 1004 (1988) (failure to warn of nuclear testing discretionary).

150. Hans v. Louisiana, 134 U.S. 1 (1890).

151. 209 U.S. 123 (1908).

152. Edelman v. Jordan, 415 U.S. 651 (1974).

the plaintiff claimed a violation of a Presidential executive order.[153] The Court noted that the plaintiff sought far-reaching and invasive relief which would shift substantially all benefits of ownership and control of vast areas from the state to the tribe. Under these circumstances, the Court held, the state may rely on its Eleventh Amendment immunity, and may insist on responding to these claims in its own courts, which are open to hear and determine the case.

Congress, the Court has also held, may not confer jurisdiction on the federal courts in violation of the Eleventh Amendment.[154] This decision overruled an earlier ruling allowing suits against the state as operator of hazardous waste sites under the Comprehensive Environmental Response, Compensation and Liability Act (CERCLA).[155] See the discussion in § 7.06[B][3][a][v].

It must be remembered that in order for suit against a state agency or official to lie under *Ex Parte Young*, there must be a claimed violation of the United States Constitution or a federal statute. Suits grounded in state law remain barred by the Amendment.[156] However, suits contending a state officer acted tortiously beyond the scope of his or her authority are not barred by the Eleventh Amendment at all.[157]

---

153. Coeur d'Alene Tribe v. Idaho, 521 U.S. 261 (1997).
154. Seminole Tribe of Fla. v. Florida, 517 U.S. 44 (1996).
155. Pennsylvania v. Union Gas Co., 491 U.S. 1 (1989).
156. Pennhurst State Hospital v. Halderman, 465 U.S. 89 (1984).
157. Scheuer v. Rhodes, 416 U.S. 232 (1974).

Chapter 2

Policy Issues

§ 2.01 Costs and Benefits: Balancing Environmental Economic Facts; Risk Assessment

[A] Weighing Economic and Environmental Costs

An issue pervading environmental law relates to the extent to which government agencies are permitted, or required, to weigh economic considerations along with environmental concerns in setting standards. Environmental regulatory statutes require agencies to decide how much risk of harm to tolerate in permitting discharges of air or water pollutants,[1] in ordering remediation of hazardous waste sites,[2] and in licensing pesticides[3] and electric power plants.[4] This involves risk assessment: determining how great a risk there is to health or the environment in permitting the activity. To what extent (if at all) should economic cost be weighed in deciding these questions?

[B] Risk Assessment: Pro and Con

Risk assessment requires the agency to "defin[e] the conditions of exposure, identify[] adverse effects, determin[e] the probabilistic relationships between exposure and effect[,] and calculat[e] overall risk."[5] It involves the complex task of weighing the risk of exposure and the likelihood of injury or illness from that exposure to decide what requirements should be imposed. Concerns have been raised that this process may overestimate risk to the public:

> [T]he typical risk assessment takes a trivial emission source, pretends that people are pressed up against the fenceline of the course 24 hours a day for 70 years, gauges the toxicity of the pollutant released by exposing ultrasensitive rodents to huge doses in the laboratory, and then uses the most "conservative" dose-response model to estimate a risk to humans at the most low ambient exposures of interest.[6]

Others view risk assessment as a critically needed component of environmental decisions and controls, and point out that in safeguarding health, the burden should be on those imposing the risks and not those seeking to reduce them.[7] This is closely analogous to the "precautionary principle" employed in international treaties to protect the environment.[8] It is not always easy to quantify precisely the risks of exposure to toxic substances. Some have pointed out the difficulty, and cost, of removing "the last 10 percent" of a pollutant.[9] At the other extreme are those who distrust risk assessment as "'publicly-sanctioned Russian roulette,' a convenient way to put a clean face on the sacrificing of lives and ecosystems for private profit."[10]

---

1. *See* 42 U.S.C. §7412(i)(6) (Clean Air Act); 33 U.S.C. §1311(b)(2)(A) (Clean Water Act).

2. *See* 42 U.S.C. §9606(c).

3. *See* 7 U.S.C. §136w(a)(1); 21 U.S.C. §346a.

4. *See* 42 U.S.C. §2134(b).

5. Clayton P. Gillette & James E. Krier, *Risks, Courts, and Agencies*, 138 U. Pa. L. Rev. 1027, 1062 (1990).

6. Report of the Carnegie Commission on Science, Technology, and Government, *Risk and the Environment, Improving Regulatory Decisionmaking* 76 (1993).

7. Donald A. Brown, *Superfund Cleanups, Ethics, and Environmental Risk Assessment*, 16 B.C. Envtl. Aff. L. Rev. 181 (1988).

8. *See* §13.01.

9. *See* Stephen Breyer, Breaking the Vicious Circle: Toward Effective Regulation (1993).

10. Adam M. Finkel, *A Second Opinion on an Environmental Misdiagnosis: The Risky Prescriptions of Breaking the Vicious Circle*, 3 N.Y.U. Envtl. L.J. 295, 301 (1994).

Despite this crossfire, risk assessment is the chief basis for determining how to deal with environmental hazards. It is unrealistic to seek to eliminate all exposure to pollutants or other risks, and no alternate means of deciding how best to reduce that exposure is available or likely to surface.

[C] Cost-Benefit Analysis

Cost-benefit analysis has been proposed on occasion as an alternative to risk assessment. This concept was, ironically, first used by environmental advocates opposing dams and river channelization projects as too costly in relation to their benefits. The idea has been adopted (or commandeered) by some opponents of environmental regulation who argue that controls ought to be imposed only when shown to be "cost-effective." But how is government or industry to measure the cost-effectiveness of reducing the risk of exposure to carcinogenic substances?

[D] Environmental Regulation Adopts Risk Assessment

Environmental statutes generally adopt a risk-assessment approach and eschew cost-benefit analysis. The Clean Air Act imposes standards such as "best available control technology."[11] See § 5.03[A][1]. Similarly, the Clean Water Act speaks of the "best available technology economically achievable."[12] See § 6.03. In pesticide regulation, the Delaney clause of the federal Food, Drug and Cosmetic Act, requiring that any additive to processed food must be banned if found to be carcinogenic to animals, has been replaced by a requirement that there be a "reasonable certainty that no harm will result from aggregate exposure to the pesticide chemical residue...."[13] See § 8.01.

In a pair of decisions construing the Occupational Safety and Health Act (OSHA),[14] the Supreme Court upheld federal risk assessment practices. That statute mandates setting workplace exposure to toxic materials at a standard "which most adequately assures, to the extent feasible, ... that no employee will suffer material impairment of health...."[15] The Court first ruled that the agency must make a threshold finding that a significant risk to health existed and could be reduced.[16] In the later case, it held that once the threshold finding is made, the standard did not require a cost-benefit analysis.[17]

The Supreme Court explicitly rebuffed a claim that the Clean Air Act requires EPA to weigh costs against benefits in setting national air quality standards.[18]

---

11. 42 U.S.C. § 7412(i)(6).
12. 33 U.S.C. § 1311(b)(2)(A).
13. 21 U.S.C. § 346a(b)(2)(A)(ii).
14. 29 U.S.C. §§ 651–678.
15. 29 U.S.C. § 655(b)(5).
16. Industrial Union Dept. AFL-CIO v. American Petroleum Institute, 448 U.S. 607 (1980).
17. American Textile Mfrs.' Institute v. Donovan, 452 U.S. 490 (1981).
18. Whitman v. American Trucking Ass'ns, 531 U.S. 457 (2001).

§ 2.02 Technology:
Conflict between Setting High Technological Standards and the Availability of the Technology to Meet Those Standards

[A] Mandating Technological Improvements

As noted in § 2.01[D], environmental statutes generally mandate risk assessment as a means of setting standards based on the best available technology. This marks a dramatic change from the reluctance of courts at common law to direct technological improvement. In a well-known and typical private nuisance action, *Boomer v. Atlantic Cement Co.*,[19] New York's highest court declined to enjoin the emission of air pollutants by a cement plant damaging the homes of numerous plaintiffs without proof that technology existed to halt the pollution without closing the plant.

In contrast, many environmental regulatory statutes mandate improvements in technology. The Clean Air Act and Clean Water Act provide for the issuance of permits to discharge pollutants at technology-based levels. This compels sources to apply state-of-the-art technology — and if necessary to create it — in order to achieve those levels. For example, the Clean Water Act required sources to achieve a "best practicable technology" standard by 1977 and a stricter "best available technology economically achievable" by 1983 (later extended).[20] *See* § 6.03. The Clean Air Act increased the standards imposed on emissions sources from a "will endanger" to "may reasonably be anticipated to endanger" public health test in its 1977 amendments.[21] *See* §§ 5.01, 5.04. Inability to meet these standards is not a defense.[22]

The Clean Water Act retains its original, somewhat quixotic, "national goal that the discharge of pollutants into the navigable waters [of the United States] be eliminated by 1985[.]"[23] In truth, though, the Act calls for technology-based standards for permits to discharge pollutants.[24]

[B] Cost-Benefit Approach to Hazardous Waste Cleanup

Although risk assessment is the generally adopted standard for environmental regulation, a cost-benefit approach has intruded in some areas. For instance, if contamination can be contained and some economic viability of the contaminated property retained for limited uses, the question arises whether a costly total elimination of contaminants is warranted. In hazardous waste site remediation, controversy has

---

19. 257 N.E.2d 870 (N.Y. 1970).

20. 33 U.S.C. § 1311(b)(2)(A).

21. 42 U.S.C. § 7545c(2)(C).

22. *See* Chemical Mfrs.' Ass'n v. Natural Resources Defense Council, Inc., 470 U.S. 116 (1985); Train v. Natural Resources Defense Council, Inc., 421 U.S. 60 (1975).

23. 33 U.S.C. § 1251(a)(1).

24. *See* 33 U.S.C. § 1311.

arisen over the extent to which cleanup is necessary (the "brownfields" controversy). *See* § 7.07. One view holds that such sites ought to be remediated to the fullest extent possible, including mandating the development of new technology where necessary.[25] A strict application of the relevant statute, CERCLA,[26] discussed in § 7.06, already has encouraged the development of an entire range of cleanup and monitoring technology. But this adds greatly to the cost of cleanup, and the contrary view is that sites in industrial areas ought not to be held to such a strict standard.[27] Brownfields advocates maintain that insisting on virtually total cleanup will make remediation less likely, leading in turn to new industry relocating outside the cities in areas less appropriate from an environmental viewpoint and less accessible to urban workforces. This controversy is linked to concerns over environmental justice, discussed at § 2.06.

§ 2.03 The Carrot or the Stick? "Command and Control" Regulation versus Incentives to Foster Voluntary Compliance

Another dispute of long duration relates to the efficacy of mandatory controls as against financial incentives. The major environmental regulatory statutes incorporate the view that enforcement of standards is the most effective means of achieving environmental goals. The typical regimen calls for requiring permits for the discharge of pollutants and imposing penalties for violating the standards in these permits. This principle undergirds the Clean Air Act, Clean Water Act, and Resource Conservation and Recovery Act (RCRA) (regulating solid and hazardous waste).[28] It is driven in part by the view that environmental law, like tax law, securities law, and labor law, is most effective when violators are punished, in Napoleon's phrase, to encourage the others. The statutory and common law antecedents of modern environmental regulation — hunting and fishing laws, zoning regulation, and public nuisance — have long employed this approach.

However, a view has been advanced that environmental goals are better achieved by economic incentives. One approach is to tax polluters to encourage compliance.[29]

---

25. *See, e.g.,* 42 U.S.C. § 9607(a)(1) (imposing strict liability on current owners and operators of a previously contaminated site).

26. The Comprehensive Environmental Response, Compensation and Liability Act, 42 U.S.C. §§ 9601–75.

27. *See, e.g.,* James T. O'Reilly, *Environmental Racism, Site Cleanup and Inner City Jobs: Indiana's Urban In-Fill Incentives*, 11 YALE J. ON REG. 43 (1994); Georgette C. Poindexter, *Addressing Morality in Urban Brownfield Redevelopment: Using Stakeholder Theory to Craft Process*, 15 VA. ENVTL. L.J. 37 (1995).

28. *See* 33 U.S.C. §§ 1311–30 (Clean Water Act); 42 U.S.C. §§ 7413, 7420 (Clean Air Act); 42 U.S.C. § 6928 (RCRA).

29. *See* Richard B. Stewart, *Economics, Environment, and the Limits of Legal Control*, 9 HARV. ENVTL. L. REV. 1 (1985).

According to its proponents, this saves government resources, and also minimizes cleanup costs since "[f]irms with relatively high abatement costs would control less and pay more in fees, while firms with low abatement costs would control more and pay less in fees."[30] A related technique is that of transferable rights to discharge pollutants. A source that reduces pollutants earns credits that it may sell to others, offering market-based incentives to achieve the goals of the statute and disincentives to those who fail to meet those goals.

The 1990 Clean Air Act amendments adopted this latter approach through an allowance trading program for sulfur dioxide, a prime contributor to acid rain. Sources may sell the credits earned through sufficient reduction of discharges.[31] This issue is discussed at § 5.03. Advocates of emissions trading and similar incentives view the market as capable of achieving environmental targets without the costs and burdens of direct regulation.[32] The proponents of government controls respond that incentives alone are unlikely to result in attainment of environmental standards.[33]

Emissions trading has been analogized to the use of transferable development rights (TDRs) in land use controls, a technique enabling a landowner to use, or sell, the right to develop on property other than the regulated parcel. *See* §§ 6.04[C] (aquifer protection), 11.04 (historic preservation). However, those who favor direct enforcement question the validity of the analogy. They point out that TDRs are an effective device for the regulatory agency to avoid a de facto taking claim, i.e., that a control has deprived the owner of all reasonable use of the parcel. This, however, is an issue that is inapplicable to controls on air and water pollution.

§ 2.04 Criminal and Civil Sanctions

[A] Both Criminal and Civil Penalties Employed

Environmental statutes typically provide for criminal as well as civil enforcement.[34] Whether criminal penalties are appropriate in the environmental area is an issue that is occasionally debated but has essentially been resolved. The overwhelming view is that criminal sanctions should exist as the ultimate deterrent to environmental violators.[35] When to invoke those sanctions is a more difficult question.

Criminal penalties existed in the earliest environmental statutes — those related to fishing and hunting. The first significant federal statute protecting navigable waters,

---

30. *Id.* at 11.

31. *See* 42 U.S.C. § 7651b.

32. Eric T. Mikkelson, *Earning Green for Turning Green: Executive Order 12291 and Market-Driven Environmental Regulation*, 42 KAN. L. REV. 243 (1993).

33. *See generally* Pat Leyden, *The Price of Change: The Market Incentive Revolution in Air Pollution Regulations*, 12 NAT. RESOURCES & ENV'T 160 (1998).

34. *See, e.g.*, 33 U.S.C. § 1319(c), (d) (Clean Water Act); 42 U.S.C. § 7413(c), (d) (Clean Air Act).

35. *See, e.g.*, Judson W. Starr, *Countering Environmental Crimes*, 13 B.C. ENVTL. AFF. L. REV. 379 (1986).

the 1899 Rivers and Harbors Act,[36] discussed at § 6.02[A][2], contains criminal penalties.[37] Federal and state agencies have great discretion in deciding whether to refer violations for criminal prosecution, and generally weigh factors such as the severity of the violation, the nature of the environmental injury it caused, the violator's history, and his or her willingness to cooperate.[38]

The major environmental statutes also provide for civil penalties recoverable by the agency without having to sue in court.[39] These penalties are, the courts have held, civil in nature, and do not trigger criminal law concerns such as self-incrimination, double jeopardy, and the Fourth Amendment's exclusionary evidence rule.[40]

[B] Criminal Penalties Raise Constitutional Issues

When criminal penalties are sought, constitutional issues come into play. It has been made clear that searches of business premises in furtherance of statutes with criminal penalties are subject to the Fourth Amendment's requirements of probable cause and a warrant.[41] Exceptions are made when the government can show exigent circumstances, such as imminent danger to public health, or likely destruction of evidence.[42] The Supreme Court has also ruled that measuring pollutant discharges from parking lots and other areas outside buildings lies within the "open fields" exception to the requirement of a warrant.[43] Similarly, aerial photography, which through infra-red pictures often can reveal the presence and nature of pollutants, has been upheld.[44] In addition, closely regulated businesses, such as auto dismantlers and coal mine operators, have been held to have a diminished expectation of privacy so that no warrant is needed, even for an interior search.[45] It should be noted, however, that the states may impose warrant requirements under state constitutional provisions for open-field searches and searches of auto dismantlers and similar businesses.[46]

Self-incrimination issues have arisen in connection with prosecutions involving oil spills, when the Clean Water Act requires dischargers to report such spills.[47] Only

---

36. 33 U.S.C. §§ 401–18.

37. *See* 33 U.S.C. § 406.

38. As to prosecutorial discretion and case selection, see Henry Habicht II, *The Federal Perspective on Environmental Criminal Enforcement: How to Remain on the Civil Side,* 17 ENVTL. L. REP. (Envtl. L. Inst.) 10478 (1987).

39. *See, e.g.,* 33 U.S.C. § 1319(g) (Clean Water Act); 42 U.S.C. § 7420 (Clean Air Act).

40. United States v. Ward, 448 U.S. 242 (1980) (self-incrimination).

41. Camara v. Municipal Court, 387 U.S. 523 (1967).

42. *Id.*

43. Air Pollution Variance Bd. v. Western Alfalfa Corp., 416 U.S. 861 (1974).

44. Dow Chemical Co. v. United States, 476 U.S. 227 (1986).

45. New York v. Burger, 482 U.S. 691 (1987); Donovan v. Dewey, 452 U.S. 598 (1981).

46. *See* People v. Scott, 593 N.E.2d 1328 (N.Y. 1992) (open-field search); People v. Keta, 593 N.E.2d 1328 (N.Y. 1992) (auto dismantler).

47. 33 U.S.C. § 1321(b)(5).

individuals, not corporations, are protected by the Fifth Amendment's bar to self-incrimination.[48] And even as to individuals, the inevitable discovery rule has been held to defeat a self-incrimination claim on the theory that the discharge would inevitably have been discovered in any event.[49] But a mere requirement to report discharges of pollutants to the Environmental Protection Agency (EPA), as many statutes mandate, does not implicate the Fifth Amendment when no criminal prosecution is involved.[50]

[C] Criteria for Civil Penalties and Abatement Orders

Civil sanctions include abatement orders and penalties recoverable by the enforcing agency, as well as injunctive relief obtainable in court. Some statutes authorize EPA or state agencies to issue a summary abatement order, halting pollutant discharges immediately when public health demands it.[51]

EPA has developed criteria for civil penalties, which consist of economic benefit and gravity-based components.[52] Economic benefit penalties are designed to offset the economic gain the source obtained from its failure to control pollutant discharge: the cost of the equipment needed to comply, plus the interest on the money saved through non-compliance. The gravity-based portion of the penalty is determined by weighing the severity of the discharge, the violator's record and willingness to cooperate, and the like.[53] Many state agencies employ similar factors in setting penalties.

§ 2.05 Federal versus State and Local Enforcement

[A] Congress Generally Has Not Preempted State Regulation

Prior to the 1970s, environmental regulation was almost totally at the state level. A few federal statutes existed, such as the Rivers and Harbors Act,[54] discussed at § 6.01, but neither level of government provided for comprehensive controls or permits

---

48. Braswell v. United States, 487 U.S. 99 (1988).

49. Hazelwood v. State, 912 P.2d 1266 (Alaska 1996).

50. United States v. Tivian Laboratories, Inc. 589 F.2d 49 (1st Cir. 1978), *cert. denied*, 442 U.S. 942 (1979).

51. 33 U.S.C. § 1321(c)(2) (Clean Water Act); 42 U.S.C. § 7603 (Clean Air Act).

52. 40 C.F.R. § 89-1006(b)(2).

53. ENVIRONMENTAL PROTECTION AGENCY, EPA GENERAL ENFORCEMENT COMPENDIUM (1980).

54. This 1899 Act, 33 U.S.C. §§ 401–18, prohibits obstructing or placing refuse in navigable waterways.

to discharge pollutants. This picture changed dramatically with enactment of the Clean Air Act in 1970, followed by the Clean Water Act, the Resource Conservation and Recovery Act (RCRA), and several other federal laws imposing thorough regulatory programs.

Although Congress surely could have preempted state law in these areas, for the most part it chose not to. Instead, Congress passed legislation preempting some specific areas — emissions from new automobiles and aircraft, for example — but most federal environmental statutes coexist with, and even encourage, state enforcement. This is accomplished in a variety of ways. The Clean Air Act empowers EPA to set national standards for air pollutants and mandates the states to adopt implementation plans for each of these pollutants, setting forth the state's requirements for attaining the Act's standards.[55] These state plans must be approved by EPA, and once approved have the effect of federal law. They are required to describe in detail the state's permit program, emission limitations, enforcement, monitoring of discharges, and related issues. *See* § 5.02.

The Clean Water Act and RCRA take a different tack. States may, but need not, seek authority to implement those statutes within their borders. If a state satisfies EPA as to its ability to administer the permit program established by these Acts, and enforce it against violators, EPA may delegate the program to that state.[56] *See* §§ 6.03[D], 7.04.

A third approach is to condition federal spending on a state adopting environmental controls. This technique was used to encourage states to inspect emission systems on motor vehicles in regions exceeding the Clean Air Act's standards for automotive exhaust pollutants.[57] *See* § 5.04.

[B] Factors Governing Federal or State Enforcement

Is federal, or state and local, environmental enforcement more appropriate? The federal Acts resulted from two major concerns. First, pollution does not respect state boundaries. Air and water travel from one state to another, making state regulation of out-of-state sources difficult. Second, states often competed in enticing industrial and commercial developers to move where controls were lenient. This practice made it harder for other states to enforce their environmental laws. Federal legislation was needed to restore a level playing field. However, federal controls are costly, and are perceived by some as impositions on the states' ability to decide how much weight to give environmental protection. Further, federal control, if it preempts state law, deprives that state of the ability to regulate the environment more strictly. The com-

---

55. 42 U.S.C. §§ 7409, 7410.
56. 33 U.S.C. § 1342(b) (Clean Water Act); 42 U.S.C. § 6926 (RCRA).
57. *See* 23 U.S.C. § 149.

promise that has frequently emerged, as in the Clean Water Act,[58] establishes nationwide standards but permits individual states to impose more stringent requirements.

[C] Land Use Regulation Chiefly Local

Local governments also play a role in environmental law, especially with regard to land use. Zoning is a local function, performed by municipal governments pursuant to state enabling legislation delegating zoning power to localities. Localities often regulate the preservation of historic buildings, as well as wetlands, noise, and pesticide use, again generally under state enabling laws.

In the land use area, a tension between state and local controls parallels the federal-state tension described in [B], *above*. Most states have retained, or recaptured, authority over critical areas like wetlands, and environmentally sensitive uses like power plants, where the stakes are so high as to transcend local concerns. In several states, large-scale development requires a state permit, or requires the locality to follow state-imposed standards in reaching land use decisions as to such development.[59] *See* § 11.03. Underlying these approaches is a tension between local autonomy, or home rule, and a perceived need for statewide decision-making to resolve competition among localities. Alternatively, some states have imposed state permit requirements or other land use controls only in portions of the state deemed especially sensitive, such as scenic areas like Chesapeake Bay, Lake Tahoe and New York's Adirondack region, or areas vital for water supply like New Jersey's Central Pine Barrens.[60]

§ 2.06 Environmental Justice

A growing concern in recent years is that of environmental justice, also referred to as environmental racism. It is well documented that landfills, incinerators, and similar environmentally problematic facilities are disproportionately sited in low-income communities. Racial minorities and, notably, Indian reservations, bear much of this burden. It has been shown, for example, that the proportion of the total population residing near a commercial hazardous waste site is double for racial minorities.[61] These concerns were recognized in an executive order issued by President Clinton in 1994, mandating that all federal agencies take environmental justice into

---

58. *See* 33 U.S.C. § 1251.

59. *See, e.g.*, HAWAII REV. STAT. § 205, *et seq.*; ME. REV. STAT. ANN. tit. 38 § 481, *et seq.*; OR. REV. STAT. § 197.005, *et seq.*

60. *See, e.g.*, N.J. STAT. ANN. § 13:18A-1, *et seq.*; N.Y. EXEC. L. § 801.

61. Commission for Racial Justice, United Church of Christ, *Toxic Wastes and Race in the United States* (1987).

account in their decision-making.[62] Much has been written about the issue since then.[63]

It is, however, easier to diagnose this problem than to cure it. Little can be done about existing active waste sites. As for future siting, the fact that government permits are required for virtually every hazardous waste or nuclear waste site brings into play the Constitution's Equal Protection Clause.[64] But to show that government has denied the equal protection of the laws in violation of that clause, one must prove that the government intended to discriminate. A disparate impact on one group is not enough.[65] In the context of locating a landfill or the like, proving intent on the part of the governmental agency licensing the facility to discriminate based on race or national origin is an almost insuperable burden. Thus, for example, in a major decision involving a landfill challenged on equal protection grounds, the court found the plaintiffs had not met the burden of proving intent to discriminate.[66]

The Presidential Executive Order has been used with some success in opposing the siting of facilities. The Nuclear Regulatory Commission's Atomic Safety and Licensing Board has denied a permit to construct a nuclear power plant in Louisiana on these grounds. The utility has appealed to the full Commission, and the appeal is pending.[67] Others have claimed a violation of Title VI of the Civil Rights Law of 1964,[68] which bars discrimination in federally-assisted programs. This approach may be taken where the state environmental agency rendering the decision receives federal funds. However, the Supreme Court has held that suits under Title VI require proof of intent to discriminate.[69] EPA and some other federal agencies have adopted regulations implementing Title VI that require only a showing of discriminatory effect, but the Court held in the same case that only the government, and not private citizens, may sue to enforce those regulations.[70]

Some states have followed the Presidential Executive Order's approach and adopted rules mandating greater public participation and agency scrutiny of the siting of facilities raising environmental justice concerns.[71]

---

62. Exec. Order No. 12,898, 59 Fed. Reg. 7629 (1994).

63. *See, e.g.*, Symposium, *Urban Environmental Justice*, 21 FORDHAM URBAN L.J. 425 (1994).

64. U.S. CONST., Amend. XIV. Although the clause by its terms applies to the states, the courts use the Due Process Clause of the Fifth Amendment to hold the federal government to the same standards. Washington v. Davis, 426 U.S. 229 (1976).

65. Washington v. Davis, 426 U.S. 229 (1976).

66. Rozar v. Mullis, 85 F.3d 556 (11th Cir. 1996).

67. Michael B. Gerrard & Monica Jahan Bose, *The Emerging Arena of "Justice,"* N.Y.L.J., July 25, 1997, at 3.

68. 42 U.S.C. §§ 2000d to 2000d-7.

69. Alexander v. Sandoval, 532 U.S. 275 (2001)

70. *Id.*; *see also* South Camden Citizens in Action v. New Jersey Dep't of Envtl. Prot., 274 F.3d 771 (3d Cir. 2001), *cert. denied*, 536 U.S. 939 (2002).

71. *See, e.g.*, New York's Draft Environmental Justice Policy (2003), *available at* www.dec.state. ny.us/website/ej/index.html.

Environmental justice concerns should be distinguished from broader arguments based on "NIMBY" (Not In My Back Yard), an acronym embodying opposition to environmentally (or otherwise) unwanted facilities for reasons ranging from health and safety to bias against groups such as the homeless or mentally retarded.[72]

§ 2.07 SLAPP Suits (Strategic Lawsuits against Public Participation)

[A] Suits Aimed at Deterring Opponents of Projects

In the 1980s, there was a proliferation of suits against those who sought to challenge development on the basis that it was environmentally harmful. Designed to inhibit individuals and citizen groups from voicing opposition to developers' proposals, these became known as SLAPP suits: Strategic Lawsuits Against Public Participation.[73] These suits are based on defamation, abuse of process, and related torts, and are actually an adaptation of an older technique used to inhibit civil rights advocates and others.[74] Even if the plaintiffs do not succeed in court, the suits themselves — typically seeking sizable damage awards — are a deterrent to opponents of action viewed as damaging to the environment. At a minimum, those who are sued for speaking out must retain counsel and spend many hours in depositions and preparation for trial. Liability insurance usually does not indemnify policyholders for intentional torts like defamation.

[B] First Amendment Protection for Project Opponents

The Supreme Court has recognized immunity for "legitimate petitioning of the government,"[75] based on the First Amendment's express protection of the right "to petition the Government for a redress of grievances."[76] Specifically, the Court has imposed the requirement that plaintiffs prove malice, as defined in *New York Times v. Sullivan*:[77] that the defendant spoke with knowing falsity or with a reckless disregard for truth or falsity. But malice is easy to allege, and SLAPP suits often survive motions by defendants for summary judgment. One court has gone so far, however, as to hold a SLAPP suit valid only where the defendant's real purpose was not to obtain governmental action but specifically to injure the plaintiff.[78]

---

72. *See* Michael B. Gerrard, *The Victims of NIMBY?*, 21 FORDHAM URBAN L.J. 495 (1994).

73. The acronym was coined by Penelope Canan and George W. Pring in *Studying Strategic Lawsuits Against Public Participation: Mixing Quantitative and Qualitative Approaches*, 22 L. & SOC'Y REV. 385 (1988).

74. *See* New York Times Co. v. Sullivan, 376 U.S. 254 (1964).

75. United Mine Workers v. Pennington, 381 U.S. 657 (1965); Eastern R.R. Presidents Conf. v. Noerr Motor Freight, Inc., 365 U.S. 127 (1961).

76. U.S. CONST. amend. I.

77. 376 U.S. 254 (1964).

78. Sierra Club v. Butz, 349 F. Supp. 934 (N.D. Cal. 1972).

[C] State Statutes Restricting SLAPP Suits

Some state statutes furnish a privilege for speech during legislative or judicial proceedings.[79] In addition, courts may impose sanctions under Rule 11 of the Federal Rules of Civil Procedure or parallel state laws for suits brought to harass.

Furthermore, several states have expressly enacted legislation to deter SLAPP suits. New York, for example, requires applicants or permit holders seeking damages from one who opposed or challenged their permit to show a substantial basis for their suit, or incur dismissal.[80] More broadly, California bars suits for damages based on the right of petition or free speech "in connection with a public issue."[81] One writer has imaginatively suggested that suit might be brought under that all-purpose federal civil rights statute, 42 U.S.C. § 1983, against attorneys bringing SLAPP suits.[82] He argues that the requirement of that statute, that the defendant acted "under color of state law," would be met by considering the attorney as an officer of the court—a view supported by Supreme Court decisions holding peremptory challenges to jurors based on race or gender by private attorneys to constitute state action.[83]

In approving New York's statute designed to curb these actions, Governor Mario Cuomo aptly noted that "[t]he aim of SLAPP suits is simple and brutal. The individual is to regret ever having entered the public arena to tell government what she thinks about something directly affecting her."[84]

Yet, SLAPP suits continue to be brought, and not only corporate developers, but even governmental agencies have employed this weapon.[85] The chilling effect of SLAPP suits has been well documented and is indeed self-evident.[86] Even though SLAPP defendants generally avoid liability in the end, they are obliged to incur prodigious legal expenses that greatly inhibit speaking out on environmental and similar topics. Legislation to curb SLAPP suits does not readily address these economic concerns. Some have urged more severe sanctions on SLAPP plaintiffs to further deter such suits.[87] The counter argument is that legislators ought not lightly deprive citizens of their day in court. But the SLAPP suit is itself a weapon to deny others their right to be heard.

---

79. *See* CAL. CIV. CODE § 47(b); *see generally* James W. Harper, *Attorneys as State Actors: A State Action Model and Argument for Holding SLAPP-Plaintiffs' Attorneys Liable Under 42 U.S.C. § 1983,* 21 HAST. CONST. L.Q. 405 (1994).

80. N.Y. CIV. RTS. LAW § 76-a.

81. CAL. CODE CIV. PROC. § 425.16(b).

82. *See* James W. Harper, *Attorneys as State Actors: A State Action Model and Argument for Holding SLAPP-Plaintiffs' Attorneys Liable Under 42 U.S.C. § 1983,* 21 HAST. CONST. L.Q. 405 (1994).

83. Georgia v. McCollum, 505 U.S. 42 (1992); Edmonson v. Leesville Concrete Co., Inc., 500 U.S. 614 (1991).

84. MCKINNEY's 1992 N.Y. SESSION LAWS 2911.

85. Greenwich Citizens Committee, Inc., v. Counties of Warren and Washington Industrial Dev. Agency, 77 F.3d 26 (2d Cir. 1996).

86. David J. Abell, *Exercise of Constitutional Privileges: Deterring Abuse of the First Amendment—"Strategic Lawsuits Against Political Participation,"* 47 S.M.U. L. REV. 95, 111–13 (1993).

87. *Id.* at 129–130 (1993).

Chapter 3

Common Law Remedies

§ 3.01 Nuisance

[A] Introduction

Environmental law, while largely implemented by statutes conferring regulatory jurisdiction on administrative agencies, has its roots in a variety of common law causes of action, notably the action for nuisance. These remedies have, for the most part, not been preempted by the enactment of statutes establishing administrative agency permit programs. If anything, nuisance and related causes of action have gained in popularity in recent decades, with heightened public concern over environmental issues. These remedies often furnish effective relief in situations not readily amenable to permit program enforcement, or when government fails to act. The remedy of nuisance, like many common law torts, had its origin in criminal sanctions long before civil suits for damages and injunctive relief were available. Indeed, most states retain criminal nuisance provisions in their statutes. A typical statute makes it a misdemeanor to unlawfully, knowingly, or recklessly create or maintain a condition that endangers the health or safety of a considerable number of persons.[1] Other criminal nuisance statutes prohibit the use of premises for unlawful conduct such as prostitution, gambling, and the like.[2] However, the chief use of nuisance, especially in the environmental arena, lies in civil actions, to which we now turn.

[B] Public and Private Nuisance

The tort of nuisance has long been divided into public and private nuisance actions. Although these were famously described by Dean Prosser's classic text on torts as having "almost nothing in common," so that "it would have been fortunate if they had been called from the beginning by different names,"[3] there are in fact more similarities than differences between public and private nuisance. One might usefully think of the two torts as fraternal twins developing from closely linked antecedents.

Public nuisance is an unreasonable interference with rights held by the public in general,[4] while private nuisance is an unreasonable interference with the rights of one with a possessory interest in land.[5] Both give rise to a suit for damages, as well as an injunction abating the nuisance — an unusual remedy for a tort. Thus, a plaintiff in a public nuisance case must prove the defendant's conduct to be an unreasonable interference with public rights,[6] while a plaintiff in a private nuisance case must show an unreasonable interference with the plaintiff's private rights.[7] A minority of states,

---

1. N.Y. PENAL LAW § 240.45(1).

2. N.Y. PENAL LAW § 240.45(2); N.Y. PUB. HEALTH LAW §§ 2320–34.

3. PROSSER, TORTS 618 (5th ed.).

4. Philadelphia Electric Co. v. Hercules, Inc., 762 F.2d 303 (3d Cir. 1985), *cert. denied*, 474 U.S. 980 (1985).

5. Lussier v. San Lorenzo Valley Water Dist., 206 Cal. App. 3d 92, 253 Cal. Rptr. 470 (6th Dist. 1988).

6. State of New York v. Shore Realty Co., 759 F.2d 1032 (2d Cir. 1985).

7. Wood v. Picillo, 443 A.2d 1244 (R.I. 1982).

including New York, further require a private nuisance plaintiff to prove the defendant's conduct to have been either negligent, intentional, or involving an abnormally dangerous activity, which would give rise to strict liability.[8] The intent need not be specific intent to damage the plaintiff; the ordinary tortious intent — that one intends the normal consequences of his or her acts — will suffice.[9]

A public nuisance action may be brought by the state, acting through its attorney general,[10] or by a significant number of private plaintiffs.[11] But private plaintiffs have standing to commence a public nuisance action only if their injury differs in kind — not merely in degree — from that of the public at large.[12] Thus, economic loss from a transit strike, or noise from subway trains, are too generalized to confer standing on private plaintiffs seeking to bring public nuisance actions.[13] In contrast, commercial fishermen have standing to sue in public nuisance to recover from water pollution assertedly rendering the fish they catch inedible and therefore unsellable.[14] Some states hold this specialized injury no longer necessary when the plaintiffs seek an injunction to abate a public nuisance, as opposed to seeking damages.[15]

A minority of states do not permit public nuisance suits by private plaintiffs against the state or a municipality.[16]

Private nuisance actions must be brought by one with a possessory interest in land: an owner or tenant.[17] A prior owner may recover damages, but may not obtain an injunction abating the nuisance.[18]

[C] Liability

[1] Nuisance Is an Unreasonable Interference with Rights in Land

As noted in [B], *above*, plaintiffs in public nuisance actions must prove an unreasonable interference with rights enjoyed by the public, while those in private nuisance must prove unreasonable interference with their private rights in land. Nuisance litigation over the years has involved an extraordinary variety of factual settings. Nui-

---

8. Copart Industries, Inc. v. Consolidated Edison Co., 362 N.E.2d 968 (N.Y. 1977); Patterson v. Peabody Coal Co., 122 N.E.2d 48 (Ill. App. 4th Dist. 1954).

9. Dingwell v. Litchfield, 496 A.2d 213 (Conn. App. 1985).

10. Philadelphia Electric Co. v. Hercules, Inc., 762 F.2d 303 (3d Cir. 1985), *cert. denied*, 474 U.S. 980 (1985).

11. Armory Park Neighborhood Assoc. v. Episcopal Community Services, 712 P.2d 914 (Ariz. 1985).

12. Mangini v. Aerojet-General Corp., 230 Cal. App. 3d 1125, 281 Cal. Rptr. 827 (3d Dist. 1991).

13. Burns Jackson Miller Summit & Spitzer v. Lindner, 451 N.E.2d 459 (N.Y. 1983); Abrams v. Metropolitan Transp. Auth., 355 N.E.2d 239 (N.Y. 1976).

14. Leo v. General Electric Co., 538 N.Y.S.2d 844 (App. Div. 1989).

15. Ozark Poultry Products v. Garman, 472 S.W.2d 714 (Ark. 1971).

16. Connerty v. Metropolitan Dist. Comm'n, 495 N.E.2d 840 (Mass. 1986).

17. Drouin v. Ridge Lumber, Inc., 619 N.Y.S.2d 433 (App. Div. 1994).

18. Irvine v. City of Oelwein, 150 N.W. 674 (Iowa 1915); Filson v. Crawford, 5 N.Y.S. 882 (Sup. Ct. 1889).

sances may consist of air pollution,[19] odors,[20] water pollution,[21] salt pollution of an aquifer,[22] and numerous other activities.

Just as the Supreme Court in a well-known case described a nuisance as "a pig in the parlor instead of the barnyard,"[23] the courts take the view that animal odors, mosquito-laden ponds, and similar natural conditions are generally not nuisances when confined to rural areas.[24] In fact, some states codify this result by statute.[25]

A defendant who conveys the property remains liable for a nuisance created earlier, as was held where a developer sold vacation homes with faulty septic systems that polluted a lake. It was no defense in a suit by the state, or presumably by any party other than a purchaser, that the defendant no longer owned the homes.[26] On the other hand, a purchaser is generally precluded from suing the seller of the parcel in private nuisance. The courts hold the purchaser limited to his or her rights under the contract of sale.[27] But at least one court has permitted a public nuisance action by a purchaser against a seller, holding the considerations different in public nuisance.[28]

[2] Private Nuisance and the Requirement of Fault

A California court has noted that when injury is alleged to be caused by a natural condition, the imposition of liability on a theory of nuisance, as a practical matter, generally requires a finding that there was negligence in dealing with the injury-causing condition. Thus, the worlds of nuisance and negligence overlap.[29] In New York, as noted in [B], *above*, private nuisance requires proof of negligence, intent, or the sort of abnormally dangerous activity for which strict liability is imposed.[30] One New York court has held that storing gasoline is not an abnormally dangerous activity.[31]

[3] Nuisance Must Reach the Property

The courts have held that a private nuisance, to be actionable, must reach the plaintiff's property. Recovery is not allowed for a reduction in property value stemming from concern over nearby hazardous waste.[32] This view stands in contrast to decisions

---

19. Boomer v. Atlantic Cement Co., 257 N.E.2d 850 (N.Y. 1970).
20. Spur Industries, Inc. v. Del E. Webb Development Co., 494 P.2d 700 (Ariz. 1972).
21. Commonwealth v. Barnes & Tucker Co., 319 A.2d 871 (Pa. 1974).
22. Miller v. Cudahy Co., 567 F. Supp. 892 (D. Kans. 1983).
23. Village of Euclid v. Ambler Realty Co., 272 U.S. 365, 388 (1926).
24. Lichtman v. Nadler, 426 N.Y.S.2d 628 (App. Div. 1980).
25. *See, e.g.*, N.Y. AGRIC. & MKTS. LAW § 308.
26. State v. Ole Olsen, Ltd., 324 N.E.2d 886 (N.Y. 1975). *But see* Dartron Corp. v. Uniroyal Chemical Co., 917 F. Supp. 1173 (N.D. Ohio 1996) (contra).
27. Pinole Point Properties, Inc. v. Bethlehem Steel Corp., 596 F. Supp. 283 (N.D. Cal. 1984).
28. Nashua Corp. v. Norton Co., 1997 U.S. Dist. LEXIS 5173 (N.D.N.Y. 1997).
29. Lussier v. San Lorenzo Valley Water Dist., 206 Cal. App. 3d 92, 253 Cal. Rptr. 470 (6th Dist. 1988).
30. Copart Industries, Inc. v. Consolidated Edison Co., 362 N.E.2d 968 (N.Y. 1977).
31. 750 Old Country Rd. Realty Corp. v. Exxon Corp., 645 N.Y.S.2d 186 (App. Div. 1996).
32. Adkins v. Thomas Solvent Co., 487 N.W.2d 715 (Mich. 1992).

not involving nuisance which, for example, have allowed recovery for reduced value caused by the fear of illness from electric transmission lines.[33] The courts are also quite reluctant to find a nuisance on purely esthetic, or visual, grounds, because of the subjectivity of such determinations.[34]

[D] Defenses

[1] Objective Standard

Nuisance recovery is confined to the injury that a reasonable plaintiff would suffer. Thus, a hypersensitive plaintiff, operating a business requiring unusually bucolic surroundings, or who is unusually susceptible to air pollution, will be denied recovery.[35] For similar reasons, courts generally will not find a structure to be a nuisance on esthetic grounds, because of the subjectivity of the judgment involved.[36]

[2] Limitations and Laches

The doctrine of continuing nuisance finesses the statute of limitations defense by deeming a nuisance actionable even though it commenced beyond the period of limitations, as long as the nuisance continues.[37] New York, however, applies the continuing nuisance doctrine only to actions seeking injunctions, not damages.[38] Laches are generally not a defense to nuisance actions.[39]

[3] Coming to the Nuisance

What if the nuisance were present before plaintiff obtained its property, and it was the plaintiff who "came to the nuisance"? Should that be a defense, since the plaintiff presumably knew, or should have known of the nuisance, and doubtless paid less for the property because of it? Relief has sometimes been denied in such circumstances. However, courts in other cases have expressed the contrary view, reasoning that if coming to the nuisance were a defense, it would immunize nuisances forever, in effect giving the offending party a permanent easement to continue its harmful activity.[40] Most courts have held that coming to the nuisance is not a complete defense, but an element to be weighed in deciding whether to issue an injunction.[41]

---

33. Criscuola v. Power Auth. of State of N.Y., 621 N.E.2d 1195 (N.Y. 1993).
34. United States v. County Board of Arlington County, 487 F. Supp. 137 (E.D. Va. 1979).
35. Lunda v. Matthews, 613 P.2d 63 (Or. App. 1980).
36. United States v. County Board of Arlington Co., 487 F. Supp. 137 (D. Va. 1979).
37. Miller v. Cudahy Co., 567 F. Supp. 892 (D. Kans. 1983).
38. Jensen v. General Electric Co., 623 N.E.2d 547 (N.Y. 1993).
39. Commonwealth v. Barnes & Tucker Co., 319 A.2d 871 (Pa. 1974).
40. *See* Weida v. Ferry, 493 A.2d 824 (R.I. 1985).
41. *See* Patrick v. Sharon Steel Corp., 549 F. Supp. 1259 (W. Va. 1982); Greater Westchester Homeowners Ass'n v. City of Los Angeles, 603 P.2d 1329 (Cal. 1979), *cert. denied*, 446 U.S. 933 (1980); Lawrence v. Eastern Air Lines, Inc., 81 So. 2d 632 (Fla. 1955).

[4] Effect of Regulatory Statutes

As noted in [A], *above*, the existence of regulatory statutes imposing permit requirements does not preempt state-law nuisance actions.[42] When the plaintiff and defendant reside in different states, as when the defendant is charged with polluting an interstate river or lake, the law of the state where the defendant pollution source is located governs.[43] The Supreme Court has held that it would be inappropriate to use the law of the plaintiff's state, since such an approach would subject the defendant, alone among sources in its state, to the law of another state.[44]

If a defendant is meeting the effluent standards contained in its permit, most courts view this as evidence of reasonable conduct, but not a complete defense to a nuisance action.[45] On the other hand, exceeding or violating a permit is proof of the nuisance in most jurisdictions.[46] Compliance with local zoning laws is not generally a defense to a nuisance action, since the courts sensibly view the issues of zoning compliance and whether the conduct of the operation constitutes a nuisance as separate.[47]

Some courts adopt the view that a nuisance action will not lie to challenge a discretionary governmental decision to site a landfill or similar facility, although a suit would be permitted to question its method of operation.[48]

A nuisance action involving aircraft noise at an airport is preempted by the federal Aviation Act as to the use of airspace,[49] but not as to land use concerns such as the location and use of runways and the shielding from noise of nearby homes.[50]

An odd decision has dismissed a public nuisance action seeking to require EPA to regulate carbon dioxide as an air pollutant under the Clean Air Act because of its impact on climate change. The court dismissed the suit as raising a political question beyond the courts' jurisdiction.[51]

[E] Remedies

[1] Damages for Permanent or Temporary Nuisance

Damages for a nuisance vary with regard to whether the nuisance is permanent or temporary in nature. Compensatory damages for a permanent nuisance are based

---

42. Miotke v. City of Spokane, 678 P.2d 803 (Wash. 1984); State v. Schenectady Chemicals, Inc., 479 N.Y.S.2d 1010 (App. Div. 3d Dept. 1984).

43. International Paper Co. v. Ouellette, 479 U.S. 481 (1987).

44. *Id.*

45. Village of Wilsonville v. SCA Services, Inc., 426 N.E.2d 824 (Ill. 1981).

46. Miotke v. City of Spokane, 678 P.2d 803 (Wash. 1984); Branch v. Western Petroleum, Inc., 657 P.2d 267 (Utah 1982). *But see* State v. Chemical Waste Storage and Disposition, Inc., 528 P.2d 1076 (Or. 1974) (contra).

47. Bruskland v. Oak Theater, 254 P.2d 1035 (Wash. 1953).

48. Warren County v. North Carolina, 528 F. Supp. 276 (E.D.N.C. 1981).

49. *See* 49 U.S.C. § 47506.

50. Greater Westchester Homeowners Ass'n v. City of Los Angeles, 603 P.2d 1329 (Cal. 1979), *cert. denied*, 446 U.S. 993 (1980).

51. Connecticut v. American Electric Power Co., 406 F. Supp. 2d 265 (S.D.N.Y. 2005).

on the reduction in the market value of the plaintiff's property caused by the nuisance, together with any special damages, such as medical expenses or costs of shielding the plaintiff's property from the nuisance.[52] In the case of a temporary nuisance — one ended by an injunction, or by the defendant's voluntary cessation of its conduct — compensatory damages consist of the reduction in the property's rental value during the period of the nuisance, again coupled with any special damages.[53]

[2] Punitive Damages and Their Limits

Punitive damages are available in nuisance actions when the defendant has acted maliciously or recklessly.[54] One court has ruled, however, that punitive damages were not available as against a defendant who dumped hazardous chemical waste in steel drums during the 1940s and 1950s, since such conduct was unregulated at that time.[55] This decision appears to ignore the fact that the defendant surely should have been aware that the steel drums would eventually corrode and release the wastes.

In nuisance, as in any other tort action, punitive damages may be challenged as excessive, and the United States Supreme Court has set aside punitive damages as violative of due process when they were so grossly excessive as to violate the Fourteenth Amendment.[56]

[3] Injunction Available to Abate Nuisance

Nuisance, both public and private, differs from most other torts in the availability of an injunction to abate the nuisance. In this, the law of nuisance is a common-law precursor of the regulatory statutes that today govern much of environmental law. The court, in effect, functions in the same manner as do the administrative agencies that implement these statutes, but on an individual case-by-case basis.

Plaintiffs may seek a preliminary injunction, halting a nuisance pending determination of the action, as well as a permanent injunction after proving the nuisance. A preliminary injunction is usually sought by motion at, or shortly after, commencement of the action. To obtain a preliminary injunction, plaintiff must show irreparable injury and the probability of success on the merits.[57] A permanent injunction requires the plaintiff to show that there is no adequate remedy at law (such as damages) and that an injunction abating the nuisance is appropriate.[58]

---

52. Rebel v. Big Tarkio Drainage Dist., 602 S.W.2d 787 (Mo. App. 1980).

53. Bates v. Quality Ready-Mix Co., 154 N.W.2d 852 (Iowa 1967).

54. Branch v. Western Petroleum, Inc., 657 P.2d 267 (Utah 1982).

55. United States v. Hooker Chemicals & Plastics Corp., 850 F. Supp. 993 (W.D.N.Y. 1994).

56. State Farm Mutual Ins. Co. v. Campbell, 538 U.S. 408 (2003) (punitive damages should generally not exceed nine times the compensatory damages, and the wealth of the defendant should not be a factor in determining punitive damages); BMW of North America v. Gore, 517 U.S. 559 (1996).

57. Greyhound Lines, Inc. v. Peter Pan Bus Lines, Inc., 845 F. Supp. 295 (E.D. Pa. 1994).

58. Pate v. City of Martin, 614 S.W.2d 46 (Tenn. 1981).

[4] Courts Balance the Equities in Issuing Injunctions

In determining whether to issue a permanent injunction, courts balance the equities, weighing the plaintiff's need for injunctive relief against the social utility of the defendant's activity, and the costs to the defendant of abating the nuisance.[59] Another factor to be weighed is whether the plaintiff came to the nuisance. See [D][3], *above*. In many cases, of course, the nuisance may be abated without closing down the defendant's operations entirely. There is often a technological accommodation possible, or a change in the hours or location of the activity.[60]

Courts have broad discretion in fashioning injunctions,[61] stemming from the powers of the Chancellor to relieve parties from the burdens of common law remedies under the English legal system. In one well-known instance, the Arizona case of *Spur Industries, Inc. v. Del E. Webb Development Co.*, the plaintiff contended it was unable to sell residences because of odors from an adjacent cattle feedlot. The court required the feedlot to move, but ordered the developer to pay for the move.

The New York courts deny that they balance the equities in nuisance actions, but in fact they seem to do so. While insisting that victorious plaintiffs are entitled to an injunction as of right, the court in one leading case nonetheless engaged in a balancing process and ended by enjoining air pollution from a large cement plant only if the defendant failed to pay damages.[62] The defendant, predictably, paid the damages and avoided the injunction.

An injunction and permanent damages may not both be awarded, since they are inconsistent remedies.[63] However, a plaintiff may obtain temporary damages for injuries suffered prior to the injunction taking effect.[64]

The United States Supreme Court has made clear that an injunction abating a nuisance is not a de facto taking of the defendant's property, even if it deprives the owner of all reasonable investment-based expectations. The Court first so stated, in dicta, in *Mugler v. Kansas*,[65] an 1887 decision holding that a statute prohibiting the manufacture of alcoholic beverages did not effect a taking of the plaintiff's brewery. In so holding, the Court analogized the statute to an injunction to abate a nuisance. More recently, in *Lucas v. South Carolina Coastal Council*,[66] discussed at § 1.05[C][3][c], the Court held that a statute barring construction along the shorefront, if it denied the owner all reasonable use, would be a compensable taking, unless the state's common law of nuisance or of property would have enabled the state to enjoin the activity anyway. The Court furnished two examples of construction enjoinable

---

59. *Id.*

60. *See, e.g.*, Corp. of Presiding Bishop v. Ashton, 448 P.2d 185 (Idaho 1968).

61. People ex rel. Sorenson v. Randolph, 99 Cal. App. 3d 183, 160 Cal. Rptr. 69 (1st Dist. 1979).

62. Boomer v. Atlantic Cement Co., 257 N.E.2d 850 (N.Y. 1970).

63. Antonik v. Chamberlain, 78 N.E.2d 752 (Ohio 1947).

64. City of Northlake v. City of Elmhurst, 190 N.E.2d 375 (Ill. Ct. App. 1963); McNichols v. J.R. Simplot Co., 262 P.2d 1012 (Idaho 1953).

65. 123 U.S. 623 (1887).

66. 505 U.S. 1003 (1992).

at common law: (1) storing water so as to jeopardize adjacent property, and (2) building a nuclear power plant astride an earthquake fault. Clearly, enjoining such construction would not constitute a compensable taking.

[F] Federal Nuisance

[1] Federal Nuisance Approved in 1972
Supreme Court Decision

Nuisance has traditionally been a state common law remedy, brought in state courts, or occasionally in federal courts where there was diversity of citizenship between the parties. In such cases, the federal courts employ state law.

In 1972, however, the United States Supreme Court held in *Illinois v. City of Milwaukee*[67] that a federal common law of nuisance existed, at least as to discharges into interstate waters. The State of Illinois sued Milwaukee over effluent from that city's sewage treatment plant that was being discharged into Lake Michigan. The Illinois state courts would likely not have had jurisdiction over a tort committed in another state, and a Wisconsin court would doubtless not have been receptive to a suit by Illinois seeking costly upgrading of the treatment plant by Milwaukee's taxpayers. Therefore, Illinois asserted a federal cause of action to abate a nuisance caused by discharges into interstate waters.

The Supreme Court agreed, citing the long history of federal concern over interstate waterways, commencing with the Rivers and Harbors Act of 1899 (see § 6.02[A][2]) and continuing to the 1972 Clean Water Act (see § 6.03), then being debated in Congress. However, the Court rejected Illinois' claim that the action should be heard as an original jurisdiction case in the Supreme Court itself. Under Article III of the United States Constitution, the Supreme Court has original and exclusive jurisdiction over actions between states, and original (though not exclusive) jurisdiction over suits to which a state is a party.[68] Since this suit was by a state against a city, the Court declined to hear it and remanded it to be tried in federal district court under the federal common law of nuisance.

[2] Supreme Court Later Held Federal
Nuisance Preempted

After Illinois obtained its injunction in the lower federal courts, Milwaukee sought review in the Supreme Court. This time the Court overturned the injunction and held federal nuisance involving water pollution to be superseded by the Clean Water Act, which Congress had enacted in 1972.[69] The Court noted that the Act furnished a remedy through Milwaukee's obligation to obtain a permit specifying, and reducing, its discharges. Illinois, it pointed out, had the right to participate in the permit

---

67. 406 U.S. 91 (1972).
68. *See 28 U.S.C. § 1251.*
69. City of Milwaukee v. Illinois, 451 U.S. 304 (1981).

process. As for the Act's supplanting of nuisance actions, Illinois vainly argued that § 505 of the Act explicitly provided that "[n]othing in this section shall restrict any right which any person ... may have under ... common law to seek enforcement of any effluent standard or limitation or to seek any other relief...."[70] But the Court concluded that this language merely means nothing in "this section" — § 505, the Act's citizen-suit provision — and barred a common law action. It was not the section but the Act itself, the Court ruled, that precluded such suits. The dissent portrayed this as a tortured reading, at odds with the Congressional intent to preserve common law actions.

Later decisions have expanded this ruling, to hold that federal nuisance is supplanted by the Clean Air Act and other legislation.[71] However, the Supreme Court made clear in a later case that state-law nuisance actions are not so supplanted.[72] Although the Court's earlier reading of the statute might logically preempt state-law actions as well as federal actions, the Court refused to paint with so broad a brush, doubtless because of a sensible reluctance to derail a traditional state-law remedy. It thus reached a result that is in keeping with the intent of Congress.[73]

§ 3.02 Trespass

The ancient tort of trespass has been used in recent decades to seek redress for environmental injuries. Like nuisance (see § 3.01), trespass is a tort cause of action in which an injunction is available.[74] Trespass actions have expanded from the traditional entry onto the plaintiff's property by the defendants or their livestock to encompass air emissions and the discharge of water pollutants.[75] But a physical invasion of the plaintiff's property, a basic element of a trespass, must exist.[76] Thus noise, unlike the deposit of actual particles of air or water pollutants, does not constitute a trespass unless some actual physical invasion takes place.[77]

Trespass actions have been brought to enjoin noise from aircraft overflights, where a physical invasion by the aircraft is present. However, the courts have found common law tort actions to enjoin overflights to be preempted by federal law, which exclusively governs the use of airspace by aviation.[78]

---

70. 33 U.S.C. § 1365(e).

71. New England Legal Foundation v. Costle, 632 F.2d 936 (2d Cir. 1980); United States v. Price, 523 F. Supp. 1055 (D.N.J. 1981), aff'd, 688 F.2d 204 (3d Cir. 1982).

72. International Paper Co. v. Ouellette, 479 U.S. 481 (1987).

73. See 33 U.S.C. § 1251(b).

74. Chicago Title & Trust Co. v. Weiss, 605 N.E.2d 1092 (Ill. App. 1992).

75. Borland v. Sanders Lead Co., 369 So. 2d 523 (Ala. 1979) (air); B. & R. Luncheonette v. Fairmont Theater Corp., 103 N.Y.S. 2d 747 (App. Div. 1951), lv. app. denied, 100 N.E. 2d 194 (N.Y. 1951) (water).

76. Wilson v. Interlake Steel Co., 649 P.2d 922 (Cal. 1982).

77. Id.

78. Alleghney Airlines v. Village of Cedarhurst, 132 F. Supp. 871 (E.D.N.Y. 1955), aff'd, 238 F.2d 812 (2d Cir. 1956).

The tort of trespass is a strict liability cause of action. Plaintiffs need not prove negligence on the part of the defendant,[79] although some cases suggest that proof of unreasonable conduct (as in nuisance) is required.[80] Trespass actions normally lie against the present owner of the property from which the invasion emanates, although some courts hold they may also be brought against a previous owner.[81] However, the plaintiff in trespass must be a current owner in possession of the property.[82]

§ 3.03 Strict Liability in Tort

The concept of strict liability, eliminating the need for a plaintiff to prove negligence or intentional conduct, stems from the well-known nineteenth-century English decision in *Rylands v. Fletcher*.[83] In this case, which today would be deemed an environmental tort action, the defendant was held to be strictly liable for storing large quantities of water on his property, which flooded the plaintiff's land.

Strict liability has been held to apply to inherently dangerous activities, such as blasting,[84] and in recent decades, to activities representing environmental hazards, like the storage or transport of hazardous waste.[85] Driving the concept of strict liability for ultra-hazardous (or in current parlance abnormally dangerous) activity is the notion that conduct of this sort is fraught with risk that ought to be borne by the party engaging in the activity. Thus, a plaintiff injured as a result of defendant's abnormally dangerous activities need not prove the defendant to have been at fault—i.e., negligent or acting intentionally. Furthermore, the plaintiff's contributory negligence is not a defense to a strict liability tort.[86]

Exactly what environmentally hazardous conduct gives rise to strict liability has been the subject of much recent litigation. For example, the storage of gasoline has been held not to trigger strict liability.[87] Some courts have taken the view that if, in the exercise of due care, the hazard could have been averted, then by definition the activity was not one giving rise to strict liability.[88]

Since strict liability is defined as limited to abnormally dangerous conduct, courts have found conduct not to be abnormally dangerous if it occurs with some frequency in the particular area. Thus, drilling for oil, surely not abnormal conduct in Texas,

---

79. Scribner v. Summers, 84 F.3d 554 (2d Cir. 1996).

80. *See, e.g.*, Bradley v. American Smelting & Refining Co., 709 P.2d 782 (Wash. 1985).

81. Chatham v. Clark Laundry, Inc., 191 S.E.2d 589 (Ga. App. 1972) (yes); Dartron Corp. v. Uniroyal Chemical Co., 917 F. Supp. 1173 (N.D. Ohio 1996) (no).

82. LaRue v. Crown Zellerbach Corp., 512 So. 2d 862 (La. App. 1987).

83. L.R. 1 Ex. 265 (1866), *aff'd*, 3 H.L. 330 (1868).

84. O'Malloy v. Lane Construction Corp., 194 A.2d 398 (Vt. 1963).

85. United States v. Northeastern Pharmaceutical & Chem. Co., 579 F. Supp. 823 (W.D. Mo. 1984).

86. Shields v. Morton Chem. Co., 518 P.2d 857 (Idaho 1974).

87. 750 Old Country Rd. Realty Corp. v. Exxon Corp., 645 N.Y.S.2d 186 (App. Div. 1996).

88. Fox v. McCoy Electronics Co., Inc., 21 Envt. Rptr. Cases (BNA) 1945 (M.D. Pa. 1984).

might be so in, say, Connecticut. This makes location a critical element.[89] This notion of abnormality is closely linked to the rule in the law of nuisance that a hypersensitive plaintiff may not recover.[90] See the discussion at § 3.01[D][1].

§ 3.04 Negligence

The foundation of most of the law of torts is of course the concept that one is liable for negligent activity. As noted in § 3.01[C], in some jurisdictions, negligence is an element — as may also be intent and strict liability for abnormally dangerous activity — of private nuisance. Nuisance aside, negligent conduct forms the basis for much of the law of toxic torts, discussed in detail at § 8.03.

§ 3.05 Riparian Rights

[A] Common Law Riparian Rights

[1] Riparian Right to Reasonable Flow

At common law, an owner of streamside, or riparian, property, had a right to the absolute, unimpeded flow of water, and could obtain damages from an upstream owner interfering with that right or an injunction halting that interference.[91] Since the industrial revolution, with water used first to power mills and more recently for myriad manufacturing processes, as well as for irrigation of farm land, a downstream owner no longer has a riparian right to an absolute flow, but rather to a reasonable flow.[92] This right is not limited to state law, but has been enforced as federal common law by the federal courts as well, with regard to interstate waterways.[93] Indeed, the Supreme Court has held that under federal law, including some treaties with Indian tribes, certain waters have been "reserved" and are therefore not available for state or private use.[94]

Actions to enforce riparian rights have predictably become a significant area of environmental law. Downstream property owners have sued to obtain damages for, or to enjoin, a panoply of water diversions and polluting activities, including the discharge of industrial effluent from steel mills, mining and chemical manufacturing, along with the agricultural use of pesticides and defoliants (weedkillers).[95]

---

89. *See* RESTATEMENT (SECOND) of TORTS § 520(e).

90. *See* Lunda v. Matthews, 613 P.2d 63 (Or. Ct. App. 1980).

91. *See* POWELL ON REAL PROPERTY § 65.06[4][a] (Matthew Bender).

92. Harris v. Brooks, 283 S.W.2d 129 (Ark. 1955).

93. United States v. Willow River Power Co., 324 U.S. 499 (1945).

94. Arizona v. California, 373 U.S. 546 (1963).

95. *See, e.g.,* Harris v. Brooks, 283 S.W.2d 129 (Ark. 1955); Thompson v. Enz, 188 N.W.2d 579 (Mich. 1971).

[2] No Riparian Right to Pollute

The courts have held that there is no riparian right to pollute.[96] An upstream owner may divert and use a reasonable quantity of water, but must furnish downstream property owners a reasonable amount. It should be noted that riparian rights are no longer limited to riverside landowners but apply equally along a lake shore.[97]

In one notable decision, a federal court ruled a city not liable to a downstream owner for pollution from defendant's sewage treatment plant.[98] The city acquired the plaintiffs' marina in eminent domain. The owners claimed their land had been devalued by sewage in the river from the treatment plant and were thus entitled to a higher condemnation award. But the court rejected their claim, holding that the public right of the city to operate its treatment plant took precedence. Thus, the adage that there is no riparian right to pollute, while valid as a rule, must not be taken literally in every case. Other courts have found malfunctioning sewage treatment plants to have interfered with downstream owners' riparian rights.[99]

In determining whether to enjoin an interference with riparian rights, courts balance the equities in much the same way as in nuisance actions, taking into account the economic and social importance of each party's use of the water, the degree of interference caused by the defendant, and similar concerns.[100] One court has ruled a landowner's riparian rights encompass access to the waterway for commercial purposes and that these rights may override the municipality's restrictions on dredging of its underwater lands.[101]

[B] Prior Appropriation

In the Rocky Mountain states and much of the West, courts employ, in place of riparian rights, the prior appropriation doctrine. Derived from Spanish law, this rule enables the first user (or "appropriator") of water to continue that use without hindrance.[102] Thus, a downstream rancher may not obtain damages from, or enjoin, an upstream mining operation if the mine was there first. As can be seen, this is a development-oriented doctrine.

Today, many of the western states have enacted legislation implementing, and tempering, the prior appropriation doctrine through the issuance of permits to divert or otherwise use water — a device consonant with the arid nature of most of the area.[103]

---

96. *See, e.g.*, Thompson v. Enz, 188 N.W.2d 579 (Mich. 1971).

97. Harris v. Brooks, 283 S.W.2d 129 (Ark. 1955).

98. Ancarrow v. City of Richmond, 600 F.2d 443 (4th Cir. 1979), *cert. denied*, 444 U.S. 992 (1979).

99. *See, e.g.*, Stoddard v. Western Carolina Regional Sewer Auth., 784 F.2d 1200 (4th Cir. 1986).

100. Harris v. Brooks, 283 S.W.2d 129 (Ark. 1955).

101. Town of Oyster Bay v. Commander Oil Co., 759 N.E.2d 1233 (N.Y. 2001).

102. Martinez v. Cook, 244 P.2d 134 (N.M. 1952); State ex rel. Crowley v. District Ct., 88 P.2d 23 (Mont. 1939).

103. *See* POWELL ON REAL PROPERTY § 65.09[3][b].

In Texas and California, a hybrid system has developed under which prior appro-priation generally applies to water rights based on use of the water before those states entered the Union, when Spanish law prevailed. Rights accruing since that time in those two states are governed by common law riparian rights law.[104]

[C] Rights to Groundwater

Rights to groundwater (i.e., water pumped from wells, as distinguished from surface water) are governed by legal doctrines closely analogous to riparian rights and prior appropriation law.[105] At common law, an owner had the right to draw all water from beneath the parcel. As with riparian rights to surface water, this became unrealistic, as parcels became more closely bounded and water use increased. It would hardly do for one homeowner to have the legal right to remove all the water from an aquifer serving a million residents. So here too, just as with riparian rights, the law shifted from an entitlement protecting absolute use to a doctrine of reasonable use.[106]

As with surface waters, much of the West (as well as some of the Midwest) employs a prior appropriation approach to groundwater — "first in right."[107]

Permit requirements to remove groundwater in significant quantities now overlay these traditional rules. Most states now require developers to obtain water supply permits.[108] In addition, the federal Safe Drinking Water Act imposes important re-strictions on groundwater use (see § 6.04[C]).[109]

§ 3.06 Public Trust Doctrine

[A] Public Has Right to Underwater Lands

Stemming originally from Roman law but incorporated from that source into Eng-lish common law, the public trust doctrine provides that underwater land is held in trust for the public good. The Crown's responsibility as trustee of these lands has be-come the responsibility of the states.

Over a century ago, the United States Supreme Court held in a dramatic decision that such lands cannot lawfully be conveyed for a private corporation's profit-seeking use. *Illinois Central R.R. v. Illinois*[110] involved the conveyance by that state's legislature

---

104. *In re* Water of Hallett Creek Stream System, 749 P.2d 324 (Cal. 1988); *In re* Adjudication of Water Rights of Upper Guadalupe Segment of Guadalupe River Basin, 642 P.2d 438 (Tex. 1982).

105. *See* POWELL ON REAL PROPERTY § 65.08.

106. Higday v. Nickolaus, 469 S.W.2d 859 (Mo. 1971).

107. Metropolitan Utilities District of Omaha v. Merritt Beach Co., 140 N.W.2d 626 (Neb. 1966).

108. *See, e.g.,* FLA. STAT. § 373; N.Y. ENV. CONS. L. § 15-1527; VA. CODE ANN. § 62.1-258.

109. *See* 42 U.S.C. § 300h, *et seq.*

110. 146 U.S. 387 (1892).

of the downtown Chicago waterfront to a railroad company for its private use. A subsequent legislative session annulled the conveyance, and the railroad sued, claiming the state had impaired the obligation of its contract in violation of the United States Constitution.[111] The Supreme Court, however, ruled that under the public trust doctrine the state never had the power to convey these underwater lands for private use. The Court noted that under English common law, underwater lands subject to the tides were covered by the public trust doctrine. It expanded the doctrine to apply to all lands under navigable waters, whether or not tidal. The Supreme Court has since ruled that lands are subject to the public trust doctrine if they were under water when the state entered the union, even if they are no longer underwater today.[112]

States can convey underwater lands to local governments, and to private parties as well, as long as the conveyance is for a public purpose, such as for a marina open to the public.[113]

In some states, in addition to underwater lands, wetlands and shorefront, as well as park lands, are held in public trust.[114] One noted California decision applied the public trust doctrine to water in lakes and streams.[115] Some courts have held that under the doctrine the state retains ownership of wetlands dependent on salt water, on the theory that those grasses are seaward of the mean high water mark.[116]

[B] Any Citizen of State Has Standing

Since any member of the public is a beneficiary of the public trust doctrine, any citizen of the state in question has standing to challenge an asserted violation.[117] The courts in some states take the view that the public trust doctrine guarantees public access to beaches by any resident of the state, a view some other courts have expressly rejected.[118]

---

111. U.S. Const. art. I, § 10, cl. 1.

112. Phillips Petroleum Co. v. Mississippi, 484 U.S. 469 (1988).

113. City of Jersey City v. New Jersey Dept. of Environmental Prot., 545 A.2d 774 (N.J. App. Div. 1988), *cert. denied*, 546 A.2d 551 (1988).

114. McQueen v. South Carolina Coastal Council, 580 S.E.2d 116 (S.C.), *cert. denied*, 540 U.S. 982 (2003) (wetlands); Just v. Marinette County, 201 N.W.2d 767 (Wis. 1972) (same); Friends of Van Cortlandt Park v. City of New York, 750 N.E.2d 1050 (N.Y. 2001) (parks); Ackerman v. Steisel, 480 N.Y.S.2d 556 (App. Div. 1984), *aff'd*, 489 N.E.2d 261 (N.Y. 1985) (parks).

115. National Audubon Society v. Superior Court of Alpine County, 658 P.2d 709 (Cal. 1983), *cert. denied sub nom.* City of Los Angeles Dept. of Water and Power v. National Audubon Society, 464 U.S. 977 (1983).

116. City of Newark v. Natural Resources Council, 414 A.2d 1304 (N.J. 1980), *cert. denied*, 449 U.S. 983 (1980). *But see Dolphin Lane Assocs. v. Town of Southampton*, 333 N.E.2d 358 (N.Y. 1975) (contra).

117. *See* National Audubon Society v. Superior Court of Alpine County, 658 P.2d 709 (Cal. 1983).

118. Borough of Neptune City v. Borough of Avon-by-the-Sea, 294 A.2d 47 (N.J. 1972) (public access); Bell v. Town of Wells, 557 A.2d 168 (Me. 1989) (contra).

[C] Statutes Codify Public Trust Doctrine

Several states have codified the public trust doctrine in statutes or constitutional provisions. Notably, California's Constitution guarantees public access to that state's extensive shorefront.[119] In pursuance of this goal, the state created a Coastal Commission and requires a permit from that body for any construction along the state's lengthy shoreline. It was a permit issued by that agency that led to the Supreme Court's holding in *Nollan v. California Coastal Commission*[120] that there must be a substantial nexus, or linkage, between the purpose of a land use regulation and the means employed to attain that purpose. The Commission conditioned its permit to build a shorefront residence on the owners allowing public passage across their beach-front parcel. As the Court held, there was an insufficient nexus between this requirement and the state's goal of ensuring public access to shorefront. Thus, the regulation amounted to a de facto taking of the owners' parcel in violation of the United States Constitution, as discussed in § 1.05[C], even though it did not deny the owners all their reasonable investment-based expectations.

[D] Regulation Under Public Trust Not a Taking

The United States Supreme Court revisited the impact of the public trust doctrine in the context of de facto taking claims in *Lucas v. South Carolina Coastal Council*[121] (also discussed at §§ 1.05[C][3][c] and 11.02[B][1]). A state statute barred constructing any permanent structure along the shorefront, and the owner contended this deprived him of all reasonable investment-based expectations with regard to the parcel. The Supreme Court ruled that if the statute did so deprive the owner, it would amount to a compensable de facto taking of his parcel in violation of the Constitution unless the state, at common law, could have enjoined the construction anyway. It remanded for the state's Supreme Court to decide whether the state's law of nuisance, public trust doctrine, or similar rules could have barred the construction. On remand, the South Carolina Supreme Court held the state could not have blocked the development under its common law, so that a de facto taking had occurred, entitling the owner to compensation.[122]

The courts in some states, however, have held that the public trust doctrine, where it applies to a parcel, allows the state or a local government to regulate its land use without concern over a de facto taking claim.[123] This interpretation would lead to a different result from the South Carolina court's holding in *Lucas* on remand, which did not involve a wetland.

---

119. CAL. CONST. art. XV, §§ 2, 3.
120. 483 U.S. 825 (1987).
121. 505 U.S. 1003 (1992).
122. 424 S.E.2d 484 (S.C. 1992).
123. McQueen v. South Carolina Coastal Council, 580 S.E.2d 116 (S.C.), *cert. denied*, 540 U.S. 982 (2003); Just v. Marinette County, 201 N.W.2d 761 (Wis. 1972).

Chapter 4

Environmental Quality Review

[B] Common Law Privileges Inapplicable
[C] State Privilege Statutes and EPA Ruling

§ 4.01 National Environmental Policy Act (NEPA)

[A] Importance and Origins

[1] Act Requires Federal Agencies to Weigh Impacts

Perhaps the single most dramatic and far-reaching change worked by environmental law has been the advent of statutes requiring government agencies to weigh the impacts of their actions before activities under their jurisdiction are performed, funded, or permitted. These laws, known generally as environmental quality review (or environmental impact review) legislation, exist both at the federal and state level. The first and most significant of these to be enacted was the National Environmental Policy Act (NEPA),[1] passed by Congress in 1969.[2] Since that time, about half the states have enacted similar legislation, discussed at § 4.02. NEPA requires federal agencies to consider the environmental impacts of activities they perform, fund, or permit, as well as alternatives to those activities and ways to mitigate, or lessen, those impacts.[3] The prime mechanism to achieve this is the environmental impact statement, or EIS, which the agency with responsibility over the action must prepare.[4]

NEPA commences with a broad statement of Congressional purposes:[5]

> To declare a national policy which will encourage productive and enjoyable harmony between man and his environment; to promote efforts which will prevent or eliminate damage to the environment and biosphere and stimulate the health and welfare of man; to enrich the understanding of the ecological systems and natural resources important to the Nation[.]

NEPA also directs that "to the fullest extent possible ... the policies, regulations, and public laws of the United States shall be interpreted and administered in accordance with the policies set forth in this chapter...."[6] This language might well suggest that NEPA mandates all federal agencies to act in furtherance of the Act's environmental goals, but in fact, as discussed in [E][2], *below*, the courts have declined to interpret NEPA as requiring substantive adherence to environmental protection. The

---

1. 42 U.S.C. §§ 4321–4370d.
2. Pub. L. 91-190, Jan. 1, 1970, 83 Stat. 852.
3. *See* 42 U.S.C. § 4332.
4. 42 U.S.C. § 4332(C).
5. 42 U.S.C. § 4321.
6. 42 U.S.C. § 4332(C).

Act has been construed as procedural rather than substantive.[7] But its procedural mandates, that federal agencies consider environmental impacts, alternatives, and mitigation measures, have been taken seriously by government, and have been enforced by the courts.[8] Statutes like NEPA have altered the course of federal programs, as well as the development of real property requiring permits from federal agencies, in several important respects. First, these agencies are obliged to weigh the effects on the environment, including air and water pollution, solid waste disposal, traffic, and noise, before embarking on a project. This has resulted in many actions being modified, and some even abandoned, once their impacts became evident. Second, requiring environmental impact assessment means that federal agencies that previously had no legal duty to consider environmental concerns are now obliged to do so. Third, agency decision-making is, as a result of environmental impact legislation, open to public scrutiny through participation in the EIS process.[9] And finally, whether an agency has complied with NEPA is judicially reviewable (see [F], *below*), and actions found to be in violation of law may be enjoined.[10]

[2] Origins of Act in Earlier Court Decisions

NEPA's origins can be traced to increasing concern over environmental degradation in the 1960s, exemplified by a series of federal court decisions that halted projects with substantial adverse impacts on the environment—projects that in an earlier day would likely have easily survived judicial challenge. In 1965, the United States Court of Appeals for the Second Circuit overturned a permit awarded by the Federal Power Commission allowing construction of a power plant that would have disfigured part of New York's Hudson Highlands and damaged the Hudson River's fishery. In *Scenic Hudson Preservation Conference v. Federal Power Commission*,[11] the court ruled that the agency had violated the Federal Power Act in licensing the proposed hydroelectric plant, since that Act mandated that the Commission take into account the plant's consistency with a comprehensive plan for the river that included recreational values. Later, in *Citizens to Preserve Overton Park v. Volpe*,[12] the United States Supreme Court vacated a decision by the Secretary of Transportation to build a federally-funded interstate highway through a heavily-used park in Memphis. The Court found that the agency had run afoul of a statute that barred placing federally-financed

---

7. *See* Robertson v. Methow Valley Citizens Council, 490 U.S. 332 (1989); Strycker's Bay Neighborhood Council, Inc. v. Karlen, 444 U.S. 223 (1980).

8. *See* Sierra Club v. U.S. Army Corps of Engineers, 701 F.2d 1011 (2d Cir. 1983); Environmental Defense Fund, Inc. v. Corps of Engineers, 470 F.2d 289 (8th Cir. 1972), *cert. denied*, 412 U.S. 931 (1973).

9. *See, e.g.*, 23 C.F.R. § 771.111(h) (Federal Highway Administration regulation requiring public hearings during environmental evaluation process); Robertson v. Methow Valley Citizens Council, 490 U.S. 332 (1989).

10. Coeur D'Alene Lake v. Kiebert, 790 F. Supp. 998 (D. Idaho 1992).

11. 354 F.2d 608 (2d Cir. 1965), *cert. denied*, 384 U.S. 941 (1966).

12. 401 U.S. 402 (1971).

roads through parks unless there was no feasible or prudent alternative. It rejected the Secretary's claim that because it would have been more costly and time-consuming to build around the park his decision was consistent with the statute. (*Overton Park* was actually decided by the Supreme Court after NEPA's enactment but the dispute antedated the Act.)

These decisions turned on the express wording of the substantive statutes involved, which the federal agencies were found to have violated. In each case, the agency ignored a Congressional mandate to consider environmental impacts. However, many statutes empowering federal agencies to act contain no language of this sort. Even when federal laws do require the agency to weigh a particular environmental concern, such as a highway's bisecting a park, those statutes do not mandate that the agency consider other impacts. NEPA, enacted in the wake of decisions like *Scenic Hudson*, was designed to require all federal agencies to address every significant environmental impact, along with alternatives and mitigation measures.[13] Actually, NEPA as originally drafted did not include an EIS requirement. It simply directed federal agencies to prepare findings as to environmental impact, without prescribing a specific mechanism. However, the mandates that agencies prepare and circulate EISs and consider alternatives to actions were added during the legislative process, and now effectively drive the statute.[14]

It is important to keep in mind that NEPA only governs actions taken, funded, or licensed by agencies of the federal government.[15]

[B] Environmental Impact Statement (EIS)

[1] Draft and Final EIS

At the core of NEPA is the requirement that federal agencies prepare, and circulate to other involved agencies as well as to interested members of the public, an environmental impact statement (EIS) before proceeding with any "major federal action significantly affecting the quality of the human environment."[16] Each EIS is prepared in draft form and circulated for comments. The agency may then respond to these comments, and the draft, responses, and comments together comprise the final EIS, or FEIS. A copy of every FEIS is sent to the Council on Environmental Quality (CEQ), a small but important agency with jurisdiction to implement NEPA through regulations and to advise the President as to environmental policy. The CEQ rules apply to all federal agencies unless an agency adopts rules equally or more protective of the environment.[17] Early in NEPA's existence some agencies, notably the former

---

13. 42 U.S.C. § 4332(C), (E).

14. *See* House Report No. 91-378 and Conference Report No. 91-765 (1969 U.S. Code Cong. and Adm. News 2751).

15. *See* People, by and through Cal. Dept. of Transp. v. City of So. Lake Tahoe, 466 F. Supp. 527 (D.C. Cal. 1978).

16. 42 U.S.C. § 4332(C).

17. 40 C.F.R. § 1507.3(a).

Atomic Energy Commission (now known as the Nuclear Regulatory Commission), adopted rules that took an unduly narrow and hostile view of their obligations under the Act. The courts made clear early on that rules of this sort violated NEPA.[18]

[2] Environmental Assessment to Decide Need for EIS

To determine whether an EIS is needed, the federal agency (or its consultant) first prepares an environmental assessment. Agencies may also permit the project sponsor to prepare the environmental assessment.[19] If the agency decides that no EIS needs to be prepared, it issues a finding of no significant impact (FONSI).[20] If it finds to the contrary, it must then prepare a draft EIS.[21] The CEQ rules contain time limits and restrictions on the length of EISs, designed to forestall the use of the process for delay. These are discussed in [C], *below*.

[3] Context and Intensity of Impacts Determine Whether EIS Is Necessary

Under the CEQ rules implementing NEPA's requirement that agencies prepare an EIS for major federal action significantly affecting the human environment, agencies are to take into account both the context in which the action will occur and the intensity of its impact on the environment.[22] Context refers to the degree to which the action will alter the existing environment within the setting of the proposed action.[23] For example, a new high-rise apartment-house development in an urban area will likely not significantly alter the present land use pattern, whereas the same development in a rural or suburban town would alter land use substantially. In contrast, intensity of environmental impact measures the severity of the action on air and water quality and the like.[24] Even when the context would permit a project to proceed, the addition of one more polluting entity may threaten harm. Thus, an assessment may be required to insure, in the words of one court, that the action will not be "the straw that breaks the back of the environmental camel."[25] The CEQ regulations make clear that the word "major" simply reinforces "significant," and there is no independent requirement that the federal action in fact be a "major" one.[26]

Hanly v. Kleindienst[27] illustrates the context and intensity tests. In that case, the government prepared an environmental assessment for a new house of detention for federal prisoners in Manhattan. Nearby residents challenged the assessment's finding

---

18. Calvert Cliffs' Coordinating Committee v. United States Atomic Energy Comm'n, 449 F.2d 1109 (D.C. Cir. 1971).

19. 40 C.F.R. § 1507.2.

20. 40 C.F.R. § 1501.4(e).

21. 40 C.F.R. § 1502.9(a).

22. 40 C.F.R. § 1508.27.

23. *See* 40 C.F.R. § 1508.27(a).

24. *See* 40 C.F.R. § 1508.27(b).

25. Hanly v. Kleindienst, 471 F.2d 823, 831 (2d Cir. 1972), *cert. denied*, 412 U.S. 908 (1973).

26. 40 C.F.R. § 1508.18.

27. Hanly v. Kleindienst, 471 F.2d 823, 831 (2d Cir. 1972).

of no significant impact on the ground that it failed to take into account increased risk of crime, rioting, and drug traffic surrounding the new jail. The court agreed and ordered a new assessment, but it stopped short of ruling an EIS was needed. As with most judicial review of agency decisions, the court held that the appropriate test is whether the agency findings were arbitrary or capricious.[28] It found that the failure of the assessment to make findings regarding the impact of a drug maintenance program at the site, and the increased risk of crime that might result from operation of the jail required further investigation of these issues. The court noted, however, that the residents' fear of crime, as opposed to the possible heightened risk of crime, was essentially subjective and thus not a measurable environmental impact.[29] The United States Supreme Court later adopted the same view in litigation over the reopening of the Three Mile Island nuclear power plant, ruling that area residents' fears over the reopening (in contrast to the actual risks) were psychological and not environmental impacts.[30]

One court has ruled that moving the main post office in Rochester, New York from downtown to the outskirts required an EIS because of likely increases in motor traffic and land use development around the new site.[31] Likewise, an EIS was held to be needed before the Interstate Commerce Commission could approve a proposal to abandon a substantial rail line, since that would doubtless cause passenger and freight traffic to shift to the area's highways.[32] The leasing of space in a private office building by a federal agency was also held to require an EIS, where over 2,000 employees would have to commute to the building by automobile, even though other tenants would doubtless have occupied the same space.[33]

On the other hand, it has been held that where the prime impacts of federal action are socio-economic rather than environmental, as with loss of employment and relocation of personnel when a military base is shifted, no EIS will be needed.[34]

An agency may require parties to an administrative proceeding to affirmatively raise environmental issues in order to meet a "threshold test" triggering an EIS.[35]

The halting of federal activity may constitute an action requiring assessment under NEPA, such as discontinuing the purchase of helium,[36] but the failure to take action in cases in which the government has discretion to do so has been deemed not to

---

28. *Id.* at 829.

29. *Id.* at 833.

30. Metropolitan Edison Co. v. People Against Nuclear Energy, 460 U.S. 766 (1983).

31. City of Rochester v. United States Postal Service, 541 F.2d 967 (2d Cir. 1976).

32. Harlem Valley Transp. Ass'n v. Stafford, 500 F.2d 328 (2d Cir. 1974).

33. Southwest Neighborhood Assembly v. Eckard, 445 F. Supp. 1195 (D.D.C. 1978).

34. Jackson County v. Jones, 571 F.2d 1004 (8th Cir. 1978).

35. Vermont Yankee Nuclear Power Corp. v. Natural Resources Defense Council, Inc., 435 U.S. 519 (1978).

36. National Helium Corp. v. Morton, 486 F.2d 995 (10th Cir. 1973).

constitute major federal action under the statute. For example, where the Secretary of the Interior, although he had authority to intervene and prohibit a state-authorized wolf-killing program, declined to act, the court ruled there was no federal action within the meaning of the statute.[37]

Similarly, where the Department of Transportation (DOT), acting under a Presidential directive implementing the North American Free Trade Agreement (NAFTA), planned to allow trucks registered in Mexico to enter the United States, without the requisite authority to regulate the trucks' impacts on air quality and other issues besides safety, the Supreme Court ruled no EIS was required.[38]

[4] Some Actions Fall Outside NEPA

Certain federal actions have been found beyond the reach of NEPA. These include an agency's budget requests to Congress,[39] listing a species as endangered,[40] and acquiring property by eminent domain.[41] The common thread is that these steps do not themselves incur environmental effects, although they may lead to them through subsequent actions that might well require an EIS. Similarly, entering into the GATT and NAFTA treaties did not trigger NEPA review, since the environmental impacts were too remote and speculative.[42]

Where the Navy planned to store weapons at a facility near environmentally sensitive areas, but refused for reasons of security to disclose whether nuclear weapons would be stored there, the Supreme Court ruled no EIS would be required, since the EIS could not discuss the impact of storing nuclear materials. The project's opponents requested an EIS that hypothetically assumed those weapons were present, but the Court held "[u]ltimately, whether or not the Navy has complied with NEPA 'to the fullest extent possible' is beyond judicial scrutiny in this case."[43]

EPA permit issuance under the Clean Air Act and Clean Water Act is generally exempt from NEPA review on the theory that EPA is required by those statutes to weigh environmental impacts anyway.[44] However, one court has held that a new source permit under the Clean Air Act required an EIS.[45] The registering of a pesticide

---

37. Defenders of Wildlife v. Andrus, 627 F.2d 1238 (D.C. Cir. 1980).

38. Department of Transportation v. Public Citizen, 541 U.S. 752 (2004).

39. Andrus v. Sierra Club, 442 U.S. 347 (1979).

40. Pacific Legal Foundation v. Andrus, 657 F.2d 829 (6th Cir. 1981).

41. United States v. 0.95 Acres of Land, 37 Envtl. Rptr. Cases (BNA) 1478 (9th Cir. 1993).

42. Public Citizen v. Office of U.S. Trade Rep., 804 F. Supp. 385 (D.D.C. 1992) (GATT); Public Citizen v. United States Trade Rep., 5 F.3d 549 (D.C. Cir. 1993), *cert. denied*, 510 U.S. 1041 (1994) (NAFTA).

43. Weinberger v. Catholic Action of Hawaii, 454 U.S. 139, 146 (1981). *But see* San Luis Obispo Mothers for Peace v. Nuclear Regulatory Comm'n, 449 F.3d 1016 (9th Cir. 2005), *cert. denied*, 127 S. Ct. 1124 (2007) (possibility of terrorism at nuclear waste storage facility required an environmental impact statement, even though results of analysis may be immune from disclosure).

44. Municipality of Anchorage v. United States, 980 F.2d 1320 (9th Cir. 1992).

45. Manasota-88 Inc. v. Thomas, 799 F.2d 687 (11th Cir. 1986).

under federal law does not mandate an EIS,[46] but spraying pesticides on federal land does.[47] EPA funding for a sewage treatment plant has also been deemed federal action included under NEPA.[48] However, the courts are divided as to whether the designation of a critical habitat for endangered species is action within the Act.[49]

Certain federal statutes explicitly exempt projects from NEPA review. This was done with regard to the Alaska oil pipeline after NEPA review had led to significant design modifications. Also expressly exempted were the construction of facilities to detain asylum-seeking Cuban and Haitian refugees.[50] Another line of cases holds NEPA inapplicable when Congress has itself already weighed the environmental impacts of an action it authorized, such as exporting nuclear material[51] or deciding on certain Amtrak passenger-train routes.[52] Similarly, if a federal agency does no more than furnish overall funding to a state or local government entity, with no federal responsibility for particular actions taken by the state or local agency, some courts hold that NEPA does not apply.[53] However, if a federally funded action by a state is subject to NEPA, the state may not exclude it from NEPA by shifting the federal funds away from the project in mid-stream.[54]

The CEQ rules exempt agencies from NEPA's EIS requirements in emergency actions, after the agency first consults with the CEQ.[55] NEPA has been held to apply to federal agency actions beyond the United States' borders, such as constructing an incinerator in Antarctica.[56] This decision, however, described Antarctica as a "global common" without sovereignty, and it is far from clear how a court would rule as to a federal agency's action in another country.

An EIS is not enforceable as a contract.[57] To so hold would inhibit the ability of agencies to discuss freely possible environmental impacts and solutions.

---

46. Merrell v. Thomas, 807 F.2d 776 (9th Cir. 1986), *cert. denied*, 484 U.S. 848 (1987).

47. Southern Oregon Citizens Against Toxic Sprays, Inc. v. Clark, 720 F.2d 1475 (9th Cir. 1983), *cert. denied*, 469 U.S. 1028 (1984).

48. Shanty Town Assoc. Ltd. Partnership v. Environmental Prot. Agency, 843 F.2d 782 (4th Cir. 1988).

49. Catron County Bd. of Commissioners v. United States Fish and Wildlife Service, 75 F.3d 1429 (10th Cir. 1996) (yes); Douglas County v. Babbitt, 48 F.3d 1495 (9th Cir. 1995), *cert. denied*, 516 U.S. 1042 (1996) (no).

50. *See* Colon v. Carter, 633 F.2d 964 (1st Cir. 1980).

51. Natural Resources Defense Council, Inc. v. Nuclear Regulatory Comm'n, 647 F.2d 1345 (D.C. Cir. 1981).

52. Kansas v. Adams, 608 F.2d 861 (10th Cir. 1979), *cert. denied sum nom.* Spannaus v. Goldschmidt, 445 U.S. 963 (1980).

53. *See, e.g.*, Atlanta Coalition on Transportation Crisis, Inc. v. Atlanta Regional Commission, 599 F.2d 1333 (5th Cir. 1979).

54. Ely v. Velde, 497 F.2d 252 (4th Cir. 1974).

55. 40 C.F.R. § 1506.11.

56. Environmental Defense Fund v. National Science Foundation, 986 F.2d 528 (D.C. Cir. 1993).

57. City of Blue Ash, Ohio v. McLucas, 596 F.2d 709 (6th Cir. 1979).

[5] Programmatic and Site-Specific EISs

Agencies may be obligated to prepare a programmatic EIS for an entire nationwide project as well as site-specific EISs dealing with particular locations. For example, a programmatic EIS would be appropriate for the general impacts of offshore oil drilling and alternatives to that program, while site-specific impact statements would be needed to address concerns in particular geographic areas. This practice is known as "tiering," and is encouraged by the CEQ rules.[58] However, the courts frown on attempts by agencies to divide a project — say, a highway — into so many discrete segments that no one of them has sufficient environmental impacts to warrant preparing an EIS.[59] The test is whether there are genuine environmental concerns justifying an EIS for a particular segment.[60] However, the Supreme Court has held that with respect to leasing federal lands for coal mining, a nationwide programmatic EIS and individual site-specific statements sufficed, so that there was no need to prepare a mid-level EIS addressing environmental concerns regarding coal leases on the Northern Great Plains.[61]

[6] EIS Limited to Reasonably Foreseeable Impacts

CEQ regulations provide that an EIS needs to discuss only reasonably foreseeable impacts with "credible scientific evidence," not those based on "pure conjecture."[62] This means that an EIS should discuss catastrophic impacts, even if their probability is low.[63] But it need not discuss impacts that are purely speculative.[64]

[7] Lead Agency Responsible for EIS

[a] Preparation of EISs

An EIS is to be prepared by the "responsible official."[65] In practice this means the federal agency with control, or jurisdiction, over the action. But what if more than one such agency exists? In such circumstances, the "lead agency" has responsibility to prepare the EIS. This will generally be the agency with the most involvement and expertise. Courts accord considerable discretion to agencies in sorting this out. Thus, when the Navy applied to the Army Corps of Engineers for a permit to dredge a river, the court upheld the Navy's, rather than the Army's, preparation of the EIS.[66] Federal agencies that frequently interact usually enter into lead agency

---

58. 40 C.F.R. §§ 1502.20, 1508.28.

59. Clairton Sportsmen's Club v. Penn. Turnpike Commission, 882 F. Supp. 455 (W.D. Pa. 1995).

60. Sierra Club v. Callaway, 499 F.2d 982 (5th Cir. 1974).

61. Kleppe v. Sierra Club, 427 U.S. 390 (1976).

62. 40 C.F.R. § 1502.22(b).

63. *Id.*; *see* San Luis Obispo Mothers for Peace v. Nuclear Regulatory Comm'n, 449 F.3d 1016 (9th Cir. 2006), *cert. denied*, 127 S. Ct. 1124 (2007) (terrorism at nuclear waste storage facility).

64. Robertson v. Methow Valley Citizens Council, 490 U.S. 332 (1989).

65. 42 U.S.C. § 4332(C).

66. Natural Resources Defense Council, Inc. v. Callaway, 524 F.2d 79 (2d Cir. 1975).

agreements determining which is to prepare the impact statement in particular situations. Agencies may retain consultants to draft EISs, as long as the agency retains final responsibility for the document.[67] But private project sponsors may not prepare an EIS.[68]

The one case in which entities other than federal agencies (or their consultants) may prepare an EIS occurs when a state agency with statewide jurisdiction receives federal funding; for example, a state department of transportation to construct a federally-financed highway. In that case the state agency may prepare the EIS, although the financing federal agency retains ultimate responsibility for it.[69]

[b] Timing of EISs

An EIS must be done in time to genuinely help the agency decide whether to go forward with the action, or to modify it. Prepared too late in the process, the EIS is likely to merely rationalize a decision already made. But preparing an EIS too soon can hamstring agencies' planning. The CEQ rules spell out that impact statements should be prepared at the "go-no go" stage of a project.[70] For permit or funding applications, the EIS is to be commenced when the application is received, or if possible sooner.[71] In agency adjudication, the final EIS should "precede the final staff recommendation and that portion of the hearing related to the impact study."[72] And in agency rule-making the draft EIS should accompany the proposed rule.[73]

[C] Procedures in Preparing EIS

[1] Publication of Notice of Intent

Once an agency determines, as described in [B][3], *above,* that an EIS needs to be prepared, the agency must publish its notice of intent to prepare an EIS in the Federal Register, a document published daily that lists the proposed regulations and other activities of all federal agencies.[74] The notice of intent briefly describes the proposed action and possible alternatives as well as the agency's proposed scoping process.[75]

---

67. *See* Seattle Audubon Society v. Lyons, 871 F. Supp. 1291 (W.D. Wash. 1994), *aff'd,* 80 F.3d 1401.

68. *See* Sierra Club v. Lynn, 502 F.2d 43 (5th Cir. 1974), *cert. denied,* 421 U.S. 994 (1975) (agency may not rubber stamp EIS prepared by developer, but must independently perform review, analysis, and judgment function).

69. 42 U.S.C. § 4332(D).

70. 40 C.F.R. § 1502.5(a).

71. 40 C.F.R. § 1502.5(b).

72. 40 C.F.R. § 1502.5(c); *see* Greene County Planning Bd. v. Federal Power Comm'n, 455 F.2d 412 (2d Cir. 1972).

73. 40 C.F.R. § 1502.5(d).

74. 40 C.F.R. § 1501.7.

75. 40 C.F.R. § 1508.22.

[2] Scoping

"Scoping" is the next step, defined in the CEQ rules as "an early and open process for determining the scope of issues to be addressed and for identifying the significant issues related to a proposed action."[76] Agencies are to invite comments from affected federal, state, or local agencies, the project sponsor, and other interested persons, specifically including opponents.[77] They are then to determine the scope of the action — that is, its range, alternatives, and impacts — and the significant issues with which the EIS will likely deal.[78] Scoping also entails eliminating insignificant concerns, assigning EIS preparation to a lead agency, and identifying related EISs and other environmental review requirements, such as those under state law.[79] The agency may, though it need not, hold a scoping meeting, at which the issues may be narrowed, as at a pre-trial conference in litigation.[80]

[3] Draft EIS; Time Limits; Other Requirements

The lead agency (or its consultant) then prepares and circulates a draft EIS[81] and receives and responds to comments,[82] as described in [B][1], *above*. Preparing an EIS is often subject to time limits imposed by agencies. The CEQ rules resist setting universal time limits, recognizing that the relevant issues vary greatly from one agency to another. However, they encourage agency time limits based on the action's potential environmental harm, size, public need, degree of controversy, and similar factors.[83]

Time limits may include limits on determining scope, preparing a draft EIS, reviewing comments on the draft, preparing the final EIS, and deciding on the action itself.[84]

Agencies are to designate a person as a contact to expedite the NEPA process.[85] In preparing an EIS, agencies must take into account the cumulative impact of related actions.[86] The courts require reasonably related cumulative impacts to be discussed; speculative ones need not be.[87] When circumstances have changed, an agency must prepare a supplemental EIS.[88]

---

76. 40 C.F.R. § 1501.7.
77. 40 C.F.R. § 1501.7(a)(1).
78. 40 C.F.R. § 1501.7(a)(2).
79. 40 C.F.R. § 1501.7(a)(3)–(7).
80. 40 C.F.R. § 1501.7(b)(4).
81. 40 C.F.R. § 1502.9(a).
82. 40 C.F.R. § 1503.1.
83. 40 C.F.R. § 1501.8(b)(1).
84. 40 C.F.R. § 1501.8(b)(2).
85. 40 C.F.R. § 1501.8(b)(3).
86. 40 C.F.R. § 1508.25(a)(2), (3).
87. City of Carmel-by-the-Sea v. United States Dept. of Transportation, 95 F.3d 892 (9th Cir. 1996); Coalition for Canyon Preservation v. Bowers, 632 F.2d 774 (9th Cir. 1980).
88. Hickory Neighborhood Defense League v. Skinner, 893 F.2d 58 (4th Cir. 1990).

[4] *Record of Decision*

Finally, the agency must prepare a record of decision (ROD) upon completion of the EIS, indicating its determination with regard to the project as well as alternatives and mitigation measures.[89] The ROD must specifically "[s]tate whether all practicable means to avoid or minimize environmental harm from the alternative selected have been adopted, and if not, why they were not."[90]

[D] Alternatives

NEPA requires federal agencies to weigh alternatives to actions they are considering. This mandate actually appears both in the provisions regarding the contents of an EIS and in the general wording of the Act,[91] so that agencies need to consider alternatives whether or not an EIS is required.

Under the CEQ regulations, consideration of alternatives "is the heart of the environmental impact statement."[92] "[A]ll reasonable alternatives" must be evaluated, including those outside the lead agency's own jurisdiction.[93]

The leading court decision on alternatives in an EIS made clear that an agency must consider alternatives even though some of them may be outside that agency's jurisdiction to direct. In an EIS prepared by the Department of the Interior as to offshore oil drilling, the court held that the agency had to consider as alternatives increasing oil imports and using nuclear energy to generate electricity[94] — both beyond the Department's jurisdiction. But, as the court noted, EISs by federal agencies are sent to the CEQ, which may recommend alternatives to the President. The court rejected, however, the project opponents' claim that the EIS also should have discussed obtaining oil from shale or using geothermal energy, concluding that these alternatives were too remote and speculative.[95] That decision was rendered in 1972. A court today might well find these alternatives more practical and reasonable than they seemed more than a quarter century ago.

One court has adopted the view that consideration of alternatives where no EIS is required may properly be limited to those alternatives within the agency's own control. In that case the court held that the Secretary of Transportation, in adopting rules over truck transport of nuclear waste, need not consider the alternative of shipping the waste by barge, which was beyond the agency's jurisdiction.[96]

---

89. 40 C.F.R. § 1505.2.

90. 40 C.F.R. § 1505.2(c).

91. 42 U.S.C. § 4332(C)(iii), (E).

92. 40 C.F.R. § 1502.14.

93. 40 C.F.R. § 1502.14(a), (c).

94. Natural Resources Defense Council, Inc. v. Morton, 458 F.2d 827 (D.C. Cir. 1972).

95. *Id.* at 837.

96. City of New York v. United States Department of Transportation, 715 F.2d 732 (2d Cir. 1983), *cert. denied*, 465 U.S. 1055 (1984).

[E] Mitigation Measures

[1] Agency Must Discuss, but Need Not Adopt, Mitigation Measures

Along with weighing impacts and alternatives (discussed in [B]–[D], *above*), a third requirement imposed by NEPA consists of mitigation measures — steps to reduce the environmental impacts identified in the EIS. The CEQ rules spell out the following five aspects of mitigation:[97]

- Not taking the action;

- Limiting its magnitude;

- Restoring the environment;

- Preservation and maintenance; and

- Replacing injured resources.

Although agencies plainly must discuss mitigation in an EIS, the Supreme Court has ruled that an agency need not necessarily adopt those measures under the Act. The Court's decision in *Strycker's Bay Neighborhood Council, Inc. v. Karlen*[98] ended years of controversy by holding that NEPA has no substantive mandate, aside from its concededly vital procedural role. *Strycker's Bay* concerned federally-financed housing in Manhattan. The financing agency, the Department of Housing and Urban Development (HUD), was not obliged to prepare an EIS, and did not, but it did consider alternatives to the predominantly low-income project. In the end, however, HUD decided to implement the project as planned. Its opponents argued that NEPA required HUD to choose the more environmentally benign alternative. But the Court rejected that view, holding that "once an agency has made a decision subject to NEPA's procedural requirements, the only role for a court is to insure that the agency has considered the environmental consequences; it cannot 'interject itself within the area of discretion of the executive as to the choice of the action to be taken.' "[99]

An earlier Supreme Court decision, *Vermont Yankee Nuclear Power Corp. v. Natural Resources Defense Council, Inc.,*[100] had foreshadowed this result. There, the plaintiffs, challenging a rule adopted by the Nuclear Regulatory Commission's predecessor agency regarding nuclear waste, had argued that NEPA required a report on the safety of nuclear reactors to be rewritten in terms "understandable to a layman." The Court rejected that argument, holding that NEPA established "significant substantive goals for the Nation, but its mandate to the agencies is essentially procedural."[101]

---

97. 40 C.F.R. § 1508.20.

98. 444 U.S. 223 (1980).

99. *Id.* at 227–228.

100. 435 U.S. 519 (1978).

101. *Id.* at 558.

Since *Strycker's Bay*, the Supreme Court has specifically ruled that NEPA's mandate that agencies consider mitigation measures in an EIS does not require the agency to carry out the measures it discusses. In *Robertson v. Methow Valley Citizens Council,*[102] the Court held that the agency need not adopt a mitigation plan to protect wildlife or air quality while permitting a ski resort in a national forest.

[2] Criticism of Act's Limitation to Procedural Requirements

The view that NEPA is, in effect, a procedural statute only, has been criticized as being counter to the admittedly elusive Congressional intent.[103] NEPA does plainly state that "it is the continuing responsibility of the Federal Government to use all practical means, consistent with other essential considerations of national policy, to improve and coordinate Federal plans, functions, programs, and resources [to] attain the widest range of beneficial uses of the environment without degradation, risk to health or safety, or other undesirable consequences[.]"[104] NEPA further enjoins federal agencies to "identify and develop methods and procedures ... which will insure that presently unquantified environmental amenities and values may be given appropriate consideration in decisionmaking along with economic and technical considerations[.]"[105] It also "directs that, to the fullest extent possible[,] the policies, regulations, and public laws of the United States shall be interpreted and administered in accordance with the policies set forth in this Act[.]"[106]

These provisions arguably demonstrate a substantive dimension to NEPA in agency decision-making. Despite some dicta in early cases suggesting this,[107] the Supreme Court's holdings in *Strycker's Bay* and *Methow Valley* make clear that the Act requires only that agencies follow its procedural demands: impact statements and consideration of alternatives and mitigation measures — as opposed to actually being mandated to adopt the most environmentally suitable action.

[F] Judicial Review

[1] Available under Administrative Procedure Act; Standing

Although NEPA contains no explicit provision for judicial review, the courts have made clear that review of agency compliance with NEPA is available under the Administrative Procedure Act.[108] Since NEPA has no citizen suit provision, a plaintiff must show it is aggrieved to have standing to challenge an agency's failure to comply

---

102. 490 U.S. 332 (1989).

103. See Justice Marshall's dissent in *Strycker's Bay Neighborhood Council, Inc. v. Karlen*, 444 U.S. 223, 228 (1980).

104. 42 U.S.C. § 4331(b)(3).

105. 42 U.S.C. § 4332(B).

106. 42 U.S.C. § 4332.

107. *See* Calvert Cliffs' Coordinating Committee v. United States Atomic Energy Commission, 449 F.2d 1109 (D.C. Cir. 1971).

108. 5 U.S.C. § 704; *see* Salmon River Concerned Citizens v. Robertson, 32 F.3d 1346 (9th Cir. 1994).

with NEPA. This may be achieved by alleging either environmental injury or economic injury.[109] Environmental injury suffices because it brings the plaintiff within the zone of interests NEPA is designed to protect, which, coupled with the threat of imminent actual injury, provides standing.[110] Economic injury (or the threat of such injury) historically suffices to furnish standing to a plaintiff.[111]

However, the courts are reluctant to allow NEPA to be used to challenge general regulations of an agency without reference to threatened harm at a particular site.[112] Since the President is not an "agency" under NEPA, a plaintiff lacks standing to bring suit for asserted Presidential non-compliance with the Act.[113]

[2] Standard of Review

The standard of judicial review under NEPA is whether the agency acted arbitrarily or capriciously.[114] An agency may be enjoined from proceeding with an action upon a showing that it acted in violation of the Act.[115] In addition, other entities, such as private project sponsors or contractors, may be enjoined as well.[116]

[3] Injunctive Relief

The federal courts diverge as to whether a failure to comply with NEPA alone constitutes irreparable injury sufficient to support a preliminary injunction halting a project. (The requisite probability of success is shown by proof of non-compliance with NEPA.) Some courts hold that a violation of the Act is itself irreparable injury because of the statute's public importance.[117] Others require separate, independent proof of irreparable injury.[118]

Similarly, some courts will issue a permanent injunction on proof of a violation of NEPA without the traditional balancing of the equities,[119] while others, at least in unusual situations, require a balancing of the need for the injunction against the harm the defendant will undergo if enjoined.[120] In one well-known case the court declined to issue an injunction after annulling as violative of NEPA a dredge-and-fill permit under Clean Water Act § 404, holding the applicant was free to reapply

---

109. See City of Los Angeles v. National Highway Traffic Safety Admin., 912 F.2d 478 (D.C. Cir. 1990) (environmental injury); Shiffler v. Schlesinger, 548 F.2d 96 (3d Cir. 1979) (economic injury). But see Central South Dakota Cooperative Grazing Dist. v. Secretary of U.S. Dep't of Agr., 266 F.3d 889 (8th Cir. 2001) (only economic injury, not environmental, furnishes standing).

110. See, e.g., Save the Courthouse Committee v. Lynn, 408 F. Supp. 1323 (D.C.N.Y. 1975).

111. See, e.g., Goos v. I.C.C., 911 F.2d 1283 (8th Cir. 1990).

112. Michigan v. United States, 994 F.2d 1197 (6th Cir. 1993).

113. Public Citizen v. United States Trade Rep., 5 F.3d 549 (D.C. Cir. 1993), cert. denied, 510 U.S. 1041 (1994).

114. Hanly v. Kleindienst, 471 F.2d 823 (2d Cir. 1972), cert. denied, 412 U.S. 908 (1973).

115. Coeur D'Alene Lake v. Kiebert, 790 F. Supp. 998 (D. Idaho 1992).

116. Foundation on Economic Trends v. Heckler, 756 F.2d 143 (D.C. Cir. 1985).

117. See, e.g., Scherr v. Volpe, 466 F.2d 1027 (7th Cir. 1972).

118. See, e.g., Environmental Defense Fund v. Marsh, 651 F.2d 983 (5th Cir. 1981).

119. See, e.g., Save Our Ecosystems v. Clark, 747 F.2d 1240 (9th Cir. 1984).

120. See, e.g., Alpine Lakes Protection Society v. Schlapfer, 518 F.2d 1089 (9th Cir. 1975).

for the permit upon correcting the violation of NEPA.[121] Injunctions halting activity for violation of NEPA may be fashioned to apply not only to the defendant, but also to persons acting in participation with the defendant.[122]

§ 4.02 State Environmental Quality Review Statutes

[A] Broad Adoption of Statutes Patterned on NEPA

About half the states have adopted statutes patterned on NEPA requiring environmental review of actions by state or municipal government. The most useful approach to understanding these laws is to examine New York's (see [B][1], *below*), which is in many ways typical, and then to note the differences in California's (see [B][2], *below*). Since these statutes vary considerably in scope and interpretation, the reader must examine the law, if any, in his or her own state. Also, note that the requirements for standing to sue under these statutes, as well as the applicable statute of limitations, may vary from one state to another.

[B] Examples

[1] New York

New York's State Environmental Quality Review Act (SEQRA) was enacted in 1975.[123] Like NEPA, which served as its model, SEQRA requires agencies to prepare EISs and consider alternatives and mitigation measures before performing, funding, or permitting actions.[124] The statute applies to both state and local government agencies.[125] However, SEQRA differs from NEPA in several important respects. Most significantly, SEQRA is substantive, not merely procedural, in nature. That is, it requires agencies to actually mitigate environmental impacts, not just to discuss mitigation measures.[126] In addition, environmental impact is defined broadly, and explicitly includes "patterns of population concentration" and "community or neighborhood character."[127]

Environmental impact statements must be written for actions that "may have a significant effect on the environment" — in contrast to NEPA's "significantly affect-

---

121. Sierra Club v. United States Army Corps of Engineers, 776 F.2d 383 (2d Cir. 1985), *cert. denied*, 474 U.S. 1084 (1986).

122. Fed. R. Civ. Pro. 65(d); Biderman v. Morton, 497 F.2d 1141 (2d Cir. 1974).

123. N.Y. ENVTL. CONSERV. LAW §§ 8-0101 to 8-0117.

124. N.Y. ENVTL. CONSERV. LAW § 8-0109.

125. N.Y. ENVTL. CONSERV. LAW § 8-0105(3).

126. Town of Henrietta v. Department of Envtl. Conserv., 430 N.Y.S.2d 440 (App. Div. 1980).

127. N.Y. ENVTL. CONSERV. LAW § 8-0105(6).

ing" the environment — a lower threshold in the state law for mandating EIS preparation.[128] EISs must discuss, in addition to the environmental impacts dealt with under NEPA, the effects of the proposed action on energy use and conservation and groundwater protection.[129] The draft EIS, in contrast to the practice under NEPA, may be prepared by a private applicant or project sponsor.[130] Certain activities are expressly excluded from SEQRA's EIS requirements, such as power plant siting and determinations under the Adirondack Park Act (both governed by separate statutes under which environmental concerns are to be weighed).[131] In addition, emergency actions are exempt under the state agency rules implementing the Act, a provision some courts have interpreted to encompass housing for homeless persons as well as prison construction.[132] New York courts have made clear that agencies with responsibility for an action may not delegate EIS preparation to another agency that lacks that responsibility.[133]

[2] California

Like the New York statute, California's Environmental Quality Act (CEQA)[134] also applies to both state and local government actions and private developments subject to review by public agencies.[135] Indeed, CEQA specifically mandates the same level of review for public and private projects.[136] Certain actions, such as local government coastal planning, are exempted from CEQA,[137] as are urban housing and related commercial facilities built pursuant to a comprehensive plan.[138] One California decision held that rescinding an already-planned project requires no environmental impact report (EIR), the California equivalent of an EIS.[139]

CEQA provides for a master EIR in the case of general plans or actions subject to multiple stages of review.[140] Although CEQA, like New York's SEQRA, requires substantive measures to mitigate environmental harm,[141] one leading case has held

---

128. N.Y. ENVTL. CONSERV. LAW § 8-0109(2); *see* Onondaga Landfill Systems, Inc. v. Flacke, 440 N.Y.S.2d 788 (App. Div. 1981).
129. N.Y. ENVTL. CONSERV. LAW § 8-0109(2)(h), (j).
130. N.Y. ENVTL. CONSERV. LAW § 8-0109(3), (4).
131. N.Y. ENVTL. CONSERV. LAW § 8-0111(5)(b), (c).
132. Board of Visitors-Marcy Psychiatric Center v. Coughlin, 453 N.E.2d 1085 (N.Y. 1983); Spring Gar Community Civic Ass'n v. Homes for the Homeless, Inc., 540 N.Y.S.2d 453 (App. Div. 1989).
133. Coca-Cola Bottling Co. of N.Y., Inc. v. Board of Estimate of City of New York, 532 N.E.2d 1261 (N.Y. 1988).
134. CAL. PUB. RES. CODE §§ 21000–21177.
135. Friends of Mammoth v. Mono County, 502 P.2d 1049 (Cal. 1972).
136. CAL. PUB. RES. CODE § 21001.1.
137. CAL. PUB. RES. CODE § 21080.9.
138. CAL. PUB. RES. CODE § 21080.7.
139. City of National City v. State of California, 140 Cal. App. 3d 598, 189 Cal. Rptr. 682 (Ct. App. 1983).
140. CAL. PUB. RES. CODE § 21157.
141. CAL. PUB. RES. CODE §§ 21002, 21002.1.

that preserving the rotunda and dome of a historic and architecturally unique department store, while permitting demolition of the building itself, was sufficient mitigation.[142]

§ 4.03 Environmental Audits

[A] Purpose of Audits

Much controversy surrounds the preparing of environmental audits by private industry to determine whether a particular facility is in compliance with the law. The major environmental regulatory statutes, such as the Clean Air Act, Clean Water Act, and Resource Conservation and Recovery Act (RCRA) regulating waste disposal, all require sources to keep records and monitor their emissions or discharges.[143] Since these Acts impose heavy penalties for violations, sources frequently conduct audits of their own compliance, using their own personnel or a consultant. Predictably, government enforcement agencies seek the data elicited in these audits, and just as predictably, sources and their consultants seek not to turn over the information.

[B] Common Law Privileges Inapplicable

The traditional evidentiary privileges do not generally shield environmental audits from disclosure. The attorney-client privilege only applies to confidential disclosures by a client to an attorney,[144] and environmental audits are usually not prepared for an attorney.[145] (In contrast, audits performed by a law firm itself to uncover fraud within a client corporation have been ruled privileged.[146]) Nor is the work-product privilege applicable to environmental audits, since that privilege covers only material prepared for anticipated litigation.[147]

Some courts have ruled environmental audits to be within a qualified "critical self-analysis" privilege designed to encourage institutions to critique their own activities.[148] This recently-recognized privilege derived from hospitals' evaluations of their treatment of patients, railroads' investigations of accidents, and the like, and is justified by the courts as fostering "[c]onstructive professional criticism."[149] However, the precise scope of this privilege, and its applicability to environmental audits, are unclear.

---

142. Foundation for San Francisco's Architectural Heritage v. City and County of San Francisco, 106 Cal. App. 3d 893, 165 Cal. Rptr. 401 (Ct. App. 1980).

143. See 42 U.S.C. § 7414 (Clean Air Act); 33 U.S.C. § 1318 (Clean Water Act); 42 U.S.C. § 6924 (RCRA).

144. Fisher v. United States, 425 U.S. 391, 403 (1976).

145. Super Tire Engineering Co. v. Bandag, Inc., 562 F. Supp. 439 (E.D. Pa. 1983).

146. Spectrum Systems International Corp. v. Chemical Bank, 581 N.E.2d 1055 (N.Y. 1991).

147. United States v. Adlman, 68 F.3d 1495 (2d Cir. 1995).

148. Reichhold Chemicals, Inc. v. Textron, Inc., 157 F.R.D. 522 (N.D. Fla. 1994).

149. Bredice v. Doctors Hospital, 50 F.R.D. 249 (D.D.C. 1970); Richards v. Maine Central R.R., 21 F.R.D. 590 (D. Me. 1957).

[C] State Privilege Statutes and EPA Ruling

Nearly a score of states have enacted statutes creating an evidentiary privilege for environmental audits.[150] These are generally limited to audits voluntarily performed, and in some states do not protect audits by repeated environmental violators.[151] Other states authorize prosecutors to override the privilege on a showing of compelling need.[152] A few states go beyond affording a privilege, and actually immunize from penalties violations voluntarily disclosed in an audit.[153]

In contrast, EPA issued a Policy Guidance Document in 1995, in which it provided no privilege or immunity, but agreed not to seek gravity-based penalties (those based on the severity of the environmental harm and the prior history of the violator) for violations revealed by voluntary audits.[154] To qualify, violations must be promptly corrected, and repeat violations, or those seriously endangering public health, do not gain this protection. EPA's policy governs proceedings before that agency and is not binding on the states. The United States Department of Justice has adopted a generally parallel policy in which voluntarily disclosed information regarding environmental violations is taken into account as an element of mitigation in deciding whether to prosecute violators criminally.

Those favoring a privilege for data in environmental audits argue that such a policy encourages the greater use of audits and fosters environmental cleanup. Opponents of a privilege take the view that it impedes enforcement and allows environmental violators to profit from their skirting of the statutes' regulatory requirements.[155]

---

150. *See, e.g.*, ILL. COMP. STAT. ANN., ch. 415, § 52.2; TEX. REV. CIV. STAT., art. 4447cc.

151. 1991 MICH. PUB. ACTS 132, Part 148, § 14804(d); UTAH CODE ANN., § 19-7-104(d).

152. *See, e.g.*, COLO. REV. STAT. § 13-25-126.5(c); IND. CODE ANN. § 13-10-3-5(a)(2)(D).

153. *See, e.g.*, TEX. REV. CIV. STAT., art. 4447cc; VA. CODE ANN. § 10.1-1199.

154. Incentives for Self-Policing: Discovery, Disclosure, Correction and Prevention of Violations, 60 Fed. Reg. 66,706 (1995).

155. *See Legal Privilege for Audit Information Continues to Frame Debate, Panelists Say*, 26 ENVTL. L. REP., July 21, 1995, at 605.

Chapter 5

Air Quality

[4] Notice Requirements

[5] Costs and Fees

[6] No Preemption of Other Statutory or Common Law Claims

§ 5.01 The Clean Air Act: Standards

[A] Overview of Act

[1] Reasons for Federal Legislation

Although air quality issues have been the subject of public and private nuisance actions since the nineteenth century (see discussion in § 3.01), state legislation to safeguard air quality was, until relatively recently, rudimentary. In the 1960s, public concern over both industrial air pollution and urban smog from motor vehicle exhaust became serious enough to attract the attention of Congress.

Air quality, Congress realized, is a particularly apt subject for federal control for several important reasons. First, air pollution does not respect state borders. Factories and traffic in one state frequently impact on air quality in neighboring states. In addition, states may be reluctant to regulate air pollutant emissions stringently, lest industrial sources move their operations to other, more lenient, states. Finally, any serious attempt to regulate air quality means imposing significant controls on the automotive and oil industries, which had until that time been largely successful in resisting such controls at the state level. If such controls were to be enacted, Congress alone had the political reach and power to do so.

These converging concerns, coupled with the general increase in environmental awareness during the late 1960s, resulted in the Clean Air Act,[1] the first of a series of major comprehensive environmental regulatory statutes to be enacted by Congress. Many of the approaches and features of the Clean Air Act were to be incorporated into the later Clean Water Act,[2] the Resource Conservation and Recovery Act,[3] and other laws to be examined later in this work.

The agency established to administer the Clean Air Act was the Environmental Protection Agency (EPA), created for this purpose by Presidential Executive Order.[4] Since 1970, EPA has been clothed with additional jurisdiction to enforce much of the Clean Water Act, together with numerous other environmental statutes relating to solid and hazardous waste, pesticides, toxic chemicals, and other subjects, dealt with in subsequent chapters. *See* Chapters 7 and 8.

---

1. 42 U.S.C. § 7401, *et seq.*

2. 33 U.S.C. § 1251, *et seq.*

3. 42 U.S.C. § 6901, *et seq.*

4. *See* Reorg. Plan No. 3 of 1970, 84 Stat. 2086 (1970), reprinted in 5 U.S.C. App. at 389.

[2] Federal and State Tandem Regulation

Congress first had to decide how much of the vast subject of air quality it ought to regulate. On the one hand, Congress clearly had authority under the Commerce Clause[5] to legislate in this area and, indeed, to preempt state laws completely. As discussed in § 1.04[A], the United States Supreme Court has, since the 1930s, interpreted the congressional power to regulate commerce under Article I, § 8 of the U.S. Constitution as broad enough to encompass control over any activity substantially related to commerce between the states.[6] On the other hand, controlling air quality is a classic exercise of the states' police power to protect the health, safety, and welfare of their citizens — even though the actual exercise of that power was scant. Further, preempting the field through federal legislation would have deprived the states of jurisdiction over an important area and likely would have been met with intense political resistance. In addition, total federal control and enforcement would have required the allotment of enormous resources.

There were, though, weighty countervailing concerns. The oil, aircraft, and automotive industries did not want to be subject to 50 potentially conflicting state air quality requirements. If they were to be closely regulated, they preferred uniform controls. Besides, the reasons for federal intervention in this area — air pollution crossing state boundaries, and the prospect of states enticing industry into their borders with offers of lenient air quality rules — were reasons for uniform federal rules and enforcement.

In the end, the Clean Air Act was a compromise between these opposing viewpoints. As a consequence, the Clean Air Act has been described as "an experiment in cooperative federalism."[7] This relationship is central to the nation's reduction of air pollution and cannot be circumvented by other legal remedies. On this basis, the Supreme Court struck down an attempt to control emissions crossing state lines under federal common law theories,[8] although claims for in-state emissions grounded in trespass, nuisance and the like under state law that do not contravene the Clean Air Act may be permissible.[9] What if emissions from an upwind state by crossing state lines place a downwind state in potential violation of the statute or the downwind state's own State Implementation Plan? Although the downwind state may be deprived

---

5. U.S. Const. art. I, § 8.

6. *See* Gonzales v. Raich, 545 U.S. 1 (2005); United States v. Lopez, 514 U.S. 549 (1995); Wickard v. Filburn, 317 U.S. 111 (1942).

7. Luminant Generation Co. LLC v. Environmental Protection Agency, 675 F.3d 917, 921 (5th Cir. 2012).

8. American Electric Power Co., Inc. v. Connecticut, 564 U.S. 410 (2011). *See* Native Village of Kivalina v. ExxonMobil Corp., 696 F.3d 849 (9th Cir. 2012); State of North Carolina ex rel. Cooper v. Tennessee Valley Authority, 615 F.3d 291 (4th Cir. 2010).

9. 42 U.S.C. § 7416; Bell v. Cheswick Generating Station, 734 F.3d 188 (3d Cir. 2013), *cert. denied* 134 U.S. 2696 (2014). However, state law theories would not be available to sue for emissions from another state which, of course, cross state lines. North Carolina ex rel. Cooper v. Tennessee Valley Authority, 615 F.3d 291 (4th Cir. 2010).

of a remedy, EPA under its Transport Rule can enforce a Federal Implementation Plan in the upwind state to offset the relevant emissions.[10]

Three areas, newly manufactured motor vehicles, aircraft, and vehicle and aircraft fuels, are expressly preempted by federal requirements. These are described in § 5.04. The remaining fields of clean air regulation, including smokestacks and other stationary sources of pollutants, as well as vehicles in use, are left to be controlled by the states, but subject to federal standards. The mechanism to achieve these standards is the State Implementation Plan (SIP) that each state must submit for federal approval with regard to each of the major regulated air pollutants (see § 5.02).

[B] Federal Criteria and Standards

Congress did not attempt to specifically enumerate all of the air pollutants to be regulated in the original 1970 Clean Air Act. In keeping with the usual pattern of delegating specific responsibilities to an administrative agency, it mandated that EPA list each air pollutant whose emissions "may reasonably be anticipated to endanger public health or welfare."[11] Thereafter, it became the responsibility of EPA to issue air quality criteria for each named pollutant, indicating its anticipated effects on public health and welfare.[12] These pollutants, referred to as "criteria pollutants," are sulfur dioxide (SO_2), nitrogen oxide (NO_x), carbon monoxide (CO), the photochemical oxidants (ozone) that cause smog, particulates (soot, fly ash, and the like), and lead. EPA is free to add to this list but has not done so. Hazardous air pollutants — those likely to result in death or serious illness, including lead — are separately dealt with in § 112 of the Act,[13] described in § 5.03[D].

After announcing criteria for each pollutant, EPA is required to prescribe a standard "requisite to protect the public health ... with an adequate margin of safety" for that pollutant, specifying the maximum quantity that should be permitted in the air. This standard is the *primary* national ambient air quality standard (NAAQS) for that pollutant.[14] A *secondary* NAAQS is to be set representing the maximum quantity of that pollutant consistent with public welfare, which must be protected "from any known or anticipated adverse effects."[15] This can include injury to soil, water, crops, vegetation, animals, wildlife, weather, visibility, climate, buildings and other property damage, economic damage, and the like but also, more vaguely, effects on "personal comfort and well-being."[16] These standards must reflect a balance between the reduction of air pollution and the need to avoid imposing excessive costs to achieve that goal. As characterized by the Supreme Court, EPA's standards must be "sufficient,

---

10. Environmental Protection Agency v. EME Homer City Generation LP, 572 U.S. 489 (2014).
11. 42 U.S.C. § 7408(a)(1)(A).
12. 42 U.S.C. § 7408(a)(2).
13. 42 U.S.C. § 7412.
14. 42 U.S.C. § 7409(a), (b)(1)(a). National Association of Manufacturers v. Environmental Protection Agency, 750 F.3d 921 (D.C. Cir. 2014).
15. 42 U.S.C. § 7409(a), (b)(1)(2).
16. 42 U.S.C. § 7602(h).

but not more than necessary."[17] For instance, a challenge to the EPA standard for particulates contending that Congress had given insufficient guidance to the Agency, and therefore had unconstitutionally delegated its legislative authority, was rejected by the Supreme Court.[18] On remand, the standard was upheld as reasonably based on the Act's mandate that standards be requisite to protect the public health.[19] However, the Act's requirements also work in the reverse. When EPA took the position that it lacked the statutory authority to regulate greenhouse gases, the Supreme Court effectively mandated EPA to exercise that statutory responsibility.[20] Both criteria and standards must be periodically reviewed by EPA and an independent scientific review committee.[21] Within these parameters, EPA has significant discretion. Its promulgation of standards, or its decision to defer revising a particular standard so that it can develop a better scientific basis, will often be upheld if scientifically supported.[22]

§ 5.02 State Implementation Plans

[A] Requirement to Prepare Plans

As noted, the Clean Air Act is rooted in federalism, whereby the federal government delegates significant regulatory and enforcement authority to the states. A key provision of the Clean Air Act calls upon each state to prepare an implementation plan for *each* of the criteria pollutants. The plan, known as a State Implementation Plan, or SIP, must provide "for the implementation, maintenance, and enforcement of [the] primary standard."[23] An additional SIP must be prepared with regard to the secondary standard.[24] *See* § 5.01[B]. The goal is for the state, on its own terms, to come into *attainment* with the federal standards. If the SIP conforms to the federal standards, EPA's approval becomes ministerial in that the state has the authority to decide how it will implement federal requirements. If the SIP is consistent with EPA's minimal standards for a pollutant, the state may also include additional state require-

---

17. Whitman v. American Trucking Association, Inc., 531 U.S. 457 (2001).
18. Whitman v. American Trucking Association, 531 U.S. 457 (2001).
19. American Trucking Association v. Whitman, 283 F.3d 355 (D.C. Cir. 2002).
20. Massachusetts v. Environmental Protection Agency, 549 U.S. 497 (2007).
21. 42 U.S.C. § 7409(d). The Act directs EPA at five-year intervals to thoroughly review the criteria pollutants set forth in 42 U.S.C. § 7408, as well as the related national ambient air quality standards, and either revise or issue new standards as is necessary. 42 U.S.C. § 7409(d); Communities for a Better Environment v Environmental Protection Agency, 748 F.3d 333 (D.C. Cir. 2014). However, if necessary, EPA also may do so without waiting for a full five-year period.
22. Center for Biological Diversity v. Environmental Protection Agency, 749 F.3d 1079 (D.C. Cir. 2014); National Association of Manufacturers v. Environmental Protection Agency, 750 F.3d 921 (D.C. Cir. 2014).
23. 42 U.S.C. § 7410(a)(1); New York Public Interest Research Group v. Whitman, 321 F.3d 316 (2d Cir. 2003).
24. 42 U.S.C. § 7410(a)(1).

ments without violating the Act.[25] If federal rules or standards change after EPA has approved a SIP, however, EPA can require the SIP to come into compliance.[26]

[B] Contents of State Plans

Each SIP, adopted after public notice and hearings, must contain the following:[27]

- Enforceable emission limitations and other control measures;
- Schedules for attaining compliance;
- Procedures to monitor air quality;
- Enforcement measures;
- Prohibitions of emissions that will lead to non-attainment of the standards; and
- Assurances that the state has adequate legal authority, funding, and personnel to enforce the Act.

[C] Submission of Plans

Each SIP must be submitted to EPA, and once approved by that agency, becomes federal law and is codified in the Code of Federal Regulations.[28] EPA's minimum standards are not uniform national standards, nor does the national minimum standard preempt state standards that exceed the federal standard. Rather, states are free to exceed EPA's standards in the exercise of their police power to protect health and safety.[29] The Supreme Court, in an early ruling dating to the early days of the Clean Air Act, held that EPA may reject a SIP as too lenient, but may not reject one as too stringent.[30] Another early Supreme Court decision upheld the right of a state to provide in its SIP for variances for individual sources or categories of sources where warranted by special circumstances.[31] Courts will dismiss lawsuits, even those seeking environmentally beneficial results, that interfere with enforcement of the emissions standards in a SIP, or even with the SIPs in nearby states.[32] Moreover, even federal agencies must show that their transportation-related activities conform with the relevant SIP.[33]

---

25. 42 U.S.C. § 7410(k)(3); Luminant Generation Co. LLC v. Environmental Protection Agency, 675 F.3d 917, 921 (5th Cir. 2012); State of Texas v. Environmental Protection Agency, 690 F.3d 670 (5th Cir. 2012).

26. 42 U.S.C. § 7410(k)(5); US Magnesium v. Environmental Protection Agency, 690 F.3d 1157 (10th Cir. 2012).

27. 42 U.S.C. § 7410(a)(2).

28. 42 U.S.C. § 7410(k).

29. Exxon Mobil Corp. v. Environmental Protection Agency, 217 F. 3d 1246 (9th Cir. 2000).

30. Union Electric Co. v. Environmental Protection Agency, 427 U.S. 246 (1976).

31. Train v. Natural Resources Defense Council, Inc., 421 U.S. 60 (1975).

32. State of North Carolina v. Tennessee Valley Authority, 615 F.3d 291 (4th Cir. 2010).

33. 42 U.S.C. 7506(c)(1); Environmental Defense, Inc. v. Environmental Protection Agency, 2007 U.S. App. LEXIS 28559 (D.C. Cir. 2007); cf. South Coast Air Quality Management District v. Federal Energy Regulatory Commission, 621 F.3d 1085 (9th Cir. 2010).

[D] Time for Attaining Primary Standard

Under the statute, SIPs were required to provide for attaining the primary standard, in general, by November 15, 1993, although later dates govern SIPs for photochemical oxidants (i.e., smog) in non-attainment areas (areas that have not achieved either the primary or secondary standard).[34] Many states continue to lag in satisfying the federal standards, especially in and around large cities.

[E] Revisions of State Plans

States may revise SIPs to reflect technological advances or other changed circumstances, but the existing plan remains in effect until a revision is approved by EPA.[35] In addition, EPA may not approve a revision that "would interfere with any applicable requirement concerning attainment and reasonable further progress."[36] Nor may a state with an approved SIP thereafter interpret its terms in a manner that effectively implies a revision that is inconsistent with the SIP's actual requirements.[37]

[F] SIPS Addressed to Parks and Wilderness Areas

In recent years EPA has promulgated a Regional Haze Rule applicable to states which have mandatory federal Class 1 areas.[38] By 2007, those states had to submit a Regional Haze SIP to EPA, with revisions allowed up to 2018, after which SIP revisions were due every ten years. The Regional Haze SIP must show how the state will consistently improve visibility in the designated areas. Should the state fail to comply, EPA must prepare a Federal Implementation Plan, a FIP, for the mandatory Class 1 areas, basically parklands and wilderness areas for which pristine air quality is sought, in that state.[39] Older sources[40] emitting pollutants in certain

---

34. 42 U.S.C. §§ 7410(n)(2), 7502.

35. Montana Environmental Information Center v. Thomas, 902 F.3d 971 (9th Cir. 2018).

36. 42 U.S.C. § 7410(l); Safe Air for Everyone v. Environmental Protection Agency, 475 F.3d 1096 (9th Cir. 2007), amended by 488 F.3d 1088 (9th Cir. 2007).

37. Safe Air for Everyone v. Environmental Protection Agency, 475 F.3d 1096 (9th Cir. 2007), amended by 488 F.3d 1088 (9th Cir. 2007).

38. 42 U.S.C. § 7491; 40 C.F.R. § 51.308. Class I areas, which may not be in every state, usually are comprised of wilderness areas and parklands. 42 U.S.C. § 7472(a). See 40 C.F.R. Part 51, app. Y, for EPA's list.

39. 42 U.S.C. § 7410(c)(1)(A); National Parks Conservation Association v. Environmental Protection Agency, 788 F.3d 1134 (9th Cir. 2015).

40. An "older source" is one that preexists the relevant regulation. Older sources may be treated to a more lenient standard in recognition of the economic costs of retrofitting up to current standards. "New sources," discussed in § 5.03[A], are those falling under current regulations when the relevant operations begin. Presumably, it is more reasonable to expect a new source to be engineered to meet heightened standards. If an older source changes its operations or undertakes new construction in such a manner that current regulations are invoked, then it is usually treated as a new source for that purpose. In this manner, older sources may be able to economically survive under a lighter regulatory burden, but since industry inevitably upgrades, triggering new source compliance, the more stringent CAA standards increasingly apply nationwide.

quantities[41] in mandatory Class 1 areas, when they are modified, will fall under a standard of Best Available Retrofit Technology (BART) set forth in the Regional Haze SIP to reduce the pollutants that are detrimental to visibility. The SIP's restrictions on those emissions must balance various factors, including the extent to which pollution controls have already been implemented by the source, its useful life still remaining, and the environmental effects plus or minus, such as energy usage, which may result from retrofitting to comply with the SIP. For these "BART eligible" sources, a source's compliance costs, and, as against these factors, the reasonably anticipated visibility benefit of compliance, must also be evaluated.[42]

§ 5.03 Stationary Sources

[A] New Source Regulation

[1] New Sources Subject to Stringent Controls

The Clean Air Act divides sources of air pollutants into three broad categories. "Stationary sources" consist of smokestacks located at factories, power plants, incinerators, and similar facilities.[43] "Mobile sources" (see § 5.04) are motor vehicles, aircraft, and other moving sources of emissions. "Indirect sources" include a highway, shopping center, or other facility that "attracts, or may attract, mobile sources of pollution."[44]

Since stationary sources are not part of the three federally-preempted areas of new motor vehicles, aircraft, and fuels (see § 5.01[A]), they are controlled by state regulation, as set forth in the SIPs, but, again, subject to EPA approvals and oversight. See § 5.02. The chief exception is control of hazardous air pollutants, which is discussed in [D], *below.*

The Act distinguishes between new and existing stationary sources.[45] See [B], *below,* for discussion of existing sources. New sources are defined as sources that either commenced discharging pollutants after the Act prescribed a performance standard for that type of source, or increased their emissions since that time.[46] New stationary sources in non-attainment areas, defined as areas that have not attained either the primary or secondary standard, are required to meet the stringent LAER (Lowest Achievable Emission Rate) standard, mandating the use of the most effective technology. Such sources must achieve "the most stringent emission limitation which is contained in the [SIP] for such class or category of source," unless that limit is not

---

41. *See* § 40 C.F.R. § 51.301.
42. 42 U.S.C. § 7491(g)(2); 40 C.F.R. Part 51, App. Y, "Regional Haze Regulations and Guidelines for BART Determinations." Facilities that significantly rely on fossil fuels may be subject to stricter requirements. 42 U.S.C. § 7491(b)(2)(B); 40 C.F.R. § 51.308(e)(1)(ii)(B).
43. 42 U.S.C. § 7411(a)(3).
44. 42 U.S.C. §§ 7410(a)(5)(C), 7602(z).
45. 42 U.S.C. § 7411(a)(2), (6). See discussion in n. 40, supra.
46. 42 U.S.C. § 7411(f).

achievable, or meet the most stringent limit achieved in practice, whichever is more stringent.[47]

New sources in attainment areas are held to a somewhat less stringent BACT (Best Available Control Technology) standard. This mandates "the maximum degree of reduction of each pollutant[,] taking into account energy, environmental, and economic impacts," that is achievable through available methods and techniques.[48] This means that the regulatory agency is to take cost into account along with other factors, although BACT is plainly a far more stringent regime than cost-benefit analysis (discussed in § 2.01). BACT is a reflection that air quality presents a less urgent problem, even if still a concern, in areas that are already in attainment with the CAA.

Although EPA's regulation in furtherance of clean air clearly is in the driver's seat, there is a flip side to its authority that must be taken into account which may occasionally provide relief to regulated parties. As a standard principle of administrative law, EPA may regulate only to the extent that Congress, by statute, authorizes it to do so. By way of example, EPA regulations adopted in 2002 attempted to narrow the definition of a new source and thus exempt some sources from the more stringent requirements of new source review, but these rules were successfully challenged as exceeding EPA's authority under the Clean Air Act.[49]

[2] Permit Requirements

The Clean Air Act, from its enactment, has required new sources to obtain permits. Permits are issued by state environmental agencies pursuant to the SIP adopted by that state. See § 5.02. Even federal instrumentalities that are stationary sources — military installations, federally-operated power plants, and the like — are subject to state permit requirements under the Act.[50] This provision represents an unusual congressional grant of authority to the states to regulate federal entities, and in fact superseded an earlier Supreme Court decision holding that the original Act did not bestow such power.[51] Under the Act, state permit programs must be conducted under strict guidelines, including the imposition of fees that must equal or exceed a specified minimum amount. If a state fails to meet this requirement, EPA may impose higher fees.[52] EPA has authority to override a state-issued permit if it finds it inconsistent with the Act or unreasonable in light of the Act's goals.[53]

---

47. 42 U.S.C. § 7501(3).

48. 42 U.S.C. § 7479(3).

49. See New York v. Environmental Protection Agency, 413 F.3d 3 (D.C. Cir. 2006), cert. denied, sub. nom. Environmental Protection Agency v. New York, 550 U.S. 928 (2007) (exemption for sources replacing equipment amounting to up to 20% of source's value found invalid); Environmental Defense v. Duke Energy Corp., 549 U.S. 561 (2007) (exemption for sources increasing hours of operation, as long as hourly emission rate does not increase, found invalid).

50. 42 U.S.C. § 7418.

51. Hancock v. Train, 426 U.S. 167 (1976).

52. 42 U.S.C. § 7661a(b)(3).

53. Alaska Department of Environmental Conservation v. Environmental Protection Agency, 540 U.S. 461 (2004) (citing 42 U.S.C. § 7607(b)(1)).

[3] Performance Standards

New sources are subject to performance standards specified in the Act. EPA has adopted these standards for various categories of sources.[54] A limited waiver of the standards is available from EPA in order to test an innovative emission control technique.[55]

[4] Prevention of Significant Deterioration of Air Quality

May a new source be built that will significantly impair air quality in an attainment area? This issue turns on whether the Act should be construed to bar such sources since it is aimed at protecting and enhancing air quality, as its congressional statement of purposes specifies,[56] or whether the Act's goals are essentially met once the standards have been attained in a particular area. This controversy over prevention of significant deterioration ("PSD") reached the United States Supreme Court in an early case but was not firmly resolved in that forum since the Court divided evenly on the issue.[57] In such a case, the Court writes no opinion, and its affirmance of the lower court's judgment does not constitute a precedent.

The issue was ultimately resolved in the Act's 1977 amendments, which required states to revise their SIPs so as to divide attainment areas into three zones allowing varying amounts of new source construction. Class I areas allow no significant deterioration, and Class II a reasonable degree, while in Class III zones new sources may emit pollutants as long as the area remains within the limits of the primary standard.[58] The limits are subject to caps, with emissions measured in increments.[59] The zones established by the states, like all SIP revisions, must be approved by EPA. The sole express requirement of these provisions is that states must include national parks and national monuments in Class I regions.[60] New sources must use Best Available Control Technology (BACT) as defined by EPA for each new source in order to prevent significant deterioration of regional air quality.[61]

The extent to which a new source may offset reductions in air emissions from existing sources (the "bubble concept") is examined in [B], *below.*

[B] Existing Sources and the Bubble Concept

In contrast to new sources, existing sources are held to a lesser standard of Reasonably Available Control Technology (RACT), if they are in a non-attainment area.[62] This

---

54. 42 U.S.C. § 7411(b); *see* 40 C.F.R. Part 60.

55. 42 U.S.C. § 7411(j).

56. 42 U.S.C. § 7401(b)(1).

57. Fri v. Sierra Club, 412 U.S. 541 (1973).

58. For a more extensive discussion, *see* ROBINSON, ENVIRONMENTAL REGULATION OF REAL PROPERTY § 16.05 (Law Journal Press updated to 2022).

59. Clean Water Action Council of Northeastern Wisconsin v. Environmental Protection Agency, 765 F.3d 749 (7th Cir. 2014).

60. 42 U.S.C. §§ 7471–75.

61. Sur Contra La Contaminacion v. Environmental Protection Agency, 202 F.3d 443 (1st Cir. 2000).

62. 42 U.S.C. § 7502(c)(1).

level takes into account the greater economic burden of mandating that existing sources install pollution controls, as opposed to imposing such requirements on new sources. Since the 1990 amendments to the Clean Air Act, existing sources, like new sources, are required to obtain permits.[63] Moreover, any significant physical modification of a facility requires a permit,[64] which will subject the facility to a new source review.

Operators of stationary sources advanced the argument from the passage of the Act that a source ought to be permitted to offset increased emissions from a new facility against improvements in air quality achieved at an existing outlet. This approach has become known as the "bubble concept." It envisages a huge imaginary bubble placed over both the new and the existing chimney. If, on balance, the total emissions from both achieve a reduction in pollutant discharges, the argument goes, then the Act's mandate is satisfied without the need to impose stricter limits on either of the metaphorical chimneys.

After much discussion, the bubble concept was embodied in an EPA rule, adopted first for attainment areas and later extended to non-attainment areas as well.[65] The rule broadens the definition of a source to encompass an entire plant or facility, so that gains may be used as offsets against increased emissions as long as there is no resultant net loss in air quality. The Supreme Court in the oft-cited *Chevron* case[66] upheld the regulation as a reasonable construction of the Act's definition of a source, holding that a reviewing court should give considerable deference to EPA's regulations construing the statute that the agency administers.

In the wake of *Chevron*, Congress and EPA extended the concept of offsets to authorize emission trading between sources. The Act now explicitly allows new sources to offset "increased emissions of any air pollutant by obtaining emission reductions of such air pollutant from the same source or other sources."[67] This is closely linked to the practice of marketing emission allowances, discussed generally in § 2.03 and specifically as employed in reducing acid rain, discussed in [C], *below.*

[C] Acid Rain

[1] Origins of Acid Rain

In the 1970s scientists observed fish kills in lakes and streams in the northeastern United States and eastern Canada that had no evident water pollution-related cause. Proof began to mount showing that the culprit was in fact acid precipitation resulting from sulfur dioxide and nitrogen oxide entering these watercourses through rain and

63. 42 U.S.C. §§ 7502(b)(6), 7503.

64. 42 U.S.C. § 7475(a)(4); 40 C.F.R. § 52.21; United States v. Cynergy Corp., 458 F.3d 705 (7th Cir. 2006); New York v. Environmental Protection Agency, 413 F.3d 3 (D.C. Cir. 2005).

65. 40 C.F.R. § 60.2.

66. Chevron USA, Inc. v. Natural Resources Defense Council, Inc., 467 U.S. 837 (1984).

67. 42 U.S.C. § 7503(c).

snow in the form of sulfates. This process has now been thoroughly documented and has long since become known as acid rain.[68]

[2] Effects of Acid Rain; Causes

Acid rain has far-reaching adverse effects beyond killing fish. It damages forests, stained-glass windows, and stonework on buildings, and depletes soil by acidifying it. Its impacts are not limited to North America, and are quite severe in Europe as well. Its chief cause has been shown to be sulfur dioxide and nitrogen oxide emissions from power plants and other stationary sources burning high-sulfur coal, although nitrogen oxide emissions from vehicles also play a significant role.

[3] Attempts to Reduce Acid Rain

In the late 1970s, several states and localities made ultimately unsuccessful attempts to compel EPA to curb acid rain stemming from power plants in other states. The Clean Air Act contains provisions requiring SIPs to identify new and existing sources of interstate air pollution and to notify affected states.[69] These states may then seek an EPA determination that these sources will contribute significantly to those states' non-attainment of the standards. If EPA so finds, the source is in violation of the Act.[70] However, EPA under the earlier text of the Act failed to so rule with regard to the power plants, on the ground that there was insufficient proof that the acid rain was caused by any one particular source. The courts upheld these EPA determinations.[71]

Similarly, the Act enables EPA to direct a state found to be causing international air pollution to amend its SIP so as to eliminate the danger.[72] This provision only applies if the injured country has given similar rights to the United States. Although EPA did so order some Midwestern states at the petition of Canada in 1980, the order was withdrawn by a subsequent EPA administrator. The validity of the withdrawal was likewise sustained by the courts.[73]

The 1990 Clean Air Act amendments brought relief. The statute now expressly limits sulfur dioxide emissions from offending sources, and requires EPA to set nitrogen oxide limits from those sources.[74] Those limits have been established and upheld on judicial review.[75] A noteworthy feature of this legislation allows sources to

---

68. For a more comprehensive discussion of acid rain regulation, see Communities for a Better Environment v. Environmental Protection Agency, 748 F.3d 333 (D.C. Cir. 2014).

69. 42 U.S.C. § 7426(a).

70. 42 U.S.C. § 7426(c).

71. *See* Air Pollution Control Dist. of Jefferson County v. Environmental Protection Agency, 739 F.2d 1071 (6th Cir. 1984); Connecticut v. Environmental Protection Agency, 696 F.2d 147 (2d Cir. 1982).

72. 42 U.S.C. § 7415.

73. Environmental Defense Fund v. Thomas, 870 F.2d 892 (2d Cir. 1989), *cert. denied sub nom.* Alabama Power Co. v. Environmental Defense Fund, 493 U.S. 991 (1989).

74. 42 U.S.C. § 7651b, 7651f.

75. 40 C.F.R. §§ 70.5, 70.6, upheld in Appalachian Power Co. v. Environmental Protection Agency, 135 F.3d 791 (D.C. Cir. 1998); *see also* Appalachian Power Co. v. Environmental Protection Agency, 249 F.3d 1032 (D.C. Cir. 2001) (EPA may impose controls on Midwestern sources of nitrogen oxide directly upon findings they lead to air pollution in Northeast).

market their emission reductions that exceed their mandated reductions under the statute. Each coal-fired utility producing substantial quantities of sulfates is granted an allowance of sulfur dioxide emissions, measured in tons per year. Reductions in emissions in excess of these allowances are marketable and may be sold.[76] This is designed to provide financial incentives to reduce emissions to an extent greater than the Act would otherwise require.

[D] Hazardous Air Pollutants

[1] Background

Hazardous air pollutants are strictly controlled under the Clean Air Act — far more strictly than the criteria pollutants. Section 112 of the Act establishes a separate regime for hazardous pollutants, originally defined in the 1970 Act as those that cause or contribute to air pollution reasonably anticipated to result in greater mortality or serious illness.[77] The 1990 amendments omitted this succinct definition and replaced it with a list of 189 pollutants expressly found by Congress to be hazardous.[78]

The 1970 Act required EPA to name hazardous air pollutants meeting the statutory definition and then, within six months of naming a pollutant, to adopt emission standards for that substance. Standards had to provide an ample margin of safety to protect public health. This statutory arrangement, in contrast to that for the less lethal criteria pollutants (see §§ 5.01, 5.02), required EPA to itself establish emission standards. It did not, however, preempt the states from establishing stricter standards.

This system faltered because the statutory criterion of an ample margin of safety to protect public health placed EPA on the horns of a dilemma. An emission standard of that severity would impose prodigious costs on major industries like oil refining and copper smelting. A lesser standard would arguably violate the Act. As a result, few hazardous air pollutants were identified, and few standards were set.

[2] Act's Current Approach

The 1990 amendments sought to break the impasse. First, as noted in [1], *above*, the Act now directly identifies a "starter list" of the hazardous pollutants, which include benzene, chlorine, and cyanide compounds.[79] EPA is also required to periodically review the list and add others or to delete substances.[80] If a major source of hazardous air pollutants is listed, EPA must regulate the source as to those emissions to reduce any threat to public health. Its failure to do so will constitute a violation of the Act.[81]

---

76. 42 U.S.C. §§ 7651b, 7651c.

77. Former 42 U.S.C. § 7412(a)(1).

78. 42 U.S.C. § 7412(b)(1).

79. 42 U.S.C. § 7412(b)(1).

80. 42 U.S.C. § 7412(b)(2), (3).

81. 42 U.S.C. § 7412(e)(1)(E); Sierra Club v. Environmental Protection Agency, 895 F.3d 1 (D.C. Cir. 2018). For a more comprehensive discussion of the subject, see ROBINSON, ENVIRONMENTAL REGULATION OF REAL PROPERTY § 16.03(3) (Law Journal Press 2021).

If EPA determines that a category of sources cause the emissions of hazardous air pollutants, it is required to apply emissions restrictions for the entire category.[82] Once a hazardous air pollutant is listed, it cannot be de-listed by EPA unless EPA can make findings on the basis of compelling scientific evidence that there are no sources emitting that pollutant at levels that will endanger public health or that will result in environmental consequences.[83] In addition, the statute imposes a standard of Maximum Achievable Control Technology (MACT), defined as "the maximum degree of reduction in emissions..., taking into consideration the cost[,] achievable."[84] EPA is to report to Congress on the risk to public health from pollutants subject to these standards.[85] EPA can also conclude that there are no safe emissions level for a hazardous air pollutant, as it has for lead. In the case of ambient lead, EPA was able to show on the basis of ample scientific and medical evidence population studies that there is a direct correlation between lead emissions and a reduction of IQ and other cognitive defects in children.[86]

[3] Work Practice Standards

EPA, in addition, may establish work practice standards regarding hazardous air pollutants when appropriate.[87] This provision, originally added in the 1977 amendments, was aimed at overcoming a Supreme Court decision holding that EPA lacked authority to set work practice standards.[88] That ruling set aside an EPA rule requiring demolition contractors to spray water on asbestos to prevent it from blowing into the air. The Court held that regulation not to be an emission standard (such as a rule limiting emissions to a maximum amount) but a work practice standard, which EPA was then without power to enact.

[4] Accidental Releases

Another important provision of § 112 is designed to prevent accidental releases of hazardous air pollutants, such as the devastating occurrence at Bhopal, India (discussed in § 8.04[D][2]) when methyl isocyanate was discharged from a factory and many deaths resulted. EPA is to promulgate a list of 100 substances known or reasonably thought to be dangerous if accidentally released. It may add or delete substances from the list.[89] In addition, EPA may adopt rules to prevent accidental releases, including work practice controls, monitoring and reporting requirements, and design and equipment rules.[90]

---

82. 42 U.S.C. § 7412(c), (d).

83. 42 U.S.C. 7412(c)(9); State of New Jersey v. Environmental Protection Agency, 517 F.3d 574 (D.C. Cir. 2008) (EPA's attempt to de-list mercury emissions from utilities' electricity generated steam facilities that utilized fossil fuels was invalidated.)

84. 42 U.S.C. § 7412(b), (d)(2).

85. 42 U.S.C. § 7412(f).

86. See 73 Fed. Reg. 66,964 (Nov. 12, 2008); Coalition of Battery Recyclers Association v. Environmental Protection Agency, 604 F.3d 613 (9th Cir. 2010).

87. See 42 U.S.C. § 7412(h).

88. Adamo Wrecking Co. v. United States, 434 U.S. 275 (1978).

89. 42 U.S.C. § 7412(r)(3). The list is in 40 C.F.R. § 68.130.

90. 42 U.S.C. § 7412(r)(7).

The accidental release provisions dovetail with the requirements of the Emergency Planning and Community Right-to-Know Act,[91] discussed at § 7.08.

§ 5.04 Mobile Sources

[A] Introduction

Subchapter II of the Clean Air Act[92] governs EPA regulation of motor vehicles and their engines. Restrictions are imposed on emissions from these "mobile sources" as well as the fuels and fuel additives they use. See [E], *below*. These rules apply to both domestic vehicles and imports.

The applicability of emissions standards to vehicles turns on the vehicle's "model year," determined by the manufacturer's annual production period, which may or may not be a calendar year.[93] If an engine is manufactured before a regulatory standard takes effect and is incorporated later into a new vehicle, or vice versa, for purposes of evading the stricter new standard, EPA is empowered to define model year differently to defeat an industry evasion of this kind.[94]

Emissions standards set by EPA have been characterized as "technology forcing"[95] in that manufacturers and fuel producers have been forced to develop technological means of reducing emissions, particularly of hydrocarbons, carbon monoxide, and nitrogen oxides, by statutory deadlines. For an early dramatic example, promulgated towards the end of the environmentally friendly Carter administration, vehicles for model year 1981 and thereafter were required to meet a 90 percent reduction in hydrocarbon and carbon monoxide emissions measured from the standard applicable for model year 1970.[96] Any revision in standards must require a reduction of emissions, although the reductions may be phased in.[97] The Act since its early history has required EPA to consistently enhance standards, resulting in a correlating reduction in air pollution. However, while many of these measures are exacting, Congress also incorporated enough flexibility into times and manners of compliance to minimize economic disruption.[98] The maximum degree of emission reduction achievable is measured by what is generally achievable in the industry broadly speaking, rather than the level of technology achieved by an industry leader.[99] Fuels are also subject to regulation if they pose public health threats; as noted in [E][1][b], *below*, leaded fuel is now legally unmarketable.

---

91. 42 U.S.C. §§ 11001–50.

92. 42 U.S.C. §§ 7521–51.

93. 42 U.S.C. § 7521(b)(3)(A)(i).

94. 42 U.S.C. § 7521(b)(3)(A)(ii).

95. International Harvester v. Ruckelshaus, 478 F.2d 615 (D.C. Cir. 1973).

96. 42 U.S.C. § 7521(b)(1)(A).

97. 42 U.S.C. § 7521(b)(1)(C).

98. Natural Resources Defense Council v. Environmental Protection Agency, 655 F.2d 318 (D.C. Cir. 1980), *cert. denied*, 454 U.S. 1017 (1981).

99. Natural Resources Defense Council v. Thomas, 805 F.2d 410 (D.C. Cir. 1986).

[B] Emission Standards for New Vehicles and Engines

[1] Requirements Generally Applicable

[a] Vehicle Categories

EPA must promulgate standards for pollution emissions from new classes of new motor vehicles or engines that in EPA's judgment contribute to air pollution. The Clean Air Act differentiates between light-duty (i.e., 6,000 pounds or less gross weight) vehicles (see [2], *below*),[100] which have been interpreted to include passenger cars,[101] heavy-duty (i.e., over 6,000 pounds gross weight) vehicles,[102] and light-duty trucks (one class 6,000 pounds or below, and another from 6,000 pounds to 8,500 pounds). Standards are applicable for the useful life of the vehicle.[103]

[b] Pollutants Regulated

The Clean Air Act regulates hydrocarbons, carbon monoxide, and nitrogen oxides as motor vehicle emissions.[104]

When EPA, claiming that it lacked the statutory authority, declined to regulate carbon dioxide or methane as automotive pollutants, the Supreme Court held that the Agency has authority to do so for carbon dioxide, since it contributes significantly to climate change (*see* § 13.02[A]), unless EPA found that scientific uncertainty precluded it.[105] Despite, or because of, EPA's failure to control carbon dioxide, several states started to do so. For heavy-duty engines or vehicles[106] and some light-duty trucks, particulate matter emissions are also regulated. Of course, with new information on greenhouse gases, the regulation of all hydrocarbon emissions is given greater force. EPA, in promulgating new standards, must consult with the National Academy of Sciences, which conducts feasibility studies.[107]

[c] Averaging of Emissions among a Manufacturer's Vehicle Classes

EPA, rather than imposing standards as to each vehicle, uses an "averaging" methodology, in which average emissions for entire classes of a vehicle are utilized, and the class is determined to be in or out of compliance.[108]

---

100. 42 U.S.C. § 7521(g).

101. International Harvester v. Ruckelshaus, 478 F.2d 615, 640 (D.C. Cir. 1973).

102. 42 U.S.C. § 7521(b)(3).

103. 42 U.S.C. § 7521(d).

104. 42 U.S.C. § 7521(b)(1).

105. Massachusetts v. Environmental Protection Agency, 127 S. Ct. 1438 (2007).

106. *See* Natural Resources Defense Council v. Environmental Protection Agency, 655 F.2d 318, 327 (D.C. Cir. 1980), *cert. denied*, 454 U.S. 1017 (1981) (particulate matter emissions regulated only for heavy-duty, rather than light-duty, vehicles and engines).

107. 42 U.S.C. § 7521(c).

108. 48 Fed. Reg. 33,456 (July 21, 1983); 50 Fed. Reg. 10,606 (March 15, 1985). The methodology has been upheld. *See* National Resources Defense Council v. Thomas, 805 F.2d 410 (D.C. Cir. 1986).

[d] Time Period before Revised Standards Apply

Congress, weighing economic feasibility, required EPA to allow a sufficient time period for the development and application of the new technology, taking into account compliance costs.[109] EPA must identify the new and improved technology it thinks is feasible and respond to industry inquiries about its use, identify what steps are necessary to develop and refine the technology, and explain why the deadline it imposed is adequate for the development and implementation of the new technology.[110] In short, EPA must weigh "the risks of economic impacts against the environmental risk."[111] Although this lead time benefits industry, it also benefits EPA by giving it greater flexibility to modify standards that do not measure up to expectations.[112]

[e] Temporary Waiver of Standards

EPA may grant a waiver of nitrogen oxide standards for up to four model years if the following requirements are met:[113]

- It will not endanger public health — meaning that it will not increase emissions;
- There is a substantial likelihood that the vehicle or engine will be in compliance at the end of the waiver period; and
- The technology potentially has a long-term air quality benefit, and will meet or exceed the applicable fuel economy standard for the vehicle class.

[2] Light-Duty Vehicles

The Act sets forth mandatory standards to reduce emissions from light-duty vehicles and light-duty trucks up to 6,000 pounds. The new emission standards are phased in over three years.[114]

Manufacturers are required to install diagnostic systems in light-duty vehicles and light-duty trucks, able to detect malfunctioning in the catalytic converter that might result in a violation of emissions standards and alert the owner to the need for repairs and provide access to information required by EPA.[115]

[3] Heavy-Duty Vehicles and Engines

In contrast to light-duty vehicles (see [2], *above*), heavy-duty vehicles or engines (including motorcycles)[116] must achieve the most emission reduction achievable by

---

109. 42 U.S.C. §7521(a)(1), (2).

110. *See* Natural Resources Defense Council v. Environmental Protection Agency, 655 F.2d 318, 331–32 (D.C. Cir. 1980).

111. International Harvester v. Ruckelshaus, 478 F.2d 615, 641 (D.C. Cir. 1973).

112. Natural Resources Defense Council v. Environmental Protection Agency, 655 F.2d 318 (D.C. Cir. 1980).

113. 42 U.S.C. §7521(b).

114. 42 U.S.C. §7521(h).

115. 42 U.S.C. §7521(m).

116. 42 U.S.C. §7521(a)(3)(E).

the best technology available, taking into account cost, energy, and safety.[117] Nitrogen oxide emissions from heavy duty trucks must be even further reduced.[118] Buses have been held to a standard that sharply reduces emissions of particulate matter.[119] As a practical matter, by the third decade of the 21st century, many urban buses have been converting to alternative energy.

[4] Manufacturers Have a Four-Year Lead Time to Comply with New Standards

Standards may be revised upward, but manufacturers of heavy-duty vehicles and engines are given a four-year lead time — the standards are applicable starting with the model year four years after revision — and remain applicable for at least three model years.[120]

[C] Ensuring Manufacturers' Compliance

[1] Testing and Certification for New Vehicles and Engines

Manufacturers are required to submit new vehicles and engines to EPA, which must test them for compliance with these emissions standards.[121] EPA uses sample vehicles or engines for testing. For vehicles, this means that a prototype of a vehicle family must be tested during assembly, and re-tested every 5,000 miles up to 50,000 miles. If the vehicle or engine complies, then EPA must certify it as such, for up to a one-year period.[122]

[2] Testing and Certification for Older Vehicles and Resales

EPA also must test to establish that vehicles for model years already on the road remain in compliance.[123] For resales, certification depends on the vehicle using the same parts as those upon which the original certification was based. The vehicle will be out of compliance if different emissions control equipment is installed, even if there is no sum effect on actual emissions.[124] Testing initially proved to be less than accurate in that it was done under ideal conditions, assuming regular maintenance. Testing now must account for actual driving conditions. Any light-duty vehicle that cannot pass additional EPA testing procedures devised to incorporate varying fuel characteristics and ambient temperatures, and short waiting periods rather than a full warm-up before tests are performed, may not be given a certificate of compliance.[125]

---

117. 42 U.S.C. §7521(a)(3)(A).
118. 42 U.S.C. §7521(a)(3)(B).
119. 42 U.S.C. §7521(n).
120. 42 U.S.C. §7521(a)(3)(C).
121. 42 U.S.C. §7525.
122. 42 U.S.C. §7525(a)(1).
123. 42 U.S.C. §7541.
124. United States v. Chrysler Corp., 591 F.2d 958 (D.C. Cir. 1979).
125. 42 U.S.C. §7525(a)(4).

[3] Hearing Requirement for Vehicles or Engines That
   Fail to Comply

If a vehicle or engine fails to comply, and EPA either declines to grant or revokes certification, the manufacturer is entitled to a hearing to evaluate whether the tests were properly devised or conducted or sampling was properly done. If an actual controversy arises as a result of this hearing, then the manufacturer may appeal to the Circuit Court of Appeals.[126]

For noncomplying heavy-duty vehicles, the manufacturer may pay a nonconformance penalty in lieu of certification suspension or revocation.[127] However, certifications may not be issued if the number of noncomplying vehicles in a class exceeds a percentage established by EPA.[128]

[4] Testing of Emission Control Systems

Manufacturers must submit emission controls systems for EPA testing, after which EPA must verify compliance with emissions control standards for the vehicle class into which the system will be incorporated.[129]

[5] Recall of Noncomplying Vehicles

EPA may recall vehicles found not to comply, or it may even prevent an entire class of vehicle from being marketed. For instance, early in the Act's history, EPA required Chrysler to recall some 208,000 1975 vehicles in 1978 because of excessive carbon monoxide emissions.[130] This served as a dramatic warning to industry for the future.

[6] Warranties and Certifications by Industry

Manufacturers of every new vehicle or engine must warrant to ultimate purchasers that it will conform to emissions controls at the time of sale and during its useful life.[131] For light-duty vehicles manufactured in model year 1995 or later, the warranty must also extend for a statutory warranty period of two years/24,000 miles.[132] Manufacturers are responsible for warranty service performed by their authorized dealers.[133]

For a vehicle or engine part, the manufacturer or rebuilder must certify for purposes of the sale that the use of the part will not cause the vehicle or engine to fail to comply with emissions standards.[134]

---

126. 42 U.S.C. § 7525(b).
127. 42 U.S.C. § 7525(g).
128. 42 U.S.C. § 7525(g)(2).
129. 42 U.S.C. § 7525(a)(2).
130. Chrysler Corp. v. Environmental Protection Agency, 631 F.2d 865 (D.C. Cir. 1980).
131. 42 U.S.C. § 7541(a)(1).
132. 42 U.S.C. § 7541(a)(1). *See* 42 U.S.C. § 7541(d) for warranty period.
133. Automotive Parts Rebuilders Association v. Environmental Protection Agency, 720 F.2d 142 (D.C. Cir. 1983).
134. 42 U.S.C. § 7541(a)(2).

For defective emissions controls parts of light-duty vehicles, such as catalytic converters, the Act requires that the manufacturer bear replacement costs,[135] regardless of age or mileage.[136]

[7] Manufacturer Is Required to Provide Information

Manufacturers of new vehicles or engines, or parts of either, must maintain records and submit relevant information required by EPA to determine the manufacturer's compliance.[137] As with other federal environmental statutes, with the exception of trade secrets, records generally are available to the public. Confidential information must be supplied to EPA, although it may be protected from third party disclosure.[138]

[8] Site Inspections

As with most federal environmental statutes, facility inspections are allowed. EPA may enter manufacturers' premises at reasonable times to conduct tests or inspect records, processes, and controls.[139]

[D] State Standards

Generally, the Clean Air Act preempts states from adopting their own emissions standards.[140] However, Congress gave EPA the authority to waive its exclusive jurisdiction over mobile source regulation for states that had adopted their own standards prior to 1966 if those standards "in the aggregate" are at least as stringent as federal standards.[141] Hence, a state's standards could trade off more stringent restrictions on some emissions while being more flexible on others, depending on that state's particular environmental needs. However, vehicles meeting the state standards but, because of that flexibility on some emissions, not federal standards, may not be placed in commerce outside of that state.[142]

Originally, only California was authorized to adopt standards,[143] although New York[144] and Massachusetts[145] had moved to adopt their own standards. The Act re-

---

135. 42 U.S.C. § 7541(a)(3).

136. General Motors Corp. v. Ruckelshaus, 742 F.2d 1561 (D.C. Cir. 1984), *cert. denied*, 471 U.S. 1074 (1985).

137. 42 U.S.C. § 7542(a).

138. 42 U.S.C. § 7542(c).

139. 42 U.S.C. §§ 7525(c), 7542(b).

140. 42 U.S.C. § 7543.

141. 42 U.S.C. § 7543(b).

142. *See* Ford Motor Co. v. Environmental Protection Agency, 606 F.2d 1293, 1300 (D.C. Cir. 1979).

143. 42 U.S.C. § 7543(e)(2).

144. *See* Motor Vehicle Manufacturers Association v. New York Department of Environmental Conservation, 17 F.3d 521 (2d Cir. 1994).

145. American Automobile Manufacturers Association v. Commissioner, 31 F.3d 18 (1st Cir. 1994).

quires that other state standards must conform to the California standards,[146] in order not to subject the industry to multiple requirements. Although there has been occasional political pushback against the dominance of the California standards, particularly during the Trump Administration, the doctrine survives. Interestingly, among the opponents of scrapping reliance on the California standards were automobile manufacturers, who rely on the existence of a uniform set of standards.

Deviation from the California standards will result in another state's standard being struck down.[147]

A rule adopted by California's South Coast Air Quality Management District limiting the purchasing of diesel trucks and buses by fleet owners, though, was held preempted by the Clean Air Act since the District is a regional, not a statewide, agency.[148] California and other states have limited CO2 emissions from vehicles, a move that was challenged. California also imposed strict controls over trucks' emissions of diesel particulates. Approved by EPA, the new state standards are being phased in by model year. Evidence in support projects an 85% reduction in deaths associated with particular cancers by 2020 at the cost of $3,000 to $5,000 for each truck that is now required to come into compliance, a price that EPA considered to be reasonable. Upon a challenge by the trucking industry, the standards were judicially found to be justified by compelling circumstances arising from the state's drastic air pollution.[149]

State emission standards must be distinguished from state authority to establish inspection and maintenance (I&M) programs for motor vehicles. States had always been free to conduct I&M, which today is a prominent feature of motor vehicle ownership and operation throughout the states.[150] But as a prod, Congress enacted a provision in the 1977 amendments, repealed in 1990, that required EPA and the Department of Transportation to withhold certain federal funding if I&M programs were not set up for non-attainment metropolitan areas.[151]

[E] Regulation of Fuel

[1] Regulation of Fuels by EPA

[a] EPA May Prohibit Commerce in Harmful Fuels

Congress has given EPA authority to prohibit the sale or distribution of any fuel or fuel additive until it is registered with EPA.[152] Before registration, EPA may require

---

146. 42 U.S.C. §7543(e)(2)(B).

147. American Automobile Manufacturers Ass'n v. Cahill, 152 F.3d 196 (2d Cir. 1998).

148. Engine Manufacturers Ass'n v. South Coast Air Quality Management Dist., 541 U.S. 246 (2004).

149. American Trucking Associations v. Environmental Protection Agency, 600 F.3d 624 (D.C. Cir. 2010).

150. 42 U.S.C. §7416.

151. Former 42 U.S.C. §7506(a).

152. 42 U.S.C. §7545(a).

the manufacturer to provide comprehensive information on any additives and their concentrations, descriptions of testing methods, and any other necessary information. The manufacturer also may be required to conduct tests to determine potential health effects of the fuel or additives.[153]

EPA may prohibit the sale of particular fuels or fuel additives on two grounds. First, EPA may conclude that they cause emissions that may reasonably be anticipated to endanger public health. This does not require a showing of actual existing harm or even that the fuel or additive, alone, may cause the harm; the harm may be cumulative. This involves a policy judgment rather than a finding of harm to an exact scientific certainty.[154] Second, if the fuel or additive impairs the performance of emission control devices in general use, its sale may be prohibited. Lead, for instance, prohibited on health grounds, also has byproducts that interfere with catalytic converters.[155]

[b] Lead

Lead was traditionally incorporated into gasoline to reduce engine "knocking." However, the serious health consequences of lead inhalation and ingestion are now incontrovertible (see § 8.07). EPA determined that leaded gasoline is harmful and adopted a regulation phasing out its sale and use as early as the 1970s.[156] Congress specifically provided that after 1995, it is illegal for "any person" to sell, supply, dispense, transport, or introduce into commerce any gasoline containing lead or lead additives.[157] The relevance of the prohibition has lapsed with the passage of time, since after model year 1992, engines requiring leaded gasoline may not even be manufactured, sold, or introduced into commerce.[158]

[c] Reformulated Gasoline in Ozone Nonattainment Areas

Reformulated gasoline is required in designated ozone nonattainment areas.[159] "Reformulated" simply means that it meets certain requirements designed to improve air quality, whereas "conventional" gasoline does not.[160] The designated areas are nine nonattainment areas for ozone, although the Act provides a mechanism to add other areas.[161] Reformulated gasoline must have the greatest achievable reduction in emissions of ozone-forming volatile organic compounds, as measured during the high ozone season, and of emissions of toxic air pollutants such as benzene and

---

153. 42 U.S.C. § 7545(b).

154. Ethyl Corp. v. Environmental Protection Agency, 541 F.2d 1 (D.C. Cir. 1976), *cert. denied*, 426 U.S. 941 (1976).

155. *See* Amoco Oil Co. v. Environmental Protection Agency, 501 F.2d 722 (D.C. Cir. 1974).

156. Ethyl Corp. v. Environmental Protection Agency, 541 F.2d 1 (D.C. Cir. 1976).

157. 42 U.S.C. § 7545(n). For EPA's regulations also prohibiting marketing leaded gasoline, see 40 C.F.R. Part 80.

158. 42 U.S.C. § 7553.

159. 42 U.S.C. § 7545(k).

160. 42 U.S.C. § 7545(k)(1), (10)(E), (F).

161. 42 U.S.C. § 7545(k)(6), (10)(D).

formaldehyde measured year-long.[162] Nitrogen oxide levels must not exceed those of conventional gasolines; oxygen content generally is held to a high level; benzene content is held to a low level; hydrocarbons may not exceed 25 percent of the gasoline mixture; and heavy metals, especially lead, are prohibited.[163] The reformulated gasoline is required to contain detergents[164] to prevent the accumulation of deposits in engines or fuel lines that cause emissions during burn-off. Reformulated gasoline must be certified as in compliance with the Act by EPA.[165]

One additive adopted as a reformulated gasoline, MTBE (methyl tertiary butyl ether), proved to be a severe water pollutant and was later banned by an EPA rule, which has been sustained in the courts.[166]

[d] Carbon Monoxide Nonattainment Areas

Any state containing a nonattainment area for carbon monoxide must revise its SIP to require that oxygenated gasoline be sold in that area.[167] During the part of the year most prone to carbon monoxide high ambient concentrations (but no less than four months), the gasoline must be blended to contain increased levels of oxygen.[168] If the area is designated a Serious Nonattainment Area, then the oxygen level may be increased further.[169]

States cannot require oxygenated gasoline in attainment areas. However, if a nonattainment area is redesignated as attainment for carbon monoxide, the requirement stays in effect as long as is necessary to ensure continuing attainment.[170]

Ethanol, made from corn, sugar and other farm products, has become a popular additive to oxygenate gasoline.

[2] New Fuels

Marketing new fuels or additives requires EPA approval.[171] There are also restrictions on the sulfur content of diesel fuels.[172] EPA, however, may exempt new fuels or additives that are shown not to affect emissions control devices during the vehicle's useful life, and which do not interfere with satisfaction of emission standards.[173]

---

162. 42 U.S.C. §7545(k)(3)(B).
163. 42 U.S.C. §7545(k)(3)(A).
164. 42 U.S.C. §7545(l).
165. 42 U.S.C. §7545(k).
166. George E. Warren Corp. v. U.S. Environmental Protection Agency, 159 F.3d 616 (D.C. Cir. 1998).
167. 42 U.S.C. §7545(m).
168. 42 U.S.C. §7545(m)(2).
169. 42 U.S.C. §7545(m)(7).
170. 42 U.S.C. §7545(m).
171. 42 U.S.C. §7545(f)(1)(B).
172. 42 U.S.C. §7545(i).
173. 42 U.S.C. §7545(f).

The advent of hybrid vehicles, consuming far less fuel since they run partly on electricity, has dramatically changed the automobile fuel scene in the past few years. *See* § 12.05.

[3] Preemption of State Regulation

If EPA does not prohibit a fuel or additive, states may not do so.[174] If EPA prohibits or in some other manner controls a fuel or additive, states are limited to imposing only identical controls. However, states may regulate fuels as part of a state emission control program stricter than EPA's, as in California (see discussion in § 5.04(D), *supra*), or if such regulation is provided for in any EPA-approved SIP.

[F] Urban Buses

Urban buses, historically a major source of emissions, are held to heightened clean air standards.[175] Using the best available technology, but taking into account costs, safety, energy, lead time, and other relevant facts, buses must meet all requirements applicable to heavy-duty vehicles.[176] Additionally, urban buses must accomplish a 50 percent reduction in particulate matter emissions — a severe air pollutant from diesel buses.[177] As a practical matter, the bus fleets in many major metropolitan areas have been converting to cleaner fuels in recent decades.

If EPA's sampling indicates noncompliance during buses' useful lives, it may revise standards in large metropolitan areas to require the exclusive use of low polluting fuels such as ethanol, methanol, propane, or natural gas.[178]

[G] Clean Fuel Vehicles

[1] Types of Clean Fuels; Standards

The Clean Air Act imposes detailed minimum standards for "clean fuel" vehicles that run exclusively on certain types of low-polluting fuels.[179] Clean fuels include methanol, ethanol, or other alcohols, reformulated gasoline (see [E][1][c] and [d], *above*), natural gas, liquefied natural gas, hydrogen, and electricity (see [E][2], *above*).[180] The statute contemplates the establishment of clean fuel fleets (i.e., at least 10 vehicles owned or operated by a single person).[181] The distinction between light-duty and heavy-duty vehicles and trucks is carried over,[182] as is the requirement that standards

---

174. 42 U.S.C. § 7545(c)(4); *see* Exxon Corp. v. City of New York, 548 F.2d 1088 (2d Cir. 1977) (setting aside municipal reduction of lead in gasoline before EPA restricted lead).

175. 42 U.S.C. § 7554.

176. 42 U.S.C. § 7554(a).

177. 42 U.S.C. § 7554(b).

178. 42 U.S.C. § 7554(f)(2).

179. 42 U.S.C. Part C.

180. 42 U.S.C. § 7581(2).

181. 42 U.S.C. §§ 7586, 7581(5), (6).

182. 42 U.S.C. §§ 7583 (light-duty clean fuel vehicles), 7585 (heavy-duty clean fuel vehicles).

continue for the vehicle's useful life.[183] There are procedures applicable to vehicle conversions from the use of conventional fuels to clean fuels, but conversion is not required for existing gasoline or diesel-powered vehicles.[184] By 2022, market forces have been facilitating the increased use, and hence the increased production, of clean fuel vehicles.

[2] California's Pilot Program

A pilot program run by EPA in California, which revised its SIP accordingly, demonstrated the effectiveness of clean-fuel vehicles in controlling air pollution, especially in ozone nonattainment areas. There are incentives to manufacturers and consumers. There also are disincentives imposed on conventional fuel vehicles, such as a state registration fee of 1 percent of vehicle cost. EPA also must develop opt-in programs for other states.[185]

[3] Conversion of Vehicle Fleets

The Act contemplates the conversion of federal fleets, except certain Department of Defense vehicles.[186] In addition, many companies and government agencies have begun to convert buses, taxis, and delivery vehicles to natural gas and other clean fuels. In 2022, an issue arose when the Post Office leadership proposed purchasing large numbers of gasoline powered trucks rather than the electric vehicles as a cost saving measure. As of this writing, that conflict between the agency and the Biden Administration has not yet been resolved. However, the attention given to the controversy reflects the extent to which the conversion by federal fleets to clean fuels is being taken seriously.

§ 5.05 Enforcement

[A] Air Quality and Emission Limitations

Whenever EPA finds that any person has violated a SIP (see § 5.02) or permit requirement (see § 5.03[A][2]), upon notice to the violator and the state, it must do one of the following:[187]

- Order compliance;
- Impose an administrative penalty; or
- Commence a civil action.

---

183. 42 U.S.C. § 7582.
184. 42 U.S.C. § 7587.
185. 42 U.S.C. § 7589.
186. 42 U.S.C. § 7588. See also the Energy Policy Act of 1992, 42 U.S.C. § 13257, requiring federal fleets to switch to alternate fuels.
187. 42 U.S.C. § 7413(a)(1).

If EPA commences a civil action, it may seek injunctive relief and civil penalties against the owner or operator of the affected source, major emitting facility, or major stationary source.[188]

Criminal penalties are available for knowing violations of SIPs, abatement or compliance orders, or permits, as well as for knowing misrepresentations on required documents, failure to notify or report, or tampering with any monitoring device.[189] Criminal penalties are also available for the negligent emission of any listed hazardous air pollutant or extremely dangerous substance, if the release places another person in imminent danger of death or serious bodily injury.[190] There is an affirmative defense if the endangered person consented to the possible exposure and the risks were reasonably foreseeable job related hazards or were risks associated with medical treatment or scientific experimentation.[191]

[B] Prevention of Significant Deterioration

EPA, or the state, must enjoin the construction or modification of any major emitting facility that violates air quality standards, or significantly impairs air quality in an attainment area not subject to a SIP.[192] The Supreme Court has held that EPA may determine whether a facility has impermissibly modified its operations, resulting in an increase in emissions by utilizing the facility's annual emissions as a baseline for measurement.[193]

[C] Mobile Sources

[1] Violations, Generally

Violations involving mobile sources generally fall into one or more of the following four categories:[194]

- Placing nonconforming vehicles, engines, or parts of either in commerce;
- Warranty and certification violations;
- Informational violations; and
- Tampering with any emissions control device or diagnostic system.[195]

---

188. 42 U.S.C. § 7413(b).
189. 42 U.S.C. § 7413(c).
190. 42 U.S.C. § 7413(c).
191. 42 U.S.C. § 7413(c).
192. 42 U.S.C. § 7477.
193. Environmental Defense v. Duke Energy Corp., 549 U.S. 561 (2007).
194. 42 U.S.C. § 7522(a).
195. Although a dealer or manufacturer may remove emissions control equipment while the vehicle remains in its custody, without violating the Act, once custody of the vehicle or engine is relinquished without ensuring the operability of the equipment, the Act is violated. Early cases provided warnings for shops that might be tempted to circumvent the requirements. *See* United States v. Haney Chevrolet, Inc., 371 F. Supp. 381 (D. Fla. 1974). Tampering occurred, for instance, when a repair shop replaced three-way catalytic converters that reduced nitrogen oxide emissions with a two-way

[2] Violations for Vehicles Imported and Exported

If a vehicle or engine in violation of the Clean Air Act is imported, the Secretary of the Treasury (i.e., Customs) and EPA may require measures to bring the vehicle or engine into conformity. If the Act cannot be satisfied, the vehicle or engine must be properly re-exported or, failing that, will be disposed of by the Treasury Department.[196] If the vehicle or engine is intended for export it still must comply, and, if the recipient country has emissions controls standards, it also must satisfy those standards.[197]

[3] Exemptions

EPA may exempt new vehicles or engines for various reasons, including research, investigation, studies, demonstrations, training, or national security.[198]

[4] Injunctive Relief

EPA, in addition to civil penalties (see [5], *below*), may seek to enjoin violations in a federal court action.[199] An injunction also could be granted to prevent importation of nonconforming vehicles.[200] Injunctive relief might consist of enjoining future sales, which could have drastic effects on the defendant's business.

[5] Civil Penalties

EPA may either assess civil penalties administratively, subject to judicial review, or commence a penalty action in federal court.[201] The amount of the penalty will depend on the gravity of the violation, the economic benefit to the violator resulting from the violation, the size of the violator's business, the violator's history of compliance, the action taken to remedy the violation, and the effect of the penalty on the violator's ability to stay in business.[202] If the Attorney General, on behalf of EPA, must commence a collection proceeding, then the penalty is not subject to judicial review, quarterly sanctions of 10 percent are added on to the base penalty, and the defaulting violator must also pay attorneys' fees and costs incurred by the United States.[203]

[D] Emergency Powers

If pollution sources present an imminent danger to public health or the environment, EPA may immediately seek a restraining order in federal court or take any

---

converter that was less effective at doing so. *See* United States v. Economy Muffler & Tire Center, Inc., 762 F. Supp. 1242 (E.D. Va. 1991). Dealers are responsible for tampering by their mechanics. United States v. Haney Chevrolet, Inc., 371 F. Supp. 381 (D. Fla. 1974).

196. 42 U.S.C. §7522(b)(2).
197. 42 U.S.C. §7522(b)(3).
198. 42 U.S.C. §7522(b)(1).
199. 42 U.S.C. §7523.
200. United States v. Holtzman, 762 F.2d 720 (9th Cir. 1985).
201. 42 U.S.C. §7524.
202. 42 U.S.C. §7524.
203. 42 U.S.C. §7524.

other necessary action. If that is not a practicable remedy, then EPA may issue any orders, including summary abatement orders, effective for 60 days, necessary to protect public health or the environment.[204]

[E] Citizen Suits

[1] Introduction

In addition to administrative, civil, and injunctive remedies available to EPA, the Clean Air Act, like most other federal environmental statutes, provides for citizen suits.[205] These actions are discussed generally in § 1.03. As with several of these statutes, however, the Clean Air Act provisions have nuances of their own.

[2] Types of Citizen Suits

Citizen suits as contemplated by the Clean Air Act and certain other federal environmental statutes are a device to ensure that the Act is enforced if the government is derelict in this duty. Citizen plaintiffs, in effect, act as private attorneys general in bringing an action against a party violating the Act. Citizen plaintiffs may sue anyone in federal court for violations of the Act, including individual states and even the United States as a polluter, although the latter would be subject to Eleventh Amendment restrictions. *See* § 1.05[E]. The action may seek to enjoin a violation of either an emission standard or a state or federal order related to an emission standard.[206] A state also may be sued in a federal citizen suit for failure to enforce its own SIP,[207] or for utilizing a classification scheme that evaded requirements of the Act.[208] However, a citizen suit does not create a private cause of action — hence, a citizen plaintiff cannot recover damages or other common law remedies within the context of a citizen suit under the Act — and it is not a vehicle to sue a facility for claims falling outside of the SIP or a permit.[209]

Citizen plaintiffs may also sue EPA for *failure* to perform a nondiscretionary duty.[210] They may not sue, however, to challenge *how* the duties are performed.[211] This is an important distinction which reflects the deference usually accorded by courts to EPA, recognizing that EPA and not judges are the experts in the realm of reducing air pollution, involving how the agency exercises its *discretion* in deciding how to discharge its statutory obligations. Nevertheless, the statute imposes various specific obligations on the agency which, to a degree that the statute directs, must

---

204. 42 U.S.C. § 7603.

205. 42 U.S.C. § 7604.

206. 42 U.S.C. § 7604(a)(1).

207. American Lung Association of New Jersey v. Kean, 871 F.2d 319 (3d Cir. 1987).

208. Weiler v. Chatham Forest Products, 370 F.3d 339 (2d Cir. 2004).

209. McEvoy v. IEI Barge Services, 622 F.3d 671 (7th Cir. 2010) (citizen suit was not a vehicle to sue a neighboring owner for spread of coal dust onto plaintiff's property).

210. 42 U.S.C. § 7604(a)(2).

211. Wisconsin's Environmental Decade, Inc. v. Wisconsin Power & Electric Co., 395 F. Supp. 313 (W.D. Wis. 1975).

be undertaken. The failure to perform such a *mandatory* duty can be the basis for a citizen suit. For instance, EPA's failure to timely review proposed revisions to a SIP is a valid basis to compel EPA's action,[212] although a challenge to EPA's approval of a SIP, inherently discretionary, would not be.[213]

Citizen plaintiffs also may sue to enjoin the construction of new or modified major emitting facilities lacking permits required in connection with significant deterioration of air quality or nonattainment.[214] Compare this with the Resource Conservation and Recovery Act citizen suit provisions that do not allow a challenge to facility siting.[215] If a permit was granted, citizen plaintiffs likewise may raise violations of a permit condition.[216]

[3] Disposition of Penalties

Penalties are paid into a special fund in the United States Treasury dedicated to financing compliance and enforcement activities. However, unlike some other environmental statutes, the court may allow EPA to use civil penalties for beneficial mitigation projects consistent with the Act.[217]

[4] Notice Requirements

EPA, acting within budgetary and numerous practical limitations, has a degree of discretion as to how it prioritizes its enforcement decisions. Citizen suits are a valuable device for ensuring that the Act and its regulations are enforced when EPA fails to take action against particular violations owing to the regional office or even agency headquarters being overworked, distracted by too many cases, understaffed or for less defensible reasons. However, Congress did not intend that citizen suits be used as a subterfuge for interfering with EPA or other governmental operations by the device of a flurry of ongoing lawsuits. Hence, the Act imposes certain conditions precedent that must be satisfied before citizens may commence an action against an alleged violator.

Initially, an action to challenge a violation is barred unless 60 days' notice is given to EPA, the state, and the violator. The notice document must be specific as to the time, place and manner of the violation. This can draw EPA's attention to the violation and thereby allow it to take enforcement action, and it provides a grace period for the violator to address the violation. Then, once the sixty days has passed after adequate notice was provided, the action will still be barred if EPA has commenced and is diligently prosecuting a civil action or administrative proceeding. The notice and

---

212. United States v. General Motors Corp., 876 F.2d 1060 (1st Cir. 1989), *aff'd*, 496 U.S. 530 (1989).

213. West Penn Power Co. v. Train, 522 F.2d 302 (3d Cir. 1975), *cert. denied*, 426 U.S. 947 (1976).

214. 42 U.S.C. § 7604(a)(3).

215. 42 U.S.C. § 6972.

216. 42 U.S.C. § 7604(a)(3).

217. 42 U.S.C. § 7604(g). States may recover penalties against federal sources. United States v. Tennessee Air Pollution Control Bd., 185 F.3d 529 (6th Cir. 1999).

the resulting EPA enforcement action accomplish the statutory goal and makes the citizen suit unnecessary. The manner in which EPA enforces, though, is discretionary. As long as it is reasonable and moderately effective, EPA's choice of enforcement actions will be immune from further citizen suits.

If the plaintiff sues EPA rather than a violator on a theory that it has failed to satisfy a statutory obligation, 60 days' notice to EPA is required, unless the action is to enjoin emissions of hazardous air pollutants, a matter of urgency, or to require compliance with a SIP.[218]

[5] Costs and Fees

Courts may award costs, including reasonable attorney and expert witness fees, to "any party" whenever the court determines that it is appropriate, typically but not exclusively to a prevailing party.[219] Courts pay attorneys at rates commensurate with prevailing community standards for the particular type of work.[220]

[6] No Preemption of Other Statutory or Common Law Claims

The citizen suit provisions of the Clean Air Act do not preempt any other statutory or common law rights to seek enforcement.[221] Hence, while citizen plaintiffs may not recover damages for injuries to persons or property as a remedy within a citizen suit, that would not bar them from separately suing for nuisance, negligence or other common law or state law remedies in connection with harm caused by the violation. Nor do the citizen suit provisions prevent state or local authorities from enforcing state or local law.[222]

---

218. 42 U.S.C. § 7607(f). For actions involving hazardous air pollutants for which the extended notice period may be dispensed with, see 42 U.S.C. § 7412(i)(3)(A). For SIP enforcement, see 42 U.S.C. § 7413(a).

219. 42 U.S.C. § 7607(f).

220. Save Our Cumberland Mountains, Inc. v. Hodel, 857 F.2d 1516 (D.C. Cir. 1988).

221. 42 U.S.C. § 7604(e); United States v. Atlantic-Richfield Co., 478 F. Supp. 1215 (D. Mont. 1979).

222. 42 U.S.C. § 7604(e).

Chapter 6

Water Pollution

> [2] Statutory Exempt Activities
> > [a] Agriculture/Silviculture
> > > [i] "Normal" Farming, Silvicultural, or Ranching Use
> > > [ii] Farming, Silvicultural, or Ranching Use Must Be "Ongoing"
> > [b] Ponds or Ditches Relating to Agriculture
> > [c] Farm, Forest, and Mining Roads
> > [d] Structures in the Water: Maintenance and Repair
> > [e] Sedimentation Basins at Construction Sites
> [3] When Statutory Exemptions Are Inapplicable
> > [a] New Use of Water Body
> > [b] Activity Impairs Flow or Circulation
> [4] Certain Government Projects Are Exempted
> [G] Nationwide or "General" Permits

§ 6.01 Overview of Provisions Regulating Water Pollution

Water pollution is regulated, in the main, under three federal statutes and the regulations promulgated thereunder, or by state programs approved by EPA. The Clean Water Act (CWA)[1] regulates the discharge of pollutants into the "navigable waters of the United States," reflecting its legislative background as a navigation-protection device.[2] Regulation of wetlands also has been grafted onto the Clean Water Act. However, the Act does not regulate the discharge of pollutants into ground waters,[3] or some types of runoff, and has only limited effect on discharges into the ocean. The Safe Drinking Water Act[4] regulates groundwater sources of drinking water and recharge areas, as well as public water systems. The Marine Protection, Research and Sanctuaries Act[5] regulates, and essentially prohibits, ocean dumping, reflecting its background as a conservation statute. The statute which has the broadest reach and receives the greatest attention, though, is the Clean Water Act.

---

1. 33 U.S.C. §§ 1251–1387. As with other environmental statutes which are also known by common names, there are two sets of numeration: the U.S. Code section numbers; and section numbers as denoted in the original Act. Hence, 33 U.S.C. § 1251, the prefatory clause of the Act, is also FWPCA [hereinafter "CWA"] § 101.

2. Tellingly, the Clean Water Act, or Federal Water Pollution Control Act as it officially is entitled, is included in Title 33 of the U.S. Code, which specifically is dedicated to regulating Navigation and Navigable Waters.

3. This general exclusion of ground waters from regulation under the Clean Water Act has some caveats. One possible device for CWA enforcement has been termed the conduit theory, whereby pollutants are discharged subsurface, such as by an injection well, and travel by means of groundwater or the subsurface geology to an ultimate discharge into a water body that falls within the CWA. This is an evolving theory on which Circuit Courts have divided and as to which the United States has been taking only incremental steps. See the discussion in § 6.03[B][1][b] and [d], *below*.

4. 42 U.S.C. §§ 300(f) to 300j-26.

5. 33 U.S.C. §§ 1401–1445.

It is helpful to understand the history of regulation in each of these areas in order to appreciate their reach and congressional intentions of these acts, the nature of the enforcement programs, and the respective jurisdiction of federal, state, and local governments, as well as some of the regulatory assumptions which are incorporated into each act.

§ 6.02 Legislative History of Federal Water Pollution Statutes

[A] Early Federal Attempts to Control Water Pollution

[1] Historical Background

Historically, industry was sited along water courses, which provided a means of egress and ingress for commerce and for populations. Water courses also provided an inexpensive means of disposing of wastes. Early attempts to control water pollution were fitful, and often required reliance on common law remedies such as nuisance.[6] However, with the passage of time, and the increasingly intensive industrialization of erstwhile rural regions, discharges into water bodies became a recognized threat to navigation as well as to public health.

The modern Clean Water Act has two distinct antecedents: (1) the Rivers and Harbors Act, which prohibited obstructions to navigation but not strictly speaking pollution; and (2) a series of federal water pollution measures, starting with the 1948 Federal Water Pollution Control Act (see [4], [5], *below*), which ostensibly addressed water pollution, but encompassed little enforcement power, and which, until enactment of the Clean Water Act (see [D], *below*), essentially left regulation of the field to the states.

[2] Rivers and Harbors Act

[a] Overview of the Act

Several nineteenth century enactments, variously codified as the "Rivers and Harbors Act" or the "Refuse Act" within Title 33 of the United States Code, approached the problem of what we now term pollution from the standpoint of how to minimize interference with navigation, reflecting the economic paradigm of the day, rather than how to minimize contamination of water quality, the overriding modern concern. The United States Supreme Court recognized early that there was no common law of the United States which prohibited obstruction of navigable waterways (as contrasted with actions based on nuisance as a remedy for infringements on private or public lands, discussed in § 3.01).

Congress responded by enacting the Rivers and Harbors Act of 1890, which was amended by the Refuse Act in 1899,[7] although the statute is still known, and is still

---

6. See discussion in § 3.01.
7. 33 U.S.C. §§ 403–407.

effective, as the Rivers and Harbors Act. The Rivers and Harbors Act generally prohibits "the creation of any obstruction, not affirmatively authorized by law, to the navigable capacity" of any of the "waters of the United States."[8] This provision also prohibits excavation or filling that could alter or modify the course, location, condition, or capacity of a navigable waterway,[9] which has echoes in §404 of the Clean Water Act, relating to dredging and filling (see §6.07). However, under the Rivers and Harbors Act, the Department of the Army (originally the War Department) was empowered to grant permits, a function now subsumed under the Clean Water Act (see §6.03[C] and [D]).

The Rivers and Harbors Act prohibits the disposal of "refuse" into national water bodies, which might obstruct navigation, except for liquid wastes released from sewers and streets.[10] Violations of these provisions, which are still valid law, are misdemeanors.[11]

[b] Supreme Court Cases Construing the Rivers and Harbors Act: Antecedents to Enactment of Federal Water Pollution Policy

The United States Supreme Court in *United States v. Republic Steel*[12] gave support to a broad reading of congressional intent to prohibit — and to require abatement of — pollution of the nation's waterways. The respective opinions in that case underscored some of the ambiguities of the Rivers and Harbors Act which had rendered it historically ineffective prior to *Republic Steel* as a prohibition of pollution. The majority and dissent also foreshadowed many of the divisions which were to arise from subsequent environmental legislation.

The majority opinion interpreted "obstruction" broadly, to reach not only structures, but any impediment to navigation, noting that an earlier Court had found the Rivers and Harbors Act to provide authority to prohibit even a reduction of water level.[13] The dissent, noting that the basic congressional purpose was only to facilitate navigation, read the statute to apply only to specified structures. What was meant by "refuse" under the Act? Again, the split bench in *Republic Steel* provided insights into the ineffectiveness of early congressional attempts to regulate the condition of waterways. What if industrial solids were included in a liquefied waste stream, such as in sewage? The question still arises for the definition of "solid" waste in modern environmental law.[14] The majority, narrowly interpreting a congressional intent to provide an exception, concluded that if the wastes were in solution, then the exception provided by §13 of the Act applied; if they were in suspension, they

---

8. 33 U.S.C. §403(1).
9. 33 U.S.C. §403(3).
10. 33 U.S.C. §407.
11. 33 U.S.C. §§406, 411.
12. 362 U.S. 482 (1960).
13. *See* Sanitary District v. U.S., 266 U.S. 405, 429 (1925); *accord* Wisconsin v. Illinois, 278 U.S. 367, 414 (1929).
14. See §7.02, in connection with RCRA, and §7.06, in connection with CERCLA.

remained solids, and the discharge was prohibited. Even if the wastes were entirely liquid, but they were not discharged from sewers or streets, the discharge was still prohibited.[15] The dissent noted the unlikelihood that a nineteenth century congress would have distinguished the nature of dissolved solids in sewage, or would have differentiated between domestic and industrial sewage, considering the primitive level of sewer facilities then available, especially when the original purpose was only related to navigability.

The Supreme Court returned to the term "refuse" in 1966, in *United States v. Standard Oil Co.*,[16] a prosecution arising from the discharge of oil. The majority again read the Rivers and Harbors Act expansively, finding congressional intent to prohibit the discharge of any refuse matter into navigable waterways except for liquid sewage; the discharge of oil, not fitting that exception, could be prosecuted. The dissent again focused on the physicality of refuse matter which might affirmatively obstruct navigation, rejecting the majority's broad prohibition of any discharges except liquid sewage. The dissent, conceding the importance of concerns over water pollution, which it characterized in terms of nuisance, nevertheless found no congressional intent to reach so broadly with the Rivers and Harbors Act, and concluded that there was no comprehensive national law which provided relief for what all members of the bench recognized to be a national problem.

What remedy was available to the government to abate the pollution aside from criminal prosecution? The *Republic Steel* Court again divided: the majority found the Rivers and Harbors Act to imply congressional intent to confer on the Department of Justice the power to seek injunctive relief when the provisions of the Act were violated; the dissent found the remedies to be much more narrow, generally limited to criminal penalties. The dissent conceded the aptness of the result desired by the majority, but found that "this old piece of legislation [did not] fit modern-day conditions...."[17]

The Supreme Court dissent in the *Standard Oil* case made another telling observation: why would the Court grant to the federal government, absent explicit congressional authority, powers ordinarily and historically exercised by states in connection with regulating discharges into water bodies? These were the questions that launched the legislative activity eventually codified as the Clean Water Act.

[c] Permitting Scheme

The Rivers and Harbors Act had another feature which also foreshadowed the Clean Water Act: unlike other early federal efforts at curbing water pollution, it authorized a federal permitting scheme. However, the scheme was little enforced. It was not until 1966 that a permitting program was developed, when the Army Corps

---

15. U.S. v. Republic Steel Corp., 362 U.S. 482, 489 (1960) (dissent per Frankfurter and Harlan, JJ.).

16. 384 U.S. 224 (1966) (dissent per Harlan, Black and Stewart, JJ.).

17. United States v. Republic Steel Corp., 362 U.S. 482, 510 (1960).

of Engineers was given permitting authority by executive order.[18] The Corps at that time, however, was not structured to assume such broad administrative burdens.[19] There were additional weaknesses: the Rivers and Harbors Act, unlike the current Clean Water Act, vested sole permitting authority in the federal government, eliminating a state role, and was inapplicable to municipal dischargers, a major source of water pollution. Although not repealed, it largely has been superseded by the Clean Water Act as a viable means of restricting discharges into navigable waters. Unpermitted discharges, however, continue to be a violation of the Rivers and Harbors Act should they fall within that statute.[20]

[3] Congressional Preferences for State Regulation of Water Pollution

Under the modern Clean Water Act, states assume a great degree of responsibility for establishing and enforcing state water quality standards, and — utilizing national rather than state standards — technology-based limitations, subject to EPA approval.[21] This congressional preference for a state role has roots in the early regulatory scheme. During much of the twentieth century, states had been the primary regulatory authority over pollution discharges, with the federal government's role relegated to research and providing financial and technical assistance to the states.[22]

[4] Water Pollution Control Act

Congress enacted the first national legislation purporting to regulate water pollution in 1948, the Federal Water Pollution Control Act (FWPCA).[23] This Act, using the power of the purse, was directed mainly at encouraging the construction of municipal sewage treatment plants rather than establishing national water quality standards. Although the federal government provided scientific guidance for the establishment of state standards, the Act provided little enforcement power even if federal authorities had been inclined to assert a federal prerogative. Nevertheless, that Act, significantly amended, is the forebear of the current Clean Water Act.

[5] Water Quality Improvement Act of 1965

With enactment of the Water Quality Improvement Act in 1965, Congress required states to adopt water quality standards for interstate navigable waters, loosely subject to approval by the now-defunct Federal Water Pollution Control Administration. Although that agency took steps to coordinate state water quality standards, and to

---

18. Exec. Order No. 11,288, 31 Fed. Reg. 9261 (1966).

19. STEVER & DOLIN, ENVIRONMENTAL LAW AND PRACTICE, § 3.01, n.7 (CBC).

20. 33 U.S.C. § 407.

21. The distinction between "water quality standards" and "technology-based" or "effluent limitations" is explained at § 6.03[B][2][b].

22. See STEVER & DOLIN, ENVIRONMENTAL LAW AND PRACTICE, § 3.01[1].

23. 62 Stat. 1155. The FWPCA also was known as the Water Quality Act.

encourage the adoption of effluent limitations,[24] as an alternative to general water quality standards, federal efforts at persuasion generally were not successful. Local industrial interests responsible for discharges of pollutants into water bodies could often use as leverage a threat to move to another less restrictive state to persuade the home state to relax water quality standards.

[B] Early State Attempts to Control Water Pollution — Promulgation of Water Quality Standards for Different Classifications of Water Bodies

Before 1972, the usual manner by which states sought to manage water pollution was to classify water bodies within the state by type of use, and then promulgate ambient water quality standards for each classification. The appropriate water quality standards then would be applied to water bodies which received discharges of contamination and industrial wastes. Water bodies generally were divided into four classifications, which have echoes in the current Clean Water Act. A "Class A" water body contained potable sources of water. A "Class B" water body was "fishable and swimmable," i.e., not necessarily fit for drinking, but acceptable for recreational uses. A "Class C" water body was polluted, but still might be viable as a habitat. A "Class D" water body was so polluted as to be essentially devoid of non-microbial aquatic life and not useful for any purpose other than sewage disposal.[25] Typically, state water quality standards were imposed to maintain the existing classification rather than to upgrade a water body. Under industry pressure, water bodies might even be downgraded to a lesser use, with a correlating relaxation of standards. Notably, the modern CWA has an anti-degradation provision prohibiting the downgrading of use (see § 6.03[B][2]).

Water quality standards utilized by the states typically imposed numerical limits on oil and grease, pH, total suspended solids (TSS), biochemical oxygen demand (BOD), coliform bacteria, turbidity, phenols, chromium, and other heavy metals. However, many other pollutants were not specified in state water quality standards, or else small quantities of potentially toxic pollutants evaded regulation.[26] In contrast with the modern Clean Water Act, if the pollutant was not specified, it was not included. Moreover, water quality often was measured, not at the "end of the pipe," as in the CWA, but rather in "mixing zones" downstream from the discharging facility.

As an evaluation of genuine water quality, however, measuring pollutants in a designated mixing zone often was ineffective: larger mixing zones, by diluting the proportion of pollutants discharged into the water body, might conceal total quantities

---

24. Effluent is waste material discharged into the environment. Effluent limitations refer to "any restriction … on quantities, rates and concentrations of chemical, physical, biological, and other constituents which are discharged from point sources into navigable waters…." 33 U.S.C. § 1362(11); CWA § 502(11); see also ROBINSON, ENVIRONMENTAL LAW LEXICON (Law Journal Press 2016).

25. See STEVER & DOLIN, ENVIRONMENTAL LAW AND PRACTICE, § 3.01[3].

26. Id. § 3.01[3][c].

discharged; discharges in the immediate vicinity of the pipes could create pockets of significant pollution, deadly to ecosystems, which would not be reflected downstream at the mixing zone; the parameters of the mixing zones were arbitrary from a biological perspective; the discharge of warm or hot water in one location might have unpredictable consequences with respect to a water body's thermocline in other locations.[27] And, of course, the size and location of the mixing zones were always susceptible to negotiation at the administrative level, as well as politically. Most significantly for enforcement, if there were multiple dischargers, discharging similar pollutants in a water body, it was difficult to identify which discharger was responsible when water quality standards were not met.[28] Further, the interstate locations of many streams and rivers, and even some lakes, created jurisdictional uncertainties.

The significant increase in the pollution of water bodies across the nation, particularly in populated areas, underscored the ineffectiveness of a system relying on the states' monopoly over regulation of water pollution. It also demonstrated the need for a new national policy emphasizing the interrelatedness of pollution sources and environmental consequences, as well as the interstate nature of the problem. The result is the modern Clean Water Act.

[C] Delay in Enacting National Policy Can Have Serious Consequences

A half century of enforcement under the Clean Water Act has now passed, and the benefits of enforcement under nationwide standards is increasingly obvious as many water bodies have been consistently upgraded. However, gaps that the original legislation left unaddressed have allowed some clusters and types of water pollution to persist and even expand in the absence of timely water quality controls. Since there often is a time lag between a polluting act and its consequences, many of the effects of the absence of a national policy for so long are still with us today, despite great general improvement in the nation's water quality. Just one dramatic example makes the point. Discharges which historically have entered the Mississippi watershed, which drains 40 percent of the land area of the contiguous United States, have had extensive, and currently advancing, biochemical effects on the Gulf of Mexico. The Mississippi River releases 580 cubic kilometers of water into the Gulf annually. Between 1960 and the first edition of this book, the amount of dissolved nitrogen tripled, and phosphorous levels doubled at the receiving end, mostly from agricultural sources spread across the Midwest. Both chemicals have excessively stimulated the growth of phytoplankton in the Gulf, whose feces and skeletons increasingly have littered the marine floor, spawning, in lower but rising water columns, a thick mat of bacteria which consume them but which also reduce oxygen levels. The consequence has been the creation — and expansion — of a massive dead hypoxic zone, inhabited by in-

27. *Id.* § 3.01[3][d].
28. *Id.* § 3.01[4], [5].

creasing quantities of sulfur-oxidizing bacteria, and decreasing numbers of other sea life — with surviving aquatic life greatly stressed. This is in a region that provides the United States with over 40 percent of its commercial fisheries. Oceanographers are convinced of the links between the increased nitrification, the hypoxia in the lower water columns, and the consequential ecological changes.[29] However, agricultural sources remain largely exempt from Clean Water Act regulation (see § 6.03[B][1][d], *below*). In the third decade of the 21st century, the problem persists, in recent years coupled with massive oil spills which have created their own hypoxic zones in the Gulf of Mexico.[30]

[D] Federal Water Pollution Control Act of 1977 — Modern Clean Water Act (CWA)

Effective federal enforcement of water quality on a national scale arrived with en-actment of the 1972 Federal Water Pollution Control Act,[31] significantly amending the prior statute. Primary regulatory authority was vested in the fledgling Environmental Protection Agency. The 1977 amendments to the 1972 Act constituted the Clean Water Act (CWA), which was amended again by the 1987 Water Quality Act. Although the legislation is still identified as the Federal Water Pollution Prevention and Control Act in the United States Code, it commonly is termed, *in toto*, the Clean Water Act.

The new legislation directed a shift away from sole reliance on water quality stan-dards to the additional use of technology-based standards, or "end of pipe" limita-tions, on the discharge of a broad range of pollutants. Although states still employ their own water quality standards for particular water bodies, these standards may not supplant, but may only supplement, the federally mandated technology-based standards (see §§ 6.03[B][2], 6.03[D]). The CWA, although still vesting significant oversight responsibility and enforcement authority in the states, nevertheless placed state regulation under the umbrella of a comprehensive national permitting system. With enactment of the CWA, Congress was not content to seek maintenance of the status quo. Rather, in a sharp change from the former inchoate policy, the CWA affirmatively manifests Congress's intent to inexorably improve water quality. The CWA subjects all polluters, at a minimum, to nationally applicable limitations devised to upgrade the nation's waters. Although states may employ a state tech-nology-based permitting system as a substitute for the national permitting system (see § 6.03[D]), the state scheme is subject to EPA approval and must be as stringent as, or more exacting than, the federal standards. The role of federalism is a major feature of the modern CWA.

---

29. Scientific American, Nov. 1997, at 17–20. See, also, https://ocean-today.noaa.gov>dead-zonegulf-2021. See, also, EPA, "Northern Gulf of Mexico Hypoxic Zone," (2019), at EPA.gov.

30. The oil spills have also inflicted significant damage on the shorelines of Gulf states and on the marine wetland ecologies that are integral to the open sea's biological health. See, generally, § 6.07[B], [D][2], *below*.

31. 33 U.S.C. §§ 1251–1387.

This regulatory scheme was a reaction to the prior half century of unsuccessful state management of water pollution. The Act recognizes the need, not so much to analyze the pollution problem from the perspective of where the pollution is received, but rather to control how much is sent. The theory is that if the discharge of pollutants is restricted at the inception, then water quality necessarily will improve over time. The validation of this theory, as well as the efficacy of federal control over standards and, ultimately over enforcement, has become self-evident.

The CWA also regulates the discharge of dredge and fill material, formerly, and still, within the jurisdiction of the Army Corps of Engineers, now under the aegis of CWA § 404 (see discussion in § 6.07). This jurisdiction, which is shared in part with EPA, is a relic of the Rivers and Harbors Act, as referenced in § 6.02[2]. Ocean dumping and other discharges, except for oil discharges, subject to certain geographic limits, fall under § 403 of the CWA (see discussion in § 6.05[B]). Maritime oil discharges are regulated by CWA § 311, as amended by the Oil Pollution Act of 1990 (see discussion in § 6.06[B]), which also has substantive provisions of its own, regulating spills (see § 6.06[C]). The Ports and Waterways Safety Act (see § 6.06[E]), imposing design and operation requirements on oil tankers, complements the Oil Pollution Act. Offshore and gas drilling are governed by the Outer Continental Shelf Lands Act (see § 6.06[D]).

Other federal environmental statutes, some derived from other enactments, also followed in the wake of the Clean Water Act. The Safe Drinking Water Act (see discussion in § 6.04[C]), derived from the 1944 Public Health Services Act, was enacted in its present form in 1974, and was substantially amended in 1986. The original statute, as the name implies, was a public health measure. Its restructuring into an environmental statute grafted on concepts used for water pollution controls.

The Resource Conservation and Recovery Act (RCRA), otherwise discussed in Chapter 7, also applies to contamination of groundwater by underground storage tanks (see discussion in § 6.04[D]). Viewed *in toto*, these statutes, and others mentioned in this chapter, operate together to impose permitting requirements and other restrictions and prohibitions on contamination of the nation's, and in part, the world's waters.

§ 6.03 Clean Water Act (CWA)

[A] Scope and Legislative Background of CWA

[1] CWA Regulates Discharges of Pollutants into Surface Waters

The CWA regulates direct as well as some indirect[32] discharges of pollutants into surface waters. Discharges generally come from the following three sources:

---

32. An indirect discharge would occur, for instance, when a polluter discharges non-domestic waste (i.e., not household sewage) to a treatment plant, rather than directly to a water body, and the treatment plant subsequently discharges to a water body. 40 C.F.R. § 122.2.

(1) Commercial/industrial sources;

(2) Sewage and other discharges from municipal water treatment plants, also known as "publicly owned treatment works" or "POTWs"; and

(3) Agricultural and stormwater runoff.

Categories (2) and (3), however, often evade CWA regulation. The CWA also regulates the dredging and filling of wetlands, discussed in § 6.07. Filling in or destruction of wetlands not only adds potential contaminants, but also threatens to impede the viability of wetlands as fresh water recharge zones, as natural devices for absorbing or at least slowing down flood waters, and as ecological nurseries. Although it is broad in scope, the CWA does not universally regulate water quality. It has some limitations, discussed below, which were built into the legislative definitions.

[2] Legislative Purposes of the CWA

Congress stated that the purpose of the CWA was to "restore and maintain the chemical, physical and biological integrity of the nation's waters."[33] To achieve this ideal, Congress established some lofty, but ambitious, goals. It was a "national goal" to eliminate the discharge of pollutants by 1985, and to enhance water quality nationally to a "fishable/swimmable" level by 1983.[34] Needless to say, the work goes on. Less ambitiously, Congress stated that it was now national policy to prohibit the discharge of *toxic* pollutants in toxic amounts;[35] to require states to develop and implement area-wide waste treatment management planning processes; and to have the nation support the research into, and development of, the technology required to eliminate the discharge of pollutants into navigable waters, the contiguous zone, and the ocean.[36] Generally, the CWA directly regulates pollution only from point sources (see definition in [B][1][d], *below*). However, Congress also stated a goal of developing and implementing programs "in an expeditious manner" to control pollution from both point sources and non-point sources.[37]

Congress also stated its intention of recognizing, preserving, and protecting "the primary responsibilities and rights of states" in pollution reduction, prevention and elimination.[38] This was a carry-over from the Act's former history (see § 6.02[A][3]). However, since all states were now subject to national technology-based standards, the inefficiency previously created by different and even conflicting state water quality standards theoretically would be eliminated. Although Congress stated its intention of allowing states to implement permit programs, the innovation of the CWA was

---

33. 33 U.S.C. § 1251(a); *see also* Catskill Mountains Chapter of Trout Unlimited v. City of New York, 273 F.3d 481 (2d Cir. 2001).

34. 33 U.S.C. §§ 1251(a)(1), (2).

35. 33 U.S.C. § 1251(1)(a), (3). For a listing of toxic pollutants, see 33 U.S.C. § 1317(a). For toxic pollutant standards, see 40 C.F.R. § 129.1, et seq. For permitting regarding toxic pollutants, see [C][2], below.

36. 33 U.S.C. § 1251(a)(3)–(6).

37. 33 U.S.C. § 1251(a)(6).

38. 33 U.S.C. § 1251(b).

to mandate that state permitting be at least as stringent as the CWA. Congress also wanted to encourage uniformity in state laws,[39] and interstate cooperation, extending to regional compacts,[40] so long as federal law and national standards remain paramount. The result is that there is less than meets the eye in terms of actual state independence in carrying out water pollution policy. For instance, the power of states to promulgate their own effluent limitations translates only into those limitations which exceed federal regulations, and state water quality standards may only coexist with, and not substitute for, effluent limitations.[41] Thus, states have been relegated more to the administrative realm, rather than the total regulatory realm which they formerly had enjoyed.

Congress also targeted the cleanup of specified water bodies, which had come to symbolize uncontrolled pollution run amok by the 1970s, such as the Hudson River, Chesapeake Bay, and Great Lakes.[42] The provision of funding for the construction of water treatment facilities was carried over from former law (see §6.02[A][4]). However, with a likely nod to Western states, the CWA may not interfere with a state's authority to allocate water resources within the state.[43]

[3] International Aspirations of the CWA

The CWA also includes a broad and essentially indefinite grant of power to the President to seek to achieve the prevention, reduction and elimination of water pollution internationally.[44] The ironic result, likely underscoring Congress's serious environmental concerns during that time period, was to direct the President to exercise powers — which he lacked beyond national borders — internationally, in furtherance of a statute having no international effectiveness. However, the grant of power will likely facilitate the authority of the President to enter into international agreements to reduce ocean pollution.

[4] EPA's Authority under the CWA

EPA is granted general administrative authority to carry out the provisions of the CWA, except as provided otherwise within the CWA itself.[45] EPA also is charged with a broad range of scientific and engineering research and development (R&D)

---

39. 33 U.S.C. §1253(a).

40. 33 U.S.C. §1253(b).

41. 33 U.S.C. §1313.

42. 33 U.S.C. §§1266–1268.

43. 33 U.S.C. §1251(g). However, to the extent that this section is inconsistent with specific substantive sections of the statute, the substantive sections prevail. Riverside Irrigation District v. Andrews, 758 F.2d 508 (10th Cir. 1985). Hence, state allocation of water resources is to be accommodated, but subject to a CWA permit. In this case, the state entity wanted to construct a dam, but this would have impacted on a downstream population of whooping cranes, which also triggered concerns under the Federal Endangered Species Act.

44. 33 U.S.C. §1251(c).

45. 33 U.S.C. §1251(d). For instance, the Army Corps of Engineers is also given authority with respect to dredge and fill permits (see §6.07) and navigation-related problems.

responsibilities, in addition to its regulatory and enforcement responsibilities,[46] in furtherance of which it has the authority to make R&D grants, subject, of course, to congressional largesse. For the attorney, however, the primary interest in the CWA is in its permitting scheme (see § 6.03[C]) and enforcement (see § 6.03[E]).

[B] Basic Terms Defined

[1] Terms Triggering Applicability of the CWA

[a] Terms Interlock and Are Interpreted Broadly

To understand when and how the CWA operates, it is essential to grasp its nuts-and-bolts. The most basic components of the CWA are its threshold terms, whose meanings are not always self-evident. In its most basic role, the CWA addresses pollution, which it defines as "the man-made or man-induced alteration of the chemical, physical, biological, and radiological integrity of water."[47]

The CWA applies to any *discharge* of a *pollutant* from a *point source* into the *navigable waters of the United States.* The definitions of these terms interlock quite a bit. Courts generally have interpreted them broadly to effectuate congressional intent. If these circumstances exist, then any discharge must comply with a NPDES or SPDES permit, respectively EPA and state-issued discharge permits (see discussion in [C] and [D], *below*).[48]

[b] Discharge

A "discharge" is "any addition of any pollutant to navigable waters from any point source [or to] waters of the contiguous zone[49] of the ocean from any point source other than a vessel or other floating craft."[50] Note that a discharging vessel may directly trigger the CWA's permit requirements in other navigable waters, although not in the contiguous zone. The CWA, though it defines "discharge" and other relevant terms, does not define "addition." Courts have divided on the meaning to be accorded the term.[51] The "addition" must be made *by* the point source.[52] Hence, a dam through which pollutants, already in the stream, flow does not add the pollutants

---

46. 33 U.S.C. § 1254, 1254a.

47. 33 U.S.C. § 1362(19).

48. 33 U.S.C. § 1311(f). For a more comprehensive discussion of EPA's jurisdiction under the CWA, see ROBINSON, ENVIRONMENTAL REGULATION OF REAL PROPERTY § 12.02 (Law Journal Press 2021).

49. *See* 33 U.S.C. § 1362(9). The contiguous zone is the entire zone established by the U.S. in the Convention of the Territorial Sea and Contiguous Zone, Article 24.

50. 33 U.S.C. § 1362(12).

51. *See* Catskill Mountains Chapter of Trout Unlimited v. City of New York ("*Catskill II*"), 451 F.3d 77 (2d Cir. 2006), *cert denied*, 549 U.S. 1252, 127 S. Ct. 1373 (2007).

52. United States *ex rel.* Tennessee Valley Authority v. Tennessee Valley Water Quality Board, 717 F.2d 992, 998 (6th Cir. 1983).

to the downstream flow.[53] As a practical matter, one could not expect the dam operator to stop the river flowing while a permit is issued, and the operator has no control over the existence of the pollutants in the water, so that this application of the rule makes sense. By comparison, dirt returned by placer miners to a stream "discharged" through a sluice thereby was added to the stream.[54] In 2008, EPA adopted the so-called "unified waters" rule during the waning years of the administration of George W. Bush. The theory proposed that no addition, and thus no discharge, occurs when a pollutant is simply moved, or allowed to move, from one part of a water system to another.[55] This interpretation of the statute, of course, would have significant consequences for permitting involving many complex water bodies. However, the doctrine triggered an extensive round of litigation which injected considerable uncertainty about its enforceability. This provides an example of how the intrusion of politics into environmental policies that should rely on science can sometimes distort achievement of the statutory goals.[56] Another recent development in evaluating whether a discharge has occurred within the CWA, that is, from a point source into navigable waters of the United States, is the conduit theory. This theory proposes that an underground discharge subsequent to which pollution travels to a water body within federal jurisdiction could trigger the CWA. The Supreme Court majority, in *County of Maui, Hawaii v Hawaii Wildlife Fund*,[57] allowed that a subsurface discharge thereby could occur within the meaning of the statute if the point source was close in proximity to the location where the pollutant stream entered the water body and occurrence was close in time to the discharge from the point source.[58]

---

53. National Wildlife Federation v. Gorsuch, 693 F.2d 156 (D.C. Cir. 1982). However, other courts have concluded that the logic of *National Wildlife Federation v. Gorsuch* has been "severely eroded," and that the movement of water and its sediments through a dam is an addition to the receiving water. *See* Greenfield Mills v. Macklin, 361 F.3d 934 (7th Cir. 2004); *see also* Catskill Mountains Chapter of Trout Unlimited v. City of New York, 273 F.3d 481 (2d Cir. 2001).

54. Rybachek v. Environmental Protection Agency, 904 F.3d 1276 (9th Cir. 1990).

55. The underlying theory, proposed years earlier, was initially challenged prior to formal rule making either as contrary to the statutory intent, or as impracticable under many circumstances. The Second Circuit, upon reargument in *Catskill II, supra* n. 51, the First Circuit (DuBois v. Department of Agriculture, 102 F.3d 1273, 1296 [1st Cir. 1996], *cert. denied*, 521 U.S. 1119 [1997]) and the Ninth Circuit (North Plains Resource Council v. Fidelity Exploration and Development, 325 F.3d 1115, 1163 [Cir. 2003], *cert. denied*, 540 U.S. 967 [2003], in rulings preceding EPA's rule, found the unified waters doctrine untenable, while the Supreme Court equivocated under the facts of the case in *South Florida Water Management District v. Miccosukee Tribe of Indians*, 541 U.S. 95 (2004). One significant difficulty, of course, pertains to how one defines a water system, and how unified it must be.

56. For further discussion as to how the water body was to be defined, see § 6.03[B][f].

57. ___ U.S. ___, 140 S. Ct. 1462, 206 L. Ed. 2d 640 (2020), *vacating and remanding* 886 F.3d 737, *modifying* 881 F.3d 754 (9th Cir. 2019).

58. In this case, a waste stream was deposited in an injection well, from which pollutants seeped into ground water which entered vents opening into the floor of the Pacific Ocean. Rather than imposing more specific standards as to either criterion, the Supreme Court remanded for further fact-finding along these lines. Nevertheless, the conduit theory espousing a possible subsurface hydrological connection as a basis for CWA jurisdiction was ratified in the Court's abrogation of two paired Sixth Circuit rulings, *Tennessee Clean Water Network v. Tennessee Valley Authority*, 905 F.3d 436 (6th Cir.

For some pollutants, however, such as radiological, chemical or biological warfare agents, or high-level radioactive or medical wastes, no permit will be given and the discharge is illegal per se.[59]

[c] Pollutant

A pollutant is anything introduced into the water that alters its physical, chemical or biological integrity.[60] Examples provided by the statute include "dredged spoil, solid waste, incinerator residue, sewage, garbage, sewage sludge, munitions, chemical wastes, biological materials, radioactive materials,[61] heat, wrecked or discarded equipment, rock, sand, cellar dirt and industrial, municipal and agricultural waste discharged into water."[62] The list is non-exclusive. Hence, "chemical oxygen demand" was found by a court to be a pollutant, since it fit the definition of pollution in that it altered the chemical, physical and biological integrity of the water.[63] A substance need not even be waste, strictly speaking. New York City adds chlorine to water pumped from the Hudson River and from its upstate reservoirs to render it safe for human consumption; however, chlorine-treated water released back into a reservoir or river would be a pollutant.[64] Pesticides, even if legally registered and applied in compliance with FIFRA (see 8.01), would be pollutants subject to CWA enforcement when they drain into a water body.[65] Even natural materials, not innately contaminating, which are shed during transportation by water can be pollutants if they alter the physical or biological characteristics of the water.[66]

"Pollutant" does not include sewage from vessels discharged into the ocean, which is regulated under the Marine Protection Act (see discussion in § 6.05), although it does include marine sanitation devices.[67] It also does not include certain liquid or

---

2018), and *Kentucky Waterways Alliance v. Kentucky Utilities Co.*, 905 F.3d 925 (6th Cir. 2018), which had rejected reliance on a hydrological connection. A prior Fourth Circuit ruling found a basis for CWA jurisdiction as to polluted surface water which seeps into groundwater from which it then enters navigable waters of the United States. *See* Forever v. Kinder Morgan Energy Partners, 887 F.3d 637 (4th Cir. 2018). As of this edition, these important issues need further clarification.

59. 33 U.S.C. 1311(f).

60. 33 U.S.C. § 1362(1).

61. However, the EPA administratively excludes many radioactive materials, specifically radium and accelerator-produced isotopes, from enforcement under the CWA despite its statutory authority, in favor of regulation by the Nuclear Regulatory Commission. 40 C.F.R. § 122.2. *See* Train v. Colorado Public Interest Research Group, 426 U.S. 1, 6 (1976) (finding administrative exclusion to be valid).

62. 33 U.S.C. § 1362(6).

63. FMC Corp. v. Train, 539 F.2d 973 (4th Cir. 1976).

64. *See* Hudson River Fishermen's Association v. City of New York, 751 F. Supp. 1088 (S.D.N.Y. 1990), *aff'd without opinion*, 940 F.2d 649 (2d Cir. 1991).

65. Peconic Baykeeper v. Suffolk County, 600 F.3d180 (2d Cir. 2010); The National Cotton Council of America v. Environmental Protection Agency, 553 F.3d 927 (6th Cir. 2009).

66. Natural Resources Defense Council v. Environmental Protection Agency, 279 F.3d 1180 (9th Cir. 2002). The example here was bark scraped off of bundled logs being floated out of roadless wilderness areas which, while seemingly harmless, can bioaccumulate on stream bottoms and interfere with the riverine ecology.

67. 33 U.S.C. § 1322.

gaseous products used in connection with "injection wells," injected into the ground to facilitate production of oil or gas, also regulated elsewhere (see § 6.06). This has become a more significant, and more controversial, exemption with the rapid development of hydrofracking, especially in the northeastern states where the Marcellis Shale formations are found. With hydrofracking, substantial volumes of water and chemical treatments are injected into subterranean areas where natural gas deposits have been found to exist. The pressure of the injections pulverizes the sedimentary rock and releases the gas, which is then brought to the surface. The injections, however, have heightened concerns for adverse impacts on water quality. The CWA also does not reach water "derived in association" with oil or gas production, which is disposed of in a well, when the well is used to facilitate production, or when the well is used for disposal purposes, so long as state approval was given for such disposal.[68] In order to approve the disposal in a well, the state has to determine that injection into the well or disposal in the well does not degrade either ground or surface water.[69] However, EPA may not, by rule making, create exemptions that are not specified in the statute.[70]

The term "pollutant" necessarily includes "toxic pollutants," which are "those pollutants or combinations of pollutants, including disease-causing agents, which after discharge and under exposure, ingestion, inhalation, or assimilation into any organism, either directly from the environment or indirectly by ingestion through food chains, will, on the basis of information available to the Administrator, cause death, disease, behavioral abnormalities, cancer, genetic mutations, physiological malfunctions (including malfunctions in reproduction), or physical deformations, in such organisms or their offspring."[71] Congress's eventual goal is to preclude the discharge of any toxic pollutant into the environment. Thus, toxic pollutants are controlled more strictly than others (see discussion in [C][2], *below*).

[d] Point Source

The discharge into navigable waters must be from a point source in order to directly trigger the CWA, although states are expected to implement programs to control non-point source pollution. A "point source" is "any discernible, confined and discrete conveyance, including but not limited to any pipe, ditch, channel, tunnel, conduit, well, discrete fissure, container, rolling stock, concentrated animal feeding operation,[72] or vessel or other floating craft, from which pollutants are or may be

---

68. 33 U.S.C. § 1362(6).

69. 33 U.S.C. § 1322.

70. The National Cotton Council of America v. Environmental Protection Agency, 553 F.3d 927 (6th Cir. 2009).

71. 33 U.S.C. § 1362(13).

72. An animal feeding operation is defined as a lot or facility in which animals are stabled, or confined, or fed or maintained for 45 days or more within a twelve-month period; and the lot or facility is not used for crops or for growing forage. Whether the operation is "concentrated" depends on the size of the animal population, the nearness to waters of the United States, the amount of wastes reaching these waters, the manner in which waste is conveyed to these waters, and the slope, vegetation, rainfall, and other factors affecting the likelihood of a discharge of the animal wastes into such waters.

discharged."[73] The regulations also specifically add "concentrated aquatic animal production facilities"; discharges into aquaculture projects;[74] silvicultural point sources;[75]
and stormwater discharges, as further defined in the regulations,[76] as point sources
under the CWA.[77] The point source does not have to be the point of origin for the
pollutants, but need only be the point of discharge. Hence, a water tunnel, which
conveys water from one water body to another,[78] a dam,[79] a sewer outfall that merely
discharges accumulated runoff originating elsewhere in a stormwater collection system,[80] and a pumping facility that conveys water from a canal into a water conservation
area[81] are point sources, through which water-borne pollutants flow and from which
they may be discharged. The term is broadly construed to contemplate some discrete
conveyance; by contrast, one court has held that a human being tossing out medical
waste does not fit the definition.[82] However, the conveyance need not itself be man-

---

The designation whether the operation is "concentrated," and hence defined to be a point source for
CWA purposes, may be done on a case-by-case basis. 40 C.F.R. § 122.23.

73. 33 U.S.C § 1362(14).

74. "Aquaculture" generally refers to projects which are designed for the production of food in
a managed aquatic system. *See* ROBINSON, ENVIRONMENTAL LAW LEXICON. An aquaculture project is
defined as a "defined managed water area which uses discharges of pollutants into that designated
area for the maintenance or production of harvestable freshwater, estuarine, or marine plants or animals." 40 C.F.R. § 122.25. Although the general concept suggests a beneficial recycling of pollutants
for a biologically beneficial use, there are environmentally adverse results if the process is not carefully
managed. With the decline of valuable species of salmon from the Pacific Northwest, salmon fisheries
have become commercially valuable enterprises. Notwithstanding that the industry relieves some
pressures from overfished wild stocks, these fisheries have also become a notorious concentrated
source of pollution from salmon feed and feces. They also threaten still-wild salmon stocks which,
with hybridization, can lose the homing instinct specific to particular rivers that are so critical to
their breeding success.

75. Silvicultural point sources include "any discernible, confined and discrete conveyance related
to rock crushing, gravel washing, log sorting, or log storage facilities which are operated in connection
with silvicultural activities and from which pollutants are discharged into the waters of the United
States." Silvicultural activities may also include non-point sources, which do not trigger CWA requirements. Such non-point sources include nursery operations, site preparation, reforestation and
subsequent cultural treatment, thinning, proscribed burning, pest and fire control, harvesting operations, surface drainage, or road construction and maintenance from which there is only natural
runoff. 40 C.F.R. § 122.27. However, even some of these activities may trigger the need for a CWA
permit, such as under CWA § 404 (33 U.S.C. § 1344) for the discharge of dredge and fill materials.

76. 40 C.F.R. § 122.26.

77. 40 C.F.R. § 122.1(b)(2).

78. Catskill Mountains Chapter of Trout Unlimited v. City of New York, 273 F.3d 481 (2d Cir.
2001).

79. Greenfield Mills v. Macklin, 361 F.3d 934 (7th Cir. 2004). In this case, the dam acted as a
point source as the water level behind it was being lowered, causing the accumulation of sediment
and debris rather than unchanged river water to pass through the dam.

80. National Resources Defense Council v. County of Los Angeles, 2011 U.S. App. LEXIS 14443
(9th Cir. 2011).

81. South Florida Water Management District v. Miccosukee Tribe of Indians, 541 U.S. 95, 105
(2004).

82. United States v. Plaza Health Labs, Inc., 3 F.3d 643, 649 (2d Cir. 1993), *cert. denied*, 512 U.S.
1245 (1994).

made: an eroded gully or a ditch carrying leachate is a point source.[83] Nor need it be intended to be a conveyance: a hazardous waste lagoon which overflows would be a point source.[84] Likewise, overflowing ponds, leaking collection tanks and eroded berms are all point sources,[85] as is a pile of coal mining waste from which leachate flows.[86] A liquid manure storage and spreading operation, which conveyed manure through pipes to fields to be fertilized, was a point source from which liquefied manure inadvertently seeped into ditches from which it entered a stream.[87] For a designated pollutant, such as munitions, shipboard artillery which fires the shells is the point source.[88]

However, the mode of conveyance for the waste stream should involve channeling of some kind in contrast to unchanneled surface runoff, the latter constituting a non-point source.[89] An injection well into which pollutants are deposited which results in a subsurface seepage into ground water or permeable subsurface geologic strata which eventually enters waters of the United States could be a point source. This presents the further question, though, whether it would constitute a discharge directly into waters of the United States requiring NPDES or SPDES permitting under the CWA. The United States Supreme Court has allowed that the CWA would be triggered if the pollutants were thereby conveyed by subsurface hydrology or geology close in time and proximity to waters of the United States, although as of the time this edition is being written, no bright-line qualifying criteria have been defined.[90]

Agricultural stormwater discharges and "return flows" from irrigated agriculture are specifically exempted from the definition of point source.[91] Although these sources otherwise would fit the general notion of what a point source is, and significant nitrification doubtless originates from these sources, Congress evidently found it ex-

---

83. Sierra Club v. Abston Construction Co., 620 F.2d 41 (5th Cir. 1980).

84. United States v. Oxford Royal Mushroom Products, Inc., 487 F. Supp. 852 (E.D. Pa. 1980).

85. O'Leary v. Moyer's Landfill, Inc., 523 F. Supp. 642, 654 (E.D. Pa. 1981).

86. Rayle Coal Co. v. West Virginia Dept. of Natural Resources, 401 S.E.2d 682 (W. Va. 1990). This conclusion, however, may no longer be good law. *See* Sierra Club v. Virginia Electric & Power Co., 903 F.3d 403 (4th Cir. 2018). See also Upstate Forever v. Kinder Morgan Energy Partners LP, 887 F.3d 637 (4th Cir. 2018), which was abrogated by County of Maui, Hawaii v. Hawaii Wildlife Fund, ___ U.S. ___, 140 S. Ct. 1462, 206 L. Ed. 2d 640 (2020), *vacating and remanding* 886 F.3d 737, *modifying* 881 F.3d 754 (9th Cir. 2019), with no clear standards yet emerging from the Supreme Court.

87. Concerned Area Residents for the Environment v. Southview Farms, 34 F.3d 114 (2d Cir. 1994), *cert. denied*, 514 U.S. 1082 (1995).

88. Romero-Barcelo v. Brown, 643 F.2d 835 (1st Cir. 1981), *rev'd on other grounds sub. nom.* Weinberger v. Romero-Barcelo, 456 U.S. 305 (1982).

89. Cordiano v. Metacon Gun Club, Inc., 575 F.3d 199 (2d Cir. 2009); Sierra Club v. Virginia Electric & Power Co., 903 F.3d 403 (4th Cir. 2018).

90. County of Maui, Hawaii v. Hawaii Wildlife Fund, ___ U.S. ___, 140 S. Ct.1462, 206 L. Ed. 2d 640 (2020), *vacating and remanding* 886 F.3d 737, *modifying* 881 F.3d 754 (9th Cir. 2019). The point of the remand order was for the lower court to make findings regarding the distance between the point of discharge and the Pacific Ocean in this case and the time that it took for a waste stream to cover that distance.

91. 33 U.S.C § 1362 (14).

pedient to accommodate the nation's agricultural sector in this regard.[92] However, in the example given above, the liquid manure distribution system was found not to be exempt, either as stormwater runoff, when rain washed effluent into ditches, or as agricultural runoff.[93] Congressional intent, as manifested in the statutory language, prevails, of course, over agency goals. If the conveyance fits within the statutory definition of a point source, an agency lacks the power to define it, by regulation, as a non-point source. For example, a court has found that aerial spraying fits the statutory definition of a point source for the subsequent runoff of pesticides into a water body; neither the Forest Service nor EPA could define it, by regulation, as an exemption related to silvicultural activities.[94]

[e] Non-Point Source Pollution/Stormwater Runoff

Originally, runoff, such as stormwater runoff from streets, roads, and parking lots, often containing heavy metals and other toxic pollutants, or runoff from agricultural fields, forestry or mining operations, or runoff from construction sites, did not fall within reach of the Clean Water Act, since these are not point sources. However, if runoff was channeled through or contained by a point source, from which the pollutant-containing runoff was discharged into navigable waters, then the CWA was triggered.

Now, although some discharges composed entirely of stormwater (i.e., surface runoff or stormwater runoff which discharges to surface water) may not require a permit, this exclusion is significantly limited.[95] Stormwater runoff which is associated with industrial[96] or commercial activity is defined in the regulations as emanating from a point source (i.e., the entire facility or site is deemed to constitute a point source) and must be under permit. Stormwater runoff from parking lots or buildings which happen to be on an industrial site may not require a permit, but any mixing of such runoff with any other runoff (e.g., process wastewater) on that site triggers the permit requirement. Industrial facilities may apply for inclusion within a general or group permit, such as when a single company owns several facilities or a trade as-

---

92. For a critique of point source as well as non-point source agricultural exclusions, especially insofar as agricultural sources add considerably to the pollution load of nearby water bodies, see Susan E. Schell, *The Uncertain Future of Clean Water Act Agricultural Pollution Exemptions After Concerned Area Residents for the Environment v. Southview Farms*, 31 LAND & WATER L. REV. 113 (1996).

93. Concerned Area Residents for the Environment v. Southview Farms, 34 F.3d 114 (2d Cir. 1994), *cert. denied*, 514 U.S. 1082 (1995).

94. League of Wilderness Defenders/Blue Mountain Biodiversity Project v. Forsgren, 309 F.3d 1181 (9th Cir. 2002).

95. *See generally* 40 C.F.R. § 122.26.

96. EPA categorizes several types of facilities or activities as "industrial," at 40 C.F.R. § 122.26(b)(14), a degree of detail that is beyond the purview of this book. The point to note, however, is that discharges from these facilities presumably require a permit, even if there is no demonstrated contact between the runoff and the industrial operation. An exception exists for runoff from parking lots and buildings, as noted.

sociation seeks to include all similar member facilities under the same permit, although EPA reserves the right to require an individual permit, especially if the discharges of stormwater runoff threaten water quality standards.[97]

A stormwater discharge from a medium or large municipal "separate storm sewer system" (i.e., street and curb runoff which is not discharged to a POTW) requires a permit. Medium systems are those serving a population of 100,000 or more, while large systems serve in excess of 250,000 people. The discharge for those purposes is the water exiting the system, rather than storm water entering the system. Very large systems may be hindered in controlling the flow of pollutants, especially if there are numerous points of entry, but they remain responsible for staying in compliance with permit limitations on discharges. The substantial and complex Los Angeles County wastewater system illustrates not only the difficulties of, but also the mandate for, NPDES compliance.[98] The system operator may apply for a system-wide permit covering the entire system. Conversely, EPA still may require individual permits for different types of discharges within the system.[99]

Operators of construction sites also may be subject to permitting for runoff.[100] In addition, EPA is given statutory authority to determine that under some circumstances, stormwater runoff, even if otherwise exempted, contributes to a violation of a water quality standard or significantly adds pollutants to waters of the United States, in which case a permit will be required.[101]

[f] Navigable Waters of the United States

"Navigable waters" traditionally were given an extremely broad reading by courts, although the United States Supreme Court has narrowed the interpretation in recent years. The statute defines navigable waters simply as the "waters of the United States" — without further qualification — including the territorial seas. The territorial seas are "the belt of the seas measured from the line of ordinary low water along that portion of the coast which is in direct contact with the open sea and the line marking the seaward limit of inland waters, and extending seaward to a distance of three miles."[102] No mention is made of actual navigability.

Historically, navigability was equated with waters subject to the ebb and flow of the tide, which had been a jurisdictional element of the Rivers and Harbors Act. Alternatively, the waters could be "navigable in fact ... when they form in their ordinary condition by themselves, or by uniting with other waters, a continued highway" between states, usable by commerce.[103] Although the definition of "navigability" was

---

97. *See* 55 Fed. Reg. 47,803; 55 Fed. Reg. 48,022.
98. Natural Resources Defense Council v. County of Los Angeles, 636 F.3d 1235 (9th Cir. 2011).
99. *See* 40 C.F.R. § 122.26(a)(3)(ii).
100. 40 C.F.R. § 122.26(c)(1)(G).
101. 33 U.S.C. § 1342(p)(1), (2).
102. 33 U.S.C. § 1362(8).
103. The Daniel Ball, 77 U.S. 557 (1870).

expanded by early caselaw to reach waters which could become navigable with reasonable improvement,[104] pre-CWA federal jurisdiction historically still was limited to the water's potential for interstate transportation.

With the CWA, however, Congress wanted the definition to be accorded its "broadest constitutional interpretation"[105] to ensure that the legislation could "repudiate limits that had been placed on federal regulation by earlier water pollution control statutes," extending federal jurisdiction over waters considered to be up to this time non-navigable.[106] Hence, despite the reliance of the CWA on the Commerce Clause,[107] federal jurisdiction for the CWA became essentially de-linked from actual navigation as a necessity for commerce. Thus, whether or not a water body is actually navigable is not a jurisdictional pre-condition.

EPA defines the term "navigable waters" in the Code of Federal Regulations as including: all waters currently used, or ever used, or which could be used in interstate or foreign commerce, including, in addition, all waters subject to the ebb and flow of the tide; all wetlands which are adjacent to waters of the United States; all other waters, even if intrastate, including lakes, rivers, streams (including intermittent streams, which are common in the West), mudflats, sandflats, wetlands, sloughs, prairie potholes, wet meadows, or natural ponds which "would affect or could affect" interstate or foreign commerce.[108] EPA also deems waters to be covered by the CWA if these waters could be used by interstate or foreign travelers for recreational or other purposes; or are waters from which fish or shellfish could be taken and sold in interstate or foreign commerce; or which could be used by industries in interstate commerce for industrial purposes. The CWA is also deemed by EPA to reach all "impoundments of waters" when those waters are taken from waters of the United States or their tributaries.[109]

Courts, in applying EPA's definitions, have found that the CWA governs discharges into non-navigable tributaries of navigable streams,[110] to intermittent streams,[111] to wetlands which, while not navigable, are in reasonable proximity to other waters of

---

104. United States v. Appalachian Electric Power Co., 331 U.S. 337 (1940).

105. See remarks of Rep. Dingell at 118 Cong. Rec. 33,757.

106. United States v. Riverside Bayview Homes, 474 U.S. 121 (1985).

107. *See, e.g.*, Hoffman Homes, Inc. v. Environmental Protection Agency, 999 F.2d 256 (7th Cir. 1993) (widespread use of wetlands for hunting, fishing, bird observation and other potentially interstate revenue-related activities triggered federal jurisdiction under the Commerce Clause).

108. 40 C.F.R. § 122.2. Some of these broad regulatory terms, though, have been clarified by the Supreme Court in recent years to better accord with the statutory text so that an exclusive reliance on the regulatory terminology may present interpretive risks.

109. 40 C.F.R. § 122.2. This addresses the practice of some facilities which create internal streams within a large site for wastewater processing or for cooling purposes.

110. United States v, Hubenka, 438 F.3d 1026, 1034 (10th Cir. 2006); Headwaters, Inc. v. Talent Irrigation District, 243 F.3d 526, 533 (9th Cir. 2001); United States v. Texas Pipeline Co., 611 F.2d 345 (10th Cir. 1979).

111. United States v. Phelps Dodge Corp., 391 F. Supp. 1181 (D. Ariz. 1975); Avoyelles Sportsmen's League v. Alexander, 511 F. Supp. 278 (W.D. La. 1981), *aff'd in part sub. nom.* Avoyelles Sportsmen's League v. Marsh, 715 F.2d 897 (5th Cir. 1983).

the United States,[112] to an artificial water body connected to navigable waters only by irrigation and flood control structures,[113] and even to man-made streams within a facility created for the discharge of wastewater.[114] Early courts found the CWA to apply even when a water body was seasonally dry,[115] or man-made.[116] If a water body had been historically navigable, then that designation remains so for CWA purposes, even if navigational access thereafter was blocked.[117] Earlier caselaw held that even a water body entirely contained within a state, not used for commercial navigation, and not connected by surface waters to any interstate water body, was considered "waters of the United States" if it was a habitat for migratory water fowl or potentially attracts hunters or other recreationists from across state borders because of the potential for interstate commerce.[118]

However, the Supreme Court in recent decades has incrementally started to restrict agency jurisdiction that relied on strained assertions of jurisdiction over water bodies that are isolated from navigable waters, which may place in doubt the continuing viability of some earlier case law. In *Solid Waste Agency of Northern Cook County v. U.S. Army Corps of Engineers*,[119] the Supreme Court invalidated the "migratory bird rule" which the Army Corps of Engineers, by regulation in 1986, had used as a basis to assert jurisdiction over isolated, intrastate, water bodies, and wetlands that contained avian habitat. The asserted predicate for EPA's jurisdiction in these cases was that there existed a federal interest in protecting the habitat of migratory birds. The Court noted that it had upheld prior assertions of federal jurisdiction because the regulated water body or wetland, even if it was entirely intrastate and was not itself navigable, nevertheless had been adjacent to waters of the United States. However, the Court found that the text of the CWA did not support federal jurisdiction over isolated water bodies that had no significant nexus with navigable waters of the United States, even those that undoubtedly were habitats for migratory birds.

More tellingly, the Supreme Court returned to the issue of adjacency in 2006 in its divergent opinions in *Rapanos v. United States*.[120] Although the *Rapanos* context

---

112. United States v. Riverside Bayview Homes, 474 U.S. 121 (1985). However, as will be discussed below with respect to the ruling in *Rapanos v. United States*, 547 U.S. 715 (2006), the relationship between the subject wetland and an "adjacent" water of the United States requires greater clarification for the CWA to apply. The CWA also directly regulates dredge and fill operations in wetlands, as distinct from discharges of pollutants. *See* § 6.07.

113. United States v. Akers, 651 F. Supp. 320 (E.D. Cal. 1987).

114. Texas Municipal Power Agency v. Environmental Protection Agency, 836 F.2d 1482 (5th Cir. 1988).

115. Leslie Salt Co. v. United States, 896 F.2d 354 (9th Cir. 1990), *cert. denied*, 498 U.S. 1126 (1991).

116. *Id.* (man-made salt pits at abandoned mine which were alternatively dry and wet depending on the season, at which migratory waterfowl stopped).

117. Lykes Brothers, Inc. v. U.S. Army Corps of Engineers, 64 F.3d 630 (11th Cir. 1995).

118. Hoffman Homes, Inc. v. Environmental Protection Agency, 999 F.2d 256 (7th Cir. 1993).

119. 531 U.S. 159 (2001).

120. 547 U.S. 715 (2006).

was that of wetlands, the ruling likely has ramifications for the CWA, generally.[121] The plurality, notably not itself a majority, concluded that federal agency jurisdiction under the CWA depended on whether the water body subjected to regulation had a physical, continuous, connection to a water body that was actually navigable. However, that plurality conclusion, to date, is not the law. Rather, Justice Kennedy authored a concurring opinion which, with the plurality, constituted a majority. Kennedy's concurrence, then, became the standard that was relied on by many later courts. The concurrence also required that the water bodies be connected, but was more flexible in the nature of the connection. It allowed for a hydrological relationship that might be transient between the water body as to which federal jurisdiction was being challenged and a navigable-in-fact water body. Justice Kennedy even contemplated an ecological connection in which one water body, being sufficiently "adjacent," played a beneficial role in the filtration of pollutants or served flood control purposes in relation to the other water body as to which the CWA clearly applied. Some subsequent Circuit Court decisions have construed Justice Kennedy's plurality opinion to establish the governing standard.[122] The relevant considerations for CWA applicability, and

---

121. A brief summary is submitted here solely to alert readers to what had been a controversy resulting from dueling agency rules which in their details are beyond the scope of this book but which may cause some confusion. Between 2015, when EPA issued a Rule ostensibly clarifying the *Rapanos* ruling, and 2020, when President Biden succeeded President Trump, substantial rulemaking, litigation and counter rulemaking occurred with respect to defining waters of the United States. The earlier EPA Rule issued during the Obama administration (80 Fed. Reg. 37,054 (June 29, 2015)) was stayed by the Sixth Circuit, although the Supreme Court vacated the stay on jurisdictional grounds in *National Association of Manufacturers v. Department of Defense*, ___ U.S. ___, 138 S. Ct. 617, 199 L. Ed. 2d 501 (2018). Meanwhile, EPA and the Army Corps of Engineers, pursuant to President Trump's Executive Order (Executive Order No. 13778 (Feb.28, 2017)), issued a subsequent joint Rule, repealing the 2015 Rule and defining waters of the United States in accordance with the narrower *Rapanos* plurality decision rather than Kennedy's concurrence (84 Fed. Reg. 56,626 (Oct. 22, 2019)), which itself subsequently was repealed pursuant to President Biden's Executive Order (No. 13990 (Jan. 20, 2021)), which implemented EPA's and the Army Corps of Engineer's rule defining waters of the United States in a manner that essentially restored their 2015 rule. (85 Fed. Reg. 22250.) A more comprehensive summary of the proceedings is set forth in ROBINSON, ENVIRONMENTAL REGULATION OF REAL PROPERTY § 12.02(2)(b)(iv). The present agency position can be reviewed at EPA, "Definition of 'Waters of the United States': Rule Status and Litigation Update," available at https://www.epa.gov/wotus/definition-waters-united-states-rule-status-and-litigation-update.

122. United States v. Gberke Excavating, Inc., 464 F.3d 723 (7th Cir. 2006); Northern California River Watch v. City of Healdsburg, 457 F.3d 1023 (9th Cir. 2006); United State v. Bailey, 571 F.3d 791 (8th Cir. 2009); United States v. Robison, 505 F.3d 1208 (11th Cir. 2007), *rehearing en banc*, 521 F.3d 1319 (11th Cir. 2008). The Ninth Circuit later reaffirmed its position in *United States v. Robertson*, 875 F.3d 1281 (2017). Other courts have declined to find the Kennedy standard to provide exclusive authority when the facts in their cases satisfied both the Kennedy and the plurality standards. *See* United States v. Cundiff, 555 F.3d 200 (6th Cir. 2009); United States v. Lucas, 516 F.3d 316, 327 (5th Cir. 2008). The Fifth Circuit subsequently reaffirmed the position that either the plurality or the Kennedy standard could provide a basis for federal jurisdiction under the CWA in *United States v. Lipar*, 665 Fed. Appx. 322 (5th Cir. 2016). This remains an evolving jurisdictional doctrine. However, as a practical matter, parties and district courts, now alerted to the need for better factual development of the connection between the water bodies, likely will establish a sufficient record as to render the matter largely academic in many cases.

how far the Kennedy standard reaches, doubtless will be clarified in the factual contexts of case law as it evolves.

The Supreme Court returned to the issue of adjacency, although in a different context, in *County of Maui, Hawaii v. Hawaii Wildlife Fund* by construing that a point source could be sufficiently connected by subsurface hydrology to a navigable water of the United States as to be functionally adjacent for purposes of bringing a discharge within the CWA (see discussion in 6.03[B][1][b]).[123] However, as of this writing the further ramifications of the majority opinion in *County of Maui* are still evolving.

Even the broadest use of the term "navigable waters" has long been understood to not encompass ground waters not connected in some way to navigable waters.[124] Discharges into ground water do not elude federal regulation though; they are subject to the Safe Drinking Water Act (see § 6.04[C]) and the Resource Conservation and Recovery Act (see § 7.05). Waste treatment systems, including treatment ponds or lagoons such as might be found in a treatment plant, are not waters of the United States.[125]

[g] Permit

A "permit" includes a NPDES "general permit," but it does not include a draft permit or a proposed permit (i.e., a permit prepared at the close of the public comment period), which has not been the subject of final agency action.[126] A general permit authorizes a category of discharges within a geographic area, usually corresponding to geographic or political boundaries. General permits may be used to control stormwater point sources or treatment works treating domestic sewage. The treatment works within the covered region must involve substantially similar operations, discharge the same types of waste, or engage in the same type of sludge disposal practices, and require similar monitoring in order to qualify for a general permit. The fact that a discharger qualifies for a general permit, however, does not preclude EPA from requiring it to also apply for an individual permit.[127]

For NPDES permitting, see the discussion in § 6.03[C]. States having programs that have received EPA approval can also administer the state's clean water program

---

123. County of Maui, Hawaii v. Hawaii Wildlife Fund, ___ U.S. ___, 140 S. Ct. 1462, 206 L. Ed. 2d 640 (2020), *vacating and remanding* 886 F.3d 737, *modifying* 881 F.3d 754 (9th Cir. 2019). Here, the dispute pertained to an injection well into which liquid wastes were disposed which seeped into groundwater which exited in the Pacific Ocean. However, having held that the hydrological connection could be adequate, the majority ruling did not conclude whether it was and remanded for findings as to whether the point of discharge was sufficiently close in time and location to the point of entry into the ocean.

124. Exxon Corp. v. Train, 554 F.2d 1310 (5th Cir. 1977); Village of Oconomowoc Lake v. Dayton Hudson Corp., 24 F.3d 962 (7th Cir. 1994), *cert. denied*, 513 U.S. 930 (1994). However, *County of Maui, Hawaii, supra*, and caselaw subsequently relying on it, as well as the ramifications from its abrogation of Circuit Court caselaw addressing surface pollutants leaching through ground water, should be carefully considered.

125. 40 C.F.R. § 122.2.

126. *Id.*

127. *Id.*; 40 C.F.R. § 122.28.

pursuant to which they can issue State Pollution Discharge Elimination System permits (SPDES) in lieu of EPA involvement (see § 6.03[D]).

[h] Source, Outfall, and New Source

A "source" is any building, structure, facility or installation from which there is or may be a discharge.[128] The term "outfall" sometimes is used to connote a point source from a facility. A "new source" is any source which is constructed after new regulations are promulgated containing standards of performance.[129] As to such a regulation, the new facility, new part of an older facility, or a new operation triggering the CWA, is a new source. Of course, a facility is not necessarily a new source for all purposes, since its discharges in one area may be subject to prior permitting. New sources often are treated differently in terms of permit applications and conditions and generally are subjected to the stricter requirements imposed by the new or newly amended regulation.

[2] Water Quality Standards versus Effluent Limitations

[a] Water Quality Standards

Effluent limitations — or technology-based limitations — are different from water quality standards. The manner in which they are different is important to understand if one is to grasp the strategy of the NPDES program.

Historically, "water quality standards"[130] were the means by which the end result — the quality of a water body — was evaluated. The CWA places primary reliance for developing water quality standards on the states.[131] The CWA requires NPDES permits to impose limitations that ensure that state water quality standards are satisfied. (See § 6.03[C][4].)[132] In fact, the CWA requires states to establish and regularly review water quality standards for each water body in the state.[133] State water quality standards still must be satisfied under the NPDES program. If a state's water quality standard for a water body cannot be reached solely by effluent limitations established in a permit targeted at the particular process or pollutants, the water quality-based approach must be utilized. That is, the standard pollutants that threaten water quality must be reduced until the receiving body of water reaches the designated purity level.

Water quality standards correlate with the designated use of the water (e.g., for fishing, swimming, drinking, etc....). (See § 6.02[B].) "Water quality criteria," often expressed in concentration levels, are used to describe the water body by its chemical,

---

128. 33 U.S.C. § 1316(3).

129. 33 U.S.C. § 1316(2).

130. *See generally* 40 C.F.R. § 131.

131. Scott v. City of Hammond, 741 F.2d 992, 994 (7th Cir. 1984).

132. 33 U.S.C. § 1313(b)(1)(C); CWA § 301(b)(1)(C). Water quality standards must be satisfied for the state of the discharge as well as for other states which the discharge impacts. Arkansas v. Oklahoma, 503 U.S. 91 (1992).

133. 33 U.S.C. § 1313(c); CWA § 303(c).

biological or physical characteristics as they relate to the designated use. If water quality becomes unacceptably diminished in relation to its classification of use (e.g., if dissolved oxygen was necessary at a certain level for fish life, but did not meet that threshold for the water body), then the state must reduce the quantity — the Total Maximum Daily Loads (TMDLs)[134] — of the standardized pollutants which industry may discharge into that water body to avoid violation of water quality standards. States are required to identify those water bodies in the state that fall within the CWA but do not meet the relevant water quality standards, prioritize them, and then develop a TMDL for each pollutant affecting each water body or segment that is appropriate for that water body's location and classification of use.[135] Water quality standards set upper limits on the amount of each pollutant which may be found in the water body, without distinguishing among sources, although TMDLs may be allocated among sources discharging into the water body. Under the NPDES system, the permit is the device which determines a particular point source's maximum allocable share of a pollutant which must comport with the state's water quality standards (see §6.03[C][7]).

Water quality standards historically have been expressed in narrative terms (i.e., that the water must be free of certain pollutants in certain quantities which interfere with designated uses), although the CWA requires states to adopt numerical criteria for toxic pollutants. Water quality criteria also may be expressed in terms of "lethal concentrations" or a bioassay scale determining the relative toxicity of particular concentrations to aquatic life. EPA has published water quality criteria for all listed toxic pollutants. EPA reviews and approves or disapproves state water quality standards.[136] EPA has imposed an antidegradation policy on states,[137] related to the anti-backsliding provisions of the CWA prohibiting states from adopting water quality standards which do not protect existing uses.[138] If EPA disapproves a state water quality standard, it must promulgate its own water quality standard for that state.[139]

Federal energy projects, such as hydropower projects or those requiring water drawn from local water bodies for cooling purposes, are subject to federal licensing by the Federal Energy Regulatory Commission (FERC), which in most respects pre-

---

134. A TMDL includes the best estimates of pollution from point sources as well as from non-point sources and natural background sources, and must take into account seasonal variations. 40 C.F.R. §130.3(1). Courts differ, though, on whether the standard of measurement is necessarily a "daily" basis, or whether a daily average, calculated on the basis of a longer time frame, is permissible. *Compare* Friends of the Earth v. Environmental Protection Agency, 446 F.3d 140 (D.C. Cir. 2006), *with* Natural Resources Defense Council v. Muszynski, 268 F.3d 91, 98 (2d Cir. 2001).

135. 33 U.S.C. §1313(d)(1); Sanitary Board of Charleston, West Virginia v. Wheeler, 918 F.3d 324 (4th Cir. 2019).

136. 40 C.F.R. §131.3; El Dorado Chemical Co. v. U.S. Environmental Protection Agency, 763 F.3d 950 (8th Cir. 2014); Natural Resources Defense Council v. Environmental Protection Agency, 279 F.3d 1180 (9th Cir. 2002).

137. 40 C.F.R. §131.12.

138. 33 U.S.C. §1342(o).

139. 33 U.S.C. §1313(c)(4); 40 C.F.R. §131.5(e).

empts state laws and regulations. However, these projects must obtain certification from the state where the utility is operating that it complies with that state's water quality standards as a precondition for FERC licensing (see § 6.03[C][4]).[140]

[b] Effluent Limitations or Technology-Based Standards

"Effluent limitations" or "technology-based standards," by contrast, do not depend on the particular quality of the receiving water, but assume that a stringent and progressively strict reduction of all discharges of pollutants inevitably will improve water quality to a purer level. Effluent limitations are just that — limitations on *effluent* or *discharges* — which are imposed prior to the wastewater leaving the facility. Effluent limitations are said to be *technology-based*. The standards employed focus on how advanced the available technology is for reducing the particular pollutant or reducing the pollutant load of particular industrial processes. EPA promulgates effluent discharge guidelines for various types of industrial facilities. The guidelines set forth the effluent limitations applicable to the particular class or subclass of facility, which then will be incorporated into permits for facilities that fall under the particular guideline. If an applicable guideline has not been promulgated, then the Agency will utilize the same factors used in establishing nationwide effluent limitations to derive an appropriate discharge limitation. There are complicated types of standards generally using the "best" facilities as a baseline measurement for other facilities, to be applied to different industries and processes which are beyond the scope of this book.[141] The basic point, however, is that EPA's regulations, by restricting the discharge of pollutants to progressively lower levels, with subsequent permitting or permit renewals incorporating stricter controls over specific effluent waste streams, typically drive the development of better technology. The statutory device has been characterized as "technology forcing," since industry and other polluters must anticipate the need for progressively cleaner processes.[142] Hence, water quality standards and technol-

---

140. 33 U.S.C. § 1341; Hoopa Valley Tribe v. Federal Energy Regulatory Commission, 913 F.3d 1099 (D.C. Cir. 2019). For a discussion on the procedure, see Constitution Pipeline Co. LLC v. New York State Department of Environmental Conservation, 868 F.3d 87 (2d Cir. 2017), *cert denied*, ___ U.S. ___, 138 S. Ct. 1697 (2018). The state agency has a one-year deadline within which to deny certification or to grant it, potentially with conditions. Appropriate conditions relating to water quality issues will be incorporated into the FERC license. 33 U.S.C. § 1341(d). If the state fails to act within one year, the certification requirement is waived. New York State Department of Environmental Conservation v. Federal Energy Regulatory Commission, 991 F.3d 87 (2d Cir. 2021).

141. The various "best" standards applicable in different circumstances take into account the best practicable control technology that is currently available and, alternatively, the best achievable control measures and practices, which includes a consideration of whether the technology that is demanded is economically achievable at the present time or under the facility's particular circumstances. 33 U.S.C. § 1314(b). EPA by regulation may also define best management practices for categories of industrial point sources. 33 U.S.C. § 1314(e). EPA is required to devise performance standards to reduce effluent from new sources in particular industrial categories. 33 U.S.C. § 1316(b). See § 6.03[C][7][c], [d].

142. Natural Resource Defense Council v. U.S. Environmental Protection Agency, 808 F.3d 556 (2d Cir. 2015). The factor of competition can also play a role, that a competitor having invested in

ogy-based standards are complementary devices. But if water quality deteriorates with respect to a particular pollutant, CWA goals can be met by increasingly restricting effluent containing that pollutant from sources that discharge into that water body.[143] Since the CWA prohibits backsliding, the water quality standards applicable to that water body for the subject pollutant will have to be upgraded to bring the water body into compliance. (See § 6.03[B][2][a]).[144]

If the applicable effluent limitations happen not to be adequate to protect a receiving body of water, the state in which the discharge occurs still may employ its own water quality standards. This may occur when the water body is particularly polluted, so that national standardized effluent limitations do not suffice to clean up — *restore* — the water body. Similarly, if a downstream state is insufficiently protected by the applicable effluent limitations, its water quality standards may be used by EPA in a NPDES permit.[145] Typically, permits will reference effluent limitations, as well as water quality standards, and may fine-tune the permit with conditions to more effectively achieve its goals, such as when the water quality standards may have a seasonal variable (e.g., the effect of certain pollutants may be different during summer months than during the winter).[146]

[C] National Pollutant Discharge Elimination System (NPDES) Program

[1] NPDES Permits Are Required for Discharges of Pollutants, and Are Subject to Other Environmental Laws

The National Pollutant Discharge Elimination System (NPDES) Program is the centerpiece of the Clean Water Act. It is defined as "the national program for issuing, modifying, revoking and reissuing, terminating, monitoring and enforcing permits, and imposing and enforcing pretreatment requirements."[147]

NPDES permits are the regulatory hook upon which enforcement efforts hang. A discharge of a pollutant from a point source without a permit, or contrary to the

cleaner technology may receive a permit renewal more favorable than a procrastinating facility and thereby achieve an economic advantage.

143. 33 U.S.C. § 1312.

144. 33 U.S.C. § 1342(o).

145. Arkansas v. Oklahoma, 503 U.S. 91 (1992).

146. Courts have disagreed on whether seasonal considerations can be accounted for by Total Maximum *Daily* Loads. *See* Natural Resource Defense Council v. Muszynski, 268 F.3d 91 (2d Cir. 2001) (phosphorous levels in the New York City watershed varied by seasons, so a more flexible timeline was permissible to achieve statutory goals); Friends of the Earth v. Environmental Protection Agency, 446 F.3d 140 (D.C. Cir. 2006) (CWA text referenced only "daily," precluding seasonal variations for TMDLs); American Farm Bureau Federation v. U.S. Environmental Protection Agency, 792 F.3d 281 (3d Cir. 2015) (in the absence of statutory specificity, court deferred to EPA's flexible interpretation).

147. 40 C.F.R. § 122.2.

conditions of a permit, is a violation of the CWA.[148] The issuance of any permit, however, must be on notice to the public and is subject to hearing[149] and public comment requirements.[150]

The NPDES program requirements supersede any authority relied on by other federal agencies which issue permits or licenses having water quality conditions.[151] However, the NPDES permit nevertheless will be subject to the requirements of other laws. For instance, if the legislative or administrative concerns of the Wild and Scenic Rivers Act, the National Historic Preservation Act, the Endangered Species Act, the Coastal Zone Management Act, or the Fish and Wildlife Coordination Act are triggered by virtue of the issuance of a NPDES permit, the permittee must follow those laws, which may result in specific conditions being incorporated into the NPDES permit. Additionally, the issuance of a NPDES permit may trigger NEPA (see Chapter 4), with the consequential preparation of an EIS.[152]

[2] Obtaining Permits for Toxic Wastes

The discharge of toxic pollutants is governed by CWA § 307 (33 U.S.C. § 1317). EPA maintains a list of toxic pollutants[153] that qualify for listing on the basis of their toxicity, persistence, and degradability of the toxin, the usual or potential presence of affected organisms in any waters, the importance of the organisms, and the nature and extent of the toxin's effect on the organisms. Toxic pollutants often, but not necessarily, may be found in process wastes, unavoidably resulting from manufacturing processes.[154]

When a toxic pollutant is listed, EPA deems it to be injurious to health,[155] subjecting it to effluent limitations resulting from the application of the best available technology economically achievable for the applicable point source.[156] The effluent limitations may be incorporated into a permit,[157] although they also may be directly enforceable.[158]

---

148. 33 U.S.C. § 1311(a). If the discharge is of dredged or fill material, a CWA § 404 permit is necessary. *See* § 6.07.

149. *See* Natural Resources Defense Council v. Environmental Protection Agency, 279 F.3d 1180 (9th Cir. 2002).

150. 33 U.S.C. § 1342 (a)(1).

151. For instance, the Nuclear Regulatory Commission and the Federal Energy Regulatory Commission issue licenses which have water quality requirements. *See* National Wildlife Federation v. Consumers Power Co., 862 F.2d 580 (6th Cir. 1987); American Rivers, Inc. v. F.E.R.C., 129 F.3d 99 (2d Cir. 1997); Scenic Hudson Preservation Conference v. Callaway, 370 F. Supp. 162 (S.D.N.Y. 1973), *aff'd*, 499 F.2d 127 (2d Cir. 1974). Hence, a permittee may not evade CWA goals by relying on less onerous water quality conditions in other permits issued under other statutes. The EPA has administratively exempted many radioactive wastes from the CWA and has ceded jurisdiction to the Nuclear Regulatory Commission. The administrative exemption was upheld in an early Supreme Court decision. Train v. Colorado Public Interest Research Group, 426 U.S. 1, 6 (1976).

152. 40 C.F.R. § 122.49.

153. *See* 40 C.F.R. §§ 129.4, 129.100–129.105.

154. 40 C.F.R. § 129.2(n).

155. 40 C.F.R. § 129.5(c)(1).

156. 33 U.S.C. § 1317(a).

157. 40 C.F.R. § 129.1.

158. *Cf.* Inland Steel Co. v. Environmental Protection Agency, 574 F.2d 367 (7th Cir. 1978).

The limitations utilize an ambient water criterion, meaning the concentration of a toxic pollutant in navigable water that will not result in an adverse impact on important aquatic life or consumers of seafood, and will not significantly place a human population at risk.[159] Owners or operators of the discharging source are subject to monitoring, sampling, recording, and reporting conditions.[160] More stringent effluent limitations also may be required in permits by approved state programs.[161] If the source discharges to navigable waters as well as a POTW (see [3], *below*), then its mass emissions are subject to the less restrictive standard (i.e., the direct discharge standard or the pretreatment standard), but it may not exceed the toxic pollutant limitations standard for a direct discharge to navigable waters.[162] If the ambient water criterion is not met, EPA may impose more stringent effluent limitations.[163] Thus far, EPA has promulgated toxic effluent standards for only six pollutants: aldrin, DDT, endrin, toxophene, benzidine, and PCBs.[164]

The CWA also requires states to restrict discharges of toxic pollutants that violate water quality standards.[165] States must identify "toxic hot spots" and subject point sources discharging into those waters[166] to "individual control strategies," including permit limitations on toxic pollutants to ensure compliance with water quality standards.[167] EPA also may include in permits toxicity-based limitations on waste streams *in toto*, as contrasted with numerical limitations on individual toxic pollutants,[168] a policy upheld on judicial challenge.[169] This may be accomplished by referencing bioassay methods measuring toxicity by the proportionate mortality of test organisms in water samples. EPA may also incorporate numerical limitations in NPDES permits to ensure compliance with general narrative toxicity criteria from state water quality standards,[170] which have also been upheld on judicial review.[171]

No permits are available for the discharge of certain highly toxic wastes into waters of the United States,[172] or generally for discharges of oil.[173]

---

159. 40 C.F.R. § 129.2(g).

160. 40 C.F.R. § 129.5(d).

161. 40 C.F.R. § 129.5(e).

162. 40 C.F.R. § 129.5(f).

163. 40 C.F.R. § 129.7.

164. 40 C.F.R. §§ 129.100–129.105.

165. 33 U.S.C. § 1314(l).

166. 54 Fed. Reg. 246 (1989); 54 Fed. Reg. 23,868 (1989).

167. 40 C.F.R. § 123.46.

168. 40 C.F.R. § 125.3(c)(4).

169. Natural Resources Defense Council v. Environmental Protection Agency, 859 F.2d 156 (D.C. Cir. 1988).

170. 40 C.F.R. § 122.44(d).

171. American Paper Institute v. Environmental Protection Agency, 996 F.2d 346 (D.C. Cir. 1993).

172. These include: radiological, chemical or biological warfare agents; high-level radioactive wastes; medical wastes. 33 U.S.C. § 1311(f). Medical wastes include "isolation wastes"; infectious agents; human blood and blood products; pathological wastes; sharps; body parts; contaminated bedding; surgical wastes; potentially contaminated laboratory wastes; dialysis wastes; and whatever additional medical wastes the EPA reaches by regulation. 33 U.S.C. § 1362(20).

173. *See* 33 U.S.C. § 1321.

[3] Discharges from Publicly Owned Treatment Works (POTWs)

[a] Direct Discharges

The NPDES permit system restricts discharges by point sources directly into navigable waters, but does not govern discharges from industrial facilities into "publicly owned treatment works" (POTWs). POTWs are systems constructed to collect, store, treat, and then dispose of municipal waste, including stormwater runoff or industrial waste, including waste in combined stormwater and sanitary sewer systems.[174] POTWs that receive wastes from other sources must have a permit, as point sources, to discharge the effluent into navigable waters.[175]

The Clean Water Act provides for federal construction grants, but municipalities also must provide financing methods, such as user charges.[176] Federal grant funds may be withheld from nonconforming POTWs,[177] but discharges of effluent in violation of the POTW's permit also constitute a § 301 violation.[178]

[b] Indirect Discharges

Rather than being subject to a national permit program, indirect dischargers — those who discharge into the POTW rather than directly in navigable waters of the United States — are subject to pretreatment standards under CWA § 307(b). This provision prohibits the discharge of any pollutants into or through the treatment works that interfere with, or otherwise are incompatible with it.[179] EPA imposes categorical restrictions for categories of industrial sources. Limitations are imposed for pollutants that EPA determines will not be adequately removed but will "pass through" a POTW,[180] placing the POTW in violation of its own permit.[181] Indirect dischargers also are prohibited from introducing pollutants into a POTW that create a hazard of fire or explosion at a POTW, cause structural damage as a consequence of corrosivity, obstruct the flow of wastewater in a POTW, thus "interfering" with the POTW, or contain sufficient heat to interfere with a POTW.[182] The interference and pass-through regulations have been upheld on judicial challenge.[183] If a POTW can successfully treat a toxic pollutant, the indirect discharger may receive a "removal credit"

---

174. 33 U.S.C. § 1292(2)(B).

175. *See* 40 C.F.R. § 122.21.

176. See discussion in Middlesex County Utilities Authority v. Borough of Sayreville, 690 F.2d 358 (3d Cir. 1982), *cert. denied*, 460 U.S. 1023 (1983).

177. City of New Brunswick v. Borough of Milltown, 686 F.2d 120 (3d Cir. 1982), *cert. denied*, 459 U.S. 1201 (1984).

178. Township of Franklin Sewerage Authority v. Middlesex County Utilities Authority, 787 F.2d 117 (3d Cir. 1986), *cert. denied*, 479 U.S. 828 (1986).

179. 33 U.S.C. § 1317(b); County Sanitation District No. 2 of Los Angeles County v. Inland Container Corp., 803 F.2d 1074 (9th Cir. 1986).

180. 45 Fed. Reg. 9416.

181. 40 C.F.R. § 403.3(n).

182. 40 C.F.R. § 403.5(b).

183. Arkansas Poultry Federation v. Environmental Protection Agency, 852 F.2d 324 (8th Cir. 1988).

allowing some relief from pretreatment requirements,[184] although the removal credit may not be granted if toxic metals discharged to POTWs, ending up in POTW sludge, prevent compliance with sludge use or disposal requirements. Although, in the interest of cost-efficiency, EPA allows facilities to combine waste streams from different industrial categories to a central waste treatment plant,[185] facilities may not seek to evade categorical standards by the expedient of diluting the waste streams with more process water.[186] POTWs also may develop their own local limits, either on an individual pollutant basis, or on the basis of particular industries, or for individual facilities,[187] in addition to EPA's categorical limits, to prevent interference and pass-through violations.[188] Dischargers subject to pretreatment standards must submit various monitoring reports and compliance reports after promulgation of standards.[189]

[c] Secondary Treatment

The POTW, at a minimum, must practice "secondary treatment."[190] Secondary treatment consists either of biological treatment (which utilizes oxidation ponds, lagoons or trickling filters)[191] or chemical treatment (which utilizes sediment settlement, aeration, and bacterial treatment). Both treatments also require chlorination of the discharged waters. Parties who introduce the wastes into a POTW are subject to pretreatment standards.[192] A POTW that fails to provide adequate secondary treatment to meet the relevant effluent limitations in its permit, thereby allowing unpermitted or excessive discharges into navigable waters, violates § 301.

[d] Sludge Is Regulated as an End-Product of POTW Wastewater Treatment

An end-product of POTW treatment of wastewater is sludge, the disposal of which is a growing problem. EPA estimates that some 40 percent of sludge is disposed of in municipal landfills (see discussion in § 7.03), 20 percent is incinerated (see discussion in § 7.02), and the rest is applied to land as fertilizer or soil conditioner (see discussion in § 7.02). The Clean Water Act requires EPA to develop standards for the use and disposal of sludge generated by treatment works.[193] Sludge, as noted above, also is regulated under other statutes. If sludge use or disposal from a treatment

184. 33 U.S.C. § 1317(b)(1); 40 C.F.R. § 403.7.

185. *See* 40 C.F.R. § 403.6(e).

186. 40 C.F.R. § 403.6(d).

187. 51 Fed. Reg. 21,459 (1986).

188. 40 C.F.R. § 403.5(c).

189. 40 C.F.R. § 403.12(b), (d), (e).

190. 40 C.F.R. § 133.102. Secondary treatment addresses biological oxygen demand (B.O.D.) and pH, and, under some circumstances, chemical oxygen demand (C.O.D.) and total organic carbon (T.O.C.), factors which may reduce dissolved oxygen. *See* 40 C.F.R. §§ 133.104, 133.105.

191. 33 U.S.C. § 1314(d)(4).

192. 33 U.S.C. § 1317(b); *see* 40 C.F.R. Part 403.

193. 33 U.S.C. § 1345.

works does not fall under another statute, the NPDES permit must require compliance with EPA's sludge management procedures.[194]

[4] State Certification of Compliance with Water Quality Standards Is Required

When the applicant seeks a NPDES permit, or intends to construct or operate facilities which may result in discharges, CWA § 401 requires the permitting agency to obtain from the state where the discharge will occur certification that the discharge complies with the relevant federal and state effluent limitations and water quality standards. This provides great leverage to the states, even when a particular state might lack an approved State Pollutant Discharge Elimination System (SPDES) program (see [D], *below*). The state is likewise authorized to add conditions to its certification, which then become conditions in the permit.[195]

This right of the state to impose its own conditions under the CWA seems to be impervious to challenge by other federal agencies acting in furtherance of their own statutory mandates. The issue was addressed by the Supreme Court in *PUD No. 1 of Jefferson County v. Washington Department of Ecology*.[196] In that case, the Federal Energy Regulatory Commission was involved in licensing proceedings in connection with the diversion of water for a hydroelectric project, which would have altered the stream flow in that part of the state. The FERC licensing process required state CWA certification as a component of the FERC approval of the project. However, the state agency determined that the consequential reduction of water flow would impact on breeding populations of salmon and trout, and conditioned certification on a higher level of water flow. The FERC objected that this condition involving water levels did not involve water quality. The FERC claimed that the state's refusal to certify absent inclusion of this condition in the permit was unauthorized under the CWA, triggering preemption issues by the FERC when it acted within its statutory domain. The Supreme Court, however, found the condition to be an appropriate state law requirement and permissible under the CWA.

If there are no applicable state effluent limitations or state water quality standards, the state has to certify that fact and standards have to be promulgated. If the state

---

194. 33 U.S.C. § 1345; *see* 40 C.F.R. § 122.21.

195. *See* PUD No.1 of Jefferson County v. Washington Department of Ecology, 511 U.S. 700 (1994). The inclusion of conditions by the state may not be administratively challenged, but may only be judicially challenged. *See* American Rivers, Inc. v. F.E.R.C., 129 F.3d 99 (2d Cir. 1997). Note, though, that "discharge" for purposes of state certification under § 401 takes on a broader meaning that under § 402, in which a NPDES permit is required for "discharge of a pollutant." The qualifying language under § 402 means that the triggering event requires the addition of a pollutant to the water body (see discussion in § 6.03[B][1][b], *above*), whereas, for purposes of state certification, a discharge can occur even if the same water, unadulterated by pollutants, flows through a conveyance such as a dam. *See* S.D. Warren Co. v. Maine Board of Environmental Protection, 126 S. Ct. 1843 (2006).

196. 511 U.S. 700 (1994); *see also* Alcoa Power Generating, Inc. v. Federal Energy Regulatory Commission, 643 F.3d 963, 2011 U.S. App. LEXIS 9041 (D.C. Cir. 2011).

denies certification, the permit may not be issued.[197] If the state fails to act on a request for certification within one year, it is deemed to have waived any objections under the state's water quality standards, although various factors may influence when that one-year period starts and ends.[198]

The CWA also provides for State "SPDES" programs, and contemplates that most enforcement responsibility will eventually be assumed by states.[199] However, state SPDES programs must be approved by EPA, and must provide as much enforcement as, or in excess of, the CWA's basic requirements.[200] These SPDES programs are discussed at [D], *below*. Even for non-approved state water quality programs, states may impose more stringent regulations than are required for an approved SPDES program, which will be enforced by EPA in connection with NPDES permits.[201]

[5] Persons and Conduct Covered by NPDES

The NPDES requirements are set forth in CWA § 402;[202] the general statutory framework is fine-tuned in the Code of Federal Regulations.[203]

EPA generally is authorized to issue NPDES permits for the discharge of pollutants into navigable waters.[204] There are exceptions, as follows, when a NPDES permit is not required:

- Discharge of dredge and fill material to specified disposal sites is governed by CWA § 404, discussed in § 6.07.[205]

- Agricultural irrigation return flows are exempted.[206]

---

197. 33 U.S.C. § 1341.

198. 33 U.S.C. 1341(a)(1); Alcoa Power Generating, Inc. v. Federal Energy Regulatory Commission, 643 F.3d 963 (D.C. Cir. 2011); AES Sparrows Point LNG v. Wilson, 589 F.3d 721 (4th Cir. 2009); FPL Energy Maine Hydro LLC v. Maine Department of Environmental Protection, 2007 Me. 97, 926 A.2d 1197 (2007).

199. "State" includes the 50 states, the District of Columbia and the territories. 33 U.S.C. § 1362(3). A Native American tribe also may qualify as a "state" if the relevant criteria are satisfied. These include a governing body carrying out substantial governmental duties and powers; the tribe's program must be intended to manage and protect water resources within tribal territory; and the tribe is capable of carrying out the provisions of the CWA. The tribe's program will then be submitted for approval to the EPA. 33 U.S.C. § 1377(e); 33 U.S.C. § 1251(g); 40 C.F.R. §§ 122.2, 131.8(a); *see* Fed. Reg. 64,339; William C. Galloway, *Tribal Water Quality Standards Under the Clean Water Act: Protecting Traditional Cultural Uses*, 70 WASH. L. REV. 177 (1995).

200. 33 U.S.C. § 1370. The EPA's certification of water quality standards issued by a Native American tribe exceeding federal standards and even exceeding state standards for water bodies flowing through tribal territory and impacting on upstream dischargers has been upheld. City of Albuquerque v. Browner, 97 F.3d 415 (10th Cir. 1996), *cert. denied*, 522 U.S. 965 (1997).

201. 40 C.F.R. § 122.1(f).

202. 33 U.S.C. § 1342.

203. 40 C.F.R. Part 123.

204. 33 U.S.C. § 1342(a).

205. *See* 33 U.S.C. § 1344.

206. 33 U.S.C. § 1342(l)(1).

- Stormwater runoff from oil, gas and mining operations are exempted.[207]

- Stormwater runoff from non-point source agricultural and silvicultural activities does not require an NPDES permit. These include stormwater runoff from orchards, cropland, pastures, range lands, and forest lands. These do not include concentrated feeding operations, discharges from concentrated aquatic animal production facilities, discharges from silvicultural point sources, or discharges to aquacultureprojects.[208]

- Although EPA may permit the discharge of specific pollutants under controlled conditions in connection with an approved aquaculture project, this is handled under separate authority.[209]

- A discharge of sewage from a vessel or effluent incidental to the proper functioning of the vessel does not need a NPDES permit. However, the exclusion does not apply to trash or garbage; nor does it apply if the vessel is used for purposes other than transportation (e.g., as a seafood processing facility, or as a mining, energy, or storage facility).[210]

There also are exceptions when a permit will not be issued:

- Certain toxic wastes, including medical wastes, may not be discharged into navigable waters, even by permit.[211]

- No permit may be issued if the conditions to be imposed cannot ensure compliance with the state's applicable water quality standards, as required by CWA § 401 (see [C][4], *above*).[212] If the state otherwise fails to provide certification (see [C][4], *above*), a permit will not be issued.[213]

- If the Secretary of the Army determines that the proposed discharge will substantially impair anchorage or navigation in any of the waters of the United States, a permit will be denied.[214]

- If EPA objects to the issuance of a permit, the state may not issue one.[215]

[6] Permit Application: Contents and Procedures

[a] Filing the Application

The NPDES process begins with the application. The application process is rigorous and information-driven. In a sense, the application is one of the most important components of the NPDES program, insofar as all discharges are governed by the

207. 33 U.S.C. § 1342(l)(2).
208. 40 C.F.R. § 122.3. See discussion at [B][1], *above*.
209. *See* 33 U.S.C. § 1328.
210. 40 C.F.R. § 122.3(a).
211. 33 U.S.C. § 1311(f); *see also* 33 U.S.C. § 1362(20) (range of what is considered to constitute medical wastes).
212. 40 C.F.R. § 122.4(d).
213. 40 C.F.R. § 122.4(b).
214. 40 C.F.R. § 122.4(e).
215. 40 C.F.R. § 122.4(c).

permit, and the permit is substantially determined by the completeness and specificity of the application.

The Code of Federal Regulations sets forth detailed and specific application requirements and procedures for NPDES permits.[216] Although an attorney representing a discharging facility would be well advised to review these provisions with great care, for present purposes many of these requirements need not be addressed. Rather, a summary of general application requirements will suffice.

Generally, the proposed discharger must apply 180 days before the discharge, but EPA may be flexible and allow for a later date. If a new discharge is expected in an existing, permitted facility, then the 180-day period must precede the date of the new discharge. If the facility proposes a new discharge of stormwater associated with industrial activities, the application period also is 180 days. If new construction is the basis for the permit, or other stormwater discharges, the time period is 90 days.[217]

[b] Contents of Application

The application must set forth information which basically identifies the applicant and the business. The information filed with the application must be maintained by the applicant for five years after filing. Applicants also must supply extensive information about the entire operation and all possible environmental consequences of the discharge. This includes a geographic layout of the facility so that EPA can identify and evaluate potential discharge points. The applicant must provide a topological map extending one mile beyond the source's property boundaries, depicting the following:[218]

- The facility and each of its intake (i.e., where the water is coming from) and discharge structures.
- Each of its hazardous waste treatment, storage and disposal facilities, if any.
- Each well, if any, where facility fluids are injected underground.
- All wells, springs or other surface water bodies.
- Drinking water wells listed in public records or otherwise known to the applicant in the map area (i.e., the wells may be outside the applicant's property).

EPA will also want to know the regulatory landscape, so to speak, in which the applicant is operating. The applicant must include a listing of all permits or construction approvals applied for or received under any of the following:[219]

- RCRA;
- The Safe Drinking Water Act;
- The CWA NPDES program;
- The Clean Air Act;

---

216. 40 C.F.R. § 122.21.
217. *Id.*
218. 40 C.F.R. § 122.21(f)(7).
219. 40 C.F.R. § 122.21(f)(6).

- The national emission standards for hazardous pollutants preconstruction approval under the Clean Air Act;

- Ocean Dumping permits under the Marine Protection Research and Sanctuaries Act;

- Dredge or fill permits under CWA § 404; and

- Any other relevant environmental permits, including state permits.

Manufacturing, mining and silvicultural dischargers also must provide specification of outfall locations, drawings diagraming water flow, average flows from each source, intermittent flows, and effluent characteristics.[220]

The regulations also require that the applicant report quantitative data for every outfall for certain pollutants which were typical variables under water quality standards, including: biological oxygen demand (BODs); chemical oxygen demand; total organic carbon; total suspended solids; ammonia; temperature, specified by season; and pH. For facilities discharging domestic sewage, information about fecal coliform, total residual chlorine, oil and grease, and discharge flow also must be provided. The data must be collected over 365 days, and must include the maximum daily value and average daily value. If the applicant is a "new discharger" there are additional requirements, but it will have two years to submit information about these effluents and effluent characteristics.[221]

Specific information also must be provided for a range of pollutants set forth in appendices to the regulations. If the applicant knows or should know of biological toxicity tests performed within the past three years, the results must be reported. If a contract laboratory or consulting firm performed chemical analyses, the laboratory must be identified. If EPA directs further testing, such as bioassays to evaluate the relative toxicity of the discharges to aquatic life, the results must be included in the application. The applicant also must describe the frequency of flow and the duration of discharges which occur only intermittently or seasonally. Additionally, the applicant must identify the treatment system used for pollutants.[222]

If pollutants are present in intake water, the applicant must identify them. If the applicant can demonstrate that such pollutants are present solely because they are in the intake water, EPA may waive the requirement of providing quantitative data as to those pollutants.

[c] Specific Types of Applications

[i] Concentrated Animal Feeding Operation and Concentrated Aquatic Animal Production Facility

If the application is for a concentrated animal feeding operation or concentrated aquatic animal production facility, each operation must be fully described in terms

220. 40 C.F.R. § 122.21(g), (h).
221. 40 C.F.R. § 122.21(h)(4).
222. 40 C.F.R. § 122.21(g)(11).

of the type and number of animals, the size of the facility or operation, and provide feeding and effluent information.[223]

[ii] Publicly Owned Treatment Works (POTWs)

If the applicant is a POTW, there are specific requirements. For instance, if a POTW is designed to discharge more than one million gallons of effluent per day or has a pretreatment program, the applicant must provide the results of "whole effluent biological toxicity testing" (i.e., the aggregate toxic effect of its effluent). Even for other POTWs, EPA still may require the testing and production of the results. The testing either must comply with EPA's own methodology or else be scientifically defensible and sufficiently sensitive to detect aquatic toxicity.[224]

[7] NPDES Permits: Terms and Conditions

[a] Overview

Certain conditions must be made a part of all permits, either by being directly noted or incorporated by reference. The permittee must agree to comply with all conditions, and must acknowledge that any permit noncompliance is a violation of the CWA, as well as grounds for an enforcement action or for termination, revocation, or modification of the permit (see [b], *below*).[225] The NPDES permit must contain conditions that reference the applicable effluent limitations.[226] If the permittee wants to continue the permitted activity when the permit term lapses, it has an obligation to reapply.[227] The permittee also must agree to mitigate permit violations. Permits also require proper operation and maintenance of the facility. The permittee must allow inspection and entry, subject to Fourth Amendment requirements. There are data and information collection requirements (i.e., monitoring), record keeping obligations, and requirements that violations be reported within 24 hours after the discharger becomes aware of a violation.[228] All of these requirements will be set forth as conditions of the permit. The permit also may include whatever additional conditions EPA determines to be appropriate.[229]

Permits must be for a fixed term, but not exceeding five years.[230] The term may be renewed. Generally, the old permit remains in effect until issuance of the renewal permit.[231]

The issuance of a permit does not confer on the permittee any property right in the permit, or any exclusive privilege.[232] Hence, any civil action seeking to prevent EPA from modifying or terminating a permit will be barred.

---

223. *See 40 C.F.R. §§ 122.23, 122.24.*
224. *See 40 C.F.R. § 122.21(d)(3).*
225. 40 C.F.R. § 122.41(a).
226. 40 C.F.R. § 122.41(a)(1).
227. 40 C.F.R. § 122.41(a)(3).
228. 40 C.F.R. § 122.41(l)(6).
229. 33 U.S.C. § 1342(a)(1)–(3); 40 C.F.R. § 122.43.
230. 40 C.F.R. § 122.46(a).
231. See 40 C.F.R. § 122.6 for criteria for continuing expiring permits.
232. 40 C.F.R. § 122.5(b).

Moreover, the CWA contains an "anti-backsliding" clause. As a general rule, a permit may not be renewed, reissued, or modified so as to allow the source to discharge greater quantities of effluent. The effluent limitations in the new permit may not be less stringent than the "comparable" effluent limitations in the original permit.[233] However, there are exceptions[234] by which Congress sought to give EPA some discretion to be fair to a permittee, reflecting changed circumstances which materially relate to the conditions of the original permit, so long as the pollution load of the receiving water body is not significantly affected. However, the modification may not reduce the effluent limitation below that specified in an effluent guideline,[235] or violate a water quality standard.[236] The exceptions may be available in the following circumstances:[237]

- After the permit is issued, new information becomes available which would have justified a less stringent effluent limitation in the first instance. This new information requirement, however, is not satisfied by a mere revision in the regulations or a guideline, or new test methods; or

- EPA determines that technical mistakes were made, or law was misinterpreted, in connection with the issuance of the original permit. This exception applies when EPA imposed a permit condition, in the discretion of the Administrator, in lieu of formal regulatory authority, or when a relevant regulation has not yet been implemented; or

- Events occur over which the permittee has no control, and for which there is no reasonably available remedy, which might warrant a reduction in an effluent limitation.

Permits can be terminated[238] or modified[239] for cause. The source is entitled to an evidentiary hearing. A non-exclusive list of reasons for termination or modification includes the following:[240]

- A condition of the permit has been violated.

- The discharger obtained the permit by misrepresentation.

- The discharger failed to fully disclose all relevant facts in applying for and obtaining the permit.

- There has been a change of circumstances that calls for either a temporary or permanent reduction of a discharge, or for its elimination altogether.

- There are material and substantial alterations to the facility after issuance of the permit which bear on discharges.

---

233. 33 U.S.C. § 1342(o)(1); CWA § 402(o)(1).
234. 33 U.S.C. § 1342(o)(2).
235. An "effluent guideline" is a regulation published by EPA to adopt or revise effluent limitations under CWA § 304(b).
236. 33 U.S.C. § 1342(o)(3); CWA § 402(o)(3).
237. 33 U.S.C. § 1342(o)(2).
238. 40 C.F.R. § 122.64.
239. 40 C.F.R. § 122.62. See 40 C.F.R. § 122.63 for minor modifications of permits.
240. 40 C.F.R. § 122.62.

A permit does not authorize any tortious activity or an invasion of someone else's private rights. Nor does possession of a permit give the permittee the right to violate state or local laws or regulations.[241]

Permits also may be transferred to new owners, subject to notice to EPA, and a written acknowledgment of responsibilities, liabilities and operative dates for the transfer, executed between transferor and transferee.[242] EPA may block the transfer if it concludes that the transferee is unable to comply with the permit requirements.[243]

[b] Effluent Limitations May Be Set Out in the Permit in Different Ways

Quantifying effluent limitations is not for the mathematically challenged. However, a few basic principles are important to understand. How might effluent limitations for particular pollutants be expressed in the permit? The most common means of expressing a limitation is by mass or volume per defined unit of time (e.g., the permit might authorize the discharge of 50 pounds or gallons of the pollutant per day), or per unit of production (e.g., 10 pounds of the pollutant per barrel). The environmental benefit of a mass limitation is that a discharger cannot utilize dilution as a means of evading limitations, which was one of the flaws of former law. Some pollutants, of course, such as thermal pollution or pH, do not lend themselves to expression in terms of mass and have to be addressed separately.[244] EPA also uses other expressions of effluent limitations, often in addition to limitations expressed by mass.[245] For instance, the permit may employ concentration limitations, such as by setting a ceiling on discharges of a specified pollutant to 100 milligrams per liter, or other liquid measurement. However, permittees may not try to substitute concentration limitations, which potentially allow for dilution of pollutants, for applicable mass concentrations. Hence, many permits restrict discharges by mass as well as by concentration. Additionally, permits may limit discharges in terms of their acute (i.e., immediate) or chronic (i.e., prolonged) toxicity in relation to the effect of a toxin on specific organisms or ecosystems in the receiving water. The measurement of toxicity may be expressed in terms of concentration of toxic substance per unit of water. The effluent limitation could also be expressed in terms of the toxic consequences which are acceptable (e.g., a specified morbidity of a target species may be defined as acceptable) which equates with a particular toxic concentration. Permits also may use "indicator" pollutants as a correlate of the intended pollutant. This limitation is employed when the intended pollutant is difficult to measure from a technological or economic standpoint, but its similarity to other — indicator — pollutants provides a useful baseline for the intended pollutant. That is, by requiring

---

241. 40 C.F.R. § 122.5(c).

242. 40 C.F.R. § 122.61(b).

243. 40 C.F.R. § 122.61(b).

244. 40 C.F.R. § 122.45(f)(1)(i), (ii), (iii).

245. *See* 40 C.F.R. § 122.45(f)(2).

technological control of the discharge of the indicator pollutant, the intended pollutant is expected to be similarly controlled.[246]

A "daily discharge" is measured by the total discharge during a calendar day or any 24-hour period that reasonably represents a calendar day for purposes of sampling. If the permit defines the limitation in units of mass, then there is a "daily average" calculated on the basis of the total mass of the pollutant discharged over the course of the day; if another unit of measurement is used, then the variable is a "daily discharge" which equates with the average measurement of the pollutant over the course of the day. The "maximum daily discharge limitation" is the highest allowable daily discharge. "Average weekly limitation" is deemed to be the highest allowable average of "daily discharges" over the calendar week. The variable is computed by adding together all seven daily discharges for the week, then calculating the average for a daily discharge.[247] The "average monthly discharge" limitation is the highest allowable average of daily discharges over a calendar month. Again, the daily discharges for a month are added, and then averaged, to calculate the basic unit.[248]

All permit effluent limitations must be established for each outfall or discharge point of the permitted facility[249] (unless, of course, a general permit is applicable to the entire operation). If an outfall eventually is discontinued, this can be addressed by a minor modification in the permit.[250] For POTWs, limitations are measured against "design flow."[251]

[c] Standard of Performance for Dischargers Requires Use of Best Available Demonstrated Control Technology

Dischargers generally are held to a standard of utilizing Best Management Practices, or "BMPs." These standards govern the scheduling of activities, the prohibition of practices, maintenance procedures, and other management practices aimed at preventing or reducing water pollution. BMPs also govern treatment requirements, operating procedures, and practices to control plant site runoff, spillage or leaks, sludge or waste disposal, or drainage from raw material spillage.[252] However, the CWA defines the standard of performance in terms of the greatest possible reduction of

---

246. See discussion in ENVIRONMENTAL LAW PRACTICE GUIDE § 18.03[3][a] (Gerrard, ed., Matthew Bender).

247. 40 C.F.R. § 122.2.

248. Id.

249. 40 C.F.R. § 122.45.

250. 40 C.F.R. § 122.63(e)(2).

251. 40 C.F.R. § 122.45.

252. EPA by regulation may also define best management practices for categories of industrial point sources. 33 U.S.C. § 1314(e). See 40 C.F.R. § 122.2.

effluents achievable by the "best available demonstrated control technology" (BAT), including, whenever possible, a standard prohibiting any discharge of pollutants.[253]

[d] Other Conditions Apply to Different Classes of Discharges and Categories of Pollutants

There are numerous detailed conditions specifically related to different classes of dischargers and different categories of pollutants, as well as particular effluent limitations, particular standards, and the impact of state requirements. These, however, are beyond the scope of this book.[254]

[8] Monitoring and Reporting Requirements

[a] Primary Monitoring Responsibilities Are Imposed on Permittee

One of the features of the CWA, as with many environmental statutes, is that it imposes primary monitoring responsibilities on the permittee, who must self-monitor, rather than on EPA or the state agency.[255] This has proven to be cost effective for the government, in that the permittee has the financial responsibility for monitoring, for reporting violations, and for correcting the violation, as well as paying penalties. The permittee fills out a "discharge monitoring report," which is a uniform national form used by EPA as well as the states.[256]

[b] Public Disclosure Is Required with Limited Protection for Trade Secrets

There is some limited "trade secret" protection afforded in consequence of the often sensitive nature of the information which a discharging facility must disclose. Information submitted with the application may be treated as confidential if the applicant specifically requests confidentiality.[257] However, most information submitted to EPA is public. For instance, although information relating to production processes might be confidential, effluent data that must be reported to EPA is not

---

253. 33 U.S.C. § 1316(a)(1). The various "best" standards applicable in different circumstances take into account the best practicable control technology that is currently available and, alternatively, the best achievable control measures and practices, which includes a consideration of whether the technology that is demanded is economically achievable at the present time or under the facility's particular circumstances. 33 U.S.C. § 1314(b). *See* Southwestern Electric Power Co. v. U.S. Environmental Protection Agency, 920 F.3d 999 (5th Cir. 2019).

254. EPA is required to devise performance standards to reduce effluent from new sources in particular industrial categories. 33 U.S.C. § 1316(b). *See* 40 C.F.R. § 122.44.

255. However, in order for a state program to receive EPA approval, it must demonstrate a capacity for monitoring independent of the permittee's self monitoring. See [D][2], *below*.

256. 40 C.F.R. § 122.2.

257. 40 C.F.R. § 122.7; *see* 5 U.S.C. § 552.

thereby protected unless it clearly reveals production processes.[258] Furthermore, EPA requires disclosure of the "production rate" to the extent that a pretreatment standard applicable to a facility limits discharge of a pollutant per unit of production.[259] Even if a competitor might glean information about production processes from the disclosure of the monthly production rate data, it is not protected information.[260] If a facility's effluent data is reported to EPA and is subject to public disclosure, competitors may utilize the Freedom of Information Act to obtain this information.[261]

[c] General Record Keeping Requirements and Reporting Obligations

Samples and measurements taken for purposes of monitoring must be representative of the permitted activity. Monitoring records must be kept for three years; if the activity is sewage sludge use and disposal, the records must be kept for five years. Monitoring records must specify the date, place and time of the sampling or measurements, the individual who performed the sampling or measurements, the date that analyses were performed, the individual who performed the analyses, the analytical methodology, and the results of the analyses.[262] EPA specifies the acceptable testing procedures.[263] All reports and information must be signed and certified by the permittee. Tampering with, falsifying, or knowingly rendering inaccurate any monitoring device,[264] or knowingly making misrepresentations or false certifications,[265] is a criminal offense.

In addition, the permittee must report planned physical alterations or additions to the facility that brings the permittee within the requirements for new sources (e.g., a new waste stream), or that could significantly change the pollutants discharged, increase the amount discharged, or significantly change the permittee's sludge use or disposal practices. Any planned changes in the facility that may result in noncompliance with the present permit must be reported in advance.[266]

The reporting obligation may be accelerated to 24-hour notice after the occurrence of an event.[267] This would occur if an unanticipated bypass or an upset should exceed any effluent limitation in the permit. A "bypass" is the intentional diversion of waste

---

258. *See* 33 U.S.C. § 1318(b).

259. 40 C.F.R. § 421.135(b).

260. RSR Corp. v. Browner, 924 F. Supp. 504 (S.D.N.Y. 1996), *aff'd*, 1997 U.S. App. LEXIS 5523 (2d Cir. 1997).

261. *See* 5 U.S.C. § 552.

262. 40 C.F.R. § 122.41(j).

263. 40 C.F.R. Parts 136, 503.

264. 40 C.F.R. § 122.41(j)(5). United States v. Long, 450 Fed. Appx. 457 (6th Cir. 2011); United States v. Panyard, 403 Fed. Appx. 17 (6th Cir. 2010).

265. 40 C.F.R. § 122.41(k)(2). United States v. Panyard, 403 Fed. Appx. 17 (6th Cir. 2010); States v. Holden, 557 F.3d 698 (6th Cir. 2009).

266. 40 C.F.R. § 122.41(l)(1).

267. 40 C.F.R. § 122.41(l)(6).

streams from any portion of a treatment facility.[268] A bypass is prohibited unless it is unavoidable to prevent loss of life, injuries, or severe property damage,[269] there is no feasible alternative, and the permittee provided advance notice. An "upset" is a temporary and unintentional noncompliance with a permit's effluent limitations, that is beyond the permittee's control. Operational errors, or noncompliance resulting from either design defects or lack of preventative maintenance (theoretically within the permittee's control) are not upsets, and in fact, the facility must prove the absence of these factors.[270] If an upset can be proved, it is an affirmative defense to the discharge in excess of effluent limitations, as well as for a violation of state water quality standards.[271]

Manufacturing, commercial, mining, and silvicultural dischargers must report the discharge of any toxic pollutant, even if that pollutant is not limited in the permit (recall that certain toxic pollutants may never be discharged).

The reporting obligation is triggered as soon as the permittee knew, or should have known, of the discharge. If the discharge is infrequent, there are higher thresholds.[272] In the event of an unexcused noncompliance, the violation still must be reported, although it may result in modification, termination, or revocation of the permit, or an enforcement action.

[d] Additional Reporting Obligations for Publicly Owned Treatment Works (POTWs)

A POTW has additional reporting obligations for which there is no specified reporting period, but as to which notice to EPA must be "adequate." Adequacy is determined by the specificity of the information given, including the quantity and quality of the effluent received, and the anticipated effect on the quantity and quality to be discharged by the POTW.[273] The POTW must notify EPA in either of the following circumstances:

- There is any new introduction of pollutants into the POTW from an indirect discharger that would have required a NPDES permit if the pollutants had been directly discharged into the waters of the United States.

- A source which had been introducing pollutants into the POTW at the time the permit was issued substantially changes the volume or character of the pollutants being introduced.

---

268. 40 C.F.R. § 122.41(m).

269. Courts differ as to what constitutes severe property damage. *See* American Petroleum Institute v. Environmental Protection Agency, 661 F.2d 340 (5th Cir. 1981); Marathon Oil Co. v. Environmental Protection Agency, 564 F.2d 1253 (9th Cir. 1977).

270. 40 C.F.R. § 122.41(n).

271. NRDC v. Environmental Protection Agency, 859 F.2d 156 (D.C. Cir. 1988).

272. 40 C.F.R. § 122.42.

273. 40 C.F.R. § 122.42(b).

Recall that indirect dischargers sending wastewater to a POTW generally will not need their own NPDES permit (although they must meet pretreatment standards), since that is not a discharge into the waters of the United States.

A "municipal separate storm sewer system" (i.e., storm runoff, as distinct from domestic sewage) has annual reporting obligations, basically tantamount to the providing of a status report.[274]

[D] State Pollutant Discharge Elimination System (SPDES) Programs

[1] Overview of State Permitting Programs

The CWA contemplates that, subject to federal review and regulations, states may exercise significant responsibilities to control water pollution. About 35 states have approved state permitting programs, or State Pollutant Discharge Elimination System (SPDES) programs. If a SPDES program is approved by EPA, then EPA relinquishes its primary enforcement authority (except for extant EPA issued permits, over which EPA may retain jurisdiction),[275] and delegates permitting and enforcement authority to the "approved" state. An approved state then carries out the terms of the CWA and federal regulations by delegation. The state may seek approval of a partial or a phased program in lieu of a full program.[276] If the state satisfies all CWA requirements to qualify for state enforcement as is discussed in [2], *infra*, and it certifies that it has the ability and legal authority to operate a program, then EPA must transfer permitting and enforcement authority to the state.[277] Most provisions and definitions pertinent to the federal NPDES program apply also to state programs.[278] SPDES permits also may be coordinated with the issuance of permits under CWA § 404 (see § 6.07), other NPDES permits, and RCRA.[279]

For these purposes, Native American tribes also may apply for and carry out EPA-approved programs.[280] In that event, although tribal areas are carved out from state jurisdiction, the state is not precluded from obtaining approval of a full state program.[281]

A state is authorized to regulate in excess of federal regulation. Hence, an approved state may impose requirements that are more stringent than federal requirements. However, to the extent that state regulation exceeds that required by the CWA or

---

274. 40 C.F.R. § 122.42(c).

275. 40 C.F.R. § 123.1(d)(1).

276. 40 C.F.R. § 123.1(g)(2).

277. National Association of Home builders v. Defenders of Wildlife, 551 U.S. 644, 127 S. Ct. 2518, 2525, 2532–2533, 168 L. Ed. 2d 467 (2007).

278. 40 C.F.R. § 123.2.

279. 40 C.F.R. § 123.3.

280. 40 C.F.R. § 123.1(d)(2). The regulations utilize the same standards as the CWA regarding eligibility of tribes. *See* 40 C.F.R. §§ 123.31, 123.32.

281. 40 C.F.R. § 123.1(h).

the federal regulations, the additional requirements are not part of the federally approved program.[282]

If a state proposed program is not approved, or if EPA approval is withdrawn, then the NPDES program is re-imposed for discharges within that state.

[2] State Program Requires EPA Approval: Process and Requirements

To be approved, a state program, at a minimum, must prohibit all discharges of pollutants from point sources, or into aquaculture projects, as well as sludge disposal which leads to a discharge, except as would be authorized by a NPDES permit.[283] However, EPA regulations impose more specific informational and programmatic requirements on applicant states. Approval and maintenance of state programs is driven by extensive information requirements and assurances of the state's diligent enforcement. EPA seeks to ensure that an approved state will carry out all aspects of a NPDES program. If the state fails, EPA must carry out the CWA responsibilities. If EPA fails to do so, it will likely be subject to a citizen suit (see § 6.03[F][5]).[284]

The state must first complete a "program submission" to EPA, including a formal letter from the Governor or relevant tribal authority, a complete program description (discussed below), an Attorney General's statement, a Memorandum of Agreement with EPA, and copies of all applicable state statutes and regulations. EPA will inform the state (or tribe) within 30 days whether the submission is complete, after which the 90-day review period[285] commences.

The "program description" consists of: a narrative description of the scope, structure, coverage, and processes of the state program;[286] a jurisdictional and organizational description of the state agencies that will exercise administrative responsibilities for the state program, identifying the "lead" agency; and an assurance that each agency exercises statewide jurisdiction with respect to its particular responsibility.[287] The state also must include an in-depth description of its agency's staffing,[288] anticipated administrative costs,[289] and agency resources and funding sources.[290] EPA also requires information regarding the applicable state procedures, including permitting procedures, and administrative and judicial review procedures.[291] The state is required to have judicial review procedures for challenges to both the grant and denial of a permit,

---

282. 40 C.F.R. § 123.1(i).
283. 40 C.F.R. § 123.1(g)(1).
284. See discussion in § 6.03[F].
285. See 40 C.F.R. § 123.44.
286. 40 C.F.R. § 123.22(a).
287. 40 C.F.R. § 123.22(b).
288. 40 C.F.R. § 123.22(b)(1).
289. 40 C.F.R. § 123.22(b)(2).
290. 40 C.F.R. § 123.22(b)(3).
291. 40 C.F.R. § 123.22(c).

which are broad enough to allow challenges by parties other than the permittee. EPA wants to encourage public participation.[292]

EPA will want to look at the state's proposed standard application form, permit form, and monitoring form. Generally, state forms need not be identical to EPA's standard forms, but they must be substantially similar. EPA encourages states to use uniform national forms, although modified to use the state rather than EPA letterhead. The exception is that states *must* use EPA's standard Discharge Monitoring Reports.[293]

EPA also requires details of the state's compliance tracking and enforcement program.[294] If the state wishes to manage a sludge program as part of its SPDES program, the state will have to identify its sludge inventory.[295] If the applicant is a tribe, and the state has been authorized by EPA to issue permits on the reservation, EPA will want to see a Memorandum of Agreement between the state and the tribe, addressing how authority would be transferred from state to tribe regarding pending permit applications, existing permits, and the transfer of supporting files.[296]

The state Attorney General's letter must ensure that the *existing* state laws are adequate to carry out the SPDES program. Thus, no conditional promises of prospective legislation will suffice. If the state intends to implement a general permit program, the Attorney General must certify that the state has adequate legal authority to issue and enforce general permits. If the state asserts authority over discharges on tribal land, the Attorney General must analyze the basis of state authority to do so.[297]

The next step is a Memorandum of Agreement (MOA) between the state and EPA.[298] The MOA must include provisions for the prompt transfer of pending permit applications and existing EPA-issued permits and related documents from EPA to the state.[299] EPA has suggested that one means of transfer might be for the state to issue a permit identical to the existing federal permit, and the federal permit would then be terminated simultaneously with issuance of the state permit. If EPA has approved state issuance of permits on tribal land and the tribe seeks program approval, the MOA must describe how it will transfer to the tribe pending applications, permits and related information.[300] The MOA also must specify permit classes and categories, and proposed permits must be sent to EPA for review and comment. If EPA objects, the permit will not be issued.[301] The MOA also must specify the frequency and content

---

292. 40 C.F.R. § 123.30.
293. 40 C.F.R. § 123.22(d). For reference to DMR's, see [C][8][a], *above*.
294. 40 C.F.R. § 123.22(e).
295. *See* CWA § 405(f); 40 C.F.R. § 123.22(f). See 40 C.F.R. § 501.12(f) for inventory requirements.
296. 40 C.F.R. § 123.22(g).
297. 40 C.F.R. § 123.23.
298. 40 C.F.R. § 123.24.
299. 40 C.F.R. § 123.24(b)(1)(i).
300. 40 C.F.R. § 123.24(b)(1)(ii).
301. 40 C.F.R. § 123.29.

of reports, documents and other information which the state is required to submit to EPA. EPA and the state are required to share information without restriction.[302] The MOA must provide for routine EPA inspection of state records, reports and files relevant to administration and enforcement of the approved state program,[303] and for monitoring and enforcement by the state, setting forth how EPA and the state will coordinate their interests and efforts.[304] Since facilities may need EPA-issued permits as well as state permits for various activities, the MOA must address joint processing procedures.[305]

As has been seen, a major component of the NPDES program is compliance evaluation, consisting of monitoring and reporting obligations by permittees. In order for a state program to receive EPA approval, the state program must also have procedures for monitoring and reporting.[306] However, the state program may not rely solely on self-monitoring by permittees: the state must ensure EPA that it will have detailed independent sources of information provided by inspection and surveillance,[307] as well as the ability to investigate information provided by the public.[308] The state's compliance officers must be able to enter and inspect any regulated premises, and to demand and copy records therefrom,[309] subject to Fourth Amendment requirements. In seizing evidence, compliance officers must ensure the integrity of the evidence by maintaining a proper chain of custody.[310]

States must have adequate enforcement authority, encompassing the full range of remedies available under the CWA, including: cease and desist orders; judicial injunctive relief, available without the need to initially revoke the permit; and civil and criminal penalties and sanctions, including fines. Specifically, states legally must be able to recover adequate civil penalties for violation of any permit condition or any filing requirement, any violation in connection with inspection, entry or monitoring, or any violation of an administrative order. Criminal fines must be available for negligent, grossly negligent or strict liability offenses, and for knowing misrepresentations or false statements or certifications in any permit form or report, or for knowingly rendering inaccurate any monitoring device or methodology.

EPA also recommends, but does not require, that states enact procedures for recovery by the state for destruction of wildlife or aquatic life or habitat.

As a component of its SPDES program, a state must also have authority to issue permits to control the disposal of pollutants into wells.[311] Notably, permitting of dis-

---

302. 40 C.F.R. §§ 123.41, 123.42.
303. 40 C.F.R. § 123.24(b)(3).
304. 40 C.F.R. § 123.24(b)(4).
305. 40 C.F.R. § 123.24(b)(5).
306. 40 C.F.R. § 123.26(a).
307. 40 C.F.R. § 123.26(b).
308. 40 C.F.R. § 123.26(b)(4).
309. 40 C.F.R. § 123.26(c).
310. 40 C.F.R. § 123.26(d).
311. 40 C.F.R. § 123.28.

charges into groundwater is not covered by the CWA's own NPDES program (see § 6.04[B], covering federal groundwater regulation).

The regulations also require states to file quarterly, semi-annual, and annual reports to EPA fully itemizing information about each permittee.[312]

[3] SPDES Programs May Be Revised by the State or EPA

State programs may be revised by either the state or by EPA after approval is granted and the programs are running. Revisions usually are necessitated by amendments to the CWA, state statutes, or regulations. However, revision also will be necessary if the original approved program included state regulation of discharges on tribal land, and the tribe has subsequently received EPA approval for conducting a SPDES program.[313] Program revision also may be necessary if responsibilities are shifted among state agencies in a manner different from that specified in the original submission.[314]

[4] EPA Approval of SPDES Programs May Be Withdrawn

EPA may withdraw program approval if the state program no longer conforms to EPA requirements and the state fails to take corrective action.[315] This can arise in a number of circumstances. The state may have failed to enact or promulgate new laws to conform to changes in federal regulations, or the state legislature or courts may have restricted existing state authority to less than is necessary to comply with federal regulations.[316] For instance, a state in an approved program is required to promulgate adequate TMDLs (see [B][2][a], *above*) in connection with its water quality standards for excessively polluted waters; a failure to do so may result in withdrawal of approval. The state may still have the necessary authority, but fail in the operation of its program by not controlling discharges, by not issuing permits, by issuing too many permits which do not conform to federal requirements, or by restricting public participation contrary to federal requirements.[317]

The state may fail to act on violations, fail to seek or collect adequate penalties, or fail to inspect or monitor.[318] Withdrawal also may result when a state fails to promulgate adequate water quality-based effluent limitations for inclusion in its SPDES permits.[319]

EPA's decision in these respects has been characterized as discretionary rather than mandatory, so that it may decline to withdraw approval from the state in favor

---

312. 40 C.F.R. § 123.45.
313. 40 C.F.R. § 123.62(a). For procedural requirements of revision, see 40 C.F.R. § 123.62(b).
314. 40 C.F.R. § 123.62(c).
315. 33 U.S.C. § 1342(c)(3); 40 C.F.R. § 123.64(b)(1).
316. 40 C.F.R. § 123.63(a)(1).
317. 40 C.F.R. § 123.63(a)(2).
318. 40 C.F.R. § 123.63(a)(3).
319. 40 C.F.R. § 123.63(a)(5).

of other measures which it concludes will better achieve the statutory goals.[320] Nevertheless, if EPA fails to withdraw approval, a citizen suit may force that result on the theory that the there is no prospect of state compliance under the circumstances of the case, such that the end result is that the CWA is not being enforced (see [F][5], *below*).[321]

[E] Enforcement

[1] Overview

[a] Enforcement Goals

There are a variety of enforcement strategies ranging from a cease and desist notice up to civil and even criminal penalties. The remedies may be monetary or injunctive. The underlying point of the enforcement authority granted by Congress in the CWA is, first, to abate the discharge, and second, to discourage its recurrence, either by the particular discharger or by others in the regulated community.

[b] How Violations Occur

Violations typically result when a permit condition is not satisfied or an effluent limitation in the permit has been exceeded (which technically also constitutes violation of a permit condition). A CWA violation also may occur when a party wrongfully introduces pollutants into a treatment works, in which case the owner or operator of the treatment works is made a party to the action.[322] Unpermitted discharges also are violations of the CWA.[323]

[c] Discharge of Pollutants into a Treatment Works May Place Treatment Works in Violation

If a discharger has wrongfully introduced pollutants into treatment works, it may place the treatment works in violation of its own permit. In such cases, the notice of violation will be given by EPA to the treatment works as well as the state.[324]

---

320. Cahaba Riverkeeper v. Environmental Protection Agency, 938 F.3d 1157 (11th Cir. 2019).

321. *See, e.g.*, Sierra Club v. Hankinson, 939 F. Supp. 865 (N.D. Ga. 1996); Idaho Sportsmen's Coalition v. Browner, 951 F. Supp. 962 (W.D. Wash. 1996); Natural Resources Defense Council v. Hevesi, 909 F. Supp. 153 (S.D.N.Y. 1995). More recent caselaw, while acknowledging that there may be a point where the state's failure to discharge its responsibilities is so systemic that EPA's failure to withdraw may be an abdication of its statutory responsibilities, nevertheless dismissed a citizen suit on the basis that, in this case, EPA had been acting within its statutory discretion. Cahaba Riverkeeper v. Environmental Protection Agency, 938 F.3d 1157 (11th Cir. 2019).

322. *See* 33 U.S.C. § 1319(f).

323. 33 U.S.C. § 1311(a).

324. 33 U.S.C. § 1319(f).

[2] Enforcement Authority

[a] State Has Enforcement Authority Under SPDES Program; Otherwise, EPA Enforces

In the first instance, once it has been determined that there is a violation, it must be determined who has primary enforcement authority. If the violation of a permit condition or limitation occurs under the aegis of an EPA-approved state program (see [D], *above*, as to State Pollutant Discharge Elimination System (SPDES) Programs) and EPA has information that there is a violation, EPA will issue a notice of violation to the discharger as well as providing notice to the state. The state will then assume enforcement authority.

If there is no EPA-approved state program and EPA issued the permit, or if the state program has been suspended, then EPA will exercise enforcement authority.[325] While the choice of strategies is left to EPA, the agency is mandated by the statute to enforce.[326]

[b] State Has Limited Time Period to Undertake Enforcement

The expectation is that the state will generally assume enforcement responsibility. However, the state has a limited window of thirty days to do so (given the nature of many pollution discharges, which present environmental dangers and may well be continuous or repetitive, Congress wanted to ensure speedy state action). If the state does not act by the thirtieth day after notification, EPA must issue an order compelling compliance with the condition or limitation. In the alternative, EPA may dispense with the administrative order and commence a civil action.[327]

[c] Systematic Nonenforcement by the State; EPA's Resumption of Enforcement Authority

If, under the circumstances described in [b], *above*, EPA determines that the violations are so widespread that they indicate a systematic failure by the state to enforce its permit conditions or effluent limitations effectively, then EPA must give notice to the state of its intent to withdraw approval, which triggers another thirty day period. If the failure continues beyond the thirtieth day, EPA must hold a public hearing, after appropriate notice, to inquire into the state's dereliction of its duty under the CWA. Until such time thereafter that the state satisfies EPA that it will resume its enforcement responsibilities, EPA will reassume enforcement authority and will be able to issue administrative compliance orders or commence civil actions.[328]

---

325. 33 U.S.C. § 1319(a)(3).

326. *Id.*

327. 33 U.S.C. § 1319(a)(1).

328. 33 U.S.C. § 1319(a)(2). See § 6.03[D][4] regarding withdrawal of the EPA approval from derelict state programs and whether EPA must withdraw approval or has discretion in this regard.

[3] Enforcement Options

[a] Compliance Order; Notice of Violation

When EPA issues an order to compel compliance, the violator has thirty days to comply. A copy of the order is sent to the state and "other affected states." If the violator has wrongfully introduced pollutants into a treatment works, EPA also may seek injunctive relief against the treatment works, requiring the owner or operator to come into compliance with the CWA.[329]

The violator must be personally served. If it is a corporation, then an appropriate corporate officer must be served. The notice also must specify the nature of the violation and, within the 30-day compliance period, specify a time for compliance.

EPA retains statutory authority to extend the compliance period in the event that the violator cannot timely cure the violation despite good faith efforts, evidenced by a commitment of resources in the form of contracts or other means of security. EPA will take into account the seriousness of the violation and the possible environmental consequences.[330]

[b] Administrative Enforcement

[i] Public Notice; Public's Opportunity to Comment

On giving notice of a violation, and before assessing a penalty, EPA must provide public notice and an opportunity for comment in connection with the violation and proposed penalty.[331] Any person who comments will then be provided notice of any subsequent evidentiary hearing at which that person will have a reasonable opportunity to present evidence.[332] If no hearing is conducted with respect to assessment of the penalty, any person who commented during the public comment period may petition for a hearing regarding the penalty within thirty days after the issuance of an order assessing penalties. If the evidence is material, then a hearing must be held; if the petition is denied, EPA must provide written reasons to the petitioner, which will also be published in the Federal Register.[333]

[ii] Public Hearing; Witnesses May Be Subpoenaed

If a hearing of any kind is held, EPA may subpoena witnesses and require production of the relevant records and documents. If a party refuses to comply with a subpoena, EPA may seek a judicial order compelling the appearance, production or disclosure of relevant records and documents. A violation of the court order is punishable by contempt.[334] On a finding of a permit violation, EPA will issue a compliance order and assess penalties.

---

329. *See* 33 U.S.C. § 1319(f).
330. 33 U.S.C. § 1319(a)(5).
331. 33 U.S.C. § 1319(g)(4)(A).
332. 33 U.S.C. § 1319(g)(4)(B).
333. 33 U.S.C. § 1319(g)(4)(C).
334. 33 U.S.C. § 1319(g)(10).

[iii] Penalties

Violations are of two degrees: Class I or Class II, providing different avenues of judicial review, with the latter resulting in higher penalties.[335] A single operational upset[336] which leads to simultaneous discharges of more than one pollutant is, nevertheless, treated as a single violation.[337]

In determining how much of a penalty to impose, EPA will consider the nature and circumstances of the violation, its extent and gravity, the violator's ability to pay, the economic benefit potentially realized by the violator as a result of the offense, the violator's history of infractions, if any, and degree of culpability.[338] Unless the violator petitions for judicial review, the EPA compliance order becomes final thirty days after the order is issued.[339] If the violator fails to pay the penalty, the Attorney General may sue in federal court for the amount assessed plus stiff penalties, including attorneys' fees and court costs.[340]

[c] Civil Remedies

Under any circumstances in which EPA has authority to issue a notice of violation and an administrative compliance order, the agency also has the authority to bring a civil court action. Such an action is commenced in the federal district court where the violator is located, or resides, or is doing business (or, if appropriate, where the treatment works is located). State courts do not have jurisdiction to hear EPA enforcement actions. Nevertheless, EPA must give notice of commencement of the action to the "appropriate" state.[341] EPA may seek civil penalties or injunctive relief. The injunction may be temporary or permanent,[342] but injunctive relief is not available if a civil penalty is imposed.[343] Of course, EPA retains the right to modify, terminate or revoke the permit upon a finding that its terms or conditions have been violated.

The court may impose civil penalties for violation of any permit condition or effluent limitation, whether the permit is issued by EPA or by a state; or for violation of any requirement imposed in an approved pretreatment program; or for violation of any administrative compliance order issued by EPA. Penalties are often imposed on a per diem basis—i.e., per day of violation, rather than per instance of violation (especially since a violation may extend over several days). The aggregate penalty can be significant,

---

335. 33 U.S.C. § 1319(g)(2).

336. An upset is an exceptional incident that is an unintentional and temporary noncompliance with a permit's effluent limitations. It must result from factors beyond the permittee's reasonable control. It cannot result, however, from operational error, improperly designed or inadequate treatment facilities, a lack of preventative maintenance or carelessness — all of which are within the permittee's control. *See* 40 C.F.R. § 42(n).

337. 33 U.S.C. § 1319(g)(3).

338. *Id.*

339. 33 U.S.C. § 1319(g)(5).

340. 33 U.S.C. § 1319(g)(9)(A).

341. 33 U.S.C. § 1319(b).

342. *Id.*

343. Weinberger v. Romero-Barcelo, 456 U.S. 305 (1982).

an inducement to a violator to take swift remedial action or otherwise to abate the violation expeditiously. However, was noted in [b][iii] above, a single operational upset[344] involving more than one pollutant will be treated as a single violation.[345] This moderate approach accords with the necessarily unanticipated nature of an upset beyond the permittee's control. Many of the same factors that govern the assessment of administrative penalties are also considered by the court when determining civil penalties, and a defaulting violator faces similar additional costs.[346]

Although earlier law held that persons receiving an EPA compliance order had no right to judicial review prior to enforcement, the Supreme Court has since rejected that perspective. A compliance order is final agency action, providing for judicial review under the federal Administrative Procedure Act.[347]

[d] Criminal Enforcement

[i] Overview

EPA also may seek criminal penalties, consisting of fines and/or incarceration under some circumstances. Fines are imposed on a per diem basis. As with civil penalties, a single operational upset is treated as a single violation.[348] The CWA punishes negligent and intentional violations, as well as knowing endangerment. The Act also criminalizes any coverup. Any person may also be prosecuted for knowingly making any false material statement, representation, or certification in any of the documents filed in connection with the permit; or for knowingly falsifying, rendering inaccurate, or tampering with any monitoring device or monitoring method.[349]

[ii] Criminal Negligence

A violator may be prosecuted for criminal negligence for a permit violation, or for noncompliance with a pretreatment program requirement, or for a negligent discharge into a sewer system or a publicly owned treatment works (POTW), when the discharger knew or should have known that the particular pollutant could cause personal injury

---

344. *See* 40 C.F.R. § 42(n).

345. 33 U.S.C. § 1319(d).

346. 33 U.S.C. § 1319(g)(9)(B).

347. Sackett v. Environmental Protection Agency, 566 U.S. 120 (2012). The Court recognized a due process problem in that the party subjected to the order either had the Hobson's choice of either complying, which could likely moot judicial review, or declining to comply and then face the consequences if it was wrong. The Supreme Court recognized that the alleged violator should have the opportunity to challenge the legality of the order or its enforceability before making its informed decision. Hence, parties subject to the order may now request a jurisdictional determination — basically a request that the agency explain the basis of its determination — which, if the objection to jurisdiction is denied, will be subject to judicial review. If the order lacked a jurisdictional basis, compliance would itself become moot.

348. 33 U.S.C. § 1319(c)(5).

349. 33 U.S.C. § 1319(c)(4). United States v. Long, 450 Fed. Appx. 457 (6th Cir. 2011); United States v. Panyard, 403 Fed. Appx. 17 (6th Cir. 2010); States v. Holden, 557 F.3d 698 (6th Cir. 2009).

or property damage.[350] A negligent discharge into a treatment works, which then causes the treatment works to be in violation of its own permit, is also a crime.[351]

[iii] Knowing Violations

A knowing violation is punished more severely than a negligent violation.[352] Scienter in these cases does not require knowledge that the conduct is criminal, nor even that the permit was violated.[353] Rather, a much criticized Circuit Court ruling, *Weitzenhoff v. United States*,[354] concluded that the discharger need only know that the discharge occurred for criminal liability to attach under a scienter theory. Some commentary argues that such an approach effectively creates strict liability offenses without real regard to *mens rea*,[355] while other commentary sees this result as consistent with the Act's legislative history.[356] Nevertheless, criminal prosecution has been constitutionally upheld even though the statute does not define the conduct to which "knowing" would apply.[357]

[iv] Knowing Endangerment

A discharger may be prosecuted on a theory of knowing endangerment.[358] This offense is based on an allegation that the discharger knew that the violation placed another person in imminent danger of death or serious bodily injury.[359]

---

350. The government may rely on general negligence principles: that the defendant failed to use the care that a reasonably prudent person would have used under the circumstances. Hence, negligence occurred when the defendant's inattention contributed to the collapse of an old oil storage tank, discharging substantial quantities of oil into a river. U.S. v. Ashland Oil, 705 F. Supp. 270 (W.D. Pa. 1989).

351. 33 U.S.C. § 1319(c)(1)(B).

352. 33 U.S.C. § 1319(c)(2).

353. *See generally* Christine L. Wettach, *Mens Rea and the "Heightened Criminal Liability" Imposed on Violators of the Clean Water Act*, 15 STAN. ENVTL. L.J. 377 (1996).

354. 35 F.3d 1275 (9th Cir. 1994), *cert. denied*, 513 U.S. 1128 (1995); *see also* United States v. Schallom, 998 F.2d 196 (4th Cir. 1993), and United States v. Cooper, 482 F.3d 658 (4th Cir. 2007), where the defendant claimed to be unaware that the stream receiving the discharge was connected to navigable waters of the United States, since the knowing discharge, and not the result of the discharge, was the statutory element. Subsequently, *Weitzenhoff* was followed by *United States v. Hopkins*, 53 F.3d 533 (2d Cir. 1995), also finding the CWA to be only a general intent statute in which the defendant need only knowingly engage in conduct, rather than codifying a specific intent culpability. For perspectives on this approach, see discussion in Kevin Phillip Cichetti, United States v. Weitzenoff: *Reading Out The "Knowingly Violates" in the Clean Water Act*, 9 ADMIN. L.J. AM. U. 1183 (1996).

355. *See* Patrick W. Ward, *The Criminal Provisions of the Clean Water Act as Interpreted by the Judiciary and the Resulting Response from the Legislature*, 5 DICK. J. ENVTL. L. & POL'Y 399 (1996).

356. See Christine L. Wettach, *Mens Rea and the "Heightened Criminal Liability" Imposed on Violators of the Clean Water Act*, 15 STAN. ENVTL. L.J. 377 (1996), noting that congressional drafters of the 1987 amendments substituted "knowingly" for the original mens rea "willfully," which would have suggested purposeful activity. The commentator concludes that congress wanted to preclude a defense that the discharger did not act purposefully to violate the law. Even under pre-1987 law, the CWA was not a specific intent statute. United States v. Baytank (Houston), Inc., 934 F.2d 599 (5th Cir. 1991).

357. United States v. Long, 450 Fed. Appx. 457 (6th Cir. 2011).

358. 33 U.S.C. § 1319(c)(3).

359. "Serious bodily injury" has its usual meaning in criminal statutes: a substantial risk of death, unconsciousness, extreme physical pain; protracted and obvious disfigurement; or protracted loss or impairment of the function of a bodily member, organ or mental faculty. 33 U.S.C. § 1319(c)(3)(B)(iv).

There are some procedural safeguards: if the defendant is an *individual* (including any responsible corporate officer)[360] rather than a corporation or another entity, he or she will be held responsible only for his or her actual awareness or belief; knowledge possessed by other persons will not be imputed to the individual defendant. However, knowledge may be proved circumstantially, and, moreover, the defense will be unavailable if the defendant took affirmative steps to be shielded from the necessary information comprising knowing endangerment.[361]

There is an affirmative defense available to the defendant if the endangered person consented to the charged conduct, and the conduct and consequential danger were reasonably foreseeable hazards of the occupation, business, or profession. The affirmative defense also is available if the hazard results from medical treatment or scientific experimentation conducted by professionally approved methods, that the endangered person was aware of the risks prior to giving consent, and that he or she then gave consent. The affirmative defense must be proved by a preponderance of the evidence.[362]

[F] Citizen Suits

[1] Overview; Purpose Is to Ensure Compliance with the CWA

As is true with several other environmental statutes, and as described in § 1.03, the CWA authorizes citizen suits.[363] Citizen suits are a means by which "citizen" plaintiffs — perhaps individuals, but usually organizations — seek enforcement of the CWA when they conclude that the appropriate regulatory authority has failed to diligently carry out its enforcement duties. The citizen suit is a vehicle for a court to order the relief necessary to secure prompt compliance with the CWA when the designated federal authorities fail to take the initiative.[364] Citizen plaintiffs may sue to enforce a permit condition, or effluent limitation or standard, or to enforce a related civil or administrative order, or to require that penalties be paid.

However, since the goal of a citizen suit is limited — enforcement rather than personal recovery — the basis for the citizen suit is defeated if, in fact, the appropriate governmental actor is acting "diligently." This bar to commencement of the suit is discussed in [8], *below.*

The CWA citizen suit provisions apply only to actions in federal court to redress a violation of a NPDES[365] (federal) or SPDES[366] (state) permit. The point is to provide a substitute avenue to enforce the CWA when federal or state authorities fail to act. A citizen suit under the CWA does not confer a private right of action, so that there is no private remedy or recovery of damages.

---

360. 33 U.S.C. § 1319(c)(6).

361. 33 U.S.C. § 1319(c)(3)(B)(i).

362. 33 U.S.C. § 1319(c)(3)(B)(ii).

363. 33 U.S.C. § 1365.

364. Weinberger v. Romero-Barcelo, 456 U.S. 305, 320 (1982).

365. See § 6.03[C] for discussion of National Pollutant Discharge Elimination System.

366. See § 6.03[D] for discussion of State Pollutant Discharge Elimination System.

[2] Enforcement Goals: Violations of Permit, Effluent Limitations, Water Quality Standards, Compliance Orders

Typically, citizen plaintiffs seek to redress a discharger's violation of a condition in the permit, or of a national effluent limitation or standard, or disobedience of an administrative order, such as a compliance order.[367] Case law has allowed enforcement by citizens of a state effluent limitation which may be incorporated as a condition in the NPDES permit, although there is divided authority on the point.[368] The law also is unsettled as to whether state water quality standards, as contrasted with effluent limitations, may be enforced by citizen suits.[369] There is case law, however, which has limited citizen suits to occasions when an effluent standard or limitation is explicitly incorporated in the permit, disallowing the action when a pollutant, although discharged, has not been specified in the permit, on the theory that the permit had not been violated.[370]

[3] Citizen Suits May Address Only Present Violations

Citizen suits may address only an ongoing or imminent violation. CWA citizen suits may not be maintained for wholly past violations which are not likely to be repeated.[371]

[4] Statutory and Common Law Remedies May Still Be Pursued

By commencing a citizen suit the plaintiffs do not foreclose their other available common law or statutory remedies, such as nuisance, negligence and trespass.[372]

---

367. 33 U.S.C. § 1365(a)(1).

368. In favor, see Northwest Environmental Advocates v. Portland, 56 F.3d 979, 985–990 (9th Cir. 1995), *cert. denied*, 518 U.S. 1018 (1996). For case law ruling that state regulations incorporated as permit conditions may not be enforced in a citizen suit, see Atlantic States Legal Foundation, Inc. v. Eastman Kodak Co., 12 F.3d 353, 358–59 (2d Cir. 1993), *cert. denied*, 513 U.S. 811 (1994).

369. See discussion in Northwest Environmental Advocates v. Portland, 11 F.3d 900, *reconsidered at* 56 F.3d 979, *cert. denied*, 518 U.S. 1018 (1996).

370. *See* Atlantic States Legal Foundation, Inc. v. Eastman Kodak Co., 12 F.3d 353 (2d Cir. 1994), *cert. denied*, 513 U.S. 1018 (1996).

371. Steel Company v. Citizens for a Better Environment, 523 U.S. 83 (1998). The statutory phrasing is that citizen suits may be brought against any person who "is in violation ..." (CWA § 505(a)), which has been interpreted to address only ongoing or current violations. *See also* Gwaltney of Smithfield, Ltd. v. Chesapeake Bay Foundation, Inc., 484 U.S. 49, 64 (1987). Although recovery may not be had for a wholly past violation, such as a discharge that occurred before the violator obtained a permit, that would not bar a citizen suit against the same violator for failing to monitor later discharges at the time the citizen suit was filed. *See* Parker v. Scrap Metal Processors, Inc., 386 F.3d 993 (11th Cir. 2004).

372. 33 U.S.C. § 1365(e); Concerned Area Residents for the Environment v. Southview Farms, 34 F.3d 114 (2d Cir. 1994), *cert. denied*, 514 U.S. 1082 (1995). The discharge of liquefied manure from a manure spreading operation into a ditch and thence into waters of the United States was the basis for the CWA citizen suit. However, the plaintiffs also joined nuisance, trespass and negligence claims under the state's common law. See discussion in Chapter 3 for common law theories of recovery for environmental harm.

[5] EPA May Be Sued for Its Failure to Comply with the CWA

Citizen plaintiffs may sue EPA, claiming that it failed to perform a nondiscretionary duty, such as when the Agency fails to promulgate regulations or standards despite statutory obligations to do so, or fails to act when states fail to enforce state programs.[373] The CWA also allows state governors to sue EPA when a discharge crosses state borders and the Agency fails to enforce an effluent limitation or permit condition.[374] Under such circumstances, the state, alleging damage to state waters, may also intervene in a citizen suit already properly commenced against EPA challenging its failure to promulgate the necessary standards.[375] In these cases, EPA is being challenged for its failure to perform a nondiscretionary duty. However, citizen plaintiffs have been less successful in suing EPA with respect to how it exercised its discretion under the statute. Such citizen suits have been dismissed when EPA decided not to enforce as to an alleged violation.[376] The recourse of citizen plaintiffs then is to sue the alleged violator for the violation rather than to sue EPA to compel its enforcement (see § 6.03[F][8], *infra*).

[6] Standing

As a threshold requirement, the plaintiff must have standing.[377] This is defined in the CWA, in contrast to other citizen suit provisions in federal environmental statutes, as an interest that is affected or may be affected by the challenged conduct (the Clean Air Act, RCRA and other citizen suit statutes do not have this language).[378] Case law has required that the citizen plaintiff must have suffered, or will suffer, an injury-in-fact. That is, the citizen plaintiff must show: (1) the invasion of a legally protected interest; (2) that the injury is concrete and particularized; and (3) that the injury is actual and imminent, rather than conjectural or hypothetical.[379] Interestingly, showing injury to the environment, although necessary for a citizen plaintiff to prevail on the merits, is not a requirement of citizen standing.[380] If the contamination of the water body interferes with the citizen plaintiff's use, including recreational use, of the water,

---

373. 33 U.S.C. § 1365(a)(2); Natural Resources Defense Council v. Environmental Protection Agency, 542 F.3d 1235 (9th Cir. 2008).

374. 33 U.S.C. § 1365(h).

375. Natural Resources Defense Council v. Environmental Protection Agency, 542 F.3d 1235 (9th Cir. 2008).

376. Sierra Club v. Whitman, 268 F.3d 898 (9th Cir. 2002). For a discussion of the distinction between lawsuits challenging EPA for its failure to perform a nondiscretionary duty versus its exercise of discretion, see Our Children's Earth Foundation v. Environmental Protection Agency, 506 F.3d 781 (9th Cir. 2007).

377. For a more comprehensive discussion of standing, generally, under the CWA, see ROBINSON, ENVIRONMENTAL REGULATION OF REAL PROPERTY § 12.07 (Law Journal Press 2021).

378. 33 U.S.C. § 1365(g).

379. *See* Friends of the Earth v. Laidlaw Environmental Services, 528 U.S. 167 (2000); Steel Co. v. Citizens For a Better Environment, 523 U.S. 83 (1998).

380. Friends of the Earth v. Laidlaw Environmental Services, 528 U.S. 167 (2000).

the necessary injury to the plaintiff may be established.[381] If recreational injury has been established, in that the plaintiff demonstrates that because of the pollution he uses the water body less often for swimming, fishing, boating, or even for aesthetic enjoyments such as bird watching, the frequency of the former use is not a dispositive factor.[382] When recreational or aesthetic injury is asserted as the basis for CWA standing, however, there is a critical distinction between these actual uses of the water body into which pollutants are discharged, and uses that are merely speculative or remote from the point of discharge.[383] If an organizational plaintiff is involved, the requirements of organizational standing also must be met.[384] The citizen plaintiff also must establish a causal connection between the challenged conduct and the injury, and that the injury can be judicially redressed.[385] A violation that is not ongoing, but is entirely in the past, cannot be judicially addressed (see [I][3], *infra*) and would defeat standing.

[7] Target of Suit; Suit Subject to Eleventh Amendment

If standing is established, the next step is for the plaintiff to establish that the particular target may be sued. The statute allows suit against "any person," which includes the United States and any other governmental unit, as well as private dischargers of pollutants.[386] While this requirement is easily satisfied in the case of most dischargers, it becomes more complicated, in view of the Eleventh Amendment (see discussion

---

381. *Id.*; Friends of the Earth v. Gaston Copper Recycling Corp., 204 F.3d 149 (4th Cir. 2000); Sierra Club et al. v. U.S. Army Corps of Engineers et al., 645 F.3d 978 (8th Cir. 2011) (although environmental harm was alleged, the citizen plaintiffs, including a hunting club and an avian enthusiast organization also sufficiently alleged recreational and aesthetic harm allowed by the permitted filling of wetlands and construction activity to establish their standing).

382. Ecological Rights Foundation v. Pacific Lumber Co., 230 F.3d 1141 (9th Cir. 2000).

383. An illustration of the distinction between claims are minimally adequate and those that are excessively remote or where the actual use of the water body of its vicinity remains only speculative, has been made in two Seventh Circuit decisions issued close in time to each other. *See* Sierra Club v. Franklin County Power of Illinois, 546 F.3d 918 (7th Cir. 2008); Pollack v. United States Department of Justice, 577 F.3d 736 (7th Cir. 2009). In the latter decision, rejecting standing, the court drew the distinction with Friends of the Earth v. Gaston Recycling Corp., in note 381, supra.

384. See discussion in § 1.02; Sierra Club v. Morton, 405 U.S. 727 (1972) (established the basic rules for organizational standing. One or more of the organization's members must actually use the water body or be affected by its contamination). See also Sierra Club v. SCM Corp., 747 F.2d 99 (2d Cir. 1984). Because an organization's standing depends on at least one of its members having standing, the question arises whether organizational standing can survive should a sole member having standing does not survive the citizen suit. In Friends of the Earth v. Gaston Copper Recycling Corp., 629 F.3d 387 (4th Cir. 2011), a later phase of the litigation referenced in note 381, supra, the citizen suit remained viable because another member of the organization, who had individual standing, could be substituted upon the death of the only member who previously asserted individual standing. The lesson to be learned is to have multiple members who individually can assert standing.

385. Steel Co. v. Citizens For a Better Environment, 523 U.S. 83 (1998); Lujan v. Defenders of Wildlife, 504 U.S. 555 (1992) (under Endangered Species Act); Public Interest Research Group of New Jersey v. Powell Duffryn Terminals, Inc., 913 F.2d 64 (3d Cir. 1990), *cert. denied*, 498 U.S. 1109 (1991).

386. 33 U.S.C. § 1365(a)(1).

in § 1.04), when the plaintiff sues a state actor in federal court. The citizen suit provisions explicitly are made subject to the Eleventh Amendment, although, of course, even if they were not, the Eleventh Amendment would still apply. Although state agencies[387] or a state regional water quality control board[388] may be sued in federal court for prospective injunctive relief, a state itself may not be sued by citizen plaintiffs in federal court for a CWA violation.[389]

[8] Bar to Commencement of Suit: 60 Days Notice; Contents of Notice; EPA Diligently Prosecuting Enforcement Action

Congress provided for citizen suits only to ensure that permitting authorities do not backslide in their enforcement efforts. Citizen suits were not intended to be an open-ended vehicle for relief. Congress did not intend to subject a discharger to multiple suits at once, nor did it want the commencement of a citizen suit to interfere with pending or prospective enforcement actions. For this reason, the CWA contains a statutory pre-condition to commencement of a citizen suit: a citizen suit may not be commenced if an enforcement action is pending or imminent.[390] To ensure that investigations are not interfered with, the citizen plaintiff must give sixty days' notice of the alleged violation to EPA, to the state, and to the alleged violator.[391] However, the pre-condition is not jurisdictional, so that a party's failure to challenge insufficient notice may constitute a waiver.[392] The notice letter, at a minimum, should identify the date and place of the violation, the identity of the violator, the particular outfall or other location[393] where the alleged violation occurred, the specific violation, the pollutant discharged,[394] and the names of all plaintiffs.[395] Courts generally impose a standard of "reasonable specificity" rather than to require notice of every detail of every violation.[396] The point is to provide all necessary information to all parties so that the alleged violation may be resolved speedily. As one court stated, "the target

---

387. Mancuso v. New York State Thruway Authority, 909 F. Supp. 133, 135 (S.D.N.Y. 1995), aff'd, 86 F.3d 289 (2d Cir. 1996); Pennsylvania Environmental Defense Fund v. Mazurkiewicz, 712 F. Supp. 1184, 1189 (M.D. Pa. 1989).

388. Committee to Save Mokelumne River v. East Bay Utility District, 13 F.3d 305, 309–10 (9th Cir. 1993), cert. denied, 513 U.S. 873 (1994).

389. Burnette v. Carothers, 192 F.3d 52 (2d Cir. 1999), cert. denied, 531 U.S. 1052 (2000); Seminole Tribe of Florida v. Florida, 517 U.S. 44 (1996).

390. For a more comprehensive discussion of the procedural requirements for CWA citizen suits, see ROBINSON, ENVIRONMENTAL REGULATION OF REAL PROPERTY § 12.07 (Law Journal Press 2021).

391. 33 U.S.C. § 1365(b)(1); see also 33 U.S.C. § 1319(g)(6); Armstrong v. ASARCO, Inc., 138 F.3d 382 (8th Cir. 1998).

392. Lockett v. Environmental Protection Agency, 319 F.3d 678 (5th Cir. 2003).

393. Center for Biological Diversity v. Marina Point Development Co., 535 F.3d 1026 (9th Cir. 2008) (mere reference to the discharge of fill in a wetland, without further specifying the particular wetland, was inadequate notice).

394. Public Interest Research Group of New Jersey v. Hercules, Inc., 50 F.3d 1239 (3d Cir. 1995).

395. Cf. Washington Trout v. McCain Foods, Inc., 45 F.3d 1351 (9th Cir. 1995) (failure to list all plaintiffs and provide addresses rendered notice letter defective).

396. Catskill Mountains Chapter of Trout Unlimited v. City of New York, 273 F.3d 481, 488 (2d Cir. 2001); accord San Francisco Baykeeper v. Tosco Corp., 309 F.3d 1153 (9th Cir. 2002). However,

[of the notice letter] is not required to play a guessing game."[397] The citizen suit provisions are not enacted to benefit a particular class of persons, but are intended to provide another means of ensuring compliance with the CWA. It is not intended that the plaintiffs be given a litigation advantage by withholding information which may facilitate the goals of the CWA.

After the required notice is provided, the next step is to determine whether the citizen suit would be redundant to an official enforcement action. If an enforcement action already has been commenced and is being "diligently" prosecuted, then the citizen suit will be barred.[398] However, the question arises, "What is diligent?" Diligent does not necessarily equate with successful. So long as the regulatory agency is doing something by way of enforcement, courts likely will defer to its exercise of discretion in selecting strategies. By way of illustration, a county was the discharger in one case, but the state regulatory agency seldom commenced civil actions to recover fines from a county, preferring to rely on consent orders. In this case, the strategy did not work— the violations recurred. However, the court concluded that the state agency had not been lacking in diligence at the time of the original violation, but only that the county had failed to abide by an order. It was not necessary for the agency to seek fines to establish that it had acted with diligence.[399] A so-ordered consent decree entered by the violator and EPA that addresses most of the locations giving rise to violations may be adequate to bar commencement of a citizen suit, even if some sites are omitted. The statutory goal is to resolve the violation, which could be undermined if violators, fearing subsequent citizen suits as to minor omissions, might decline to enter such consent decrees.[400] Similarly, a citizen suit will be dismissed when the agency extracts from the violator a binding agreement to implement specific measures that address the violation.[401]

On the other hand, a citizen plaintiff may ordinarily establish a lack of diligence in connection with enforcement efforts by showing a dilatory pattern of laxness.[402] There also is a concern that the government may have started an action for the very

---

in a multi-claim action, claims as to which no notice is provided will be dismissed (*Catskill Mountains Chapter of Trout Unlimited*).

397. Center for Biological Diversity v. Marina Point Development Co., 535 F.3d 1026 (9th Cir. 2008).

398. 33 U.S.C. § 1365(b)(1)(B).

399. Orange Environment, Inc. v. County of Orange, 860 F. Supp. 1003 (S.D.N.Y. 1994). Other courts, however, have looked to whether a penalty was paid in determining whether there actually was an enforcement action which would bar a subsequent citizen suit. *See also* Citizens for a Better Environment v. Union Oil Co. of California, 83 F.3d 1111 (9th Cir. 1996), *cert. denied*, 519 U.S. 1101 (1997).

400. Karr v. Hefner, 475 F.3d 1192 (10th Cir. 2007).

401. Friends of Milwaukee's Rivers v. Milwaukee Metropolitan Sewerage District, 556 F.3d 603 (7th Cir. 2009).

402. Connecticut Fishermen's Association v. Remington Arms Co., Inc., 777 F. Supp. 173, 183 (D. Conn. 1991), *aff'd in part*, 989 F.2d 1305 (2d Cir. 1993).

purpose of barring a citizen suit. This would provide another basis for a court to evaluate the extent of the government's diligence.[403] However, as was noted 6.03[F][5], *supra*, a distinction must be drawn between claims that EPA has failed to exercise its discretion to enforce, in which case the citizen plaintiff may be substituted as the enforcer under the CWA, and claims that EPA is failing perform a duty required by the statute, in which case the appropriate vehicle is to sue EPA directly to compel it to perform a nondiscretionary duty.[404]

The statute specifies that EPA or the state regulatory authority must be diligently prosecuting a civil or criminal court "action." Some courts do not construe a mere administrative compliance proceeding to be an actual enforcement action so as to trigger the bar,[405] whereas other courts interpret "enforcement action" broadly to include an administrative compliance proceeding.[406]

[9] Intervention

If the citizen suit is dismissed, the citizen plaintiff may still seek to intervene as of right in the pending enforcement action.[407] Conversely, if the citizen suit is maintained, EPA may intervene as of right.[408]

[10] "Substantially" Prevailing Plaintiff May Recover Attorney and Expert Witness Fees

If the citizen plaintiff substantially prevails in an action against the government, when the government's role is either that of a lax enforcement authority or of a discharger, the CWA specifically provides for an award of reasonable attorneys' and expert witnesses' fees.[409] If the citizen plaintiff prevails against a private party, despite

---

403. Certainly, actions by state administrative agencies which were not initiated until after the filing of a citizen's suit have been deemed to show a lack of diligence. *See Sierra Club v. Simkins Industries, 617 F. Supp. 1120 (D. Md. 1985); Conn. Fund for Environment v. Job Plating Co., 623 F. Supp. 207 (D. Conn. 1985).*

404. For a discussion of the distinction, see Our Children's Earth Foundation v. Environmental Protection Agency, 506 F.3d 781 (9th Cir. 2007).

405. Jones v. City of Lakeland Tennessee, 224 F.3d 518 (6th Cir. 2000) (state administrative proceeding); Washington Public Interest Research Group v. Pendleton Woolen Mills, 11 F.3d 883 (9th Cir. 1993); Citizens For a Better Environment v. Union Oil Co. of California, 83 F.3d 1111 (9th Cir. 1996), *cert. denied,* 519 U.S. 1101 (1997). For instance, both RCRA (42 U.S.C. § 6972(b)(2)(B)(iv)) and CERCLA (42 U.S.C. § 9659(d)(2)) specifically bar citizen suits in the event of pending compliance actions or abatement orders, by contrast with the CWA, which specifies that the bar applies to "enforcement" actions. Hence, a strict reading of 33 U.S.C. § 1365 when contrasted with these other statutes could support the conclusion that Congress intended the bar to be applied narrowly according to the statutory terms. *See Jones, supra.*

406. North & South Rivers Watershed Association v. City of Scituate, 949 F.2d 552 (1st Cir. 1991).

407. 33 U.S.C. § 1365(b)(1)(B).

408. 33 U.S.C. § 1365(c)(2).

409. 33 U.S.C. § 1365(d). For how "reasonable" fees are computed, see Public Interest Research Group of New Jersey v. Windall, 51 F.3d 1179 (3d Cir. 1995).

the usual provisions of the American rule, the "substantially prevailing" plaintiff may recover "appropriate" legal and expert witness fees if the remedy directly contributes to the goals of the CWA.[410] The CWA does not explicitly allow a substantially prevailing defendant to recover fees from the non-prevailing plaintiff, and there is a cogent argument that such was not the statutory goal. Nevertheless, some courts have allowed prevailing defendants to recover attorneys fees when the citizen plaintiff's action was frivolous, unreasonable, or lacking a legitimate foundation.[411]

[11] Penalties Are Paid to U.S. Treasury; Some Courts Allow Earmarking for Environmental Projects

The funds paid as penalties are deposited in the United States Treasury, although the penalties sometimes are earmarked for cleanups.[412] If the recovery is denoted civil penalties, most courts have required that the funds be deposited in the Treasury,[413] although disposal of settlement funds that are not denoted penalties is not so constricted.[414] One court has suggested that there is a "middle ground" where penalties may permissibly be paid to environmental groups as a remedy for the wrong,[415] while another court, finding such penalty payments impermissible, would have authorized a similar result as an incident to injunctive relief.[416]

---

410. 33 U.S.C. § 1365(d). By contrast, if the fees are for duplicative actions, so that the action did not, itself, advance the goals of the CWA, or the citizen plaintiff played only a secondary role in existing enforcement litigation (*see* California Public Interest Group v. Shell Oil Co., 1996 WL 33982 (N.D. Cal. 1996)), the application for fees will be denied. See, also, in a NEPA context, Citizens for Better Forestry v. U.S. Department of Agriculture, 567 F.3d 1128 (9th Cir. 2009) (no relief on the merits, hence no award of fees). However, absent a sound reason not to award fees, many courts find that the award of fees to a substantially prevailing party itself advances the goals of the CWA since it facilitates statutory enforcement by citizen plaintiffs. The Ninth Circuit is especially disposed to do so. St. John's Organic Farm v. Gem County Mosquito Abatement District, 574 F.3d 1054 (9th Cir. 2009).

411. Paolino v. J.F. Realty LLC, 830 F.3d 8 (1st Cir. 2016); Bentley v. Fanguy, 396 Fed. Appx. 130 (5th Cir. 2010); City of Santa Clarita v. United States Department of the Interior, 249 Fed. Appx. 502 (9th Cir. 2007) (court, finding an inherent common law right to do so, awarded fees to defendants as a sanction for plaintiff's several vexatious actions commenced over the years that lacked merit or were barred by the statute of limitations or were collaterally estopped).

412. *See* Quan B. Nghiem, *Using Equitable Discretion to Impose Supplemental Environmental Projects Under the Clean Water Act*, 24 B.C. ENVTL. AFF. L. REV. 561 (1997); David S. Mann, *Polluter-Financed Environmentally Beneficial Expenditures: Effective Use or Improper Abuse of Citizen Suits Under the Clean Water Act?*, 21 ENVTL. L. 175 (1991).

413. Public Interest Research Group of New Jersey v. Powell Duffryn Terminals, Inc., 913 F.2d 64 (3d Cir. 1990), *cert. denied*, 498 U.S. 1109 (1991).

414. Northwest Environmental Defense Center v. Unified Sewerage Agency of Washington County, 1990 U.S. Dist. LEXIS 13349 (D. Or. 1990); Sierra Club v. Electronic Controls Design, 909 F.2d 1350 (9th Cir. 1990).

415. Friends of the Earth v. Archer Daniels Midland Co., 1990 U.S. Dist. LEXIS 9152 (N.D.N.Y. 1990).

416. Public Interest Research Group of New Jersey v. Powell Duffryn Terminals, Inc., 913 F.2d 64 (3d Cir. 1990), *cert. denied*, 498 U.S. 1109 (1991).

§ 6.04 Water Resources

[A] Background

[1] What Are the Sources of Ground Water Contamination?

Drinking water, generally, is drawn from two sources: surface water and ground water. Approximately half of the country's population relies on ground water for drinking water supplies; in rural areas, this may reach 90 percent.[417] Ground water pollution derives from numerous and diverse sources. There are over 100,000 landfills throughout the country, many of which have leached contamination into ground water over the decades. The existence of some ten million underground storage tanks, containing petroleum products and industrial chemicals, creates the statistical likelihood that large quantities of contaminants have leaked from these sources over the years, an assumption which is becoming overwhelmingly supported empirically. Injection wells, in which liquid wastes, many of them hazardous, are placed, have been used for years as a method of disposal. These often leak into geological strata containing ground water. Mineral and oil extraction also have played a historical role in ground water contamination. Hundreds of millions of pounds of pesticides are applied annually across the country, in addition to many products containing hazardous constituents used by households to clean, paint, and even weed the garden. These have resulted in significant seepage into ground water. Road salting and runoff of heavy metals from road surfaces and parking lots also play a role in ground water contamination when runoff enters fresh water recharge zones.[418] Leaking or poorly designed septic tanks are one of the most significant sources of groundwater contamination. Ponds for wastewater storage and disposal also leak significant amounts of contaminants into the ground annually.[419] More recently, the rush to exploit natural gas reserves, particularly in the Northeastern shale deposits, with the use of the new technology of hydrofracking, is presenting concerns for groundwater resources. Hydrofracking utilizes the high-pressure injection of water and chemicals into deeply subsurface formations, which is anticipated to fracture the rock and release gas pockets that previously were unreachable by conventional engineering methods. The pressure also facilitates the movement of the gas deposits to the surface. However, it is feared, the often uncertain science of subsurface hydrology cannot fully account for the dispersal of the fluids that cannot be recaptured and for their impact on aquifers.

The source of pollution in a given area usually turns on the land uses in that area, so that nationwide generalizations are hard to make. On the other hand, the migratory patterns of ground water contamination complicate the correlation between land use

---

417. SIERRA CLUB LEGAL DEFENSE FUND, THE POISONED WELL: NEW STRATEGIES FOR GROUNDWATER PROTECTION, at xvii (Jorgensen, ed., 1989) [hereinafter THE POISONED WELL].

418. *Id.*

419. STEVER & DOLAN, ENVIRONMENTAL LAW AND COMPLIANCE § 3.12, n.9 (and cites therein).

and pollution in many regions, so that local projections often must rely on an understanding of hydrologic dynamics on a fairly broad map.

[2] How Does the Hydrologic Cycle Affect Ground Water Contamination?

One reason why water bodies historically were useful for disposal of wastes is that water tends to keep moving, hence apparently minimizing the on-site consequences of pollution. However, the very fact of hydrologic dynamics has meant that contamination that was historical in origin, and is still ongoing, tends to have drastic, often imprecise, and geographically far ranging effects.[420] This is especially true for ground water. Although ground water is one of the least visible sources of water, and hence its contamination is less publicly apparent, it is second only to the oceans and the polar ice caps in volume of water. Of all the available fresh water in this country, 96 percent is ground water.[421]

Ground water, originating in precipitation or in some instances from water bodies, filters down through the soil to fill spaces in the rock layers, finding its way to the water table. The water table fluctuates seasonally with plant hydration and evaporation. Saturated rock formations that retain large quantities of water are aquifers. Aquifer borders may be permeable or impermeable, depending on the degree to which aquifers may interconnect, which in turn depends on the porosity of the rock or the positioning of clay layers. Permeability becomes very important when an aquifer becomes contaminated, and the geologic characteristics of the rock layers will determine whether, or where, the contamination will travel farther afield. The direction of the flow of contaminated ground water is called a flume.[422]

Contamination often arises in an aquifer's "recharge" zone. Water exits from the aquifer through a "discharge" area, which may be a surface water body or a well. The recharge zone is a surface drainage area through which precipitation washes and then percolates into the soil until it reaches the aquifer. This is where many surface-based contaminants originate, especially in agricultural or industrial areas, but also from such commonplace sources as highway and street runoff. Although recharge zones often are located directly above the affected aquifer, this is not always the case. Alternating rock layers and various gradients may complicate and diversify the downward water flow, which at times may be largely lateral. Hence, many aquifers may become contaminated by pollution in recharge zones significant distances from the aquifer's discharge area. This geologic factor may render land use regulation alone ineffective at times, and hence may force reliance on statutes imposing quantitative restrictions on discharges or releases of pollutants.[423]

---

420. THE POISONED WELL, *supra* note 417, at 3.
421. *Id.*
422. *Id.*
423. *Id.*

[B] Ground Water Contamination Is Regulated by Several Statutes

Several federal environmental statutes operate independently or together to protect drinking water. Surface water pollution generally is governed by the Clean Water Act, discussed in § 6.03. The Clean Water Act does not regulate ground water, unless there is some discernible flow from surface water regulated under that Act into ground water, so that pollution of the former leads to pollution of the latter.[424] Ground water pollution is regulated directly under certain provisions of the Resource Conservation and Recovery Act (RCRA, discussed more fully in Chapter 7) and the Safe Drinking Water Act, discussed *below*. Ground water also is protected under the Surface Mining Control and Reclamation Act (see § 12.04[A]), which requires permits to protect ground water from mine drainage. Ground water also is regulated indirectly under other federal statutes, including the Toxic Substances Control Act (TSCA; see discussion in § 8.02) and the Federal Insecticide, Fungicide, and Rodenticide Act (FIFRA; see discussion in § 8.01). These latter statutes often raise a question of federal preemption of an area of law otherwise regulated by states, so that federal protections, including protections of ground water, may prevail over less stringent or more parochial state regulations. The Comprehensive Environmental Response, Compensation, and Liability Act (CERCLA; see discussion in § 7.06) mandates cleanups of hazardous substances and provides a cost recovery scheme for ground water contamination not involving petroleum products.

Ground water regulation also is an area in which states historically have had a significant presence. Particularly in the West, water rights restricting the withdrawal and use of ground water are codified and amply litigated, and state common law rights also are a source of much litigation (see discussion in § 3.05[A]). However, many states, not limited to the West, employ permitting systems for the use of groundwater. Restrictions on use do not directly relate to pollution controls, but to the extent that aquifer depletion exceeds the pace of water replacement, relatively increasing the contamination of ground water supplies as the concentration of contaminants increase, these restrictions have an indirect effect. Correlating with ground water use, many states also restrict land uses in significant aquifer areas when particular uses, such as landfills, are incompatible with the continued potability of water supplies.[425]

---

424. Note, though, that the Supreme Court decision in *County of Maui, Hawaii v. Hawaii Wildlife Fund*, ___ U.S. ___, 140 S. Ct. 1462, 206 L. Ed. 2d 640 (2020), establishing a line of jurisprudence which likely will see further development, allows for regulation and enforcement and may require permitting under the CWA when pollutants migrate from a point source such as injection wells to a nearby water body under federal jurisdiction by means of a ground water connection. See the discussion in § 6.03[B][b] and [d].

425. *See, e.g.*, N.Y. ENVTL. CONSERV. LAW § 15-0514 (Long Island designated a primary water supply aquifer area); FLA. STAT. ANN. § 373.0395; Moviematics Industrial Corp. v. Board of County Commissioners, 349 So. 2d 667 (Fla. App. 1977).

In this section, however, we will focus on those federal statutes which directly regulate ground water, the Safe Drinking Water Act and those provisions of RCRA regulating underground storage tanks.

[C] Safe Drinking Water Act

[1] Background and Jurisdiction

The Safe Drinking Water Act is officially known as the Public Health Service Act.[426] The Act, in its antecedent provisions, dates back to the Public Health Services Act enacted in 1944. It was substantially amended in 1974 to create the Safe Drinking Water Act, and again in 1986 to give it its present structure and reach.

This Act has had a comprehensive effect on preventing ground water pollution. Yet its actual statutory reach is restricted to ground water that is a drinking water source. The Act principally affects drinking water sources in two broad manners: (1) by requiring water purity within a water system itself; and (2) by imposing general land use requirements affecting ground water. For the former, the Act regulates "public water systems"[427] by imposing national standards protecting water quality by means of maximum contaminant levels (MCLs), subject to specified variances[428] and exemptions.[429] For the latter, the Act operates by protecting "sole source aquifers"[430] and by requiring EPA to regulate the underground injection of wastes.[431] The 1986 amendments to the Act also prohibit the use of lead pipes, solder, or flux in any public water system or in any plumbing associated with drinking water derived from public water systems.[432]

Congress envisaged that primary enforcement responsibility would be exercised by states,[433] subject to EPA's establishment of minimum requirements. As with many environmental statutes which accord much administrative authority to the states, this means that states may regulate, but such regulations may not be less stringent than the federal regulations.[434] Most states now have programs under the Act. If a state does not, then EPA assumes regulatory authority for that state. Native American tribes have also assumed increasing responsibilities for SDWA permitting enforcement within their reservations,[435] although it is sometimes difficult to delineate sovereign tribal lands from territory falling under state jurisdiction.[436]

---

426. 42 U.S.C. §§ 300f to 300j-26.

427. 42 U.S.C. §§ 300g, 300g-1.

428. *See* 42 U.S.C. § 300g-4.

429. *See* 42 U.S.C. § 300g-5.

430. 42 U.S.C. § 300h-6.

431. 42 U.S.C. § 300h-3.

432. 42 U.S.C. § 300g-6.

433. 42 U.S.C. § 300h-1.

434. 42 U.S.C. § 300h.

435. 42 U.S.C. 300j-11; 59 Fed. Reg. 64339 (Dec. 14, 1994); *see, e.g.,* Navajo Nation: Underground Injection Control (UIC) Program: Primary Approval, 73 Fed. Reg. 65,556-01, at 65,558–65,560 (Nov. 4, 2008).

436. *See* Hydro Resources, Inc. v. Environmental Protection Agency, 608 F.3d 1131 (10th Cir. 2010); Hydro Resources, Inc. v. Environmental Protection Agency, 198 F.3d 1224 (10th Cir. 2000)

[2] Regulation of Public Water Systems: Water Quality Requirements

[a] Maximum Contaminant Levels

[i] Drinking Water Regulations

The major method by which the Act operates is in the establishment of maximum contaminant levels that create minimum water purity criteria for drinking water sources. These are based on national standards promulgated by EPA. These standards impose restrictions on listed contaminants, such as barium, cadmium, chromium, lead, mercury, and coliform bacteria, as well as any other contaminant that may adversely affect human health and is known or anticipated to be found in public water systems.[437] A "contaminant" is "any physical, chemical, biological or radiological substance or matter in water."[438] A "maximum contaminant level" is the maximum permissible level of a particular contaminant in water that is delivered to any user of a public water system.[439] The point is that when water reaches the user, there should be a monitoring report that indicates exactly what level of purity it has achieved.

Regulatory policy divides into primary — essentially health oriented — and secondary — essentially aesthetic — drinking water regulations. The water company or utility must regularly monitor the water supply in accordance with the EPA criteria, or the more stringent criteria established by the state, and the records of the monitoring must be available for public inspection.

[ii] Primary Drinking Water Regulations

For the primary regulation of each such contaminant, EPA will promulgate maximum contaminant level goals. These goals are standardized objectives against which contaminant levels in individual public water systems are to be measured. These goals correlate with the level at which "no known or anticipated adverse effects on the health of persons occur and which allows a margin of safety."[440] EPA will either impose an enforceable maximum contaminant level for a public water system that comes as close as is feasible to a maximum contaminant level goal, or seek by other means to reduce the contaminant's presence to near the ideal threshold of public safety. The choice of options is determined in part by knowledge that a particular contaminant is present and will have adverse health consequences, and in part by the ability to control and monitor that contaminant. This latter consideration is gov-

---

(addressing the jurisdictional quandaries on checkerboard reservations, where tribal territories are often interspersed with formerly tribal properties that have passed into non-tribal private ownership and now fall under state jurisdiction).

437. 42 U.S.C. §§ 300f(1), 300g-1.

438. 42 U.S.C. § 300f(6). Although the CWA and SDWA have many points of correspondence, they are not identical in their definitions of contaminants. Hence, although turbidity might be considered to be a pollutant under the CWA, it is not a contaminant under the SDWA. See United States v. White, 270 F.3d 356 (6th Cir. 2001); Catskill Mountains Chapter of Trout Unlimited v. City of New York, 273 F.3d 481, 488 (2d Cir. 2001).

439. 42 U.S.C. § 300f(3).

440. 42 U.S.C. § 300g-1(4).

erned by whether the imposition of a national standard is "economically and technologically feasible."[441] That is, if by the use of the best available technology, it is economically and technologically feasible to ascertain the level of a contaminant in a public water system and to evaluate its effect on public health, the public water system's strategy will be measured against the maximum contaminant level goal promulgated for the contaminant. If EPA concludes that the level of a particular contaminant cannot be feasibly ascertained or the goal cannot feasibly be met, then a "known" treatment technique must be utilized to reduce the contaminant's presence to a level that will not adversely affect public health.[442] There are some specific exceptions, such as the parasite cryptosporidium, where no MCL is permissible and the contaminant must be removed from the water systems regardless of cost.[443]

Choosing a mode that is feasible depends on the use of the best available technology and treatment techniques, and on results. EPA will determine feasibility on the basis of field conditions as well as laboratory results.[444] For instance, the use of granulated activated carbon is deemed to be feasible as a means of controlling synthetic organic chemicals. In order to also be feasible, any alternative best available technology or treatment technique must be equally effective.[445] Filtration and disinfection are commonly used treatment techniques.

For primary drinking water regulations, EPA establishes criteria and devises procedures, including quality control and testing procedures to monitor compliance, to ensure that drinking water supplies "dependably" comply with maximum contaminant levels. EPA will establish requirements as to each public water system regarding the minimum quantity of water that may be taken into the system, and the location of new public water system facilities.[446]

[iii] Secondary Drinking Water Regulations

Secondary drinking water regulations also apply to public water systems and impose maximum contaminant levels.[447] However, here EPA regulates in a more general sense for the public "welfare" rather than solely for public health. The secondary drinking water standards will be applied to any contaminant that may adversely affect the odor or appearance of drinking water so that a substantial number of users may discontinue their use of that public water system. However, the odor/appearance criteria are only one specified predicate for EPA action; any results of contamination that adversely affect the public welfare also will authorize the application of secondary standards.[448] EPA has established criteria for chloride, color, cor-

---

441. 42 U.S.C. §§ 300f(1)(c), 300g-1(b)(7).

442. Id.

443. 42 U.S.C. 300g-1(b)(6)(C); City of Portland v. Environmental Protection Agency, 507 F.3d 706 (D.C. Cir. 2007).

444. 42 U.S.C. § 300g-1(b)(5).

445. Id.

446. 42 U.S.C. § 300f(1)(D).

447. 42 U.S.C. § 300f(2); 40 C.F.R. § 143.3.

448. 42 U.S.C. § 300f(2).

rosiveness, fluoride, foaming, pH (acidity), sulfates, total dissolved solids, and other agents.[449]

[b] What Is a Public Water System?

A public water system generally provides piped water for public consumption. Such a system must have at least fifteen service connections, or serve regularly at least twenty-five people to qualify for inclusion within the Act.[450] If this threshold is passed, then the term also includes any collection, treatment, storage or distribution facilities under the control of the system's operator, or pretreatment storage facilities not necessarily under the operator's control, if they are used primarily in connection with the system.[451] EPA defines water systems meeting these minimum criteria on a year-round basis to be "community" systems, which are fully subject to all Safe Drinking Water Act requirements.[452] "Noncommunity" water systems, which operate for the minimum number of users only part of the year, may be accorded more flexible treatment by EPA.[453]

The maximum contaminant levels apply only to "public water systems," although EPA interprets its statutory mandate to extend to regulation of contaminants in any drinking water, including private wells, surface water, and other ground water.[454] A "public" water system need not be publicly owned; it need only service a minimal number of members of the public.[455] Nor does the location where the drinking water is made available necessarily have to be regularly open to the public. Thus, a prison, while hardly a place accessible by the public, falls within the category of public water system, assuming that the other criteria are satisfied.[456]

[c] Variances

The Act allows for variances from national primary drinking water regulations for particular contaminants or multiple contaminants in carefully circumscribed situations.[457] Although the public water system may be allowed to comply with alternative requirements — hence the variance — this allows only a postponement of compliance with regulations. The permitted noncompliance will not be indefinite. Although the Act allows states to grant variances to state drinking water regulations, EPA still retains overall control over the criteria to be employed.

Generally, the Act allows consideration of the nature of the "raw water resources which are reasonably available" to the particular system when such water cannot

---

449. 40 C.F.R. § 143.3.
450. 40 C.F.R. § 143.2(c).
451. 42 U.S.C. § 300f(4).
452. 40 C.F.R. § 141.2.
453. 40 C.F.R. §§ 141.11, 141.13, 141.14.
454. 50 Fed. Reg. 46,941–46,943 (Nov. 13, 1985).
455. Spotts v. United States, 613 F.3d 559 (5th Cir. 2010).
456. Spotts v. United States, *id.*
457. 42 U.S.C. § 300g-4.

meet maximum contaminant levels.[458] However, to qualify for a variance, the system first must utilize the best available technology or treatment, or other means which EPA finds to be available.[459] In evaluating what is best and what is available, costs may be taken into account, and the evaluation will vary, depending on the number of persons served by the system or by engineering feasibility.[460] The state then must find that the proposed variance will not result in an unreasonable risk to health.[461] If the variance is to be granted, the state will provide the water system with a compliance schedule as to each contaminant level requirement for which the variance is sought, and an implementation schedule for whatever additional control measures the state determines to be necessary to eventually comply with maximum contaminant levels. The additional control measures remain in effect until the date of compliance.[462] Prior to the schedule's effective date, the state must provide public notice and an opportunity for a public hearing.[463]

Variances also may be given when the nature of the "raw water resource" renders a particular treatment technique set forth in a primary drinking water regulation unnecessary to protect public health; the burden of proof in such cases remains on the applicant.[464] This type of variance may be conditioned on monitoring, or any other requirement imposed by the agency. Again, public notice and an opportunity for a hearing must precede the variance taking effect.[465]

In either event, if EPA determines that the authority to grant variances is being abused by a state, EPA may step in, after public notice and an opportunity for a hearing, and rescind the variance or impose appropriate schedules.[466]

[d] Exemptions

The Act also authorizes states to grant exemptions from state Safe Drinking Water programs under limited circumstances, subject, again, to EPA oversight.[467] A state may also issue a temporary exemption of SDWA standards on an emergency basis in response to so-called acts of God. The Texas emergency exemption was triggered after a devastating hurricane when a prison, deprived of its electrical power along with its drinking water for more than a month, provided alternative drinking water to inmates that did not conform to certain SDWA standards.[468] The state must find that due to compelling factors, which may include cost, a public water system within

---

458. 42 U.S.C. § 300g-4; 40 C.F.R. § 142.40(a).
459. 42 U.S.C. § 300g-4(a)(1)(A); 40 C.F.R. § 142.42(c).
460. 40 C.F.R. § 142.42.
461. 42 U.S.C. § 300g-4(a)(1)(A).
462. Id.
463. Id.
464. 42 U.S.C. § 300g-4(a)(1)(B); 40 C.F.R. §§ 142.40(b), 142.42(d).
465. 42 U.S.C. § 300g-4(a)(1)(B).
466. 42 U.S.C. § 300g-4(a)(1)(G).
467. 42 U.S.C. § 300g-5.
468. Spotts v. United States, n.455, supra.

state jurisdiction is unable to comply with a maximum contaminant level or a treatment technique requirement.[469] To qualify for the exemption, however, the public water system must have been in operation prior to the promulgation of the contaminant level or requirement for which the exemption is sought.[470] For a new system, the only predicate for granting the exemption is that no reasonable alternative source of drinking water is available.[471] In any case, the state must find that an exemption will not result in an unreasonable risk to health.[472] Then, as with variances, the state must provide a schedule for eventual compliance and implementation of other control measures pending compliance.[473] Again, EPA may rescind an exemption in the event of abuse by the state and implement additional control measures.[474]

[3] Regulation of Ground Water Sources of Drinking Water

[a] Restrictive Land Use Regulation

Another means by which the Safe Drinking Water Act protects drinking water is by restrictive land use regulations in areas that are sources of underground drinking water supplies. The Act regulates[475] ground water chiefly by means of addressing drinking water sources such as wellheads (see [d], *below*) and aquifers (see [b], *below*); it also directly regulates actual incursions into the ground which may cause leaching into ground water, such as injection wells (see [c], *below*). In all three cases, the Act essentially delegates regulatory and enforcement jurisdiction to the states, subject, however, to EPA's establishment of minimum standards and its oversight authority. EPA may always deny program approval for a state if the state's program fails to achieve the Act's goals.[476] The extent of regulation often turns on whether contamination will affect a "sole source aquifer"[477] (see [b], *below*). The Act does not effectively protect all aquifers. Some states have supplemented the Act with their own regulations, while others have failed to do so.

[b] Protection of Sole Source Aquifers

A sole source aquifer is a single or principal drinking water source for an area which, if contaminated, would create a significant hazard to the public health.[478] Once EPA determines that an area depends on a sole source aquifer, the determination will be published in the Federal Register, and federal funds will be cut off for any

---

469. 42 U.S.C. § 300g-5(a)(1); 40 C.F.R. § 142.50(a).

470. 42 U.S.C. § 300g-5(a)(2); 40 C.F.R. § 142.50(b).

471. 42 U.S.C. § 300g-5(a)(2).

472. 42 U.S.C. § 300g-5(a)(3); 40 C.F.R. § 142.50(c).

473. 42 U.S.C. § 300g-5(b).

474. 42 U.S.C. § 300g-5(d).

475. *See generally* 42 U.S.C. §§ 300h to 300h-7.

476. *See* 42 U.S.C. § 300h-1(b), (c) (underground injection), 300h-7(c) (wellheads), 300h-6(i) (aquifers).

477. 40 C.F.R. § 149.2(d).

478. 42 U.S.C. § 300h-3(a)(1).

project which threatens to contaminate that aquifer.[479] The area served by a sole source aquifer may be designated a Critical Aquifer Protection Area.[480] In reaching that determination, EPA will look to the aquifer's vulnerability to contamination, the number of people relying on the aquifer for drinking water, and the relative costs and benefits of protecting the designated area.[481]

A federal grant program, the Sole Source Aquifer Demonstration Program,[482] provides up to 50 percent, or up to $4 million, per aquifer annually, to qualifying states for developing programs to protect critical aquifer protection areas.[483] To qualify, local planning authorities must map borders and undertake protective land use measures leading to the promulgation of a comprehensive management plan for any development in the designated area. The objective of such comprehensive planning is to maintain, to the maximum extent possible, the natural vegetative and hydrological conditions of the area.[484] The area must be mapped, and existing and potential point sources, as well as non-point sources of ground water degradation must be identified. The plan must relate land uses and water quality. Management practices designed to prevent contamination must be implemented.[485] Interestingly, Congress specifically restricted comprehensive planning requirements so as not to interfere with any rights to withdraw quantities of water when those rights have been established by interstate compacts, the Supreme Court, state laws, or other environmental laws.[486] This savings provision likely has the greatest significance for water rights carved out in Western states. Compacts and Supreme Court decisions have divided the waters of the Colorado, the Delaware, and numerous other rivers.

[c] Injection Wells

The use of underground injection started in the 1930s with the petroleum industry, which used underground injection of fluids to increase underground pressure as a means of impelling petroleum toward oil wells. The by-products of the oil extraction often were used for the injection, and since the injection often went into geological layers from which potable water was not drawn — especially petroleum-rich strata — no impact on drinking water supplies was anticipated. As was noted in § 6.04[A][1], *supra*, the recently increasing use of hydrofracking, in which pressurized fluids are injected into the ground to fracture rock formations and thereby release natural gas, which is forced to the surface, is causing concerns that underground drinking water

---

479. 42 U.S.C. § 300h-3(e).
480. 42 U.S.C. § 300h-6(b); 40 C.F.R. § 149.3.
481. 42 U.S.C. § 300h-6(d); 40 C.F.R. § 149.3(b).
482. 42 U.S.C. § 300h-6.
483. THE POISONED WELL, *supra* note 417.
484. 42 U.S.C. § 300h-6(f).
485. 42 U.S.C. § 300h-6(f)(1).
486. 42 U.S.C. § 300h-6(m).

supplies will be infiltrated and thereby contaminated. There is the additional concern that no feasible treatment methodology can mitigate the contamination. During the 1950s, the petroleum industry diversified into petrochemical products such as plastics, which created a new realm of waste by-products needing disposal, and industrial wastes, including many toxins, were simply disposed of in the same manner. Now, annually, hundreds of millions of tons of toxic, hazardous, radioactive, and other liquid wastes are deposited directly into the earth in hundreds of thousands of waste disposal wells. Generally, this waste disposal method is used by the chemical, petroleum, metals, minerals, aerospace, and wood preserving industries. It has contaminated ground water in many states as a result of improperly constructed wells or leakages, as pressure is increased in existing and often aging wells. Additionally, agricultural, automotive, and septic wastes historically were frequently disposed of in shallow, poorly constructed wells, of which there may be one million around the country.[487]

The Safe Drinking Water Act makes the connection between underground injection of wastes and the contamination of drinking water. The Act is triggered by contamination of ground water which is used for public water systems resulting in a system's failure to comply with national primary drinking water regulations, or otherwise affecting human health.[488] EPA may prohibit new injection wells in sole source aquifer areas.[489] Permits may be granted for new injection wells only if it can be determined that the aquifer will not be contaminated.[490]

EPA regulations classify injection wells into five classes. Class I wells are used by hazardous waste treatment, storage and disposal facilities[491] (see discussion in § 7.05[E]), as well as for disposal of nonhazardous municipal and industrial wastes. There are probably 200 injection wells for hazardous wastes, and 400 injection wells for nonhazardous wastes, operating under permit.[492] Injection of hazardous wastes within one quarter mile of an underground source of drinking water is prohibited unless the wastes can be injected below the aquifer. Class II wells are used in connection with oil and gas extraction, usually to reinject salt water derived from extraction activities back into the ground.[493] There are more than 160,000 of these wells.[494] Class III wells are used in connection with mining and utilities' activities.[495] There are about 10,000 of these wells.[496] These three classes are heavily regulated. In Class IV wells, radioactive and hazardous wastes used to be injected, either above or

---

487. THE POISONED WELL, *supra* note 417, at 29.

488. 42 U.S.C. § 300h(d).

489. 42 U.S.C. § 300h-3(a).

490. 42 U.S.C. § 300h-3(b)(3).

491. 40 C.F.R. § 146.5(a)(2).

492. THE POISONED WELL, *supra* note 417, at 249.

493. 40 C.F.R. § 146.5(b)(1); Legal Environment Assistance Foundation v. Environmental Protection Agency, 276 F.3d 1253 (11th Cir. 2001), *cert. denied*, 537 U.S. 989 (2002).

494. THE POISONED WELL, *supra* note 417, at 249.

495. 40 C.F.R. § 146.5(c).

496. THE POISONED WELL, *supra* note 417, at 249.

even into aquifers. These wells are now mostly banned.[497] Class V wells include just about everything else: septic wells or cesspools serving multiple family or industrial users, drainage wells, and other wells. These wells tend to be shallow, and construction may be simple. Although they are not designed — or permitted — for disposal of hazardous wastes, many hazardous constituents of other wastes are likely to find their way into many of these wells. Class V injection wells likely number in excess of a million, although large numbers may never have been mapped, and they are essentially unregulated at the federal level.[498]

For any permissible use of injection wells (i.e., except for Class V), a permit must be acquired. As with much of the Safe Drinking Water Act, states with approved programs tend to be the permitting authorities, albeit under EPA criteria. However, this approval of state programs does not contemplate a regulatory role for local governments, since state law may be preemptive.[499] If a state lacks an approved program, EPA is the permitting authority. The goal of any permitting system is to ensure that underground injection of wastes does not create a significant hazard to drinking water sources.[500] Conversely, the regulations do not extend to aquifers that are not usable for drinking water or to those that are usable for mineral, hydrocarbon, or geothermal energy production.[501]

[d] Wellhead Protection

The wellhead protection program grew out of the 1986 amendments to the Safe Drinking Water Act. Basically, this, too, is a state-regulated and state-enforced program, subject to EPA's overall authority to set standards. States are required to develop programs to protect the area around public water supply wells from which a public water system's well-water is drawn. Although ground water is the focus of such a program, it is not the exclusive focus, since surface waters also may be drawn into the well field. Generally, the areas of focus are the pumping area, the surrounding area which contributes to the pumping area, and the associated recharge areas.[502] State programs are supposed to track the potential routes of contaminant infiltration, evaluate the rate of travel under various hydrological conditions, detail how such contamination can be prevented, and implement contingency planning.[503] This requires an evaluation of what contaminants are in the system or are expected to enter the system, and a knowledge of how rapidly they move generally in ground water, and how they are expected to move under the particular geological and hydrological conditions of the particular wellhead area. Not all of this assessment relies on na-

---

497. 40 C.F.R. §§ 146.5(c), 146.5(d).
498. THE POISONED WELL, *supra* note 417, at 250.
499. EQT Production Co. v. Wender, 870 F.3d 322 (4th Cir. 2017).
500. 42 U.S.C. § 300h-1(b)(1)(B)(3).
501. 40 C.F.R. § 146.4.
502. 42 U.S.C. § 300h-7(e).
503. 42 U.S.C. § 300h-7(a), (e).

ture—the faster well water is withdrawn, the faster contaminants are drawn into the wellhead.

[D] Underground Storage Tanks

RCRA has had a significant effect on regulation of pollutants that end up contaminating ground water. (RCRA is more completely discussed in Chapter 7.) However, RCRA's regulation of underground storage tanks (USTs) properly belongs in a discussion specific to drinking water contamination and brief mention may be made here. There probably are millions of old USTs around the country, many of which have been abandoned. The existence of a UST may remain unknown until a due diligence inspection is conducted on a site. By the 1980s, EPA came to recognize the danger to ground water posed by leaking USTs. Many of these tanks had been poorly constructed, or corroded over time, or leaked and the leaks went unattended. Many had been used for the storage of gasoline and other petroleum products, since underground storage reduced the risks of fire. However, CERCLA (see § 7.06) excludes cost recovery for cleanups of petroleum products.[504] This has consequences for cleanups of ground water. Many leaking USTs also contained solvents and other hazardous products that were still in use, and hence were not wastes, so that the tanks evaded RCRA regulation. Although leakage of these hazardous substances could trigger CERCLA, the contaminants already were in the ground, which created a regulatory gap. The result was enactment of new RCRA proscriptions specifically addressing leaking underground storage tanks (LUSTs).[505] As with many ground water regulations discussed *above*, EPA establishes national standards, but states are given administrative and enforcement authority for programs approved by EPA.

Two definitions are relevant to the question of whether the LUST provisions of RCRA are triggered: what is an underground tank and does it contain a regulated substance? An underground storage tank is either a single tank, or a combination of tanks. The term also includes connecting pipes. In order to qualify, the volume of the tank—and volume takes into account the pipes themselves—must be at least 10 percent underground.[506]

The statutory definition specifically excludes certain types of tanks.[507] The excluded tanks generally are those associated with consumer use by individuals or families, or else they are not considered to be USTs since they are regulated under other statutes. Hence, farm tanks or residential tanks which do not exceed 1,100 gallons are excluded, as are tanks in which heating oil for on-site use is stored, as well as septic tanks. Surface impoundments, pits, lagoons, and stormwater or wastewater collection systems, even if below ground, are excluded, although these might fall under other pro-

504. 42 U.S.C. §§ 9601(14), 9604(a)(2).
505. 42 U.S.C. §§ 6991-6991g. This is Subtitle I of RCRA.
506. 42 U.S.C. § 6991(1).
507. *Id.*

visions of RCRA, the Clean Water Act, or the Safe Drinking Water Act. These various containers also may be regulated under state law. Some types of underground traps or facilities associated with oil or gas operations are excluded. If a tank would seem to qualify as a UST since it is below grade, but it is at or above floor level on an underground area, it is still excluded.[508]

To qualify, the tank must contain a "regulated substance." A regulated substance includes petroleum, as well as any of the many hazardous substances that trigger CERCLA liability.[509] The LUST program now closes the gap created by CERCLA by providing for cleanups of petroleum leakages from USTs.[510] CERCLA is available for cleanup operations in connection with leakages of non-petroleum hazardous substances.

The regulatory treatment of a UST depends on whether it is a "new" tank or an "old" tank. New tanks are those placed in operation after May 8, 1985, which, as a practical matter, may constitute most USTs remaining in use by the third decade of the 21st century. Old tanks are those that pre-date 1985 and are still in operation, or else were taken out of operation after 1973. The structural integrity of old tanks, which may have been subject to lesser manufacturing standards or may have corroded after decades of exposure to subsurface soil or hydrology conditions, raises environmental concerns. As to all such tanks, the owners and operators have extensive notification obligations. They must provide the appropriate agency with information on the type, volume, and age of each tank, as well as provide its location.[511] Any deposit of a regulated substance in a UST triggers additional notice requirements, and sellers must give notice to buyers of relevant performance criteria.[512] Tanks taken out of operation before January 1, 1974 do not trigger notification requirements.[513] However, historic leakage of hazardous substances from those tanks exempt from notification requirements may still trigger cleanup responsibilities as noted above, warranting due diligence inspections for a property being conveyed or leased and for operations on the premises (see § 7.06[B]).

Owners and operators must satisfy criteria in connection with the detection of leaks, the need for corrective action, including cleanup operations, closure requirements, and financial responsibilities for these actions. Owners and operators are also bound by extensive monitoring and reporting requirements.[514] Although EPA establishes the criteria, state programs may substitute their own criteria, as long as the state program is more stringent than federal requirements.[515]

---

508. 42 U.S.C. § 6991(1).

509. 42 U.S.C. § 6991(2); *see* CERCLA § 101(14) at 42 U.S.C. § 9601(14).

510. 42 U.S.C. § 6991b(h)(2).

511. 42 U.S.C. § 6991a(a)(2).

512. 42 U.S.C. § 6991a(a)(5), (6).

513. 42 U.S.C. § 6991a(a)(2)(A).

514. 42 U.S.C. § 6991c(a).

515. If the state program provides less environmental protection than RCRA's UST requirements, it will not be approved by EPA. *See* Boyes v. Shell Oil Products Co., 199 F.3d 1260 (11th Cir. 2000).

§ 6.05 Marine Protection

[A] Generally

Pollution of the ocean has been a growing threat to the domestic as well as the international environment. The ocean consists of numerous interlocking ecosystems whose dynamics and remote effects are only poorly understood. As a consequence, the ramifications of widespread pollution, disrupting local ecosystems, but also, in all probability, the entire network of ecosystems, remain indefinite. Nor is the ocean an impermeable unit, a physical feature of the earth's geography which is segregated from the land — and from terrestrial pollution. To the contrary, the effects of pollution on land, notably runoff, but also pollution loads carried in the atmosphere originating on land, are increasingly appreciated as having significant deleterious effects on marine environments. Since the ocean provides the bulk of the world's fisheries, and hence is a dramatically important food source, and also is a sink for carbon and other greenhouse gases, the importance of regulating the discharge of pollution into its waters is critical. Of course, there are other benefits to reducing the pollution load of the ocean, as any beachgoer or shore side summer business knows; these benefits inure to aesthetics, human health, and economic vitality. Areas of the sea bed have potential for mineral extraction. The ocean also is a significant, if not yet significantly exploited, source of scientific information, the value of which could be diminished by widespread pollution.

Ocean pollution is approached from various angles. The Clean Water Act, § 403,[516] governs discharges of pollutants from point sources on land into the ocean, the territorial seas, or the contiguous zone. The Marine Protection, Research, and Sanctuaries Act[517] — or the "Ocean Dumping Act" — as it descriptively is termed, governs ocean dumping, as the name indicates. Ocean "dumping" historically consisted of disposing of trash, garbage, sludge, and industrial wastes.

There also are a variety of other federal statutes that address aspects of ocean pollution. These include the Deep Water Port Act;[518] the Prevention of Pollution from Ships Act;[519] the Public Vessel Medical Waste Anti-Dumping Act;[520] the Shore Protection Act;[521] the Fishery Coastal Zone Management Act;[522] and the Ports and Waterways Safety Act.[523] The United States also has entered the London Dumping Convention,[524] although international controls over ocean pollution, relying essentially on a nation's agreement to be bound by them, historically have been difficult to enforce.

---

516. 33 U.S.C. § 1343.
517. 33 U.S.C. §§ 1401–1445.
518. 33 U.S.C. §§ 1501–1524.
519. 33 U.S.C. §§ 1901–1911.
520. 33 U.S.C. §§ 2501–2504.
521. 33 U.S.C. §§ 2601–2623.
522. 16 U.S.C. §§ 1451–1464.
523. 46 U.S.C. § 391a.
524. Convention on the Prevention of Marine Pollution by Dumping of Wastes and Other Matter, Aug. 30, 1975, 26 U.S.T. 2403, T.I.A.S. No. 8165, ENVTL. L. REP. (Envtl. L. Inst.) STATUTES 40329 (1988).

In this chapter, we will focus on the restrictions on ocean discharges included in the Clean Water Act, the structure and working of which already has been discussed *above*, and the Marine Protection Act.

[B] Point Source Discharges

[1] Relationship between § 403 and Other Provisions of the Clean Water Act

Section 403[525] of the Clean Water Act governs discharges of pollutants from a land-based point source into the marine environment. A permit is required for such discharges. This section carves out from the Act a specialized arena for CWA permits, and in many respects, the general provisions of the Act may be applied, albeit within the specific regulatory framework promulgated under § 403.

However, § 403, like § 404,[526] governing dredge and fill discharges (see discussion in § 6.07), is somewhat set apart from other provisions of the Clean Water Act. It is not internally clear whether § 403 overrides other provisions when there is an overlap. For instance, § 301(h) governs discharges by POTWs into marine waters, subject to compliance with water quality standards, enforcement of pretreatment standards, monitoring of the marine biota, and other requirements. Thermal discharges are governed by § 316.[527] Does this mean that these more specific provisions override the more general provisions of § 403 — a normal canon of statutory construction — when such a discharge is made into the ocean? Section 301(a) states that except in compliance with several other provisions — omitting mention of § 403 — the discharge of any pollutant is unlawful. Does this mean that § 403 is subordinate to the general technology-based standards of the Clean Water Act? Or, as the more specific provision, does § 403 supersede § 301(a)? The prevailing view is that all relevant parts of the Clean Water Act applying standards for discharges must be satisfied for any given discharge, effectively requiring that the stricter standards must be met.[528]

Oil discharges are prohibited under § 311 of the Act[529] (see discussion in § 6.06[B][1]), which necessarily applies equally to restrict the issuance of permits under § 403.

Unlike permitting under other sections of the Clean Water Act, however, for which inadequate information can always be rectified by additional studies, or by mitigation or safeguards, Congress was concerned with the inadequate state of information about the ocean and the resulting potential for unintended and perhaps drastic results. Therefore, the Act states that in "any event where insufficient information exists on

---

525. 33 U.S.C. § 1343.

526. 33 U.S.C. § 1344.

527. 33 U.S.C. § 1326.

528. Pacific Legal Foundation v. Quarles, 440 F. Supp. 316, 322–26 (C.D. Cal. 1978), *aff'd sub nom.* Kilroy v. Quarles, 614 F.2d 225 (9th Cir. 1979), *cert. denied*, 449 U.S. 825 (1980).

529. 33 U.S.C. § 1321.

any proposed discharge to make a reasonable judgment on any of the guidelines established [by EPA] … no permit shall be issued.…"[530]

[2] Where NPDES Permits under § 403 Operate

Section 403 prohibits unpermitted discharges into the territorial sea, the waters of the contiguous zone, and the oceans.[531] The territorial sea is "the belt of seas measured from the line of ordinary low water along that portion of the coast which is in direct contact with the open sea and the line marking the seaward limit of inland waters, and extending seaward a distance of three miles."[532] The contiguous zone technically is 12 miles, by reference to the 1958 Convention of the Territorial Sea and the Contiguous Zone.[533] For the ocean, dumping is more generally regulated by the more restrictive Marine Protection Act, although point source discharges also remain under the aegis of § 403. (See [C], *below*.)

[3] Criteria Governing Issuance of Marine Discharge Permits

[a] Congress' Concerns

Section 403 is skeletal as a regulatory mechanism, likely reflecting the uncertain state of knowledge about the ocean environment when § 403 was added to the Act in 1972. Most of the substance of the permitting scheme is set forth in EPA's regulations, promulgated in 1980, or else requires reference to the general permitting provisions of the Clean Water Act. Congress was concerned with degradation of the ocean environment but recognized that ocean discharges would have to be subjected to some permitting scheme. As such, Congress specified several criteria which significantly circumscribe EPA's regulations and its ability to issue permits.[534] These criteria track some of the general criteria for water quality set forth in § 304(a).[535] These general concerns include the following:

- The effect of the disposal of pollutants on human health, as well as the ecosystem, including the effect on plankton, fish, shellfish, wildlife, shorelines, and beaches;

- The effect on marine life. This criterion includes a concern for how pollutants, or their by-products, move through biological, physical, or chemical processes, how such might adversely impact on ecosystem diversity, productivity, and stability, and how marine populations might respond;

- The effects on esthetic, recreational, and economic values;

---

530. 33 U.S.C. § 1343(c)(2).

531. 33 U.S.C. § 1343(a).

532. 33 U.S.C. § 1362(8).

533. 33 U.S.C. § 1362(9). Although the 1982 Law of the Sea Convention extended national contiguous zones to 24 miles, the United States was not a signatory to that convention, leaving the contiguous zone somewhat indefinite under the Clean Water Act.

534. 33 U.S.C. § 1343(c).

535. 33 U.S.C. § 1314(a).

- How persistent or permanent any effects might be;

- What alternatives there are to ocean disposal, including recycling and land-based alternatives; and

- How ocean disposal of pollutants will affect other ocean uses, such as mineral exploitation and scientific study.

[b] How EPA Evaluates the Permit Application

[i] If There Is an Unreasonable Degradation of the Marine Environment, the Permit Will Be Denied

EPA's standard in evaluating whether to grant or deny a permit application is more general than elsewhere in the Clean Water Act. If there is an "unreasonable degradation of the marine environment," then the permit will be denied.[536] Tracking the Congressional criteria, EPA defines unreasonable degradation in terms of "significant adverse changes in ecosystem diversity, productivity and stability of the biological community within the area of discharge and surrounding biological communities."[537] Unreasonable degradation may also be manifested by threats to human health as a consequence of direct personal exposure to the subject pollutants. Threats to swimmers posed by discharging caustic or acidic wastes would be such a threat. Readers may also recall that the discharge of medical waste is prohibited by the Clean Water Act (see discussion in § 6.03), yet this was a major concern on many East Coast beaches during the early 1990s. Threats to human health through consumption of exposed sea life, when the subject pollutant enters the food chain, also constitutes an unreasonable degradation of the marine environment.[538] Note that the definition does not include threats to property, per se. However, there is a category of environmental detriments which, on the basis of a balancing, may constitute an unreasonable degradation of the marine environment: this exists when the benefit derived from the discharge is outweighed by the loss of aesthetic, recreational, scientific, or economic values,[539] presumably including damage to property.

[ii] Factors Considered by EPA in Determining Whether There Is an Unreasonable Degradation

EPA uses a list of factors in reviewing a permit application to determine whether the effect of the discharge on the marine environment will constitute an unreasonable degradation.[540] The following are included in the list of factors:

- The physical and chemical properties of the pollutant.

- The nature, significance and vulnerability of the biological communities being affected.

---

536. 40 C.F.R. § 125.122(a).
537. 40 C.F.R. § 125.121(e).
538. Id.
539. Id.
540. 40 C.F.R. § 125.122(a).

- Human recreational, aesthetic, and health values being impacted by the discharge.

- The impact on commercial fishing.

- Whether a coastal zone management plan applies.

- The effect on marine water quality criteria, noted *above*, as set forth in § 403(a).

EPA will require that certain conditions be included in the permit. The discharger must implement a monitoring program to evaluate the impacts of the discharge with reference to the above criteria. Additionally, the permit will provide for revocation whenever it is determined that an unreasonable degradation is occurring. The permit also will incorporate requirements under the Marine Protection Act relating to concentrations of diluted pollutants in the designated mixing zone, the concentration of solid wastes, and limiting solid waste discharges to avoid the buildup of toxic materials in the human food chain.[541]

The applicant will be required to conduct all necessary studies to evaluate the chemical, physical, and biological impacts of the discharge, as well as to plot dispersion routes.[542] EPA may require the submission of reasonable alternatives, such as a reduction of wastes, or land based disposal or dumping at an approved dump site, regulated under the Marine Protection Act.[543]

[C] Ocean Dumping

[1] Background

The Marine Protection, Research and Sanctuaries Act (Marine Protection Act) arose in conjunction with the London Convention of 1975. The Convention signatories, including the United States, committed themselves to "take effective measures individually, according to their scientific, technical and economic capabilities, and collectively, to prevent marine pollution caused by dumping and harmonize their policies in this regard."[544] The Convention mandated signatories to prohibit the dumping of specified toxins unless they were made harmless by natural marine processes.[545] It included a prohibition regarding other specified materials, including heavy metals, toxins, acids, alkalis, and low level radioactive wastes, unless they were disposed of under permit.[546] The Marine Protection Act is the permitting regime instituted by the United States pursuant to the Convention.[547]

---

541. *See* 40 C.F.R. § 227.27.

542. 40 C.F.R. § 125.124.

543. *Id.*

544. Convention on the Prevention of Marine Pollution by Dumping of Wastes and Other Matter, Aug. 30, 1975, 26 U.S.T. 2403, at 2407, T.I.A.S. No. 8165, ENVTL. L. REP. (Envtl. L. Inst.) STATUTES 40329 (1988).

545. *Id.*

546. *Id.*

547. *See* 40 C.F.R. § 220.1(b).

[2] Jurisdiction

[a] Purpose and Prohibitions

[i] What Did Congress Intend the Act to Accomplish?

Congress has declared that the "[u]nregulated dumping of material into ocean waters endangers human health, welfare, and amenities, and the marine environment, ecological systems, and economic potentialities."[548] With the Marine Protection Act, Congress declared national policy to include the regulation of "dumping of all types of materials into ocean waters and to prevent or strictly limit the dumping into ocean waters of any material" that would threaten such dangers.[549]

The types of disposal activities regulated under the Act are those that otherwise would be regulated under a number of discrete environmental laws if land disposal or discharges into the waters of the United States, or into the air, were involved.[550] When ocean disposal is involved, all such activities fall under the umbrella of the Marine Protection Act.

Any dumping undertaken without a permit, or contrary to a permit, is a violation of the Act.[551]

[ii] What Is "Dumping"?

"Dumping" is defined generally as a "disposition of material"[552] (see discussion in [3][a], *below*, regarding what "material" is included) at sea (for geographic reach of the Act, see [2][b], *below*). EPA, or in some cases other agencies, may issue permits authorizing the dumping of specified materials, subject to criteria discussed in [3], *below*. EPA is authorized to designate recommended sites or times for dumping. If EPA finds it necessary to protect critical areas, it may also exclude specified sites or times from dumping.[553]

However, the term excludes the discharge of effluent from outfall structures which fall directly under §301 of the Clean Water Act (see §6.03[B][1][h], [C]), or of such dredged and fill materials that fall under §404 of the Clean Water Act (see §6.07). It also excludes the routine discharge of effluent incidental to the operation of vessels, or dispositions regulated under the aegis of the Atomic Energy Act of 1954.[554] "Dumping" also does not include the construction of fixed structures or artificial islands or

---

548. 33 U.S.C. §1401(a).

549. 33 U.S.C. §1401(b).

550. For instance, waste disposal companies sometimes incinerate hazardous wastes at sea. The issue arose whether a RCRA permit or a permit under the Marine Protection Act was required. The EPA, by regulation, classifies this type of disposal to fall under the Marine Protection Act, under which authority it sharply restricts ocean incineration and disposal activities. 40 C.F.R. §228.4(b).

551. 33 U.S.C. §1411.

552. 33 U.S.C. §1402(f); 40 C.F.R. §220.2(e).

553. 33 U.S.C. §1412(c).

554. 33 U.S.C. §1402(f).

the non-disposal placement of devices, when these activities are regulated under other state or federal programs.[555]

[b] Geographic Jurisdiction

The Marine Protection Act was enacted to regulate two broad classes of activity: (1) transportation of materials to be dumped, and (2) the actual dumping. The first activity addresses the transportation of material from the United States to any location for purposes of ocean dumping. If an American vessel, aircraft, or an American agency is involved, then the Act's jurisdiction extends to any such transportation even from a location outside of the United States. The second activity addresses the dumping of any material in the United States territorial sea or contiguous zone, that is, within twelve miles of our shores (see definitions in [B][2], *above*) if such material was transported from a location outside of the United States.[556] The objective is to regulate the dumping of wastes anywhere in the marine environment if the waste originated in the United States, and to regulate the dumping of waste from anywhere if it is discharged into American territorial waters or the contiguous zone. Note that the Act does not confer jurisdiction over dumping into inland waters,[557] which would fall under the Clean Water Act or the Rivers and Harbors Act (see discussion in § 6.03 as to regulation of wastewater discharges in these waters and § 6.07 regarding regulation of the discharge of dredged and fill materials in these waters).

Since a linchpin between congressional jurisdiction and prohibited conduct is American territorial sovereignty, Congress defined the "United States" to include the fifty states and the District of Columbia, Puerto Rico, the Trust Territory of the Pacific Islands, and the several other territories and possessions.[558] The term also includes the Canal Zone, although in light of the treaty ceding jurisdiction over the Canal Zone to Panama, this territorial outpost may no longer be a basis of national jurisdiction.

[c] Regulatory and Enforcement Jurisdiction

EPA is the designated administrative[559] and permitting[560] authority under the Act. However, if the activity is transportation of dredged materials (see discussion in

---

555. *Id.*

556. 33 U.S.C. § 1401(c).

557. However, it is not always clear what constitutes an inland water. For instance, the Act specifically addresses dumping in Long Island Sound (33 U.S.C. § 1416(f)) and the courts have found Long Island Sound to be within the ambit of the Act (*see* Town of Huntington v. Marsh, 859 F.2d 1134 (2d Cir. 1988)). The Sound also has been found for other purposes, such as ownership of submerged lands, to be inland waters rather than waters under the direct jurisdiction of the United States (*see* United States v. Maine, 469 U.S. 504 (1985)).

558. 33 U.S.C. § 1402(d).

559. 33 U.S.C. § 1402(a).

560. 33 U.S.C. § 1412.

§ 6.07) for the purpose of ocean dumping, then the Army Corps of Engineers is the permitting authority.[561] The Army Corps must first notify EPA if a permit is to be issued, and EPA is given veto power by the Act over any Army Corps decision.[562] Conversely, if dumping of other than dredged or fill materials is involved, then the Army Corps may veto an EPA permit under three circumstances: when the dumping is likely to adversely affect navigation in the territorial seas; when it occurs in any approach to a harbor of the United States; or when it may create an artificial island on the continental shelf.[563] In all other cases, the criteria for issuing a permit are those set forth in [4], *below.*

States are accorded a limited role. A state may propose criteria relating to dumping into ocean waters within state jurisdiction or dumping that may have an effect on such waters. EPA may adopt the recommended criteria, so long as they do not conflict with the Act. States, however, may not regulate contrary to the Act.[564]

Since neither EPA nor the Army Corps of Engineers have a fleet of ships at their disposal for purposes of surveillance and apprehension, surveillance and enforcement often is undertaken by the Coast Guard, although other federal and state agencies also may be utilized by EPA or the Army Corps for these purposes.[565] EPA and the Army Corps, within their respective jurisdictions, are also empowered to delegate responsibility for reviewing permit applications and the authority to issue decisions thereon to other federal departments or agencies.[566]

[3] Scope of Coverage

[a] Materials Subject to Permitting Requirements

The Marine Protection Act regulates the dumping of "materials," and defines the term broadly. It includes "matter of any kind or description," although some exceptions are carved out.[567] As noted above, the type of materials or types of disposal or discharge would have triggered a number of other environmental laws if land disposal or non-marine discharges were involved. However, if marine disposal is involved, these "materials" all fall under the aegis of the Marine Protection Act. Examples include dredged material, solid waste, incinerator residue, garbage, sewage, sewage sludge, munitions, radiological, chemical and biological warfare agents, radioactive materials, chemicals, biological laboratory waste, wreck or discarded equipment, rock, sand, excavation debris, and industrial, municipal, agricultural and other waste.[568] The dumping of fish wastes, such as from fishing boats, ordinarily does not require a permit, unless they are deposited in a harbor or enclosed coastal waters, or if EPA

561. 33 U.S.C. § 1413(a).
562. 33 U.S.C. § 1413(c).
563. 33 U.S.C. § 1416(c).
564. 33 U.S.C. § 1416(d).
565. 33 U.S.C. § 1417(a), (c).
566. 33 U.S.C. § 1417(b).
567. 33 U.S.C. § 1402(c); 40 C.F.R. § 220.2(d).
568. 33 U.S.C. § 1402(c).

determines that the deposits thereby could endanger health, the environment, or ecological systems.[569]

Specifically excluded from the term, and hence from the Marine Protection Act, is ordinary sewage from vessels that is incidental to the vessel's operation.[570] That type of waste remains under the Clean Water Act's regulation of marine sanitation devices.[571]

Some materials are subject to strict restrictions or will require particular treatment before they may be dumped under permit. These include: benzene and its compounds; low level radioactive materials; viral or microbial life material, or higher life forms; highly acidic or alkaline wastes; and oxygen consuming wastes.[572] Some toxic wastes may be dumped, but a mixing zone will be designated and the wastes must be diluted to a specific concentration.[573]

For the dumping of dredged spoil, if it has toxic characteristics, EPA may require capping, which requires the further task of locating clean capping material — usually sand or clay — within a reasonable proximity to the dump site.[574]

[b] Materials for Which No Permit May Be Granted

The dumping of some of the itemized list of materials within the Act is illegal per se; no permit may be issued.[575] This prohibition parallels the prohibition against discharges of these materials in the Clean Water Act (see discussion in § 6.03). These materials include radiological, chemical, and biological warfare agents, high level radioactive wastes, and medical waste.[576] The regulations also prohibit permits if the subject materials have unknown effects, or may result in flotsam, and hence become navigational hazards, or may wash up on shore.[577]

There are other designated materials for which permits will usually be denied, unless the disposal consists of only trace amounts and bioassays indicate that the particular compounds will not bioaccumulate and will not cause adverse effects within the meaning of the statutory criteria (see discussion in [4], *below*). These compounds include known or scientifically suspected carcinogens, mutagens, and teratogens;

---

569. 33 U.S.C. § 1412(d).

570. 33 U.S.C. § 1402(c).

571. See CWA § 312, regulating the discharge of human wastes from vessels.

572. 40 C.F.R. § 227.7.

573. 40 C.F.R. § 227.27(a).

574. See generally 40 C.F.R. Part 230, and particularly subpart H (§§ 230.70–230.76) for actions to minimize contamination at disposal sites. 40 C.F.R. § 230.72(b) provides for capping of contaminated material. See also 40 C.F.R. § 227.13, and 40 C.F.R. § 228.4(e), for discharge of dredged material.

575. 33 U.S.C. § 1412(a).

576. "Medical waste" means isolation wastes, infectious agents, human blood and blood products, pathological wastes, sharps, body parts, contaminated bedding, surgical wastes, potentially contaminated laboratory wastes, dialysis wastes, and any additional items that the EPA includes by regulation. 33 U.S.C. § 1402(k).

577. 40 C.F.R. § 227.5.

organohalogens; mercury and mercury compounds; and cadmium and cadmium compounds.[578]

[c] Dumping of Sewage Sludge and Industrial Waste: Forbidden by the Statute

Except on an emergency basis, which is very narrowly construed,[579] ocean dumping of sewage sludge and industrial waste was prohibited after 1991.[580] These types of material were a principal component of the municipal waste burden of many cities. Coastal cities, in particular, historically relied on ocean dumping beyond the territorial sea. For example, the City of New York used a so-called "106 mile ocean waste dump site"[581] to dispose of such wastes. The closing of the ocean dump sites and the elimination of this waste disposal option has had significant impacts on other disposal methods, especially land filling and incineration (see discussion in Chapter 7).

[4] Permitting Criteria

[a] Dumping May Not Unreasonably Degrade Marine Environment or Endanger Human Health

The Marine Protection Act, like the marine discharge provisions of § 403 of the Clean Water Act (see [B][1], *above*), has an anti-degradation criterion. For the permit to be issued, EPA (or the Army Corps) must first affirmatively determine that the proposed dumping will not unreasonably degrade the marine environment, ecological systems, or economic potentialities, and that it will not endanger human health, welfare, or amenities.[582]

[b] General Criteria

The Act imposes threshold considerations on EPA's (or the Army Corps') authority to promulgate regulations and issue permits. These criteria also must be considered when the agency designates a particular dump site. These criteria essentially track, with minor differences, those enacted for § 403 of the Clean Water Act relating to marine point source discharges pursuant to NPDES permits (see discussion at [B][3], *above*) and to a lesser extent the general water quality criteria in the Clean Water Act.[583] However, the means of applying the criteria differ somewhat, in that EPA is

---

578. 40 C.F.R. § 227.6.

579. 33 U.S.C. § 1412a. A qualifying emergency requires "a marked degree of urgency." Further, emergency dumping of these wastes may take place only if there is no feasible alternative, in that any alternative poses an unacceptable risk to human health.

580. 33 U.S.C. § 1414b(a)(1)(B).

581. *See* 33 U.S.C. § 1414a(b).

582. 33 U.S.C. § 1412(a).

583. *See* CWA § 401. The EPA requires consideration of the applicable water quality standards in determining whether the proposed dumping will impact on esthetic, recreational, and economic values. *See* 40 C.F.R. § 227.18(c).

generally given a freer hand under the Marine Protection Act in evaluating the criteria. The Act specifies that no permit may be issued which violates applicable water quality standards.[584] EPA also is directed to try to accommodate the London Convention, so long as such accommodation does not result in a relaxation of the Act's general criteria.[585]

These criteria are non-exclusive; EPA (or the Army Corps) may provide further restrictions by regulation. If a consideration of the criteria leads to a determination of unreasonable degradation, the permit will be denied.[586] Congress required, at a minimum, consideration of the following:[587]

- The need for the proposed dumping.

- The effect of such dumping on human health and welfare, including economic, esthetic, and recreational values.[588]

- The effect on fisheries resources, plankton, fish, shellfish, wildlife, shorelines, and beaches.

- The effect on marine ecosystems. More specifically: the effect caused by the transfer, concentration, or dispersion of the dumped wastes, and possible by-products through biological, physical and chemical processes; potential changes in marine ecosystem diversity, productivity, and stability; and species and community population dynamics.

- The persistence and permanence of the effects of the dumping.

- The specific effect of dumping particular volumes and particular concentrations of the subject materials.

- What locations and methods of recycling or disposal are appropriate? Land-based alternatives also must be considered. When all alternatives are considered, their relative probable impacts on values affecting the public interest also must be considered.

- The effect of the dumping on alternate uses of the ocean also must be considered. These alternate uses include scientific study, fishing, and other resource exploitation.

[c] Dump Site Designation in Permit

EPA is authorized to designate recommended sites for ocean dumping. The Act directs that in designating dump sites, EPA must utilize locations beyond the edge of the continental shelf wherever feasible.[589] EPA often designates locations that historically were used as dump sites. EPA tends to avoid fishing grounds, areas containing

---

584. 33 U.S.C. § 1412(a).
585. *Id.*; 40 C.F.R. § 220.1(b).
586. 40 C.F.R. § 227.3.
587. 33 U.S.C. § 1412(a).
588. *See* 40 C.F.R. § 227.18(c).
589. 33 U.S.C. § 1412(a).

shellfish beds, and navigation lanes, and to prefer locations removed from beaches and shore lines.[590] If EPA finds it necessary to protect "critical areas" — which are undefined — it may also exclude specified sites.[591] Dumping of dredged material must meet specific requirements, and is generally prohibited unless it will have no adverse impact on the aquatic ecosystem.[592]

[5] Issuance of Permit

[a] Public Notice

As with many environmental permitting statutes, there is a public notice prerequisite to the issuance of an ocean dumping permit. The public must be placed on notice and there must be an opportunity for a public hearing.[593]

[b] Permit Conditions

As with many environmental permits, the face of the permit will contain general conditions relating to compliance with the Marine Protection Act and other appropriate statutes, as well as specific conditions pertinent to the particular activity for which the permit is sought.

EPA often relies on general permits for ocean dumping, which will have many standardized conditions. The Act requires that for general permits, the dumping must have a minimal adverse environmental impact.[594] Special permits authorizing nonrecurring dumping,[595] emergency permits authorizing the dumping of otherwise prohibited materials,[596] research permits,[597] and incineration permits[598] may occasionally also be issued.

Each permit must provide certain information, including the following:[599]

- The type of material being transported for dumping or to be dumped.

- The amount of material.

- The location where the transporting for dumping will terminate or where the dumping will occur.

- The duration of the permit and the expiration date.

---

590. 40 C.F.R. § 228.5.
591. 33 U.S.C. § 1412(c).
592. *See* 40 C.F.R. Part 230.
593. 40 C.F.R. §§ 222.3–222.13.
594. 33 U.S.C. § 1414(c).
595. 40 C.F.R. § 220.3(b).
596. 40 C.F.R. § 220.3(c). The emergency must pose an unacceptable risk to public health, and there must be no other feasible alternative to ocean dumping.
597. 40 C.F.R. § 220.3(e).
598. 40 C.F.R. § 220.3(f).
599. 33 U.S.C. § 1414(a).

- Any special provision necessary for monitoring and surveillance.
- Any other condition that the agency deems necessary.

Permits must be regularly reviewed by the agency to ensure continuing compliance with the criteria and any other factors which bear on marine water quality. Permits may be revised whenever necessary. EPA (or the Army Corps, if appropriate) is authorized to limit, partially revoke, or revoke *in toto*, any permit when the dumping does not consistently comply with the criteria. However, before any such adverse action is taken, notice and an opportunity to be heard must be accorded the permittee.[600]

[c] Public Record

Any information received during the permitting process must be made available to the public at every stage of the process.[601] Once a final determination is made by the agency, this, too, must be available to the public.[602]

[6] Enforcement and Penalties

[a] Generally

Civil and criminal penalties are authorized, all subject to notice and hearing requirements. Injunctive relief is also available, as the equities of the case may require.[603] Each day of a continuing violation is a separate offense, as is each dumping episode from each of several vessels.[604] Civil penalties may be assessed by EPA; for the dumping of medical waste, the penalty ceiling is increased.[605] A knowing violation exposes the violator to criminal enforcement, subject to a fine, one-year incarceration, or both.[606] The dumping of medical waste, again, receives special treatment, with an increased fine and/or five years incarceration. In either case, the Act contains a property forfeiture provision. Additionally, the vessel may be liable in rem for any penalty assessed or fine imposed.[607]

[b] Emergency Dumping: No Enforcement Sanctions

If, in an emergency, materials must be dumped without a permit, or in contravention of a permit, then enforcement is barred. "Emergency" conditions occur in the context of a need to safeguard life at sea. Although sanctions may not be imposed, the emergency dumping must be reported to EPA.[608]

---

600. 33 U.S.C. § 1414(d).
601. 33 U.S.C. § 1414(f).
602. *Id.*
603. 33 U.S.C. § 1415(d).
604. 33 U.S.C. § 1415(c).
605. 33 U.S.C. § 1415(a).
606. 33 U.S.C. § 1415(b).
607. 33 U.S.C. § 1415(e).
608. 33 U.S.C. § 1415(h).

[c] Citizen Plaintiffs

As with several other environmental statutes, citizen suits are authorized under the Marine Protection Act.[609] Notice to enforcement authorities must be filed 60 days prior to commencement of a citizen suit. The suit may be maintained if the enforcement authority fails to diligently prosecute a civil or criminal action in court to require compliance, or has failed to commence a penalty action or permit revocation or suspension proceedings. (For analogous examples of what constitutes "diligent prosecution," *see* the discussion of the citizen suit provisions of the Clean Water Act at § 6.03[F].)

Reasonable litigation costs, including attorney fees and expert witness fees, may be awarded.[610]

As with other environmental statutes, the citizen suit provisions do not operate to bar such individual common law or statutory rights as may be available.[611]

§ 6.06 Oil Discharge and Liability

[A] Background

Oil is defined in the Clean Water Act as any kind of petroleum product, including fuel oil, sludge, oil refuse, and oil mixed with other wastes (except for dredged spoil).[612] Oil pollution of water bodies has, for several decades, been regulated under CWA § 311.[613] Section 311 was enacted to establish oil and hazardous substance liability for cleanups, and it remains viable with regard to oil pollution prevention and removal.[614] However, the provision was largely ineffective in addressing compensation issues. This gap was brought to the attention of the public, as well as Congress, most vividly with the crash and resulting oil spill of the Exxon Valdez in March of 1989. Additionally, accidental discharges from tankers, storage facilities, tank trucks, railway tank cars, and pipelines, with consequential environmental destructiveness, had been occurring with increasing frequency. In August of 1990, Congress unanimously enacted the Oil Pollution Act of 1990 (OPA), which had been extensively debated for more than a decade. The OPA now performs the CERCLA-like function of assigning liability for cleanups, requires financial assurances from the oil production and shipping industries in connection with responses to potential cleanups, and imposes construction requirements, notably double hulls for oil tankers. It also significantly

---

609. 33 U.S.C. § 1401; MPRSA § 105(g).

610. 33 U.S.C. § 1415(g)(4).

611. 33 U.S.C. § 1415(g)(5).

612. 33 U.S.C. § 1321(a)(1).

613. 33 U.S.C. § 1321.

614. *See* Charles Openchowski, *Federal Implementation of the Oil Pollution Act of 1990*, 21 ENVTL. L. REP. (Envtl. L. Inst.) 10,605, n.3 (1991). However, § 311 had not addressed issues of compensation and remedial liability.

expands criminal liability. The OPA amended parts of § 311, but also created a new chapter 40 in Title 33 of the United States Code.[615] Many states also have enacted their own oil spill legislation, which often tends to be stricter than federal legislation.

[B] Regulation under the Clean Water Act

[1] "Discharges" Covered by § 311

The Clean Water Act regulates "discharges" of oil and hazardous wastes. Although the Act chiefly deals with the discharge of oil, these terms are generally used together in the statute. "Discharge," of course, is a pivotal term elsewhere in the Clean Water Act (see discussion in § 6.03[B][1][b]). Discharges permitted under § 402 are excluded from regulation under § 311.[616] For oil pollution, a discharge includes any spilling, leaking, pumping, pouring, emitting, emptying or dumping of oil, but this list is non-exclusive.[617] Generally, in determining if the discharge is harmful, EPA's "sheen test" is utilized — any discharge, even a de minimis one, causing a sheen triggers § 311.[618] Hazardous waste has the same meaning utilized in CERCLA (see discussion in §§ 7.05[B][1], 7.06); it also would include the discharge of a vessel's bilge water which contains hazardous substances.[619]

In § 311, Congress declared it to be national policy to prohibit discharges of oil into the waters of the United States, adjoining shorelines, waters of the contiguous zone, or waters under the outer continental shelf where discharges might adversely affect natural resources under exclusive American jurisdiction.[620] However, since it only deals with penalties and cleanup costs, § 311 explicitly does not preempt local authorities from imposing their own prohibitions or requirements with respect to removal actions for discharges within state waters.[621]

[2] Liable Parties Include Owners and Operators of
Vessels and Facilities

Liable parties include the owner, operator, or "person in charge" of any vessel, onshore facility, or offshore facility,[622] as well as any party liable under the Oil Pollution Act of 1990.[623] There have been occasions when courts have pierced the corporate veil to impose liability on a parent corporation for discharges caused by wholly owned subsidiaries, when each subsidiary owned a vessel, and the parent corporation derived

---

615. 33 U.S.C. § 2701, *et seq.*
616. 33 U.S.C. § 1321(a)(2)(A).
617. 33 U.S.C. § 1321(a)(2).
618. Orgulf Transport Co. v. United States, 711 F. Supp. 344 (W.D. Ky. 1989).
619. *See, e.g.*, Pickens v. Kanawha River Towing, 916 F. Supp. 702 (S.D. Ohio 1996).
620. 33 U.S.C. § 1321(b)(1).
621. 33 U.S.C. § 1321(o).
622. 33 U.S.C. § 1321(b)(6).
623. 33 U.S.C. § 1321(c)(6).

income from the operations of these companies.[624] An "operator" is a party that has the capacity to timely discover discharges, had the authority to direct the activities which caused the pollution, had the capacity to have prevented the discharge, or has the capacity to abate the damage.[625] Hence, when a barge being towed crashed into a bridge and discharged oil, since the tugboat had exclusive control over the barge at the time of the discharge, the tugboat's owner was liable as an operator of the barge which was the source of the discharge.[626] The owner or operator is strictly liable for removal costs up to certain maximum amounts spelled out in the statute.[627] However, in contrast to CERCLA (in which past and present owners and operators are liable, *see* § 7.06[B][3]), that status is determined by reference to the date of the discovery of the discharge.[628]

[3] "Person in Charge" Must Immediately Notify Coast Guard of Discharge of Oil

Any "person in charge" is required to immediately notify the United States Coast Guard as soon as he or she knows of any illegal discharge of oil.[629] "Person in charge" is not defined in § 311, but has been construed to also include corporations or other entities.[630] Hence, an employer, as well as its employee, could be liable for failing to report an oil spill.[631] Note that corporations, unlike individuals, may not assert the Fifth Amendment's privilege against self-incrimination.[632] On being notified by the person in charge, the Coast Guard will then immediately notify the relevant state agency of any state that would be adversely affected. Any violation of the reporting obligation subjects the violator to criminal penalties.[633] However, the notification provides a reporting individual with immunity from prosecution in connection with the information timely reported, unless he or she can be prosecuted on the basis of information entirely derived from a nonimmunized independent source.[634]

---

624. United States v. Ira S. Bushey & Sons, 487 F.2d 1393 (2d Cir. 1973), *cert. denied*, 417 U.S. 976 (1974).

625. Beartooth Alliance v. Crown Butte Mines, 904 F. Supp. 1168 (D. Mont. 1995).

626. United States v. Nature's Way Marine LLC, 904 F.3d 416 (5th Cir. 2018). In *United States v. American Commercial Lines, LLC*, 875 F.3d 170 (5th Cir. 2017), the owner of the tugboat contracted with a third party to operate the tugboat which was towing the barge which discharged oil upon a collision. The operator was criminally prosecuted and convicted, but the tugboat owner remained civilly liable. The court found that the statute did not allow the owner to escape liability simply because the operator was convicted.

627. Montauk Oil Transportation Co. v. Tug El Zorro Grande, 54 F.3d 111 (2d Cir. 1995); *In re* Oriental Republic of Uruguay, 821 F. Supp. 928 (D. Del. 1992).

628. Quaker State Corp. v. U.S. Coast Guard, 681 F. Supp. 280 (W.D. Pa. 1988).

629. 33 U.S.C. § 1321(b)(5).

630. United States v. Hougland Barge Line, Inc., 387 F. Supp. 1110 (D. Pa. 1974); United States v. General American Transportation Corp., 367 F. Supp. 1284 (D.N.J. 1973).

631. Apex Oil Co. v. United States, 530 F.2d 1291 (8th Cir. 1976), *cert. denied*, 429 U.S. 827 (1976).

632. United States v. White, 322 U.S. 694 (1944).

633. 33 U.S.C. § 1321(b)(5).

634. State of Alaska v. Hazelwood, 866 P.2d 827, *on remand*, 912 P.2d 1266 (Alaska App. 1993), *rev'd on other grounds*, 946 P.2d 875 (Alaska 1997).

[4] Penalties for Discharge or Failure to Comply with Cleanup Order

An illegal discharge, or a failure to comply with cleanup orders, subjects the violator to administrative[635] and court-imposed civil[636] penalties. In addition, removal costs may be recovered from the owner or operator of the source of the discharge.[637] Generally, civil penalties are subject to caps, although the responsible party may be subject to the entire cleanup cost in the event of gross negligence or willful misconduct.[638] If penalties are owed, a vessel may be prevented from proceeding or leaving port by order of the Treasury Department.[639]

[5] Boarding Vessels, Entry of Facilities; Inspections

Law enforcement authorities enjoy broad powers to board and inspect vessels on navigable waters or in the contiguous zone, or to enter facilities, and to arrest any person who violates any provision of §311 in the view or presence of that officer.[640]

[6] Removal and Mitigation

The federal government enjoys broad powers to ensure the immediate and effective removal of spilled oil, to require mitigation, or to prevent a substantial threat of discharge, in compliance with the National Contingency Plan (NCP). There is an NCP specific to marine discharges of oil or hazardous wastes.[641] Generally, the cleanup must adhere to the NCP, although deviation is possible if another plan of action ensures a more effective response.[642] The federal government's powers include the actual removal — directing or monitoring of any federal, state or private removal action — and the removal or destruction of the discharging vehicle.[643] If the discharge, or substantial threat of discharge, poses a substantial threat to public health or welfare, then the federal government must direct the immediate removal of the oil or hazardous wastes. Threats to fish, shellfish, wildlife, other natural resources, public and private beaches, and shorelines would satisfy this criterion. In that case, the government is relieved of the ordinary contracting procedures or employment regulations usually restricting government work.[644] If the federal government conducts the cleanup, the funds are provided in the first instance from the Oil Spill Liability Trust Fund, which will be reimbursed upon cost recovery from liable parties. The trust fund also is replenished by financial penalties received from responsible parties.[645] The Attorney

635. 33 U.S.C. §1321(b)(6).
636. 33 U.S.C. §1321(b)(7).
637. 33 U.S.C. §1321(b)(10).
638. 33 U.S.C. §1321(f)(1).
639. 33 U.S.C. §1321(b)(12).
640. 33 U.S.C. §1321(m).
641. 33 U.S.C. §1321(c) (setting forth the general outlines of the NCP).
642. 33 U.S.C. §1321(c)(3).
643. 33 U.S.C. §1321(c)(1).
644. 33 U.S.C. §1321(c)(2).
645. 33 U.S.C. §1321(s).

General may be directed to "secure any relief from any person" to ensure abatement of the danger.[646] Furthermore, federal district courts are given the power to order "any relief ... that the public interest and equities of the case may require."[647]

The statute provides that any person, except a responsible party, who is engaged in a removal action that is consistent with the NCP, or which is otherwise authorized, is exempt from liability for response costs or damages resulting from his or her actions or omissions. This protection does not apply to a CERCLA cleanup, or for gross negligence or willful misconduct, nor does it exempt the non-responsible party from liability for personal injuries or wrongful death.[648] Further, any exemption under § 311 does not affect liability under the Oil Pollution Act of 1990.

[7] Third Party Liability; Defenses; Cost Recovery by Innocent Owner or Operator

The statute has provisions similar to the defenses often found elsewhere in environmental laws. Although the owner or operator of the discharging source cannot escape removal responsibilities, it can seek cost recovery from the United States if it can prove that the discharge was caused solely by an act of God, an act of war, the negligence of the United States, or an act or omission of a third party.[649] In the latter case, whether or not the third party's act or omission was negligent is not relevant to the availability of the defense to the owner or operator who is primarily liable.[650] If the owner or operator can demonstrate third party liability, then the third party becomes liable for cleanup costs; the primarily liable party is entitled to subrogation to all rights of the government to cost recovery from the third party. However, the third party has available the same right of reimbursement from the government in the event that its liability arises from an act of God, act of war, or act or omission of a fourth party.[651] The primarily liable party may also seek cost recovery directly from the liable third party.[652]

However, the mere fact that another party was tangentially involved in the operation leading to the spill does not create third party liability absolving the discharger of liability. For instance, a river pilot who directs the vessel is not a third party for this purpose when a collision causes a discharge.[653] A tug pushing a barge is not a third party relieving the discharger from liability.[654] However, a tug pushing a barge

---

646. 33 U.S.C. § 1321(e)(1)(A).
647. 33 U.S.C. § 1321(e)(2).
648. 33 U.S.C. § 1321(c)(4).
649. 33 U.S.C. § 1321(i).
650. Id.
651. 33 U.S.C. § 1321(g).
652. 33 U.S.C. § 1321(h).
653. In re Oriental Republic of Uruguay, 821 F. Supp. 928 (D. Del. 1992).
654. United States v. LeBeouf Bros. Towing Co., 621 F.2d 787 (5th Cir.), cert. denied, 452 U.S. 906 (1981).

may itself be responsible for a discharge it causes.[655] If the owner or operator shares liability with the third party, then the defense is unavailable.[656] If the discharge resulted from natural causes, but the owner or operator still could have prevented the discharge by the exercise of reasonable care, the "act of God" defense will be unavailable.[657] There is case law that the term "third party" excludes the United States government.[658]

[8] National Response System Facilitates Prevention and Speedy Cleanups

To facilitate speedy and effective cleanups, the 1990 amendments established a national response system, involving the Coast Guard as well as other federal agencies, which also requires tank vessel and facility response plans.[659] Facilities can be onshore or offshore, and can include oil pipelines. The national response system envisages procedures, methods, and equipment requirements to ensure prevention, speedy detection, and response to discharges; vessel inspections; coordination between the Coast Guard and local authorities; comprehensive data collecting and retrieval; and other prevention and response measures.[660] The tank vessel and facility response plans must include preparation for a "worst case scenario" to the maximum extent practicable.[661] A worst case scenario would contemplate the possibility that a vessel may lose its entire cargo of oil, or that a facility may have the largest foreseeable discharge during adverse weather conditions.[662] If the response plan satisfies the statutory requirements, it must be approved, although it must also be subject to periodic reviews.[663] The Coast Guard may board and inspect vessels to ascertain the existence

---

655. Frederick E. Bouchard, Inc. v. United States, 583 F. Supp. 477 (D. Mass. 1984). If the tugboat operator is in complete control of a barge which discharges the oil during a collision, the tugboat operator is liable for the spill. United States v. Nature's Way Marine LLC, 904 F.3d 416 (5th Cir. 2018). *See also* United States v. American Commercial Lines, LLC, 875 F.3d 170 (5th Cir. 2017) (convicted third-party operator of the tugboat was bankrupt, but tugboat's owner remained liable as an owner).

656. Quaker State Corp. v. United States Coast Guard, 716 F. Supp. 201 (W.D. Pa. 1989).

657. Total Petroleum, Inc. v. United States, 12 Ct. Cl. 178 (1987) (oil pipeline crossing stream cracked during heavy flooding; but monitoring of the site would have revealed the extent of the pre-flood erosion which contributed to the cracking; moreover, the company's failure to timely stop the flow also contributed to spill); Liberian Poplar Transports, Inc. v. United States, 26 Ct. Cl. 223 (1992) (if vessel had monitored weather reports, it would have been advised of the approaching storm; discharge of oil being transferred during storm did not result from act of God).

658. *In re* Glacier Bay, 71 F.3d 1447 (9th Cir. 1995).

659. 33 U.S.C. § 1321(j).

660. 33 U.S.C. § 1321(j)(1)–(4).

661. 33 U.S.C. § 1321(j)(5).

662. 33 U.S.C. § 1321(a)(24). Further authority has been granted to the Department of Transportation, Department of the Interior, the Coast Guard and EPA to respond to worst case scenarios. Executive Order 12777, §§ 2(b)–(d) (March 15, 2013).

663. 33 U.S.C. § 1321(j)(5)(D)(iii), (iv). If approval is mandated by the act, the agency lacks any discretionary authority to burden the response plan with additional conditions not required by Section 311, even if other environmental statutes otherwise would warrant additional responsibilities. National Wildlife Federation v. Secretary of the United States Department of Transportation, 960 F.3d 872 (2020).

of a response plan as well as the vessel's capacity to carry it out.[664] If a response plan has not been approved, the vessel or facility, with limited exceptions, is prohibited from handling, storing or transporting oil.[665]

[C] Oil Pollution Act of 1990

[1] Introduction

Aside from amending § 311 of the Clean Water Act, the Oil Pollution Act of 1990 (OPA)[666] also has numerous substantive provisions of its own. The Act expanded the federal response authority already contained in § 311 (see [A], *above*). It also mandated an expansion of the existing regulatory programs for contingency planning and the prevention of discharges of oil. The OPA created a $1 billion trust fund available for removal and for compensation for property damage resulting from oil spills, and also provided for the recovery of restoration costs and other damages to natural resources, including the costs of acquiring replacement natural resources.[667]

[2] Responsible Parties Include Owners and Operators of Vessels, Facilities, and Pipelines

Under the OPA, responsible parties include the owner or operator of a vessel, or the party that charters the vessel, as well as the owner or operator of onshore or off-shore facilities. Governmental units are explicitly exempted from liability as an owner when the government transfers the possession and right to use the facility to another party by lease, assignment or permit. The owner or operator of a pipeline also is a responsible party.

What if the vessel or facility is abandoned? In such case, the party who would have been responsible immediately before abandonment remains responsible for spills.[668] However, when the discharge is under permit, it is exempt from OPA liability.[669]

[3] Third Party Liability; Defenses

As with § 311 of the Clean Water Act, there is third party liability (see [B][7], *above*), and cost recovery and subrogation rights are available to a primarily responsible party when the spill is caused solely by a third party, an act of God, or an act of war.[670] However, unlike § 311 of the Clean Water Act, the OPA relieves the statutorily responsible party of cleanup obligations in the first instance when the spill is caused entirely by a third party. The party claiming the defense must show that it

---

664. 33 U.S.C. § 1321(m)(1).

665. 33 U.S.C. § 1321(j)(5)(E), (F).

666. 33 U.S.C. §§ 2701–2761.

667. *See generally* Charles Openchowski, *Federal Implementation of the Oil Pollution Act of 1990*, 21 ENVTL. L. REP. (Envtl. L. Inst.) 10,605 (1991).

668. 33 U.S.C. § 2701(32).

669. 33 U.S.C. § 2702(c).

670. 33 U.S.C. § 2702(d).

exercised due care with respect to the oil which was spilled, and took precautions against foreseeable acts or omissions by third parties.[671] However, an employee or agent of the party claiming the defense is excluded from the definition of a third party. The defense also is unavailable if the act or omission that caused the spill was caused by one with a contractual relationship with the party claiming the defense.[672] Hence, when the spill occurred at a fuel terminal, and the operator of a vessel receiving fuel from the terminal under contract was a responsible party under the statute, the vessel owner could not avail itself of the third party defense.[673]

The statutory limits on amounts of recovery from a third party apply unless the third party was grossly negligent or acted willfully.[674] Even if a defense is not available, however, a responsible party may seek contribution from other responsible parties.[675]

[4] Indemnification Agreements Are Enforceable, but Are Not a Statutory Defense

The OPA does not preclude enforcement of a valid indemnification agreement, contractually protecting a responsible party from the liability of others. Indemnification contracts are in the realm of common law remedies, which the OPA does not bar as between the contracting parties. However, an indemnification agreement cannot shift *statutory* liability from the responsible party to anyone else; the responsible party remains liable to the government under the statute, despite its contractual rights against another party.[676]

[5] Responsible Party Is Liable for Removal Costs and Damages

When oil is discharged, or a discharge is substantially likely, into navigable waters or adjoining shorelines, or in the exclusive economic zone, then the responsible party is liable for removal costs and damages. Removal costs are the same costs for which recovery is allowed in § 311 of the Clean Water Act.

[6] Recoverable Costs Include Natural Resource Damages; Subsistence Use of Natural Resources

Damages cover a broad area under the OPA, and particular attention is paid to natural resource claims, especially because of the devastating ecological results of

---

671. 33 U.S.C. § 2703(a)(3).

672. *Id.* In *United States v. American Commercial Lines, LLC*, 875 F.3d 170 (5th Cir. 2017), the owner of the tugboat contracted with a third party to operate the tugboat which was towing the barge which discharged oil upon a collision. The operator was criminally prosecuted and convicted, but the tugboat owner remained civilly liable.

673. International Marine Carriers v. Oil Spill Liability Trust Fund, 903 F. Supp. 1097, *recons. denied*, 914 F. Supp. 149 (S.D. Texas 1994).

674. National Shipping Co. of Saudi Arabia v. Moran Trade Co., 122 F.3d 1062 (unpub.), 1997 U.S. App. LEXIS 29237 (4th Cir. 1997), *cert. denied*, 523 U.S. 1021 (1998).

675. 33 U.S.C. §§ 2709, 2717.

676. 33 U.S.C. § 2710.

several oil spills during the late 1980s. Hence, recoverable costs include injury to natural resources, including the reasonable cost of assessing the damage, and loss of subsistence use of natural resources, recoverable by users. Natural resources are broadly defined to include land, fish, wildlife, biota, air, water, ground water, drinking water supplies, and any other similar public resources.[677] The parties entitled to recover natural resource damages include the federal and state governments, Indian tribes, and even foreign governments for injuries to their natural resources.[678] Damages consist of the costs of restoration, replacement, or acquisition of the equivalent natural resources.[679] Costs that are recovered are deposited in the trust fund, making it a revolving fund for coverage of other cleanups.[680]

Statutory damages also include loss of "subsistence" use of natural resources; however, these need not be resources under government control, and the particular ownership or management of the resource is immaterial to proving the user's entitlement to recovery.[681]

[7] Additional Recoverable Costs: Lost Tax Revenues; Lost Profits; Cost of Public Services

The OPA permits recovery of governmental losses of tax revenues, royalties, and the like, and lost profits by private entities, as well as the net costs of providing additional public services as a consequence of the spill.[682]

[8] Monetary Limitations on Damages

As with Clean Water Act § 311 (see [B][4], *above*), there are monetary limits on liability under OPA, but the limits do not apply if the responsible party was grossly negligent, the misconduct was willful, or the conduct violated federal safety, construction, or operating regulations.[683]

One court has ruled punitive damages are not available under the OPA.[684]

A separate statute established the Trans-Alaska Pipeline Liability Fund, governing discharges from that pipeline and from tankers transporting Alaska oil to United States ports.[685] This statute dealt with the notorious Exxon Valdez spill, which also resulted in tort litigation awarding substantial compensatory and punitive damages.[686]

---

677. 33 U.S.C. §§ 2701(20), 2702(b)(2)(A).

678. 33 U.S.C. § 2706(a).

679. 33 U.S.C. § 2706(d).

680. 33 U.S.C. § 2706(f).

681. 33 U.S.C. § 2702(b)(2)(C).

682. 33 U.S.C. § 2702(b); Maritrans Operating Partners v. Port of Pascagoula, 73 Fed. App'x. 733, 2003 U.S. App. LEXIS 17719 (5th Cir. 2003).

683. 33 U.S.C. § 2704.

684. South Port Marine, LLC v. Gulf Oil Ltd., 234 F.3d 58 (1st Cir. 2000).

685. 43 U.S.C. § 1653.

686. *In re* Exxon Valdez, 490 F.3d 1066 (9th Cir. 2007).

[D] Oil and Gas Drilling on the Outer Continental Shelf: Outer Continental Shelf Lands Act

[1] Congressional Purpose

The outer continental shelf (OCS) is a vital national resource reserve held by the federal government for the public. Congress views this region as an economic resource, that should be "made available for expeditious and orderly development, subject to environmental safeguards, in a manner which is consistent with the maintenance of competition and other national needs."[687] The outer continental shelf, however, has significant impacts on coastal states, which may be less than enthusiastic about offshore oil and gas operations.[688] Unrestrained production of oil and gas from offshore hydrocarbon-bearing geological areas could result in a number of harmful national effects, including unnecessary drilling, the construction of unnecessary facilities, environmental damage, such as discharges that kill fish and wildlife and clog harbors and beaches, economic waste, and the depletion of resources.[689] There is a correlating national interest in the effective management of the marine, coastal, and human environments.[690] As a consequence of these often competing interests, Congress enacted the Outer Continental Shelf Lands Act, based on an earlier 1953 statute.[691] This Act, rather than maritime law, generally governs the regulation of oil and gas operations in the outer continental shelf,[692] although the law of the coastal state will govern common law claims.

Recognizing the fragility of the environment, the Act requires that operations in the outer continental shelf "should be conducted in a safe manner by well-trained personnel using technology, precautions, and techniques sufficient to prevent or minimize the likelihood of blowouts, loss of well control, fires, spillages, physical obstruction to other users of the waters or subsoil or seabed, or other occurrences which may cause damage to the environment or to property, or endanger life or health."[693]

[2] Federal versus State Roles

Congress wanted to preserve a consultative role for affected coastal states, and to provide funding, financed in part by paying coastal states 27 percent of the licensing fees generated by outer continental shelf oil and gas exploration.[694] This funding helps states mitigate the adverse economic and environmental effects of offshore oil and gas activities. Although Congress authorized the sharing of exploration rights

---

687. 43 U.S.C. § 1332(3).

688. *See, e.g.*, Note, *"Not on My Beach:" Local California Initiative to Prevent Onshore Support Facilities for Offshore Oil Development*, 38 Hastings L.J. 957 (1987).

689. 43 U.S.C. § 1334(j).

690. 43 U.S.C. § 1332(4).

691. 43 U.S.C. § 1331, *et seq.*

692. Offshore Logistics, Inc. v. Tallentire, 477 U.S. 207 (1986), *on remand*, 800 F.3d 1390 (5th Cir. 1986).

693. 43 U.S.C. § 1331(6).

694. 43 U.S.C. § 1331(4).

with the states,[695] the Department of the Interior still retains substantial discretion over the allocation of funds, and the federal government is not required to enter exploration-sharing agreements.[696]

The United States retains control over the areas and resources of the continental shelf regions,[697] while states retain authority over areas and resources under navigable waters within the territory of the respective states,[698] defined to extend up to three miles seaward from the coastline[699] (10 miles in the Gulf) except as to areas ceded to or otherwise retained by the federal government.[700] The federal government retains rights involving navigation in all maritime areas, but authority over leasing turns on which government retains property interests in the particular locale.[701] This subsection addresses oil and gas leasing in the area of the outer continental shelf, principally by the federal government.

The "outer continental shelf" (OCS) includes all submerged lands under the jurisdiction of the United States, lying seaward and outside of the areas of lands under "navigable waters"[702] which extend to the three mile boundary.[703] The federal government exclusively[704] issues oil and gas leases for areas on the outer continental shelf under the aegis of the Department of the Interior.[705]

[3] Lease Program

Leases are issued after competitive bidding.[706] The Department of the Interior maintains a lease management program for the outer continental shelf, which must take into account economic, social and environmental values of the resources of the OCS, and the potential impact of oil and gas drilling on other resource values of the OCS, as well as on the marine, coastal, and human environments.[707] The leases permit exploration, development, and production.[708] In particular, the timing and location of exploration, development and production of oil and gas must take into account: existing information about the geographic, geological, and ecological characteristics of the region; an equitable sharing of development benefits and environmental risks

---

695. State of Alabama v. U.S. Dept. of the Interior, 84 F.3d 410 (11th Cir. 1996).
696. State of Louisiana *ex rel.* Guste v. United States, 832 F.2d 935 (1987), *cert. denied*, 485 U.S. 1033 (1987).
697. 43 U.S.C. §§ 1301, 1302.
698. 43 U.S.C. § 1311.
699. 43 U.S.C. § 1312.
700. 43 U.S.C. § 1313.
701. 43 U.S.C. § 1314.
702. 43 U.S.C. § 1331(a).
703. 43 U.S.C. § 1301(a).
704. United States v. Maine, 420 U.S. 515 (1975).
705. 43 U.S.C. § 1331(b).
706. 43 U.S.C. § 1337.
707. 43 U.S.C. § 1344(1).
708. 43 U.S.C. § 1340.

among various regions of the OCS; the location of these operations in relation to fisheries, navigation and other uses; and the environmental sensitivity and marine productivity of a particular region in relation to other regions of the OCS.[709]

"Exploration" includes the use of geophysical surveys utilizing magnetic, gravity, seismic, or other means to detect minerals and oil and gas deposits.[710] "Development" refers to any activities following discovery of deposits, including geophysical activity, drilling, platform construction,[711] and the operation of on-shore support facilities necessary for production of the resources.[712] "Production" includes the activities which are necessary for removal of the resources, including field operations, the transfer of the resources to shore, operation monitoring, maintenance, and work-over drilling.[713] "Operation" requires some nexus with the oil or gas exploration, development, or production.

The issuance of the lease is subject to environmental regulation by the Department of the Interior.[714] The lessee is required to submit a development and production plan, which then must be approved by the Department. Prior to issuing a lease, the Department must conduct an environmental study of the area to assess the impacts on the human, marine, or coastal environments. The environmental study must indicate whether marine biota may suffer from either chronic low-level pollution or from spills, and what impact the introduction of drilling muds and drill cuttings, and the laying of pipe will have.[715] If more studies are called for, then the Department is obliged to perform them,[716] although the Department may rely on environmental information provided by other agencies.[717] In making lease decisions, the Department must utilize any relevant environmental information.[718] Health and safety studies also must be done in connection with operations, drilling, and even underwater diving.[719] The Secretary of the Interior must report back annually to Congress. Congress also wanted to ensure the agency's continuing accountability for the outer continental shelf. The report must provide an accounting of all funds spent and received, a detailed accounting of all exploration and drilling related activities for the year, a summary of management, supervision, and enforcement activities for the year, and recommendations for improvement.[720]

---

709. 43 U.S.C. § 1344(2).

710. 43 U.S.C. § 1331(k).

711. Tennessee Gas Pipeline Co. v. Houston Gas Co., 881 F.2d 245 (W.D. La. 1995), *reh'g denied*, 95 F.3d 1151 (1996). Construction of fixed platform on the outer continental shelf 35 miles from coast was an "operation" triggering federal regulation.

712. 43 U.S.C. § 1331(l).

713. 43 U.S.C. § 1331(m).

714. 43 U.S.C. § 1351.

715. 43 U.S.C. § 1346(a).

716. 43 U.S.C. § 1346(b).

717. 43 U.S.C. § 1346(c).

718. 43 U.S.C. § 1346(d).

719. 43 U.S.C. § 1347.

720. 43 U.S.C. § 1343.

Every three years, the Department must report to Congress on the cumulative environmental impacts of all outer continental shelf leasing programs on the human, marine, and coastal environments. This report must be available to the public.[721]

[4] Development and Production Plans

Lessees must submit development and production plans to the Department of the Interior for approval prior to conducting these activities.[722] Any plan will be submitted to affected states and local governments, and must be available to relevant interstate regional entities and to the public.[723] The Department may not issue any lease that fails to require compliance with the relevant plan.[724] The plan must detail the facilities and operations in the lease area on the outer continental shelf, even if they are neither owned nor operated by the lessee, including specifications as to size, location, and the economic and energy needs of the facility or operation. The plan also must detail: (1) the environmental and safety safeguards necessary; (2) how they will be implemented; and (3) the expected rate of development and production.[725] If the lease will impact the coastal zone of any state with a coastal zone management program (see discussion in § 11.02[B][2]), then that state or the Secretary of Commerce must certify the plan's consistency with the Coastal Zone Management Act.[726] If the lessee fails to submit a valid plan, the lease must be canceled.[727]

The Department may approve, disapprove, or require modification of the plan.[728] Approval of a plan may be a major federal action[729] requiring preparation of an environmental impact statement, which must be distributed to the appropriate governors and local governments (see discussion in § 4.01[B], [C]).[730] If it is not found to be a major federal action, states and local governments still have an opportunity to submit comments and make recommendations.[731]

Disapproval is required if: the lessee cannot demonstrate its ability to comply with all requirements and regulations; it is out of compliance with a state program adopted under the Coastal Zone Management Act (see § 11.02 [B][2]); or, the plan impinges on national security. The plan also must be disapproved on environmental grounds if there are exceptional geological conditions in the leased area or exceptional resource values in the marine or coastal environment, or for other exceptional circumstances. Grounds for disapproval are also established if the plan's implementation would "probably" cause serious harm to aquatic life, or the marine, coastal or human en-

---

721. 43 U.S.C. § 1346(e).
722. 43 U.S.C. § 1351(a)(1).
723. 43 U.S.C. § 1351(a)(3).
724. 43 U.S.C. § 1351(b).
725. 43 U.S.C. § 1351(c).
726. 43 U.S.C. § 1351(d); see 16 U.S.C. § 1456(c)(3)(B)(i)–(iii).
727. 43 U.S.C. § 1351(j).
728. 43 U.S.C. § 1351(h).
729. 43 U.S.C. § 1351(e)(1).
730. 43 U.S.C. § 1351(f).
731. 43 U.S.C. § 1351(g).

vironments, the threat is likely to remain viable, and the benefits of disapproval out-weigh the benefits of approval. If the plan is disapproved, the lessee has no right to compensation — it is not a taking (see § 1.05[C]).[732] Approved plans may be revised, but the revision still must protect the human, marine, and coastal environments.[733]

The Act also requires that all lessees and permittees,[734] and government agencies,[735] provide the Department with access to all data obtained from their activities in con-nection with oil and gas. Affected states have a right to a summary of whatever data the Department collects.[736] However, there is protection for confidential information,[737] and information provided to states may disguise locations or lessees' names, so as to protect the competitive position of those parties providing the information.[738]

[5] Citizen Suits

The Outer Continental Shelf Lands Act provides for citizen suits. These provisions parallel those in many other environmental statutes (see § 1.03). Standing is defined in terms of an adverse effect on any person's valid legal interest.[739] The citizen plaintiff may sue any government entity,[740] subject to the limitations of the Eleventh Amendment (see discussion in § 1.05[E]). However, there is the usual notice requirement, in this case 60 days, to the Secretary of the Interior, to "any other appropriate Federal official," to the state where the violation occurs and to the alleged violator. If the Attorney General or the state has commenced and is diligently prosecuting a civil action, then the citizen suit will be dismissed, although the citizen plaintiff can intervene as of right.[741] There is an exception permitting immediate commencement of an action if the alleged violation constitutes an imminent threat to public health or safety, or would "immediately" affect the plaintiff's legal interest.[742] If the citizen suit may be maintained, then the Attorney General may intervene as of right.[743] As with other environmental statutes, the court may award plaintiff costs and attorneys' fees.[744] There is no require-ment that the party seeking the award prevail, or even substantially prevail.[745]

---

732. 43 U.S.C. § 1351(h).
733. 43 U.S.C. § 1351(i).
734. 43 U.S.C. § 1351(a)(1).
735. 43 U.S.C. § 1351(a)(2).
736. 43 U.S.C. § 1352(b)(2).
737. 43 U.S.C. § 1352(c), (e), (f), (g), (i).
738. 43 U.S.C. § 1352(d).
739. 43 U.S.C. § 1349(a)(1).
740. 43 U.S.C. § 1349(a)(1).
741. 43 U.S.C. § 1349(a)(2).
742. 43 U.S.C. § 1349(a)(3).
743. 43 U.S.C. § 1349(a)(4).
744. 43 U.S.C. § 1349(a)(5).
745. See, e.g., *Conservation Law Foundation of New England, Inc. v. Secretary of the Interior*, 790 F.2d 965 (1st Cir. 1986), in which the plaintiff sought to enjoin the sale of offshore drilling leases in an area which subsequently was determined to belong to Canada, as to which bids for the leases had not even been submitted. The court awarded attorneys' fees despite dismissing the action on grounds of mootness.

Challenges may be brought to the Department's approval of a lease program or action taken with regard to exploration, development, or production plans, but only after exhaustion of administrative remedies.[746] In this case, citizen suits are specifically barred.[747]

[6] Enforcement

Enforcement authority may be exercised by the Department of the Interior, the Army, and the Coast Guard.[748] Permittees must comply with the Occupational Safety and Health Act (OSHA), and other relevant health and safety and environmental regulations; in this connection, permittees must allow inspectors prompt access, and must provide relevant documents upon request.[749] Enforcement authorities must conduct annual on-site inspections of all facilities on the outer continental shelf for regulatory compliance, including equipment inspections.[750] Every major fire and spill (defined to be a spill of over 200 barrels of oil within a 30 day period) must be investigated,[751] as must every death or serious physical injury,[752] although lesser incidents also may be investigated. Investigators enjoy broad discovery and subpoena powers.[753] Every investigation must be detailed in the annual report to Congress (see [3], above).[754]

Enforcement options include injunctions and civil penalties. Criminal sanctions are available for the knowing and willful violation of the Act, its regulations, or of a lease, license or permit. False statements or certifications in any required documentation, tampering with monitoring devices, falsifying required records, or unlawfully disclosing confidential information, are also subject to criminal sanctions.[755]

[E] Tanker Design and Operation

[1] The Ports and Waterways Safety Act

Complementing the Oil Pollution Act's provisions governing liability for oil discharges are the requirements of the Ports and Waterways Safety Act (PWSA)[756] dealing with tanker design and other statutes dealing with maritime traffic.

---

746. 43 U.S.C. § 1349(c)(3).
747. 43 U.S.C. § 1349(c)(4); Amerada Hess Corp. v. Department of Interior, 170 F.3d 1032 (10th Cir. 1999).
748. 43 U.S.C. § 1348(a).
749. 43 U.S.C. § 1348(b).
750. 43 U.S.C. § 1348(c)(1).
751. 43 U.S.C. § 1348(d)(1).
752. 43 U.S.C. § 1348(d)(2).
753. 43 U.S.C. § 1348(f).
754. 43 U.S.C. § 1348(g).
755. 43 U.S.C. § 1350.
756. 46 U.S.C. §§ 3701–3718.

The PWSA, originally enacted in 1972, applies to all tank vessels of over 500 gross tons of domestic or foreign registry. However, it exempts foreign vessels simply passing through United States waters.[757] PWSA empowers the Secretary of Transportation to prescribe rules for the design, construction, operation and manning of tankers, as well as for navigation and vessel safety. The statute specifies that regulations "shall include requirements" about hulls, cargo tanks, "propulsion machinery" (engines and propellers), the handling of cargo, fire protection, crew qualifications and training, the elimination of oil discharges during deballasting, and several other related topics.[758] Deballasting relates to the practice of filling the cargo holds of tankers with water to act as ballast and thus stabilize the vessel when it is not carrying oil. When the tanker is prepared to load its cargo of oil it must discharge the water, or deballast.

The Secretary of Transportation was designated by Congress to administer this program since the Department of Transportation encompasses the Coast Guard, which historically has supervised harbor traffic and vessel safety and inspection.

[2] Preempts State Laws on Tanker Design

Despite the broad mandate of PWSA, the Coast Guard and Secretary of Transportation adopted few regulations of significance regarding tanker design and traffic during its first decade. When the completion of the Trans-Alaska oil pipeline led to a vast increase in tanker traffic between Alaska and the ports of Seattle and Tacoma, the State of Washington enacted a series of statutes regulating tankers. These included requiring tankers of over 40,000 tons to have twin propellers and double bottoms (so that puncturing the outer hull will not necessarily cause the cargo to spill). The state also mandated tug escorts for tankers not meeting these design requirements, and barred all tankers of over 125,000 tons from its waters.

The State of Washington's concern stemmed from the prospect of greater tanker traffic in Puget Sound, a body of water studded with islands, heavily used by fishing craft and ferries, and often fog-bound.

The statutes were successfully challenged in *Ray v. Atlantic Richfield Co.*,[759] which found them to be preempted by the PWSA. The Supreme Court ruled that the congressional intent was to assure uniformity in tanker design and equipment. The Ports and Waterways Safety Act empowering the Coast Guard to adopt rules on these subjects served to bar state regulations even where the Coast Guard failed to adopt controls. The Court assumed that the Coast Guard's failure to mandate twin propellers or double bottoms meant that the agency had considered these regulations, but rejected them as unnecessary. The state-imposed maximum size limit was similarly held to be a design requirement and preempted. Only the tug escort requirement was found not to be preempted by federal law, since the Coast Guard had not adopted

---

757. 46 U.S.C. §§ 3702, 3710, 3711.
758. 46 U.S.C. § 3703.
759. 435 U.S. 151 (1978).

such a rule. Unlike the design and size regulations, where Congress mandated uniformity, the Court held the state tug escort rule was valid at least until the Coast Guard either adopted such a requirement or expressly determined not to do so.[760]

A portion of the *Atlantic Richfield* opinion dealing with a state law mandating pilots on tankers is discussed in [F], *below*.

[3] Double Hulls Required by 1990 Amendment

It was not until the 1989 *Exxon Valdez* oil spill, which devastated much of the Alaska coast, that Congress finally acted to expressly require some of the chief safety features involved in *Atlantic Richfield*. In the same torrent of legislation that enacted the Oil Pollution Act (discussed in [C], *above*), Congress amended the PWSA to require double hulls. The Act, as amended in 1990, now mandates double hulls on all new tankers of 5,000 tons or more.[761] New tankers are defined as those under construction as of 1990. Existing vessels are furnished a phase-out period extending to 2010, depending on the age of the ship.[762]

Two other major safety requirements, double sets of radar, and segregated ballast (separate holds for oil and for the water carried as ballast), were enacted in the 1983 amendments to the PWSA.[763] Segregated ballast eliminates concern over discharges of oil while the vessel is deballasting, discussed earlier in this subsection.

[4] Proof of Compliance and Penalties

Vessels must provide evidence of compliance with PWSA. Vessels of United States registry must have a certificate of inspection, and foreign vessels in United States waters (unless merely passing through these waters) must have a certificate of compliance with the PWSA.[764] All vessels subject to the Act are to be inspected at least once a year, and ships over ten years old are subject to a "special and detailed inspection of structural strength and hull integrity."[765] There are civil and criminal penalties for violations, as well as injunctive relief. In addition, the Secretary of the Treasury, at the request of the Secretary of Transportation, may refuse or revoke clearances needed for a vessel to sail from a United States port.[766]

Particularly strict Coast Guard rules control tankers carrying liquefied natural gas, which must be transported at extremely low temperatures to reduce the risk of fire. All such vessels must have double hulls.[767]

---

760. *Atlantic Richfield Co.*, 435 U.S. at 171–73.
761. 46 U.S.C. § 3703a(a).
762. 46 U.S.C. § 3703a.
763. 46 U.S.C. §§ 3705, 3708(1).
764. 46 U.S.C. §§ 3710, 3711.
765. 46 U.S.C. § 3714.
766. 46 U.S.C. § 3718.
767. 46 C.F.R. §§ 32.63-5(b)(2), 38.05-1(f).

[5] State Laws on Deballasting and Tanker Performance

The authority of states to legislate regarding oil tanker practices came to the fore in two cases of importance after *Atlantic Richfield*. In one case, an Alaska statute, prohibiting all deballasting in that state's waters was challenged as preempted by a Coast Guard rule that bars discharging ballast that leaves a visible trace of oil. The court upheld the state law, holding that unlike the design requirements in *Atlantic Richfield*, there was no congressional intent to require nationwide uniformity with regard to the act of deballasting.[768] However, in a second case, a Washington law, requiring inspection of tankers, monitoring of their crews' performance, and reporting of collisions and near-collisions, was found to be preempted by the PWSA, as in *Atlantic Richfield*.[769]

[F] Pilotage

Federal law for many years has required vessels engaged in coastal trade, between United States ports, to "be under the control and direction of pilots licensed by the Coast Guard" when entering or leaving harbors.[770] This statute does not apply to vessels in foreign trade, which traditionally have been subject to state laws requiring state-licensed pilots.[771] The validity of these state laws was upheld by the Supreme Court in the well-known case of *Cooley v. Board of Wardens of Port of Philadelphia*,[772] decided in 1851. In *Cooley*, the Court rejected a claim that the state lacked authority to require licensing of pilots because the Commerce Clause gave such power to Congress.

This old issue resurfaced in the *Atlantic Richfield* case, other facets of which are described in [E], *above*. The State of Washington required all oil tankers in its waters to take on a state-licensed pilot to reduce the likelihood of collisions and resulting discharges of oil in heavily-trafficked Puget Sound. However, a federal statute expressly provides that "[n]o State ... shall impose upon pilots of ... vessels any obligation to procure a State or other license in addition to that issued by the United States."[773] The Court predictably ruled that this statute precluded the state from requiring state-licensed pilots on coastal vessels, for which federal law mandates a Coast Guard-licensed pilot. The state, it went on to hold, is free to mandate state-licensed pilots on foreign-trade vessels, where the federal law is silent. This, however, was a Pyrrhic victory for the state, since the vast bulk of the oil shipped into its ports is loaded in Alaska and is thus part of the coastal trade.

---

768. Chevron USA, Inc. v. Hammond, 726 F.2d 483 (9th Cir. 1984), *cert. denied*, 471 U.S. 1140 (1985).

769. United States v. Locke, 529 U.S. 89 (2000).

770. 46 U.S.C. § 364.

771. *Atlantic Richfield Co.*, 435 U.S. at 170–71.

772. 53 U.S. 299 (1851).

773. 46 U.S.C. § 215.

[G] International Agreements

There is an international treaty of limited effectiveness imposing requirements on oil tankers. In 1973 the Marine Pollution Convention (MarPol)[774] was negotiated, and has been signed by nations representing over 90% of the world's merchant tonnage. It mandates double hulls for tankers built since 1993 and navigation standards for designated "special areas" including the Mediterranean and Baltic Seas. There are limits on the discharge of oil, and certification required for all tankers of over 150 tons. MarPol is enforceable by coastal states as well as port states (those with ports used by tankers), and has been implemented in the United States by legislation.[775] Although the Law of the Sea Convention's article 211 in general terms provides for agreements such as MarPol, that Convention, which originally was to specifically encompass tanker safety and oil discharges, was diverted from these topics and, as finally enacted, chiefly governs the extraction of minerals from undersea lands, the right of innocent passage, and other unrelated subjects.[776] The International Maritime Organization, a United Nations agency, administers MarPol, but this agreement is limited by the fact that tankers, like other ocean vessels, tend to be registered in countries (flag states) not necessarily reflective of the vessel's actual ownership. Flag states have an interest in limiting liability for spills as well as not requiring more than minimal safety equipment, to keep shipowners' costs low. Maritime states, those whose resident corporations own the vessels or that depend heavily on shipping, as well as oil producing and oil importing countries, likewise favor the fewest restrictions on tankers and the least liability for discharges. Coastal states, in contrast, with beaches, harbors and fishing grounds, support greater liability and stricter safety and equipment standards. However, as noted, the United States and some other countries have implemented and are enforcing MarPol.

§ 6.07 Dredge and Fill Operations

[A] Introduction

[1] "Dredge" and "Fill" Definitions

The primary goal of the Clean Water Act is to "maintain the chemical, physical, and biological integrity of the Nation's waters."[777] Dredge and fill operations are regulated under § 404 of the Clean Water Act,[778] and require a permit from the Army Corps of Engineers. "Fill" is defined to be a pollutant in the Clean Water Act.[779] If

---

774. 17 Int'l Legal Mats (I.L.M) 546 (1978).

775. 33 U.S.C. §§ 1901–1915.

776. United Nations Convention on the Law of the Sea, 21 I.L.M. 1261 (1982). The United States has not ratified this treaty.

777. 33 U.S.C. § 1251; CWA § 101.

778. 33 U.S.C. § 1344.

779. 33 U.S.C. § 1362(6).

statutory criteria are met, and a regulatory exemption does not apply (see [F], *below*), then the operation must be done under permit.

Although the terms "dredged" materials and "fill" materials are often used simultaneously, they are not synonymous, having potentially different origins and often used for different purposes. The end result is the same, however, under § 404: material placed in navigable waters to change depth or to convert it to dry land is deemed to constitute a unique type of pollutant.

"Dredging" refers to the removal of dirt or other accumulated materials, including the excavation of rock, from the bottom of water bodies, usually using a mechanical scooper. Siltation and ecosystem disturbance often results.[780] "Dredged material" is the material removed or excavated from navigable waters of the United States.[781]

"Filling" is the depositing of dirt and mud, often raised by dredging, into swamp areas or waterways.[782] Historically, filling was done to "reclaim" marshes for agricultural purposes or for reasons of public health. In more recent times, filling has been done to accommodate real estate development. "Fill material" is any pollutant which replaces portions of waters of the United States with dry land, or which changes the bottom elevation of a water body for any purpose.[783] Since fill, especially dredge spoil, may contain toxic pollutants, where it is deposited becomes environmentally critical.

[2] Dredge and Fill Activities Are Governed by § 404 of the Clean Water Act

As noted in [1], *above*, dredge and fill activities require the issuance of a permit under § 404 of the Clean Water Act. Ordinarily, if the application for a "404" permit is denied, no compensation is due the applicant. However, as discussed in § 1.05, the denial of the 404 permit may constitute a compensable taking under some circumstances if it deprives the owner of all reasonable investment-based expectations.

Although § 404 commonly is thought of as governing wetlands protection, the statute does not specifically so provide. Rather, the Code of Federal Regulations applies the Clean Water Act so as to regulate wetlands which are adjacent to waters of the United States.[784] Adjacent wetlands are those that border, or in some other manner are contiguous to, other waters of the United States. This basis for federal jurisdiction under the Clean Water Act has undergone a more probing analysis by the Supreme Court in recent years. Although they may be separated from other water bodies by dikes, berms, dunes, or other barriers, such wetlands may still fall within Army Corps jurisdiction, despite the absence of navigability.[785] A ground water con-

---

780. *See* ROBINSON, ENVIRONMENTAL LAW LEXICON, *Dredging* (Law Journal Press), citing United States v. H.G.D. & J. Mining Co., Inc., 561 F. Supp. 315 (S.D. W. Va. 1983).

781. 33 U.S.C. § 1402 (Ocean Dumping Act/Marine Protection Act); 40 C.F.R. § 232.2.

782. *See* ROBINSON, ENVIRONMENTAL LAW LEXICON, *Filling* (Law Journal Press).

783. 40 C.F.R. § 232.2.

784. 33 C.F.R. § 328.3(a)(2), (7).

785. 40 C.F.R. § 230.3(b).

nection between a wetland and navigable waters also is a basis for direct regulation over discharges of dredged and fill materials by the Army Corps.[786] In 2006, the Supreme Court allowed that the nature of the significant nexus between a wetland and waters of the United States so as to bring it within the purview of the CWA might be broadly interpreted, but not as broadly as had been the case previously in applying the Army Corps of Engineer's regulatory definitions.[787]

By contrast, discharges of dredged and fill materials in "isolated" waters or wetlands do not directly trigger § 404 permitting.[788] Isolated waters are non-tidal waters of the United States that are not part of a surface tributary system to interstate or navigable waters, and are not adjacent to tributary waters.[789] However, if the isolated wetland has some effect on interstate commerce[790] (see discussion in § 1.04[A]) then the agency may acquire jurisdiction. Formerly, federal jurisdiction was found to exist on the

------

786. United States v. Riverside Bayview Homes, 474 U.S. 121, (1985); United States v. Tilton, 705 F.2d 429 (11th Cir. 1983). Whether this decision remains good law *in toto* as a consequence of the *Rapanos* ruling, **n. ***___, *infra*,** is subject to question.

787. Rapanos v. United States, 126 S. Ct. 2208 (2006). The plurality opinion required that in order for a water body to be adjacent to the wetland, that water body itself must fit within the definition of "waters of the United States," being a permanent water body that is navigable-in-fact or connected to navigable waters, and it must have a continuous surface connection to the wetland. This jurisdictional term is discussed in § 6.03[B][1][f]. The concurring opinion by Justice Kennedy, providing the fifth vote, did not necessarily require a surface connection or that it be permanent, and allowed for a more indirect hydrological, or even an ecological, connection, just so sufficient relatedness between the water bodies could be demonstrated. The concurring opinion, though, required the existence of a "substantial nexus" between the water body and the ostensibly adjacent wetland for federal authority under the CWA. Relying on the congressional goals of the CWA, Justice Kennedy reasoned that the requirement could be satisfied by a showing that the wetlands in question had demonstrated value in maintaining the chemical, biological, or physical integrity of the adjacent water body, such as controlling floods, acting as a reservoir for water storage or in filtering pollutants. But this was only one vote on a bench of nine Justices, so how was the *Rapanos* outcome to be applied prospectively? Subsequent Circuit Court rulings have concluded that Justice Kennedy's opinion, insofar as it added the critical vote and thereby established the majority holding, articulates the governing standard. *See* United States v. Robertson, 875 F.3d 1281 (9th Cir. 2017); Northern California River Watch v. City of Healdsburg, 457 F.3d 1023 (9th Cir. 2006); United States v. Gerke Excavating, Inc., 464 F.3d 723 (7th Cir. 2006); United States v. Bailey, 571 F.3d 791 (8th Cir. 2009); United States v. Robison, 505 F.3d 1208 (11th Cir. 2007), *rehearing en banc*, 521 F.3d 1319 (11th Cir. 2008). The Fourth Circuit in two decisions for the same case exemplified when the respective wetlands were not, and were, functionally related to the water body to a sufficient degree to satisfy the significant nexus test. *See* Precon Development Corp, Inc. v. United States Army Corps of Engineers, 633 F.3d 278 (4th Cir. 2011), and the subsequent analysis at 603 Fed. Appx. 149 (4th Cir. 2015). Other courts have avoided addressing which standard applies when the facts satisfied Kennedy's standard as well as that of the plurality. *See* United States v. Cundiff, 555 F.3d 200 (6th Cir. 2009). In *United States v. Lucas*, 516 F.3d 316, 327 (5th Cir. 2008), *cert. denied*, ___ U.S. ___, 129 S. Ct. 116, 172 L. Ed. 2d 36 (2008), the Fifth Circuit, affirming the defendant's conviction under the CWA, found that all three *Rapanos* standards were satisfied. As a practical matter, in jurisdictions where any question continues as to whether the Kennedy standard applies, the government will likely now seek to establish a factual basis broad enough to also incorporate at least the plurality's standard in order to avoid jurisdictional uncertainty.

788. 33 C.F.R. § 330.2(e).

789. *Id.*

790. 33 C.F.R. § 328.3(3).

basis that isolated wetlands, unconnected to waters of the United States, were used by migratory birds. However, the Supreme Court rejected the Army Corps' "migratory bird rule" with respect to wetlands, unless there exists a "significant nexus" to waters of the United States.[791]

In view of some of the jurisdictional uncertainty involving CWA jurisdiction over wetlands as is noted above, a property owner wishing to develop property having wetlands characteristics can avail itself of a jurisdictional determination by the Army Corps of Engineers prior to undertaking the expense, delays and uncertainty which permitting likely will involve. The jurisdictional determination constitutes final agency action informing the property owner that the Army Corps of Engineers either has § 404 jurisdiction over the project, or does not. Earlier law held that if the agency asserted jurisdiction with a compliance order bringing the project under § 404, which might require the property owner to remove fill or otherwise undo components of the project already implemented, that was not subject to judicial review. If the property owner protested jurisdiction and failed to comply, it faced the risks of enforcement. Only then, with sanctions imposed, could the property owner seek judicial review. The process was replete with risks. The property owner was on the horns of a dilemma — either undergo expensive and onerous permitting even if it ultimately would have been unnecessary, or risk enforcement. The Supreme Court has rejected the doctrine that a property owner challenging CWA 404 jurisdiction is not entitled to pre-enforcement review.[792] Now, the property owner can seek a determination from the Army Corps of Engineers at the outset, or upon the issuance of a compliance order, whether the project will fall under CWA § 404. If the Army Corps issues a positive final determination, that the project falls within the purview of CWA § 404, the property owner can challenge that in court before proceeding further.[793]

Typically, § 404 becomes relevant to projects such as construction and maintenance of shipping channels, port development, use of landfilling to create development sites, flood control projects, and construction or maintenance of reservoirs. However, the importance of § 404 in reducing the loss of wetlands is significant. It has been estimated that only half of the wetlands which existed at the end of the eighteenth century still exist, with most destruction occurring during the latter half of the twentieth century.[794] For a discussion of wetlands and how they are delineated, and an analysis of land use issues attendant thereto, *see* § 11.02[A].

---

791. *See* Solid Waste Agency of Northern Cook County v. Army Corps of Engineers, 531 U.S. 159 (2001).

792. Sackett v. Environmental Protection Agency, 566 U.S. 120 (2012).

793. 33 C.F.R. § 320.1(A)(2), (6); United States Army Corps of Engineers v. Hawkes, ___ U.S. ___, 136 S. Ct. 1807, 195 L. Ed. 2d 77 (2016); National Association of Home Builders v. Environmental Protection Agency, 786 F.3d 34 (D.C. Cir. 2015). A more informal guidance termed a preliminary, in contrast to final, jurisdictional determination, though, is not a judicially reviewable final agency action. *See* 33 C.F.R. § 331.2.

794. *See* Phillip M. Bender, *Slowing the Net Loss of Wetlands: Citizen Suit Enforcement of Clean Water Act 404 Permit Violations*, 27 ENVTL. L. 245 (1997) (citing Dahl et al., U.S. Dept. of the Interior, *Wetlands: Status and Trends in the Coterminous United States 1780s to 1980s*, at 1 (1990)); Steven

Section 404 may apply under circumstances where a NPDES permit is not required; conversely, despite the fact that a party is regulated by a §404 permit, there may be circumstances when a NPDES permit also is necessary. There also may be circumstances when a 404 permit will not be issued and the party must seek appropriate relief under the NPDES program, such as for the discharge of toxic materials and when pretreatment standards apply.

[B] Army Corps of Engineers Is Primary Regulatory and Enforcement Agency

[1] Overlapping Jurisdiction with Rivers and Harbors Act

Dredge and fill operations may trigger the Rivers and Harbors Act of 1899 (discussed at §6.02[A][2]) if the project involves placement of a structure, or other "obstructions," such as dredge and fill, which would interfere with navigation.[795] Although the historic focus of the Rivers and Harbors Act was on navigability, and that Act is limited to actually navigable waters, in 1960 the Army Corps of Engineers, the permitting and enforcement authority under that Act, initiated wetlands protection measures under the Act.[796] This historic role of the Army Corps to maintain navigation was continued in §404(t) of the Clean Water Act. However, particular permit applications may still trigger permit requirements under the Rivers and Harbors Act as well as CWA §404.[797]

[2] Overlapping Jurisdiction with EPA

The Army Corps of Engineers is the primary administrative, regulatory, and enforcement authority for dredge and fill operations under §404 of the Clean Water Act.[798] The Army Corps describes itself as a very de-centralized organization. Most of its administrative authority is delegated to its 36 district engineers and 11 division engineers, who make final decisions which are administratively non-reviewable, so long as the agency's regulations were followed.[799] Judicial review, of course, remains available (see discussion in §1.01[B]).

The Army Corps, as an essentially engineering-oriented agency, sees its mission in a context that differs from that of many conservation-oriented agencies: it is neither a proponent nor an opponent of any permit proposal; its primary interest is in efficiently processing permit applications pursuant to its regulations.[800] This adminis-

---

W. Watkins, *Congressional Attempts to Amend the Clean Water Act: American Wetlands Under Attack*, 72 N.D. L. REV. 125 (1996) (cites included).

795. 33 U.S.C. §401, *et seq.*

796. *See* 33 U.S.C. §403.

797. 33 C.F.R. §320.1(6). Note, though, that the Army Corps may apply definitions that differ as between §404 and the Rivers and Harbors Act. United States v. Milner, 583 F.3d 1174 (9th Cir. 2009) (remanded for further fact-finding as to whether the site in question was historically wet or dry).

798. 33 U.S.C. §1344(d).

799. 33 C.F.R. §320.1(2).

800. 33 C.F.R. §320.1(4).

trative distinctiveness is reflected in the Army Corps' regulations, as contrasted with EPA's regulations: the Army Corps gives itself a lot of discretion in permitting determinations; the application process is less onerous than the NPDES process (compare [D] & [E], *below*, with § 6.03[C]); the Army Corps is more flexible than EPA in issuing authorizations; and the Army Corps' regulations tend to be stated more generally than is typical for EPA's regulations.

For dredge and fill permits, the Army Corps' jurisdiction is not exclusive. Its own regulations specifically leave unaffected EPA oversight authority under the Clean Water Act.[801] EPA is specifically given the authority to overturn the Army Corps' § 404 decisions granting permits, after "consulting" with the Army Corps, when EPA concludes that the proposed activity will adversely affect municipal water supplies, shellfish beds, fishery areas, wildlife, or recreational areas.[802] However, the Supreme Court, by a sharply split bench, upended the easy assumption that EPA's supervisory authority gave it the power to vacate a § 404 permit issued by the Army Corps when the Army Corps was acting within the scope of its statutory authority. The Army Corps permit allowed the discharge of mining slurry that would raise a lake bottom — thus the Army Corps' determination that it was fill — which EPA defined as toxic effluent as to which EPA exercised exclusive authority. However, because EPA had not previously promulgated standards defining effluent limitations for fill material, it could not trump the Army Corps' jurisdiction to issue fill permits. Thus, the gap in EPA's own regulations created a loophole that the dissent found to be perverse — that simply by the expedient of defining a material, generally, as fill, the Army Corps, and its permittee, could frustrate the goals of the NPDES system.[803]

[3] State Jurisdiction versus Army Corps Jurisdiction

Although states retain jurisdiction over dredging and filling of in-state wetlands, provisions in § 404 ensuring a state role regarding in-state wetlands are self-limiting to the extent that they "shall not be construed as affecting or impairing the authority of the Secretary [of the Army] to maintain navigation."[804] However, the Army Corps prefers to avoid duplication of state and federal regulatory programs, and seeks to coordinate its efforts with states and other agencies.[805]

A state may apply to administer its own permit program. The state must submit to EPA a description of the proposed state program; this applies, too, if the proposed program is to be administered under an interstate compact. Additionally, the state,

---

801. 33 C.F.R. § 320.1(6).

802. 33 U.S.C. § 1344(c).

803. Coeur Alaska, Inc. v. Southeast Alaska Conservation Council, 557 U.S. 261, 129 S. Ct. 2458, 174 L. Ed. 2d 193 (2009). On the jurisdictional prerogatives of the respective agencies regarding the discharge of sediment and fill into waters of the United States, see Ohio Valley Coalition v. Aracoma Coal Co., 556 F.3d 177 (4th Cir. 2009). For the Army Corps permitting the depositing of fill in river valleys as disposal sites which may have environmentally detrimental results, see Mingo Logan Coal Company v. Environmental Protection Agency, 829 F.3d 710 (D.C. Cir. 2016).

804. 33 U.S.C. § 1344(t).

805. 33 C.F.R. § 320.1(5).

or the interstate compact, must submit a legal statement that it has adequate authority to administer the proposed program. The Army Corps, and the Department of the Interior acting through the Fish and Wildlife Service, may submit written comments.[806] EPA will then issue a determination after a public hearing. If the program is approved, the permit program essentially must track the requirements of the federal program.[807] If the state fails to comply with the § 404 requirements or guidelines promulgated thereunder, then, after another public hearing, and an opportunity for correction, EPA must withdraw approval.[808]

[C] Statutory Criteria Triggering Need for a Permit

[1] Basic Requirements: Discharge into Waters of the United States

As with the Clean Water Act in general, § 404 addresses "discharges" into "navigable waters" of the United States[809] (see definitions in § 6.03). Unlike the interchangeable-ness of the terms "waters of the United States" and "navigable waters" elsewhere in the Clean Water Act, the Army Corps clearly distinguishes the terms for purposes of § 404. Navigable waters are "navigable in the traditional sense" while waters of the United States specifically are not so limited.[810] When the Army Corps carries out its historical role of enforcing the Rivers and Harbors Act, basically that of protecting against impediments to navigation, it uses the term "navigable waters," since the Rivers and Harbors Act is limited to navigable waters (see § 6.02[A][2]). When carrying out its duties under § 404, it utilizes the term "waters of the United States," since the Clean Water Act itself conflates the terms. Thus, for § 404 permits, many non-navigable waters fall under Army Corps jurisdiction. (See discussion in § 6.03[B][1][f].)

The type of discharge governed by § 404 is that of "dredged or filled materials," which must be placed at specified disposal sites. If the discharge is one covered by § 404, then a "404" permit must be obtained from the Army Corps of Engineers; a failure to obtain the permit, or a violation of its conditions, is a violation of the Clean Water Act.

[2] "Discharge" of Dredged or Fill Materials: How Construed

[a] Addition Required

"Discharge" under § 404 is related to disposal-type activities. Going back to the standard definition of "discharge" in the Clean Water Act (see definition in § 6.03[B][1][b]), a discharge for § 404 purposes contemplates an "addition" of dredged or fill materials to navigable waters.[811]

---

806. 33 U.S.C. § 1344(g).
807. 33 U.S.C. § 1344(h).
808. 33 U.S.C. § 1344(i).
809. 33 U.S.C. § 1344(a).
810. 33 C.F.R. § 320.1(d).
811. 33 C.F.R. § 323.2(d).

[b] Dredging Itself Not Covered

It is important to note that while § 404 regulates the "discharge" of dredged and fill materials, it does not regulate the actual dredging activities,[812] as contrasted with the disposal of dredge spoil. Dredging results in the removal of material rather than an addition to the water body, as when dredge spoil or other fill is deposited.

[3] Activities Traditionally Not Treated as Discharges

[a] Land Clearing

Initially, land clearing of a wetland area—consisting of the removal of vegetation and even planting activities, which nevertheless resulted in some discharges of excavated materials—was not included within § 404 jurisdiction. The theory was that materials actually were being taken away from, rather than added to, navigable waters.[813] Hence, an operation in which a 20,000 acre wetland was cleared of timber and vegetation at or just above ground level, and brush was raked away, by itself might not have constituted an "addition" of fill materials. However, the additional factors that the wetland was intentionally being converted to farmland, and timber was burned, and ashes and brush were plowed into the soil, constituted a redepositing of materials. The ash, stumps, and brush, constituting fill, were added, triggering § 404.[814]

Similarly, clearing vegetation from a wetland by mechanical digging, using a marsh plow to turn excavated material into the ground, fell within § 404.[815] Land clearing activities that resulted in redepositions and actual leveling of a wetland area were an "addition,"[816] whereas chain-sawing trees, windrowing them and leaving them to deteriorate naturally were not an addition of fill material, especially when there was no intent to convert the wetland to farmland.[817]

In 1990, however, the Army Corps issued a guidance directing that mechanized land clearing is deemed to result in a "redeposition" of dredged or fill materials, except for the clearing of trees solely by cutting them above ground level.[818] In 1993, this was promulgated as a regulation. The regulation now defines mechanized land clearing operations in a wetland to result in the addition of dredged or fill materials

---

812. American Mining Congress v. Army Corps of Engineers, 951 F. Supp. 267 (D.D.C. 1997), *adhered to at* 962 F. Supp. 2 (D.D.C. 1997), *aff'd*, 145 F.3d 1399 (D.C. Cir. 1998); *see also* 51 Fed. Reg. 41,210.

813. RGL No. 84-1, *Regulatory Jurisdiction Over Vegetative Operations*, Jan. 10, 1984, reprinted at 56 Fed. Reg. 2408.

814. Avoyelles Sportsmen's League, Inc. v. Marsh, 715 F.2d 897, 922–24 (5th Cir. 1983).

815. United States v. Huebner, 752 F.2d 1235, 1242 (7th Cir. 1985), *cert. denied*, 474 U.S. 817 (1985).

816. Salt Pond Associates v. United States Army Corps of Engineers, 38 Env't Rep. Cas. (BNA) (D. Del. 1993).

817. Save Our Wetlands, Inc. v. Sands, 711 F.2d 634 (5th Cir. 1983).

818. RGL No. 90-5, *Landclearing Activities Subject to Section 404 Jurisdiction*, July 18, 1990, reprinted at 56 Fed. Reg. 2408.

to the wetland, but excludes from the definition vegetation-cutting above ground level if the roots are not disturbed.[819]

[b] Draining of Water Bodies or Wetlands

In the same sense that dredging, per se, is not included within § 404, draining, per se, does not require a § 404 permit: something is being taken away rather than being added.[820] Draining typically is accomplished by ditching alongside a wetland to facilitate runoff. However, the Army Corps will assert regulatory and enforcement authority if any addition of dredged or fill material to, or redeposit into, navigable waters occurs during the ditching operation, no matter how minor or limited in duration the operation is.[821]

[c] Pilings

One might easily construe the placement of a piling in navigable waters to constitute fill. The Army Corps had not originally taken that position, except when the pilings were being used as fill or were placed so densely in combination that they effectively replaced portions of a water body.[822] However, when developers started to use pilings, rather than actual fill, as foundations for buildings, so as to evade § 404 regulation, the Army Corps defined such pilings to constitute fill.[823] Currently, if the pilings effectively act as fill, in that they are the foundation for a building or another structure, or if they are arranged in such a manner as to cause increased sedimentation, or if they are placed so densely together that they effectively displace a significant amount of water, then they are treated as fill and a 404 permit is required for their placement.[824]

[4] Specification of Disposal Sites

Generally, the Army Corps specifies where a permittee's disposal site will be. However, EPA actually promulgates the guidelines for the selection process.[825] EPA may

---

819. 58 Fed. Reg. 45,037 (1993).

820. Save Our Community v. Environmental Protection Agency, 971 F.2d 1155 (5th Cir. 1992). The Circuit Court declared that draining, per se, does not trigger § 404. It reversed a district court decision which had ruled in favor of § 404 regulation on the theory that the fact of draining threatened significant alteration or destruction of the wetland, hence triggering the wetlands protection purpose underlying § 404. The District Court declined to reach the issue whether a de minimis discharge during a draining operation constitutes a discharge.

821. 58 Fed. Reg. 45,008, 45,037 (1993).

822. RGL No. 88-14, *Applicability of Section 404 to Piles*, Nov. 3, 1988, reprinted at 56 Fed. Reg. 2408 (1991).

823. RGL No. 90-8, *Applicability of Section 404 to Pilings*, Dec. 14, 1990, reprinted at 56 Fed. Reg. 2409 (1991).

824. 58 Fed. Reg. 45,038 (1993).

825. 33 U.S.C. § 1344(b).

even veto or restrict the designation of any defined area as a disposal site.[826] A disposal site must be designated as to each permit.[827]

[D] General Policies for Evaluating Permit Applications

The Army Corps relies on general policies, such as evaluating the public interest dimension of any permit (see [1], *below*) and several environmental impacts (see [2]–[4], [7], *below*), as threshold criteria in determining whether to grant a permit. If a denial is not required for the reasons discussed in [C], *above*, then a balancing analysis is applied. Some examples of factors considered by the agency, examined *below*, will suffice to provide a sense of the scope of the review of § 404 applications.

[1] Public Interest Review

The agency will consider probable individual as well as cumulative impacts of both the proposed discharge and the intended use of the project on the public interest. Then, it will balance the reasonably expected benefits against reasonably foreseeable detriments before issuing a determination. The public interest review is comprehensive, although the facts vary from project to project. There is no hard and fast rule governing how the Army Corps comparatively weighs each factor among projects. However, the Army Corps must give some weight to the various informed comments during the public comment stage of the application process.

These factors include the effects on conservation, economics, esthetics, general environmental concerns, wetlands, historic properties, fish and wildlife values, flood hazards, floodplains values, land use, navigation, shore erosion and accretion, recreation, water supply and conservation, water quality, energy needs, safety, food and fiber production, mineral needs, considerations of property ownership, and, in general, the needs and welfare of people. The Army Corps also looks to the extent of the real need for the project, and the practicality of reasonable alternatives. If the proposed discharge fails to comply with EPA's guidelines and criteria under § 404(b)(1), then the permit must be denied. In all other cases, unless the district engineer determines that the discharge is contrary to the public interest, the permit will be granted.[828]

[2] Effect on Wetlands

The effect on wetlands is a well recognized public interest. Although the Army Corps does not have an institutional position, per se, on the appropriateness of dredge and fill operations, it does posit that the unnecessary alteration or destruction of wetlands is contrary to the public interest. Moreover, the preservation of wetlands is deemed to represent important public interests, insofar as wetlands facilitate the performance of significant biological functions in connection with the food chain, and

---

826. 33 U.S.C. § 1344(c).
827. 40 C.F.R. § 230.10.
828. 33 C.F.R. § 320.4(a)(1)–(3).

are important for spawning and habitat for terrestrial as well as aquatic species (see discussion in § 11.02[A]).

In reviewing a 404 application, the agency will also consider the importance of wetland preservation to natural drainage, sedimentation patterns, salinity distribution, and flushing characteristics, among other environmentally important functions.[829] Another factor which the agency will consider will be the effect of the project on the value of a particular wetland, especially a wetland associated with a barrier beach, in shielding land areas from wave action, erosion, or storm damage.[830] The agency will look to whether the particular wetland is important as a ground water recharge area and whether it serves important water purification functions, or whether it is unique in some manner or is scarce.[831] If the individual project constitutes only a minor alteration of a wetland, but cumulative impacts from piecemeal alterations threaten a major impairment of a wetland resource, especially when the particular wetland is part of an interconnected wetland area, such a consequence would be an important factor in balancing the benefit against the detriment.[832]

In the final analysis, if the wetland is considered to be important, a permit authorizing a discharge which would alter the wetland will be denied. The exception relies on the same balancing test noted above: the benefit of the project must clearly outweigh the detriment caused by damage to the wetland.

[3] Effect on Fish and Wildlife

The Army Corps consults with the Fish and Wildlife Service, the National Marine Fisheries Service, if appropriate, and corresponding state agencies.[833] It must "give full consideration to [their] views," to evaluate whether the discharge would adversely impact on fish or wildlife. As a consequence of that consultation, the 404 permit might be granted or denied, or conditions might be imposed.[834]

[4] Water Quality

The agency will consider whether the discharge of dredged and fill materials would be in compliance with the applicable effluent limitations and water quality standards[835] (see [B][2], above).

[5] Historic, Cultural, Scenic, and Recreational Values

The agency will consider the possible effect of the project on historic, cultural, scenic, and recreational values, many of which relate to state designated sites. The

---

829. 33 C.F.R. § 320.4(b).
830. 33 C.F.R. § 320.4(b)(2)(iv).
831. 33 C.F.R. § 320.4(b)(2)(vi), (vii).
832. 33 C.F.R. § 320.4(b)(3).
833. 33 C.F.R. § 325.2(a)(6).
834. 33 C.F.R. § 320.4(c).
835. 33 C.F.R. § 320.4(d).

agency will, as far as possible, try to accommodate these values in making its decision whether to grant the § 404 permit.[836]

[6] Effect on Property Interests

The fact that a permit is provided to fill an aquatic area does not translate into any property right. Nor does the § 404 permit authorize the discharging party to injure or invade someone else's property. Generally, the agency looks favorably on applications relating to erosion protection, unless the project may damage the property of others or adversely impact floodplains or wetlands and, in so doing, affect the property interests of others. If the project validly seeks to protect property from erosion, but in doing so, will affect the property of others, then the district engineer will suggest alternative means of protecting the applicant's property.[837]

The fill operation also may not interfere with riparian rights, or block access to navigable waters by nearby riparian landowners or by the public. In such cases, the agency likely will deny the application. Nor does the grant of a § 404 permit preclude the government from undertaking future operations for the conservation or improvement of navigation. In that event, the permittee has no claims to compensation for damages to the § 404 project which result from the government's operations.[838]

[7] Activities in Coastal Zone, Marine Sanctuary

If the § 404 permit would authorize a discharge of dredged or fill materials in a coastal zone, the applicant must submit to the Army Corps a certification of compliance with the applicable coastal zone management program, including concurrence by the appropriate state agency (see § 11.02[B]).[839]

If the project is in a marine sanctuary, the applicant must submit a certification from the Secretary of Commerce that the project is consistent with the Marine Protection, Research and Sanctuaries Act[840] (see discussion at § 6.05).

[E] Bases upon Which Permit Will Be Denied

[1] Generally

Although an applicant for a permit may satisfy the statutory criteria, this does not ensure that a permit will be granted. The Army Corps' regulations specifically note that even qualifying applications may still be subject to other regulations, including those of a state 404 agency, which might result in a denial. More generally, the Army Corps reserves to itself the authority to add requirements, depending on the seriousness of the potential for adverse impacts on aquatic ecosystems posed by specific dis-

---

836. 33 C.F.R. § 320.4(e).
837. 33 C.F.R. § 320.4(g)(1)–(2).
838. 33 C.F.R. § 320.4(g)(3)–(5).
839. 33 C.F.R. § 320.4(h).
840. 33 C.F.R. § 320.4(i).

charges of dredged and fill materials, so that unique circumstances of each case may warrant a denial, even though the standard requirements have been met.[841] As a basic principle, a 404 permit will be denied unless the applicant has taken "appropriate and practical" steps to minimize potential adverse impacts of the discharge on the aquatic ecosystem.[842]

Even if there is some mitigation, or the project's ostensible benefits balance well against detriments, the Army Corps regulations require that the application for a 404 permit must be denied under various circumstances.[843] Denial is mandated either where the discharge is not necessary, even though it may be the most convenient option for an applicant, or where the discharge triggers additional pollution or conservation concerns, despite a mitigation of § 404 concerns.[844]

[2] Practicable Alternative Has Less Impact

The § 404 permit must satisfy EPA's § 404(b)(1) Guidelines[845] which identify certain aquatic features that presumably warrant protection. As to these, the permit applicant must consider alternative sites that avoid environmental detriments but are also economically feasible.[846] The Army Corps has significant discretion in determining that a proposed alternative need not be implemented because it is not technologically feasible or is economically impracticable in light of the goals that the applicant intends to achieve.[847] In making its determination, the Army Corps must itself independently ascertain the basic purpose of the project for which a permit is sought and then find that the nature of the project is water dependent, that necessarily places it in proximity to a wetland.[848] A non-discharge option is defined to be practicable if "it is available and capable of being done after taking into consideration cost, existing technology, and logistics, in light of overall project purposes."[849] The permit applicant could even be required to purchase or otherwise expand to an area not presently owned by the applicant, if it can be reasonably obtained, to facilitate the practicable alternative.

Among practicable alternatives are the non-discharge option, or a discharge of dredged or fill materials at another location, even including aquatic locations.[850] However, here, too, a balancing analysis among economic and environmental factors is employed.[851] Furthermore, the applicant might not be required to utilize the practicable

---

841. 40 C.F.R. § 230.10.

842. 40 C.F.R. § 230.10(d).

843. *See generally* 40 C.F.R. § 230.10.

844. 40 C.F.R. § 230.10(a).

845. 40 C.F.R. § 230.

846. 40 C.F.R. § 230.10.

847. Jones v. National Marine Fisheries Service, 741 F.3d 989 (9th Cir. 2013).

848. 40 C.F.R. 230.10(a)(3). *See* Butte Environmental Council v. Army Corps of Engineers, 620 F.3d 936 (9th Cir. 2010).

849. 40 C.F.R. § 230.10(a)(2).

850. 40 C.F.R. § 230.10(a)(1)(i), (ii); Sierra Club v. Van Antwerp, 362 Fed. Appx. 100 (11th Cir. 2010).

851. Town of Norfolk v. United States Army Corp of Engineers, 968 F.2d 1438, 1454 (1st Cir. 1992).

alternative if that alternative also poses significant adverse environmental effects, albeit not on an aquatic ecosystem.[852]

The Army Corps presumes that a practicable alternative not involving an aquatic discharge will have a lesser impact on the aquatic ecosystem. Other alternatives not requiring discharges at aquatic sites are presumed to be available, and the applicant has the burden of demonstrating non-availability.[853] A failure of the applicant to analyze practical alternatives may result in denial, per se. In any event, the omission allows the agency to presume that practicable alternatives exist that have not been utilized.[854] The Army Corps' determination is accorded great deference in the event of judicial review.[855]

One means by which the Army Corps will explore the existence of practicable alternatives is to review the environmental impact statement, if one is required under NEPA (see § 4.01).[856] Environmental impact statements typically identify adverse environmental impacts which cannot be avoided, alternatives, including a no-action alternative, to the proposed action, the relationship between local short-term uses of resources or of a site and longer-term productivity, and the potential irreversibility of the project.[857]

[3] Degradation of Waters of the United States

The Army Corps must deny a § 404 permit when the proposed discharge would contribute to a "significant" degradation of waters of the United States.[858] The Army Corps will determine empirically what constitutes a significant degradation, and especially must take into account how pervasive any degradation would be, and how long it might last.[859]

Various factors contribute to significant degradation of water bodies. For 404 purposes, these factors include significant adverse effects on the following:[860]

- Human health or welfare, generally;
- Municipal water supplies;
- Plankton, fish, shellfish, wildlife and special aquatic sites;
- Life stages of aquatic life and other wildlife dependent on aquatic ecosystems. For this factor, the Army Corps will look to whether there is a transfer, concen-

852. 40 C.F.R. § 230.10(a); see Butte Environmental Council v. Army Corps of Engineers, 620 F.3d 936 (9th Cir. 2010).

853. 40 C.F.R. § 230.10(a)(3); see Greater Yellowstone Coalition v. Flowers, 359 F.3d 1257 (10th Cir. 2004).

854. O'Connor v. Army Corps of Engineers, 801 F. Supp. 185, 195 (D. Ind. 1992).

855. Town of Norfolk v. United States Army Corps of Engineers, 968 F.2d 1438, 1454 (1st Cir. 1992).

856. 40 C.F.R. § 230.10(a)(4).

857. 42 U.S.C. § 4332(c).

858. 40 C.F.R. § 230.10(c).

859. Id.

860. Id.

tration, and spread of pollutants or their by-products outside of the disposal site through biological, chemical, or physical processes;

- Aquatic ecosystem diversity, productivity, and stability. For this factor, the Army Corps will evaluate the projected loss of habitat. If the effects will be felt on a wetland, then the Army Corps will evaluate its ability to assimilate nutrients, purify water, or reduce wave energy; and

- Recreational, aesthetic or economic values.

[4] State Water Quality Standards

A § 404 permit will be denied if the proposed discharge of dredged or fill materials contributes to a violation of an applicable state water quality standard, as required by CWA § 401[861] (see § 6.03[B][2]). However, this consequence may be minimized by factoring in dilution or dispersion at a particular disposal site.[862]

[5] Toxic and Pretreatment Effluent Standards

The § 404 permit must be denied if the proposed discharge would violate any applicable toxic effluent standard or prohibition. The permit also will be denied if the proposed discharge would violate any applicable pretreatment effluent standards[863] (see § 6.03[B][2]).

[6] Adverse Effect on Regulated Species or Habitat

The Army Corps will evaluate the applicability of the Endangered Species Act (see § 10.03) in determining whether to grant a 404 permit. If the proposed discharge jeopardizes the continued existence of an endangered or threatened species which is listed under the Endangered Species Act (ESA), then the proposed discharge of dredged or fill materials must be prohibited.[864] Notably, the agency formally restricts itself to a mandatory consideration of the Federal ESA, although the agency may consider listings of applicable state conservation agencies.

If the proposed discharge would likely lead to the destruction or even the adverse modification of critical habitat, then the permit also must be denied.[865]

[7] Marine Sanctuaries

In reviewing applications for a dredge and fill discharge permit, the Army Corps is also subject to the Marine Protection, Research and Sanctuaries Act, which is administered by the Department of Commerce (see § 6.05). The Secretary of Commerce imposes requirements with regard to marine sanctuaries under that Act. If the pro-

---

861. 40 C.F.R. § 230.10(b)(1).
862. Id.
863. 40 C.F.R. § 230.10(b)(2). For toxic and pretreatment effluent standards, see 33 U.S.C. § 1317.
864. 40 C.F.R. § 230.10(b)(3).
865. Id.

posed discharge of dredged or fill material will violate any such requirement, then the discharge must be prohibited.[866]

[F] Discharges of Dredge or Fill Materials That Are Exempted from § 404 Permitting

[1] Generally

Certain activities are specifically exempt under the statute from the need for § 404 permitting.[867] These include temporary or emergency work to maintain the aquatic status quo. Other exemptions parallel the exemptions provided elsewhere in the Clean Water Act. An exempt activity is not subject to regulation under § 404, and except for toxic or pretreatment effluent standards or prohibitions,[868] the discharger also is not subject to a NPDES permit, or effluent limitations in general[869] (see discussion in § 6.03[C]).

[2] Statutory Exempt Activities

[a] Agriculture/Silviculture

[i] "Normal" Farming, Silvicultural, or Ranching Use

Normal farming, silviculture, and ranching activities are exempt from § 404.[870] This exemption comports with exemptions from the usual NPDES requirements elsewhere in the Act (see § 6.03[A]). The statute illustrates the types of activities included within the more general statutory exemption: plowing, seeding, cultivating, minor drainage, harvesting for the production of food, fiber and forest products, or upland soil and water conservation practices.[871]

Although the above list is not exclusive, the objective is to exempt activities normally associated with agriculture, silviculture, and ranching that incidentally cause discharges of material into wetlands or water bodies. However, the activity must be "normal" in terms of farming, silviculture or ranching. For example, when 30 acres of wetlands formerly used as pasture were drained by a farmer and re-planted, this was not normal farming and a § 404 permit was required.[872]

[ii] Farming, Silvicultural, or Ranching Use Must Be "Ongoing"

To qualify for this exemption, the landowner or operator must demonstrate that the agricultural, silvicultural, or ranching uses of the land are ongoing, rather than recent or prospective. To be ongoing, there must be a history of specifically exempt

---

866. 40 C.F.R. § 230.10(b)(4).
867. 33 U.S.C. § 1344(f)(1).
868. See 33 U.S.C. § 1317.
869. See 33 U.S.C. § 1311(a).
870. 33 U.S.C. § 1344(f)(1)(A).
871. Id.
872. United States v. Brace, 41 F.3d 117 (3d Cir. 1994), cert. denied, 515 U.S. 1158 (1995).

activities.[873] Hence, the clearance of a wetland formerly used for silvicultural purposes in order to convert it to agricultural purposes did not qualify: the silvicultural exemption did not apply, since the land was not to be used for silviculture, and the farming exemption did not apply, since there had been no ongoing agricultural use. Rather, the purpose of the landclearing was to permanently change the character of the land from wetlands to non-wetlands.[874]

However, changing the particular crop, in the context of an ongoing farming operation, does not, of itself, require a § 404 permit.[875] In at least one case, however, the result was different — and a 404 permit was required — when a wetland intermittently used for wetland-tolerant farming was altered so as to enable the planting of upland crops. This constituted a new use, and hence was not an ongoing operation.[876] Although farm use may be "ongoing," though intermittent, it must be shown that when the land is unused for ongoing farming, it is actually lying fallow pursuant to conventional crop rotation, and the overall operation is ongoing.[877] That explanation for fallow land, however, is unavailing once the overall operation terminates, or when the area is converted to another use.[878] One of the risks in allowing land to be fallow too long is that the site may change hydrologically, requiring that the parcel be modified hydrologically in order to commence the "ongoing" operation again. In that event, the operation is deemed to have been terminated.[879]

However, just to illustrate the complexity of what is to be deemed "ongoing," the Army Corps will still exempt activities that require changes in the hydrologic cycle when that alteration of hydrology is inherent in the nature of an ongoing operation. For instance, the use will be considered ongoing when it consists of regular crop rotation from wetland-type use to non-wetland type use because of the particular crops. An example would be when rice planting in a wetlands area is routinely rotated into use of a non-wetland crop, such as another grain, requiring de-watering, after which it will as a matter of course be converted back again to rice harvesting in a saturated area.[880]

When an ongoing wetland farming operation is expanded into adjacent wetlands not part of the traditional farming usage, then the farming use is not ongoing as to that adjacent parcel. For instance, when the owner used wetlands for its ongoing cranberry operations, no permit was required as to that parcel. However, the exemption did not apply, and a permit was required, when the owner converted adjoining wetlands acreage to cranberry plantings.[881]

---

873. United States v. Cumberland Farms of Connecticut, Inc., 647 F. Supp. 1166, 1175 (D. Mass. 1986), aff'd, 826 F.2d 1151 (1st Cir. 1987), cert. denied, 484 U.S. 1061 (1988).

874. United States v. Larkins, 852 F.2d 189 (6th Cir. 1988), cert. denied, 489 U.S. 1016 (1989).

875. United States v. Akers, 785 F.2d 814, 820 (9th Cir. 1985), cert. denied, 479 U.S. 828 (1986).

876. Id. at 819.

877. 33 C.F.R. § 323.4(a)(1)(a).

878. 33 C.F.R. § 323.4(a)(1)(ii).

879. Id.

880. 33 C.F.R. § 323.4(a)(1)(iii)(C).

881. United States v. Huebner, 752 F.2d 1235, 1243 (7th Cir. 1985), cert. denied, 474 U.S. 817 (1985).

[b] Ponds or Ditches Relating to Agriculture

When dredged or fill materials are discharged for the purpose of constructing or maintaining farm or stock ponds, or irrigation ditches, or in connection with the maintenance (but note — not the construction) of drainage ditches, no 404 permit is required.[882] If this particular activity qualifies for the § 404 exemption, then it also is exempt under approved state programs which regulate areawide waste treatment.[883] However, excavating a new drainage ditch, or deepening an existing drainage ditch, would not qualify for the exemption.[884] Nor would the ditch-construction activity qualify merely by calling a drainage ditch an irrigation ditch.[885] And even if an irrigation ditch is being constructed, an activity eligible for the exemption, the exemption still is not available if the activity is so extensive that it will change the use of the affected area, or impair the flow, or reduce the extent of the navigable waters.

[c] Farm, Forest, and Mining Roads

Under certain circumstances, a § 404 permit will not be required when dredged or fill material is discharged as a result of road construction or maintenance in connection with agricultural, silvicultural, or mining activities.[886] The exemption is limited to "farm" roads, forest roads, or "temporary" roads for moving mining equipment. The roads, to qualify, must be constructed and maintained so that the flow and circulation patterns and chemical and biological characteristics of the affected navigable waters are not impaired, the reach of the navigable waters is not reduced, and any impact on the aquatic environment is minimized. In this regard, "best management practices" must be utilized in the exempt road construction and maintenance.[887]

[d] Structures in the Water: Maintenance and Repair

Structures in a water body, or along a water body constructed to hold back the water, such as dams, dikes, levees, groins, riprap, breakwaters, causeways, and bridge abutments or approaches, as well as transportation structures, may be entitled to an exemption from a § 404 permit. If they are "currently serviceable," then they may be maintained without a permit.[888] If they have been "recently" damaged, portions may even be reconstructed on an emergency basis without a § 404 permit.[889] Of course, there are important qualifications. Reconstruction not occurring in the context of an emergency will require a permit. Similarly, work which is not maintenance, such as additions or material alterations, will require a permit.

---

882. 33 U.S.C. § 1344(f)(1)(C); Peconic Baykeeper v. Suffolk County, 600 F.3d 180 (2d Cir. 2010).
883. *See* 33 U.S.C. § 1288(b)(4).
884. United States v. Huebner, 752 F.2d 1235, 1242 (7th Cir. 1985); *see* United States v. Cundiff, 555 F.3d 200 (6th Cir. 2009).
885. *Id.* at 1242.
886. 33 U.S.C. § 1344(f)(1)(E).
887. *Id.*
888. 33 U.S.C. § 1344(f)(1)(B).
889. *Id.*

Section 404(f)(1) also exempts the activity from approved state programs in connection with areawide waste treatment management.[890]

If qualifying work creates an "obstruction," there may be a need for a permit under the Rivers and Harbors Act (see § 6.02[A][2]).

[e] Sedimentation Basins at Construction Sites

A § 404 permit will not be required when dredged or fill material gets discharged as a consequence of the construction of "temporary" sedimentation basins on a construction site. However, this exemption does not apply if the dredged or fill material is actually placed in navigable waters.[891]

[3] When Statutory Exemptions Are Inapplicable

[a] New Use of Water Body

The exemptions described in [2], *above*, become inapplicable when the project's purpose strays from that specifically contemplated by Congress in creating the exemption, and in doing so alters the status quo of the water body. That is, if the purpose of the activity is to bring an area of navigable waters into a new use, to which it had not been historically subject, then any incidental discharge of dredged or fill materials into the navigable waters will require a § 404 permit.[892]

[b] Activity Impairs Flow or Circulation

If the otherwise exempt activity nevertheless may impair the flow or circulation of navigable waters, or may reduce the reach of navigable waters, then any incidental discharge of dredged or fill material will require a § 404 permit.[893]

[4] Certain Government Projects Are Exempted

If Congress specifically authorizes a federal project, then the discharge of dredged or fill material is not regulated under either § 404, or a state program approved under § 404, or a SPDES program (see discussion in § 6.03[D]). However, the federal agency must identify the effects of a discharge, if any, in an environmental impact statement. The EIS must be submitted to Congress before the actual discharge of dredged or fill materials, and before the project is actually authorized or funded.[894] In addition, the project must still meet toxic and pretreatment effluent standards.[895]

---

890. *See* 33 U.S.C. § 1288(b)(4).
891. 33 U.S.C. § 1344(f)(1)(D).
892. 33 U.S.C. § 1344(f)(2).
893. *Id.*
894. 33 U.S.C. § 1344(r).
895. *See* 33 U.S.C. § 1317.

[G] Nationwide or "General" Permits

Nationwide permits are available to authorize the discharge of dredged and fill materials under appropriate circumstances.[896] Nationwide permits are available for certain § 404 discharges, and for activities under the Rivers and Harbors Act, and under the Marine Protection, Research and Sanctuaries Act (see § 6.05).[897] For § 404 general permits, the Army Corps must determine that the adverse environmental effects of the permitted activity will be minimal. The cumulative effects from the activity governed by a general project must also be minimal.[898] The Army Corps prefers to issue nationwide permits, and will review all individual permits to determine whether, unbeknownst to the applicant, the discharge would qualify for a nationwide permit.[899] Nationwide permits are general permits that authorize activities on a nationwide basis.[900] Rather than an individual permit being issued, the permittee receives authorization to carry out specified activities under the already existing, and generalized, nationwide permit.

The nationwide permits are fairly standardized. They are intended to regulate those activities that have minimal impact, with a minimum of paper work and delay.[901] The scale of the impact is measured in terms of the individual impact as well as the cumulative impact.[902] In order to minimize impacts so as to fall within a nationwide permit, an applicant may try to mitigate the loss of aquatic sites, or to otherwise reduce the impact of the discharge of dredged and fill materials.[903] If the adverse effects are more than minimal, then an individual permit will be required.[904]

Even if an applicant does not secure a nationwide permit, however, the activity may still be permitted under an individual permit.[905] Additionally, the permittee may receive authorization under a nationwide permit for part of a project, and individual permits for other parts of a project.[906]

The Army Corps reserves to itself the right to retroactively issue a permit and to terminate enforcement proceedings for an activity that otherwise was unauthorized,

---

896. 33 U.S.C. § 1344(e); 33 C.F.R. Part 330.

897. 33 C.F.R. § 330.1(g).

898. Black Warrior Riverkeeper, Inc. v. United States Army Corps of Engineers, 833 F.3d 1274 (11th Cir. 2016). A project's future impacts on wetlands may presently be speculative, which differs from presently ascertainable cumulative effects. In that case, the future impact analysis can be deferred until such time as it is ascertainable. Sierra Club, Inc. v. Bostwick, 2015 U.S. LEXIS App. 8995 (10th Cir. 2015).

899. 33 C.F.R. § 330.1(f).

900. 33 C.F.R. § 330.2(b).

901. 33 C.F.R. § 330.1(b).

902. 33 C.F.R. § 330.1(e)(2); Sierra Club U.S. Army Corps of Engineers, 508 F.3d 1332 (11th Cir. 2007).

903. 33 C.F.R. § 330.1(e)(3).

904. *Id.*

905. 33 C.F.R. § 330.1(c).

906. 33 C.F.R. § 330.6(d).

so long as the project is modified to conform to nationwide permit requirements.[907] On the other hand, if the discharge authorized under a nationwide permit will impact adversely on the aquatic environment or will adversely affect the public interest, then the authorization can be further restricted, additional conditions may be imposed, or the permit may be suspended, modified, or even revoked.[908]

Nationwide permits do not substitute for other federal, state, or local requirements, which remain binding on the applicant.[909] Nationwide permits do not create property rights, and do not confer exclusive privileges. Nor do they authorize any injury to the property or rights of others, nor allow interference with federal projects.[910]

Before a nationwide permit will be issued, the applicant must secure a state 401 water quality certification or the state's waiver of certification (see discussion in § 6.03[C]).[911] If the state has included conditions with its § 401 certification, then the Army Corps will incorporate those conditions into the permit.[912] If the state denies certification, then all nationwide permitted activities within that state which would result in a discharge of dredged and fill materials remain unauthorized.[913] This impasse is sidestepped, of course, once the state issues or waives a 401 water quality certification. These provisions reflect the importance of state certification in the Clean Water Act.

Nationwide permits do not extend to any activity that is likely to jeopardize the continued existence of a threatened or endangered species listed or proposed for listing under the Endangered Species Act (see Chapter 10), or that would adversely affect critical habitat.[914] If a regulated species is likely to be affected, or is seen in the vicinity of the project, then the permittee is required to notify the Army Corps and to suspend work until authorized by the agency to continue.[915]

Similar rules apply if the project may affect properties listed or eligible for listing on the National Register of Historic Places.[916] Additionally, the permittee must notify the agency if he or she encounters a historic property that is unlisted and has not been determined to be eligible for listing, but he or she has reason to believe might be eligible.[917]

---

907. 33 C.F.R. § 330.1(c).
908. 33 C.F.R. § 330.1(d); Sierra Club U.S. Army Corps of Engineers, 508 F.3d 1332 (11th Cir. 2007).
909. 33 C.F.R. § 330.4(a), (b)(2).
910. 33 C.F.R. § 330.4(b)(3)–(5).
911. 33 C.F.R. § 330.4(c).
912. 33 C.F.R. § 330.4(c)(2).
913. 33 C.F.R. § 330.4(c)(3).
914. 33 C.F.R. § 330.4(f).
915. 33 C.F.R. § 330.4(f)(2).
916. 33 C.F.R. § 330.4(g).
917. 33 C.F.R. § 330.4(g)(3).

Chapter 7

Solid and Hazardous Wastes

[D] Transporters
   [1] Custody and Tracking of Hazardous Waste Shipments
   [2] Spills During Transport
[E] Treatment, Storage, and Disposal (TSD) Facilities
   [1] Definitions
      [a] "Facility"
      [b] "Storage"
      [c] "Disposal"
      [d] "Treatment"
   [2] TSD Permits
[F] TSD Facility Standards
   [1] Tracking and Identification
   [2] Safety
   [3] The "Land Ban"
   [4] Groundwater Protection, Monitoring, and Corrective Action
      [a] Groundwater Protection Obligation
      [b] Detection Monitoring
      [c] Compliance Monitoring
      [d] Corrective Action
   [5] Financial Assurance
[G] Closure and Post-Closure Requirements
[H] Inspections, Reporting, and Monitoring
[I] Delegation to States
[J] Enforcement
   [1] Administrative and Civil Enforcement
   [2] Criminal Penalties
   [3] Abatement Orders for Imminent Hazards
   [4] Citizen Suits
      [a] Bases for Suits; Remedies
      [b] Notice Requirements
      [c] When Suits Are Barred
      [d] Fees to Prevailing Party
§ 7.06 Hazardous Waste Sites: Comprehensive Environmental Response,
   Compensation and Liability Act (CERCLA)
[A] Remediation under CERCLA
   [1] Introduction
   [2] Facility Defined
   [3] Release, Threatened Release, or Disposal; Exclusions
   [4] Section 106 Orders
   [5] Use of CERCLIS, Preliminary Assessments, the Hazard Ranking
      System, and the NPL
   [6] Remediation: Response Actions, Removal, Monitoring, and Mitigation
      [a] Definitions
      [b] Remedial Investigation, Feasibility Study, and Record of Decision
      [c] What Remediation Involves

§ 7.01 Introduction to Solid and Hazardous Wastes

[A] Background

This chapter addresses the very broad category of how we handle and dispose of our solid and hazardous wastes. This is an increasingly important topic nationally and locally. Many people may still remember television images of wandering garbage barges that were not allowed into ports, local protests at hazardous waste sites, rusted drums of chemicals emerging from athletic field turf, and alarming statistics of children — suspiciously clustered regionally — being diagnosed with strange maladies.

From these experiences, where otherwise obscure legal principles were brought home to the public during the late twentieth century, the twenty-first century public has been increasingly engaged in supporting safe and hygienic waste disposal, even if other environmental laws sometimes enjoy less robust public support. Industry, of course, is less enamored of cleanup obligations but by the third decade of the 21st century, industry has basically conceded the major legal requirements, even if reluctantly, so that the legally compliant and safe handling and disposal of wastes, whether conventional or toxic, has become a routine part of industrial and commercial operations. However, legacy problems remain.

The pervasiveness of the many problems associated with waste handling and disposal, and the drastic consequences of historic indifference to the connections between chemical waste, environmental contamination, and public health, prompted unprecedented federal intervention during the 1970s and 1980s into what formerly had been controlled by local authorities. Like polluted water and air, and often because of those media, contamination from many solid wastes does not respect state boundaries. Historically, rigorous local regulation often encouraged industry — and its jobs and taxes — to relocate to more legally accommodating states. As with other federal environmental statutes, the solid and hazardous waste statutes, and the regulations promulgated thereunder, have significantly recast the constitutional and political paradigm of traditional federalism.

However, while Congress has provided the regulatory superstructure governing the handling and disposal of wastes, the implementation of federal programs often still remains the responsibility of state and local governments. The two main federal solid waste statutes, the Resource Conservation and Recovery Act (RCRA)[1] and the Comprehensive Environmental Response, Compensation and Liability Act (CERCLA),[2] repose significant authority in qualifying states, as do the Clean Water Act (see § 6.03)[3] and Clean Air Act[4] (see Chapter 5). RCRA and CERCLA specifically do not preempt state law,[5] although the federal statutes, the focus of this chapter, will apply in the absence of adequate state law.

[B] Definitions

The term "solid" waste is disingenuous; as will be discussed elsewhere in this chapter (see § 7.02[A][1]), "solid" waste often is liquefied or even gaseous. As such, activities that trigger these statutes also may come within reach of the Clean Water Act and similar statutes, discussed in Chapter 6, and the Clean Air Act, discussed in Chapter 5.

---

1. 42 U.S.C. §§ 6901–6992k.
2. 42 U.S.C. §§ 9601–9675.
3. 33 U.S.C. § 1251, *et seq.*
4. 42 U.S.C. § 7401, *et seq.*
5. 42 U.S.C. § 9614 (CERCLA); 42 U.S.C. §§ 6926, 6929 (RCRA).

Hazardous wastes are a category of solid wastes. Hazardous wastes are comprised of hazardous substances, discussed elsewhere in this chapter (see § 7.05), but also may result from the manufacture, processing, distribution, or use of various toxic substances, discussed in Chapter 8. Hence, there is considerable overlap with other environmental statutes. Some wastes, such as radioactive materials, are excluded from the statutes discussed in this chapter, but are regulated elsewhere (see Chapter 12).

[C] RCRA and CERCLA Complement Each Other

The statutes covered in this Chapter complement one another. They not only re-quire certain conduct with regard to waste handling and cleanup,[6] but also require the compilation of a national inventory of information about where wastes originate, where they end up, and how they got there.[7] This reflects the Congressional intention of constructing a tightly weaved net capturing all aspects of hazardous waste handling and disposal under federal standards. This is the so-called "cradle to grave" framework in which hazardous substances are regulated, and documented, from inception to their final safe, disposal.

[D] Regulatory Structure of RCRA and CERCLA

RCRA generally sets standards for all solid waste management and disposal, es-pecially municipal landfills, in its Subtitle D regulations, addressed in §§ 7.02, 7.03, and 7.04. RCRA's Subtitle C regulations govern the generation, transport, treatment, storage, and disposal of hazardous wastes, discussed in § 7.05. One goal of RCRA is to eliminate future unregulated, and thus unsafe, hazardous waste disposal sites.

Cleanup responsibilities for historic hazardous waste sites are governed by CER-CLA, discussed in § 7.06. CERCLA, significantly amended in 1986, incorporates the Superfund program, initially intended to provide seed capital for cleanups of the most dangerous sites, to be reimbursed by cost recovery from liable parties (see § 7.06[A][1]). The sheer number of hazardous waste sites, and their remediation, though, have expanded well beyond Superfund's original assumptions and its funding. Today, cleanups increasingly are funded by private parties. The role of private parties is an outgrowth of CERCLA's draconian regime imposing joint and several liability on certain categories of "responsible parties," without regard to their individual fault. For reasons discussed in § 7.06, it often makes economic sense for private parties to assume responsibility for devising and carrying out cleanup strategies, and to implead all other responsible parties to share the costs, although within regulatory guidelines and subject to EPA supervision.

An unintended consequence of CERCLA's heavy hand, though, is that many mod-erately contaminated sites, for which full scale cleanups may not be necessary, have

---

6. *See* 42 U.S.C. § 9621.
7. *See* 42 U.S.C. §§ 6933, 6937.

been abandoned or otherwise left unproductive, and remain essentially unmarketable. The result is that land still appropriate for commercial or industrial use disappears from local tax rolls as businesses shut down, jobs are lost, and new businesses, fearing ownership of contaminated property, end up developing the very type of pristine land that should be preserved. One response to the quandary thus posed is the "Brownfields" proposal, discussed in § 7.07, encouraging redevelopment of moderately contaminated sites, which has met with significant success in recent decades under federal as well as various state and local brownfield programs. The 1986 CERCLA amendments also included the Emergency Planning and Community Right-to-Know Act (EPCRA).[8] EPCRA, discussed in § 7.08, is a two-part statute requiring local community and business preparedness for hazardous substance releases, and detailed information-gathering and disclosure about hazardous substances used and stored locally.

Hence, the federal statutes covered in this chapter collectively are comprehensive in scope, covering wastes, as noted, from "cradle to grave," imposing responsibilities for the cleanup of historic wastes in hundreds of thousands of sites around the country, many of which we do not yet know about; imposing requirements with regard to handling and disposal of wastes whose existence legally must be disclosed; and constructing an informational matrix, accessible locally and nationally, that is part of the growing national data base telling us how and where the nation handles its dangerous chemicals.

§ 7.02 Federal Regulation of Solid Waste

[A] Basic Terms

[1] How Solid Is "Solid" Waste?

The term "solid waste" is very broadly construed in RCRA. The criteria for what are considered to be solid wastes under RCRA, and hence for determining which solid waste disposal facilities and practices may pose adverse effects on health or the environment,[9] are set forth in 40 C.F.R. Part 257. Except as specifically excluded (see [B], *below*), solid waste is defined to specifically include any garbage, refuse, sludge from a waste treatment plant, waste from a water supply treatment plant, and waste from an air pollution control facility.[10]

"Solid" waste is not always solid. It may be dissolved. It also includes "other discarded material," including solid, liquid, semi-solid, or "contained gaseous material" from industrial, commercial, mining, and agricultural operations.[11] "Leachate" is liquid that passes through or emerges from solid wastes, carrying with it soluble, sus-

---

8. 42 U.S.C. §§ 11001–11050.
9. 40 C.F.R. § 257.1(a).
10. 42 U.S.C. § 6903(27).
11. *See* 42 U.S.C. § 6903(27); 40 C.F.R. § 257.2.

pended, or miscible materials from the wastes.[12] "Domestic septage" is either liquid or solid material which is removed from septic tanks, cesspools, and toilet devices, including treatment works that receive only domestic sewage. But for purposes of regulation under EPA's Part 257 rules, it does not include septage that is only commercial or industrial in origin.[13] Part 257 applies generally to non-hazardous industrial solid waste disposal facilities. Part 258, discussed in § 7.03, carves out municipal landfills for somewhat different treatment, although many of the basic concepts of Parts 257 and 258 parallel one another.

"Sludge" is a solid waste, although its regulation under Part 257 depends on certain circumstances (see [C][2][e], *below*). Sludge generally refers to any solid, semisolid, or liquid waste from a municipal, commercial, or industrial wastewater treatment plant, water supply treatment plant, or air pollution control facility. It also can include any other waste having similar characteristics and effects.[14] "Sewage sludge" refers to the residue generated during the treatment of domestic sewage in a treatment works, but not the grit and screenings removed during preliminary treatment, nor the ash generated when sludge is incinerated. The term can include domestic septage, noted *above*. It can also include scum or solids removed during wastewater treatment processes. Material derived from sewage sludge remains sewage sludge for definitional purposes.[15]

"Industrial solid waste" can be generated by industrial or manufacturing processes, but the term excludes mining waste or oil or gas waste.[16] If it is hazardous, it falls under the stricter RCRA Subtitle C regulation (discussed in § 7.05) and not under Part 257. "Commercial solid waste" is that generated by stores, offices, restaurants, and warehouses, but is not residential or industrial waste.[17]

[2] Disposal Activities and Facilities

Disposal comes in many forms, only some of which trigger Part 257 regulation. Generally, "disposal" implicates the common usage of the term. However, in order to avoid disposals that might surreptitiously slip through the regulatory sieve, the regulations describe disposals as including the discharge, deposit, injection, dumping, spilling, leaking, or placing of solid waste onto, or into, land or water in such a manner that its constituents enter the environment. In this regard, the environment includes land, air, and water, including surface as well as ground water, leaving no real outdoor geography excluded from the regulatory reach.[18]

Various types of structures may be solid waste disposal facilities for purposes of Part 257, although some that evade Part 257 regulation fall under Part 258 regulation,

12. 40 C.F.R. § 257.2.
13. *Id.*
14. *Id.*
15. *Id.*
16. 40 C.F.R. § 258.2.
17. *Id.*
18. 40 C.F.R. § 257.2.

under some circumstances (see § 7.03). A "facility" includes all contiguous land structures, other appurtenances, and improvements on land used for the disposal of solid wastes.[19] One of the more common types of solid waste disposal facilities is a "landfill," defined as a land area or excavation where wastes are placed for permanent disposal.[20] However, it is not just any such area. A "surface impoundment" is separately defined as a facility comprised of a natural topographic depression or a human-made excavation, or as a diked area that is designed to hold liquid wastes. This type of facility includes storage, settling, and aeration pits, ponds, and lagoons. However, the definition of a surface impoundment does not incorporate injection wells, which, as the name suggests, are subsurface disposal sites.[21] Nevertheless, leaking injection wells do not escape regulation, since they can trigger CERCLA remediation if hazardous wastes are released into the subsurface environment and the Clean Water Act (by application of recent Supreme Court caselaw referenced in § 6.03[B][1]) if a subsurface structure discharges into surface waters. Readers will also recall that injection wells also may trigger the Safe Drinking Water Act, discussed in § 6.04[C].

A "sanitary landfill" is required by Part 257, which prohibits an "open dump," and requires fill to be placed on top of the waste[22] (see [C], *below*).

A "municipal solid waste landfill" unit is governed by Part 258 (see discussion in § 7.03) rather than Part 257 regulation. It essentially is a solid waste facility operated by a local government that receives household waste.[23] A qualifying municipal solid waste landfill may also receive other RCRA Subtitle D wastes, such as commercial or industrial solid waste and non-hazardous sludge. A "municipal" facility may be either privately or publicly owned.[24]

Readers should note that RCRA is not the exclusive legal regime for regulating solid waste facilities and disposal, although it establishes the baseline requirements. State and local laws which are minimally consistent with the federal requirements must also be considered where applicable.[25]

[B] Wastes Excluded from Federal Regulation of Solid Waste Disposal

By being specifically defined as not being "solid waste," certain wastes are effectively excluded from regulation under RCRA, although they do not necessarily escape regulation under other environmental statutes. The following wastes are excluded from the Part 257 criteria:

---

19. *Id.*
20. *Id.*
21. *Id.*
22. 42 U.S.C. § 6903(14), (26); 40 C.F.R. § 257.2.
23. 40 C.F.R. § 257.2.
24. *Id.*
25. *See, e.g.,* New York Environmental Conservation Law Art. 27.

- Domestic sewage (e.g., non-hazardous household septic wastes), whether solid or consisting of dissolved constituents.[26]

- The land application of domestic sewage or treated domestic sewage.[27] Septic tanks are not themselves regulated under RCRA, as to location or operation; but if the septic wastes are removed from the septic tank (as contrasted with normal dispersal through a leaching field), then they are more akin to sewage sludge and constitute a solid waste falling within RCRA.[28] Land application of sludge from domestic sewage is governed by 40 C.F.R. Part 503, not Part 257 regulation.[29]

- Agricultural wastes, such as manure and crop residues, which are reintegrated into the soil as fertilizer or soil conditioners,[30] as well as solid or dissolved material in irrigated return flows.[31]

- Industrial discharges[32] which fall under Clean Water Act § 402 (see § 6.03) and materials that fall under Atomic Energy Act regulation[33] (see § 12.02).

- Mining overburden that is returned to the mine.[34]

Although "solid waste" subsumes a subcategory of hazardous waste,[35] hazardous wastes are separately regulated under RCRA Subtitle C (see discussion in § 7.05). In addition, as noted in [A][2], *above,* disposal of solid waste in underground injection wells is formally regulated under the Safe Drinking Water Act (see discussion in § 6.04[C]),[36] although leachate which escapes containment might also trigger other environmental laws.

[C] Sanitary Landfills

[1] Open Dumping Is Prohibited

Solid waste disposal facilities generally, though not exclusively, are landfills (formerly and colloquially known as dumps). Historically, landfills were simply the location to which local garbage was brought and simply "dumped," typically with little thought given to aesthetics or pests, let alone surface or ground water contamination. Regulation of such "open dumps" was minimal, with deleterious health and environmental consequences. RCRA and its implementing regulations seek to correct

---

26. 40 C.F.R. § 257.1(c)(3).

27. Id.

28. 40 C.F.R. § 257.1(c)(4); 44 Fed. Reg. 53,440 (1979).

29. 40 C.F.R. § 257.1(c)(1).

30. Id.

31. 40 C.F.R. § 257.1(c)(5).

32. 40 C.F.R. § 257.1(c)(6).

33. 40 C.F.R. § 257.1(c)(7).

34. 40 C.F.R. § 257.1(c)(2).

35. 40 C.F.R. § 257.1(c)(8).

36. 40 C.F.R. § 257.1(c)(9). See 40 C.F.R. Part 146, implementing the Underground Injection Control Program under the Safe Drinking Water Act at 42 U.S.C. § 3007, *et seq.*

these conditions at already existing dumps and to prevent their occurrence at modern landfills. The engineering design and operation of the landfill, as well as the nature of the wastes disposed of there, will determine whether it is a lawful "sanitary" landfill or an unlawful "open dump."

An open dump is simply any solid waste disposal facility (excepting hazardous waste disposal facilities, which are separately regulated under RCRA Part C) that cannot meet the requirements of a sanitary landfill.[37] However, the definition of "open dump" is not limited to typical landfills. It could be any facility where trash is disposed of, such as a junk yard, if the construction or operation does not satisfy the requirements for a sanitary landfill.[38] Open dumping is now prohibited.[39] Existing open dumps must be closed or brought into compliance with RCRA's sanitary landfill requirements. To achieve this, states are required to inventory all open dumps and promulgate plans (see § 7.04[A]) to bring the dumps into compliance with EPA regulations.[40]

[2] Criteria Governing Sanitary Landfills

[a] Sanitary Landfill Defined

A "sanitary" landfill is a solid waste disposal facility which satisfies the RCRA criteria that requires no reasonable probability of adverse effects on health or the environment.[41] The term sanitary landfill is not limited to a landfill, but incorporates other disposal methods (see [A][2], *above*). The landfill operator must obtain, and renew as is necessary, permits required under state and local laws for every kind of non-hazardous waste stream.[42] The RCRA criteria, which impose requirements and restrictions regarding locations and disposal activities, are set forth in [b] through [g], *below*.

[b] Flood Plains

The siting, location, and operation of disposal facilities such as landfills in flood plains are restricted. The facility must not impede the flow of the "base flood," or reduce the temporary water storage capacity of the floodplain.[43] The base flood is "a flood that has a one percent or greater chance of occurring in any year or a flood of a magnitude that is equaled or exceeded once in 100 years on the average,"[44] a so-

---

37. 42 U.S.C. § 6903(14).
38. Parker v. Scrap Metal Processors, 386 F.3d 993 (11th Cir. 2004).
39. 42 U.S.C. § 6945(a).
40. *Id.*
41. 43 U.S.C. § 6944.
42. Griffin v. Town of Unionville, 338 Fed. Appx. 320 (4th Cir. 2009).
43. 40 C.F.R. § 257.3-1(a).
44. 40 C.F.R. § 257.3-1(b)(1).

called 100-year flood. Nor may the siting or construction allow a washout of wastes during a flood that would threaten human health or the environment.[45]

[c] Wildlife Habitat

Solid waste disposal methods or siting of facilities may not intrude upon endangered or threatened species' critical habitat. Such a disposal facility would not be a sanitary landfill and thus would constitute a RCRA violation.[46] If it resulted in a "taking" of the species (see § 10.03[C]), it also might constitute a violation of the Endangered Species Act.

[d] Water

[i] Surface Water

A discharge of solid waste that violates the Clean Water Act also violates the RCRA criteria.[47] A violation at the facility designated under either § 402 or § 404 of the Clean Water Act (see § 6.03) converts a facility into an open dump.[48] A discharge of non-point source pollutants that violates an approved water quality management plan under § 208 of the Clean Water Act (see § 6.03) also violates the Part 257 criteria.[49]

[ii] Groundwater

Solid waste may not be disposed of so as to contaminate an underground drinking water source, or aquifer, beyond the solid waste boundary or an "alternative boundary."[50]

Contamination occurs when the concentration of any substance in the waste exceeds a maximum contaminant level (MCL)[51] under the Safe Drinking Water Act (see discussion in § 6.04[C]).

[iii] Wetlands

New solid waste facilities may not be located in wetlands, subject to some exceptions under the Clean Water Act.[52] Initially, the presumption in § 404 that a practicable alternative to wetlands use exists (see discussion in § 6.07[E][2], *supra*) must be clearly rebutted. The construction or operation of the facility must also not do any of the following:[53]

---

45. 40 C.F.R. § 257.3-1(a).
46. 40 C.F.R. § 257.3-2.
47. 40 C.F.R. § 257.3-3.
48. 46 Fed. Reg. 47,050 (1981).
49. 40 C.F.R. § 257.3-3(c).
50. 40 C.F.R. § 257.3-4.
51. *See* 40 C.F.R. § 257.3-4(c)(2) for MCLs.
52. 40 C.F.R. § 257.9, added by 61 Fed. Reg. 34252 (July 1, 1996) (eff. Jan. 1, 1998).
53. 40 C.F.R. § 257.9(a)(4).

- Violate any state water quality standard or any toxic effluent standard under Clean Water Act § 307 (see § 6.03);

- Violate the Endangered Species Act (see § 10.03); or

- Degrade the wetlands.

[e] Agricultural Use of Sewage Sludge

[i] Toxic Substances

As sewage sludge becomes more difficult to dispose of safely, especially since ocean dumping is now banned (see § 6.05[C]), its use as fertilizer has increased. When sludge is essentially biologically organic, then, subject to eradicating pathogenic contamination (see [ii], *below*), its use as fertilizer has significant environmental, as well as commercial, potential as a disposal method. However, what if the sludge contains heavy metals and other toxins? Will these contaminants be absorbed into the food crops or crops intended for animal feed and, entering the food chain, defeat the very purpose of environmental regulation?

The problem remains partially unaddressed. Currently, sludge wastes containing cadmium applied to food cropland (as well as tobacco) are subject to cumulative and annual limits.[54] But as applied to feed cropland, there are no particular limits,[55] although there are pH requirements (6.5 or greater) regarding the soil to which the cadmium may be applied. In that case, the use of cadmium must be recorded in the deed along with a warning that food crops should not be grown at that location.[56]

Polychlorinated biphenyls — PCBs — in sludge-fertilizer being applied to cropland are regulated above threshold levels of concentration.[57] However, pesticides, lead, and other toxins in sludge fertilizer are unregulated.[58] The reader may want to review Chapter 8 for coverage of the direct regulation of these toxic substances.

[ii] Pathogens

Disposal of sewage sludge as fertilizer creates another problem — the possible presence of pathogenic constituents, especially those that can spread disease through vectors, such as rodents, flies, and mosquitoes.[59] This practical reuse of a biological waste product also presents other risks. The Federal Food and Drug Administration has

---

54. 40 C.F.R. § 257.3-5(a)(1). Cadmium tends to bio-accumulate in cereal crops, leafy greens, various vegetables, including roots and potatoes, pulses such as peas and beans, nuts and their oils, and animals which feed on these crops. However, cadmium can also infiltrate soil and crops from water and ambient air contaminated by manufacturing, mining and other activities. *See* Agency for Toxic Substances and Disease Registry, Environmental Health and Medicine Education, "Cadmium," at atsdr.cdc.gov.

55. 40 C.F.R. § 257.3-5(a)(2).

56. *Id.*

57. 40 C.F.R. § 257.3-5(b).

58. *See* 44 Fed. Reg. 53,449 (1979).

59. 40 C.F.R. § 257.3-6(c)(2).

required several recalls of grocery produce in recent years because of contamination by listeria, salmonella and other pathogens which have been traced to contaminated fertilizer.

Disease vectors must be minimized by adding cover material, such as soil, or other appropriate techniques[60] to cover wastes at the end of each operating day, or as is necessary.[61] In addition, the sludge must be treated by an EPA-approved process to significantly reduce pathogens prior to the application, and public access to the site and its use for grazing or food crops are restricted.[62]

Processes to significantly reduce pathogens include aerobic or anaerobic digestion, air drying, heat, composting, pasteurization, addition of lime to decrease acidity, and irradiation.[63]

[f] Open Burning

Open burning of residential, commercial, institutional, or industrial waste is prohibited.[64] Open burning refers to the combustion of solid waste without sufficient control to ensure efficient and complete combustion and control of emissions.[65] However, occasional burning of agricultural or silvicultural wastes does not trigger the RCRA regulations.[66] If burning of waste results in a violation of a State Implementation Plan under the Clean Air Act (see § 5.02), it also constitutes a violation of the Part 257 criteria.[67]

[g] General Safety Hazards

The regulations also include restrictions pertaining to general safety concerns in the following four major areas:

- The concentration of explosive gases from the landfill or from the disposal method itself[68] — generally methane;

- Fire hazards arising from the facility's operation or the method of disposal;[69]

- Bird hazards caused by the landfill operation that create a threat to aircraft;[70] and

- Assurances that access to the facility is restricted.[71]

---

60. 40 C.F.R. § 257.3-6(a).
61. 40 C.F.R. § 257.3-6(c)(4).
62. 40 C.F.R. § 257.3-6(b)(1)–(3).
63. 40 C.F.R. Part 257 App. II.
64. 40 C.F.R. § 257.3-7(a).
65. 40 C.F.R. § 257.7(c).
66. 40 C.F.R. § 257.3-7(a).
67. 40 C.F.R. § 257.3-7(b); 46 Fed. Reg. 47,048 (1981).
68. 40 C.F.R. § 257.3-8(a).
69. 40 C.F.R. § 257.3-8(b).
70. 40 C.F.R. § 257.3-8(c).
71. 40 C.F.R. § 257.3-8(d).

These safety considerations are also reflected in the conditions that are imposed on the siting or operation of municipal landfills (see § 7.03).

[D] Groundwater Monitoring and Corrective Action

Subpart B of Part 257 imposes several requirements for groundwater monitoring and corrective action. However, facilities that can demonstrate no potential for hazardous constituents to enter the uppermost aquifer for the active life of the facility (running from first disposal to closure[72] plus 30 years[73]) may be exempted.[74] The uppermost aquifer is the one nearest the surface, but it also includes lower aquifers hydrologically connected to it.[75] Unless exempted, non-complying new units may not accept wastes,[76] unless permitted to do so by a state-approved program.[77] Monitoring must be done for the active life of the unit plus 30 years — although EPA relaxes the temporal requirement if the facility can demonstrate no threat to health or the environment.[78] Monitoring must be conducted by a qualified groundwater scientist, as that term is defined in the regulation.[79]

The regulations include detailed requirements for the monitoring systems,[80] sampling and analysis requirements,[81] the detection monitoring program,[82] the assessment monitoring program,[83] the assessment of corrective measures,[84] and the implementation of corrective measures[85] that are beyond the scope of this book.

Small facilities may be treated more flexibly, in that some of the monitoring requirements may be modified or suspended. However, to qualify, a small facility must (1) dispose of less than 20 tons of non-municipal waste daily, (2) have no evidence of groundwater contamination, and (3) serve a community that either has an annual interruption of surface transportation exceeding three months that prevents access to a regional waste management facility (e.g., parts of Alaska), or serves a community that has no practical alternative and receives 25 inches or less of annual precipitation (e.g., parts of the Southwest).[86] These criteria parallel those for small municipal solid waste disposal facilities (see § 7.03[B][3]). Having qualified, the small facility can rely

---

72. 40 C.F.R. § 258.2.
73. 40 C.F.R. § 257.21(b).
74. *Id.*
75. 40 C.F.R. § 258.2.
76. 40 C.F.R. § 257.21(c)(2).
77. 40 C.F.R. § 257.21(d).
78. 40 C.F.R. § 257.21(e).
79. 40 C.F.R. § 257.21(f).
80. 40 C.F.R. § 257.22.
81. 40 C.F.R. § 257.23.
82. 40 C.F.R. § 257.24.
83. 40 C.F.R. § 257.25.
84. 40 C.F.R. § 257.26.
85. 40 C.F.R. § 257.28.
86. 40 C.F.R. § 257.21(h).

on alternative, less onerous, monitoring methodologies[87] until contamination is detected.[88] If the contamination is detected in the unsaturated zone (i.e., not in the water table), corrective measures must be taken.[89] If monitoring indicates that contamination from the facility has reached the saturated zone — the part of the earth's crust where all voids are water saturated[90] — groundwater monitoring wells must be installed and operated for sampling.[91]

§ 7.03 Municipal Solid Waste Disposal Facilities

[A] Governing Rules

The EPA's Part 258 rules[92] specifically govern municipal solid waste disposal facilities. They establish minimum criteria for all municipal solid waste landfill units under RCRA and, if sewage sludge is accepted, under the Clean Water Act.[93] However, states with approved programs control landfills under their own rules, discussed in § 7.04.

Constructing or operating a municipal landfill in a manner inconsistent with the EPA criteria converts the landfill into a prohibited open dump, in violation of RCRA. Part 258 imposes design, operating, and groundwater monitoring requirements for municipal landfills. Those near drinking water intakes are subject to stringent groundwater monitoring.[94] If the landfill is located in a state which has a state wellhead protection program under the Safe Drinking Water Act (see § 6.04[C]), there may be additional requirements.[95] Part 258 also contains financial assurance requirements[96] and corrective action obligations.

As usual, new facilities or lateral expansion of existing facilities are subject to stricter requirements than existing facilities.

[B] Facilities Included

[1] What Is "Municipal" Solid Waste?

Municipal solid waste is basically household waste, such as garbage, trash, and septic tank waste, derived from households of all types. Households include single

---

87. 40 C.F.R. § 257.21(i)(1).
88. 40 C.F.R. § 257.21(i)(2).
89. 40 C.F.R. § 257.21(i)(2)(ii).
90. 40 C.F.R. § 258.2.
91. 40 C.F.R. § 257.21(i)(2)(i).
92. 40 C.F.R. §§ 258.1–258.74.
93. 40 C.F.R. § 258.1(a).
94. 40 C.F.R. § 258.50(c).
95. 40 C.F.R. § 258.16, Note.
96. 40 C.F.R. § 258.70(b).

and multiple residences, hotels, motels, campgrounds, picnic grounds, and day-use recreational areas.[97]

[2] Municipal Solid Waste Management Units: Definition and Requirements

Municipal solid waste management units are landfills, which may be publicly or privately owned.[98] As with many environmental laws, regulations govern both owners and operators.[99] The major qualification is that the facility receives household (i.e., domestic) wastes.[100] However, it also may receive some commercial solid waste, nonhazardous sludge, industrial solid waste and the like, but not hazardous waste.[101]

[3] Exclusion of Small Landfills

Some "small" municipal landfills are exempt from many of the Part 258 regulations. These landfills receive less than 20 tons daily of municipal solid waste and serve certain types of small or isolated communities.[102] In addition, there must be no evidence of ground water contamination from the facility.[103] If contamination is discovered at a small landfill, the owner or operator must report it, and the exemption will be lost. If neighboring drinking water sources are contaminated, the owner and operator must also take corrective action, in addition to assuming the full range of design and groundwater monitoring responsibilities applicable to municipal land-fills.[104]

[4] Municipal Incineration of Solid Waste

Incineration of household waste, though not regulated in Part 258, also is a method by which communities dispose of solid waste. Incineration, aside from preserving land fill space, provides the additional advantage of generating energy that can be used for co-generation and other beneficial uses. Incineration releases two by-products: (1) gases, including particulates, and (2) ash. The air emissions require a Clean Air Act permit and must satisfy National Air Quality Standards (see § 5.03[A], [B]) and, potentially, National Emission Standards for Hazardous Air Pollutants (see § 5.03[D]). Even if an incineration facility accepts only household waste, ordinarily exempting it from permitting requirements as a generator of the waste, the exemption is lost and a permit is required if the ash residue contains hazardous constituents. However, the exemption does not apply in the first place if the facility accepts hazardous waste,

---

97. 40 C.F.R. § 258.2.
98. 40 C.F.R. § 257.1(b).
99. 40 C.F.R. § 258.1(b).
100. See 40 C.F.R. § 261.4(b)(1) for definition of household waste.
101. 40 C.F.R. § 258.20.
102. 40 C.F.R. § 258.1(f)(1).
103. *Id.*
104. 56 Fed. Reg. 50,990.

which then subjects the incinerator's ash to the full range of RCRA TSD permitting (see § 7.05[E]).[105]

[C] Limitations that Apply to a Municipal Landfill's Siting and Location

[1] Wetlands

New municipal landfills and lateral expansions of existing units generally may not be constructed in wetlands.[106] If a state has an EPA-approved permitting program, an exception may be made[107] under certain conditions:

- There is a presumption under § 404 of the Clean Water Act (see § 6.03) that a practicable alternative to wetland construction is available (see discussion in § 6.07[E][2], *supra*). This presumption must be rebutted for construction of a new facility or lateral expansion in a wetland, even in a state with an approved permitting program.[108]

- The applicant must demonstrate that approval of the construction or the subsequent operation of the municipal landfill will not cause or contribute to violations of water quality standards or Clean Water Act § 307 toxic effluent limitations (see § 6.03), or injure threatened or endangered species or their critical habitat under the Endangered Species Act (see § 10.03).[109]

- The applicant must demonstrate that the construction or expansion will not result in significant degradation of the wetlands.[110]

- The applicant must demonstrate its efforts to prevent any net loss of wetlands, in compliance with Clean Water Act § 404 (see §§ 6.03, 11.02[A]), and relevant state laws.[111]

[2] Flood Plains

As in the Part 257 rules regarding solid waste facilities in general (see § 7.02[A][1]), a municipal landfill, whether existing, new, or an expansion, must demonstrate that it will not restrict the flow of a 100-year flood, or reduce the temporary water storage capacity of that flood plain. It also must demonstrate that its construction or operation will not result in a washout that might threaten human health or the environment.[112] If existing units cannot so demonstrate, they must have closed by 1996, although an

---

105. *See 42 U.S.C. § 6921(i); City of Chicago v. Environmental Defense Fund, 511 U.S. 328 (1994).*
106. 40 C.F.R. § 258.12(a).
107. 56 Fed. Reg. 51,004.
108. 40 C.F.R. § 258.12(a)(1).
109. 40 C.F.R. § 258.12(a)(2).
110. 40 C.F.R. § 258.12(a)(3).
111. 40 C.F.R. § 258.12(a)(4).
112. 40 C.F.R. § 258.11.

approved state can extend the deadline if there is no alternative disposal site and no immediate threat to health or the environment.[113]

[3] Seismic Zones

New landfills, or the lateral expansion of existing facilities, in seismic impact zones are prohibited.[114] However, a state with an EPA-approved permitting program may approve the project if the facility shows that it is designed to resist earthquakes.[115]

Similarly, new landfills, including expansion of existing units, are barred within 200 feet of a fault line that has had any activity since the end of the Pleistocene epoch (35,000 years ago), unless the applicant can demonstrate that an alternative setback of less than 200 feet will protect the landfill's structural integrity, as well as human health and the environment.[116]

[4] Airports

Landfills notoriously attract flocks of birds, particularly sea gulls. Municipal landfills located near airports often must demonstrate that they will not create a hazard to aircraft by attracting birds. This requirement applies for municipal landfills within 5,000 feet of any airport runway-end used by propeller aircraft, or within 10,000 feet of an airport runway-end used by jets.[117] Landfills in violation must have closed by 1996, although an approved state can extend the deadline if there is no alternative disposal site and no immediate danger.[118] In addition, new landfill units, or the expansion of existing units, within five miles of an airport require notification to the airport and to the Federal Aeronautics Administration.[119]

[5] Unstable Areas

EPA defines an "unstable area" in terms of the earthen underpinnings of the landfills, such as those with poor foundation conditions, or those susceptible to mass movements of ground.[120] Any municipal landfill—existing or new—in an unstable area must demonstrate that it is engineered in such a manner "that the integrity of the structural components of the ... unit will not be disrupted."[121] Existing units that could not make these demonstrations had to have been closed after 1996, although there was a narrow window for an approved state to extend the deadline if there was no alternative disposal site and no immediate threat to health or the environment.[122]

---

113. 40 C.F.R. § 258.16.
114. 40 C.F.R. § 258.14(a).
115. *Id.*
116. 40 C.F.R. § 258.13.
117. 40 C.F.R. § 258.10(a).
118. 40 C.F.R. § 258.16.
119. 40 C.F.R. § 258.10(b); 56 Fed. Reg. 51,004.
120. 40 C.F.R. § 258.15(b)(1).
121. 40 C.F.R. § 258.15(a).
122. 40 C.F.R. § 258.16.

[D] Design and Operating Requirements

[1] Design Criteria

The landfill's design must be approved by EPA or by an approved state, so as to prevent leaching of waste into groundwater or surface water, taking into account hydrology, climate, and characteristics of the leachate it may produce.[123] The design must ensure that concentrations of heavy metals and other toxic wastes will not exceed specified levels in the uppermost aquifer, or must include a composite liner and leachate collection system.[124] A composite liner must have a polyethylene flexible membrane liner over a layer of compacted soil at least two feet thick.[125]

[2] Operating Restrictions

The Part 258 rules direct how municipal landfills may operate. At the end of each operating day, or more frequently if necessary, the waste must be covered with at least six inches of earthen or similar material to control disease vectors, fires, odors, blowing litter, and scavengers.[126] The landfill has an affirmative obligation to prevent or control disease vectors independent of the requirement of covering.[127] The landfill also must limit or monitor methane accumulations in excess of specific levels.[128]

Municipal landfills may not violate a State Implementation Plan under the Clean Air Act (see § 5.02), and open burning (see § 7.02[C][2][f]) is prohibited, except for the occasional burning of agricultural or forest wastes, land clearing debris, diseased trees, or debris from emergency cleanups.[129]

Landfills must use natural or man-made barriers to control unauthorized access, especially to prevent illegal dumping.[130] The danger of hazardous waste dumping in municipal landfills is a serious one, and poses the additional risk of CERCLA liability (see § 7.06).

Generally, bulk or non-containerized liquid waste may not be placed in a municipal landfill, unless it is non-septic household waste, or leachate, where the landfill has a composite liner and leachate collection system.[131] Containers of liquid waste may not be placed in municipal landfills unless they are small, consist of only household waste, and are not storage containers.[132] Municipal landfills may not cause discharges in violation of Clean Water Act § 402[133] or non-point source discharges violating an ap-

---

123. 40 C.F.R. § 258.40(a), (c).
124. 40 C.F.R. § 258.40(a).
125. 40 C.F.R. § 258.40(b).
126. 40 C.F.R. § 258.21(a), (b).
127. 40 C.F.R. § 258.22.
128. 40 C.F.R. § 258.23(a).
129. 40 C.F.R. § 258.24.
130. 40 C.F.R. § 258.25.
131. 40 C.F.R. § 258.28(a).
132. 40 C.F.R. § 258.28(b).
133. 40 C.F.R. § 258.27(a).

proved water quality management plan (see § 6.03).[134] Municipal landfills also must construct run-on control systems to prevent flow on to the landfill during the peak discharge from a 25-year storm, and run-off controls to collect and contain water volume from such a storm.[135]

[3] Recordkeeping

Municipal landfills must maintain detailed records, including inspection records, training and notification procedures, monitoring and testing results, proof of financial assurance, and closure and post-closure plans, including monitoring and analysis.[136] When records are added, the director of an approved state program must be notified, and the records must be readily available for inspection.[137]

[4] Groundwater Monitoring

Municipal landfills have extensive groundwater monitoring requirements. Existing units within two miles of drinking water intakes must be brought into compliance with the Part 258 rules,[138] and new units, or lateral expansions of existing units, must be in compliance before accepting any waste.[139] Groundwater monitoring must be maintained throughout the active life and post-closure care period of the unit.[140]

As with other requirements, groundwater monitoring may be suspended or modified by the director of an approved state program, upon a showing of no potential migration of hazardous constituents into the uppermost aquifer, during both the active life of the unit and the post-closure period.[141]

A groundwater monitoring system consists of wells at various locations and depths, so as to yield samples from the uppermost aquifer. These samples must represent the quality of uncontaminated background water as well as downgradient water at the unit boundary or some other designated point.[142] There are numerous technical requirements for sampling and analysis,[143] detection monitoring,[144] the assessment of corrective measures,[145] selection of a remedy,[146] and the implementation of a corrective action program.[147]

---

134. 40 C.F.R. § 258.27.
135. 40 C.F.R. § 258.26.
136. 40 C.F.R. § 258.29(a).
137. 40 C.F.R. § 258.29(b).
138. 40 C.F.R. § 258.50(c)(1)–(3).
139. 40 C.F.R. § 258.50(c)(4).
140. 40 C.F.R. § 258.50(f).
141. 40 C.F.R. § 258.50(b).
142. 40 C.F.R. § 258.51(a).
143. 40 C.F.R. § 258.53.
144. 40 C.F.R. § 258.54.
145. 40 C.F.R. § 258.56.
146. 40 C.F.R. § 258.57.
147. 40 C.F.R. § 258.58.

[E] Closure and Post-Closure Requirements

[1] Purpose of Requirements

There are detailed closure and post-closure requirements for municipal solid waste disposal facilities. These requirements are designed to ensure continued containment of the waste, to prevent threats to health or the environment, and to restrict future use that might interfere with this goal. These plans must be in place even before waste is disposed of on-site.

[2] Cover System

For closure, a final cover system, even more impermeable than the bottom liner, must be designed to minimize infiltration and erosion. There must be at least 18 inches of earthen material, topped by an erosion layer of at least six inches of soil, capable of sustaining plant growth, to prevent wind and water erosion.[148] Approved states can authorize alternative designs that achieve the same purpose.[149]

[3] Closure Plan and Other Closure Requirements

The landfill owner or operator must submit a closure plan, detailing the composition of the cover, the maximum area of the facility used for waste disposal during its active life, and a schedule for completion,[150] which then must be placed in the operating record prior to the first acceptance of waste.[151] Closure must commence shortly after the last acceptance of waste.[152] The state agency must be notified before closure commences,[153] and it must be completed within 180 days, subject to extensions granted by the state agency.[154] Closure must be certified for compliance by the state agency or by an independent registered professional engineer.[155] A notation must be placed in the deed, notifying potential purchasers of this prior use, and of potential restrictions on future use,[156] although the notation may be removed if all the waste is removed.[157]

[4] Post-Closure Care

The period following closure is termed post-closure, which, absent an extension or a contraction of the period by the state director,[158] lasts for 30 years.[159] Post-closure

---

148. 40 C.F.R. § 258.60(a).
149. 40 C.F.R. § 258.60(b).
150. 40 C.F.R. § 258.60(c).
151. 40 C.F.R. § 258.60(d).
152. 40 C.F.R. § 258.60(f).
153. 40 C.F.R. § 258.60(e).
154. 40 C.F.R. § 258.60(g).
155. 40 C.F.R. § 258.60(h).
156. 40 C.F.R. § 258.60(i).
157. 40 C.F.R. § 258.60(j).
158. 40 C.F.R. § 258.61(b).
159. 40 C.F.R. § 258.61(a)(1).

care consists of maintaining the integrity and effectiveness of the final cover, and responding to settlement, subsidence, erosion, or other threats to containment of the wastes, generally to prevent run-on and run-off from damaging the cover.[160] Groundwater monitoring, including maintenance of the leachate collection system, and gas monitoring remain necessary during the post-closure period.[161] All of these activities must be evaluated and recorded in a post-closure plan. The plan must also project the post-closure use of the property, subject to restrictions on use that would disturb the cover, or any components of the containment system.[162] Post-closure use restrictions must also be placed in the operating record prior to acceptance of waste.[163] Completion of post-closure also requires certification,[164] similar to that for completion of closure.

[F] Financial Assurances

[1] General Requirements

A municipal landfill owner or operator must demonstrate a financial ability to undertake all steps necessary to protect health and the environment at every stage of the active life of the landfill, and thereafter through post-closure. Readers should recall that municipal landfills may be privately owned or operated. The financial assurance obligations rest on any municipal landfill owner or operator, except for those landfills run by state and federal governmental entities.[165]

[2] Estimates

For closure, the landfill must place in the operating record and provide the state agency with a written estimate, annually adjusted, of the cost of hiring a third party to close and cover the facility, and provide financial assurance equal to the cost.[166] Similarly, a post-closure estimate must be prepared and annually updated, projecting the maximum necessary work to be done by a third party, which information must be maintained in the operating record on notice to the state agency.[167]

In anticipation of corrective action, the landfill must likewise furnish an estimate, and a showing of financial capacity.[168]

[3] Financing Mechanisms

EPA provides numerous financing mechanisms from which landfill owners or operators may choose to cover the costs of closure, post-closure, and corrective action.

---

160. 40 C.F.R. § 258.61(a)(2).
161. 40 C.F.R. § 258.61(a)(2)–(4).
162. 40 C.F.R. § 258.61(c).
163. 40 C.F.R. § 258.61(d).
164. 40 C.F.R. § 258.61(e).
165. 40 C.F.R. § 258.70.
166. 40 C.F.R. § 258.71.
167. 40 C.F.R. § 258.72.
168. 40 C.F.R. § 258.73.

These include establishing a trust fund,[169] purchasing a surety bond,[170] an irrevocable letter of credit,[171] insurance,[172] bonds,[173] local government written guarantees,[174] an assumption of financial responsibility by the state,[175] or any other mechanism approved by the state that meets the financial assurance criteria.[176]

§ 7.04 State and Local Control of Solid Waste Disposal

[A] State Plans

[1] Federal Encouragement of State Plans

As noted in § 7.01, the federal government, with the enactment of RCRA, did not preempt the field of solid waste disposal.[177] Rather, Subchapter IV of RCRA,[178] addressing state or regional solid waste plans, contemplates that states will assume significant programmatic and enforcement authority. Although it is not mandatory that states have a plan, significant federal inducements encourage it. Congress has provided for federal technical and financial assistance[179] to states or regional authorities for comprehensive planning, pursuant to the federal guidelines governing solid waste disposal (discussed in §§ 7.02 and 7.03). Federal assistance is also available for small rural communities, defined as having a population of less than 5,000, or for counties with less than 10,000 in population, for solid waste management facilities to meet the minimum requirements and to eliminate open burning.[180] Congress also intended, ambitiously, to encourage state plans that would facilitate the conservation and recycling of materials that otherwise would become waste, and the conversion of waste to energy.[181]

[2] Minimum Requirements of State Plans

A state must meet certain minimum requirements for its proposed plan to be approved by EPA. The plan must do all of the following:[182]

- Identify the respective local, state, and regional responsibilities in the implementation of the state plan;

---

169. 40 C.F.R. § 258.74(a).
170. 40 C.F.R. § 258.74(b).
171. 40 C.F.R. § 258.74(c).
172. 40 C.F.R. § 258.74(d).
173. 40 C.F.R. § 258.74(f).
174. 40 C.F.R. § 258.74(h).
175. 40 C.F.R. § 258.74(j).
176. 40 C.F.R. § 258.74(i).
177. City of Philadelphia v. New Jersey, 437 U.S. 617 (1978).
178. 42 U.S.C. §§ 6941–6949a.
179. *See* 42 U.S.C. §§ 6947, 6948.
180. 42 U.S.C. § 6949.
181. 42 U.S.C. §§ 6941, 6941a.
182. 42 U.S.C. § 6943.

- Identify the distribution of federal funds to the authorities responsible for the development and implementation of the state plan;

- Identify the means for coordinating regional planning and implementation under the state plan;

- Prohibit the establishment of new open dumps within the state, and require that solid waste be utilized for resource recovery or else disposed of in sanitary landfills, or disposed of otherwise in an environmentally sound manner (see § 7.02[C]);

- Provide for either the upgrading or closure of all existing dumps in the state;

- Provide for the establishment of state powers necessary to implement the plan; and

- Provide that state or local governments may not be legally prohibited from:

- Entering long-term contracts for the supply of solid wastes to resource recovery facilities;

- Entering long-term contracts to operate resource recovery facilities;

- Seeking long-term markets for material and energy thereby recovered; or

- Requiring conservation by waste reduction.

An important aspect of solid waste disposal is the reduction of the waste stream, as just noted above. Among the more viable means of accomplishing this purpose is recycling, thereby extending the useful life of many products and thus delaying the time at which they will require disposal. Many municipalities encourage or even require the recycling of beverage containers, paper, cardboard, plastics and metals. In the aggregate, these materials consume significant amounts of landfill space. At the least, separation of these wastes, many of which are not biodegradable or will not decompose quickly, facilitates the easier disposal of the remaining solid waste. However, to be truly effective, there must be a market for these separated materials so that they can be beneficially recycled. The EPA and state and local governments have been experimenting with means to create or facilitate existing markets in these recycled materials.

Some states also require by law that beverage containers be returnable to vendors for reuse or recycling deposit, and require that the purchasers pay a deposit to encourage the return.[183]

[3] Additional Components of State Plans

[a] Open Dumps

As noted in [2], *above*, the state plan must require that open dumps be closed or upgraded or, in rare instances where there is no immediate practicable alternative,

---

183. See, e.g., New York's "bottle bill" codified in Environmental Conservation Law Article 27, Title 10. New York's bottle bill was substantially expanded in 2010 to create a comprehensive network of functions to accommodate the recapture of used and empty bottles from the stream of commerce, with the goal that the bottles be recycled for beneficial uses and thereby reduce the waste stream, but also reduce the environmental costs of utilizing new resources to manufacture new bottles.

that they meet a compliance schedule which includes appropriate remedial measures.[184] The state must inventory open dumps within its borders. EPA must also maintain and publish a national inventory of open dumps.[185]

The state inventory requirement caused some uncertainty initially, since the mere listing of a facility in such an inventory was seen to equate the facility's operation with a RCRA violation. The state plan could not be approved until the state listed all such facilities and required immediate upgrades or closures. EPA addressed the problem by treating the listing as a mere planning tool rather than as the finding of a violation.[186] EPA also may conditionally approve state plans notwithstanding the existence of open dumps, as long as the state issues a schedule by which open dumps eventually will be brought into compliance.[187]

The state must also implement a permit program covering solid waste management facilities receiving hazardous household wastes, or hazardous wastes from small quantity generators, that otherwise are not subject to treatment, storage, and disposal ("TSD") permitting (see §7.05[E]), which regulates such facilities and assures compliance with sanitary landfill criteria[188] (see §7.02[C]). If EPA is not satisfied with the adequacy of the state plan in this regard, it may require closures within the state.[189]

[b] Used Oil

State plans may encourage the use of recycled oil in an environmentally sound manner, including its use by parties that contract with the state. To accomplish this, the state may implement programs for the collection, transport, treatment, storage, reuse, or disposal of used oil.[190]

[4] Implementation of State Plans

A state plan is implemented by incorporating and carrying out the minimum responsibilities noted in [2], *above*. A plan is carried out regionally within a state: state regulations are to identify regional boundaries, taking into account urban concentrations, geographic conditions, markets, and other factors.[191] The state designates an agency to implement and oversee the plan and to decide which activities will be carried out by the state, and which by regional entities.[192] If some regions are located in more than one state, interstate regional solid waste management plans may be drafted and, on EPA approval, implemented as to those regions, subject to the nec-

---

184. 42 U.S.C. §6945(a).
185. 42 U.S.C. §6945(b).
186. 44 Fed. Reg. 47,048.
187. 42 U.S.C. §6945(a).
188. 42 U.S.C. §6945(c).
189. 42 U.S.C. §6945(c)(2)(A).
190. 42 U.S.C. §6943(b).
191. 42 U.S.C. §6946(a).
192. 42 U.S.C. §6946(b).

essary interstate agreements. However, EPA still deems the regional plan carried out within a particular state to be part of that state's plan.[193]

[B] Restrictions on State and Local Solid Waste Disposal

[1] Commerce Clause Considerations

The Commerce Clause of the United States Constitution provides the constitutional underpinning of most federal environmental statutes (see general discussion in §§ 1.04, 1.05). Conversely, it acts as a limitation when states and local communities try to restrict the flow of solid waste from out-of-state into local communities and when local communities, for economic reasons, try to keep local waste from bypassing local disposal facilities for more competitive facilities elsewhere. Most such restrictions have been found to discriminate against interstate commerce. These statutes or local ordinances violate the "negative" or "dormant" aspect of the Commerce Clause, which has long been recognized to deny states the power to unjustifiably discriminate against, or unduly burden, the interstate flow of articles of commerce.[194] Solid waste in the modern world is commerce, since its transportation is a commercial enterprise.[195]

The dormant Commerce Clause bars both laws that discriminate against interstate commerce and laws that impose a burden on interstate commerce that is excessive in proportion to the putative local benefits of the law. In undue burden cases, a court will look to the nature of the local benefits, and whether less restrictive means can be used to accomplish legitimate state or local purposes.[196] The test was articulated by the Supreme Court, at the dawn of the era that gave us modern environmental law, as follows:

> Where the statute regulates evenhandedly to effectuate a legitimate local public interest, and its effects on interstate commerce are only incidental, it will be upheld unless the burden imposed on such commerce is clearly excessive in relation to the putative local benefits. . . . If a legitimate local purpose is found, then the question becomes one of degree. And the extent of the burden that will be tolerated will of course depend on the nature of the local interest involved, and on whether it could be promoted as well with a lesser impact on interstate activities.[197]

Dormant Commerce Clause violations may be avoided when Congress has granted appropriate authority to the states, notwithstanding discriminatory results in the ex-

---

193. 42 U.S.C. § 6946(c).

194. U.S. CONST. art. I, § 8, cl. 3; Oregon Waste Systems, Inc. v. Department of Environmental Quality, 511 U.S. 93 (1994).

195. City of Philadelphia v. New Jersey, 437 U.S. 617 (1978).

196. C&A Carbone v. Town of Clarkstown, 511 U.S. 383 (1994).

197. Pike v. Bruce Church, Inc., 397 U.S. 137, 142 (1970).

ercise of that power. However, the grant of authority must be explicit or otherwise unmistakably clear, so that the challenged state law must have been contemplated in the grant of authority.[198] In enacting the provisions of RCRA that allow implementation of approved state solid waste programs, Congress failed to evince any intent to allow states to discriminate against or burden interstate commerce while controlling solid waste disposal.[199]

Any person who demonstrates an injury resulting from the challenged law has standing to challenge it,[200] although standing is not limited to non-residents of the regulating state,[201] a consideration increasingly important as local businesses resist local efforts to retain their waste disposal business locally.

Hence, under the dormant Commerce Clause, it has long been recognized that state or local regulations cannot discriminate against the importation of out-of-state waste on the basis of point of origin, or impose restrictions on out-of-state generators or transporters if similar restrictions are not imposed against in-state entities.[202] Accordingly, a New Jersey law that prohibited the importation of solid waste on the rationale of conserving the capacity of that state's landfill space was invalidated by the Supreme Court.[203] An Oregon law imposing substantially higher fees on out-of-state waste likewise was found to be invalid.[204] A facially neutral Minnesota law that imposed costs and indemnification requirements on all parties disposing of solid wastes in in-state landfills was held invalid, since it exempted 39 Minnesota counties, thus favoring in-state interests.[205] Similarly, a Michigan law barring out-of-county waste violated the dormant Commerce Clause since, by definition, it barred out-of-state waste as well.[206] One court recognized that "[t]he burden ... of conserving the state's remaining landfill space should not fall disproportionately on out-of-state interests,"[207] although it also has been recognized that "the commerce clause does not purport to require fairness among the states in interstate commerce,"[208] only that state laws not be anti-competitive. Local communities may impose caps on use of landfill space, as

---

198. South-Central Timber Development, Inc. v. Wunnicke, 467 U.S. 82, 91–92 (1984); Environmental Technology Council v. Sierra Club, 98 F.3d 774 (4th Cir. 1996).

199. Environmental Technology Council v. Sierra Club, 98 F.3d 774 (4th Cir. 1996).

200. Lujan v. Defenders of Wildlife, 504 U.S. 555, 560–61 (1992).

201. Oregon Waste Systems v. Department of Environmental Quality, 511 U.S. 93 (1994); Lujan v. Defenders of Wildlife, 504 U.S. 555, 560–61 (1992).

202. Chemical Waste Management, Inc. v. Hunt, 504 U.S. 334 (1992); City of Philadelphia v. New Jersey, 437 U.S. 617 (1978).

203. City of Philadelphia v. New Jersey, 437 U.S. 617 (1978).

204. Oregon Waste Systems v. Department of Environmental Quality, 511 U.S. 93 (1994).

205. National Solid Waste Management Association v. Williams, 877 F. Supp. 1367 (D. Minn. 1995).

206. Fort Gratiot Sanitary Landfill, Inc. v. Michigan Department of Environmental Resources, 504 U.S. 353 (1992).

207. Hazardous Waste Treatment Council v. State of South Carolina, 945 F.2d 781, 792 (4th Cir. 1991) (citing City of Philadelphia v. New Jersey, 437 U.S. 617 (1978)).

208. Environmental Technology Council v. Sierra Club, 98 F.3d 774 (4th Cir. 1996).

long as the caps are imposed uniformly with respect to in-state and out-of-state interests.[209] However, when the state law allows caps to be exceeded in a manner favoring local interests, the dormant Commerce Clause is violated.[210] Nevertheless, merely requiring solid waste transporters to obtain state certification, at a nominal cost, when the certification is neutral as to origin or disposal of the waste, does not result in a violation.[211]

As discussed in [2], *below*, the enactment of flow control ordinances by local communities have required the courts to deal with laws designed to fence waste in, as well as keep it out.

[2] Flow Control Ordinances: Local Attempts to Control Solid Waste Disposal

Flow control ordinances are the means by which local communities have sought to assert control over the flow of solid waste into and out of the community. Many were enacted during the 1970s and 1980s, when many landfills were being closed, and other facilities were much restricted with the enforcement of environmental laws. As a result, more communities were relying on fewer landfills, driving up operational and capital expenses and concurrently setting the stage for a competitive market for the transport and disposal of solid waste — often to a destination in other states.[212] Yet, new construction compatible with the new RCRA requirements, and often required by law, was expensive. Construction and operating costs, rather than being satisfied solely by taxes or municipal obligations, often were satisfied out of charges for waste disposal, or "tipping fees." Local landfills, although newly constructed and operating up to code, often lost solid waste disposal business to cheaper, often less environmentally benign facilities, sometimes out-of-state. This problem was especially severe with incinerators, which require a steady supply of waste to operate efficiently.

This was the reverse of the classic interstate commerce problem, where local communities sought to keep out non-community generated solid waste. As a consequence, communities started to enact "flow control" ordinances, many of which sought to maintain the profitable operation of local landfills and incinerators, even if privately owned or operated, by keeping local solid waste in town. Though these flow control

---

209. Chemical Waste Management, Inc. v. Hunt, 504 U.S. 344 (1992); Chambers Medical Technologies of South Carolina v. Bryant, 52 F.3d 1252, 1258 (4th Cir. 1995).

210. Environmental Technology Council v. Sierra Club, 98 F.3d 774 (4th Cir. 1996). In this case, the statute allowed the cap to be exceeded for in-state generated waste. It also fixed ceilings for out-of-state waste on the basis of the prior year's out-of-state quantity, but allowed a floor for in-state waste equivalent to the prior year's total disposal of in-state waste; effectively, disposal of in-state generated waste would increase over time, whereas out-of-state waste would stay static or decrease.

211. Kleenwell Biohazard Waste v. Nelson, 48 F.3d 391, 398 (9th Cir. 1995).

212. *See* Harvey & Harvey, Inc. v. County of Chester, 68 F.3d 788, 791–92 (3d Cir. 1995); Atlantic Coast Demolition & Recycling, Inc. v. Board of Chosen Freeholders, 48 F.3d 701, 704–05, 707 (3d Cir. 1995); Eric S. Petersen & David N. Abramowitz, *Municipal Solid Waste Flow in the Post-*Carbone *World*, 22 FORDHAM URB. L.J. 361, n.33 (1995).

ordinances were important mechanisms for ensuring the economic viability of many local solid waste disposal facilities,[213] they violated the dormant Commerce Clause to the extent that they favored local economic interests, such as landfills, at the expense of out-of-state disposal facilities or transporters who otherwise would ship the waste out-of-state.

The Supreme Court so held in the landmark decision *C&A Carbone v. Town of Clarkstown*.[214] The town, required by the state to close its existing landfill and construct a solid waste transfer station that would separate recyclables and dispose of the remaining waste, contracted with a private operator who agreed to finance construction and operate the facility. The operator expected to satisfy its costs, and make a profit, out of tipping fees. To ensure adequate revenue, the town guaranteed a minimum flow of solid waste, and to ensure sufficient volume to provide the revenue, enacted an ordinance requiring that all nonhazardous solid waste generated, processed, or handled within town boundaries had to be deposited at the transfer station. A local recycler seeking to ship waste out-of-town challenged the ordinance as discriminating against interstate commerce.

The Supreme Court concluded that by monopolizing waste processing in the town facility, the ordinance impermissibly discriminated against the interstate commerce in servicing and transporting waste. It also found that the town had failed to demonstrate that it had no other means to advance the local purpose; general taxes and bonds were alternative, even if less convenient, available financial measures.

Following *Carbone*, a federal circuit court invalidated a New Jersey solid waste management plan that directed each district in the state to grant one facility an exclusive franchise for that district's waste disposal. Under the plan, all nonrecyclable waste generated in the district had to be disposed of at the designated facility. Out-of-state bidders could not compete for solid waste processing or disposal in the local market, in violation of the dormant Commerce Clause.[215]

[3] Market Participation by the State

There is a distinction between anti-competitive regulation of a market, and a state's participation in that market on a competitive basis. The "market participant doctrine" has long been recognized as exempting a state from dormant Commerce Clause constraints when the state itself has entered the market in a particular commodity. The Supreme Court, in *Hughes v. Alexandria Scrap Corp.*,[216] declared that nothing in the dormant Commerce Clause forbids a state's entry into the market in particular articles of interstate commerce when the state favors its own citizens in the trade. As with any

---

213. *See* Harvey & Harvey, Inc. v. County of Chester, 68 F.3d 788, 792 (3d Cir. 1995); Eric S. Petersen & David N. Abramowitz, *Municipal Solid Waste Flow in the Post-*Carbone *World*, 22 FORDHAM URB. L.J. 361, 365, n.5 (1995).

214. 511 U.S. 383 (1994).

215. *See Harvey & Harvey, Inc. v. County of Chester, 68 F.3d 788 (3d Cir. 1995)*.

216. 426 U.S. 794 (1976).

enterprise, the state may pick its business partners.[217] The Supreme Court noted the limits of the doctrine, though, in *South-Central Timber Development, Inc. v. Wunnicke*,[218] in which Alaska required buyers who purchased timber from the state to have the timber processed within Alaska. Alaska was not a participant in the timber-processing market. If the state had merely subsidized the timber-processing industry, so that the timber purchaser had a choice that might have led it to use a local processor, the dormant Commerce Clause would not have been violated. However, the state took this choice away from the buyer. It was using its dominant position in the timber-producing market to exert influence on the timber-processing market in favor of local businesses. The Supreme Court noted that "[t]he limit of the market-participant doctrine must be that it allows a state to impose burdens on commerce within the market in which it is a participant, but allows it to go no further. The state may not impose conditions … that have a substantial regulatory effect outside of that particular market."[219]

In *United Haulers Association, Inc. v. Oneida-Herkimer Solid Waste Management Authority*,[220] the Supreme Court returned to the problem of parsing the difference between a community's unconstitutional regulation of the interstate market in solid waste, and the local laws that favor the public participant in the marketplace while treating all private businesses, in-state and out-of-state, equally. The Supreme Court noted that the challenged flow control ordinance was similar to that in *Carbone*, except for the "salient difference" that the ordinance in *United Haulers Association* required haulers to bring solid waste to facilities owned and operated by a state-created public benefit corporation, whereas the facility in *Carbone* was private. The Court found this distinction to be "constitutionally significant" since any incidental burden on interstate commerce did not outweigh the benefits to county residents, and did not violate the dormant Commerce Clause. The dissent, though, found no meaningful difference from *Carbone*, found the public-private distinction to be "illusory," and concluded that discrimination against interstate commerce exists, and is unconstitutional, regardless of whether the monopoly is public or private.

In the solid waste disposal context, a town operating a landfill has been deemed to be entitled to charge lower fees for locally generated waste; this was not a town regulation requiring town-generated garbage to be disposed of in the town-operated landfill, or discriminating against non-local waste.[221] The town was merely exercising its entrepreneurial prerogative in favor of its taxpayers who paid the landfill's operating expenses.

---

217. SSC Corp. v. Town of Smithtown, 66 F.3d 502, 510 (2d Cir. 1995), *cert. denied*, 516 U.S. 1112 (1996).

218. 467 U.S. 82 (1984).

219. South-Central Timber Development, Inc. v. Wunnicke, 467 U.S. 82, 96–97 (1984).

220. United Haulers Association, Inc. v. Oneida-Herkimer Solid Waste Management Authority, 550 U.S. 330, 127 S. Ct. 1786, 167 L. Ed. 2d 655 (2007).

221. Swin Resource Systems, Inc. v. Lycoming County, 883 F.2d 245 (3d Cir. 1989).

§ 7.05 Hazardous Waste Management: The Resource Conservation Recovery Act (RCRA)

[A] RCRA Goals

The Resource Conservation and Recovery Act (RCRA), aside from its general regulation of solid waste disposal, has also become the major part of a regulatory web governing hazardous wastes "from cradle to grave." It complements the Comprehensive Environmental Response, Compensation and Liability Act (CERCLA) (see § 7.06), which establishes financial liability for cleanup of hazardous waste sites, by providing a detailed regulatory regime to reduce hazardous waste releases and inappropriate disposal. RCRA is complemented by the Emergency Planning and Community Right to Know Act (EPCRA) (see § 7.08), which requires emergency planning for potential releases caused by, and dissemination of information about, local activities involving hazardous substances. There are also numerous state statutes modeled on RCRA. By its terms, RCRA seeks to achieve "resource conservation," meaning the reduction of solid waste volume and decreased resource consumption through resource recovery — extracting reusable material and energy from solid waste.[222] Recovered material, the waste material and byproducts recovered from solid waste, is excluded if reused within an original manufacturing process.[223] These protocols are especially applicable when the solid waste is hazardous, as defined by the statute.

RCRA addresses hazardous waste management, requiring systematic control of the collection, storage, transportation, processing, treatment, and disposal of hazardous wastes.[224] RCRA regulates generators and transporters of hazardous wastes, as well as facilities that treat, store, and dispose of hazardous wastes. RCRA is largely administered by the states under delegations similar to those under the Clean Water Act (see § 6.03). RCRA also regulates certain kinds of underground storage tanks which, when they leak, can pollute groundwater (see § 6.04[D]). EPA may delegate RCRA enforcement authority to a state upon satisfaction of certain requirements demonstrating that the state can and will carry out the federal goals (see 7.05[I]).[225] However, the state's regulatory requirements must be at least as stringent as those required by the federal program.[226] If EPA finds that the state program fails to achieve the federal goals either in implementation of its program or enforcement and thereby violates RCRA, EPA must revoke its authorization, placing that state under EPA-enforced RCRA regulations.[227]

---

222. 42 U.S.C. § 6903(22).
223. 42 U.S.C. § 6903(19).
224. 42 U.S.C. § 6903(7).
225. 42 U.S.C. § 6926(b).
226. 42 U.S.C. § 6929; *see* United States v. Richter, 796 F.3d 1173 (10th Cir. 2015); Premier Associates, Inc. v. EXL Polymers, Inc., 507 Fed. Appx. 831 (11th Cir. 2013).
227. 42 U.S.C. § 6926(e); 40 C.F.R. § 271.22, 271.23; Public Citizen, Inc. v. Environmental Protection Agency, 343 F.3d 449 (5th Cir. 2003).

RCRA's regulation of hazardous wastes, as administered by EPA, has the following three goals:[228]

- To establish a nationwide, comprehensive, tracking system, bolstered by extensive documentation and recording requirements, for the movement of all hazardous wastes from point of origin to final disposal;

- To prevent the release of hazardous wastes, and to ensure their safe disposal; and

- To ensure compliance with tracking requirements, as well as treatment, storage, and disposal (TSD) requirements, with an effective enforcement mechanism.

[B] Wastes Subject to RCRA Regulation Because They Are "Hazardous"

[1] Defining Hazardous Wastes

All hazardous wastes are regulated by RCRA. The difficulty, though, lies in determining exactly what is a hazardous waste. Hazardous waste is a category of solid waste, discussed more generally in §§ 7.02 through 7.04. A waste (which actually may be solid, liquid, or gaseous) is hazardous if it "may cause or contribute to an increase in mortality or an increase in serious irreversible or incapacitating reversible illness," or "pose[s] a substantial present or potential hazard to human health or the environment when improperly treated, stored, transported or disposed of or otherwise managed."[229]

EPA defines solid waste as "discarded material."[230] As with the definition of "disposed of" discussed in § 7.02[A][2], the common usage of the term can be applied to "discarded," but the textual definition embraces a host of synonyms in order to keep a range of activities within the regulatory reach. Some of the lawyerly creativity in early caselaw attempting to carve out exceptions for clients justified this semantic diligence. A material is "discarded" if it is "abandoned," "recycled," or "inherently waste-like."[231] A material is abandoned if it is "disposed of, burned or incinerated," or "accumulated, stored or treated (but not recycled) in lieu of disposal, burning or incineration."[232] By contrast, a material or substance that is being used as intended is not a "waste," even though it may be hazardous,[233]although a useful product, becoming exhausted and thereby losing its usefulness, may then be deemed a waste upon disposal.[234]

---

228. See generally 42 U.S.C. § 6901.
229. 42 U.S.C. § 6903(5).
230. 40 C.F.R. § 261.2(a); see 50 Fed. Reg. 614.
231. 40 C.F.R. § 261.2(a)(2).
232. 40 C.F.R. § 261.2(b).
233. Cordiano v. Metacon Gun Club, Inc., 575 F.3d 199 (2d Cir. 2009), illustrates the point under facts that could mislead the analysis if one loses sight of the useful, and thus non-wasteful, nature of the material. Lead bullets, although potentially hazardous, when shot are being used as intended, and are not thus deemed to be discarded, even if they are essentially non-retrievable.
234. See Howmet Corp. v. Environmental Protection Agency, 614 F.3d 544 (D.C. Cir. 2010), where a corrosive solution being used for mechanical cleaning became contaminated over time — and thus no longer useful as a cleaning solvent — was sold as a spent material to a fertilizer manufacturer with the intent that it would become a constituent of the fertilizer. Although that was a "use,"

[2] Hazardous Waste Criteria

EPA specifically lists numerous wastes as being hazardous, automatically bringing them within RCRA regulation.[235] In addition, an unlisted waste is hazardous if it has certain characteristics.[236] A waste must be listed as hazardous if it is any of the following:

- Ignitable, with a flash point lower than 140 degrees Fahrenheit;[237]

- Corrosive, with a pH of 2.0 or less, or 12.5 or greater;[238]

- Reactive, meaning chemically unstable, likely to detonate if heated or when introduced to water, or, when mixed with water, produces toxic emissions;[239]

- Characteristically toxic;[240] or

- Contains constituents known to have toxic, carcinogenic, mutagenic, or teratogenic effects.[241]

[3] Materials "Mixed With" Hazardous Wastes

If a nonhazardous solid waste is mixed with a listed hazardous waste, the resulting compound is hazardous[242] regardless of the relative quantity of the hazardous constituents.[243] This is designed to prevent a new, unlisted, chemical compound, formed out of hazardous constituents, from evading regulation by using the expedient of also incorporating nonhazardous constituents.[244] Regulation of the mixed compound under RCRA does not preclude regulation under other laws.[245]

[4] Exclusions

The following materials are expressly excluded[246] from the term "solid waste" (see § 7.02), and hence from "hazardous waste":

---

it was not the use for which the solution was manufactured and was discarded by being incorporated into the fertilizer. By contrast, even if the cleaning solution could no longer be used to clean a particular product, but could still be as a cleaning solution for other products, it is not, in that context, spent, and is not discarded upon being used thus. See 50 Fed. Reg. 614.

235. *See* 40 C.F.R. Part 261, Subpart D.
236. *See* 40 C.F.R. §§ 261.11, 261.20–261.24.
237. 40 C.F.R. § 261.21.
238. 40 C.F.R. § 261.22.
239. 40 C.F.R. § 261.23.
240. 40 C.F.R. § 261.24.
241. The listed toxic constituents are included in 40 C.F.R. Part 261, Appendix VIII. *See* 40 C.F.R. § 261.11(a)(3).
242. 40 C.F.R. § 261.3(a)(2)(iii), (iv).
243. B.F. Goodrich v. Murtha, 99 F.3d 505 (2d Cir. 1996); Louisiana-Pacific v. Asarco, Inc., 24 F.3d 1565, 1573 (9th Cir. 1994), *cert. denied*, 513 U.S. 1103 (1995).
244. 57 Fed. Reg. 7628.
245. For instance, the expedient of mixing radioactive material with other substances, thereby triggering RCRA regulation, would not shield the compound from regulation under the Atomic Energy Act, at 42 U.S.C. § 2011 *et seq. See* State of Washington v. Chu, 558 F.3d 1036 (9th Cir. 2009).
246. 42 U.S.C. § 6903(27).

- Domestic sewage, either solid or dissolved (untreated sanitary wastes that pass through a sewer system or a Publicly Owned Treatment Work (POTW) (see §6.03[C][3]) for treatment);[247]

- Materials in irrigation return flows;[248]

- Discharges covered by the Clean Water Act; however, on-site treatment or storage of wastewater, or sludge resulting from industrial wastewater treatment, does fall within RCRA as a solid waste;[249] and

- Nuclear materials covered by the Atomic Energy Act.[250]

EPA also has excluded household wastes[251] from hazardous waste regulation, although municipal incinerator ash waste,[252] even when derived from household wastes,[253] may be hazardous, depending on its toxicity. However, household waste exempt from RCRA may still be subject to cleanup cost actions under CERCLA (see §7.06).

Polychlorinated Biphenyls (PCBs) are exclusively regulated under the Toxic Substances Control Act (TSCA) (see §8.02[E][4]), and not RCRA,[254] unless there are PCBs within a hazardous waste stream.[255] Agricultural pesticide use, regulated under the Federal Insecticide, Fungicide, and Rodenticide Act (FIFRA) (see §8.01) is exempt from RCRA,[256] subject only to the requirement that pesticide containers be cleaned and disposed of in specified manners (e.g., farmers must triple rinse emptied containers and dispose of them on their own farm).[257]

Ambiguities still occur in how some seemingly hazardous wastes are governed. Notwithstanding their likely hazardous constituents, coal ash, fly ash, bottom ash and other end products of the generation of electricity are defined merely as solid wastes rather than the more rigorously governed hazardous wastes.[258]

---

247. 40 C.F.R. §261.4(a)(1)(ii). One court has even excluded sanitary/hazardous waste mixtures that were diverted from the intended POTW because of a cracked sewer line. *See* Comte Pro Rescate de la Salud v. Puerto Rico Aqueduct and Sewer Authority, 693 F. Supp. 1324 (D.P.R. 1988).

248. Note that the Clean Water Act has a similar exclusion (33 U.S.C. §1352(14), discussed in §6.03).

249. 40 C.F.R. §261.4(a)(2).

250. *See* Train v. Colorado Public Interest Research Group, 426 U.S. 1 (1976). However, the exclusion would not preclude RCRA regulation should radioactive material be mixed with other wastes so as to create a new hazardous waste. *See* State of Washington v. Chu, 558 F.3d 1036 (9th Cir. 2009).

251. 40 C.F.R. §261.4(b)(1).

252. *See* Environmental Defense Fund v. Wheelabrator Technologies, Inc., 725 F. Supp. 758 (S.D.N.Y. 1989), *aff'd*, 931 F.2d 211 (2d Cir. 1991), *cert. denied*, 502 U.S. 974 (1991). *But see* Environmental Defense Fund v. City of Chicago, 948 F.2d 345 (7th Cir. 1991)506 U.S. 982 (1992), *on remand*, 985 F.2d 303 (1993) (not exempt).

253. *See* E.P.A., *Characteristics of Municipal Waste Combustor Ashes and Leachates from Municipal Solid Waste Landfills, Monofills, and Codisposal Sites*, 52 Fed. Reg. 49,080 (1987).

254. Brewer v. Ravan, 680 F. Supp. 1176 (M.D. Tenn. 1988).

255. *See* 52 Fed. Reg. 25,760 (July 6, 1988).

256. 40 C.F.R. §§264.1(g)(4), 265.1(c)(8), 270.1(c)(2)(ii).

257. 40 C.F.R. §262.70.

258. 40 C.F.R. §261.4; Solvay USA, Inc. v. Environmental Protection Agency, 608 Fed. Appx. 10 (D.C. Cir. 2015). A 2015 EPA rule that directed how "coal combustible residuals" (CCRs) must be

[C] Generators

[1] Requirements

Generators include persons or facilities that produce (or import) hazardous wastes. Generators occupy the first step in RCRA's "cradle to grave" regime.

RCRA imposes broad responsibilities on generators, including record keeping obligations,[259] labeling practices,[260] use of appropriate containers,[261] and providing information about the chemical composition of wastes to transporters and TSD facilities.[262] Most importantly, generators must submit comprehensive manifests to track the wastes and state to whom they conveyed the hazardous wastes.[263] In addition, the generators must certify that they have an in-place waste-reduction program.[264]

Generators must determine whether their waste is hazardous; there is no defense of lack of knowledge.[265] Every generator must obtain an identification number as a predicate to shipping or arranging for treatment, storage, or disposal of any hazardous waste.[266] The manifest, a shipping document itemizing the nature and quantity of the waste being transported,[267] is the cornerstone of the RCRA tracking system. Copies of the manifest must travel with the waste at every step.[268] When a TSD facility receives the hazardous waste shipment, it must send a signed copy of the completed manifest back to the generator, who must maintain the record for three years from date of shipment.[269] Additionally, generators must package, label, and provide warnings on, the hazardous waste.

[2] Generators that Act as Treatment, Storage, and Disposal Facilities

Generators that treat, store, or dispose of hazardous waste on-site must comply with certain of RCRA's TSD (see [E], *below*) requirements.[270] A generator accumulating hazardous wastes at the facility in excess of 90 days is deemed to also operate a storage facility.[271]

---

disposed of also defined these materials only as solid wastes. 80 Fed. Reg. 21,302. Nevertheless, the design and operational requirements are exacting. *See* Utility Solid Waste Activities Group v. Environmental Protection Agency, 901 F.3d 414 (D.C. Cir. 2018).

259. 40 C.F.R. § 262.40.
260. 40 C.F.R. § 262.31.
261. 40 C.F.R. §§ 262.30, 262.32.
262. 42 U.S.C. § 6922(a)(4).
263. 40 C.F.R. §§ 262.20–262.23.
264. 42 U.S.C. § 6922(b).
265. 40 C.F.R. § 262.11.
266. 40 C.F.R. § 262.12.
267. 40 C.F.R. §§ 262.22, 262.23, 262.50(b)(3), (b)(4), (d), (e).
268. 40 C.F.R. §§ 262.22, 262.23.
269. 40 C.F.R. § 262.40(a).
270. 40 C.F.R. § 262.11(c).
271. 40 C.F.R. § 262.34.

[3] Small Generators

Generators of less than 100 kilograms of hazardous waste per month are exempt from the requirements set forth in [1] and [2], *above.*[272] However, if the waste is acutely hazardous, the monthly threshold for regulation is only one kilogram of waste.[273] Small quantity generators nevertheless must dispose of the wastes on-site or at an approved TSD (see [E], *below*) facility.[274]

[D] Transporters

[1] Custody and Tracking of Hazardous Waste Shipments

The transportation of hazardous wastes, which can be undertaken by truck, rail, ship and even air, has been burdened by a lengthy and complicated regulatory history. Early laws, prior to the modern era of environmental law, applied to the shipment of explosives and other dangerous substances. The shipment was often interstate, which came under the jurisdiction of the Interstate Commerce Commission. With the advent of air shipments, the Federal Aviation Administration also was vested with jurisdiction. Many of these laws continue to apply.[275]

Today, though, in the main, transporters are largely regulated under the Hazardous Materials Transportation Act,[276] administered by the Department of Transportation, rather than under RCRA. However, RCRA imposes manifest, labeling, and record keeping obligations. Transporters are responsible for ensuring that hazardous wastes are transported only to the TSD facility designated on the manifest and that the facility holds a permit.[277]

Before transporting the hazardous waste, the transporter must sign and date the manifest, giving a copy to the generator.[278] The original manifest travels with the shipment, with each subsequent transporter signing and dating a copy that is given to the prior transporter, until final delivery to the TSD facility.[279] Each transporter must maintain records for three years dating from the original acceptance of the waste.[280]

[2] Spills During Transport

Transporters must respond to a spill or discharge during transport, and must take appropriate immediate action to protect human health and the environment.[281] The

---

272. 40 C.F.R. § 261.5.
273. 40 C.F.R. § 261.5(e).
274. 40 C.F.R. § 261.5(g)(3), (f)(3).
275. For a history of this area of regulation, see *United States v. Sabretech, Inc.*, 271 F.3d 1018 (11th Cir. 2001).
276. 49 U.S.C. § 1801, *et seq.; 49 C.F.R. Subchapter C.*
277. 42 U.S.C. § 6923(a).
278. 40 C.F.R. § 263.20(b).
279. 40 C.F.R. § 263.20(c), (d).
280. 40 C.F.R. § 263.22(a).
281. 40 C.F.R. § 263.30(a).

transporter is responsible for the cleanup and must take any steps necessary to elim-inate any resulting hazard.[282]

[E] Treatment, Storage, and Disposal (TSD) Facilities

[1] Definitions

[a] "Facility"

The core of RCRA's hazardous waste regulation is the permitting system, pursuant to which hazardous wastes are treated, stored, and finally disposed of, at facilities collectively termed hazardous waste management, or "TSD" facilities. However, the manufacturer of the substance is not included as a RCRA TSD facility, unless it treats, stores or disposes of the end product.[283]

As with other federal environmental statutes that employ permitting schemes, permit obligations and liabilities are imposed on owners and operators of facilities. A "facility" is broadly defined to include "all contiguous land, and structures, other appurtenances, and improvements on the land, used for treating, storing, or disposing of hazardous waste."[284]

[b] "Storage"

"Storage" cannot serve as a disguised disposal where the "stored" hazardous waste left on-site perpetually evades the costs of a safe disposal at an appropriate disposal facility. Storage is the "containment of hazardous waste, either on a temporary basis or for a number of years, in such a manner as not to constitute disposal,"[285] although EPA restricts non-disposal storage to only "temporary periods."[286] If the storage man-ner or time period suggests disposal, the storage facility may actually be subject to permitting as a disposal facility. Storage and disposal are mutually exclusive. If an extended period of purported storage at an off-site facility begins to look as though the wastes were abandoned, they may be found to have been discarded and thus dis-posed of which, if done knowingly, may expose the defendant to criminal liability.[287] Courts will examine the substance of the conduct rather than how a defendant de-scribes the activity in determining which permit was required and whether the failure to obtain that permit was a RCRA violation.[288] Moreover, for criminal liability, the defendant only has to know that the wastes are being stored without a permit, re-

---

282. 40 C.F.R. § 263.31.
283. United States v. Union Corp., 277 F. Supp. 2d 478 (E.D. Pa. 2003).
284. 40 C.F.R. § 260.10(a).
285. 42 U.S.C. § 6903(33).
286. 40 C.F.R. § 260.10(a).
287. United States v. Evertson, 320 Fed. Appx. 509 (9th Cir. 2009).
288. *Compare* United States v. Humphries, 728 F.3d 1028 (9th Cir. 2013), *with* United States v Roach, 792 F.3d 1142 (9th Cir. 2015). Readers should note that if the illegal storage isn't terminated, it tolls the statute of limitations as a continuing crime. United States v. Tonawanda Coke Corp., 636 Fed. Appx. 24 (2d Cir. 2016).

gardless of whether he knows that a permit was necessary or that the activity violated RCRA or otherwise was illegal.[289]

RCRA also imposes comprehensive design, operating and, if a release occurs, corrective action requirements, for underground storage tanks (USTs).[290] These often store petroleum products such as fuel, but also chemicals. Given the potential for substantial consequences for groundwater and other environmental impacts should a UST leak (see § 6.04[d]), these requirements are exacting. As with other RCRA programs, EPA may approve a state's UST program, which must be at least as rigorous as federal requirements.[291] Absent EPA approval, a state UST program cannot displace federal requirements.[292]

[c] "Disposal"

RCRA defines "disposal" as the "discharge, deposit, injection, dumping, spilling, leaking, or placing of any . . . hazardous waste into or on any land or water so that such . . . waste or any constituent thereof may enter the environment or be emitted into the air or discharged into any waters, including ground waters."[293] As a practical matter, this covers any intentional or unintentional release of hazardous wastes.[294] The regulations limit the term by defining a "disposal facility" as one where hazardous waste is "intentionally placed into or on any land or water and at which waste will remain after closure."[295] Disposal facilities may consist of landfills, land treatment facilities, surface impoundments, waste piles, tanks, incinerators, or any combination of these at the same location.[296] Note that RCRA has imposed a "land ban" on the landfilling of hazardous wastes under many circumstances (see § 7.05[F][3]). However, if a hazardous material is encapsulated in such a manner that it is not likely, nor intended to enter the environment, there is no disposal of the hazardous material as waste.[297]

An unpermitted disposal under RCRA could also result in violations of the Clean Water Act if it causes an unpermitted discharge into waters of the United States (see § 6.03[B]), and the Safe Drinking Water Act if it contaminates an aquifer falling within that statute (see § 6.04[C]). However, the provisions of the various environ-

---

289. United States v. Spatig, 870 F.3d 1079 (9th Cir. 2017).

290. 42 U.S.C. § 6991, *et seq.*

291. 42 U.S.C. § 6991c.

292. Sanchez v. Esso Standard Oil Co., 572 F.3d 1 (1st Cir. 2009); Boyes v. Shell Oil Products Co., 199 F.3d 1260 (11th Cir. 2000).

293. 42 U.S.C. § 6903(3).

294. The Ninth Circuit, however, in what may be an outlier decision, concluded that emissions into the air would not fall within RCRA's definition of disposal. Center for Community Action and Environmental Justice v. BNSF Railway Co., 764 F.3d 1019 (9th Cir. 2014).

295. 40 C.F.R. § 260.10.

296. 40 C.F.R. § 264.

297. Sycamore Industrial Park Associates v. Ericsson, 546 F.3d 847 (7th Cir. 2008).

mental statutes must be cross-referenced to ensure that the administration or any enforcement action taken under RCRA does not interfere with the goals of those other statutes.[298]

[d] "Treatment"

RCRA defines "treatment" of hazardous wastes as "any method, technique or process, including neutralization, designed to change the physical, chemical or biological character or composition of any hazardous waste so as to neutralize such waste or so as to render such waste nonhazardous, safer ... or reduced in volume...."[299] This encompasses thermal treatment (incineration), land treatment, "totally enclosed" treatment, chemical, physical and biological treatment facilities, wastewater treatment units, and "elementary neutralization" units.[300] Totally enclosed treatment units refer to piping through which, for instance, acid is neutralized, and from which a release is unlikely. Elementary neutralization units are tanks in which corrosive materials are neutralized.[301]

Hazardous wastes are applied to the soil surface in land treatment facilities, but, as with other treatment facilities, they become disposal facilities if the wastes remain after closure.[302]

[2] TSD Permits

As with other environmental permits, RCRA permits are information-driven. However, in addition to the narrative type information required of permit applicants generally, RCRA applicants also must provide site histories, and must evaluate the potential for hazardous waste releases and public exposure arising from normal operation, accidents, and discharges during transportation.[303]

Permit applications, issuances, and revocations require public notice and a comment period,[304] during which interested persons may request a hearing,[305] which must be conducted if there is a "significant degree of public interest."[306] Hearings are generally non-adversarial, although cross-examination of witnesses may be conducted on request.[307] Final decision is made after the close of the comment period, or the

---

298. 42 U.S.C. § 6905(a); Ecological Rights Foundation v. Pacific Gas & Electric Co., 874 F.3d 1083 (9th Cir. 2017).
    299. 42 U.S.C. § 6903(34).
    300. 40 C.F.R. §§ 261.10(a), 270.2.
    301. 40 C.F.R. §§ 264.1(g)(5), (g)(6); 45 Fed. Reg. 76,074 (Nov. 17, 1980).
    302. 40 C.F.R. §§ 260.10(a), 270.2.
    303. 40 C.F.R. §§ 270.14–270.21.
    304. 40 C.F.R. § 124.10.
    305. 40 C.F.R. §§ 124.11, 124.13.
    306. 40 C.F.R. § 124.12(a).
    307. 40 C.F.R. § 124.12(e).

conclusion of the hearing, upon public notice, and responses to "interested" parties' comments are provided.[308] Administrative appeals are available,[309] as is judicial review upon exhaustion of administrative remedies.[310]

Permits are for a term not to exceed 10 years,[311] and may be terminated or revoked after an evidentiary hearing.[312]

If the facility seeks to transfer the permit, it may be modified to reflect the new ownership.[313] A facility may operate under interim status without a permit pending disposition of its permit application.[314] Interim status facilities are limited to accepting the type of hazardous waste for which the original permit application was made.

Permits are required during a facility's active life, closure, and post-closure.[315]

It should be noted that the activities discussed above are sometimes regulated under other statutes. For example, waste disposal may require Clean Water Act permitting if the discharge is into navigable water, or to a POTW (see § 6.03); the Marine Protection, Research and Sanctuaries Act governs ocean dumping (see § 6.05[C]); and injection wells may trigger the Safe Drinking Water Act (see § 6.04[C]). RCRA permitting is required to the extent that such other permitting schemes do not apply.[316] Persons obtaining permits under other environmental statutes for conduct otherwise covered by RCRA need not obtain a separate RCRA permit,[317] although they must satisfy some additional RCRA requirements.[318]

RCRA permits do not confer property rights or exclusive privileges on permittees, and do not authorize any violation of state statutory or common law.[319] Nor is a RCRA permit a defense to a CERCLA abatement (see § 7.06[A][4]) or cost recovery action (see § 7.06[C], [D]), or to an action to abate an imminent hazard under RCRA (see [J][3], *below*).[320]

---

308. 40 C.F.R. § 124.15.

309. 40 C.F.R. § 124.19.

310. 40 C.F.R. § 124.19(e).

311. 40 C.F.R. § 270.50.

312. 40 C.F.R. § 124.71.

313. 40 C.F.R. § 270.41(b).

314. 42 U.S.C. § 6925(e); 40 C.F.R. § 265.1; *see* 40 C.F.R. § 264.3.

315. *See* 42 U.S.C. § 6925; 40 C.F.R. §§ 264.110–264.120.

316. *See, e.g.*, Inland Steel Co. v. Environmental Protection Agency, 901 F.2d 1419 (7th Cir. 1990) (if discharge is not to navigable waters, it nevertheless may be from a solid waste management facility, triggering RCRA).

317. 40 C.F.R. § 270.60.

318. *See* 40 C.F.R. § 264.

319. 40 C.F.R. § 270.4.

320. *See* 42 U.S.C. § 6973.

[F] TSD Facility Standards

[1] Tracking and Identification

TSD facilities must provide notification when hazardous wastes are accepted from transporters pursuant to manifesting requirements.[321] They must undertake detailed chemical and physical analyses of any new hazardous waste or hazardous waste from a new generator, or whenever the facility has reason to believe that a generator's process or operation has been significantly modified.[322]

[2] Safety

TSD facility locations are restricted in seismically active areas or flood plains.[323] Facilities must restrict entry to the site and otherwise ensure that persons will not be exposed to the hazardous waste.[324] Equipment, monitoring operations, emergency equipment, and security devices must be regularly inspected, inspection records must be maintained for three years,[325] and all employees must receive emergency, security, and operational training.[326]

Waste must be treated, stored, and disposed of in a manner that will prevent reactivity or ignition.[327] A facility's design, construction, maintenance, and operation must be directed against the risk of fire, explosion, or unanticipated releases.[328] The facility also must make arrangements with local emergency authorities to deal with releases[329] (see § 7.08 for discussion of emergency planning), and have a contingency plan to address the consequences of fire, explosion, or unanticipated releases.[330]

[3] The "Land Ban"

Widespread groundwater contamination led to a prohibition on the disposal of noncontainerized hazardous wastes or free liquids contained in hazardous wastes in landfills. The landfill disposal of liquids that absorb into biodegradable material, or in materials that extrude wastes when compressed, such as normally occurs in a landfill operation, also are prohibited.[331]

RCRA also prohibits the landfill disposal of specified wastes, unless EPA determines that the disposal would not affect human health or the environment "for as long as

321. 40 C.F.R. § 264.12.
322. 40 C.F.R. § 264.13(a)(1), (3).
323. 40 C.F.R. §§ 264.14(b)(11), 270.18.
324. 40 C.F.R. § 264.14.
325. 40 C.F.R. § 264.15.
326. 40 C.F.R. § 264.16.
327. 40 C.F.R. § 264.17.
328. 40 C.F.R. § 264.31.
329. 40 C.F.R. § 264.37.
330. 40 C.F.R. §§ 270.14(b), 270.50–270.56.
331. 42 U.S.C. § 6924(c).

the waste remains hazardous."[332] In other words, these wastes may not be landfilled unless treated. EPA must take into account the persistence, toxicity, mobility, and propensity to bioaccumulate of the particular hazardous wastes and their constituents. It also must be demonstrated to a reasonable degree of certainty that the wastes will not migrate for as long as they remain hazardous.[333] The listed wastes, in specified concentrations, include cyanide, arsenic, cadmium, chromium, lead, mercury, nickel, PCBs, solvents and dioxins, and liquid acids.[334] The prohibition also extends to hazardous wastes that are mixed with radioactive waste.[335]

Treatments available to avoid the land ban include chemical destruction (usually incineration), or immobilization. EPA has rejected land treatment — incorporating the waste into the soil so as to degrade — as a viable treatment method for banned wastes.[336]

As a result of the land ban, many of these hazardous wastes either are not being generated, or are being reused and recycled, effectively eliminating much of the problem.

[4] Groundwater Protection, Monitoring, and Corrective Action

[a] Groundwater Protection Obligation

Surface impoundments and landfills have specific groundwater protection obligations, including groundwater monitoring, double liners to prevent leaching into groundwater, and a leachate collection system.[337] The protective obligations and monitoring are required, at a minimum, for the life of the facility, or in some cases for a 30 year post-closure period.[338] If groundwater has been contaminated by the facility, there may be additional requirements.[339]

[b] Detection Monitoring

Detection monitoring requires periodic sampling for "indicator parameters" and specific hazardous constituents.[340] If the hazardous constituents increase, the facility must immediately conduct sampling to determine if listed hazardous constituents are present. If hazardous constituents are found, the facility becomes subject to compliance monitoring.[341]

---

332. 42 U.S.C. § 6924(d).

333. 42 U.S.C. § 6924(d)(1).

334. 42 U.S.C. § 6924(d)(2), (e).

335. State of Washington v. Chu, 558 F.3d 1036 (9th Cir. 2009).

336. American Petroleum Institute v. Environmental Protection Agency, 906 F.2d 729 (D.C. Cir. 1990).

337. 42 U.S.C. § 6924(o)(1)(A); 40 C.F.R. §§ 264.222 (surface impoundments), 264.252 (waste piles), 264.302 (landfills).

338. 40 C.F.R. §§ 264.90(c), 264.96.

339. 40 C.F.R. §§ 264.93–264.95.

340. 40 C.F.R. § 264.98.

341. 40 C.F.R. §§ 264.98(h)(4), 264.91(a)(1), 264.99. Listed hazardous constituents are set forth in 52 Fed. Reg. 25,942 (July 9, 1987).

[c] Compliance Monitoring

Compliance monitoring requires that several wells be located by, and down gradient from, the part of the facility where hazardous constituents would have been released.[342] If the groundwater protection standard is exceeded, corrective action is required, such as excavation and removal of contaminated soil, collection of leachate, prevention or collection of runoff, extracting and treating groundwater, and preventing migration off-site. The goal is to reduce hazardous constituents to below the limits specified in the permit. Corrective action may be suspended when the groundwater protection standard has not been exceeded for three successive years.[343]

[d] Corrective Action

The statute also requires facilities to take corrective action for any contamination at the facility, regardless of when it occurred. If the corrective action cannot be completed before the issuance of a permit, the permit must incorporate a compliance schedule, and must require financial assurances that the corrective action will be completed.[344] Facilities also must take corrective action beyond facility boundaries if necessary to protect human health or the environment.[345]

[5] Financial Assurance

RCRA imposes one of the following financial responsibility requirements on TSD facilities:[346] liability insurance, self-insurance, or a corporate guarantee by a parent company.[347] For closure and post-closure, financial responsibility can be assured by trust fund, surety bond, letter of credit, insurance, self-insurance, or any combination of these.[348] Insurance coverage must include sudden as well as gradual occurrences, such as migration of pollutants into groundwater.[349]

[G] Closure and Post-Closure Requirements

All TSD facilities must comply with detailed and comprehensive closure and post-closure requirements. Facilities must submit closure and post-closure plans to EPA for approval, notify the local land use authority as to post-closure restrictions on the property, and record an instrument of title including the land use restrictions.[350] Methods of closure include capping and leachate collection, and removal and treatment of remaining hazardous wastes or constituents. Post-closure controls are re-

---

342. 40 C.F.R. § 264.99(a), (b).
343. 40 C.F.R. § 264.100(e).
344. 42 U.S.C. § 6924(u).
345. 42 U.S.C. § 6924(v).
346. 42 U.S.C. § 6924(a)(6).
347. 40 C.F.R. § 264.147.
348. 40 C.F.R. §§ 264.143 (closure), 264.145 (post-closure).
349. 40 C.F.R. § 264.140(g).
350. 40 C.F.R. §§ 264.112–264.120.

quired for 30 years, although EPA may increase or decrease the period on the basis of its determination of hazard.[351] During that period, the site must be maintained, including groundwater monitoring.[352]

[H] Inspections, Reporting, and Monitoring

Much information is made available by the manifesting system. However, the EPA and state authorities also have broad powers to acquire more targeted, on-site, information. Any generator, transporter, or TSD facility is required, on request by EPA or an authorized official of an approved state agency, to furnish information about its hazardous wastes. Regulated parties also must allow access and copying of relevant records during reasonable hours. Unless consented to, though, entry must be accompanied by a search warrant.[353] Officials also are authorized to inspect and obtain samples of wastes, and samples of hazardous waste containers and labeling.[354] However, the information requested must bear some relationship to the hazardous wastes. Although EPA may demand more than a simple description of the waste, questions about facility finances and insurance coverage during a site inspection are beyond the scope of the inspector's authority.[355] EPA, or approved states, are required to inspect every TSD facility every two years.[356]

Any records, reports, or information obtained from regulated parties must be available to the public. There is an exception for trade secrets, although even those documents are available to officials acting under color of RCRA. Unlawful disclosure of valid trade secret information subjects the violator to fines and/or incarceration. Any and all information, though, must be made available to Congress on request.[357]

Federal as well as state facilities also may be inspected by federal and state officials to ensure compliance with RCRA.

If, upon receiving information, EPA or an approved state determines either that the presence of hazardous wastes at a site, or its release, may present a substantial hazard to human health or the environment (see [J][3], *below*), it can order the facility to conduct monitoring, testing, analysis, and reporting to the extent necessary to ascertain the nature and extent of any hazard,[358] including groundwater monitoring and the like.

[I] Delegation to States

RCRA permit and enforcement authority may be delegated by EPA to qualifying states. Any state that seeks to administer and enforce a hazardous waste program

---

351. 40 C.F.R. § 264.117(a).
352. *Id.*
353. Marshall v. Barlow's, Inc., 436 U.S. 307 (1978).
354. 42 U.S.C. § 6927(a).
355. *See* United States v. Charles George Tucker Co., 642 F. Supp. 329 (D. Mass. 1986).
356. 42 U.S.C. § 6927(e).
357. 42 U.S.C. § 6927(b).
358. 42 U.S.C. § 6934(a).

may submit the proposal to EPA, after public notice and an opportunity for a public hearing. The state program must be the equivalent of the federal program, and must provide an adequate level of enforcement.[359] EPA also retains the authority to insert its own permit conditions in lieu of state conditions.[360] If the state program is approved, then action taken by the state has the same force and effect as an EPA action.[361]

If EPA determines after a public hearing that the state's administrative and enforcement efforts are inadequate, after first notifying the state and affording an opportunity for correction, EPA may withdraw approval.[362]

[J] Enforcement

[1] Administrative and Civil Enforcement

EPA has the option of the following enforcement strategies:[363]

- Administrative compliance order with a civil penalty;
- Administrative order revoking or suspending a permit; and
- Civil federal court action seeking penalties and/or injunctive relief.

A compliance order must allow the violator a public hearing upon request.[364] If the violator fails to take corrective action in the time specified in the compliance order, that failure constitutes a separate violation, and is a basis to suspend or revoke the permit.[365]

[2] Criminal Penalties

RCRA authorizes criminal enforcement, generally predicated on a knowing violation, such as being aware that one's conduct is substantially certain to cause danger of death or serious bodily injury.[366]

Criminal liability may be imposed if the defendant knowingly does any of the following:[367]

- Transports hazardous waste to a facility lacking a permit;
- Treats, stores, or disposes of hazardous waste without a permit, or in knowing violation of a permit's material condition, or regulations or standards;

---

359. 42 U.S.C. § 6925(b).
360. 40 C.F.R. § 271.19.
361. 42 U.S.C. § 6926(d).
362. 42 U.S.C. § 6927(e).
363. 42 U.S.C. § 6928(a).
364. 42 U.S.C. § 6928(b).
365. 42 U.S.C. § 6928(c).
366. 42 U.S.C. § 6928(f)(1).
367. 42 U.S.C. § 6928(d).

- Omits or misstates material information in connection with any application, label, manifest, record, report, permit, or other required document;

- Destroys, alters, conceals, or fails to file any necessary record, manifest, application, or other required document;

- Transports without a manifest identifying unlisted hazardous wastes; or

- Exports a listed hazardous waste without the recipient country's consent, or in violation of a treaty.

The defendant also will be guilty of knowing endangerment if he or she does any of the above activities, knowing at the time that he or she thereby places another person in imminent danger of death or serious bodily injury.[368] However, it is an affirmative defense that the endangered person consented, and that the danger was a reasonably foreseeable hazard of employment or medical treatment or experimentation.[369]

[3] Abatement Orders for Imminent Hazards

RCRA authorizes EPA, on notice to the affected state, to seek a federal court abatement order for past[370] or present handling, storage, treatment, transportation, or disposal of hazardous waste that presents an "imminent and substantial endangerment" to health or the environment.[371] This provision also may be a basis for a citizen suit (see [4], *below*). Although this remedy bears some similarity to a CERCLA cleanup order, it is not a vehicle for cost recovery, and proof of culpability is required.[372] Under CERCLA, by contrast, liability is strict, the contamination usually results from an historic release, and EPA's interest is in recovering cleanup costs or requiring others to expend those costs in undertaking a cleanup (see § 7.06[A][4]). Also, for a RCRA abatement order to issue, the harm must be current or impending to be "imminent"; wholly past harm is not a basis for an abatement order.[373]

Enforcement for failure to comply is venued in federal court, with penalties imposed per diem.[374] As soon as EPA knows of an imminent endangerment, it must notify the appropriate local government agency (see § 7.08 for emergency response) and post the notice.[375] If EPA decides not to sue, or settles, it must give the public notice

---

368. 42 U.S.C. § 6928(e).

369. 42 U.S.C. § 6928(f)(3).

370. Meghrig v. KFC Western, Inc., 516 U.S. 479 (1996); Craig Lyle Ltd. Partnership v. Land O'Lakes, Inc., 877 F. Supp. 476 (D. Minn. 1995) (prior owner of contaminated site could be sued for spill).

371. 42 U.S.C. § 6973(a).

372. Leister v. Black & Decker (U.S.), Inc., 117 F.3d 1414 (4th Cir. 1997) (RCRA § 7003 does not impose strict liability).

373. Leister v. Black & Decker (U.S.), Inc., 117 F.3d 1414 (4th Cir. 1997); Crandall v. City and County of Denver, 594 F.3d 1231 (10th Cir. 2010).

374. 42 U.S.C. § 6973(b).

375. 42 U.S.C. § 6973(c).

and an opportunity for a "public meeting" and comment, but the substantive decision is not a final agency action subject to judicial review.[376]

[4] Citizen Suits

[a] Bases for Suits; Remedies

RCRA has citizen suit provisions similar to those seen in many environmental statutes (see generally § 1.03; *see also* § 6.03[F]).[377] RCRA provides three bases for citizen suits. "Any person" may sue any of the following:[378]

- Any other person (including the government) for a violation of any RCRA permit, standard, regulation, or order; however, the violation must be current and actions challenging wholly past violations will be dismissed;[379]

- Any other person (again including the government) who has contributed to past or present imminent endangerment, discussed in [3] *above*; and/or

- EPA for failure to perform a nondiscretionary duty.

The citizen suit may seek enforcement, penalties (to the government), and/or injunctive relief.[380] When it is not a party, EPA may intervene as of right.[381]

However, citizen plaintiffs may not sue in connection with the siting of a TSD facility or to prevent the issuance of a TSD permit.[382]

[b] Notice Requirements

As with all environmental citizen suits, there is a jurisdictional notice period,[383] but for RCRA the provisions are more detailed. For a violation action, the citizen plaintiff must give 60 days notice to EPA, the state, and the violator. The suit is barred if the EPA or state has "commenced and is diligently prosecuting" a civil or criminal court action[384] (but not an administrative proceeding)[385] to require compliance. If the action is predicated on imminent endangerment (see [3], *above*), then 90 days notice is required, unless a violation of hazardous waste management standards (discussed in

---

376. *See* 42 U.S.C. § 6973(d).

377. 42 U.S.C. § 6972.

378. *Id.*

379. ABB Industrial Systems, Inc. v. Prime Technology, Inc., 120 F.3d 351 (2d Cir. 1997); Connecticut Coastal Fishermen's Association v. Remington Arms Co., 989 F.2d 1315 (2d Cir. 1993).

380. 42 U.S.C. § 6972(a).

381. 42 U.S.C. § 6972(d).

382. 42 U.S.C. § 6972(b)(2)(D).

383. Hallstrom v. Tillamook County, 493 U.S. 20 (1989).

384. 42 U.S.C. § 6972(b)(1).

385. Chico Service Station, Inc. v. Sol Puerto Rico Ltd., 633 F.3d 20 (1st Cir. 2011) (an administrative action does not bar a citizen suit); Orange Environment, Inc. v. County of Orange, 860 F. Supp. 1003 (S.D.N.Y. 1994).

[C] to [G], *above*) is alleged.[386] In that case, the threat of significant harm to the community resulting from a hazardous waste release supersedes the usual policy preference of according EPA a primary enforcement role.[387] Of course, the tolling period does not affect the plaintiff's right to bring common law claims.[388] If EPA is a defendant, 60 days notice is required, unless there is a violation of hazardous waste management standards.[389] The notice letter must be specific as to the hazardous wastes disposed of, the method of disposal, and how the wastes entered the environment.[390]

[c] When Suits Are Barred

Citizen suits will be barred if EPA:[391]

- Has already commenced and is diligently prosecuting an abatement action (see [3], *above*) or a CERCLA § 106 action[392] (see § 7.06[A][4]);

- Is actually engaged in a CERCLA § 104[393] removal action (see § 7.06[A][6]); or

- Has incurred costs in connection with CERCLA § 104 remediation.

In addition, if there is a CERCLA § 106 removal order or RCRA § 7003 abatement order with which the responsible party is complying, the action will be barred.[394]

However, the dismissal will be limited to those claims already being advanced in the government's RCRA enforcement action. Hence, additional RCRA claims in the citizen plaintiff's complaint that are not being asserted by the government may survive dismissal if the notice requirements are satisfied.[395]

[d] Fees to Prevailing Party

The court may award reasonable attorney and expert witness fees to the substantially prevailing party.[396]

---

386. 42 U.S.C. § 6972(b)(2); Hallstrom v. Tillamook County, 493 U.S. 20, 26–27 (1989).

387. AM International, Inc. v. Datacard Corp., 106 F.3d 1432 (7th Cir. 1997).

388. ABB Industrial Systems, Inc. v. Prime Technology, Inc., 120 F.3d 351 (2d Cir. 1997); Elmwood Village Center v. K-Mart Corp., 863 F. Supp. 309 (E.D. La. 1994) (although citizen plaintiffs were barred from seeking RCRA relief because of pending compliance action, they could sue for trespass, nuisance, and negligence).

389. 42 U.S.C. § 6972(c).

390. Brod v. OMYA, Inc., 653 F.3d 156 (2d Cir. 2011).

391. 42 U.S.C. § 6972(b).

392. 42 U.S.C. § 9604.

393. 42 U.S.C. § 9606.

394. 42 U.S.C. § 6972(b)(2)(B).

395. Adkins v. VIM Recycling, Inc., 644 F.3d 483 (7th Cir. 2011); Sanchez v. Esso Standard Oil Co., 572 F.3d 1 (1st Cir. 2009).

396. 42 U.S.C. § 6972(e). This has included defense costs when the citizen plaintiff's RCRA action is frivolous. See George v. Residorf Brothers, Inc., 410 Fed. Appx. 382 (2d Cir. 2011).

§ 7.06 Hazardous Waste Sites: Comprehensive Environmental Response, Compensation and Liability Act (CERCLA)

[A] Remediation under CERCLA

[1] Introduction

Unlike RCRA (see § 7.05), CERCLA is not a regulatory statute.[397] Rather, it provides a basis to establish financial responsibility for cleanup of hazardous waste sites—or "facilities." It also establishes the Superfund, a fund to pay for cleanups when necessary. Under CERCLA, a party conducting the cleanup of a hazardous waste site is entitled to recover the expansive category of costs thereby incurred from designated classes of responsible parties. CERCLA imposes virtually strict liability.[398] A plaintiff satisfying the following four-part test is entitled to summary judgment on liability:[399]

- The site must be a "facility," a condition generally easy to satisfy;
- The defendant must be a "responsible person" (discussed in [B], below), who is unable to prove one of the statutory defenses;
- There must be a release or threatened release of hazardous wastes; and
- The plaintiff must show that the release or threatened release caused the plaintiff to incur costs.

The Hazardous Substances Superfund, commonly known as "superfund," is a major component of CERCLA. Congress had envisioned that cleanups around the nation would be funded by two mechanisms: cost recovery (see [C], below), and taxes imposed on the chemical and petroleum industries and out of general tax revenues to be deposited into a trust fund. In this sense, superfund is a revolving fund, in theory at least, although it is chronically underfunded. The fund is available to pay for EPA cleanups pending cost recovery from responsible parties, and for cleanups where the responsible party cannot be identified or is insolvent. Congress initially created a $1.6 billion fund with CERCLA's enactment in 1980, which was increased by $8.5 billion with the 1986 enactment of SARA, and the fund was set at $5.1 billion with the 1990 reauthorization of CERCLA. Remediation of potential superfund sites may exceed $100 billion. Not every contaminated site is eligible for superfund, though;

---

397. For a more comprehensive discussion of CERCLA, itself a very complex regulatory regime, see ROBINSON, ENVIRONMENTAL REGULATION OF REAL PROPERTY §§ 22.05 to 22.09 (Law Journal Press).

398. Harley-Davidson, Inc. v. Minstar, Inc., 41 F.3d 341, 343 (7th Cir. 1994), cert. denied, 514 U.S. 1036 (1995).

399. Environmental Transportation Systems, Inc. v. ENSCO, Inc., 969 F.2d 503, 507 (7th Cir. 1992).

only sites on the National Priorities List qualify (see [5], *below*), although funding may also be available for emergency response and removal actions (see [4], *below*).[400] Because of the complexity and cost of superfund litigation, many private parties have availed themselves of alternative dispute resolution (ADR) in private cost recovery and contribution actions (see [C], *below*).

[2] Facility Defined

A "facility" under CERCLA is given a long descriptive definition, but basically it is any structure, equipment, containment, vehicle, or site where hazardous waste is placed or disposed of. The definition excludes any place where a consumer product is still in consumer use — a product still in use is not a waste and thus is not "disposed of."[401]

[3] Release, Threatened Release, or Disposal; Exclusions

CERCLA liability often turns on whether there has been a "release" or threatened release, or a "disposal," of hazardous wastes. A release is the event by which contamination escapes into the environment.[402] Here, too, the statute provides a long list of illustrations, but the point requires little elaboration. The abandonment or discarding of barrels or other closed receptacles containing hazardous residue also is deemed to be a release of the residue, a construction that has practical ramifications for many industries. The term "release" specifically incorporates disposal[403] — rather than vice versa — which has consequences for potential liability of prior owners of the site (see [B][3][a][vi], *below*). However, CERCLA explicitly excludes the following activities:[404]

- Workplace or OSHA claims;

- Engine exhaust from railroads, motor vehicles, airplanes, vessels, or pipeline pumping stations, which fall under the Clean Air Act (see Chapter 5); and

- Radioactive releases that are governed under the Atomic Energy Act (see Chapter 12).

In addition, the normal application of fertilizer is not a CERCLA release.[405] CERCLA also does not impose liability in connection with an unaltered or naturally occurring substance (e.g., uranium) or one altered only by naturally occurring processes. It also does not reach products found in the structures of buildings, or contamination of drinking water supplies caused by deterioration of the system through normal

---

400. *See* RICHARD L. REVESZ, FOUNDATIONS OF ENVIRONMENTAL LAW AND POLICY 251 *[hereinafter* FOUNDATIONS OF ENVIRONMENTAL LAW].

401. 42 U.S.C. § 9601(9).

402. 42 U.S.C. § 9601(22).

403. *Id.*

404. *Id.*

405. *Id.*

use,[406] unless any of these occurrences presents an emergency, in which case EPA may intervene.[407]

[4] Section 106 Orders

If EPA determines that there is an imminent and substantial danger to the public health or welfare, or to the environment, because of a release or threat of release, it may issue a so-called "106" order, authorized under CERCLA § 106. The order directs abatement of the danger or threat. A party who complies, completing the required action, and thereby incurs costs, may seek reimbursement from the Superfund established under CERCLA on the basis that it was not the party responsible for incurring the costs.[408] The party conducting the cleanup also may sue other responsible parties for cost recovery without waiting for the conclusion of the cleanup.[409] However, the party conducting a cleanup pursuant to a 106 order cannot challenge the order once cleanup commenced until it is completed.[410]

[5] Use of CERCLIS, Preliminary Assessments, the Hazard Ranking System, and the NPL

EPA's involvement with a hazardous waste site starts by listing the site with the CERCLA Information System (CERCLIS), currently an inventory of some 36,000 sites that may require a cleanup (remediation). EPA conducts a Preliminary Assessment analyzing the risks to health and the environment and, if necessary, a site inspection. At this point, the site may be eliminated from further consideration. If the site is preliminarily evaluated as posing risks, the risks will be assessed under standards provided in the Hazard Ranking System (HRS)[411] to determine whether the site qualifies for the National Priorities List (NPL).[412] The HRS was promulgated in 1982[413] and revised in 1990.[414] The system relies on the use of a mathematical model to measure the potential hazards caused by a given release, taking into account the specific chemicals involved and site-specific conditions; the hazards are then scaled from one to 100. If a site's scoring exceeds 28.5, it may be placed on the NPL.[415] The HRS may also utilize a "human toxicity factor" (HTF) for known toxins or carcinogens. Lead, for example, which is considered toxic at any concentration, has been accorded the

---

406. 42 U.S.C. § 9604(a)(3).
407. 42 U.S.C. § 9604(a)(4).
408. 42 U.S.C. § 9606.
409. United States Atlantic Research Corp., 551 U.S. 128, 127 S. Ct. 2331, 168 L. Ed. 2d 28 (2007).
410. City of Rialto v. West Coast Loading Corp., 581 F.3d 865 (9th Cir. 2009).
411. 42 U.S.C. § 9605(a)(8)(A), (B); 40 C.F.R. Part 300.
412. 42 U.S.C. § 9605(c). EPA's determination, if rational and it properly utilizes the HRS, is entitled to judicial deference. *See* Meriton v Environmental Protection Agency, 966 F.3d 864 (D.C. Cir. 2020).
413. 47 Fed. Reg. 31,180 (1982).
414. 55 Fed. Reg. 51,532 (1990).
415. 55 Fed. Reg. 51,532, 51,569 (1990).

highest HTF ranking available.[416] The NPL is an inventory of the most contaminated sites in the country. It now consists of more than 1,200 sites; individual cleanups, taking years, may cost $30 million.[417] Only sites on the NPL qualify for Superfund moneys.[418]

[6] Remediation: Response Actions, Removal, Monitoring, and Mitigation

[a] Definitions

The cleanup, in its many phases, is generally termed "remediation," although the initial emergency response technically is known as a "response action," and the permanent, long-term, project to return the site to its pre-contaminated state or insulate the wastes in such a manner that they no longer threaten health or the environment, is the remedial phase of the cleanup. "Removal" refers to the physical removal—the cleanup—of hazardous wastes from a site. This is coupled with whatever additional action is necessary to monitor and assess the release or threat of release, the eventual disposal of the hazardous wastes—which triggers regulation under RCRA (discussed in §7.05)—and whatever further mitigation is necessary to minimize the damage caused by the release. This might involve putting up security fencing, or providing alternative water supplies, and even temporary evacuation and housing of people placed under threat of contamination, or other emergency assistance.[419] A careful distinction must be made, however, between removal actions and remedial actions, because there are different statutes of limitations (see discussion in §7.06[C]) and different standards.[420]

[b] Remedial Investigation, Feasibility Study, and Record of Decision

The remedial action is permanent in nature. A remedial action is done instead of, or in addition to, removal actions, depending on circumstances.[421] Remediation is a

416. See discussion in RSR Corp. v. Environmental Protection Agency, 102 F.3d 1266 (D.C. Cir. 1997).

417. FOUNDATIONS OF ENVIRONMENTAL LAW, *supra* note 400 at 247.

418. 40 C.F.R. §§ 300.425(b)(1), 300.430(e)(7). This applies to sites that require remediation. Removal actions, under some circumstances, may receive Superfund moneys without being listed on the NPL. *See* United States v. W.R. Grace & Co., 429 F.3d 1224 (9th Cir, 2005).

419. 42 U.S.C. § 9601(23); Schaefer v. Town of Victor, 457 F.3d 188 (2d Cir. 2006); United States v. W.R. Grace & Co., 429 F.3d 1224 (9th Cir. 2005); Colorado v. Sunoco, Inc., 337 F.3d 1233 (10th Cir. 2003).

420. *See* discussion in Agere Systems, Inc. v. Advanced Environmental Technology Corp., 602 F.3d 204, 219–225 (3d Cir. 2010), and Commonwealth of Pennsylvania Dept. of Environmental Protection v. Beazer East, Inc., 553 Fed. Appx. 153 (3d Cir. 2014). *See also* Valbruna Slater Steel Corp. v. Joslyn Manufacturing Co., 934 F.3d 553 (7th Cir. 2019). For a more comprehensive discussion of the distinction between removal actions and remedial actions, see ROBINSON, ENVIRONMENTAL REGULATION OF REAL PROPERTY § 22.05(2)(c) (Law Journal Press).

421. 42 U.S.C. § 9601(24); Valbruna Slater Steel Corp. v. Joslyn Manufacturing Co., 934 F.3d 553 (7th Cir. 2019); MPM Silicones LLC v. Union Carbide Corp., 966 F.3d 200 (2d Cir. 2020); Pakootas v. Teck Cominco Metals, Ltd., 905 F.3d 565 (9th Cir. 2018).

multi-step process, starting with a remedial investigation and a feasibility study (RI/FS), consisting of a more detailed site analysis and a preliminary examination or response strategies, followed by a Record of Decision (ROD), in which EPA, having analyzed alternative strategies, selects one. The remedy selected must ensure protection of human health and the environment. Next, a remedial design phase follows, with the actual cleanup conducted during the remedial action phase.[422]

[c] What Remediation Involves

One goal of remediation is to prevent off-site migration of the hazardous wastes.[423] Remediation includes storage of wastes, and perimeter protection or other means of confining the wastes. Cleaning up groundwater contamination is often the most difficult, and costly, part of a remedial action. Perimeter protection can consist of dikes or trenches, and clay cover, as well as collecting leachate and other segregation of wastes, and treating or disposing of wastes on-site or off-site. Alternative sources of water may have to be provided, and monitoring to protect the public health may be necessary. In short, remediation includes all steps necessary to restrict the wastes and, if necessary, dispose of them.[424] It may also include permanent relocation of residents, businesses, and community facilities if that is more cost-effective and environmentally preferable to extensive measures at the site.[425] Response, removal, and remediation also include enforcement activities and expenses.[426]

[d] EPA versus Private Party Cleanups

Remediation may be done by EPA, utilizing Superfund resources, or by the owner or operator of the property, usually in connection with a settlement with EPA, and subject to an EPA determination that the private party is qualified and able to conduct the cleanup.[427] The private party must still reimburse the fund for any expenses incurred by EPA, and must meet the same standard of liability,[428] but private cleanups tend to be faster and more cost effective than EPA sponsored cleanups, often costing 20 percent less,[429] so they have become common.

---

422. 42 U.S.C. § 9604(a)(1). Whether opting for a removal action, which depends on speed, or remediation, which utilizes EPA's technical expertise, EPA's selection is entitled to judicial deference. Lawsuits by parties subject to enforcement which interfere with CERCLA's statutory goals will often be dismissed. *See* Giovanni v. United States Department of the Navy, 906 F.3d 94 (3d Cir. 2018).

423. 42 U.S.C. § 9601(24).

424. 42 U.S.C. § 9601(24).

425. *Id.*

426. 42 U.S.C. § 9601(25).

427. 42 U.S.C. § 9604(a)(1).

428. *Id.*

429. FOUNDATIONS OF ENVIRONMENTAL LAW, *supra* note 400, at 255.

[e] National Contingency Plan Requirements

Remediation must comply with the National Contingency Plan (NCP) set forth in EPA regulations.[430] The NCP sets forth detailed standards and procedures for responses,[431] and stringent requirements for remediation.[432] If the cleanup is conducted pursuant to an EPA order under CERCLA § 106, it is deemed to conform to the NCP.[433] When a state conducts the cleanup, it also is deemed to act consistent with the NCP, although that presumption is rebuttable.[434] When a private party selects a response strategy, it must provide public notice of it and the selection must be available for public comment.[435]

[f] Recovering Costs of Cleanup

CERCLA allows for recovery by EPA for a government-conducted cleanup, or reimbursement to a private party that incurs response or remediation costs. Given the significant expenses involved, recovery of particular costs, as well as basic liability of responsible parties, has been much litigated. These topics are discussed in [B] and [C], *below.*

[7] Notice and Record Keeping Requirements

Any owner or operator who knows of a release must notify EPA.[436] A failure to provide immediate notification, or submission of false or misleading information with the notification, may lead to criminal penalties.[437] There also must be detailed and comprehensive record keeping of facility locations and operations, and the identity, characteristics, quantities, origin, and condition of hazardous substances at the facility.[438] The records must be maintained for 50 years,[439] and any falsification, concealment, or destruction is a crime.[440]

---

430. *See* 42 U.S.C. § 9607(a)(4)(B); 40 C.F.R. Part 300; Cooper Industries, Inc. v. Aviall Services, Inc., 543 U.S. 157 (2004); United States v. W.R. Grace & Co., 429 F.3d 1224 (9th Cir. 2005).

431. 42 U.S.C. § 9605.

432. *See* United States v. W.R. Grace & Co., 429 F.3d 1224 (9th Cir. 2005).

433. 40 C.F.R. § 300.700(c)(3)(ii).

434. Regional Airport Authority of Louisville and Jefferson County v. LFG, LLC, 460 F.3d 697 (6th Cir. 2006); Washington State Dept. of Transportation v. Washington Natural Gas Co., 51 F.3d 1489 (9th Cir. 1995). *Cf.* Public Service Co. of Colorado v. Gates Rubber Co., 175 F.3d 1177 (10th Cir. 1999).

435. 40 C.F.R. §§ 300.415(n), 300.430(f)(3).

436. 42 U.S.C. § 9603.

437. 42 U.S.C. § 9603(b).

438. 42 U.S.C. § 9603(d).

439. 42 U.S.C. § 9603(d)(3).

440. 42 U.S.C. § 9603(d)(2).

[B] Responsibility for Cleanup

[1] Statutory Categories of Responsible Parties

CERCLA imposes cleanup responsibilities primarily on the following classes of potentially responsible parties (also referred to as "PRPs") involving the disposal of hazardous substances which thereupon become wastes:[441]

- Generators;
- Owners or operators of the facility where hazardous substances are disposed of (or the vessel from which they are discharged), thus converting them into wastes;
- Any party who contractually arranged for disposal or treatment;
- Any person who contractually arranged to transport the hazardous substances for disposal or treatment;
- Transporters, and
- Parties which accept the delivery of hazardous substances at a disposal or treatment facility from which there is a release or threatened release that results in response costs.

These parties, discussed in [2]–[5], *below*, are liable unless they can avail themselves of the statutory defenses available, discussed in [D], *below*.

[2] Generators

A generator, as the term indicates, is the party with whom the hazardous waste originated.[442] Removing already-disposed of wastes and relocating them also constitutes generation of those wastes. The government can be a generator. Federal agencies are subject to CERCLA in the same manner as any other responsible party,[443] and do not enjoy sovereign immunity.[444] Locally, municipalities have been major generators of land filled hazardous wastes, triggering CERCLA liability.[445] A publicly owned sewage treatment works from which a release occurs also may incur CERCLA liability as a generator.[446] Although state and local governments may be excluded from CERCLA liability for past contamination of property they involuntarily hold (see [3][a][v], *below*), the exclusion does not apply when that government unit is a generator.[447] However, the Eleventh Amendment bars suits in federal courts against states, an

---

441. 42 U.S.C. §9607(a).
442. 42 U.S.C. §6903(6).
443. 42 U.S.C. §9620.
444. United States v. Shell Oil Co., 281 F.3d 812 (9th Cir. 2002); FMC Corp. v. United States Department of Commerce, 29 F.3d 833, 835 (3d Cir. 1994).
445. Goodrich Corp. v. Town of Middlesbury, 311 F.3d 154 (2d Cir. 2002); B.F. Goodrich v. Murtha ("*Murtha I*"), 958 F.2d 1192, 1197 (2d Cir. 1992).
446. Westfarm Associates Limited Partnership v. Washington Suburban Sanitary Commission, 66 F.3d 669, 678 (4th Cir. 1995), *cert. denied*, 517 U.S. 1103 (1996).
447. 42 U.S.C. §9601(20)(D).

issue discussed generally in § 1.05[E], and with regard to CERCLA at [3][a][v], *below*. CERCLA was amended in 2002 to exempt some generators, including small businesses and households, that, before 2001, generated only de minimis quantities of hazardous wastes as a portion of their overall municipal solid waste stream.[448]

[3] Owners and Operators of Disposal Sites

[a] Owners and Operators Subject to Liability

[i] Joint and Several Liability

Both owners and operators are jointly, severally, and strictly liable,[449] although each might have indemnification rights against the others.[450] By the device of owner/ operator liability, pervasive in environmental statutes but particularly effective under CERCLA, Congress precluded defendants from engaging in a shell game with enforcement authorities whereby liability might be shifted from owner to operator and back again, and ultimately require the EPA's proof of the party's fault. Under CERCLA, the relative fault of an owner or operator is immaterial to EPA. Each is strictly, and jointly and severally, liable.

[ii] Owner and Operator Defined

The term "owner" is not technically defined under CERCLA, except by its exceptions.[451] However, it may be given its ordinary meaning.[452] "Operator" basically is left undefined. The Supreme Court, noting the statutory omission, has defined an operator in terms of one that manages, directs, or conducts operations specifically related to the leakage or disposal of hazardous wastes, or makes decisions about compliance with environmental regulations.[453]

Whether a bank or other lender may be an owner or an operator is discussed in [b], *below*.

[iii] Partnerships and Corporate "Owners" and Operators

Ownership may be individual, corporate, or by partnership.[454] For partnerships, all general partners are deemed owners.[455] Whether or not limited partners, typically

---

448. Small quantity generators include those whose hazardous wastes at a particular site are less than 110 gallons or 200 pounds, although some restrictions apply. 42 U.S.C. § 9607(o).

449. 42 U.S.C. § 9607(a).

450. *See* 42 U.S.C. § 9607(e).

451. 42 U.S.C. § 9601(20).

452. Redwing Carriers, Inc. v. Saraland Apartments, 94 F.3d 1498 (11th Cir. 1996). Even if the release on the property occurred prior to the present owner's ownership, it is still an owner as to that hazardous waste for purposes of CERCLA liability. Pennsylvania Department of Environmental Protection v. Trainer Custom Chemical LLC, 906 F.3d 85 (3d Cir. 2018). The facts of this case precluded the innocent purchaser defense discussed in § 7.06[D][4], although the present owner had remedies against prior owners and operators, as is discussed in § 7.06[C].

453. United States v. Bestfoods, 524 U.S. 51 (1998).

454. 42 U.S.C. § 9601(20) defines an owner in terms of "any person." 42 U.S.C. § 9601(21) defines "person" to include individuals, corporations, firms, partnerships, et al.

455. *See* Redwing Carriers, Inc. v. Saraland Apartments, 94 F.3d 1489 (11th Cir. 1996).

investors with rights and liability limited to their investment, are owners is determined by state law.[456] Of course, limited partners who assume managerial responsibility might be liable as operators.

Are the shareholders of a corporation personally liable as owners? Generally, no,[457] unless the corporate veil is pierced. They own the corporation, but not necessarily the site. However, if a shareholder acts in a managerial capacity, he or she will be liable as an operator. One court, however, has limited even operational liability of shareholders to instances when a shareholder had actually participated in the wrongful conduct.[458] Corporate officers who are responsible for disposal of hazardous wastes are personally liable for their own conduct, even if the conduct is performed on behalf of the corporation.[459]

The liability of a parent corporation for the CERCLA liability of a subsidiary turns on the parent's operational role, rather than its ownership role. The Supreme Court, in *United States v. Bestfoods*,[460] noted the "bedrock principle" of general corporate law that, absent a piercing of the corporate veil, a parent corporation is not liable solely on the basis of ownership; the relationship between the parent and the facility, more than the relationship between the parent and the subsidiary, will govern CERCLA liability. Hence, in *Bestfoods*, when the parent corporation actively participated in and exercised control over the operations of the subsidiary's facility, it incurred liability for releases from that facility.

Courts have looked to whether the parent had the authority to control the particular facility or site at the time of the disposal or release.[461] Some courts have required that substantial control actually be exercised.[462] Others have looked to whether the corporate veil has been pierced.[463] If the same executive officer is involved in both corporations, one of which operated the facility, a court will look at which role that executive officer exercised before imposing liability on the other corporation. The focus is on the facility at which the release occurred, the conduct of the executive officer, and which corporation he acted on behalf of, rather than on the seeming re-

---

456. Redwing Carriers, Inc. v. Saraland Apartments, 94 F.3d 1489 (11th Cir. 1996).

457. United States v. USX Corp., 68 F.3d 811, 824 (3d Cir. 1995); United States v. Kayser-Roth Corp., 910 F.2d 24 (1st Cir. 1990), *cert. denied*, 498 U.S. 1084 (1991).

458. Riverside Market Development Corp. v. International Building Products, Inc., 931 F.2d 327 (5th Cir. 1990), *cert. denied*, 502 U.S. 1004 (1991).

459. United States v. Northeastern Pharmaceutical & Chemical Co., 579 F. Supp. 823 (W.D. Mo. 1984), *aff'd in part, rev'd in part*, 810 F.2d 726 (8th Cir. 1986), *cert. denied*, 484 U.S. 848 (1987).

460. 524 U.S. 51 (1998).

461. United States v. Sterling Centrecorp, 977 F.3d 750 (9th Cir. 2020) (parent's control over the mine nominally owned by the subsidiary was pervasive, and parent had even assumed control when dam burst on a prior occasion releasing arsenic); Nurad, Inc. v. William E. Hooper & Sons Co., 966 F.2d 837, 842 (4th Cir. 1991), *cert. denied*, 506 U.S. 940 (1992).

462. Atlantic Gas Light Co. v. UGI Utilities, Inc., 463 F.3d 1201 (11th Cir. 2006); United States v. Kayser-Roth Corp., 910 F.2d 26 (1st Cir. 1990), *cert. denied*, 498 U.S. 1084 (1991); Lansford Coaldale Joint Water Authority v. Tonolli Corp., 4 F.3d 1209, 1221–1222 (3d Cir. 1993); United States v. TIC Investment Corp., 68 F.3d 1082 (8th Cir. 1995), *cert. denied*, 519 U.S. 808 (1996).

463. United States v. Cordova Chemical Co., 59 F.3d 584, 590–591 (6th Cir. 1995).

latedness of the corporations.[464] What if the degree of control exercised by the parent corporation over subsidiaries waxes and wanes over time? Will the exercise of control during one period of time *per se* pierce the corporate veil for CERCLA purposes? Several factors must be considered for piercing the corporate veil during some periods when the subsidiary may retain very limited control over operations which might not characterize other periods. Of course, a critical factor would be when a disposal or release involving property nominally owned by the subsidiary occurred.[465]

[iv] U.S. Government May Be an Owner or Operator

CERCLA operates as a partial waiver of sovereign immunity so that the United States government may be an owner or operator under CERCLA,[466] although its liability as an operator may require a showing of actual managerial control. This was the holding in a case in which the government placed orders for the production of Agent Orange, the defoliant discussed in § 8.03[A][4], on a priority basis. However, the government never supplied, owned, or controlled the raw materials, never controlled disposal of the wastes, and never participated in the operation of the plant.[467] Merely because the United States has regulatory authority over the activities that produces a toxin as well as over its treatment or disposal does not make it an operator,[468] if it does not control the production process.[469] Nor does the EPA's "control" of a site during a response action make EPA vulnerable to a CERCLA claim that it thereby assumed operational control.[470]

[v] Liability of State and Local Governments

State or local governments are not liable for contamination found on property they acquired as a result of bankruptcy, tax foreclosure, abandonment, or otherwise, by virtue of the state government's status as a sovereign. If the government entity was responsible for the release, though, the exclusion does not apply, and the government is responsible under CERCLA for its own conduct as a generator.[471] However, if the release occurs during emergency operations, as when a fire department, technically in control of the premises for that reason, responds to a fire, it benefits from the statutory defense and will not be deemed an operator.[472] It should be noted that

---

464. Raytheon Construction, Inc. v. ASARCO, Inc., 368 F.3d 1214 (10th Cir. 2003).

465. New York State Electric and Gas Corp v. Firstenergy Corp., 766 F.3d 212 (2d Cir. 2014).

466. 42 U.S.C. § 9620(a)(1); United States v. Shell Oil Co., 281 F.3d 812 (9th Cir. 2002); Cadillac Fairview v. Dow Chemical Co., 299 F.3d 1019 (9th Cir. 2002) (although the disposal of the hazardous waste was by a chemical company, the United States had owned the property during the period of disposal, as to which it was knowledgeable).

467. United States v. Vertac Chemical Corp., 841 F. Supp. 884 (E.D. Ark. 1993), *aff'd*, 46 F.3d 803 (8th Cir. 1995), *cert. denied*, 515 U.S. 1158 (1995).

468. Maxus Energy Corp. v. United States, 898 F. Supp. 399 (N.D. Tex. 1995), *aff'd*, 95 F.3d 1148 (5th Cir. 1996).

469. FMC Corp. v. United States Department of Commerce, 29 F.3d 833, 843 (3d Cir. 1994).

470. United States v. Berks Associates, Inc., 1992 WL 68346 (E.D. Pa. 1992).

471. 42 U.S.C. § 9601(20)(D).

472. 42 U.S.C. § 9607(d)(2); AMW Materials Testing, Inc. v. Town of Babylon, 584 F.3d 436 (2d Cir. 2009).

the Eleventh Amendment to the U.S. Constitution bars suits against states for damages or similar relief in federal courts (see § 1.05[E]).

[vi] Liability of Past and Present Owners and Operators

Present owners are liable under CERCLA, regardless of fault, assuming a defense is not proved.[473] But liability under CERCLA also includes past owners and operators who might have been in ownership or management at the time of the disposal or release, unless they can affirmatively prove that the contaminating event occurred after they conveyed the property.[474] Liability may also be imposed on subsequent owners or operators, unless a defense can be asserted (see [D], *below*). The inclusion of owners and operators who did not enter the picture until after the contaminating event has resulted in significant litigation, and has dramatically imposed liability on some unwary parties. However, this construction essentially keeps an unscrupulous responsible party from escaping the net of liability by legal subterfuge. It also has spawned a new generation of business practices in which due diligence inspections, usually performed by environmental consulting firms, are now the norm before purchases of property, mergers, and the like, uncovering contamination that otherwise may have lain unnoticed but dangerous.

The ownership may be very transient, yet liability will attach. A firm that held title for only one hour as an accommodation owner nevertheless was deemed an owner for CERCLA purposes.[475] Some courts have imposed liability even on trustees[476] or conservators of property,[477] although a 1996 amendment to CERCLA[478] protects fiduciaries under some circumstances (see [c], *below*). Operator's liability, again, may attach even when ownership is an insufficient predicate for CERCLA liability.

A question arises whether a lessee of property can be the equivalent of an owner for purposes of imposing cleanup responsibilities when the lessee did not qualify as an operator or as a generator for a release that occurred before or during its tenancy. Although some lower court decisions did impose liability, the Second Circuit has reasoned that the mere status of lessee is not a basis to impose liability, unless the lessee in some manner acted as a de facto owner.[479] However, the property owner

---

473. New York v. Shore Realty Corp., 759 F.2d 1032 (2d Cir. 1985).

474. *Cf.* Crofton Ventures Limited Partnership v. G&H Partnership, 258 F.3d 292 (4th Cir. 2001).

475. United States v. Carolawn, 14 Environmental Law Inst. 20698 (D. S.C. 1984). However, depending on the circumstances of the brief ownership as an accommodation, subsequent amendments to CERCLA discussed below protecting lenders and fiduciaries could supersede this lower court ruling, making it either an outlier or a legal artifact.

476. City of Phoenix v. Garbage Services Co., 816 F. Supp. 564, 567 (D. Ariz. 1993).

477. Castlerock Estates, Inc. v. Estate of Walter S. Markham, 871 F. Supp. 360 (N.D. Cal. 1994). This court noted that while trustees, who hold title by deed, do have some discretion as to use or sale of the property, justifying CERCLA liability, conservators, who have title only as a consequence of office, lack such discretionary authority, so that additional indicia of ownership are necessary to impose CERCLA liability.

478. Pub. L. 104-208, 1996 HR 3610, Subtitle E, § 2501, *et seq.*

479. Commander Oil Corp. v. Barlo Equipment Corp., 215 F.3d 321 (2d Cir. 2000), *cert denied*, 531 U.S. 979 (2000).

remains an owner for CERCLA liability purposes even when the property has been leased to a third party which causes the release.[480]

Although past owners may be relieved of liability on proving that their ownership ended prior to the contamination, termination of ownership must have preceded the actual disposal rather than only preceding the release. The release might occur long after the disposal, as might occur with later leakage from disposal containers, and the past owner might actually have been responsible for, or might have known about, the disposal that led to the release.[481]

[vii] Successor Liability

If a corporation with CERCLA liability dissolves before liability is imposed, and perhaps even before the triggering event is known, is there a corporate entity that remains liable as a former owner? The answer may depend on whether there is a successor corporation. State corporate law may also determine the outcome. Generally, courts utilize one of two tests to determine whether CERCLA liability runs to the successor entity. Under common law, a successor corporation's liability for its predecessor's obligations was governed by the "same identity" test. That is, the two corporations had to have the same shareholders, stock holdings, directors, and officers, and a complete transfer of assets, to continue the liability. Although that standard is still employed in some jurisdictions,[482] many courts today employ the "substantial continuity" test, which looks for a continuing enterprise, rather than an exact identity between the corporations. Under this test, courts look to whether the successor corporation engages in essentially the same business, with basically the same employees performing the same responsibilities, for the same customers, regardless of whether officers and directors may have been shifted around. Some courts have viewed this test as being more consistent with CERCLA's remedial purpose.[483] However, CERCLA would not preempt state laws which bar legal actions against dissolved corporations after a certain deadline.[484]

Does the successor corporation need notice of the predecessor's CERCLA liability before liability may be imposed on the successor? Courts differ, some requiring notice,[485] even if not actual knowledge,[486] while other courts have focused more on the

---

480. Burlington Northern and Santa Fe Railway Co. v. United States, 129 S, Ct. 1870 (2009).

481. See Diverse Real Estate Holdings Ltd. Partnership v. International Mineral and Chemical Corp., 1995 U.S. Dist. LEXIS 274 (N.D. Ill. 1995).

482. See, e.g., Sylvester Brothers Development Co. v. Burlington Northern R.R., 772 F. Supp. 443, 447–49 (D. Minn. 1990).

483. See, e.g., B.F. Goodrich Co. v. Murtha, 99 F.3d 505 (2d Cir. 1996); United States v. Carolina Transformer Co., 978 F.2d 832, 837 (4th Cir. 1992).

484. Marsh v. Rosenbloom, 499 F.3d 165 (2d Cir. 2007). The state limitations period might be ineffective, though, if the purchasing corporation agreed to assume the dissolving corporation's obligations and liabilities along with its assets. U.S. Bank National Association v. Environmental Protection Agency, 563 F.3d 199 (6th Cir. 2009).

485. See, e.g., Louisiana Pacific Corp. v. Asarco, Inc., 909 F.2d 1260 (9th Cir. 1990); United States v. Atlas Minerals and Chemicals, Inc., 824 F. Supp. 46, 50 (E.D. Pa. 1993).

486. Atlantic Richfield Co. v. Blosenski, 847 F. Supp. 1261, 1287 n.26 (E.D. Pa. 1994).

remedial purpose of CERCLA and its strict liability regime to reject a prerequisite of notice.[487]

What if there is a complete dissolution and distribution of corporate assets, and no successor corporation? The answer, again, depends on state law, which governs corporate existence. For example, under Maryland law, despite formal dissolution, the corporate entity continues in a shell existence, with the directors acting as trustees, until distribution of the assets. Until that distribution, CERCLA liability may continue. Even after distribution, the directors/trustees remain liable for their own personal wrongdoing after dissolution, and also might be liable as operators.[488]

[b] Secured Creditor Exemption

Section 107 of CERCLA specifically exempts from liability parties who, "without participating in management," hold "indicia of ownership" primarily to protect their "security interest" in the property.[489] These terms originally were undefined in the statute. A lending institution that forecloses on mortgaged property to protect its security interest falls into this category, although the unwary lender may wander into CERCLA liability when its ownership interest becomes more expansive or it exercises operational control. This ambiguity created panic in the lending industry following the financial chaos of the later 1980s. A 1996 amendment to the statute, discussed *below*, substantially limits creditors' liability, although under exacting conditions.[490]

Although the distinction between the foreclosing lender's exercise of financial and operational control was recognized in a 1985 case,[491] a 1986 decision concluded that the foreclosure terminated the security interest and that the bank, rather than holding mere "indicia of ownership," was subject to CERCLA as a holder of full title.[492] That ruling not only posed significant risks as to existing mortgages but also created uncertainty for lenders regarding prospective loans which could be the economic lifeblood of commerce and many communities.

Two 1990 rulings, *United States v. Fleet Factors*[493] and *In re Bergsoe Metal Corp.*,[494] created additional uncertainty, with *Fleet Factors* in particular starting alarms ringing for lenders during the turbulent economic climate of that period. The court there found the lender to be responsible under CERCLA, since it had participated in management and was capable of exercising actual operational control — even though it had not done so. In *Bergsoe Metals*, by contrast, the court held that there was no liability without actual management of the facility.

---

487. Gould, Inc. v. A&M Battery & Tire Service, 950 F. Supp. 653 (M.D. Pa. 1997); Hunt's Generator Committee v. Babcock & Wilcox Co., 863 F. Supp. 879, 884 (E.D. Wis. 1994).
488. Gould, Inc. v. A&M Battery & Tire Service, 950 F. Supp. 653 (M.D. Pa. 1997).
489. 42 U.S.C. §9601(20)(A).
490. 42 U.S.C. §9601(20)(E).
491. United States v. Mirabile, 23 ERC 1511 (not rep. in F. Supp.) (E.D. Pa. 1985).
492. United States v. Maryland Bank & Trust Co., 632 F. Supp. 573 (D. Md. 1986).
493. 901 F.2d 1550 (11th Cir. 1990), *cert. denied*, 498 U.S. 1046 (1991).
494. 910 F.2d 668 (9th Cir. 1990).

Although a 1992 EPA rule that sought to adopt the *Bergsoe* holding was invalidated on the basis that EPA lacked power to define the statutory provision,[495] a 1996 CERCLA amendment essentially adopted the rule. Now, as long as the lender has not participated in management, it is not liable under CERCLA, even if it later forecloses. The lender, however, must seek to sell at the "earliest practicable, commercially reasonable time, on commercially reasonable terms, taking into account market conditions and legal and regulatory requirements,"[496] but need not short-sell on dire terms. EPA now looks to whether the lender is actually participating in management, as contrasted with merely having the capacity to influence management, before imposing operational liability. As one court, exonerating the lender, characterized the test: the lender had not "crossed the murky line from the ability to influence operational decisions to actually making operational decisions...."[497]

[c] Fiduciary Exemption

The 1996 amendment to § 107 that clarified the secured creditor exemption (see [b], *above*) also made exempt from CERCLA liability a hitherto unprotected class of qualifying fiduciaries for property held under their care. Now, merely holding a property in a fiduciary capacity does not expose the fiduciary to CERCLA liability without additional factors, such as actual operational control or the fiduciary's own conduct. The exemption does not apply, however, if the fiduciary trust or estate was set up to circumvent CERCLA or other laws, or if the putative fiduciary acts in other than a fiduciary capacity in regard to the trust or estate; nor does the exemption apply beyond the fiduciary, such as to agents or independent contractors hired by the fiduciary.[498]

[4] Parties Who Arrange for Disposal

CERCLA imposes its responsibilities on any party who by contract, agreement, or otherwise, arranges for the disposal or treatment of a hazardous substance, or arranges with a transporter to transport the hazardous substance for disposal or treatment to a third party location.[499] This provision must be read with the provision for transporter liability[500] (see [5], *below*). CERCLA does not define "arranged for," so that case law, not always consistently,[501] has provided the scope of arranger liability. Determining the status of arranger liability as a result becomes largely an exercise in

---

495. Final rule at 57 Fed. Reg. 1834, invalidated by *Kelley v. Environmental Protection Agency*, 15 F.3d 110 (D.C. Cir. 1994).

496. 42 U.S.C. § 9601(20)(E).

497. Kelley v. Tiscornia, 104 F.3d 361, 1996 U.S. App. LEXIS 33616 (6th Cir. 1996).

498. 42 U.S.C. § 9607(n)(7), (8).

499. 42 U.S.C. § 9607(a)(3).

500. 42 U.S.C. § 9607(a)(4).

501. See *South Water Management District v. Montalvo*, 84 F.3d 402, 409 (11th Cir. 1996), rejecting the notion that absolute rules apply in determining arranger liability. For various ways of analyzing the problem, see California Department of Toxic Substances Control v. Alco Pacific, Inc., 2007 U.S. App. LEXIS 27463 (9th Cir. 2007), and Concrete Sales and Services v. Blue Bird Body Co., 211 F.3d 1333 (11th Cir. 2000), and their internal references.

how a court evaluates the facts pointing towards whether there was an arrangement and whether disposal was intended. The district court's fact-finding will often receive deference on appeal.[502]

Preliminarily, there must be an "arrangement" in connection with "disposal." At a minimum, there must be an actual arrangement, although courts will construe this requirement broadly to accomplish CERCLA's remedial purpose.[503] The putative arranger must do more than merely possess authority to dispose of the hazardous substances,[504] and the agreement must be carried out; an entirely executory disposal contract, under which the hazardous substances were never removed, does not trigger arranger liability.[505] The putative arranger actually must have participated in, or exercised control over, the conduct that resulted in the arrangement to remove the hazardous substances off-site,[506] although an abdication of responsibility to control disposal arrangements, conceivably, could be construed to impose liability.[507] However, the arranger need not possess the hazardous substances if it entered an agreement with the disposing party, arranged for transport, and selected the disposal site. For example, a broker in wastes who never possessed the material still could have arranged for their disposal.[508]

The putative arranger's intent has also been examined by the courts. Some courts have held that for liability to attach, it must be shown that the putative arranger intended disposal rather than some other result,[509] although other courts have allowed intent to be inferred,[510] and yet others found intent to be only a factor to be considered in evaluating whether there was an arrangement for disposal.[511] However, when intent

---

502. United States v. Dico, Inc., 920 F.3d 1174 (8th Cir. 2019).

503. United States v. Northeastern Pharmaceutical & Chemical Co., 810 F.2d 726, 733 (8th Cir. 1986), *cert. denied*, 484 U.S. 848 (1987).

504. United States v. Vertac Chemical Corp., 46 F.3d 803, 810 (8th Cir. 1994), *cert. denied*, 515 U.S. 1158 (1995).

505. Redwing Carriers, Inc. v. Saraland Apartments, 94 F.3d 1489 (11th Cir. 1996).

506. United States v. TIC Investment Corp., 68 F.3d 1082, 1087 (8th Cir. 1994). The United States government may also act so as to be held liable as an arranger for disposal. However, in a case arising from contamination that resulted from wartime production, a court has looked to whether the government actually exercised control over the disposal activities, rather than merely having the authority to do so. *See* United States v. Shell Oil Co., 294 F.3d 1045 (9th Cir. 2002), *cert. denied*, 537 U.S. 1147 (2003) (holding Government not liable as an arranger of hazardous waste disposal).

507. Compare General Electric Co. v. AAMCO Transmissions, Inc., 962 F.2d 281, 286–87 (2d Cir. 1992), in which the claim was made that the oil company retained an obligation to control dealers' disposal of used motor oil and, hence, its "arranger" status was inherent in the company-dealer relationship; since the court found the premise to be inaccurate, in that the company had no such responsibility, it rejected this arranger theory.

508. Gould, Inc. v. A&M Battery & Tire Service, 950 F. Supp. 653 (M.D. Pa. 1997).

509. United States v. TIC Investment Corp., 68 F.3d 1082 (8th Cir. 1994), *cert. denied*, 519 U.S. 808 (1996); Amcast Industrial Corp. v. Detrex Corp., 2 F.3d 746 (7th Cir. 1993), *cert. denied*, 510 U.S. 1044 (1994).

510. United States v. Cello-Foil Products, Inc., 100 F.3d 1227 (6th Cir. 1996); AM International, Inc. v. International Forging Equipment Corp., 982 F.2d 989 (6th Cir. 1993).

511. South Florida Water Management District v. Montalvo, 84 F.3d 402, 407 (11th Cir. 1996); Matthews v. Dow Chemical Co., 947 F. Supp. 1517 (D. Colo. 1996).

must be shown, it must qualify the conduct — disposal — rather than the particular location or manner of disposal.[512] Hence, an arranger cannot evade liability by claiming that the disposal site was not the one it selected, or that its arrangement had contemplated a legal disposal.

There also must be an actual disposal, rather than a mere release, to impose arranger liability. In this regard, caselaw has carved out a "useful product" exception.[513] The Supreme Court has distinguished the situation when a party arranges to transport a useful product, even if it has hazardous characteristics, for subsequent reuse so that it is not waste, during which a release occurs, from an intent to dispose of a hazardous product as waste.[514] Caselaw has devised a four-part test that can be applied in these and similar circumstances: (1) what is the intent of the parties to the transaction — are the products to be reused or reclaimed, and to what extent; (2) what is the commercial value of the products that were sold (i.e., is the "sale" a sham); (3) are the products being resold after use by the seller useful to the buyer (thus not a waste); and (4) what was the condition of the products when the transfer took place in terms of their hazardous constituents and the potential for a release during the transfer.[515]

A Fourth Circuit decision makes a close distinction as to how cost and value can be analyzed on both sides of the transaction to determine if it is an actual, even if low value, sale. The sale of transformers as useful products which contained hazardous PCBs did not lead to arranger liability for the seller even though the PCBs were not removed before the sale — the cost of removal would have exceeded the value of the transformers — when the price nevertheless exceeded that of scrap value. Even though a buyer later removed and disposed of the PCBs as useless, that was a commercial determination by the buyer rather than carrying out the seller's intent.[516] A manufacturer which sold dry cleaning machinery which was designed to recapture hazardous solvents after processing for beneficial, and economically beneficial, reuse was not intending disposal even when the manufacturer became aware of unanticipated releases of the solvents.[517] Again, the actual intent was to sell a useful, if unintentionally defective product. Caselaw supports the general principle that the manufacturer of a useful product that is not intended as a disposal device did not thereby arrange for disposal in the event that hazardous wastes ultimately are released with the use of the product.[518] In contrast, a party which is

512. United States v. Cello-Foil Products, Inc., 100 F.3d 1227 (6th Cir. 1996).
513. California Department of Toxic Substances Control v. Alco Pacific, Inc., 2007 U.S. App. LEXIS 27463 (9th Cir. 2007).
514. Burlington Northern and Santa Fe Railway Co. v. United States, 566 U.S. 559 (2009).
515. Consolidated Coal Co. v. Georgia Power Co., 781 F.3d 129 (4th Cir. 2015).
516. Consolidated Coal Co. v. Georgia Power Co., 781 F.3d 129 (4th Cir. 2015).
517. Vine Street LLC v. Borg Warner Corp., 776 F.3d 312 (5th Cir. 2015).
518. Three Ninth Circuit cases provide a comprehensive discussion of this useful product doctrine: Hinds Investments LP v. Angioli, 445 Fed. Appx. 917, 2011 U.S. App. LEXIS 15879 (9th Cir. 2011); Team Enterprises LLC v. Western Investments Real Estate Trust, 647 F.3d 901 (9th Cir. 2011); Team Enterprises LLC v. Western Investments Real Estate Trust (II), 2011 U.S. App. LEXIS 19881 (9th Cir. 2011).

engaged in sham sales of putatively useful products can be revealed as an arranger when the facts show that the hazardous substances have no actual market value and the intent is to incrementally dispose of the products disguised as sales.[519] The analysis returns to the useful product exception, though, for products having hazardous characteristics and little or no value to the seller for whom in a sense they may be "wastes," which will have commercial value, with reprocessing, for the purchaser. If a release later occurs, the seller will not be deemed to have been arranging for the disposal of hazardous substances.[520]

Hazardous wastes may be found in infrastructure on real property. The sale of the real property then may present complicated facts involving the seller's intent, which will require a consideration of the value of what is being conveyed. Is a sale including buildings or other structures economically sound, or is it only a surreptitious way to unload hazardous wastes, and the problem of their disposal, onto the buyer? If hazardous constituents of the property being conveyed are left behind in a still-useful condition for immediate use by the new owner, then useful products, not wastes, were conveyed and a surreptitious disposal was not being arranged.[521] However, in another case, a Circuit Court remanded for a more complete factual review where some of the infrastructure contained PCBs. The fact that steel beams in the infrastructure might have been beneficially reused by the buyer did not clarify whether the correlating transfer of PCBs was merely inadvertent or was a disguised disposal of a hazardous substance that arguably should have been properly disposed of prior to the sale.[522] The latter conclusion was drawn in yet another case where the court found that, in selling the building, the seller was also trying to surreptitiously arrange for disposal of the PCBs.[523]

The corporate form also raises questions when arranger liability is being analyzed. The corporation itself may be the arranger, or the corporate officer who directed the arrangement could be held personally liable as an arranger.[524] Moreover, a parent corporation may be liable if there is a causal connection between the parent's conduct and the subsidiary's arrangement for disposal. However, the mere fact that the arranging official of the subsidiary also serves as an official of the parent does not provide a sufficient nexus between the parent's conduct — if any — and the arrangement for disposal.[525]

[5] Parties Who Arrange for Recycling May Be Exempt from CERCLA Liability

In 1999, Congress amended CERCLA to exempt from liability in contribution actions (see § 7.06 [C][3]) parties who, under carefully defined circumstances, arranged

---

519. United States v. General Electric Corp., 670 F.3d 377 (1st Cir. 2012).

520. NCR Corp. v. George A. Whiting Paper Co., 768 F.3d 682 (7th Cir. 2014).

521. AM International, Inc. v. International Forging Equipment Corp., 982 F.2d 989 (6th Cir. 1993).

522. United States v. Tonawanda Coke Corp., 636 Fed. Appx. 24 (8th Cir. 2016).

523. United States v. Dico, Inc., 920 F.3d 1174 (8th Cir. 2019).

524. United States v. TIC Investment Corp., 68 F.3d 1082 (8th Cir. 1995).

525. Id.

for the recycling of materials. This was a response to a trend, seemingly contrary to some of RCRA's goals, whereby parties were reluctant to engage in recycling out of concern that they would be found to have arranged for disposal of hazardous wastes. The eventual disposal of recycled materials might trigger CERCLA liability if they contained hazardous constituents. As an additional result, industry was forgoing using many recycled materials in favor of new materials, thus consuming new natural resources.[526]

The exemption applies to various kinds of scrap material, and spent batteries, but not to large shipping containers that contain hazardous substances,[527] nor to materials containing PCBs in significant concentrations.[528] The party claiming the exemption, though, must show that it is not being used a ruse to escape CERCLA liability. This will require, among other things, that there be a proven recycling market for the particular materials, that the purportedly recycled materials fall within the grade of recycled materials that would be marketable, and that they are actually being recycled.[529] However, the focus is not only on the materials, but also on the intended recipient. The arranger must be in compliance with all relevant RCRA regulations[530] and must exercise reasonable diligence to ensure that the receiving facility is in compliance with all environmental laws and orders that pertain to recycled materials.[531]

[6] Transporters

Any party that accepts hazardous substances for transport to a disposal or treatment facility may be subject to transporter liability.[532] However, the transporter, to be liable, must select the destination, there must be a release or threatened release at the site, and the release must result in response costs.[533] The transporter's role in selecting the site may be circumstantially proved.[534] It does not matter whether the destination selected is a facility or just a location falling under the general rubric of "site"; the important criterion is the transporter's exercise of discretion as to destination.[535] Nor must the transporter exercise sole or controlling discretion; it need only have substantial input into,[536] or active participation in,[537] disposal site selection to be a statu-

---

526. 42 U.S.C. § 9627(a)(1).
527. 42 U.S.C. § 9627(b)(1).
528. 42 U.S.C. § 9627(b)(2) (greater than 50 parts per million).
529. 42 U.S.C. § 9627(c)(1)–(4).
530. 42 U.S.C. § 9627(d).
531. 42 U.S.C. § 9627(c)(5).
532. 42 U.S.C. § 9607(a)(4).
533. 42 U.S.C. § 9607(a)(4).
534. Action Manufacturing Co. v. Simon Wrecking Co., 287 Fed. Appx. 171 (3d Cir. 2008).
535. B.F. Goodrich v. Betkoski, 99 F.3d 505 (2d Cir. 1996); United States v. Hardage, 985 F.2d 1427, 1435 (10th Cir. 1993).
536. Tippins v. USX Corp., 37 F.3d 87, 94 (3d Cir. 1994).
537. B.F. Goodrich v. Betkoski, 99 F.3d 505 (2d Cir. 1996).

torily responsible party. Providing a recommendation could be sufficient participation, whereas merely doing the bidding of the generator, without more, would not trigger transporter liability.[538] One court has required a nexus between the transportation of the hazardous substances to the site, and the subsequent release at the site, to impose transporter liability.[539] As noted in connection with arranger liability (see [4], *above*), the intent matters. A spill during transport to a selected disposal location which as a result is not reached is an accident, not a disposal, and hence would not trigger CERCLA liability. However, as a hazardous waste release, it would still require RCRA remediation.

CERCLA was amended in 2002 to provide some relief for transporters of hazardous wastes which are only de minimis constituents of much larger quantities of non-hazardous solid waste being transported.[540]

[7] Strict, Joint, and Several Liability

CERCLA liability depends on the classification of the party — owner/operator, generator, transporter or arranger — rather than on fault. Although potentially responsible parties may litigate relative fault among themselves in contribution actions (see [C][3], *below*), their degree of fault is irrelevant to EPA or to private plaintiffs as a measure of liability for the cleanup of the site. In effect, EPA is determined in the first instance to ensure that the responsibility for a cleanup is imposed on one or more of the statutorily responsible parties and then to ensure that the cleanup is done. All other parties having some connection to contamination at the site can litigate among themselves later to apportion fault and their respective costs vis-à-vis each other.

Generally, all statutorily responsible parties are jointly and severally liable. There are some exceptions, such as when a particular responsible party, by settling with EPA, insulates itself from further liability (see [E], *below*), or the harm can be demonstrated to be divisible, so that a particular responsible party can prove its own share of costs.[541] Divisibility is a judge-created affirmative defense to CERCLA's joint and several liability available when a defendant can clearly show by reliable proof that it was responsible for only specific increments of the contamination, so that its cleanup responsibilities can be limited to that degree. However, compelling factual evidence, not equitable factors, will govern the analysis,[542] the mixing of wastes on-site as well as off-site mi-

---

538. *Id.*

539. Prisco v. State of New York, 902 F. Supp. 400 (S.D.N.Y. 1996).

540. With some restrictions, an exemption is afforded to a transporter that transports less than 110 gallons, or 200 pounds, of hazardous wastes. 42 U.S.C. § 9607(o).

541. *See* United States v. Township of Brighton, 282 F.3d 915 (6th Cir. 2002); United States and the State of New York v. Alcan Corp., 990 F.2d 711 (2d Cir. 1993); United States v. Alcan Corp., 964 F.2d 252 (3d Cir. 1992), *cert. denied*, 521 U.S. 1103 (1997). *But see* Bell Petroleum Services, Inc. v. United States, 3 F.3d 889 (5th Cir. 1993) (not allowing proof of divisibility).

542. Burlington Northern and Santa Fe Railway Co. v. United States, 566 U.S. 559 (2009).

gration can defeat the claim,[543]and successful cases have been rare.[544] A statutory defense also may be applicable (see [D], *below*). Unless an exception applies, though, all costs may be recovered by EPA or a private plaintiff from any or all responsible parties (see [C], *below*, for a discussion of cost recovery actions), leaving the responsible parties to sort out among themselves their relative share in contribution actions (see [C][3], *below*). As a practical matter, imposing joint and several liability relieves the plaintiff of the burden of proving the relative liability of any particular party. Rather, CERCLA shifts the burden of demonstrating relative liability to responsible parties, who have the incentive to undertake whatever investigative work is necessary to enlarge the pool of responsible parties and to implead them. The device is cost-effective from the government's and other plaintiffs' standpoint. Conversely, deleting the provision from CERCLA, as some commentators have recommended, would impose enormous costs on the government and innocent landowners.

CERCLA was not explicitly given retroactive reach by Congress.[545] However, as a remedial statute rather than a statute proscribing conduct, courts have consistently applied it retroactively to pre-CERCLA activity at hazardous waste sites.[546] Retroactivity may seem to be less relevant as the decades have passed since CERCLA was enacted. However, there are still many hazardous waste sites with legacy wastes which were disposed of or released there during the early and middle years of the 20th century preceding CERCLA's enactment which can bring owners, operators and others, or their successors in interest, from those early years within the CERCLA net of liability.

[C] Cleanup Costs: Who Pays Whom?

[1] Cost Recovery Actions versus Contribution Actions

CERCLA authorizes two types of action for the recovery and distribution of expenses incurred for remediation and related activities: a § 107 "cost recovery" action and a § 113(f) "contribution" action. Each kind of action is discussed in sections §§ 7.06[C][1] and [2], below. The discussion here will address to how they interrelate and how they differ, matters which have led to occasionally tangled jurispru-

---

543. Pakootas v. Teck Cominco Metals Ltd., 905 F.3d 565 (9th Cir. 2018); United States v. Vertac Chemical Corp., 453 F.3d 1031 (8th Cir. 2006). *See also* Tucker, *All Is Number: Mathematics, Divisibility and Apportionment Under* Burlington Northern, 22 FORDHAM ENVIRONMENTAL LAW JOURNAL 311 (2011).

544. United States v. Coeur D'Alenes Co., 767 F.3d 873 (9th Cir. 2014); Metropolitan Water Reclamation District of Greater Chicago v. North American Galvanizing & Coating, Inc., 473 F.3d 824, n. 3 (7th Cir. 2007). *See also* Judy, *Coming Full CERCLA: Why* Burlington Northern *Is Not the Sword of Damocles for Joint and Several Liability*, 44 NEW ENGLAND LAW REVIEW 249 (2010).

545. Boria v. Keane, 90 F.3d 36, 38 (2d Cir. 1996), *cert. denied*, 521 U.S. 1118 (1997).

546. *See, e.g.*, Virginia Properties, Inc. v. Home Insurance Co., 74 F.3d 1131 (11th Cir. 1996); United States v. R.W. Meyer, Inc., 889 F.2d 1497, 1506 (6th Cir. 1989), *cert. denied*, 494 U.S. 1057 (1990).

dence over the years. The different actions serve different purposes and can have very different results, so that it is important to bear the distinctions in mind.[547]

Cost recovery actions initially had been contemplated as a remedy for the government undertaking a cleanup, possibly drawing upon Superfund resources, so that those costs could be replenished upon recovery from parties who were liable by operation of § 107. Given the sheer number of contaminated sites throughout the nation, governmental cleanup responsibilities were quickly overwhelmed. Section 106, however, gives the government the authority to order a responsible party under § 107 to conduct the cleanup itself. The private party could then undertake the cleanup in lieu of the government.

Many private parties came to prefer conducting the cleanup themselves, subject to EPA supervision and approvals, in the belief that they could thereby better control costs and benefit from additional efficiencies, rather than being sued by the government for the recovery of its costs after EPA and government contractors undertook the cleanup. This also worked better for EPA, which could better control the outcome — the property is remediated — without assuming the direct responsibility and the up-front costs. Hence, whether in response to a § 106 order or a consent decree, many cleanups today are undertaken by private parties rather than by the government.

Section 107 determines the basic statutory liability of parties on the basis of their status, as noted in [B], *above*. Since the cleanup costs could be imposed jointly and severally, any statutorily responsible party (the shorthand commonly used has been PRP, for potentially responsible party) conceivably could be strictly liable for the entirety of the cleanup costs, regardless of individual fault. As a protection for a statutorily responsible party undertaking a cleanup, § 107 authorizes it, potentially one having little or no fault for the contamination, to recover costs it has incurred for a cleanup it has conducted from other responsible parties in a cost recovery action.[548] Section 113(f), by contrast, is a vehicle for responsible parties to apportion among themselves the costs being sought in a cost recovery action.[549] However, the manner in which these different CERCLA sections interact can be complicated, and caselaw has sometimes made fine but not always clear distinctions. The party burdened with cleanup responsibilities cannot simply choose one or the other. The fact that a responsible party is liable for all cleanup costs under § 107 does not, itself, establish its right to an equitable allocation of costs vis-a-vis other responsible parties.

That had been a gap in the initial statute. Section 113, enacted in later amendments, created a vehicle by which a party which had already incurred the cleanup costs could seek contribution, originally a tort concept, from other responsible parties to com-

---

547. See discussion addressing how the different remedies work in Niagara Mohawk Power Corp. v. Chevron USA, 596 F.3d 112 (2d Cir. 2010). For a more comprehensive treatise discussion, see Robinson, Environmental Regulation of Real Property §§ 22.05(2)(d), 22.08 (Law Journal Press).

548. 42 U.S.C. § 9607(a)(4)(B).

549. Town of Munster, Indiana v. Sherwin-Williams Co., Inc., 27 F.3d 1268, 1270 (7th Cir. 1994).

pensate for its cleanup costs on an equitable basis, subject to proof or negotiation.[550] Hence, while CERCLA's strict liability provisions impose strict, joint and several liability on statutorily liable parties can be harsh, § 113(f) authorizing contribution actions among the parties at fault for the contamination allows for some degree of equitable relief. The way that this has worked out in practice is that once a cost recovery action is commenced against a party who is liable by operation of § 107, the defendant in that action has a vehicle to seek out other responsible parties to sue for contribution. Those other responsible parties, once they are served with the § 113(f) complaint, then have an incentive to seek out additional responsible parties, and so on, in the hope of reducing their own ultimate financial contribution. As a result, a growing pool of responsible parties, and their lawyers and insurance carriers, collectively create the vehicle by which the costs incurred by the party undertaking the cleanup can be satisfied or at least mitigated. A contribution action is a private action for which EPA incurs no investigative or enforcement costs, a benefit to the government relieved of these responsibilities, and to the party which had been burdened initially with the exacting consequences of strict, joint and several liability insofar as a growing pool of responsible parties, and their insurance carriers, makes the recovery of adequate cleanup costs by the original cleanup party more feasible.

There is a necessary order which the respective actions must follow. The Supreme Court, following a period of differing Circuit Court interpretations, has ruled that a contribution action may not be commenced unless a civil action for cost recovery under CERCLA § 107, or an EPA administrative enforcement action under CERCLA § 106, has already been commenced. The Court noted that contribution actions exist only as a device to apportion liability among responsible parties once there is the likelihood of recoverable costs.[551] There had been previous uncertainty whether a "volunteer," a party that undertook a cleanup of the contaminated property, presumably for sound personal or commercial reasons but not under governmental coercion, could use § 113(f) to recoup its costs from responsible parties. The Supreme Court has since clarified that a party undertaking such a "voluntary" cleanup, in the absence of an existing cleanup order or consent decree, deprives the volunteer of the ability to recoup a portion of the cleanup costs in contribution against responsible parties.[552] However, all may not be lost for the diligent volunteer. If the volunteer

---

550. Elementis Chromium L.P. v. Coastal States Petroleum Co., 450 F.3d 607 (5th Cir. 2006); United States v. Davis, 261 F.3d 1 (1st Cir. 2001).

551. Cooper Industries v. Aviall Services, Inc., 543 U.S. 157 (2004).

552. Atlantic Research Group v. United States, 551 U.S. 128 (2007). *United States v. Atlantic Research Corp.* discusses some of the history among circuit courts that had left unsettled the question whether at-fault private parties, having "unclean hands," could commence actions in cost recovery, or were limited to seeking only contribution after being sued for cost recovery. The information herein is included as an advisement to readers who may come upon earlier, now possibly invalid, caselaw during their research. The position of a "volunteer," a party that voluntarily cleaned up a site, yet which might have been partially at fault for the contamination, had been ambiguous, given the splits among circuit courts. In *Cooper Industries, Inc. v. Aviall Services, Inc., supra,* the Supreme Court held that a contribution action could not be commenced by a party that had not yet been subjected to a cost recovery action, but had left unanswered the question whether a volunteer could com-

thereby has incurred the costs of removal or remedial action, it may be able to recover its cleanup costs in a § 107 cost recovery action against responsible parties even if it bears fault for the contamination.[553] Confusing? Yes. The logic outlined in the Supreme Court jurisprudence has to be carefully followed.

The Supreme Court has warned that for a viable action in contribution, the CER-CLA rules are strict—a contribution action cannot be independently initiated, nor can it refer back to responsibilities under a different statute. It must proceed exclusively from a prior CERCLA § 106 order or § 107 action directing a cleanup or a related consent decree. The fact that a party has taken corrective action or undertaken cleanup responsibilities under a different statute, such as RCRA or the Clean Water Act, even if done pursuant to a court or EPA order, will not qualify for purposes of a CERCLA contribution action.[554]

A party commencing a contribution action must first establish that the particular costs which it seeks to recover in a § 113 contribution action are actually recoverable under § 107. Contribution does not create a new basis for liability—the basis for liability must already exist under § 107—but only apportions already existing liability.[555] Recoverable costs are discussed in § 7.06[C], below.

Lawyers must carefully review the respective statutes of limitations for these actions. Dismissals are common for cases where lawyers misunderstood which limitations period applied. Cost recovery is subject to a three-year statute of limitations for a removal action, but six years for remediation, commencing with initiation of physical on-site construction.[556] Contribution actions have only a three-year limitations period, commencing with either the judgment or settlement date of the cost recovery action.[557]

Depending on the circumstances of the case, the particular limitations period or other factors bearing on the nature of the proceeding may be critically important, so parties may try characterizing the action as either cost recovery or contribution to suit their needs. However, courts look to the nature of the action actually being advanced rather than how it was formally pleaded. An improperly framed or commenced action will be dismissed, with possibly drastic consequences for the plaintiff.

A party barred under CERCLA for these or other various reasons is not thereby prevented from separately asserting state or common law claims.

---

mence a cost recovery action. In dicta, the Court suggested that it could, notwithstanding that it might have been precluded from seeking contribution. *Atlantic Research* resolved the issue, holding that a volunteer, even if at fault for contamination at the site, may commence a cost recovery action against PRPs under § 107.

553. United States v. Atlantic Research Corp., 551 U.S. 128 (2007).

554. Territory of Guam v. United States, ___ U.S. ___, 141 S. Ct. 1608, 209 L. Ed. 2d 691 (2021).

555. New Castle County v. Halliburton NUS Corp., 111 F.3d 1116 (3d Cir. 1997); Bancamerica Commercial Corp. v. Mosher Steel of Kansas, Inc., 100 F.3d 792 (10th Cir. 1996).

556. 42 U.S.C. § 9613(g)(2).

557. 42 U.S.C. § 9613(g)(3).

[2] Cost Recovery Actions

CERCLA § 107[558] authorizes the federal government and states in the first instance to commence actions to recover removal and remediation costs, consistent with the National Contingency Plan (NCP), from responsible parties. Costs that are incompatible with the NCP are not recoverable.[559] Section 107 actions also may include recovery of "any other necessary costs of response" incurred by "any other person," also consistent with the NCP.[560] The cleanup costs must be reasonable, not excessive, necessary, and further the goals of the remediation, to be recoverable.[561] CERCLA does not limit the class of persons who may recover response costs.[562] Natural resource damages and health assessment costs may also be recovered under the statutory terms.[563] The parties subject to cost recovery are those discussed in [B], *above.*

Recoverable costs include not only the physical expenses of remediation (see [A], *above*), but also the expenses arising from remediation studies,[564] and health assessment and surveillance costs.[565] However, some courts have precluded recovery of private medical expenses of persons exposed to hazardous wastes[566] as not being inherently "remedial."[567] This means personal injury and property damage suits may not be brought under CERCLA. They are typically brought as common law toxic tort actions (see § 8.03).

Expenses incurred during government oversight of a private party cleanup are generally construed to be recoverable as response costs.[568] Courts generally have allowed recovery of such expenses as routine monitoring costs affiliated with safe hazardous waste removal and thus inherently remedial,[569] although several have not. The costs incurred by contractors who remove the hazardous wastes for proper off-site disposal are also recoverable in that they further the remediation.[570]

---

558. 42 U.S.C. § 9607.

559. City of Colton v. American Promotional Events, Inc. — West, 614 F.3d 998 (9th Cir. 2010).

560. 42 U.S.C. § 9607(a)(4)(B).

561. Trinity Industries v. Greenlease Holding Co., 903 F.3d 333 (3d Cir. 2018); Pakootas v. Teck Cominco Metals, Ltd., 905 F.3d 565 (9th Cir. 2018).

562. OHM Remediation Services v. Evans Cooperage Co., Inc., 116 F.3d 1574, 1580 (5th Cir. 1997).

563. 42 U.S.C. § 9607(a).

564. B.F. Goodrich v. Betkoski, 99 F.3d 505 (2d Cir. 1996).

565. Hanford Downwinders Coalition v. Dowdle, 71 F.3d 1469 (9th Cir. 1995).

566. Durfey v. E.I. DuPont De Nemours Co., 59 F.3d 121 (9th Cir. 1995); Price v. United States Navy, 39 F.3d 1011 (9th Cir. 1994).

567. Daigle v. Shell Oil Co., 972 F.2d 1527 (10th Cir. 1992).

568. United States v. W.R. Grace & Co., 429 F.3d 1224 (9th Cir. 2005).

569. United States v. E.I. Dupont de Nemours Co., Inc., 432 F.3d 161 (3d Cir. 2005); United States v. Dico, Inc. v. 266 F.3d 864 (8th Cir. 2001); New York v. Shore Realty Corp., 759 F.2d 1032, 1043 (2d Cir. 1985); United States v. Lowe, 118 F.3d 399 (5th Cir. 1997); Atlantic Richfield Co. v. American Airlines, Inc., 98 F.3d 564 (10th Cir. 1996).

570. Blasland, Bouck & Lee, Inc. v. City of North Miami, 283 F.3d 1286 (11th Cir. 2002).

Pre-judgment and post-judgment interest relating to the initial outlay of expenses necessary for the cleanup may also be recoverable.[571]

Attorneys' fees incurred during litigation are generally not recoverable. However, pre-litigation, investigative attorneys' fees may be recovered on the same basis as those of other consultants, if incurred while identifying other responsible parties.[572]

Costs that may arise from the cleanup, such as the expenses of relocating, which, however, are not costs incurred to conduct the cleanup, are not recoverable.[573]

[3] Contribution Actions

The right to contribution was codified in the 1986 amendments to CERCLA, prior to which courts had recognized an implied right of contribution among responsible parties as a means of muting the harshness of its joint and several, and strict liability provisions.[574] To state a claim in contribution against another party, the plaintiff must show that the defendant is a PRP with reference to § 107, the site subject to the cleanup is a facility within the meaning of CERCLA, there was a release or threatened release of hazardous substances at that site, and as a result, the party seeking contribution suffered damages.[575]

Contribution is available for "potentially" responsible parties (PRPs). Hence, although EPA or another plaintiff must have initiated a cost recovery action as a predicate to any contribution action as is discussed in § 7.06[C][1], above,[576] a PRP may commence, or be joined in, a contribution action upon a prior finding of liability. The United States may even be subject to contribution actions if it is a PRP with reference to § 107.[577]

Any PRP may seek contribution from any other PRPs, among whom courts will allocate response costs "using such equitable factors as the court determines are appropriate."[578] Courts are relatively unfettered in their application of equity. A court may rely on many or few considerations, or even be persuaded by a single factor while ignoring other relevant factors in allocating responsibility.[579] How the court

---

571. 42 U.S.C. § 9607(a)(4); LITGO New Jersey, Inc. v. Commissioner of New Jersey Department of Environmental Protection, 725 F.3d 369 (3d Cir. 2013); B.F. Goodrich Corp. v. Town of Middlebury, 311 F.3d 154 (2d Cir. 2002).

572. Key Tronic Corp. v. United States, 511 U.S. 809 (1994); Pakootas v. Teck Cominco Metals, Ltd., 905 F.3d 565 (9th Cir. 2018).

573. Taira Lynn Marine Ltd. No. 5, LLC. v. Jas Seafood, Inc., 444 F.3d 371 (5th Cir. 2006).

574. *See* United Technologies Corp. v. Browning-Ferris Industries, Inc., 33 F.3d 96 (1st Cir. 1994), *cert. denied*, 513 U.S. 1183 (1995) (analyzing the legislative history of contribution); Lyondell Chemical Co. v. Occidental Chemical Corp., 608 F.3d 284 (5th Cir. 2010).

575. State of California v. Campbell, 319 F.3d 1161 (9th Cir. 2003).

576. *See* Cooper Industries v. Aviall Services, Inc., 543 U.S. 157, 125 S. Ct. 577, 160 L. Ed. 2d 548 (2004).

577. TDY Holdings, LLC v. United States, 885 F.3d 1142 (9th Cir. 2018), same case at 872 F.3d 1004 (9th Cir. 2017).

578. 42 U.S.C. § 9613(f)(1).

579. Bancamerica Commercial Corp. v. Mosher Steel of Kansas, Inc., 100 F.3d 792 (10th 1996).

allocates the responsibility for costs among contributors is discretionary. If the court's conclusions are reasonable and grounded in the evidence, its decision should be upheld.[580] Courts also may look to the so-called "Gore factors," articulated by then-Senator Albert Gore, as part of CERCLA's legislative history, in evaluating relative responsibility. These factors include the following:[581]

- The ability of the parties to demonstrate that their contribution is distinguishable;
- The amount of hazardous waste involved;
- The waste's toxicity;
- The party's involvement in generation, transportation, treatment, storage, or disposal;
- The degree of care exercised by the party, taking into account the waste's hazardous characteristics; and
- The party's cooperation with officials to prevent any harm to the public or to the environment.

Hazardous wastes attributable to unidentified, missing, or insolvent PRPs give rise to "orphan shares."[582] The orphan share represents the difference between a party's actual responsibility for harm and the portion of financial responsibility allocated to it. Some courts allow apportionment of orphan shares among all solvent PRPs.[583]

Unlike cost recovery actions, parties seeking contribution bear the burden of demonstrating a right to apportionment, identifying the other contaminating parties and the extent of their involvement.[584]

[D] Defenses

[1] Three Defenses, Generally

CERCLA recognizes three statutory defenses: that the release or threat of release was caused solely by one or more of the following:[585]

---

580. Ameripride Services, Inc. v. Texas Eastern Overseas, Inc., 782 F.3d 474 (9th Cir. 2015); LITGO New Jersey, Inc. v. Commissioner of New Jersey Department of Environmental Protection, 725 F.3d 369 (3d Cir. 213).

581. 126 Cong. Rec. 26,779-81 (1980). *See* ASARCO LLC v. Atlantic Richfield Co., LLC, 975 F.3d 859 (9th Cir. 2020). Since these criteria have never been legislated, they remain non-binding on courts. *See* Boeing Co. v. Cascade Corp., 207 F.3d 1177 (9th Cir. 2000).

582. Sun Company, Inc. v. Browning-Ferris, Inc., 124 F.3d 1187 (10th Cir. 1997), *cert. denied*, 522 U.S. 1113 (1998).

583. United States v. Kramer, 953 F. Supp. 592 (D.N.J. 1997); SC Holdings, Inc. v. A.A.A. Realty Co., 935 F. Supp. 1354, 1373 (D.N.J. 1996); Charter Township of Oshtemo v. American Cyanamid Co., 898 F. Supp. 506, 509 (W.D. Mich. 1995).

584. United States v. Monsanto Co., 858 F.2d 160, 168 n.13, 171–73 (4th Cir. 1988), *cert. denied*, 490 U.S. 1106 (1989); United States v. R.W. Meyer, Inc., 889 F.2d 1497, 1507–08 (6th Cir. 1989), *cert. denied*, 494 U.S. 1057 (1990).

585. 42 U.S.C. § 9607(b).

- An act of God;

- An act of war; or

- Under carefully circumscribed conditions, an act or omission of a third party.

In any case, the party asserting the defense has the burden of proving it by a preponderance of the evidence.[586] CERCLA also provides an affirmative defense to municipal and state governments and their agencies that respond to emergencies at facilities owned by other parties; a fire department responding to a fire during which hazardous wastes are released is a typical example.[587]

[2] Acts of God and War

An act of God is an "unanticipated grave natural disaster or other natural phenomenon of an exceptional, inevitable, and irresistible character, the effects of which could not have been prevented or avoided by the exercise of due care or foresight."[588] It has generally proved to be unavailing as a successful device to avoid CERCLA liability. Act of war is not defined, and there has been little opportunity to litigate the claim since the inception of CERCLA. However, in what hopefully is a unique circumstance, the Second Circuit concluded that the 2001 attack on the World Trade Center satisfied the definition and was the sole cause of the release of numerous toxins into the environment and damage to nearby buildings. Applying the defense, the court dismissed the CERCLA cost recovery action and other claims against its owners and trustees as well as against the airlines that were the subject of the terrorist attack.[589]

The mere fact that a release has occurred that has some tangential connection to international hostilities does not trigger the defense. Hence, the defense would not protect military contractors who are responsible for releases, even during a time of war, which are not a direct result of a military action.[590]

[3] Act or Omission of Third Party

The act or omission of a third party provides quite limited protection to an "innocent land owner" from the consequences of the conduct of the proverbial "midnight dumper," and also from the acts of prior owners. The third party may not be an employee or agent of the party claiming the defense. Nor may the third party be anyone with a contractual relationship (except for a common carrier), even an indirect one, with the defendant. In addition, the defendant must demonstrate that it exercised

---

586. *Id.*

587. 42 U.S.C. 9607(d)(3); AMW Materials Testing, Inc. v. Town of Babylon and North Amityville Fire Company, 584 F.3d 436 (2d Cir. 2009).

588. 42 U.S.C. § 9601(1).

589. *In re* September 11 Litigation: Cedar & Washington Associates LLC v. Port Authority of New York and New Jersey, 751 F.3d 86 (2d Cir. 2014).

590. United States v. Shell Oil Co., 294 F.3d 1045 (9th Cir. 2002), *cert. denied*, 537 U.S. 1147 (2003).

due care with respect to the hazardous substance and took precautions against fore-seeable acts or omissions of the third party.[591]

[4] Innocent Purchaser Defense

If an "innocent purchaser" defense is asserted in connection with activity by prior owners, the defendant must demonstrate that it had no reason to know of the hazardous substances on the site. For this showing, the defendant must establish that it undertook a due diligence inspection at the time of acquisition, including an inquiry into the nature of the prior ownership and prior uses of the property, consistent with good commercial practice. The court, in evaluating the validity of the defense, will consider the defendant's specialized knowledge or experience, how the purchase price relates to market value of similar uncontaminated property, whether information about the contamination was reasonably ascertainable, and whether the contamination was readily apparent.[592] A sale price which is too far below a reasonable market price should alert a diligent purchaser to the need for a deeper investigation and will likely defeat the defense. The defense is unavailable to a purchaser who was aware of the contamination prior to the purchase.[593] Nor is the defense available to an owner who, claiming it was unaware of the contamination when it purchased the property, subsequently conveyed the property without disclosing the contamination of which it is now aware.[594] Nor can the party who caused the release (as contrasted with the disposal) claim the defense.[595]

In 2002, Congress provided some limited protection for bona fide purchasers of "brownfields," or moderately contaminated properties who intend to beneficially develop the property (see § 7.07). The protection is hedged in by numerous restrictions to ensure that the prospective purchaser is not engaged in a sham transaction designed to insulate buyers and sellers from CERCLA liability. The protection is not available to parties responsible for the contamination, nor does it protect the purchaser from state laws.[596]

[E] Settlement and Protection from Contribution

The federal policy favoring settlements as a means of reducing litigation and encouraging speedy remediation has been identified with CERCLA.[597] When a responsible party settles its own liability in a judicially or administratively approved settlement with either the federal or state government, it will be protected from future contribution claims by other, non-settling, responsible parties with respect to "matters addressed in the settlement."[598]

---

591. 42 U.S.C. § 9607(b)(3).

592. 42 U.S.C. § 9601(35)(B); United States v. 150 Acres of Land, 204 F.3d 698 (6th Cir. 2000).

593. Pennsylvania Department of Environmental Protection v. Trainer Custom Chemical LLC, 906 F.3d 85 (3d Cir. 2018).

594. 42 U.S.C. § 9601(35)(C).

595. 42 U.S.C. § 9601(35)(D).

596. 42 U.S.C. §§ 9601(39), 9604(k).

597. United States v. Cannons Engineering Corp., 899 F.2d 79, 84 (1st Cir. 1990).

598. 42 U.S.C. § 9613(f)(2).

Although the provision does not elaborate on the meaning of "matters addressed in the settlement," some courts have construed the protection broadly to cover any matter reasonably related to the cleanup,[599] including separate but related sites involving the same parties.[600] However, other courts refused to extend the settlement's protection to a site not specified therein, even when there was a common identity of parties.[601] If the settlement agreement is with the state and it does not specifically incorporate potential federal CERCLA claims, this may expose the settling PRP to future federal CERCLA claims.[602] Another court looked closely to ensure that the settlement amount was proportionate to the settling party's equitable share as a predicate to approval.[603]

If the non-settling parties lose the benefit of having the settling contributor available in the contribution action, they receive some benefit in that the settlement amount is deducted from the total judgment. Of course, sometimes it cannot be determined at the time of settlement what the settlor's equitable share would have been, or what the final judgment will require, so this "benefit" to the non-settlors may be difficult to assess at the time of the settlement. If the settling party benefits from a generous settlement with the government so that, ultimately, it pays less than what might have been its proportionate share, it may likely increase the financial costs to the non-settling parties.[604] The court in approving the settlement, though, should review the evidence to ensure that it approximately allocates the relative fault of the settling party as measured against that of the non-settling parties.[605] However, from EPA's standpoint, encouraging responsible parties to seek early and advantageous settlements with the government imposes a correlating sanction on non-settling responsible parties, who thus may assume responsibility for unanticipated costs, including orphan shares.[606] The benefit from the government's perspective is that, under some circumstances, responsible parties may rush to settle so that, in a manner of speaking, they are not holding the bag and its potentially disproportionate share of costs as cases against others are resolved.

The statute authorizes the government to commence an action against responsible parties if it has "obtained less than complete relief" from a settling party,[607] suggesting

---

599. *See* Avnet, Inc. v. Allied-Signal, Inc., 825 F. Supp. 1132, 1139 (D.R.I. 1992); United States v. Asarco, Inc., 814 F. Supp. 951, 957 (D. Colo. 1993).

600. Lyondell Chemical Co. v. Occidental Chemical Corp., 608 F.3d 284 (5th Cir. 2010). However, even this broad reading of CERCLA did not lead the court to extend the scope of the consent decree to sites where the contamination had not been known when the settlement was entered.

601. City of Emeryville v. Robinson, 621 F.3d 1251 (9th Cir. 2010); Rumpke of Indiana, Inc. v. Cummins Engine Co., Inc., 107 F.3d 1235 (7th Cir. 1997).

602. New Jersey Department of Environmental Protection v. American Thermoplastics Corp., 974 F.3d 486 (3d Cir. 2020).

603. Akzo Coatings, Inc. v. Aigner Corp., 30 F.3d 761, 766 (7th Cir. 1994).

604. United States v. George A. Whiting Paper Co., 644 F.3d 368 (7th Cir. 2011); United States v. BP Amoco Oil LLC, 277 F.3d 1012 (8th Cir. 2002).

605. State of Arizona v. City of Tucson, 761 F.3d 1005 (9th Cir. 2014).

606. United Technologies Corp. v. Browning-Ferris Industries, Inc., 33 F.3d 96, 103 (1st Cir. 1994), *cert. denied*, 513 U.S. 1183 (1995); B.F. Goodrich v. Betkoski, 99 F.3d 505 (2d Cir. 1996).

607. 42 U.S.C. § 9613(f)(3)(A).

a defense for non-settlors when the exaction from the settlor satisfies cleanup costs. Given a possible mathematical uncertainty of cleanup costs at a time of early settlement, what if the settling party pays so much more than its equitable share that the settlement effectively relieves other responsible parties of liability? Does that create a disincentive for early settlement in some cases? One court has construed such a result to be an impermissible windfall inconsistent with CERCLA's early settlement policy. In that case, the court ruled on an alternative ground that the settlement amount, paid to a coalition organized to perform the remediation, rather than to the government, was unavailable to reduce the equitable shares of non-settling parties.[608]

A settlor, paying in excess of its equitable share, may still seek contribution from non-settlors.[609] One court allowed a settlor that paid more than its equitable share to seek contribution from non-settlors to the extent that the settlor paid cleanup costs attributable to other parties.[610]

Non-settling parties may intervene to challenge a consent decree that approves the settlement agreement.[611] However, they have no means of challenging a subsequent judgment approving and implementing the settlement.[612] For the protection to be lifted, the government must formally terminate the settlement agreement.[613] Non-settling parties cannot seek contribution solely because the settling party fails to perform the agreement.[614]

[F] Insurance

[1] Pollution Exclusion Clauses

The existence and extent of insurance coverage is a major practical component of most cleanups. A pollution exclusion clause was first incorporated into standard Comprehensive General Liability (CGL) policies in 1973 and lasted in that form until 1986,[615] coinciding with many activities that have significantly expanded CERCLA's reach. The exclusion remains important for those releases occurring during that time period that might have remained undiscovered until later years.

[2] "Sudden and Accidental" Releases

The pollution exclusion defined an insurable occurrence as including only "sudden and accidental" releases, terms that were not defined in the standard policy. Insurance carriers limited the term "sudden" to abrupt or short lasting events, as

---

608. B.F. Goodrich v. Betkoski, 99 F.3d 505 (2d Cir. 1996).
609. 42 U.S.C. § 9613(f)(3)(B).
610. United States v. Colorado & Eastern Railroad Co., 50 F.3d 1530 (10th Cir. 1995).
611. 42 U.S.C. § 9613(i).
612. ASARCO LLC v. Union Pacific Railroad Co., 762 F.3d 744 (8th Cir. 2014).
613. Dravo Corp. v. Zuber, 13 F.3d 1222, 1225–28 (8th Cir. 1994).
614. United States v. Colorado & Eastern Railroad Co., 50 F.3d 1530 (10th Cir. 1995).
615. See discussion in MITCHELL LATHROP, INSURANCE COVERGE FOR ENVIRONMENTAL CLAIMS, § 3.07 (Matthew Bender).

contrasted with gradual releases, not satisfied merely by being unexpected or unintended, the latter terms characterizing only the "accidental" part of the clause. Insureds, finding ambiguity, sought to construe the term against the draftsman-insurer. Given the draconian consequences of contaminating events that might have occurred years earlier, but were hard to pinpoint, raising questions as to which, if any, insurance policies applied, extensive litigation arose from differing interpretations of these words. The 1970 drafters were focused on third party tort claims arising from the migration of contamination from one party to another, rather than CERCLA cost recovery actions.[616] One court, reviewing the drafting history of the exclusion, concluded that the drafters had not fully appreciated the significance of the terms.[617]

Courts, applying state law, have divided in interpretations of the terms. Most find the terms to be clear and unambiguous. Hence, in one case, the seepage of land filled wastes into groundwater over a period of years, while accidental, was not sudden, and coverage did not apply.[618] Some courts have interpreted "sudden" to be an immediate, abrupt, instantaneous, or brief release, but have excluded gradual contamination or its migration,[619] and sudden events, such as storms, when the contamination had accrued over time.[620] However, other courts have found the term either ambiguous, or similar in meaning to accidental, meaning unexpected and unintentional.[621]

[3] "Absolute" Pollution Exclusion

As a result of the uncertainty and significant exposure in some states, the insurance industry drafted an "absolute" pollution exclusion that was incorporated in CGL policies in 1986. It defined "pollutants" broadly, and excluded injuries and damages from the discharge, dispersal, or escape of pollutants, in a wide variety of locations of activities, with no temporal limitation on the manner of contamination. Courts

---

616. *See generally* Nancer Ballard & Peter M. Manus, *Clearing Muddy Waters: Anatomy of the Comprehensive General Liability Policy Exclusion,* 75 Cornell L. Rev. 610 (1990).

617. Claussen v. Aetna Casualty & Surety Co., 676 F. Supp. 1571, 1574 (S.D. Ga. 1987).

618. Waste Management of Carolinas, Inc. v. Peerless Insurance Co., 340 S.E.2d 374 (S. Ct. N. Car. 1986).

619. *See, e.g.,* A. Johnson & Co. v. Aetna Casualty & Surety Co., 933 F.2d 66 (1st Cir. 1991) (Maine law); Northern Insurance Co. v. Aardvark Associates, Inc., 942 F.2d 189 (3d Cir. 1991) (Pennsylvania law); Olin Corp. v. Insurance Co. of North America, 762 F. Supp. 548 (S.D.N.Y. 1991); Northville Industries Corp. v. National Union Fire Insurance, 679 N.E.2d 1044 (C.A.N.Y. 1997).

620. Lumbermens Mutual Casualty Co. v. Belleville Industries, Inc., 938 F.2d 1423 (1st Cir.) (Mass. law).

621. New Castle County v. Hartford Accident & Indemnity Co., 933 F.2d 1162 (3d Cir. 1991); Lansco, Inc. v. Department of Environmental Protection, 368 A.2d 363 (N.J. App. Div. 1976), *cert. denied,* 372 A.2d 322 (N.J. Sup. Ct. 1977); Broadwell Realty Services, Inc. v. Fidelity & Casualty Co., 528 A.2d 76 (N.J. Sup. Ct. 1987); CPC International, Inc. v. Northbrook Excess & Surplus Insurance Co., 962 F.2d 77 (1st Dept. 1992) (New Jersey law); United Pacific Insurance Co. v. Van's Westlake Union, Inc., 664 P.2d 1262 (Wash. App. 1983); United States Fidelity & Guaranty Co. v. Specialty Coatings Co., 535 N.E.2d 1071 (Ill. App. 1989).

have generally given this exclusion effect,[622] although it has not been given effect if the injury or damage did not arise from actual pollution.[623] In some cases, coverage was successfully denied on this basis for damage resulting from gasoline,[624] lead paint,[625] or potentially non-toxic fumes resulting from a fiery garbage dump,[626] while mixed toxic and nontoxic fumes from a fire created an issue of fact as to whether the damage was caused by a noncovered pollution event or a covered accidental event — the fire.[627]

[G] State Cleanup Statutes

In enacting CERCLA, Congress specifically did not preempt states from imposing any additional liability or requirements regarding releases of hazardous wastes within the states,[628] and, in fact, many cleanups are conducted under state Superfund laws.

[H] Effect of Responsible Party's Bankruptcy

[1] Bankruptcy Petition Stays Actions for Money Judgments, but Not Governmental Enforcement Actions

A potentially responsible party facing drastic exposure for a spill or release could consider seeking refuge in bankruptcy. As a result, a few basic principles, applicable to CERCLA and other environmental laws, are important for an environmental lawyer to bear in mind.

First, bankruptcy proceedings, whether voluntary or involuntary, usually stay proceedings to collect on debts owed by the debtor or secured by its property, effectively enjoining such liens and judgments.[629] Cost recovery or contribution actions seeking only monetary awards could fit this category.[630]

However, there are exceptions that apply, precluding the stay, when the government commences or continues a regulatory enforcement proceeding or an action in fur-

---

622. *See, e.g.*, Guilford Industries, Inc. v. Liberty Mutual Insurance Co., 879 F.2d 853 (1st Cir. 1989) (Maine law); Hydro Systems, Inc. v. Continental Insurance Co., 929 F.2d 472 (9th Cir. 1991) (Calif. law); Alcolac, Inc. v. California Union Insurance Co., 716 F. Supp. 1546 (D. Md. 1989).

623. Titan Holdings Syndicate, Inc. v. Keene, 898 F.2d 265 (1st Cir. 1990) (bright lights and noise not pollution).

624. American States Insurance Co. v. Kiger, 662 N.E.2d 945 (Ind. 1996).

625. Atlantic Mutual Insurance Co. v. McFadden, 595 N.E.2d 792 (Mass. 1992); Sullins v. Allstate Insurance Co., 667 A.2d 617 (Md. 1995); Weaver v. Royal Insurance Co. of America, 674 A.2d 975 (N.H. 1996).

626. *In re* Hub Recycling, 106 B.R. 372 (D. N.J. 1989).

627. Reliance Insurance Co. v. Kent Corp., 896 F.2d 501 (11th Cir. 1990) (Ala. Law).

628. 42 U.S.C. § 9614(a).

629. 11 U.S.C. § 362(a); *see generally* COLLIER REAL ESTATE TRANSACTIONS AND THE BANKRUPTCY CODE, *Ch. 6 (Matthew Bender)*; ENVIRONMENTAL LAW AND PRACTICE GUIDE, *Ch. 10 (Michael B. Gerrard, ed., Matthew Bender)*.

630. Boston and Maine Corp. v. Massachusetts Bay Transportation Authority, 587 F.3d 89 (1st Cir. 2009).

therance of its police powers, or seeks enforcement of a non-monetary judgment resulting from such a proceeding.[631] Effectively, then, the filing of a bankruptcy petition does not prevent a governmental agency from enforcing environmental laws. For instance, an order directing the debtor operating a hazardous waste disposal facility to either complete its permit application or to file a closure plan was exempt from the stay.[632] Even if the debtor, still in possession of the site, must expend funds to comply with a remediation order, since there is no money judgment, the stay does not apply.[633] A government action to recover response costs has been interpreted as essentially a regulatory action exempt from the stay.[634] Directing a debtor responsible for contamination of adjacent owners' wells to provide them with alternative water sources, incidentally requiring the debtor's expenditure of funds, could be interpreted as a valid exercise of police powers, evading a stay.[635] By contrast, though, if the debtor is not in possession of the site at the time of the bankruptcy filing, then a subsequent cleanup order is not actually directing remediation efforts in connection with a site the debtor controls; rather, by requiring the expenditure, the order is akin to a money judgment and will be stayed.[636] However, even if enforcement of the eventual money judgment is stayed, the proceeding to determine a debtor's liability is not thereby stayed.[637] Once the reorganized PRP emerges from bankruptcy, however, and its CERCLA liability is established in the bankruptcy settlement, it may sue other PRPs for contribution.[638]

These exemptions only apply, though, to government agencies exercising their police powers or regulatory functions. Hence, citizen suits or other private enforcement actions will be stayed by the filing of the bankruptcy petition.

[2] Discharging Environmental Claim in Bankruptcy

A "claim" for purposes of bankruptcy is a debt that may be discharged in the bankruptcy proceeding. Claims that are outstanding at the time the bankruptcy petition is filed may be discharged as a consequence of the bankruptcy proceeding, protecting the debtor, but, if unsecured, the creditor's recovery may be minimal. Hence, it is important to determine what is a "claim" and when it arose.

A responsible party's obligation to remediate contamination that occurred prior to its filing a bankruptcy petition is dischargable as a claim only if it can be reduced to a money judgment.[639] If an order imposes affirmative obligations, such as for

---

631. 11 U.S.C. § 362(b).

632. *In re* Commonwealth Oil Refining Co., 805 F.2d 1175 (5th Cir. 1986).

633. Penn Terra Ltd. v. Department of Environmental Resources, 733 F.2d 267 (3d Cir. 1984).

634. United States v. Oil Transp. Co., 172 B.R. 834 (E.D. La. 1994); United States v. Sugarhouse Realty, Inc., 162 B.R. 113 (E.D. Pa. 1993).

635. *In re* Norwesco Development Corp., 68 B. R. 123 (W.D. Pa. 1986) (court denied stay on procedural grounds and addressed the police power issue in dicta).

636. Ohio v. Kovacs, 469 U.S. 274 (1985).

637. United States v. Nicolet, Inc., 857 F.2d 202 (3d Cir. 1988); *In re* Commerce Oil Co., 847 F.2d 291 (6th Cir. 1988); New York City v. Exxon Corp., 932 F.2d 1020 (2d Cir. 1991).

638. ASARCO LLC v. Noranda Mining Co., Inc., 844 F.3d 1201 (10th Cir. 2017).

639. Ohio v. Kovacs, 469 U.S. 274 (1985).

cleanup or restoration, that cannot be reduced to a money judgment, despite the necessity of expending funds to comply with the order, it is not dischargable and remains the obligation of the debtor.[640]

Another consideration is when a claim arises. A monetary claim arising before the bankruptcy filing is subject to discharge, while a claim arising during the bankruptcy proceeding may be construed to be an undischarged administrative expense accorded higher priority than prior claims.[641] If the release preceded the bankruptcy filing, but damages occur after the filing, there is some authority that the post-filing damages are a pre-bankruptcy debt subject to discharge.[642] If a cleanup order precedes the bankruptcy filing, though, requiring remediation after the filing of the bankruptcy petition, there is some authority construing the cost to be an administrative expense.[643] Cleanup obligations that arise after bankruptcy proceedings are concluded are not dischargable, even if the release occurred before the bankruptcy filing.[644]

§ 7.07 Brownfields: Redevelopment of Moderately Contaminated Sites

[A] Of "Brownfields" and "Greenfields"

Brownfields are "abandoned, idled, or under-used industrial and commercial facilities where expansion or redevelopment are complicated by real or perceived environmental contamination."[645] These properties, however, are not so contaminated as to qualify as Superfund sites, nor, under defined conditions, to require remediation to a pristine condition. "Brownfields" also may be defined by what they are not — they are not "greenfields," naturally pristine or totally remediated sites. CERCLA primarily seeks to return hazardous waste sites to an uncontaminated — or "green" — condition, but this has proved to be an extraordinarily costly, often unrealistic and sometimes ineffective strategy for some sites. It especially has deleterious effects for industrial or commercial parcels only moderately contaminated that otherwise could retain economic value. During the early period when the value of the beneficial redevelopment of sites that were only moderately contaminated began to be appreciated, Vice President Gore described brownfields as

> abandoned pieces of property — usually in inner city areas or surrounding communities — that are lightly contaminated from previous industrial use.

---

640. AM International, Inc. v. Datacard Corp., 106 F.3d 1342 (7th Cir. 1997); United States v. Hubler, 117 B.R. 160 (W.D. Pa. 1990).

641. 11 U.S.C. § 503.

642. *In re* Chateaugay Corp. (II), 118 B.R. 19 (S.D.N.Y. 1990), *aff'd*, 944 F.2d 997 (2d Cir. 1991).

643. *Id.*

644. *In re* Jensen, 114 B.R. 700 (E.D. Cal. 1990).

645. The Brownfields Economic Redevelopment Initiative, U.S. E.P.A., Pub. No. 500-F-97-147 (Sept. 1996).

These sites do not ... pose a serious public health risk to the community. However, because of the stigma of contamination and legal barriers to re-development, businesses do not buy the land and sites remain roped off, un-productive and vacant.[646]

"Brownfields" policies and legislation, often a compromise position among gov-ernment, environmentalists, and industry, have developed as measures to salvage economic value for these sites while ensuring only appropriate future use. One leading state policy maker of that early era termed brownfields redevelopment "one of the most important environmental issues governments face today."[647] It has been said that "perhaps the greatest barrier to industrial site reuse ... is [Superfund]."[648] CERCLA and comparable state statutes have imposed significant liabilities on many classes of contaminating persons, but particularly owners, whether or not they are at fault for the contamination of their property. Notwithstanding its success in many respects, by the 1990s, policymakers, commentators, state and local officials and the real estate industry were becoming aware that CERCLA's overreach for some sites had several adverse consequences. Cleaning up a parcel may cost more than it is worth, which may lead to its abandonment. The market value of a con-taminated property remains perpetually uncertain, but certainly less than its eco-nomic value if redeveloped. Banks are unwilling to extend loans secured by contaminated property out of a concern for their own potential liability along with, of course, the questionable value of the secured property, which often effectively precludes economic use. Many states have real property transfer statutes requiring disclosure of known contamination or even an inspection for pollution prior to conveyance, which discourage owners of some sites from either inspecting or selling, leaving the sites virtually abandoned.[649]

Even if known hazardous substances are removed from the property, residues of waste not yet recognized as hazardous may lawfully remain as time bombs. This leaves many industrial properties, even if cleaned up, unmarketable in the absence of a total, but often prohibitively expensive, cleanup. Although CERCLA and its state counterparts demand remediation, the issue remains as to the degree of cleanup they require. As contemporary Congressional testimony framed the issue, "[w]hile the vast majority of brownfields will never be subject to a Superfund investigation, the

---

646. United States Vice President Albert Gore, *The Clinton Administration's Brownfields Rede-velopment Initiative*, M2 PRESSWIRE, May 14, 1997.

647. Michael Finnegan, *Brownfields: The New Paradigm*, 17 N.Y. ENVTL. LAW. 4 (1997). The author, then-Counsel to Governor George Pataki, was instrumental in drafting the 1997 New York Environmental Quality Bond Act that had significant funding for brownfields redevelopment.

648. Charles Bartsch & Richard Munson, *Restoring Contaminated Industrial Sites*, ISSUES IN SCI. & TECH. (1994); *see also* OFFICE OF TECHNOLOGY ASSESSMENT, U.S. CONG., STATE OF THE STATES ON BROWNFIELDS: PROGRAMS FOR CLEANUP AND REUSE OF CONTAMINATED SITES 1–4, 8 (1995).

649. *See* Terry Tondro, *Reclaiming Brownfields to Save Greenfields: Shifting the Environmental Risks of Acquiring and Reusing Contaminated Land*, 27 CONN. L. REV. 789 (1995) (discussing Con-necticut and other state statutes).

perception of potential Superfund liability nonetheless creates a disinclination to sell, purchase or lend on brownfields."[650]

As a result, many moderately contaminated properties, while appropriate for continued industrial or commercial use, nevertheless suffered severely diminished value and usefulness, with a consequential reduction in potential jobs and other economic activity, thereby also reducing the local tax base. Many corner gas stations or dry cleaners that once generated local jobs faced abandonment because of releases endemic to their operations, while local manufacturing plants and shops that generated their own waste, but also sustained local economies, often could not survive the heavy hand of CERCLA. In 1996, the U.S. General Accounting Office estimated that there were some 85,000 contaminated sites covering hundreds of thousands of acres in the country, and perhaps 150,000 acres of abandoned urban industrial land.[651] Brownfields advocates contended that these sites would never be adequately cleaned up under the current CERCLA regime, yet astronomical financial resources would be devoted nonetheless to the effort. If the "polluter pays" principle was anticipated to fund cleanups, where does the funding come from when minor polluters become insolvent? This was especially so since cleanup estimates for already identified contaminated sites ranged from $75 billion to $650 billion.[652]

Meanwhile, if these sites had to be restored totally, industries would look elsewhere and develop more greenfields for new facilities, diminishing the stock of existing open areas and uncontaminated properties, and increasing air and other pollution as a consequence of new commercial and industrial development. These development strategies not only destroy pristine farmland and similar areas, but they are also apt to be inaccessible to urban work forces. The appropriate redevelopment of many brownfields, therefore, has come to serve the interests of many constituencies.

[B] The Awakening Federal Interest

Some early commentators noted that EPA had not initially involved itself in developing a framework for brownfield policies.[653] CERCLA had not contemplated leaving property in a contaminated state before redevelopment. Moreover, EPA gen-

---

650. Reclamation and Reuse of Abandoned Industrial Sites: Testimony Before the Subcommittee on Technology, Environment and Aviation of the House Committee on Science, Space and Technology, 103d Cong. 26–27 (1994).

651. Superfund: Barriers to Brownfield Redevelopment, United States General Accounting Office, Report to Congressional Requesters, GAO/RCED-96-125, at 2 (June 1996); Superfund: Proposals to Remove Barriers to Brownfield Redevelopment, Testimony Before Subcommittee of Superfund, Waste Control and Risk Assessment, Committee on the Environment and Public Works, U.S. Senate, at 3 (1997).

652. For the lower end of the range during that era, see *The Total Costs of Cleaning Up Nonfederal Superfund Sites*, United States Congress, Congressional Budget Office Report, at ix (Jan. 1994). For the higher end estimate, see Steven Lerner, *Brownfields of Dreams*, 17 AMICUS J., 15, 16 (1996).

653. Lynn Grayson & Stephen Palmer, *The Brownfield Phenomenon: An Analysis of Environmental, Economic and Community Concerns*, 25 ENVTL. L. REP. (Envtl. Law Inst.) 10,337, 10,343 (1995).

erally saw itself as a regulatory and enforcement agency and was reluctant to become a party to real estate transactions.[654] There also was a perception that EPA, which primarily seeks remediation and the recovery of response costs as opposed to redevelopment, sometimes demanded too much commitment from prospective purchasers, which, with its unduly protracted bargaining, only encouraged wary purchasers to abandon a potential brownfields project in favor of the far less complicated development of greenfields.

The Clinton Administration incorporated a brownfields initiative in its unsuccessful Superfund reform legislation in 1994,[655] followed by Congressional initiatives that also were never enacted. Despite a lack of legislative success, these initiatives nevertheless provide some insight into Congressional direction. Generally, they would have extended protection from CERCLA liability to bona fide purchasers, defined to include those who purchased after disposal occurred, who had made appropriate inquiry into prior ownerships and uses, who provided notification of releases when discovered, exercised appropriate care for hazardous substances on-site, cooperated in response actions, and had no affiliation with a potentially responsible party. Although the bona fide purchaser would not have cleanup costs imposed on it, the federal government would retain a lien on the property and recoup the costs upon subsequent sale. This approach is similar to that taken by many state voluntary cleanup programs.[656] However, brownfields as a discrete topic became lost amidst the legislative battle over CERCLA reauthorization, so that the necessary statutory amendments to make brownfields redevelopment feasible were not enacted.[657]

EPA entered the brownfields fray in 1995 with its Brownfields Action Agenda, and its publication of a Brownfields Checklist in 1996.[658] EPA, of course, is bound by CERCLA and has no authority to suspend its cleanup and financial liability provisions. However, EPA exercised some discretion during the 1990s by removing some 25,000 sites from the CERCLIS federal inventory (see § 7.06[A][5]), revisiting some cleanup and liability issues, starting 50 pilot Brownfields programs, and working cooperatively with Brownfields interests. EPA also incorporated a Guidance document on Prospective Purchaser Agreements during that early period,[659] which became the template for later brownfields policymaking. EPA's 1995 Guidance clarified its policy of entering covenants not to sue prospective purchasers, broadening the type of sites

---

654. *See* Guidance on Landowner Liability Under Section 107(a)(1) of CERCLA, De Minimis Settlements Under Section 122(g)(1)(B) of CERCLA, and Settlements with Prospective Purchasers of Contaminated Property, 54 Fed. Reg. 34,235, 34,241 (1989).

655. H.R. 3800, 103d Cong. (1994); S. 1834, 103d Cong. (1994).

656. *See generally* Brian C. Walsh, *Seeding the Brownfields: A Proposed Statute Limiting Environmental Liability for Prospective Purchasers*, 34 HARV. J. LEGIS. 191, 203–04 (1997).

657. Andrea Lee Rimer, *Environmental Liability and the Brownfields Phenomenon: An Analysis of Federal Options for Redevelopment*, 10 TULANE ENVTL. L.J. 63 (1996).

658. UNITED STATES ENVIRONMENTAL PROTECTION AGENCY, BROWNFIELDS CHECKLIST (1996).

659. EPA Guidance on Agreements with Prospective Purchasers of Contaminated Property and Model Prospective Purchaser Agreement, 60 Fed. Reg. 34,792 (June 21, 1995).

where the agency was willing to negotiate PPAs as well as the type of benefit (including indirect public benefits) it was willing to accept.[660]

CERCLA was amended in 2002 by the Small Business Liability Relief and Brownfields Revitalization Act,[661] which filled in the legislative gaps. The definition of a brownfield site — real property where the potential presence of hazardous substances, pollutants or contaminants might "complicate" its expansion, development or reuse — was expanded to include sites contaminated by petroleum or controlled substances, as well as "mine scarred" land. However, various sites were excluded, signifying that this was not designed for circumvention of environmental requirements. The exclusions applied to sites already subject to various levels of enforcement or remediation, or permitting under RCRA, the CWA, TSCA or the SDWA, or subject to closure, along with additional characteristics. Unlike many other cleanups, the NCP requirements will apply to brownfields remediation only when "relevant and appropriate." Private party contribution actions against parties participating in a brownfields program are barred, which protects those participants. A version of the innocent purchaser status and innocent landowner defense may be available under narrow conditions.[662]

In 2018 the Brownfields Utilization, Investment and Local Development Act reauthorized the federal program and expanded grants for brownfields assessments, the Brownfields Revolving Loan Fund, cleanups, job training, research, technical assistance and training in communities impacted by brownfields sites.[663] Readers may want to reference the 2021 Brownfields Federal Programs Guide[664] which provides a comprehensive discussion of numerous brownfields programs implemented by several federal agencies, outlines federal tax incentives and tax credits, and discusses the several brownfields projects that were in progress and those which were completed.

Several state programs have also been implemented which are compatible with CERCLA's remedial purposes and yet preserve the economic use of moderately contaminated sites and encourage redevelopment of abandoned sites. These proposals have shifted the paradigm that had defined the response to property contamination since CERCLA's enactment, so that brownfields theory, to use an overworn cliche, became the cutting edge of new legal policy.

By the third decade of the 21st century, brownfields programs have been widely adopted by many states and local governments. In many respects, it has been a win-win outcome for parties involved in land use, local taxes and employment, commercial banking, the real estate industry and commercial redevelopment, the environment and even in many respects for local aesthetics with the demolition of blighted sites and their replacement by new premises subject to strict environmental and land use standards. Lawyers, naturally, did well also.

---

660. Prospective Purchaser Guidance, May 25, 1995, 1995 Daily Envt. Rep. (BNA) 102 (May 26, 1995).

661. Pub. L. 107-118 (2002); see www.epa.gov/brownfields/overview-epas-brownfields-program.

662. *Id.*, section 223.

663. *See* www.epa.gov/brownfields/2018-build-act-division-n-consolidated-appropriations-act-2018.

664. www.epa.gov/system/files/documents/2021-10/2021-brownfields-federal-program-guide.

[C] Factors Relevant to Brownfields Policies and Redevelopment

[1] Protection for New Owners

As we have seen under CERCLA (see § 7.06), property owners are strictly liable for cleanup of contamination on their property. Subsequent purchasers buy that liability along with ownership. Although there may be some limited benefit provided by the innocent purchaser defense, the due diligence requirements in which the defense's elements are couched often make those benefits illusory. Since brownfields, by definition, are obviously contaminated, and the point is to encourage redevelopment of already contaminated properties, the defense is unavailable. For prospective purchasers which are not participating in a brownfields program, liability remains all too real as to moderately, but not dangerously, contaminated properties.

Absent other measures, purchasers intent on purchasing property must: (1) factor known contamination, and hence known risk, into the purchase price, but also take a chance on unknown risks; (2) rely on indemnification and hold harmless protection written into the sale contract; or (3) be willing to absorb cleanup costs and then seek contribution under CERCLA § 113(f) from the seller and other responsible parties. Without the protections afforded by brownfields redevelopment, none of these options are likely to make redevelopment of contaminated property attractive. Hence, brownfields policy starts with affording conditional protection for purchasers. One means of limiting risk for purchasers of qualifying properties is an EPA Prospective Purchaser Agreement (PPA) or a state equivalent. The purchaser, in exchange for a release of CERCLA liability for past contamination, agrees to specific financial obligations in connection with a partial cleanup under strict parameters established by EPA. EPA must certify the satisfaction of all obligations before the purchaser/redeveloper is released from liability.

[2] Financing of Brownfields Purchases

We have seen the difficult choice that often faces creditors of defaulting owners of contaminated properties. Foreclosing lenders can become owners of the property, in a technical sense, and if they are not careful, operators, presenting a potential dual basis for their CERCLA liability. Lender liability was mitigated to some extent by CERCLA's Secured Creditor Exemption discussed in § 7.06[B][3][b]. One beneficial result of the new arrangements has been an involuntary partnership between EPA and lenders, who now bear the onus for property inspections prior to closing on loans. Just as CERCLA and its amendments adding contribution actions relieved EPA of much of the responsibility for the cleanup of contaminated sites and locating other potentially responsible parties, the 1996 secured creditor protections, in effect, imposed on lenders rather than on EPA the burden of ascertaining the condition of properties in a CERCLA context for which financing is sought. Additional benefits flow from more predictable financing for the redevelopment of moderately contaminated properties.

[3] Restrictions on Future Use

Risk-based studies indicate, unsurprisingly, that health risks arising from property contamination are greater with future residential use. Conversely, commercial or industrial use does not statistically present the same risk, although the extent and type of the contamination, sources of drinking water, volatility of air-borne contaminants, and the duration of the worker's daily presence may increase the health risks. Hence, brownfields policies typically restrict future uses by barring residential, health care facilities, schools and other uses where potential pathways from subsurface contamination may pose health risks to individuals on-site for significant time periods. These concerns over future land use may be addressed by land use restrictions running with the land. The consent decree that is integral to brownfields redevelopment will typically restrict use by the immediate purchaser. In addition, restrictive covenants, equitable servitudes, and conservation easements binding the owners and subsequent purchasers are methods by which EPA can retain control over future uses. Some states authorize Environmental Use Restrictions, a form of restrictive covenant running with the land, enforceable by the state conservation agency.

[4] Public Economic Benefits

Funding is a major part of brownfields programs. The 2002 legislation initially authorized up to $200 million annually for brownfields assessments and cleanups, 25% of which was dedicated to petroleum brownfields sites. Grants up to $1 million were intended to fund revolving loans for brownfields cleanups, and conditional grants were authorized for up to $200,000 to eligible entities including non-profit organizations.[665] The federal grant program devised in the 2002 legislation expired in 2006, but as noted above, additional grant authority was created by the 2018 legislation. Grants and tax benefits can still serve as economic motivations for brownfields redevelopment by targeting sites for redevelopment that enhance job-creation and minimize environmental detriments arising from the new use.

A 2020 EPA study indicated that, for each brownfield "dollar," $20.13 was leveraged, and for each $100,000 of brownfield funds spent for site assessments, cleanups and revolving loan fund agreements, 10.3 jobs were leveraged. The study also found that the redevelopment of brownfields sites, even allowing for new local housing and job growth, led to fewer paved surfaces and fewer miles driven than would have been the case for greenfields development.[666] Several additional benefits resulting from the typical nexus between brownfields sites and urban and commercial areas include convenience to transportation hubs which, in effect, led to the reutilization of existing infrastructure rather than the development of new, environmentally costly, infrastructure.

---

665. *Id.*, § 221.
666. www.epa.gov/system/files/documents/2021-10/2021-brownfields-federal-program-guide.

[5] Coordination between State Brownfields
Redevelopments and EPA

A problem which might arise is that parties participating in a state brownfields program might still be exposed to federal CERCLA liability, and an EPA agreement with a participant might not, itself, bind states. Hence, as to either kind of program, participants should ensure that all relevant enforcement agencies are involved to a degree that if the participant complies with its obligations in the particular brownfields program, it will not face full cleanup obligations imposed by alternative programs, which would have to be parties to that or a similar agreement to accomplish the same result.

Many states have voluntary cleanup programs in which financial and other incentives induce owners and purchasers to clean up contaminated sites. A party which intends to enter a state voluntary cleanup agreement should be mindful of the importance of ensuring that EPA has a level of participation, without which there may be no assurance that EPA will abide by a state agreement.

Typically, voluntary cleanup programs are limited to "innocent" owners and prospective purchasers or developers who were not responsible for the contamination. The more complete the protection, the more successful it will be in attracting redevelopment. The protection also must be global — merely protecting the purchaser or owner from government lawsuits does not necessarily insulate that party from contribution actions or private suits, or new scientific determinations of hazards not covered in the agreement. Hence, these factors should be taken into account negotiating the agreement and also ensure a settlement of the volunteer's liability with EPA and the accompanying protection against contribution actions. For state programs, that protection under CERCLA would not apply, so that EPA's participation is important in yet another manner.

The benefit of the volunteer participating in a brownfields program pursuant to a carefully negotiated agreement is that actual remediation will likely be done. These state and local programs also have more predictability than CERCLA-type statutes, in that cleanup standards are definite and adjusted for the proposed future use, administrative procedures are streamlined, remedies are more flexible, administrative oversight is minimized, and transaction costs are reduced. The developer receives tax benefits, state contribution to the cleanup, financing incentives, and in many cases, releases from future liability.

[D] State Laws: Examples

New Jersey, a densely populated state rigorous in its treatment of contamination, has a brownfields law incorporating many of these measures. The New Jersey statute includes the following:[667]

---

667. N.J. PUB. LAW 1997, ch. 278; *see also* Larry Schnapf, *New Jersey Adopts Comprehensive Brownfields Legislation*, N.Y.L.J., Apr. 12, 1998, at 1.

- Remediation grants for "innocent" purchasers of 50 percent of remediation costs up to $1 million;

- Loans, not restricted to "innocent" parties, of up to 100 percent of cost for sites remediated under the state's Industrial Site Recovery Act;

- Tax abatements for vacant or underutilized sites in designated environmental opportunity zones; and

- Up to 75 percent reimbursement of cleanup costs to "innocent" developers who redevelop those sites, but subject to agreements with the state ensuring cleanup as well as redevelopment.

New York, a state with a long history of intensive industrial use, enacted its brownfields law in 2003.[668] New York's Department of Environmental Conservation (DEC) had previously engaged in Voluntary Cleanup Agreements pursuant to Guidance documents that had lacked the force of statutory law. The statute was modified in 2015 to extend the tax benefits of the Brownfield Redevelopment Tax Credits to December 31, 2022, and as of this writing, proposed legislation will extend the program for another ten years to the end of 2032. The goal, as with other brownfields programs, is to facilitate the remediation of hazardous waste sites, encourage beneficial redevelopment and concurrently to return those properties to the tax rolls with the prospect of economically beneficial reuse and consequential job growth.

The New York program excludes sites on EPA's National Priorities List as well as those on the Inactive Hazardous Waste Site Registry maintained by DEC, and those subject to various other enforcement mechanisms, while allowing for inclusion of only moderately contaminated sites.[669] In many respects, the New York program mirrors the federal standards.

The brownfields site cleanup agreement, among other specifications, imposes many of the administrative and technical costs on the program applicant. The agreement also requires the applicant to indemnify the state for any liabilities arising out of the cleanup, except for claims arising out of the state's own gross negligence or willful or intentional misconduct. If the applicant's compliance with the agreement fails, the state is free to terminate it. The applicant must also shoulder other investigative and public notice responsibilities, but will be protected against operator liability in connection with the implementation of the cleanup.[670] The New York statute also imposes work plan requirements[671] and numerous remediation requirements.[672] There are extensive requirements for citizen participation binding DEC as

---

668. 27 New York Environmental Conservation Law Title 14, §§ 1401–1433.

669. *Id.*, § 27-1405.

670. *Id.*, § 1409.

671. *Id.*, § 27-1411

672. *Id.*, § 27-1415

well as the applicant.[673] For a successful conclusion, the applicant must receive a certification of completion, which has an extensive checklist.[674] Once certification is provided, the applicant will be protected against future liability, with exceptions as described in the statute.[675]

§ 7.08 Emergency Planning and Community Right to Know Act

[A] Requirements and Purposes of Act

In 1986, CERCLA was amended to add the Emergency Planning and Community Right-to-Know Act (EPCRA).[676] EPCRA requires disclosure of the storage of hazardous substances,[677] response actions in the event of toxic releases,[678] and notification to the public.[679] EPCRA is another filament in the regulatory web devised to track hazardous chemicals during every stage of their lives and to ensure public disclosure of hazards. As one early court stated, the Act's two main purposes are (1) the "Right-to-Know" component, ensuring the availability of accurate, reliable information on the presence and release of toxic and hazardous chemicals in the local community, and (2) the "Emergency Planning" component, by which such information can be used to develop local emergency response plans to minimize the effects of accidental releases.[680] EPCRA does not preempt state and local laws.[681] In fact, planning and response are mainly local affairs.[682]

[B] Emergency Planning

[1] Local Responsibilities for Emergency Planning

EPCRA emphasizes local responsibilities and authority, requiring the establishment of state emergency response commissions, demarcation of local emergency planning districts, and the formation of local emergency planning committees.[683] The local committees are the first line of response, and must include elected local officials, civil defense and emergency service representatives, environmental, health and trans-

---

673. *Id.*, § 27-1417.
674. *Id.*, § 27-1419.
675. *Id.*, § 27-1421.
676. 42 U.S.C. §§ 11001–11050.
677. *See* 42 U.S.C. §§ 11002(c), 11021.
678. *See* 42 U.S.C. § 11004.
679. *See id.*
680. Citizens for a Better Environment v. The Steel Company, 90 F.3d 1237 (7th Cir. 1996), *rev'd for lack of standing*, 523 U.S. 83 (1998).
681. 42 U.S.C. § 11041(a).
682. *See* Nicholas J. Johnson, *EPCRA's Collision with Federalism*, 27 INDIANA L. REV. 549 (1994).
683. 42 U.S.C. § 11001.

portation personnel, and community group representatives, as well as owners and operators of facilities subject to the Act.[684] As a consequence, EPCRA contemplates that creativity and flexibility at the local level will ensure planning and response measures most appropriate for the area. The linchpin of planning are the emergency coordinators who will make decisions. Each local emergency planning committee must have an emergency coordinator.

[2] Emergency Response Plan

The local emergency planning committee must formulate an emergency response plan, submitted for review and recommendations by the state emergency response commission,[685] which evaluates the resources needed to implement the plan. The plan must do all of the following:[686]

- Identify every facility within the emergency planning district subject to EPCRA;
- Specify the plan of action for facilities, emergency, and medical personnel;
- Designate the community and facility emergency coordinators who will make decisions regarding implementation;
- Establish procedures to notify emergency personnel and the public of a release;
- Establish methods for determining when and where a release occurred and its extent;
- Identify and locate emergency equipment and responsible personnel;
- Draft evacuation plans; and
- Provide for training programs.

Facilities must identify to the committee their emergency planning coordinators, notify the committee of any relevant changes at the facility, and provide necessary information.[687] This information guides community planning.

[C] Emergency Notification

EPCRA is applied to extremely hazardous substances, hazardous chemicals, and toxic chemicals. Hazardous chemicals are listed by EPA,[688] but do not include substances regulated by the Food and Drug Administration, household products used by the general public, or substances used in medical research facilities.[689] EPA must

---

684. *Id.*
685. 42 U.S.C. § 11003(a).
686. 42 U.S.C. § 11003(a)–(c).
687. 42 U.S.C. § 11003(d).
688. 29 C.F.R. § 1910.1200(c).
689. 42 U.S.C. § 11021(e).

publish a list of extremely hazardous substances and establish thresholds triggering EPCRA,[690] and may revise the list.[691]

A release of an extremely hazardous substance triggers immediate EPCRA notification, specifying the nature, amount, and dangers of the release. The facility must notify the community emergency coordinator, and furnish an updated advisory of the action taken, necessary medical treatment, if any, and known or anticipated health risks.[692]

[D] Reporting Requirements

[1] Material Safety Data Sheets

Facilities must prepare "material safety data sheets" (MSDSs) under the Occupational Safety and Health Act (OSHA)[693] for hazardous chemicals, which EPCRA requires to be submitted to local planning committees, state emergency response commissions, and local fire departments.[694] The MSDSs categorize hazardous chemicals by health and physical hazards, and identify hazardous components, including new information concerning a particular chemical's danger.[695] The MSDS must remain available to the local committee and the public.[696] States and localities may require supplementation of EPCRA-required submissions.[697]

[2] Inventory Forms

Facilities required to submit MSDSs also must submit emergency and hazardous chemical inventory forms, again to the local committee, the state commission, and the local fire department. These forms also remain available to the public. They provide detailed information on the chemicals, and their quantities and manner of storage in the facility's inventory. Facilities submitting inventory forms must provide access to the local fire department for on-site inspections.[698]

[3] Toxic Chemical Release Forms

Facilities must annually submit to EPA toxic chemical release forms for each listed toxic chemical exceeding specified thresholds manufactured, processed, or otherwise used at the facility.[699] However, the facility may use readily available information, in-

---

690. 42 U.S.C. § 11002(a).
691. 42 U.S.C. § 11002(a)(4).
692. 42 U.S.C. § 11004.
693. 29 U.S.C. § 651, *et seq.*
694. 42 U.S.C. § 11021(a)(1).
695. 42 U.S.C. § 11021(d).
696. 42 U.S.C. § 11021(c).
697. 42 U.S.C. § 11041(b).
698. 42 U.S.C. § 11022.
699. 42 U.S.C. § 11023.

cluding monitoring reports under other statutes such as CERCLA or RCRA; no additional monitoring is required by EPCRA.[700]

The specific chemical identity of a hazardous chemical, extremely hazardous substance, or toxic chemical may be withheld, and identified only by its generic class or category, in the case of a trade secret.[701]

[4] Medical Emergencies

Medical emergencies require immediate reporting.[702] Medical professionals are entitled to receive specific information from facilities about the identity of any chemical to which a person was exposed and for which treatment is required.[703] Trade secret confidentiality does not apply to this information.[704] In a medical emergency, facilities must provide MSDSs, inventory forms, and toxic chemical release forms, including specific information about relevant chemical identities,[705] to health care workers and local governments.[706]

[E] EPA as a Data Clearinghouse

[1] EPA Must Maintain Records on National Movement of Chemicals

EPA is required to maintain a national toxic chemical inventory,[707] as well as records on the annual amounts of chemicals transported to, produced at, consumed at, accumulated at, released from, and transported from facilities. EPA relies on information provided by states or, if data are unavailable, on estimates based on a comparable number of facilities in other states.[708]

[2] EPA Must Maintain List of Toxic Chemicals

Toxic chemicals are listed by EPA. EPA may add to the list if a chemical is known to cause or can be reasonably anticipated to cause "significant acute human health effects at concentration levels that are reasonably likely to exist beyond facility site boundaries as a result of continuous, or frequently recurring, releases."[709]

[3] Citizens May Petition to Add a Chemical to EPA's List

"Any person," which includes state governors, may petition EPA to list a chemical on the Agency's toxic chemical list. EPA must respond to the petition either by com-

---

700. 42 U.S.C. § 11023(g)(2).
701. 42 U.S.C. § 11042.
702. 42 U.S.C. § 11043(b).
703. Id.
704. 42 U.S.C. § 11043(a).
705. 42 U.S.C. § 11043(b).
706. 42 U.S.C. § 11043(c).
707. 42 U.S.C. § 11023(j).
708. 42 U.S.C. § 11023(l).
709. 42 U.S.C. § 11023(d)(2).

mencing rule making preliminary to the listing of the chemical or by explaining why the petition is denied.[710]

[F] Enforcement

[1] Compliance Orders and Penalties

As with other federal environmental statutes, facilities that fail to fulfill emergency planning obligations are subject to EPA compliance orders, enforceable in federal district court. Violation subjects a facility to civil penalties.[711] Facilities that fail to provide emergency notification are subject to civil penalties in federal court and, upon proof of a knowing and willful failure, to criminal prosecution, fines, and incarceration.[712] Reporting violations are also subject to civil and administrative penalties.[713]

[2] Citizen Suits

[a] Grounds for Suit

As with many other federal environmental statutes, citizen suits under EPCRA are an important enforcement vehicle. Citizen plaintiffs can sue a facility owner or operator who fails to submit a follow up emergency notice or MSDS, or fails to submit an inventory form or toxic chemical release form.[714] In addition, citizen plaintiffs may sue EPA to require it to establish the national toxic chemical inventory computer database (see [E][1], *above*) or to render a timely decision on a citizen petition (see [E][3], *above*).[715] Citizen plaintiffs also may compel the EPA, states, and state emergency response commissions to comply with their obligation to provide a mechanism for the public availability of information required by EPCRA[716] or state authorities to timely respond to a request for information.[717]

[b] Notice; Suits for Past Violations

The citizen plaintiff must give 60 days notice of the alleged violation to EPA, the state, and the violator for actions against facilities, or to the EPA, state governor, and state emergency response commission if those parties are being sued.[718] If a facility is being sued, diligent action by EPA bars the citizen suit[719] as to the matter being pursued.[720]

---

710. 42 U.S.C. § 11023(e).
711. 42 U.S.C. § 11045(a).
712. 42 U.S.C. § 11045(b).
713. 42 U.S.C. § 11045(c), (d)(1).
714. 42 U.S.C. § 11046(a)(1)(A).
715. 42 U.S.C. § 11046(a)(1)(B).
716. 42 U.S.C. § 11046(a)(1)(C).
717. 42 U.S.C. § 11046(a)(1)(D).
718. 42 U.S.C. § 11046(d).
719. 42 U.S.C. § 11046(e).
720. *Cf.* Neighbors for a Toxic Free Community v. Vulcan Materials Co., 964 F. Supp. 1448 (D. Colo. 1997) (although facility and EPA had entered CERCLA consent agreement, this did not bar

Although some courts have allowed citizen suits for wholly past, or "historical" EPCRA violations,[721] even if cured,[722] at least one has precluded citizen suits for past violations cured after receipt of the 60-day notice.[723] The Supreme Court, finding no constitutional standing for the particular plaintiffs, specifically declined to resolve the conflict in *Steel Company v. Citizens for a Better Environment.*[724] In that case, the plaintiff organization was comprised of members of a local community, claiming harm arising from a facility's failure to timely file informational reports. As relief, they requested payment of penalties, attorney's fees, and prospective injunctive relief relating to timely filing. The Court concluded that none of the relief sought would remedy the claimed harm of past insufficient information, and on this basis dismissed the action without reaching the merits. Justice Stevens' concurring opinion would have rejected EPCRA citizen suit jurisdiction over wholly past violations.[725]

[c] Standing

The traditional standing requirements for individuals as well as organizations also apply to EPCRA citizen suits (see § 1.02[A] for a general discussion of standing). The citizen plaintiffs must demonstrate injury-in-fact, causation of the injury by the defendant's conduct, and a likelihood that the requested relief will redress the injury.[726]

[d] Costs and Fees; Intervention

Costs may be awarded to substantially prevailing plaintiffs if the court believes the action to be appropriate.[727] A prevailing defendant may recover costs and fees from a non-prevailing plaintiff, although this benefit is limited to when the citizen plaintiff commenced a frivolous action or proceeded in bad faith.[728] Any directly in-

---

citizen suit alleging EPCRA reporting violation, not part of the CERCLA complaint, although arising out of the same spill).

721. Idaho Sporting Congress v. Computrol, Inc., 952 F. Supp. 690 (D. Idaho 1996).

722. Neighbors for a Toxic Free Community v. Vulcan Materials Co., 964 F. Supp. 1448 (D. Colo. 1997).

723. Atlantic States Legal Foundation, Inc. v. United Musical Instruments, U.S.A., Inc., 61 F.3d 473 (6th Cir. 1995).

724. 523 U.S. 83 (1998).

725. Steel Company v. Citizens for a Better Environment, 523 U.S. 83 (1998). But note that the Supreme Court ruled that the defendant's cessation of past violations did not render moot a citizen suit under the Clean Water Act, in *Friends of the Earth v. Laidlaw Environmental Services*, 528 U.S. 167 (2000).

726. Steel Company v. Citizens for a Better Environment, 523 U.S. 83 (1998); Don't Waste Arizona, Inc. v. McLane Foods, Inc., 950 F. Supp. 972 (D. Ariz. 1997).

727. 42 U.S.C. § 11046(f).

728. *Cf.* Citizens For a Better Environment v. Steel Co., 230 F.3d 923 (7th Cir. 2000) (action for attorneys' fees subsequent to dismissal of action by Supreme Court; Circuit Court denied application for fees, since action, though dismissed, had not been frivolous).

terested person may intervene as of right.[729] If EPA or state is not a party, they may intervene.[730]

[3] Suits by State or Local Authorities

States and local governments may sue facilities in federal court for failure to do any of the following:[731]

- Provide notification to the emergency response commission;
- Submit MSDSs and required lists and inventory forms; or
- Make MSDSs available to the public upon request.

In addition, state emergency response commissions or local planning committees may sue facilities for failure to submit emergency response plans or emergency and hazardous chemical inventory forms.[732] States may also sue EPA for failure to provide, upon request, information protected as trade secrets.[733]

---

729. 42 U.S.C. § 11046(h)(2).
730. 42 U.S.C. § 11046(h)(1).
731. 42 U.S.C. § 11046(a)(2)(A).
732. 42 U.S.C. § 11046(a)(2)(B).
733. 42 U.S.C. § 11046(a)(2)(C).

Chapter 8

Toxic Substances

§ 8.01 Pesticides

[A] Regulation of Pesticides

Pesticides are governed by a comprehensive statute, the Federal Insecticide, Fungicide and Rodenticide Act (FIFRA).[1] Although pesticide regulations in some respects had been around for decades, the 1972 amendments were significant early in the environmental law era and formed the basis for the modern statute, which itself has been regularly amended in a continuing contest pitting agricultural interests and the chemical industry against public health and the environment, each with their respective congressional allies. FIFRA is largely an administrative statute with registration and labeling of pesticides at its core. Reflecting FIFRA's original agricultural focus, it originally fell under the auspices of the Department of Agriculture, but more recently, EPA has assumed primary, although not exclusive, jurisdiction.[2]

---

1. 7 U.S.C. §§ 136–136y.

2. In 2010, the internal agency responsibility was transferred from EPA's Office of Prevention, Pesticides and Toxic Substances to its Office of Chemical Safety and Pollution Prevention. EPA also has authority under the Federal Food, Drug and Cosmetic Act pursuant to which EPA establishes "tolerances" that correlate with the maximum safe residue of pesticides on food products. If a tolerance is exceeded, the FIFRA registration must be denied or revoked. For a discussion of the relationship between these complementary regulatory regimes, see *League of United Latin American Citizens v.*

Pesticides differ from most other environmentally hazardous substances in that they are intended to be destructive, unlike air and water pollutants that enter the environment as by-products of some other activity. Agriculture in the United States (and most other developed nations) today involves the deployment of vast quantities of pesticides. This imposes substantial risks on the health of people, livestock, and wildlife exposed to these chemicals, unless their manufacture and use are carefully controlled. Before FIFRA's thorough regulation took effect, broad-spectrum pesticides such as DDT were heavily used throughout much of the world. As Rachel Carson's 1962 book, *Silent Spring*, eloquently noted, these sorts of pesticides killed many forms of life along with the targeted mosquitoes and other pests. Their residue moves up the food chain from smaller to larger organisms, causing death to birds, as well as large mammals, including humans. For these reasons the FIFRA regulations now prohibit the use of DDT and other broad-spectrum pesticides.[3]

Regulatory vehicles in addition to FIFRA are also available to address pesticide toxicity. Pesticides may cause violations of the Endangered Species Act (ESA) if they disrupt the critical habitats or the breeding success of a protected species, factors which must be taken into account during the registration or re-registration processes.[4] Pesticides that are discharged into federally regulated water bodies can be pollutants that, if not compliant with permitting and other regulatory requirements, may also constitute violations of the Clean Water Act (see discussion in 6.03).[5] Harm to workers engaged in farming with pesticides or the manufacturing of pesticides may also invoke the protections of the Occupational Safety and Health Act. However, private rights of action by injured persons are unavailable under FIFRA.[6]

There also are ways to reduce the baleful effects of pesticides by reducing the need for their use. In recent years, numerous techniques for genetically modifying crops have been developed to ward off pests and resist molds, with the result that a substantial part of the nation's food chain relies on genetically modified products. This is an evolving area of agriculture and commerce which has been engendering some controversy. Although the genetic manipulation avoids the need for application of chemicals external to the crops, the long-term effects of the internal restructuring of food crops and the effects of people ingesting genetically modified foods is uncertain.

Wheeler, 899 F.3d 814 (9th Cir. 2018), and *National Corn Growers Association v. Environmental Protection Agency*, 613 F.3d 266 (D.C. Cir. 2010).

3. 40 C.F.R. § 129.4.

4. The Ninth Circuit framed out its analysis in *Washington Toxics Coalition v. Environmental Protection Agency*, 413 F.3d 1024 (9th Cir. 2005), and *National Family Farm Coalition v. EPA*, 966 F.3d 893 (9th Cir. 2020). The use of strychnine, even though it was registered under FIFRA, was found to be a violation of the ESA in *Defenders of Wildlife v. Environmental Protection Agency*, 882 F.2d 1294 (8th Cir. 1989). For a discussion of the complexity of intermeshing the different regulatory regimes, see *Center for Biological Diversity v. Environmental Protection Agency*, 861 F.3d 174 (D.C. Cir. 2017).

5. Peconic Baykeeper, Inc. v. Suffolk County, 600 F.3d 180 (2d Cir. 2010).

6. Bates v. Dow Agrosciences LLC, 544 U.S. 431 (2005); No Spray Coalition, Inc. v. City of New York, 351 F.3d 602 (2d Cir. 2003); Voss v. Saint Martin Cooperative, 376 Fed. Appx. 662 (2010).

Moreover, there are concerns that genetically modified plants and animals may interbreed with wild members of various species, and hence for the ecological consequences. Additional alternatives to extensive pesticide use include crop rotation (since many pests survive only on a particular crop), introducing natural predators, sterilizing pests chemically, and developing pest-resistant varieties of plants.

[B] Registration

[1] Registration Requirements, Generally

FIFRA requires all pesticides sold or distributed in commerce to be registered with the United States Environmental Protection Agency after the manufacturer submits proof of their safety and efficacy.[7] This has proven to be an effective way of ascertaining a pesticide's risk prior to its intended use. Registration and the necessary information submitted therewith is also intended to prevent dangers presented by off-label use. Since registrations must be renewed, the process is also designed to alert EPA and the public to dangers that may subsequently arise and information about risks that is developed subsequent to the initial registration.[8] Registration requirements not only impose controls on the use of pesticides but also on pesticide applicators and pesticides that enter the stream of commerce.

The registration process is densely informational. The applicant must provide detailed information about the pesticide's chemical makeup, its active ingredients, the intended use and how it will achieve the intended purpose, directions for use, and a list of its active ingredients.[9] A material change in any of these will likely void the registration. However, EPA takes into account that a pesticide has already been registered that is substantially similar to the pesticide for which registration is presently being applied.[10] As part of the registration process, EPA may require the applicant to submit data, test results, and additional information.[11] If the information submitted with the application is inadequate to support the safety threshold of the pesticide, it must be denied; otherwise, the EPA determination will be vacated.[12] EPA may also conditionally grant an application under circumstances where the data is incomplete but the existing data reveals, on the basis of substantial evidence, no adverse environmental risks. Such a temporary status can allow for short term use when the use of the pesticide is in the public interest.[13] In the absence of substantial evidence negat-

---

7. 7 U.S.C. § 136a.

8. 7 U.S.C. § 136d(a)(2).

9. *See* Natural Resources Defense Council v. Environmental Protection Agency, 806 F.3d 520 (9th Cir. 2019).

10. 7 U.S.C. § 136a(c)(3)(B).

11. 7 U.S.C. § 136a(c).

12. Pollinator Stewardship Council v. Environmental Protection Agency, 806 F.3d 520 (9th Cir. 2015).

13. 7 U.S.C. § 136(a)(1). *See* Natural Resources Defense Council v. Environmental Protection Agency, 857 F.3d 1030 (9th Cir. 2017).

ing risk relating to both short-term and long-term pesticide use, the conditional registration must be vacated.[14]

FIFRA applies to imported pesticides, but not to pesticides manufactured for export only.[15] In addition, states may impose their own registration requirements, and many have in fact prohibited the sale or use of some pesticides permitted by FIFRA (see [5], *below*).[16]

Pesticides that are not registered may be barred from sale, distribution, or use.[17] Pesticides are defined to include insecticides, weed killers and other defoliants, and fungicides, designed to destroy mildew, mold, rust, and the like.[18]

[2] Information Required to Achieve Registration

To achieve registration, an applicant must furnish EPA with data showing that:[19]

- The pesticide warrants the claims made by the applicant;
- The pesticide's labeling complies with FIFRA (see [C], *below*);
- The pesticide will "perform its intended function without unreasonable adverse effects on the environment"; and
- "[W]hen used in accordance with widespread and commonly recognized practice [the pesticide] will not generally cause unreasonable adverse effects on the environment."

This requires testing to show the pesticide will be effective and not unreasonably dangerous. The burden of showing compliance with FIFRA is on the applicant.[20] However, pesticides that were in use in 1978 are entitled to conditional registration after that date, as are those with similar ingredients to those pesticides.[21]

[3] Registration Is for General or Restricted Use

Pesticides may be registered for either general or restricted use. General use pesticides may be sold over the counter; restricted use pesticides are subject to added requirements.[22] Typically, pesticides may be employed only by a certified applicator — a state-licensed exterminator or similar user.[23]

---

14. Natural Resources Defense Council v. Environmental Protection Agency, 735 F.3d 873 (9th Cir. 2013); National Farm Coalition v. Environmental Protection Agency, 960 F.3d 1120 (9th Cir. 2020).

15. 7 U.S.C. § 136o.

16. *See* N.Y. ENVTL. CONSERV. LAW ART. 33; CAL. FOOD & AGR. CODE §§ 12751–14101.

17. 7 U.S.C. § 136a.

18. 7 U.S.C. § 136(f), (k), (t), (u).

19. 7 U.S.C. § 136a(c)(5).

20. *Id.*

21. 7 U.S.C. § 136a(c).

22. *Id.*

23. 7 U.S.C. § 136a(d).

[4] Original Registration Is for Exclusive Use

Since the necessary testing to satisfy FIFRA's mandates is lengthy and costly, controversy has arisen over whether an applicant ought to be protected from later manufacturers using similar ingredients, and in effect piggy-backing on the first company's investment in developing and testing its product. (Pesticides generally are not patentable.) To resolve this, FIFRA provides for a 10-year period of exclusive use by the original registrant. After that, the data developed by that registrant may be used by competitors.[24] The United States Supreme Court has upheld this provision as against a claim that it constituted a de facto taking of the original registrant's investment, holding the statute to be a reasonable compromise that does not deprive that registrant of all investment-based expectations.[25]

[5] State Registration

The states are free to enact registration requirements of their own, and to prohibit the sale or use of pesticides, even though EPA-registered, that fail to meet state health and safety requirements.[26] However, a state may not impose registration requirements that contravene EPA's, which are preemptive (see 8.01[C][2], below). Licensing, or certification, of applicators of restricted use pesticides is also conducted by the states. State procedures for certification of applicators must meet with EPA approval, and EPA performs this function in states without approved programs.[27]

[6] Suspension and Cancellation

Registration of pesticides is now for a fifteen-year period, after which the substance must be re-registered. All pesticides must be reviewed by EPA by October 1, 2022, or, for new active ingredients within fifteen years of the registration date, whichever is later.[28] FIFRA provides for the suspension or cancellation of registration when a pesticide violates FIFRA requirements, or causes unreasonable adverse environmental effects.[29] In addition, EPA may impose an emergency suspension where immediate danger is shown. Such a suspension was upheld when EPA provided proof that a defoliant was hazardous to health.[30] In all suspensions or cancellations, the burden of showing safety remains on the registrant.[31]

[7] Experimental Use Permits and Variances

Experimental use permits are available to enable an applicant to collect data to obtain registration, and variances are available to use unregistered pesticides to deal

---

24. 7 U.S.C. § 136a(c)(1)(F).
25. Ruckelshaus v. Monsanto Co., 467 U.S. 986 (1984).
26. 7 U.S.C. § 136v(a).
27. 7 U.S.C. § 136i.
28. 7 U.S.C. § 136a(g)(1)(A).
29. 7 U.S.C. § 136d.
30. 7 U.S.C. § 136d(c)(3); *see* Dow Chemical Co. v. Blum, 469 F. Supp. 892 (E.D. Mich. 1979).
31. 7 U.S.C. § 136d; Dow Chemical Co. v. Ruckelshaus, 477 F.2d 1317 (8th Cir. 1973).

with unexpected outbreaks of pests, such as unanticipated arrivals from foreign countries.[32]

[8] Public Access to Information

As with many federal environmental statutes, data on pesticide registration is available to the public, although the confidentiality of trade secrets is protected.[33]

[C] Labeling

[1] General Labeling Requirements

Key provisions of FIFRA address the labeling of pesticides. These are derived from the Insecticide Act of 1910, a direct ancestor of FIFRA, that dealt primarily with labeling, misbranding, and adulteration. Misbranding occurs when the label provides false or misleading information about the product, or if the registration number on the label is incorrect, or when the product actually mimics another pesticide. Labeling is defined to include not only the actual label, but also any writings "accompanying the pesticide or device at any time," which also may not be false or misleading.[34] Adequate directions for safe use, and warnings "adequate to protect health and the environment,"[35] must be included. If a pesticide contains any ingredient highly toxic to humans, the label must so indicate, and must prominently show the word "poison" as well as an antidote or other practical treatment.[36]

[2] Preemption

FIFRA's labeling requirements, unlike those regarding registration (see [B], *above*), preempt state laws.[37] The Congressional intent was to ensure uniformity so that registrants are not subject to differing and perhaps conflicting state labeling requirements. However, FIFRA does not specify field preemption and thus does not preempt all state pesticide laws, especially those that do not displace federal labelling requirements. Rather, the Supreme Court has recognized that the statute's text left much of the field open for state and local regulation.[38]

States may regulate the sale of pesticides or pesticide devices as long as they do not interfere with federally regulated labelling or the manner in which pesticides are packaged.[39] Local ordinances, for instance, may require permitting for pesticide uses which do not involve labelling.[40] State rules requiring signs on lawns or in buildings where pesticides have been applied have been held not to be preempted by FIFRA,

---

32. 7 U.S.C. §§ 136c, 136w.
33. 7 U.S.C. § 136h.
34. 7 U.S.C. § 136(p).
35. 7 U.S.C. § 136(p), (q).
36. 7 U.S.C. § 136(q)(2)(D).
37. 7 U.S.C. § 136v(b).
38. Wisconsin Public Intervenor v. Mortier, 501 U.S. 597 (1991).
39. 7 U.S.C. § 136v(a), (b).
40. Wisconsin Public Intervenor v. Mortier, supra, note 38.

since they do not deal with labeling as defined in the Act.[41] Likewise, state requirements that stores post signs warning of pesticide hazards are not preempted by FIFRA.[42] Nor are state or local laws regulating pesticide use, such as a law restricting pesticides in parks.[43] If the state has pesticide laws that comply with FIFRA, EPA may delegate enforcement authority to the state. This avoids preemption if the state has procedures adequate for satisfying FIFRA's goals.[44] If the state's enforcement is inadequate or otherwise fails, EPA may rescind this authority.[45] As a separate issue, state pesticide laws regulating how pesticides may be used may preempt local regulations. Just as EPA has an interest in uniform national standards for the registration and labeling of pesticides, states have an interest in uniform requirements throughout the state pertaining to how pesticides are used.[46]

Aside from the issue whether states have regulatory authority over pesticides is the question whether plaintiffs can utilize state tort law to seek relief. Much litigation has centered on whether tort actions based on a pesticide manufacturer's or applicator's failure to warn are preempted by FIFRA's labeling requirements. Some courts have differed as to this issue.[47] However, the Supreme Court has ruled that a tort action based on defective design of a pesticide is not preempted by FIFRA.[48] The same ruling reinstated claims for negligence pertaining to defective testing of the product, a breach of deceptive trade practices under state law and breach of an express warranty, insofar as the claims did not implicate labelling of the pesticide. FIFRA also did not preempt state law failure to warn claims that relied on how the manufacturer designed the product rather than how the pesticide was labelled or packaged.[49] Although FIFRA's goal is to impose uniform national labelling requirements, that goal is not contravened by state regulation of marketing literature, the goal of which is to encourage purchases. Hence, misrepresentations in sales brochures and the like are actionable under state law.[50] State law personal injury claims arising from pesticide use can which rely on the breach of a duty of care could also avoid FIFRA preemption.[51]

[D] Pesticide Residues in Foods

A major concern in pesticide regulation relates to residues of pesticides that remain in foods and in animal feed. Under the Federal Food, Drug and Cosmetic Act, "tol-

41. New York State Pesticide Coalition, Inc. v. Jorling, 874 F.2d 115 (2d Cir. 1989).

42. Chemical Specialties Mfrs' Ass'n v. Allenby, 958 F.2d 941 (9th Cir. 1992), *cert. denied*, 506 U.S. 825 (1992).

43. Wisconsin Public Intervenor v. Mortier, 501 U.S. 597 (1991).

44. 7 U.S.C. § 136w-1.

45. 7 U.S.C. § 136w-2.

46. Syngenta Seeds, Inc. v. County of Kauai, 842 F.3d 669 (9th Cir. 2019).

47. *See* Cox v. Velsicol Chemical Corp., 704 F. Supp. 85 (E.D. Pa. 1989) (not preempted); Fitzgerald v. Mallinckrodt, Inc., 681 F. Supp. 404 (E.D. Mich. 1987) (preempted).

48. Bates v. Dow Agrosciences LLC, 544 U.S. 431 (2005).

49. Adams v. United States, 449 Fed. Appx. 653 (9th Cir. 2011).

50. Indian Brands Farm, Inc. v. Novartis Crop Protection, Inc., 617 F.3d 207 (3d Cir. 2010).

51. Gass v. Marriot Hotel Services, Inc., 558 F.3d 419 (6th Cir. 2009).

erances" that correlate with the maximum safe residue of pesticides on food products are established. If a tolerance is exceeded, EPA must deny or revoke an existing FIFRA registration.[52] Tolerances must be set for both raw and processed foods, and are measured in parts per million of the pesticide residue. A food is deemed unsafe if it contains a quantity of pesticide not within the tolerance level set by EPA.

With regard to processed foods, until 1996 a controversial provision of the Food, Drug and Cosmetic Act known as the "Delaney Clause"[53] prohibited the sale of such foods containing any substance found "to induce cancer in man or animal." This provision was held by a federal appeals court to bar any amount of residue from a pesticide that might induce cancer even in animals.[54] Congress resolved this issue in the wake of that decision by replacing the Delaney Clause with a provision requiring tolerances to achieve "reasonable certainty that no harm will result from aggregate exposure" to the pesticide residue.[55]

[E] Enforcement

Enforcement of FIFRA includes civil penalties imposed by EPA, as well as criminal fines and imprisonment for knowing violations.[56] In addition, EPA may halt the sale or use, and if necessary, order the removal of pesticides found to violate FIFRA.[57] A pesticide may be subject to seizure in a federal court in rem proceeding if it has not been registered or, if registered, has been adulterated or misbranded; if the labelling is deficient; if the pesticide's use is inconsistent with the labelling or the registration; or if the use complies with the registration and labeling but it nevertheless causes unreasonable adverse effects on the environment.[58] Pesticides may also be recalled from sale or distribution by EPA order.[59]

If a pesticide's registration is suspended, canceled, or banned under the emergency provision discussed in [B][6], *above*, innocent persons who suffer economic losses as a result, such as farmers who used the pesticide while unaware of the ban, are to

---

52. 21 U.S.C. §§ 301–397; *see* 21 U.S.C. § 346a. For a discussion of the relationship between these complementary regulatory regimes, see *League of United Latin American Citizens v. Wheeler*, 899 F.3d 814 (9th Cir. 2018), and *National Corn Growers Association v. Environmental Protection Agency*, 613 F.3d 266 (D.C. Cir. 2010).

53. Former 21 U.S.C. § 348(c)(3)(A).

54. Les v. Reilly, 968 F.2d 985 (9th Cir. 1992), *cert. denied*, 507 U.S. 950 (1993).

55. 21 U.S.C. § 346a(b)(2)(A).

56. 7 U.S.C. § 136*l*. Civil penalties not to exceed $5,000 per offense are available against parties responsible for defective registrations, commercial pesticide applicators, and pesticide vendors and distributors. Manufacturers and registration applicants or registrants who knowingly violate FIFRA are subject to fines not to exceed $50,000 or incarceration up to one year, or both. Commercial applicators of restricted use pesticides who knowingly violate FIFRA may be fined up to $25,000 or incarceration up to one year or both. Private applicators who knowingly violate FIFRA may be subject to $1,000 fines, or up to thirty days incarceration, or both.

57. 7 U.S.C. § 136k(a).

58. 7 U.S.C. § 136k(b).

59. 7 U.S.C. § 136q(b).

be indemnified by the United States.[60] This may encourage enforcement by assuring that innocent parties will not be harmed. On the other hand, it might be argued that this automatic cost to the Government might impede enforcement of FIFRA.

States with EPA-approved programs have primary enforcement responsibility under FIFRA. EPA, as one would expect, has that responsibility in states without approved plans.[61]

The Supreme Court has held that control over the application of pesticides in particular areas, as opposed to their registration and sale, is a state or local government responsibility. A local law restricting the application of pesticides in parks was upheld as against a claim that FIFRA preempted such regulations.[62] Unlike most of the other major federal environmental statutes, FIFRA has no provision for citizen enforcement and confers no private right of action against alleged violators.[63]

§ 8.02 Regulating Toxic Substances: The Toxic Substances Control Act (TSCA)

[A] Purposes of Act

The importation, manufacture, processing, and distribution of toxic substances is regulated by the Toxic Substances Control Act (TSCA),[64] enacted in 1976 and substantially amended in 2016.[65] Although TSCA is both a products manufacturing regulatory statute and an environmental statute, it complements federal environmental statutes that regulate pollution by controlling chemical products prior to their entering the environment. The core of TSCA is informational: chemical manufacturers must provide EPA with information on the chemicals they produce (see [F][1], *below*). Violations generally arise when required information is not provided, or when orders seeking information are violated, although producing or distributing chemicals without providing adequate notice also may be a violation (see [H], *below*).

The findings that preface TSCA reflect Congressional concern for the environment's permeation by manufactured chemicals, many of which may present unreasonable risks of injury to human health or the environment,[66] which is TSCA's general standard. Congressional policy requires the development of adequate data by chemical manufacturers, which they must furnish EPA, but EPA is not to create "economic

---

60. 7 U.S.C. § 136m.

61. 7 U.S.C. § 136w-1.

62. Wisconsin Public Intervenor v. Mortier, 501 U.S. 597 (1991).

63. No Spray Coalition, Inc. v. City of New York, 351 F.3d 602 (2d Cir. 2003).

64. 15 U.S.C. § 2601, *et seq.*

65. Pub. L. No. 114-182, identified as the Frank B. Lautenberg Chemical Safety for the 21st Century Act.

66. 15 U.S.C. § 2601(a).

barriers to technological innovation" in excess of those needed to accomplish the goals of the Act.[67]

[B] Chemicals Included in and Excluded from TSCA

Under TSCA, chemical substances that may be toxic must be tested to determine whether they pose health risks.[68] If a chemical is toxic, EPA must provide public notice and after a rigorous evaluation of the risks may prohibit or restrict its use.[69] However, TSCA excludes several substances, including the following:[70]

- Pesticides regulated under the Federal Insecticide, Fungicide and Rodenticide Act (see § 8.01);

- Special nuclear material regulated by the Nuclear Regulatory Commission (see § 12.02); and

- Food, drug, and cosmetics products regulated by the Food and Drug Administration.

TSCA regulates chemical substances and mixtures. A "substance" is an element or similar chemical, or a combination of substances, either occurring in nature or resulting from a chemical reaction.[71] A "mixture" is a combination of two or more chemical substances that does not occur in nature, and is not the result of a chemical reaction. A "new" chemical substance is one not included on the EPA's chemical substance inventory list required under the Act.[72]

TSCA specifically addresses asbestos,[73] radon,[74] and lead,[75] which are separately covered in this Chapter (see §§ 8.04 for radon, 8.05 for asbestos, and 8.07 for lead), and PCBs (see [E][4], *below*).[76]

[C] Testing Requirements

[1] When Testing Is Required

Under certain circumstances, EPA may require testing of a substance or mixture to evaluate environmental or health effects arising from the chemical's manufacture,

---

67. 15 U.S.C. § 2601(b).
68. 15 U.S.C. § 2603(a).
69. 15 U.S.C. §§ 2603(f), 2605, 2606.
70. 15 U.S.C. § 2602(2)(B).
71. 15 U.S.C. § 2602(2)(A).
72. 15 U.S.C. § 2602(11).
73. 15 U.S.C. §§ 2641–2656.
74. 15 U.S.C. §§ 2661–2671.
75. 15 U.S.C. §§ 2681–2692.
76. 15 U.S.C. § 2605(e).

distribution, processing, use, or disposal. Testing responsibilities are imposed on manufacturers and processors.[77] Testing is required if:[78]

- Any of these activities may present an unreasonable risk of injury to health or the environment; and

- Data, as well as practical experience, are inadequate to reasonably predict the effects of these activities, and testing is necessary to develop the data.

Testing will also be required if:[79]

- The chemical may reasonably be anticipated to enter the environment in substantial quantities, or there may be significant human exposure to the chemical; and

- Data, as well as practical experience, are inadequate to reasonably predict the effects of the manufacture, distribution, processing, use, or disposal of the chemical; and testing is necessary to develop the data.

Mere "scientific curiosity" does not justify testing; there must be "an existing possibility of harm [and] reasonable and legitimate cause for concern."[80] TSCA also allows citizens to petition EPA conduct testing, or to modify an existing order relating to testing, which triggers either a public hearing by EPA or an investigation relating to the contents of the petition. If EPA denies the petition, it must make findings in support of its decision in the Federal Register. The denial then provides a basis for the citizen petitioners to commence a civil action to compel EPA to undertake the steps set forth in the petition.[81]

[2] Standards Used for Testing

When EPA requires testing, it must promulgate a rule setting forth the standards used for testing. The testing will look for possible carcinogenesis, birth defects, behavioral disorders, or other unreasonable risk of injury to health or the environment. Tests may include epidemiologic studies, in vitro tests, or animal tests, among others.[82]

An Interagency Testing Committee ("ITC"), comprised of representatives from EPA, the Department of Labor, the Department of Commerce, the Council on Environmental Quality, the National Institute for Occupational Safety and Health, the National Cancer Institute, and the National Science Foundation, among others, is authorized to make recommendations to EPA regarding which chemicals should receive priority testing.[83]

---

77. 15 U.S.C. § 2603(b)(3)(B).
78. 15 U.S.C. § 2603(a)(1)(A).
79. 15 U.S.C. § 2603(a)(1)(B).
80. Chemical Manufacturers Association v. Environmental Protection Agency, 859 F.2d 947 (D.C. Cir. 1988).
81. 15 U.S.C. 2620, 2603.
82. 15 U.S.C. § 2603(b)(2).
83. 15 U.S.C. § 2603(e).

EPA must promulgate the necessary rule for testing and establishing standards, or publish why it is rejecting the recommendation.[84] EPA failure to promptly respond has led to successful citizen action to compel performance of this mandatory obligation.[85]

[3] Actions to Prevent or Reduce Risk

If, upon receipt of the data from testing, EPA concludes that there is a reasonable basis to believe that a chemical presents a significant risk of serious or widespread harm[86] of cancer, gene mutations, or birth defects, EPA, within 180 days, must take appropriate action to prevent or reduce the risk.[87] For example, it may prohibit or limit the manufacture or use of the chemical.[88] If the hazard is imminent, and EPA concludes that it cannot await formal promulgation of a rule, it may seek a court order authorizing a seizure or injunctive relief (see [E][5], *below*).[89]

[D] Manufacturing and Processing Notices for New Chemicals or New Uses

[1] Ninety Day Notice Requirement; Exemptions

Ninety days notice to EPA, accompanied by risk assessment data (see [C][3], *above*), must precede any manufacture of a new chemical substance or significant new use of an existing chemical.[90] EPA determines what is a significant new use, based on the projected volume, its effect on the kind or duration of human or environmental exposure, and the anticipated methods of manufacturing, processing, distribution, or disposal of the chemical.[91] The chemical may be exempted, however, if the applicant can show that the proposed activity and use do not pose a health or environmental threat, or if the chemical is the equivalent of a chemical already reviewed by EPA.[92] There also is an exemption for the manufacture or processing of small quantities of a chemical for scientific experimentation or chemical research.[93]

[2] Required Contents of Notice

The 90-day notice, published in the Federal Register, must include the common or trade name of the chemical, its identity and molecular structure, its proposed use,

---

84. *Id.*

85. Natural Resources Defense Council v. Environmental Protection Agency, 595 F. Supp. 1255 (S.D.N.Y. 1984).

86. These are alternative types of risks: a significant risk of serious harm may affect only a few people, while a significant risk of widespread harm will affect many people, but possibly only mildly. *See* 49 Fed. Reg. 21,875, 21,881 (1984).

87. 15 U.S.C. § 2603(f).

88. 15 U.S.C. § 2605.

89. 15 U.S.C. § 2606.

90. 15 U.S.C. § 2604(a).

91. 15 U.S.C. § 2604(a).

92. 15 U.S.C. § 2604(h).

93. *Id.*

the amount to be manufactured or processed, data on health and environmental effects, estimates of how many people will be exposed to it in the workplace and the duration of the exposure, and how the chemical will be disposed of.[94]

[3] Issuance of Interim Order; Injunctive Relief

Upon receiving notice, EPA may issue an interim order prohibiting or limiting the manufacture, processing, distribution, use or disposal of the chemical if, in the absence of adequate information, it cannot make a definite determination, and:[95]

- It appears to be an unreasonable risk to health or the environment; or
- The substance is anticipated to enter the environment in substantial quantities or there may be significant human exposure.

If a manufacturer or processor objects, EPA must seek injunctive relief in federal district court.[96]

[E] Regulation of Hazardous Chemicals

[1] EPA's Promulgation of Rules

If EPA finds that there is a reasonable basis to conclude that the manufacture, processing, distribution, use, or disposal of a toxic chemical presents an unreasonable risk of injury to health or the environment, it must promulgate a rule:[97]

- Prohibiting or limiting the manufacture, processing, or distribution of the chemical;
- Requiring that the chemical be labeled, or that warnings and instructions be provided for use, distribution, or disposal;
- Requiring that manufacturers and processors retain records of the processes involved, and monitor or conduct tests to assure safety;
- Prohibiting or regulating a method of commercial use;
- Prohibiting or regulating any method of disposal of the chemical or any product containing the chemical; and/or
- Directing manufacturers or processors to give notice of the hazard to distributors and to allow purchasers to replace the chemical.

EPA's promulgation of a rule must be preceded by an informal hearing, meaning that interested persons may present their positions[98] and cross-examine the EPA's witnesses, although one court has held that the failure to allow cross-examination did not invalidate the rule.[99]

---

94. 15 U.S.C. §§ 2604(d), 2607(a)(2).
95. 15 U.S.C. § 2604(e)(1)(A).
96. 15 U.S.C. § 2604(e).
97. 15 U.S.C. § 2605(a).
98. 15 U.S.C. § 2605(c)(3).
99. Corrosion Proof Fittings v. Environmental Protection Agency, 947 F.2d 1201 (5th Cir. 1991).

[2] Balancing of Risks

If a chemical is to be banned, EPA must state an "understandable basis" for the rule, necessitating that the risk be balanced against social benefits lost as a consequence of the ban.[100]

If another federal law not administered by EPA could eliminate or reduce the risk, EPA must coordinate with the administrative agency enforcing the other law to determine how best to address the risk. If the other agency issues an order declaring that the chemical does not present a risk, or takes steps to address the risk, then EPA may not take further regulatory action.[101]

[3] Emergency Rule-Making Power

EPA has emergency rule-making power, not subject to judicial review, for threats of serious or widespread health or environmental injuries, preceded by prompt notice to interested persons, and a reasonable opportunity for a hearing.[102]

[4] Regulation of Polychlorinated Biphenyls (PCBs)

Under TSCA, PCBs, a highly dangerous substance formerly used in electrical equipment, may not be manufactured, processed, distributed, or used, except in a totally enclosed manner, unless EPA specifically finds that such measures are not necessary to avert health and environmental risks.[103] Additionally, EPA may take any action necessary, either under TSCA or under any other federal law, to control PCBs.[104] EPA's regulation of PCBs preempts state law,[105] and case law indicates that EPA regulations preempt the regulatory authority of other agencies in this area, such as the Department of Transportation's regulation of transportation of hazardous materials.[106] However, TSCA regulation of PCBs does not preempt a suit under the Resource Conservation and Recovery Act (RCRA) (see § 7.05[J][4]) to require cleanup of contamination caused by PCBs.[107] The courts have upheld EPA's regulations requiring parties using or storing in excess of 45 kgs of PCBs to maintain records of disposal,[108] deeming General Electric's distillation of dirty PCBs to constitute disposal,[109] and limiting disposal methods to incineration, including immediate incineration of PCB-

---

100. *Id.*

101. 15 U.S.C. § 2608.

102. 15 U.S.C. § 2605(d)(2).

103. 15 U.S.C. § 2605(e).

104. *Id.*

105. SED, Inc. v. City of Dayton, 519 F. Supp. 979 (S.D. Ohio 1981).

106. Environmental Transportation Systems, Inc. v. ENSCO, Inc., 763 F. Supp. 384 (C.D. Ill. 1991), *aff'd*, 969 F.2d 503 (7th Cir. 1992).

107. Hudson Riverkeeper Fund, Inc. v. Atlantic Richfield Co., 138 F. Supp. 2d 482 (S.D.N.Y. 2001).

108. *See* Yaffe Iron and Metal Co. v. Environmental Protection Agency, 774 F.2d 1008 (10th Cir. 1985).

109. General Electric Co. v. Environmental Protection Agency, 53 F.3d 1324 (D.C. Cir. 1995).

containing solvents.[110] However, a court set aside an EPA regulation allowing the importing of PCBs for disposal in the United States, finding it created an unreasonable risk to public health.[111]

[5] Imminent Hazards

EPA has emergency powers as to imminently hazardous chemical substances. It may obtain a court order to seize in rem "imminently hazardous" chemicals, or any article containing the chemical. EPA may also seek a temporary or permanent injunction, or it may seek notification to purchasers, public notice of the risk, a recall, or an order allowing a repurchase, against any person who manufactures, processes, distributes, uses, or disposes of the chemical.[112]

[F] Compilation of Information

[1] Reporting and Record Keeping by Regulated Parties

Manufacturers and processors must maintain and file records of the chemical substances they produce or process.[113] Manufacturers, processors, and distributors must also maintain records of significant adverse reactions to health or the environment allegedly caused by any chemical.[114] Claims of harm may be made by consumers, employees, or a range of other parties.[115] Employee records must be kept for 30 years from the date the reactions were reported to the employer; other records must be kept for five years from the date the information becomes known to the regulated party.[116]

Manufacturers, processors, and distributors also must maintain lists of health and safety studies for each regulated substance.[117] If any manufacturer, processor, or distributor obtains information that a chemical may present a substantial risk of injury to health or the environment, EPA must be immediately informed.[118]

[2] EPA's Inventory of Toxic Chemicals

EPA must maintain a current list of every chemical substance manufactured or processed in the United States. Every chemical substance reported to EPA is added to the list, although the exemption for small chemical quantities used only for scientific experimentation or chemical research applies here also.[119]

---

110. *Id.*
111. Sierra Club v. United States EPA, 118 F.3d 1324 (9th Cir. 1997).
112. 15 U.S.C. § 2606.
113. 15 U.S.C. § 2607(a).
114. 15 U.S.C. § 2607(c).
115. *Id.*
116. *Id.*
117. 15 U.S.C. § 2607(d).
118. 15 U.S.C. § 2607(e).
119. 15 U.S.C. § 2607(b).

[3] Inspections

EPA may inspect premises and facilities in which regulated chemicals are manufactured, processed, or stored. EPA also may inspect vehicles. Inspection must be preceded by written notice to the owner or operator, and must be reasonably prompt, conducted during reasonable hours, and in a reasonable manner. It may extend to everything within the premises or vehicle having TSCA consequences, except for financial, sales, pricing, personnel, or research data — unless the research data falls directly within TSCA requirements.[120]

[4] Confidential Data

As with many other environmental statutes, TSCA includes trade secret protection. Although a regulated party must disclose adequate data to EPA, EPA may not disclose it to others. Willful or knowing wrongful disclosure subjects the violator to criminal prosecution. The prohibition, however, does not extend to health and safety studies concerning chemicals to be commercially distributed, or chemicals requiring testing or data obtained by EPA from a health and safety study.[121]

[G] Exports and Imports

Unlike the Resource Conservation and Recovery Act's imposition of notice requirements on exporters of hazardous substances (see § 7.05), TSCA applies only to chemicals manufactured, processed, or distributed in the United States for use in the United States. Exports are exempt, unless EPA determines that the chemical presents an unreasonable risk of injury to health or the environment within the country.[122]

Imports must be blocked at the point of entry by the Treasury Department if the chemical violates TSCA.[123] As noted earlier, an EPA regulation permitting PCBs to be imported for disposal was annulled as violative of TSCA since it created unreasonable risk.[124]

[H] Enforcement

[1] Criminal and Civil Penalties

A knowing or willful violation of TSCA or orders or rules issued under the Act subjects the violator to criminal penalties, including fines imposed per day of violation, and incarceration, in addition to civil penalties.[125] Thus, for example, proof that a defendant removed transformers containing PCBs, knowing that the removal would release PCB solvents that would not be incinerated, was legally sufficient to support

---

120. 15 U.S.C. § 2610.
121. 15 U.S.C. § 2613.
122. 15 U.S.C. § 2611.
123. 15 U.S.C. § 2612.
124. Sierra Club v. United States EPA, 118 F. 3d 1324 (9th Cir. 1997).
125. 15 U.S.C. § 2615(b).

a conviction.[126] EPA has the right to inspect premises, or even vehicles, and subpoena records, in connection with TSCA violations.[127] A TSCA violation may arise if the target of inspection refuses EPA access to the premises or records.[128] By virtue of its right to inspection, a court has found that EPA also has the power to obtain a search warrant for premises where there is probable cause to believe a regulated substance is present, notwithstanding that TSCA does not mention search warrants.[129]

Otherwise, civil penalties are imposed by EPA per day of violation, with each day constituting a separate violation, after written notice to the violator, and an opportunity for a hearing. In imposing a penalty, EPA must take into account the nature, circumstances, extent and gravity of the violation, as well as the violator's ability to pay, the impact on its ability to continue in business, the violator's history of prior violations, if any, the degree of culpability, and other relevant factors.[130] An action seeking penalties under TSCA must be brought within five years of the violation.[131] The Act does not provide a private right of action.[132]

[2] Other Civil Remedies

Federal district courts may issue orders restraining violations, or restraining parties from engaging in prohibited acts, and compelling parties to take necessary actions under TSCA, such as cleanups.[133] Courts also may direct manufacturers and processors to advise distributors and others likely to be exposed that the chemical was manufactured or processed without notice to EPA, or in violation of a rule or regulation; or to give public notice; or to replace or repurchase the chemical. The chemical also may be subject to *in rem* seizure.[134]

[3] Citizen Suits

As with many environmental statutes, TSCA provides for citizen suits. "Any person" may sue "any [other] person," including government entities, for violations of TSCA, or EPA, to compel its performance of any nondiscretionary duty required by the Act.[135]

However, as with citizen suits in general, there is a 60-day notice period, with notice required to the violator and EPA,[136] and the action will be barred if EPA has com-

---

126. United States v. Catucci, 55 F.3d 15 (1st Cir. 1995).

127. 15 U.S.C. 2610(b).

128. 15 U.S.C. 2614.

129. United States v. M/V Sanctuary, 540 F.3d 295 (4th Cir. 2008).

130. 15 U.S.C. § 2615(a).

131. Minnesota Mining and Manufacturing Co. v. Browner, 17 F.3d 1453 (D.C. Cir. 1994).

132. Sanford Street Local Development Corp. v. Textron, Inc., 768 F. Supp. 1218 (W.D. Mich. 1991).

133. *See* United States v. Consolidated Edison Co., 620 F. Supp. 1404 (N.D. Ill. 1985).

134. 15 U.S.C. § 2616.

135. *See, e.g.*, Natural Resources Defense Fund v. Environmental Protection Agency, 595 F. Supp. 1255 (S.D.N.Y. 1984) (citizen plaintiff sued to compel the EPA to initiate rule making on chemicals recommended for listing by the Interagency Testing Committee); see also [C][2], *above*, regarding the ITC.

136. 15 U.S.C. § 2619(b)(1)(A).

menced and is diligently prosecuting an administrative or civil proceeding for a compliance order.[137] If the proceeding is commenced after notice is given, then the citizen plaintiff, while barred from independently seeking relief, may intervene as of right.[138] If the citizen plaintiff is suing EPA to require its performance of a statutory duty, then the action may proceed 60 days after notice if the duty remains unperformed.[139] Reasonable attorneys' fees may be awarded by the court if they are found to be appropriate; the plaintiff need not prevail to obtain an award of attorneys' fees.[140] Citizen plaintiffs retain all other statutory and common law rights, even if the citizen suit is barred,[141] although one court has held that conduct legal under TSCA, such as proper storage of PCBs, precludes nuisance actions or suits under a local ordinance.[142]

§ 8.03 Toxic Tort Litigation

[A] Liability

[1] Background

The advent of suits for damages based on exposure to toxic substances has given rise to a major subset of tort law known as toxic torts, or environmental torts. Although the subject matter of those suits may differ dramatically from the topics addressed in traditional tort law, the rules applicable to common-law tort actions apply in large measure. This is so even though some of these rules, like those regarding causation and burden of proof, are centuries old, and evolved in the context of lawsuits involving such bucolic events as farm and wagon accidents.

In contrast, toxic torts typically concern exposure to substances causing, or claimed to cause, diseases with long latency periods. Thus, issues in these cases regarding proof of fault, causation, duty of care to the plaintiff, and periods of limitation are far different from those arising in conventional tort actions.

Few of the rules relating to these issues have been altered by statute to accommodate the toxic tort action. Instead, for the most part, the courts have been obliged to adapt long-standing common-law rules to wholly new circumstances. Whether, and when, it is appropriate to fill these new bottles with old wine is a subject that pervades toxic tort litigation.[143]

---

137. 15 U.S.C. § 2619(b)(1)(B).

138. 15 U.S.C. § 2619(b)(1)(B).

139. 15 U.S.C. § 2619(b)(2).

140. *See* Environmental Defense Fund v. Environmental Protection Agency, 672 F.2d 42 (D.C. Cir. 1982).

141. 15 U.S.C. § 2619(c)(3).

142. Twitty v. State of North Carolina, 527 F. Supp. 778 (E.D. N.C. 1981), *aff'd*, 696 F.2d 992 (4th Cir. 1982); *see also* Arbor Hill Concerned Citizens Neighborhood Ass'n v. City of Albany, 250 F. Supp. 2d 48 (N.D.N.Y. 2003) (no private cause of action under TSCA to require remediation of lead paint in dwellings).

143. For detailed coverage of all aspects of toxic tort litigation, see MARGIE SEARCY-ALFORD, A GUIDE TO TOXIC TORTS (2006).

[2] Standards of Liability

[a] Strict Liability

Traditional tort law renders the defendant liable upon proof of negligent conduct. However, in a few select areas, the courts have imposed strict liability without proof of fault, as in the classic ultrahazardous activity involved in *Rylands v. Fletcher*.[144] There, the defendant's storage of large quantities of water, which flowed onto the plaintiff's property, was held to give rise to strict liability. Some American courts define strict liability as a consequence of abnormally dangerous, rather than ultrahazardous, activity, but under traditional tort principles, the concept is limited to blasting and similar acts.[145]

Actions based on exposure to toxic materials raise the question whether strict liability ought to apply. Some courts have applied strict liability to parties engaged in handling toxic substances.[146] Others have taken the view that strict liability should not apply where due care could have prevented the injury.[147] *See* the further discussion at § 3.03.

Whether conduct is abnormally dangerous has been held to turn, in part, on where it occurs. The storage of chemicals may be held to be abnormally dangerous in a location where such a practice is infrequent, but not to be so in an industrial area where it is more commonplace.[148] It is fair to ask whether geography should be a factor in determining liability.

[b] Negligence; Interference with Commercial Expectations; Emotional Distress

The negligence standard, traditional in tort litigation, raises the prospect of the plaintiff's culpable conduct as a defense. Some courts allow a claim for intentional infliction of emotional distress from toxic waste discharges.[149] The United States Supreme Court has, however, rejected an action for emotional distress, brought under the Federal Employers' Liability Act against a railroad, based on the plaintiff's fear of exposure to asbestos, since the plaintiff had not manifested symptoms of a disease.[150] However, the Supreme Court has ruled that plaintiffs exposed to asbestos (see § 8.05) may recover damages for fear of future asbestosis.[151]

In a leading case, the New Jersey Supreme Court upheld a judgment for medical monitoring expenses in a suit by 97 families based on toxic chemicals that were al-

---

144. L.R. 1 Ex. 265 (1866), *aff'd*, L.R. 3 H.L. 330 (1868).
145. Spano v. Perini Corp., 250 N.E.2d 31 (N.Y. 1969); *see also* 750 Old Country Rd. Realty Corp. v. Exxon Corp., 645 N.Y.S.2d 186 (App. Div. 1996) (no strict liability for gasoline storage).
146. *See, e.g.,* Jersey City Redevelopment Auth. v. PPG Industries, 655 F. Supp. 1257 (D.N.J. 1987).
147. *See, e.g.,* Indiana Harbor Belt R.R. v. American Cyanamid Co., 916 F.2d 1174 (7th Cir. 1990).
148. Northglenn v. Chevron U.S.A., Inc., 519 F. Supp. 515 (D. Colo. 1981).
149. Ewell v. Petro Processors, 364 So. 2d 604 (La. App. 1978), *cert. denied*, 366 So. 2d 575 (La. 1979); Sterling v. Velsicol Chem. Corp., 647 F. Supp. 303 (W.D. Tenn. 1986), *aff'd in part, rev'd in part, on other grounds*, 855 F.2d 1188 (6th Cir. 1988).
150. Metro North R.R. v. Buckley, 521 U.S. 424 (1997).
151. Norfolk & W. Ry. v. Ayers, 538 U.S. 135 (2003).

lowed to enter a town's water supply. But the court rejected a claim for emotional distress in that case because a statute barred such claims against municipalities in the absence of proven medical expenses.[152]

[c] Product Liability and Failure to Warn

In between strict liability and negligence lies the tort law standard in product liability suits, dispensing with the requirement of proving fault where a product is defective or the manufacturer failed to adequately warn the user.[153] The failure-to-warn issue has arisen in toxic tort actions based on the ingestion of foods exposed to pesticide residue,[154] as well as the exposure to asbestos,[155] and many other substances.[156]

Whether the pesticide labeling requirements of the Federal Insecticide, Fungicide and Rodenticide Act (FIFRA), described in § 8.01[C], preempt state-law tort actions based on the manufacturer's failure to warn, is an issue on which courts have been divided.[157]

[3] Causation

[a] Duty of Care

The complex issue of whether the defendant owes a duty of care to the plaintiff, highlighted in the landmark *Palsgraf v. Long Island Rail Road* decision,[158] pervades the law of toxic torts. Most courts take the view that one who caused a chemical spill in a waterway owes a duty to commercial fishermen deprived of a livelihood by contaminated fish.[159] On the other hand, seafood merchants are, one court has ruled, too far removed from the chemical discharge to be owed a duty of care.[160]

[b] Burden of Proof

Under traditional tort law doctrine, the plaintiff must prove by a preponderance of the evidence that the defendant's conduct caused the damage.[161] This is rendered problematic in some suits based on diseases with long latency periods and serious scientific dispute about causation — for example, cancer stemming from exposure to toxic substances. Some courts and scholars have questioned whether the traditional

---

152. Ayers v. Township of Jackson, 525 A.2d 287 (N.J. 1987).

153. *See* Enright v. Eli Lilly & Co., 570 N.E.2d 198 (N.Y. 1991), *cert. denied*, 502 U.S. 868 (1991).

154. *See* Albuquerque v. Nor-Am Agricultural Products, Inc., 88 N.M. 74, 537 P.2d 682 (Ct. App. 1975), *cert. denied*, 536 P.2d 1085 (N.M. 1975).

155. Borel v. Fibreboard Paper Products Corp., 493 F.2d 1076 (5th Cir. 1973), *cert. denied*, 419 U.S. 869 (1974).

156. *See, e.g., In re* Agent Orange Product Liability Litigation, 597 F. Supp. 740 (E.D.N.Y. 1984).

157. *See* Cox v. Velsicol Chemical Corp., 704 F. Supp. 85 (E.D. Pa. 1989) (not preempted); Papas v. Upjohn Corp., 985 F.2d 516 (11th Cir. 1993), *cert. denied*, 510 U.S. 913 (1993) (preempted).

158. 162 N.E. 99 (N.Y. 1928).

159. Leo v. General Electric Co., 538 N.Y.S.2d 844 (A.D. 1989).

160. Pruitt v. Allied Chemical Co., 523 F. Supp. 975 (E.D. Va. 1981).

161. *See* PROSSER & KEETON ON TORTS §§ 38, 41 (5th ed. 1984).

preponderance of the evidence requirement is appropriate in these situations.[162] It is arguable that when epidemiological proof exists of a less than 50 percent likelihood of causation, allowing a partial recovery is fairer than denying all damages — both in terms of recompensing the plaintiffs and deterring future misconduct.

[c] Multiple Defendants

Toxic tort actions frequently involve several defendants, raising issues as to how to apportion liability. For example, numerous parties may have shipped chemical waste to a landfill. One approach is to use a concert of action theory, relying on decisions involving joint enterprises such as drag-racing.[163] Most courts have rejected that approach in toxic tort cases, since true concert of action is unlikely to be provable.[164] A related theory, that of alternative liability, is based on the responsibility of a small number of wrongdoers whom the plaintiffs are unable to identify.[165] Here, too, courts have been reluctant to apply this theory to environmental tort cases when there is often a large group of defendants whose degree of responsibility may vary greatly.[166]

Other courts have considered market-share liability, holding each defendant liable not jointly and severally, but for that defendant's share, or proportion, of the total market. This view has been adopted in some actions involving pharmaceuticals.[167] Whether it is appropriate in suits regarding exposure to toxic substances is a largely unresolved issue.

[4] Suits against Government Bodies

The Department of Defense has been a particularly pernicious generator of toxic substances that for decades have ended up being disposed of in manners not protective of the environment or human health and safety. However, the United States government generally enjoys sovereign immunity from lawsuits arising from the tortious acts of its employees unless it waives its immunity by operation of exceptions carved out by the Federal Tort Claims Act (FTCA).[168] Even then, though, lawsuits against the United States are not viable unless the federal employee's conduct would have constituted a tort under local state law which would be analogous to a federal duty of care.[169] The claims also are circumscribed by the FTCA's exception for "discretionary acts," which include governmental policy decisions having social,

---

162. Allen v. United States, 588 F. Supp. 247 (D. Utah 1984), *rev'd on other grounds*, 816 F.2d 1417 (10th Cir. 1987), *cert. denied*, 484 U.S. 1004 (1988).
163. Pierce v. Wiglesworth, 903 P.2d 656 (Colo. 1994).
164. Sindell v. Abbott Laboratories, 607 P.2d 924 (Cal. 1980), *cert. denied*, 449 U.S. 912 (1980).
165. Summers v. Tice, 199 P.2d 1 (Cal. 1948).
166. Hymowitz v. Eli Lilly & Co., 539 N.E.2d 1069 (N.Y. 1989).
167. Sindell v. Abbott Laboratories, 607 P.2d 924 (Cal. 1980), *cert. denied*, 449 U.S. 912 (1980); Hymowitz v. Eli Lilly & Co., 539 N.E.2d 1069 (N.Y. 1989).
168. 28 U.S.C. §§ 2671–2680.
169. Hornbeck Offshore Transportation LLC v. United States, 569 F.3d 506 (D.C. Cir. 2009).

economic or political goals.[170] Conduct that falls outside of the FTCA, and thus evades governmental liability, can include discretionary decisions involving the disposal of hazardous wastes and toxic substances which can contaminate private property,[171] unless official policy mandates methods and procedures which effectively eliminate the agency's or employee's exercise of discretion.[172] For that reason, some courts have dismissed claims based on EPA remediation of a landfill and similar activities, holding them to be based on the discretionary acts of government employees.[173] In addition, the Claims Act bars punitive damages against the United States.[174] Suits against state governments are subject to similar rules. *See* the discussion in § 1.05[E].

Tort actions by members of the Armed Forces against the Government are barred by the *Feres* doctrine, based on the 1950 Supreme Court decision in *Feres v. United States*.[175] When numerous Vietnam veterans and their survivors contended that their exposure to a defoliant, Agent Orange, during that conflict resulted in injuries and death, one court ruled that the *Feres* doctrine prohibited them from suing the United States.[176] However, the plaintiffs were free to sue the manufacturers on a product liability theory, and did so. The manufacturers asserted the defense that they were immune as government contractors, an issue discussed in [C][2], *below.*

However, it must be emphasized that the doctrine of sovereign immunity as qualified by the FTCA applies to *torts* asserted as private rights of action. It does not protect the United States government from lawsuits asserting its liability arising from its violation of the various federal environmental statutes under the procedures set forth in those statutes. Even if asserted as statutory citizen suits, those are not private rights of action, and damages and/or compensation to private parties is foreclosed.

[B] Damages

Compensatory and punitive damages are available in toxic tort litigation, and in some cases medical monitoring costs are also available. Much litigation has centered on whether punitive damages are at times unconstitutionally excessive. The leading cases in this area are not toxic tort actions, but the rules they establish are particularly relevant for toxic tort suits, in which punitive damages are often recovered. Such damages are based on the need to deter future misconduct, as well as retribution for the injuries caused.

---

170. United States v. Gaubert, 499 U.S. 315 (1991).
171. OSI, Inc. v. United States, 285 F.3d 947 (11th Cir. 2002); Sanchez v. United States, 671 F.3d 86 (1st Cir. 2012).
172. Myers v. United States, 652 F.3d 1021 (9th Cir. 2011).
173. Dickerson v. United States, 857 F.2d 1577 (11th Cir. 1989).
174. City of Jacksonville v. Department of the Navy, 348 F.3d 1307 (11th Cir. 2003).
175. 340 U.S. 135 (1950).
176. *In re* Agent Orange Product Liability Litigation, 506 F. Supp. 762 (E.D.N.Y. 1980), *appeal dism.*, 745 F.2d 161 (2d Cir. 1984).

The Supreme Court in *BMW of North America v. Gore*[177] reversed a judgment for $2 million in punitive damages resulting from the defendant's failure to disclose that an automobile sold as new had in fact been repainted. The compensatory damages were a scant $4,000. The Court ruled the huge disproportion amounted to a deprivation of the defendant's property without due process of law.

The Supreme Court subsequently ruled that punitive damages should not exceed nine times the compensatory damages recovered, except in the most egregious cases, and further held that the "wealth of the defendant cannot justify an otherwise unconstitutional punitive damages award."[178]

The Court further ruled that punitive damages may not be based on injury to persons other than the plaintiffs in the particular suit.[179]

In other decisions, the courts have examined whether the trial judge's instructions to the jury regarding punitive damages were adequate to support the verdict or, again, constituted a denial of due process. One Supreme Court ruling upheld a punitive damage award against such a claim.[180] Another found that Oregon's courts did not sufficiently review the amount of punitive damages imposed by juries.[181]

In the well-known Love Canal litigation, where toxic waste was deposited on land later used for residential and school purposes, the court, in a much-criticized decision, denied punitive damages, ruling that the defendants could not be held to current standards of care when they disposed of the waste in the 1940s and 1950s.[182]

In another well-publicized case, the Supreme Court sustained an award of punitive damages to the estate of Karen Silkwood, an anti-nuclear activist, based on nuclear contamination of her clothing and apartment. It rejected the claim that the Atomic Energy Act's preemption of the regulation of nuclear radiation barred state-law punitive damages in a tort action, holding punitive damages not to be a form of regulation.[183] The decision, and the issues involved, are also discussed in § 12.02[F].

[C] Defenses

[1] Statute of Limitations

Tort law traditionally computes its period of limitations from the date of exposure to the event causing the damage or injury. This, however, was found to place a severe burden on plaintiffs in toxic tort litigation, where diseases often have long latency periods, and claimants therefore are unaware of the event that caused their injuries until long after the period of limitations — typically three years in tort suits — has

---

177. 517 U.S. 559 (1996).

178. State Farm Mutual Ins. Co. v. Campbell, 538 U.S. 408, 427 (2003).

179. Philip Morris USA v. Williams, 127 S. Ct. 1057 (2007).

180. Pacific Mutual Life Ins. Co. v. Haslip, 499 U.S. 1 (1991).

181. Honda Motor Co. Ltd. v. Oberg, 512 U.S. 415 (1994).

182. United States v. Hooker Chemicals & Plastics Corp., 850 F. Supp. 993 (W.D.N.Y. 1994).

183. Silkwood v. Kerr-McGee Corp., 464 U.S. 238 (1984).

expired. Most states have now adopted the rule that the period of limitations runs from the date when the plaintiff discovered the injury, or when a reasonable person should have discovered it.[184] One court has ruled that under such a statute, the date when the injury reasonably should have been discovered governs, even though the plaintiff was not then aware of the cause of the injury.[185]

Even under the older statutes of limitation that ran from the time of actual exposure, nuisance actions were governed by the continuing nuisance doctrine. Under this rule, discussed in § 3.01[D], a nuisance remains actionable even if the activity commenced beyond the statute of limitations, as long as it continues into the period within which the suit remains timely.[186] However, the New York Court of Appeals has held that the state's adoption of a discovery statute of limitations rendered the continuing nuisance rule inapplicable to nuisance actions seeking damages. The rule still governs nuisance suits seeking injunctive relief, since the amended statute of limitations applies only to actions for damages.[187]

[2] Government Contractor Defense

A series of federal court decisions immunizes government contractors working on government projects from tort liability arising from conduct falling under the contract as a derivative form of sovereign immunity under various circumstances.[188] This would also extend to users of defective products they manufacture in the absence of proof that the government contractor actually knew of the defect.[189] However, some courts have held this defense inapplicable to suits based on the failure to warn employees of the dangers of hazardous substances such as lead and asbestos.[190]

This issue arose in the Agent Orange litigation, described in [A][4], *above*, where the manufacturers of the defoliant argued that the government contractor defense immunized them from suit, in the absence of proof that the government lacked knowledge of the danger posed by the substances. The court initially upheld that defense,[191] but a subsequent trial judge considered reopening the question, finding a possible triable issue as to the extent of the government's awareness of the danger.

---

184. *See, e.g.*, N.Y. CIV. PRAC. LAW & RULES § 214-c.

185. *In re* New York County DES Litigation, 678 N.E.2d 474 (N.Y. 1997).

186. Miller v. Cudahy Co., 567 F. Supp. 892 (D. Kans. 1983).

187. Jensen v. General Electric Co., 623 N.E.2d 547 (N.Y. 1993); *see also* Barnes v. American Tobacco Co., 984 F. Supp. 842 (E.D. Pa. 1997), *aff'd*, 161 F.3d 127 (3d Cir. 1998), *cert. denied*, 526 U.S. 1114 (1999) (rejecting "continuous tort" theory in cases other than nuisance).

188. *In re* KBR, Inc. v. Burn Pit Litigation, 744 F.3d 326 (4th Cir. 2014); Ackerson v. Bean Dredging, Inc., 589 F.3d 196 (5th Cir. 2009); Adkisson v. Jacobs Engineering Group, Inc., 790 F.3d 641 (6th Cir. 2015). These Circuit Court rulings also provide differing views of whether the defense is jurisdictional, requiring dismissal at the outset, or non-jurisdictional, in that the government contractor has the burden of proving its relationship with the government and its entitlement to the defense.

189. Boyle v. United Technologies Corp., 487 U.S. 500 (1988).

190. Crawford v. National Lead Co., 784 F. Supp. 439 (S.D. Ohio 1989); Grispo v. Eagle-Picher Industries, 897 F.2d 626 (2d Cir. 1990).

191. *In re* Agent Orange Product Liability Litigation, 818 F.2d 187 (2d Cir. 1987), *cert. denied*, 487 U.S. 1234 (1988).

In the end, the litigation was settled. The contractor defendants then sued the government for indemnification based on the government contractor defense. The Supreme Court rejected that claim, holding the United States had never agreed to reimburse the defendants in the event of their liability to third parties.[192] The court likewise granted the government contractor defense when it dismissed a suit by Vietnamese plaintiffs against the manufacturers of Agent Orange.[193]

[3] Workplace Toxic Torts

Employers' liability to their employees in the workplace is controlled by workers' compensation statutes, which furnish an administrative remedy in place of a civil lawsuit. These statutes generally preclude tort actions by employees against their employers for workplace injuries. However, employees are free to sue the manufacturer or supplier of a substance that caused an injury in a third-party action.[194] In such actions, the defendant manufacturer may contend that the employer's failure to warn its employees of the hazard was the cause of the injury.[195] Some states have limited actions by manufacturer defendants against employers to cases involving severe injuries.[196]

In suits by injured employees against manufacturers, the defendants are generally held to the standard of knowledge of an expert with an awareness of scientific and medical advances.[197]

Another avenue that some courts have opened is to authorize direct suits by employees against their employers on the theory that workers' compensation laws do not bar suits for intentional torts. These decisions adopt the view that the employer intentionally exposed its employees to the hazardous substances it introduced into the workplace.[198] The intent required is not specific intent but rather the ordinary tort law standard of intent: that one is presumed to have intended the predictable consequences of one's acts.

[4] Bankruptcy

As is the case with litigation to remediate hazardous waste sites under the Comprehensive Environmental Response, Compensation and Liability Act (CERCLA), discussed in § 7.06, the bankruptcy of a defendant in toxic tort actions poses complex legal issues. In general, the filing of a petition for bankruptcy acts to stay all legal actions for damages against the debtor.[199] This fundamental precept of federal bank-

---

192. Hercules, Inc. v. United States, 516 U.S. 417 (1996).

193. *In re* Agent Orange Product Liability Litigation, 373 F. Supp. 2d 7 (E.D.N.Y. 2005).

194. Houk v. Arrow Drilling Co., 439 P.2d 146 (Kans. 1968).

195. Taylor v. Monsanto Co., 150 F.2d 806 (7th Cir. 1998); Beale v. Hardy, 769 F.2d 213 (4th Cir. 1985); Dole v. Dow Chemical Co., 282 N.E.2d 288 (N.Y. 1972).

196. *See* N.Y. WORKERS' COMPENSATION LAW § 227.

197. Borel v. Fibreboard Paper Products Corp., 493 F.2d 1076 (5th Cir. 1973), *cert. denied*, 419 U.S. 869 (1974).

198. Sydenstricker v. Unipunch Products, Inc., 288 S.E.2d 511 (W. Va. 1982).

199. 11 U.S.C. § 362.

ruptcy law is designed to enable the trustee in bankruptcy to marshal the debtor's assets, so they may be equitably apportioned among its creditors.

Complexity arises, however, when a debtor is beset with numerous claims at various stages of ripeness. Should the company's limited assets be divided among claimants with existing judgments or settlements against it, or should funds be set aside for pending claims? Should pending claims in litigation be given priority over those not yet in suit? Finally, what about the rights of future claimants, who may not become ill until after the bankrupt's assets are already parceled out?

In one noted action concerning the reorganization of Johns-Manville, a major asbestos producer, the court created a trust fund for future claimants under the Bankruptcy Code. But when the trust fund was depleted, the trust was suspended to enable the company to replenish its assets. The court than divided claimants into two groups according to the severity of their claimed injury. However, on appeal a court ruled that such a division violated the company's reorganization plan.[200]

The Supreme Court later rejected class actions in two major suits against asbestos manufactures, in large measure because of concerns over the differing interests of present and future claimants.[201]

[D] Procedure and Evidence

[1] Class Actions

Historically, tort law has not been hospitable to class actions. The traditional rule was that since plaintiffs typically suffer differing injuries, and may be subject to different defenses, such as their contributory negligence or the statute of limitations, class actions are inappropriate in tort litigation.[202]

Some courts have reconsidered this view in the context of mass tort litigation involving exposure to toxic substances by large numbers of people. One approach is to permit joint discovery or consolidated trials.[203] Some courts, though, have allowed class actions in a variety of toxic tort suits, where the sheer quantity of claimants has overcome their past reluctance to do so.[204] For example, the Agent Orange litigation, involving 46,000 plaintiffs, was of necessity litigated as a class action.[205] However, as noted in the discussion of bankruptcy issues (§ 8.03[C][4]), the Supreme Court has

---

200. *In re* Joint Eastern and Southern District Asbestos Litigation, 982 F.2d 721 (2d Cir. 1992), *modified on rehearing*, 993 F.2d 7 (2d Cir. 1993).

201. Ortiz v. Fibreboard Corp., 527 U.S. 815 (1999); Amchem Products Inc. v. Windsor, 521 U.S. 591 (1997).

202. Wojciechowski v. Republic Steel Corp., 413 N.Y.S.2d 70 (A.D. 1979).

203. *In re* Joint Eastern and Southern Districts Asbestos Litigation, 18 F.3d 126 (2d Cir. 1994).

204. McCastle v. Rollins Envtl. Services, Inc., 456 So. 2d 612 (La. 1984); Livingston Parish Police Jury v. Acadiana Shipyards, Inc., 598 So. 2d 1177 (La. 1992).

205. *In re* Agent Orange Product Liability Litigation, 506 F. Supp. 762 (E.D.N.Y. 1980).

rejected class actions against asbestos manufacturers because of the potentially conflicting interests of present and future claimants.[206]

[2] Jurisdiction

Whether the United States courts have jurisdiction over a mass toxic tort action occurring beyond our borders became the subject of litigation following the 1984 Bhopal disaster. In that case, Union Carbide of India, a subsidiary of an American corporation, emitted methyl isocyanate, a hazardous air pollutant, from a facility in that Indian city. Over 500,000 claimants brought suit for damages for injury or wrongful death, and sued in the United States where discovery is broader and verdicts higher than in the courts of India. Although the United States court clearly had jurisdiction over Union Carbide as an American corporation, the defendant invoked the doctrine of forum non conveniens, contending the court should not hear the case since the events took place in India and nearly all the potential witnesses were there.

However, the plaintiffs cited the advantages of broader discovery under the Federal Rules of Civil Procedure. The court dismissed the litigation on condition that the defendant agree to submit to discovery against it in the Indian courts under the Federal Rules. But the Court of Appeals held that while dismissal was correct, the discovery condition was invalid since it bound the defendant only, and not both sides. The court left it to the Indian courts to determine the extent of discovery.[207]

The litigation proceeded in the Supreme Court of India and was eventually settled with the approval of that court. An attempt to litigate the plaintiffs' claims in the United States despite the settlement was rejected by the United States Court of Appeals based on the act-of-state doctrine, which prohibits a United States court from reopening the decision of a court in a country, like India, with an impartial legal system.[208] Similar forum non conveniens concerns have led to the dismissal of suits in United States courts seeking damages for environmental harm resulting from activities by United States companies in foreign countries.[209]

[3] Discovery

As the course of the Bhopal action showed, pre-trial discovery is a vital element of toxic tort litigation — even more so than in most lawsuits, since these cases often turn on epidemiological and other scientific proof and involve large numbers of possible claimants. Defendants in toxic tort actions frequently seek protective orders from trial courts preventing plaintiffs from publicizing the results of discovery, or

---

206. Ortiz v. Fibreboard Corp., 527 U.S. 815 (1999); Amchem Products Inc. v. Windsor, 521 U.S. 591 (1997).

207. *In re* Union Carbide Corp. Gas Plant Disaster, 809 F.2d 195 (2d Cir. 1987), *cert. denied*, 484 U.S. 871 (1987).

208. Bi v. Union Carbide Chemicals & Plastics, Inc. 984 F.2d 582 (2d Cir. 1993), *cert. denied*, 510 U.S. 862 (1993).

209. Aguinda v. Texaco, Inc., 303 F.3d 470 (2d Cir. 2002) (oil drilling in Ecuador; dismissal conditioned on defendant's consent to suit in Ecuador).

sharing it with other potential claimants. Some courts have granted such protective orders, while others have denied them except as to trade secrets.[210]

EPA studies, and the testimony of EPA employees, are generally not subject to discovery, or otherwise available, in private litigation.[211]

[4] Expert Testimony

Since, as noted in [A][3][b], *above*, scientific evidence is so often crucial to toxic tort litigation, many courts have had to wrestle with the admissibility of expert testimony on scientific subjects. Essentially, admissibility turns on the reliability of the evidence. The traditional rule in the federal courts was that scientific evidence had to be "generally accepted" in the field of study involved — the so-called *Frye* rule devised in *Frye v. United States*, a 1923 decision.[212]

As environmental tort and other litigation involving scientific proof evolved, the *Frye* rule became the subject of criticism as unduly restrictive, barring much testimony that juries ought to be able to consider. In a 1993 decision, *Daubert v. Merrell Dow Pharmaceuticals*,[213] the Supreme Court significantly broadened the admissibility of scientific proof under the Federal Rules of Evidence. Under *Daubert*, scientific evidence is admissible if derived through scientific methods, subject to testing, and acceptable to a reasonable juror. However, state courts are not bound by the *Daubert* standard, and some have adhered to the older *Frye* rule.[214] Tort and other actions heard in federal courts based on the parties' diversity of citizenship employ the Federal Rules of Evidence and therefore the *Daubert* test.[215]

[E] Liability Insurance

[1] "Sudden and Accidental" Limitation

The degree to which liability insurance protects defendants in toxic tort litigation has itself created much litigation. Comprehensive general liability policies since the early 1970s have limited their coverage to "sudden and accidental" discharges to avoid liability for occurrences such as the seepage or migration of hazardous waste into water supply. The courts are divided as to whether these classic toxic tort scenarios are covered by policies containing that language.[216] The rule varies from state to state, depending on the courts' interpretation of this standard wording. In addition, some

---

210. Anderson v. Cryovac, Inc., 805 F.2d 1 (1st Cir. 1986) (granted); In re Agent Orange Product Liability Litigation, 104 F.R.D. 559 (E.D.N.Y. 1985) (denied).

211. Wehner v. Syntex Corp., 616 F. Supp. 27 (E.D. Mo. 1985).

212. 293 F. 1013 (D.C. Cir. 1923).

213. 509 U.S. 579 (1993).

214. *See* People v. Wesley, 633 N.E.2d 451 (N.Y. 1994).

215. FED. R. EVID. § 702.

216. *See* Avondale Industries, Inc. v. Travelers Indemnity Co., 887 F.2d 1200 (2d Cir. 1989) (covered); Technicon Electronics Corp. v. American Home Assurance Co., 542 N.E.2d 1048 (N.Y. 1989) (not covered).

courts take the view that the creation of a nuisance or similar condition is not an "occurrence" at all requiring indemnification under a liability policy.[217]

Some insurers have begun to offer liability policies without this limiting "sudden and accidental" provision, but at a higher premium. The insurance industry has also generated standard pollution exclusion policies containing clauses that specifically limit coverage to eliminate many environmental claims. Policies covering insurance claims can be purchased, but it can be expected that the cost of premiums will be higher in view of the carrier's potential exposure to expensive environmental cleanups.

[2] Duty to Defend

An insurer's duty to defend the insured — that is, to pay the costs of defense — is broader than its duty to indemnify the insured. Thus, insurers must furnish legal defense even in situations in which they may later be able to disclaim liability coverage if the insured is found liable.[218] However, the insurance policy under which recovery is sought must cover environmental contamination in order for the insurer to be responsible for a defense involving such claims. This warrants a careful review of the policy's terms and especially its exclusions.

[3] Liability of Insurer at Time of Exposure

Often, due to the nature of toxic tort cases, the insurer at the time of the exposure may not be the insurer at the time that symptoms of injury manifest themselves and a claim is filed. Some courts impose liability on the insurer during the exposure period, some on the subsequent insurer during the manifestation period.[219] The precise wording of the policy sometimes determines this issue.

§ 8.04 Radon

[A] Health Risks

Radon is a radioactive gas that results from the chemical breakdown of the element radium. Radon can enter buildings through air, water, or soil. Its deleterious effects on health have only recently become appreciated, but it seems clear that inhalation of radon particles is associated with lung cancer. Medical evidence suggests that 10 percent of all American households have radon levels associated with cancer risk.[220]

---

217. American States Ins. Co. v. Maryland Casualty Co., 587 F. Supp. 1549 (E.D. Mich. 1984); United States Fidelity & Guaranty Co. v. Star Fire Coals Inc., 856 F.2d 31 (6th Cir. 1988).

218. Fitzpatrick v. American Honda Motor Co., 575 N.E.2d 90 (N.Y. 1991).

219. See Insurance Co. of North America v. 48 Insulations, Inc., 633 F.2d 1212 (6th Cir. 1980)657 F.2d 814 (6th Cir. 1981), cert. denied, 454 U.S. 1109 (1981); Consolidated Edison Co. v. Allstate Ins. Co., 774 N.E.2d 687 (N.Y. 2002) (exposure period); Eagle-Picher Industries, Inc. v. Liberty Mutual Ins. Co., 682 F.2d 12 (1st Cir. 1982), cert. denied, 460 U.S. 1028 (1983) (manifestation period).

220. HARRISON'S PRINCIPLES OF INTERNAL MEDICINE 1436 (14th ed. 1998).

In view of the dearth of present information, Congressional attention has been focused on information-gathering rather than on imposing affirmative responsibilities on individuals, businesses, or states, although, as noted in [B][2], *below*, federal agencies must survey their own buildings. The focus of concern thus far has been on radon contamination of dwellings and schools. Radon's threat increases in buildings where radon enters through porous floors, subsurface walls, or structural elements, especially in basements lacking adequate ventilation where its buildup often remains unnoticed.

[B] Regulation of Radon as a Toxic Substance

[1] EPA's Responsibility to Provide Information

The limited regulatory attention radon has received is found in Subchapter III[221] of the Toxic Substances Control Act (discussed in § 8.02), addressing indoor radon abatement. However, the requirements are primarily informational. The statute only requires EPA to develop an information base and to make it available to states and the private sector, but even this requirement is carefully qualified.[222]

Congress has established a national goal of ensuring that buildings have air as free of radon as the ambient air outside.[223] The guidelines are promulgated by EPA, but implemented by the Department of Housing and Urban Development for public and multifamily housing.

EPA has published a *Citizen's Guide to Radon*, describing different levels of radon and health risks, and the cost and feasibility of reducing radon levels in buildings.

[2] Construction Standards

The health threat posed by radon can be significantly reduced by preventing its penetration of, or accumulation within, buildings. The statute requires EPA to develop model construction standards and techniques, with advice from organizations active in developing national building standards.[224]

EPA may make grants to states to develop and implement their own radon assessment and mitigation programs — surveying radon levels for residential, public, and school buildings, and adopting radon-preventative building codes.[225] States are the conduit through which funds are provided to local governments. In addition, Congress has directed EPA to conduct a nationwide study of contamination of the nation's schools, focusing on localities with elevated radon levels and school construction inadequate to prevent contamination.[226]

---

221. 15 U.S.C. §§ 2661–2671.
222. *See* 15 U.S.C. § 2665.
223. 15 U.S.C. § 2661.
224. 15 U.S.C. § 2664.
225. 15 U.S.C. § 2666.
226. 15 U.S.C. § 2667.

Finally, federal agencies are required to survey, subject to EPA design approval, and with EPA technical assistance, all of their public buildings for radon contamination.[227] Suits have been brought and damages recovered for undisclosed radon contamination.[228]

§ 8.05 Asbestos

[A] Background of Problem; Regulation under State and Federal Law

Asbestos containing material (ACM) is dangerous if it is inhaled when it becomes "friable," that is, when the fibers start separating from one another into dust, entering air flow. Unlike other substances regulated under the Toxic Substances Control Act (TSCA) (see § 8.02), the danger of asbestos clearly affects a particular organ, the lungs, and the risk of mortality is well-established. Unlike other chemicals, though, it may be readily contained if appropriate precautions are taken.

Asbestos, an effective fire retardant substance and insulation material, was installed in many work places, public and commercial buildings, and homes during the mid-20th century, before its significant health hazards were recognized. Its use was common as filler for plastic materials, in cement and tile floors, and in brake and clutch linings. In addition to everyday consumer exposure, workers involved in mining, milling, and manufacturing of asbestos products, and workers in the building trades and in shipyards, were occupationally exposed to asbestos. Even people only moderately exposed in the workplace, or even as a result of laundering clothing containing asbestos, were placed at risk.[229]

After the 1970s, asbestos was replaced by synthetic fibers such as fiberglass. Its use for insulation or as a fire retardant has been prohibited since 1997.[230] Today, most activity involving asbestos arises from its physical removal from buildings and its disposal.

Inhalation gives rise to three major diseases: lung cancer; asbestosis, a pulmonary disease; and mesothelioma, a cancer. The latter two diseases are difficult to diagnose and may have lengthy latency periods. Tobacco smoking in particular aggravates the damage (though apparently not for mesothelioma), but also may mask the causes of lung disease. Generally, these diseases, resulting from cumulative exposures, are irreversible.[231]

---

227. 15 U.S.C. § 2669.

228. Grefer v. Alpha Technical, 901 So. 2d 1117 (La. App. 2005), *rev'd on other grounds, sub nom.* Exxon Mobil Corp. v. Grefer, 127 S. Ct. 1371 (2007); Glacier Tennis Club at Summit, LLC v. Treweek Construction Co., 87 P.3d 431 (Mont. 2004).

229. HARRISON'S PRINCIPLES OF INTERNAL MEDICINE, *supra* note 220, at 1430–31.

230. 54 Fed. Reg. 29,460.

231. *See generally* ATTORNEYS' TEXTBOOK OF MEDICINE Ch. 205C (Matthew Bender).

Asbestos is regulated under federal law as well as the laws of many states,[232] some of which have licensing and training requirements,[233] and by local communities.[234] It is a hazardous substance under CERCLA,[235] triggering reporting obligations if it is released into the environment,[236] as well as disposal requirements,[237] and is addressed by Occupational Safety and Health Act regulations (see [C], *below*).[238] Demolition and renovation activities and asbestos removal are subject to national emission standards for hazardous air pollutants (see § 5.03[D]). It is a listed hazardous air pollutant under Clean Air Act § 112.[239] Asbestos also is directly regulated by TSCA (see [B], *below*).[240]

The use of asbestos was sharply reduced during the 1980s because of tort liability.[241] EPA issued a final rule in 1989 under TSCA banning asbestos use by 1997.[242]

[B] Regulation under Toxic Substances Control Act

[1] Asbestos in Schools

TSCA sets forth Congressional findings that the asbestos in schools should be regulated.[243] Congress directed EPA to promulgate regulations, which currently are contained in Title 40 of the Code of Federal Regulations. However, TSCA provisions addressing asbestos contamination do not preempt state law, and states may establish more stringent requirements or create additional liabilities.[244]

Every local educational agency must have an asbestos management plan,[245] developed by an accredited management planner[246] and submitted for state approval.[247]

---

232. *See, e.g.*, 8 CAL. CODE REG. § 5208; New York School Asbestos Safety Act, N.Y. EDUCATION LAW, Article 9-A; New Jersey School Aid for Asbestos, N.J. EDUCATION LAW, Article 5.

233. *See, e.g.*, MARYLAND TOXIC, CARCINOGENIC AND FLAMMABLE SUBSTANCES LAW § 36-401, *et seq.*; N.Y. LABOR LAW, Article 30; N.J. LABOR AND WORKMEN'S COMPENSATION LAW, N.J.S.A. § 34:5A-32.

234. *See, e.g.*, N.Y. CITY LOCAL LAW Nos. 70, 76.

235. *See* United States v. Nicolet, 857 F.2d 202 (3d Cir. 1988).

236. See *United States v. Liebman*, 40 F.3d 544 (2d Cir. 1994), affirming the conviction under CERCLA § 103 for the defendant's failure to report a release in connection with the improper disposal of asbestos removed from his property in bags dumped in a gravel pit.

237. National R.R. Passenger Corp. v. New York City Housing Auth., 819 F. Supp. 1271 (S.D.N.Y. 1993).

238. 29 C.F.R. §§ 1910.1001, 1926.

239. 40 C.F.R. Part 61, subpart M; *see* 38 Fed. Reg. 8820 (April 6, 1973).

240. 15 U.S.C. §§ 2641–2656.

241. Manufacturers were held strictly liable for the death of an insulation worker exposed to asbestos dust for 33 years in the Texas case of *Borel v. Fibreboard Paper Products Co.*, 493 F.2d 1076 (5th Cir. 1973), *cert. denied*, 419 U.S. 869 (1974). Litigation grew dramatically thereafter. *See* the cases described under Toxic Tort Litigation at § 8.03[C][4] and [D][1].

242. 54 Fed. Reg. 29,460 (July 12, 1989).

243. 15 U.S.C. § 2641; Pub. L. 99-519, Oct. 22, 1986, 100 Stat. 2970.

244. 15 U.S.C. § 2649(a).

245. 15 U.S.C. §§ 2643(i), 2644(d).

246. 15 U.S.C. § 2646(a).

247. 15 U.S.C. § 2645.

The management plan must provide blueprints or diagrams of buildings, identify where asbestos is found and whether it is friable, identify sampling areas and their square footage, and include records of inspections, sampling, and response actions.[248] EPA must provide information based on the best scientific evidence to facilitate public understanding of the relative risks of in-place management of asbestos versus removal, promote the least burdensome response actions necessary to protect health, and indicate when removal is necessary.[249] Local agencies are responsible for transporting[250] and disposing of asbestos as a hazardous air pollutant.[251]

Knowing or willful violations subject the violator to criminal prosecution.[252] If an asbestos condition poses an imminent and substantial danger to human health or the environment, injunctive relief,[253] as well as cost recovery,[254] is available to EPA.

[2] Asbestos Abatement

EPA's regulations under TSCA govern asbestos abatement projects. Areas that exceed permissible concentrations of airborne asbestos must be marked off, and access limited to authorized persons, who must wear respirators and protective clothing.[255]

Medical surveillance, paid for by the employer, is necessary for employees who work at locations that are above a specified threshold of asbestos concentration.[256] Fraudulent abatement schemes can be criminally prosecuted.[257]

[C] Occupational Safety and Health Act Regulation

The Occupational Safety and Health Act (OSHA) specifies permissible exposure levels for employees engaged in handling asbestos, and for construction and maintenance workers, as well as an occupational exposure standard applicable to office employees.[258] Above that threshold, OSHA requires medical and increased air monitoring, warning signs,[259] increased protections for breathing,[260] and protective clothing.[261]

---

248. 15 U.S.C. § 2643(i).
249. 15 U.S.C. § 2643(d)(7).
250. Transportation is governed by Department of Transportation regulations at 49 C.F.R. Part 173, subpart J.
251. *See* 40 C.F.R. Part 61, subpart M.
252. 40 C.F.R. § 763.97.
253. 15 U.S.C. § 2648; 40 C.F.R. § 763.97(d).
254. 15 U.S.C. § 2649(a)(4).
255. 40 C.F.R. § 121(e).
256. 40 C.F.R. § 121(m).
257. United States v. Thorn, 659 F.3d 227 (2d Cir. 2011); United States v. Starnes, 583 F.3d 196 (3d Cir. 2009); United States v. Ho, 311 F.3d 589 (5th Cir. 2002); United States v. Sawyer, 825 F.3d 287 (6th Cir. 2016); United States v. O'Malley, 739 F.3d 1001 (7th Cir. 2014); United States v. W.R. Grace, 504 F.3d 745 (9th Cir. 2007).
258. 29 C.F.R. Parts 1910 and 1926.
259. 55 Fed. Reg. 3724 (Feb. 5, 1990); 29 C.F.R. § 1910.1001(c)–(e).
260. 29 C.F.R. § 1910.1001(g).
261. 29 C.F.R. § 1910.1001(h).

[D] Clean Air Act

Asbestos is regulated as a hazardous air pollutant, subject to National Emission Standards[262] prohibiting visible emissions from manufacturing facilities and asbestos spraying, fabricating, and insulating. Demolition of any building with asbestos material or renovation involving the removal of significant amounts of friable asbestos requires notice to EPA and mitigation measures.[263] Similar standards apply to milling and manufacturing operations using asbestos.[264] Violators can be criminally prosecuted under the CAA for knowing releases of asbestos-containing materials even if the particular compound is not a TSCA specified compound,[265] and for failing to conduct air monitoring when they should have known that asbestos likely was present, or for filing false monitoring reports.[266]

§ 8.06 Chlorofluorocarbons (CFCs) and Other Ozone Depleting Chemicals

[A] Background of Problem

Ozone depleting substances include chlorofluorocarbons, or "CFCs," halons, carbon tetrachloride, and methyl chloroform,[267] although the primary concern is with the formerly widespread use of CFCs. CFCs are "fully halogenated chlorofluoroalkanes,"[268] that became popular as propellants for aerosol spray cans, Styrofoam and refrigerants during the second half of the twentieth century. CFCs were components of many products that the public took largely for granted, such as the propellants in confetti, health-related consumer products, containerized household products, a variety of horns, wall-mounted alarms, and as constituents of many lubricants and solvents.[269] As useful, but apparently benign, products, they had long been regulated by the Consumer Product Safety Commission.[270]

However, like some other post-war miracle chemicals, CFCs pose serious environmental risks: because of their dramatic potential to bond with upper atmospheric ozone, CFCs have been closely linked with depletion of the ozone layer that protects the earth from ultraviolet radiation. Ultraviolet radiation has been linked with increased skin cancer, cataracts, and global warming, as well as yet indefinite effects on ecosystems. Even as early as 1977, the Consumer Product Safety Commission

---

262. 38 Fed. Reg. 8820 (April 6, 1973).
263. 40 C.F.R. Part 61, subpart M.
264. 40 C.F.R. § 61.144.
265. United States v. W.R. Grace, 504 F.3d 745 (9th Cir. 2007).
266. United States v. George, 583 F.3d 196 (3d Cir. 2009).
267. See 40 C.F.R. Part 82 (generally).
268. 16 C.F.R. § 1401.3.
269. See 40 C.F.R. § 82.66 for the EPA's listing of presently nonessential CFC products and their exceptions.
270. See 16 C.F.R. Part 1401.

alerted the public to the possible link with ozone reduction, encouraged the public to make "a conscious choice" in using CFC products,[271] and required manufacturers to provide performance and technical data, and to label the product with a warning to purchasers reflecting the possible danger.[272] By 1978, the Food and Drug Administration started restricting the use of CFCs as propellants. As scientific data crystallized during the 1980s and 1990s, and regional ozone depletion lent empirical force to environmental and health concerns that previously had not generated much public discussion, both international agreements (see Chapter 13) and domestic regulatory bodies moved toward a virtual elimination of CFC production and use.

[B] Regulation under Clean Air Act

[1] CFC Listing

Ozone depleting chemicals are listed in the Clean Air Act and numerically identified by their ozone depletion potential[273] in a manner consistent with the listing in the Montreal Protocol (see § 13.03). At any time, any person may petition EPA to add a substance to the list.[274]

[2] Labeling

EPA requires labeling for permissible CFC products, which must include identification of the chemical and a warning statement.[275]

Private contractors who do business with the federal government are required by the Federal Acquisition Regulations System to label CFC-containing products.[276]

[3] CFC Ban

The Clean Air Act requires that "nonessential" CFC production be phased out. The uses as aerosol propellants and in refrigeration are nonessential uses,[277] as are many cleaning fluids containing CFCs, and other intended uses for which there are safe alternatives.[278] Exceptions are provided for essential uses of methyl chloroform — medical devices and those needed for aviation safety — to the extent that production and use is consistent with the Montreal protocol.[279] Residents of Alaska will be gratified to learn that EPA also excepts red pepper bear repellant sprays containing CFCs in solvent form.[280]

---

271. 16 C.F.R. § 1401.2.
272. 16 C.F.R. § 1401.5.
273. *See* 26 U.S.C. § 4682; 42 U.S.C. § 7671a; 40 C.F.R. Part 82, subpart A, App. A.
274. 42 U.S.C. § 7671a(c)(3).
275. 40 C.F.R. § 82.110.
276. 48 C.F.R. § 52.223-11.
277. See 40 C.F.R. § 82.66 for listing of nonessential uses and exceptions thereto.
278. 42 U.S.C. § 7671i(b).
279. 42 U.S.C. § 7671c(a)–(d).
280. 40 C.F.R. § 82.66(d)(2)(xi).

The sale or distribution in interstate commerce of any aerosols, pressurized dispensers, or plastic foam products containing listed substances is illegal, with minor exceptions for safety-related uses.[281]

CFCs are also listed as hazardous air pollutants,[282] and solvents containing CFCs are listed as hazardous wastes under the Resource Conservation and Recovery Act.[283]

Additionally, the Food and Drug Administration (FDA) has restricted CFC use in self-pressurized containers of food, drugs, and cosmetics.[284] For the few uses that are permissible, labels must indicate the destructive effects of CFCs.[285] CFC use otherwise is prohibited by the FDA.[286]

[C] Environmental Tax on CFCs

Taxes are imposed on the first sale, use, or import into the United States of ozone depleting chemicals by manufacturers or importers, based in part on their ozone-depletion potential.[287] There are limited exceptions applicable to recycling, or reuse when the ozone-depleting potential was consumed in the prior, taxable, use.[288] Some medical uses, such as inhalers, also may be tax exempt.[289]

§ 8.07 Lead

[A] Background of Problem; Regulations

The 20th century experienced the greatest historic exposure of populations to lead, as well as the most extensive scientific research on its health effects.[290] Like asbestos (see § 8.05), lead, often found in paint, plumbing, solder, batteries, and gasoline, was long considered to be a useful product, but its substantial toxicity has become appreciated only relatively recently. As with asbestos, federal regulation of lead has been imposed through the Toxic Substances Control Act (TSCA), although restrictions are also applied elsewhere. Lead contamination may come from numerous sources, but the sources presently regulated are lead-based paint, which degrades into lead-contaminated dust, and leaded gasoline that, as a consequence of gasoline exhaust, has caused lead concentrations in air and soil. Lead in soil may be passed to humans

---

281. 42 U.S.C. § 7671i(d).
282. 40 C.F.R. § 61.01(a).
283. 40 C.F.R. § 261.3(a)(1)(B).
284. 21 C.F.R. § 2.125.
285. 21 C.F.R. §§ 101.17 (food labeling), 201.320 (drug labeling), 801.63 (medical devices).
286. 21 C.F.R. §§ 189.191 (food), 300.100 (drugs), 700.23 (cosmetics), 801.417 (medical devices).
287. 26 C.F.R. § 52.4682-1.
288. 26 U.S.C. § 4682(d).
289. 26 U.S.C. § 4682(g).
290. HARRISON'S PRINCIPLES OF INTERNAL MEDICINE, *supra* note 220, at 2565–66.

by leafy green vegetables. Glazed ceramics and crystal still pose threats, though regulation of these sources remains nascent.[291]

Lead emissions from gasoline are prohibited by the Clean Air Act[292] (see § 5.04[E][1][b]). Residential lead-paint hazards are regulated by the Residential Lead-Based Paint Hazard Reduction Act,[293] which dovetails with TSCA provisions. Lead contamination also is the subject of many state and local laws. For instance, New York City landlords must correct a lead paint hazard in any multiple dwelling built before 1960 that contains peeling paint, presumptively lead-based, in which a child under the age of seven resides.[294] This regulation does not limit potential tort liability, though. The presence of lead in a dwelling unit's flaking paint chips which can be shown to have caused elevated lead levels in the child can be the basis for a personal injury claim regardless of the age of the building.[295]

The dangers posed by lead inhalation or ingestion, particularly by children, are now beyond cavil. The 1992 Congressional findings prefacing the Residential Lead-Based Paint Hazard Reduction Act (see [C], *below*) note (1) that low-level lead poisoning is widespread among American children, afflicting as many as three million under the age of six, with low-income communities disproportionately affected; (2) that even low-level lead poisoning in children causes IQ deficiencies, cognitive disabilities, and behavioral problems; and (3) that pre-1980 housing stock contains more than three million tons of lead in the form of lead-based paint, with most pre-1950 homes containing significant lead. The findings noted that household dust containing lead or chipping paint ingested by children is the most common source of the harm.[296] In 2008, at the conclusion of studies commenced in 2004 showing a statistically significant reduction in the IQ of children exposed to lead, EPA determined that there is no safe level of lead in ambient air.[297]

Scientific evidence indicates that children absorb up to 50 percent of the lead ingested (compared with 10 percent for adults), and absorption is enhanced by dietary deficiencies in calcium, iron, and zinc — a factor relevant to many low-income populations. Lead accumulates in tissues and attaches itself to red blood cells, but mostly is absorbed into bone, where its half-life of 25 years also causes long-term effects.

---

291. HARRISON'S PRINCIPLES OF INTERNAL MEDICINE, *supra* note 220, at 2565–66. Lead solder may not be placed in interstate commerce without a warning label (15 U.S.C. § 1263). Lead-based enamel, glassware, and ceramics are regulated as unsafe food additives (see 21 U.S.C. § 348, note).

292. 42 U.S.C. § 7545.

293. 42 U.S.C. §§ 4851–4856. Note, however, that the EPA's rules on lead dust are not limited to lead-based paint. National Multi Housing Council v. United States EPA, 292 F.3d 232 (D.C. Cir. 2002).

294. Local Law 1, N.Y. CITY ADMIN. CODE § 27-2013(h)(2).

295. A.L. v. New York City Housing Authority, 169 A.D.3d 40, 93 N.Y.S.3d 19 (S. Ct. App. Div. 1st Dept. 2019).

296. 42 U.S.C. § 4851.

297. 73 Fed. Reg. 66,964 (Nov. 12, 2008). See Coalition of Battery Recyclers Association v. EPA, 604 F.3d 613 (9th Cir. 2010), deferring to EPA's scientific conclusions and rejecting an industry challenge to these findings.

Lead is highly toxic, and medical dogma states that "it is absolutely essential to prevent further exposure of affected individuals to lead."[298]

[B] Lead Exposure Reduction under Toxic Substances Control Act

TSCA (see § 8.02) provides for lead exposure reduction, but these provisions are more informational than proscriptive. They were supplemented by the 1992 Residential Lead-Based Paint Hazard Reduction Act (see [C], *below*).

"Reduction" in this sense means reducing or eliminating the potential for people's exposure to lead by interim controls and abatement.[299] Interim controls for residences and federal buildings include specialized cleaning, repairs, maintenance, painting, containment, and monitoring and providing educational programs to housing management and residents.[300]

TSCA provisions address "lead-based paint activities" in "target housing."[301] Target housing generally includes residences built before 1978, when use of lead paint was prevalent, but excludes housing for the elderly or persons with disabilities.[302] Lead-based activities triggering TSCA include risk assessment, inspection, and abatement.[303] TSCA also requires the removal of lead from public or commercial buildings, bridges, and other structures built before 1978.[304] Risk assessment, discussed in Chapter 2, for lead exposure reduction requires an on-site investigation to evaluate the presence and extent of lead hazards in residences. Risk assessment also requires a determination of how old the residence is and whether children under the age of six live there, visual inspection, wipe sampling, and reporting on the outcome of the investigation.[305] Renovation and remodeling activities also trigger TSCA regulations.[306] Violators of these TSCA provisions may be sued civilly as well as prosecuted criminally.[307]

States may administer and enforce EPA's standards if the state program is as stringent as the federal program. Congress has directed EPA to develop a model state program that encourages states to use their existing certification and accreditation

---

298. HARRISON'S PRINCIPLES OF INTERNAL MEDICINE, *supra* note 220, at 2566.

299. 15 U.S.C. § 2681(13).

300. 15 U.S.C. § 2681(8).

301. 15 U.S.C. § 2682(b).

302. 15 U.S.C. § 2681(17).

303. *See* 15 U.S.C. §§ 2681(1) (definition of abatement), (16) (definition of risk assessment), 2682(b) (defining risk assessment, inspection, and abatement in target housing to constitute lead-based paint activities).

304. 15 U.S.C. § 2682(b).

305. 15 U.S.C. § 2681(16).

306. 15 U.S.C. § 2682(c).

307. 15 U.S.C. § 2689(a)(1) (civil penalties up to $25,000 per violation per day of violation); 15 U.S.C. § 2615(b) (similar fine, and/or up to one year of incarceration). If records are falsified for TSCA purposes, probation may be imposed in addition to other penalties (*see* 18 U.S.C. § 3561(c)(2)). United States v. Shimshoni, 631 Fed. Appx. 788 (11th Cir. 2015).

programs. If the state fails to carry out these responsibilities, however, EPA may withdraw approval. In the absence of a state program, EPA administers the federal program in that state.[308] Nor does TSCA interfere with other federal agencies' requirements that are as stringent as EPA's regulations.[309]

Additionally, the Department of Health and Human Services, working through the Center for Disease Control and the National Institute of Environmental Health Sciences, must conduct studies to identify the source of lead exposure in children, as well as evaluate how to reduce occupational lead exposure. EPA and these other agencies were required to establish by 1993 a National Clearinghouse on Childhood Lead Poisoning to collect and provide information, to provide advice to certified contractors, and to set up a hotline to answer questions from the public.[310]

[C] Residential Lead-Based Paint Hazard Reduction Act

[1] Purposes of Act

Congress, responding to mounting public concern, moved beyond TSCA requirements (while incorporating many of the key ingredients) with the 1992 enactment of the Residential Lead-Based Paint Hazard Reduction Act.[311] Congress noted that TSCA was too limited in reach, and its enforcement too lax, and thrust the federal government into a leadership role with this Act,[312] administered by the Department of Housing and Urban Development (HUD), with regulations promulgated by EPA. Congress now intended to develop a national strategy to eliminate lead-based paint hazards in all housing as quickly as possible.[313] The Act seeks to achieve this partially by federal HUD grants,[314] partially by establishing a joint EPA-HUD task force to evaluate contamination in private housing[315] and, like TSCA requirements, by also coordinating these agencies' informational efforts with the Center for Disease Control.[316]

The Act directs EPA and Department of Labor to seek maximum enforcement of TSCA residential lead hazard provisions and OSHA.[317] It directs HUD to research lead exposure from other sources, such as soil, and lead dust in carpets, furniture, and air ducts.[318] HUD must submit an annual report to Congress assessing progress in achieving the Act's goals, summarizing current health studies, recommending leg-

---

308. 15 U.S.C. § 2684.
309. 15 U.S.C. § 2690.
310. 15 U.S.C. § 2685.
311. 42 U.S.C. §§ 4851–4856.
312. 42 U.S.C. § 4851(7), (8).
313. 42 U.S.C. § 4851a.
314. 42 U.S.C. § 4852.
315. 42 U.S.C. § 4852a.
316. 42 U.S.C. § 4852b.
317. 42 U.S.C. § 4853a.
318. 42 U.S.C. § 4854.

islation and regulatory initiatives, and accounting for expenses.[319] The Act steps beyond providing a research and informational vehicle to require the establishment of guidelines for reduction and abatement of lead hazards.

[2] Disclosure of Lead Hazards Prior to Conveyance of Residential Target Housing

The Act requires sellers (or lessors) to disclose known lead-based paint hazards to buyers, lessees and real estate brokers in target housing offered for sale or lease.[320] The failure to disclose can lead to civil liability.[321] However, signifying that the statute is grounded more in contract than in tort theory, the right to be informed, and the corresponding right to sue for the seller's failure to disclose, extends only to buyers and lessees, and not to mere occupants of the premises.[322] The buyer must acknowledge understanding of the disclosure and the warnings,[323] and must be provided an opportunity to inspect for lead hazards prior to the conveyance.[324] The broker must ensure compliance.[325]

These requirements, however, do not affect the validity of the contract or title.[326] Nor do they impose affirmative obligations on any party to engage in lead abatement.[327] Nevertheless, this program represents an unprecedented federal intrusion into the state arena of contract law. Violation leads to civil penalties, with violators jointly and severally liable to the buyer for treble damages. It also constitutes a TSCA violation subject to TSCA penalties.[328] Courts may award the prevailing plaintiff reasonable attorneys' and expert witness fees.[329] A landlord may also be criminally prosecuted for falsifying records in this regard.[330]

[3] Accreditation

The Residential Lead-Based Paint Hazard Reduction Act imposes detailed accreditation requirements, effective in 1998 and 1999,[331] for lead-based paint abatement activities in target and child-occupied housing. These include training programs[332] and requirements for the certification of firms and individuals conducting these ac-

---

319. 42 U.S.C. § 4856(a).
320. 42 U.S.C. § 4852d(a); 40 C.F.R. § 90745.107.
321. Smith v. Coldwell Banker Real Estate Services, 122 F. Supp. 2d 267 (D. Conn. 2000).
322. Roberts v. Hamer, 655 F.3d 578 (6th Cir. 2011).
323. 40 C.F.R. § 745.113.
324. 40 C.F.R. § 745.110.
325. 42 U.S.C. § 4852d(a); 40 C.F.R. § 745.115.
326. 42 U.S.C. § 4852d(c).
327. 40 C.F.R. § 745.107.
328. 42 U.S.C. § 4852d(b)(5).
329. 42 U.S.C. § 4852d(b).
330. United States v. Shimshoni, 631 Fed. Appx. 788 (11th Cir. 2015).
331. 40 C.F.R. § 745.239.
332. 40 C.F.R. § 745.225.

tivities,[333] and workplace standards.[334] Violations constitute TSCA violations,[335] and subject violators to civil and criminal sanctions accordingly.[336]

[4] Occupational Exposure to Lead Hazards

The Residential Lead-Based Hazard Reduction Act also addresses occupational exposure to lead in the construction industry,[337] requiring that these workplaces be as safe as locations regulated under HUD guidelines,[338] and gives the Department of Labor regulations promulgated under the Act the force of OSHA standards.[339]

[D] Regulation of Lead Emissions under the Clean Air Act

EPA regulates fuels and fuel additives under the Clean Air Act (see § 5.04[E][1]).[340] Starting in the 1970s, EPA reduced the allowable lead content of gasoline as a public health risk,[341] and required the sale of unleaded gasoline.[342] Congress ultimately prohibited the sale or use of lead additives in gasoline,[343] a prohibition that EPA may not waive (in contrast to other heavy metals).[344] Transporters[345] and gasoline stations[346] are liable even for unintentional illegal activity, as are distributors who arrange for transportation from terminals to retailers[347] and refiners who fail to take reasonable steps to ensure retailers' compliance with contractual prohibition of sale of gasoline with impermissible lead content.[348] The prohibition is preemptive.[349] As was noted earlier (see § 8.07[A]), in 2008 EPA revised its National Ambient Air Quality Standards to reflect its conclusions, reached after a multi-year study correlating exposure to ambient lead and a statistically significant reduction of IQ in children, that there is no level at which ambient lead can be considered safe.[350]

---

333. 40 C.F.R. § 745.226.
334. 40 C.F.R. § 745.227.
335. 40 C.F.R. § 745.235; see 15 U.S.C. §§ 2610, 2614, 2689.
336. 40 C.F.R. § 745.235(e); see 15 U.S.C. § 2615.
337. 42 U.S.C. § 4853.
338. See 55 Fed. Reg. 38,973.
339. See 29 U.S.C. § 655.
340. 42 U.S.C. § 7545.
341. Ethyl Corp. v. Environmental Protection Agency, 541 F.2d 1 (D.C. Cir. 1976), cert. denied, 426 U.S. 941 (1977).
342. Amoco Oil Co. v. Environmental Protection Agency, 501 F.2d 722 (D.C. Cir. 1974).
343. 42 U.S.C. § 7545(n).
344. 42 U.S.C. § 7545(k)(2)(D), (3)(A)(iii).
345. National Tank Truck Carriers, Inc. v. Environmental Protection Agency, 907 F.2d 177 (D.C. Cir. 1990).
346. United States v. Schilling, 696 F. Supp. 407 (N.D. Ind. 1988).
347. United States v. Pilot Petroleum Associates, Inc., 712 F. Supp. 1077 (E.D.N.Y. 1989).
348. United States v. Sharp, 645 F. Supp. 337 (W.D. Mo. 1986).
349. Exxon Corp. v. City of New York, 548 F.2d 1088 (2d Cir. 1977).
350. 73 Fed. Reg. 66,964 (Nov. 12, 2008); Coalition of Battery Recyclers Association v. EPA, 604 F.3d 613 (9th Cir. 2010).

Chapter 9

Noise

§ 9.01 Noise Control Act

[A] Background of Act

Noise has come to be regarded as a serious health hazard, and is an important subject of environmental regulation. Excessive noise can not only cause hearing loss, but can also lead to a variety of other severe physical disorders.[1] In addition, noise exposure has serious economic impacts in terms of absenteeism, disability, and reduced property values.

---

1. Evidence of the extent of noise-related hearing loss among the American population, calculated at about 40 million people between the ages of 20 and 65, was provided in a 2012 report by the American Heritage Hearing Foundation (available at https://www.american-hearing.org/disease/common-ear-and-hearing-issues). The report reflects medical evidence that hearing loss can start with a consistent exposure to 90 decibels of sound. Traffic can generate 85 decibels, and a music concert can generate 110 decibels or greater. For an expanded discussion of the regulation of noise in an environmental and land use context, see ROBINSON, ENVIRONMENTAL REGULATION OF REAL PROPERTY, Ch. 8, *Noise Controls,* (Law Journal Press, rev. 2021).

Historically, noise gave rise to private common law actions for nuisance.[2] During the twentieth century, noise often was regulated at the municipal level through local land use laws and noise codes, discussed in § 9.02. In recent decades, states have also passed noise statutes and regulations as public health measures. In 1972, with the dawning of environmental law and against a backdrop of inconsistent and often ineffective state and local regulations, Congress enacted the Noise Control Act,[3] designed to furnish federal standards for noise. Noise was thus considered to be a be a form of polluting emissions. The federal statute was modeled on the Clean Air Act and Clean Water Act. However, the noise control statute, which by its terms has a limited reach, falls far short of the comprehensive controls over air and water provided by those acts.[4] Rather, it is directed in the main at manufactured products, equipment and vehicles which generate noise rather than more broadly at the noise itself.

[B] Congressional Finding; General Requirements of Act

The Noise Control Act commences with a Congressional finding that "inadequately controlled noise presents a growing danger to the health and welfare" and that, "while primary responsibility for [its] control ... rests with State and local governments, Federal action is essential to deal with major noise sources in commerce[,] control of which require national uniformity of treatment."[5] The Act requires the United States Environmental Protection Agency to adopt criteria for noise in consultation with other federal agencies, to identify products that are major sources of noise, and to adopt noise emission standards for those products.[6] The Act specifies construction equipment, transportation equipment (including recreational vehicles), motors and engines, and electrical or electronic equipment as products subject to noise regulation.[7] Aircraft, dealt with in other provisions (see §§ 9.03–9.05), are explicitly excluded from the Act's definition of a "product."[8] Noise emission standards are to be promulgated as required to "protect the public health and welfare, taking into account the magnitude and conditions of use of such product..., the degree of noise reduction

---

2. *See* Lime Rock Park LLC v. Planning and Zoning Commission of the Town of Salisbury, 2018 Conn. Super. LEXIS 1410 (Conn. Sup. Ct. 2018); Glass v. Town of Marblehead Board of Health, 2009 Mass. Super. LEXIS 55 (Mass. Sup. Ct. 2009). Even if the noise does not violate a local noise code, it may still be the basis for an action in nuisance. Oglethorpe Power Corp. v. Forrister, 303 Ga. App. 271, 693 S.E.2d 553 (2010).

3. 42 U.S.C. §§ 4901–4918.

4. Supporting documentation for congressional bills (S.3385, HR 3001) relating to a proposed amendment of the federal statute, the Quiet Communities Act, in 2018 and 2019, provided more modest numbers than the American Heritage Hearing Foundation, *supra*, but essentially made the same point in support of the need for a more robust federal role with EPA occupying a more central regulatory position.

5. 42 U.S.C. § 4901(a).

6. 42 U.S.C. §§ 4904, 4905.

7. 42 U.S.C. § 4905(a)(l)(C).

8. 42 U.S.C. § 4902(3)(A).

achievable through the application of the best available technology, and the cost of compliance."[9] Note that the Act uses a best available technology standard, similar to that in the Clean Water Act, discussed in § 6.03[B].

[C] Maximum Ambient Standards for Noise

The federal statute operates by imposing emission standards for products identified as major sources of noise. EPA may also regulate products that, while not identified as major sources of noise in the statute, nevertheless warrant controls.[10] In accordance with the Act, EPA has adopted maximum ambient standards for noise comparable to the national ambient air quality standards (NAAQS) promulgated under the Clean Air Act, discussed in § 5.01. Such standards are significant as benchmarks for public health, but need to be linked to emission controls for specific sources to be effective. Since the Noise Control Act took effect, EPA has produced noise emission regulations for trucks, motor homes, motorcycles, and certain construction equipment such as compressors.[11] In addition, operational railroad and motor carrier (truck) noise are subject to EPA control.[12]

[D] Warranty Requirement and State Regulation of Noise

The statute also provides a protection to consumers, in that the manufacturer of a new product falling within the federal noise regulations must warrant to any ultimate purchaser of the product that at the time of the sale it had been designed, built and equipped in accordance with the federal standards.[13] However, the Act does not otherwise regulate noise (except from trains[14] and trucks) emitted once a regulated product leaves the factory or loading dock. Thus, with the exception of railroad and motor carrier operational noise, which are regulated by the Act, control of noise in the environment itself — beyond the Act's manufacturing and warranty requirements — is left to the states. When EPA has adopted a regulation under the Act, state and local controls are preempted unless identical to the EPA's.[15] On the other hand, states and localities are expressly authorized to regulate "environmental noise" — noise emitted by sources in the environment itself — since the Act does not generally regulate such noise.[16]

---

9. 42 U.S.C. § 4905(c)(1).

10. 42 U.S.C. § 4905(b).

11. 40 C.F.R. Parts 203, 204, 205.

12. 42 U.S.C. §§ 4916, 4917.

13. 42 U.S.C. § 4905(d).

14. However, in contrast to railroad engine noise, the noise emitted by railroad whistles is not controlled by EPA regulations, which thus may fall within state regulatory jurisdiction. Southern Pac. Transp. Co. v. Public Utility Comm'n, 9 F.3d 807 (9th Cir. 1993).

15. 42 U.S.C. § 4905(e)(1); Consolidated Rail Corp. v. City of Dover, 450 F. Supp. 966 (D. Del. 1978).

16. 42 U.S.C. § 4905(e)(2).

An early court concluded that while state and local noise *standards* are preempted, preemption would not bar local controls over the *use* of a noise generating product.[17] Nor would traditional local land use controls be preempted that involve permitting or site plan review and the like which restrict activities that would emit unacceptable noise levels, nor would environmental reviews under NEPA or state mini-NEPAs when noise may pose an environmental impact be preempted.[18] Traditional land use controls would not be superseded even if a federal agency is responsible for the noise.[19]

[E] Labeling Requirements

A major component of federal regulation is addressed to product labels which must accurately reflect for the public and prospective purchasers the level of noise emissions generated by the product. EPA is empowered to adopt labeling requirements both for products causing noise and for products sold to reduce noise, which adequately inform the user of the level of noise the product emits, or its effectiveness in curbing noise.[20] States are not preempted from requiring labels, as long as the labels do not conflict with EPA's requirements, which would create a preemption problem.[21]

[F] Recordkeeping Requirements

Consistent with the Noise Control Act being product-based rather than addressed to ambient noise, manufacturers of noise-generating products that fall under the Act are required to test their products for the anticipated noise emissions and to maintain records of the testing. The manufacturer must allow EPA to access the records as well as allow EPA to also test the products.[22]

[G] Remedies

Notwithstanding that noise as a practical matter is often left to state and local controls, there are several means by which the federal Act can be violated. Tampering with noise control equipment is prohibited.[23] If a noise reduction device mandated by federal regulations is not incorporated into the product, or if it is removed or tampered with, that would violate federal law. A manufacturer who distributes in interstate commerce a new product that fails to comply with the federal regulations promulgated under the Noise Control Act also violates the Act, as would a person who imports a

---

17. Rockford Drop Forge Co. v. Pollution Control Board, 71 Ill. App. 3d 295, 389 N.E.2d 212 (1979).

18. Association for Community Reform Now (ACORN) v. Bloomberg, 52 A.D.3d 426, 861 N.Y.S.2d 325 (1st Dept. 2008), *aff'g* 13 Misc. 3d 1209[A], 824 N.Y.S.2d 752 (N.Y. Cty. S. Ct. 2006).

19. Davis v. Mineta, 302 F.3d 1104 (10th Cir. 2002); McGuinness v. United States Forest Service, 741 Fed. Appx. 915 (4th Cir. 2018).

20. 42 U.S.C. §4907.

21. 42 U.S.C. §4907(c).

22. 42 U.S.C. §4912.

23. 42 U.S.C. §4909(a)(2).

regulated product that fails to comply. If a label that the Act or its regulations requires for a product is removed, the labeling provisions of the Act are violated. EPA is authorized to issue enforcement orders. Federal standards curtail noise emitted by interstate railroads and interstate motor carriers. Manufacturers are required to maintain records evidencing compliance with the Act and its regulations.

A failure to comply with any of these requirements will constitute a violation of the Act. The Act contains provisions for injunctive relief, and civil and criminal penalties. Willful violations are subject to fines in the amount of $25,000 per day of violation and/or one year of incarceration. Civil penalties up to $10,000 per day of violations may be imposed. In addition, EPA may issue orders necessary to protect public health and welfare from violations of the Act.[24] The Act's citizen suit provision also allows for enforcement by citizen plaintiffs when federal enforcement is lax, even against EPA or the Federal Aviation Administration for the agencies' failure to administer the Act. Courts may also award attorney's fees to prevailing plaintiffs.[25]

§ 9.02 State and Local Laws

The Noise Control Act chiefly regulates the manufacture of noise-emitting products, and only minimally deals with controlling noise in the environment. State and municipal laws, however, do provide some measure of regulation in this area. Although state and local laws which establish noise standards applicable to manufactured products that differ from federal standards will be preempted, state and local laws may govern the operation and use of noise-generating products.

Some states have enacted noise legislation imposing maximum decibel levels for various types of sources. For instance, California, the preeminent automobile state, extensively regulates highway noise. although in a manner consistent with the federal Noise Control Act so as to avoid preemption. California's noise restrictions also reach to noise reduction measures for the construction of residences and hotels[26] Connecticut, too, restricts noise from cars and trucks on the state's highways. Connecticut, also venturing into land use, defines a property's "noise zone" in relation to a unit of land and prohibits excessive noise emissions beyond those boundaries.[27] Automobile noise stemming from defective mufflers is subject to specific decibel levels in virtually all states.[28] Massachusetts treats excessive noise as a kind of air pollution. It can be

---

24. 42 U.S.C. § 4910(d).

25. 42 U.S.C. §§ 4910, 4911.

26. California limits the allowable decibel levels for trucks and cars. CAL. VEHICLE CODE § 23130. California also imposes extensive statewide noise standards for building insulation (CAL. ADMIN. CODE Title 4; CAL. CODE REGS. Title 24, part 2) and establishes guidelines applicable to local land use planning relating to noise levels from proposed land uses to community expectations (CAL. ADMIN. CODE, Title 4).

27. See, e.g., CONN. GEN. STAT. ANN. §§ 22a-67, 22a-69.1.1, 22a-69-3.1.

28. See, e.g., CAL. VEHICLE CODE § 23130; N.Y. VEH. & TRAF. L. § 386. These state standards are drafted to remain consistent with the federal standards and thus avoid preemption. However, the state laws may preempt local municipal laws addressed to muffler noise or noise from vehicles lacking

abated as a nuisance if it risks harm to health or safety or if it unreasonably interferes with the enjoyment of one's property or a business being conducted.[29] New York also regulates noise from motor vehicles, with exceptions for emergency vehicles and highway construction and maintenance vehicles.[30]

Municipal noise controls tend to fall into two categories, although both methodologies may be utilized by local ordinances. One approach is to treat excessive and unreasonable noise, as defined by the ordinance, as a nuisance or prosecute it as a misdemeanor.[31] This kind of approach addresses the noise after it has occurred. To survive a challenge that the law is unconstitutionally vague, though, it must be grounded in objectively supportable baselines.[32] Laws prohibiting "unnecessary" noise have been found unconstitutionally vague, because of the inherently subjective nature of determining what degree of noise is "unnecessary."[33] Alternatively, municipalities often seek to prevent excessive and unreasonable noise from occurring in designated locations by zoning — prohibiting certain noise-generating activities in some locations while allowing them in others — or even by means of local building code restrictions. Municipal entities can control the noise generated by construction activities by limiting the hours of operation and the like, or imposing noise reduction measures such as vegetation screenings or baffle walls relating to a permissible use during site plan review. Municipalities often act by barring noise in excess of specified decibel levels. Some localities also use their zoning power to create districts in which varying degrees of noise are lawful.[34] How noise controls are achieved, though, likely will vary among the different kinds and character of municipalities. Large metropolitan areas likely will have noise tolerances that differ from suburban municipalities, as, too, might commercial and industrial hubs versus fundamentally residential communities, or suburban communities which mix intensive commercial and residential uses.[35]

---

mufflers. *See* Lime Rock Park LLC v. Planning and Zoning Commission, 2018 Conn. Super. LEXIS 1410 (Conn. Super. Ct. 2018).

29. MASS. GEN. LAWS ch. 111, § 122; Mass. Code Regs., Title 310, § 7.10. *See* Glass v. Town of Marblehead Board of Health, 2009 Mass. Super. LEXIS 55 (Mass. Super. Ct. 2009) (discussion of how, and where, exceedences are to be measured for purposes of upholding a violation).

30. 6 N.Y. CODE OF RULES AND REGULATIONS § 450.1; N.Y. VEHICLE AND TRAFFIC LAW § 386.

31. *See, e.g.*, Village of Sugar Grove v. Rich, 347 Ill. App.3d 689, 808 N.E.2d 525, 283 Ill. Dec. 559 (2004); State *ex rel.* City of Providence v. Augur, 44 A.3d 1218 (R.I. 2012).

32. Deegan v. City of Ithaca, 444 F.3d 135 (2d Cir. 2006) ("unreasonable" noise defined in local law as audible from 25 feet away invalid). *Compare* Ne Materials Group, 2018 Vt. Super. LEXIS 19 (Vt. Super. Ct. 2018) (noise which shocks the average person is a valid standard, in contrast to noise that shocks only the person, in this case, challenging a permit).

33. Jim Crockett Promotion v. City of Charlotte, 706 F.2d 486 (4th Cir. 1983).

34. *See, e.g.*, Chicago's demarcation of "noise sensitive zones" which include "quiet zones" for, inter alia, schools, public libraries, churches, hospitals and nursing homes, and "noise sensitive activities," provides for restrictions on noise levels in those areas which would interfere with the protected activity. MUNICIPAL CODE OF CHICAGO §§ 32-060, 32-120.

35. For these distinctions, compare and contrast: New York City's very comprehensive regulatory-based noise code in 24 N.Y.C. ADMINISTRATIVE CODE §§ 24-201 to 24-235, which, while recognizing the fact of urban noise in this densely populated commercial city, nevertheless articulates as its primary

As was noted above, common law nuisance actions have also been used to control noise through injunctive relief.[36] Nuisance actions concerning aircraft noise are dealt with in § 9.03[B].

§ 9.03 Aircraft Noise

[A] Inverse Condemnation Suits

As early as 1946, the Supreme Court, in *United States v. Causby*,[37] ruled that noise from overflights from an Air Force base above a chicken farm were compensable, since the physical invasion amounted to a de facto taking, or inverse condemnation, of the plaintiff's property in violation of the Fifth Amendment. The plaintiff successfully asserted this constitutional argument to avoid the barriers to a nuisance action associated with a "legalized nuisance" (discussed in § 9.02), as well as the United States Government's sovereign immunity from suit for damages. Although the Federal Tort Claims Act[38] today furnishes a plaintiff with the limited ability to sue the Government in tort, inverse condemnation actions have become an effective remedy to recover damages for overflights. Since the action is based on an actual physical invasion of the plaintiff's property, there must in fact be overflights, not mere sideline noise from aircraft.[39]

Inverse condemnation actions are limited to suits for damages. Injunctive relief is not available, and is regarded as preempted by the Federal Aviation Act.[40] Furthermore, class actions are disfavored in inverse condemnation suits since the courts view different claimants as differently situated in terms of the injury they suffer.[41]

In *Griggs v. Allegheny County*,[42] the Supreme Court held that in an inverse condemnation suit involving commercial aircraft overflights, the proper defendant is the airport proprietor. The Court rejected the proprietor's claim that the federal gov-

---

goal the public's health, safety and welfare; the noise code for Chicago, a large industrial city, set forth in its MUNICIPAL CODE, ch.8-32; the nuisance-based provisions for residential suburban Ridgewood, New Jersey, in its municipal ordinance, § 201-1, a commuter town with train links to New York City yet geographically distant from that metropolis; and the more comprehensive regulation-based noise code for the Town of Hempstead, a large mixed-use suburban municipality adjacent to New York City's borders, in the TOWN OF HEMPSTEAD TOWN CODE § 144.

36. *See, e.g.*, Lime Rock Park LLC v. Plannong and Zoning Commission of the Town of Salisbury, 2018 Conn. Super. LEXIS 1410 (Conn. Sup. Ct. 2018); Glass v. Town of Marblehead Board of Health, 2009 Mass. Super. LEXIS 55 (Mass. Sup. Ct. 2009). Even if the noise does not violate a local noise code, it may still be the basis for an action in nuisance. Oglethorpe Power Corp. v. Forrister, 303 Ga. App. 271, 693 S.E.2d 553 (2010).

37. 328 U.S. 256 (1946).

38. 28 U.S.C. §§ 2671–2680.

39. Batten v. United States, 306 F.2d 580 (10th Cir. 1962).

40. Alleghney Airlines v. Village of Cedarhurst, 132 F. Supp. 871 (E.D.N.Y. 1955), *aff'd*, 238 F.2d 812 (2d Cir. 1956).

41. Bieneman v. City of Chicago, 864 F.2d 463 (7th Cir. 1988).

42. 369 U.S. 84 (1962).

ernment was the proper defendant because of its pervasive regulation of commercial aviation and control over airspace. This decision proved to be a milestone in aircraft noise litigation, since it squarely placed the burden of financial liability on the airport operator. As shown in §§ 9.04 and 9.05, *Griggs* dramatically improved the ability of airport proprietors to adopt limits on aircraft noise, enabling them to counter arguments of federal preemption by contending that noise controls were needed to limit their liability to property owners affected by overflights.

One important restriction on inverse condemnation actions is imposed by the Aviation Safety and Noise Abatement Act.[43] This federal law, enacted in 1979, enables airports to file noise exposure maps describing the flight paths used by aircraft landing at, or taking off from, the airport. Property owners who purchase after these maps are on file may not recover damages for inverse condemnation, since they are deemed to have purchased with knowledge of the flight path over their parcel.[44] Of course, if the airport proprietor changes these flight paths it may again become liable.[45]

[B] Nuisance Actions

In addition to inverse condemnation, nuisance actions have also been employed to recover damages for aircraft noise, as well as to seek injunctive relief. Unlike inverse condemnation, nuisance does not require direct overflights. However, airport proprietors have argued that the Federal Aviation Act,[46] under which the Federal Aviation Administration has exclusive control over airspace use, preempts nuisance actions. This argument does not apply to actions for damages based on inverse condemnation, although it has been used to bar injunction actions.[47] In nuisance actions, some courts have regarded the Federal Aviation Act as preempting suits seeking to enjoin airspace use, such as suits to obtain a curfew or to require the use of quieter aircraft.[48] But nuisance actions to require airports to select runways that will inflict less noise, or to create buffer zones or shield adjacent property from noise, are viewed as valid and not preempted since they do not interfere with airspace use.[49] Nuisance and trespass actions against airlines (as opposed to airport proprietors) have been found to be preempted by the Federal Aviation Act, since those suits by definition relate to airspace use.[50]

---

43. 49 U.S.C. §§ 47501–47510.

44. 49 U.S.C. § 47506.

45. 49 U.S.C. § 47506(a)(1)(C).

46. 49 U.S.C. §§ 40101–49105.

47. *See* Alleghney Airlines v. Village of Cedarhurst, 132 F. Supp. 871 (E.D.N.Y. 1955), *aff'd*, 238 F.2d 812 (2d Cir. 1956).

48. San Diego Unified Port Dist. v. Superior Court, 136 Cal. Rptr. 557 (1977).

49. Greater Westchester Homeowners Ass'n v. City of Los Angeles, 603 P.2d 1329 (Cal. 1979), *cert. denied*, 449 U.S. 820 (1980).

50. Adams v. City of Atlanta, 322 S.E.2d 730 (Ga. 1984).

§ 9.04 Aircraft Noise: FAA Regulations

Since 1969, the Federal Aviation Administration (FAA) has controlled noise from commercial aircraft through its Part 36 regulations,[51] authorized by the Aircraft Noise and Abatement Act of 1968.[52] The regulations restrict noise to 107 decibels and apply to aircraft placed in service after 1969, known as Stage 2 aircraft. Earlier Stage 1 aircraft became subject to noise regulation in 1973 and were furnished a lengthy period within which to retrofit noise abatement equipment.[53] In practice, many of the Stage 1 airplanes simply continued to operate until the phase-out date in the regulations.

Over the ensuing years, noise abatement technology has improved, and the FAA adopted a new set of rules mandated by the Airport Noise and Capacity Act of 1990.[54] Under these regulations, Stage 2 aircraft were to be phased out by the year 2000, and replaced by quieter Stage 3 planes.[55]

The Airport Noise and Capacity Act of 1990 imposes a statutory limit on noise control by proprietors over the newer Stage 3 aircraft. Proprietors must submit their proposed noise rules to the Secretary of Transportation (as parent agency of the FAA). If the Secretary disapproves the rules, they may take effect, but the airport then becomes ineligible for federal funding for runway expansion and loses the power to charge a passenger departure tax to defray airport and access improvements. However, if the airport fails to adopt Stage 3 regulations following disapproval by the Secretary of Transportation, this renders the United States — not the airport — liable in inverse condemnation suits to the extent that the rules would have prevented liability.

A separate federal statute, the Airport and Airway Improvement Act of 1982,[56] requires airports, as a condition of receiving federal funding, to certify, in the case of runways that adversely affect nearby residents, that no feasible or prudent alternative to their construction exists.

§ 9.05 Aircraft Noise:
State and Local Airport Controls

In addition to the federal regulations discussed in § 9.04, state and municipal governments have enacted laws to reduce aircraft noise. These provisions were largely enacted while aircraft noise rapidly increased as jets replaced propeller driven airplanes and the frequency of flights continued to rise. In *City of Burbank v. Lockheed Air Terminal, Inc.*,[57] the United States Supreme Court ruled that a local law imposing a

---

51. 14 C.F.R. Part 36.
52. 49 U.S.C. § 44715.
53. 14 C.F.R. § 91.805.
54. 49 U.S.C. §§ 47521–47533.
55. 49 U.S.C. § 47528; 14 C.F.R. § 91.853.
56. 49 U.S.C. § 47106.
57. 411 U.S. 624 (1973).

curfew at a commercial airport was preempted by the Federal Aviation Act, which clothes the FAA with exclusive control of airspace use. The Court noted that a curfew would have the effect of "bunching" flights landing just before the curfew and taking off just after it ended. This in turn would require schedules of connecting flights to be altered, likely unduly burdening interstate commerce as well.

The Court expressly left open the question whether an airport proprietor — as opposed to a municipal legislature acting under the police power — may impose a curfew or otherwise reduce aircraft noise. Proprietors later successfully contended they should have that power to shield themselves from liability for inverse condemnation or nuisance.[58] Thus, federal law does not preempt a proprietor from closing its airport during late-night hours or limiting the decibels emitted by the aircraft using the facility.

However, the curfew in *City of Burbank* was also attacked as an undue burden on commerce in violation of the dormant Commerce Clause (see § 1.05[B]). Although the Court decided the case on preemption grounds, its opinion clearly reflected concern over the burden on commerce imposed by a curfew at a commercial airport, as evidenced by the Court's discussion of the "bunching" of flights and its impact on the schedules of connecting flights. This challenge to an undue burden on commerce is legally distinct from the preemption argument. It has been successfully used to overturn curfews by airport proprietors, where no federal preemption exists.[59]

After *City of Burbank*, an alternate approach to actually imposing curfews or noise limits was taken by California. That state enacted a statute requiring commercial airports to reduce aircraft noise to specified decibel limits, but affording airport proprietors a variety of options as to how to achieve these reductions.[60] Proprietors may use quieter runways, shield the airport from nearby residents, purchase land as a buffer from aircraft noise, or impose curfews or decibel limits. Since the choice is up to the airport proprietor, this scheme was upheld on judicial review.[61] As the court noted, there was no federal preemption since proprietors were free to adopt any method of curtailing noise. As for an undue burden on commerce, the court found none in the facial challenge to the statute, although it noted that particular methods a proprietor might select could give rise to such a claim.

Similarly, municipal limits on helicopter flights have been upheld where the city is acting as proprietor of the flight pad.[62]

As is discussed in § 9.03[B], nuisance actions seeking to enjoin overflights may run afoul of claims of federal preemption, as may statutes regulating aircraft noise. Finally, it should be kept in mind that municipalities, through their zoning power,

---

58. British Airways Bd. v. Port Authority of N.Y. & N.J., 558 F.2d 75 (2d Cir. 1977); National Aviation v. City of Hayward, 418 F. Supp. 417 (N.D. Cal. 1976).

59. United States v. New York, 552 F. Supp. 255 (N.D.N.Y. 1982).

60. Cal. Pub. Util. Code §§ 21669–21669.4.

61. Air Transport Ass'n v. Crotti, 389 F. Supp. 58 (N.D. Cal. 1975).

62. National Helicopter Corp. of America v. City of New York, 137 F.3d 81 (2d Cir. 1998).

may exclude an airport entirely. There is no federal preemption of municipal control over land use.[63] Of course, the power of a locality to bar an airport through zoning may not extend to airports operated by state or federal agencies.

§ 9.06 Occupational Noise

Noise is subject to regulation in the workplace under the Occupational Safety and Health Act (OSHA),[64] administered by the Occupational Safety and Health Administration within the United States Department of Labor. The OSHA rules adopted pursuant to the Act limit workplace noise exposure generally to 90 decibels, with exposure up to 110 decibels permitted for one half-hour.[65] Testing of employees is mandated if exposure exceeds 85 decibels. The main area of dispute here is between those who favor requiring employees to wear hearing protectors and those who contend hearing protectors are inadequate so that excessively noisy equipment should be replaced. Thus far, the hearing protector view has largely prevailed.[66]

The Federal Railroad Safety Act[67] preempts suits for hearing loss from railroad horns, but does not preempt suits based on failure to provide hearing protectors to employees.[68]

---

63. Garden State Farms, Inc. v. Bay, 390 A.2d 1177 (N.J. 1978).

64. 29 U.S.C. §§ 651–678.

65. *See* 29 C.F.R. § 1910.95.

66. *See In re* Collingsworth, 194 S.E.2d 210 (N.C. 1973) (employee's refusal to wear protective ear device deemed willful misconduct).

67. 49 U.S.C. §§ 20101–20153.

68. Tufariello v. Long Island R.R., 458 F.3d 80 (2d Cir. 2006).

Chapter 10

Fish and Wildlife

§ 10.01 Hunting and Fishing Laws

Controlling hunting and fishing is historically one of the oldest areas of government regulation, extending back to English common law. The familiar common-law concept was that fish and game were the property of the Crown. This made fishing and hunting without royal permission, or at least that of the feudal fief-holder, a crime. In the United States these rules evolved into the states' ownership of wildlife[1] and the early requirement of a hunting or fishing license.

As wildlife and fish became decimated by a lethal mixture of over-hunting and habitat loss, as early as the nineteenth century, states began to limit catches, and to impose seasonal restrictions as well. These measures did not serve to adequately protect the bison, passenger pigeon, grizzly bear, or numerous other species hunted to

---

1. Geer v. Connecticut, 161 U.S. 519 (1896).

extinction or near-extinction. The bison, shot from moving trains for sport, survived in the United States only because a small herd was shipped to New York's Bronx Zoo, which enabled it to reproduce in safety. The grizzly bear still appears on California's flag but has otherwise long vanished from that state.

Early in this century, the federal government entered the field. A federal statute to protect the egret, whose plumes were eagerly sought for hats, was enacted in 1913.[2] But since the legal fiction of the time insisted that wildlife were the property of the states, the law was found to violate the Tenth Amendment, reserving to the states all powers not given the federal government in the Constitution (discussed in § 1.05[D]).[3] As a result, the United States entered into its first treaty protecting wildlife, the Migratory Bird Treaty of 1916. The treaty, with Britain as the proprietor of Canada, was upheld by the Supreme Court in *Missouri v. Holland*[4] as a valid exercise of the treaty power. Writing for the Court, Justice Holmes held a treaty not subject to Tenth Amendment attack. As for the rule that wildlife, including migratory birds, were the property of the states, Justice Holmes found it to be "a slender reed," particularly since "[t]he subject-matter is only transitorily within the State and has no permanent habitat therein."

Though weakened by *Holland*, the fiction of state ownership of wildlife lingered until 1979, when the Supreme Court ruled[5] that an Oklahoma law prohibiting the export of minnows constituted impermissible state regulation of interstate commerce, in violation of the Commerce Clause.[6] The Court followed earlier cases that overturned state bars on importing or exporting various commodities,[7] and held those precedents applied to wildlife, as well as farm products or manufactured goods. (The dormant Commerce Clause issue is discussed at § 1.05[B].) To so hold, the Court in the Oklahoma minnows case had to first find wildlife an article of commerce. In so doing, it abolished the fiction of state ownership of wildlife once caught or killed. The modern rule allows Congress to regulate fish and wildlife under the Commerce Clause and limits state laws on the subject that discriminate against, or place undue burdens on, commerce with other states. Only when a state can meet the substantial burden of showing an unusual local need will such a law be upheld. An instance of this uncommon species of statute involved a Maine law barring importation of baitfish because of a parasite infecting out-of-state, but not local, baitfish. The parasite was difficult to detect. On these facts the Supreme Court sustained the statute as against the claim that it unconstitutionally discriminated against commerce — an exception that proves the rule.[8]

---

2. Act March 4, 1913, 37 Stat. 847.

3. United States v. McCullagh, 221 F. 288 (D. Kan. 1915).

4. 252 U.S. 416 (1920).

5. Hughes v. Oklahoma, 441 U.S. 322 (1979).

6. U.S. CONST. art. I, § 8, cl. 3.

7. *See* Baldwin v. G.A.F. Seelig, Inc., 294 U.S. 511 (1935); H.P. Hood & Sons, Inc. v. DuMond, 336 U.S. 525 (1949).

8. Maine v. Taylor, 477 U.S. 131 (1986).

Today, numerous federal and state laws restrict hunting and fishing in a variety of ways. The two major areas of environmental importance are deep sea fishing (see § 10.02) and the protection of endangered species (see § 10.03).

§ 10.02 Deep Sea Fishing

[A] Background

For decades, it has been recognized that deep sea fishing, historically unregulated since it was beyond the three-mile limit of national jurisdiction, must be controlled to prevent overfishing and the destruction of entire species. As long as the supply of cod, herring, and other food fish appeared virtually limitless there was scant impetus for regulation. However, with the advent of large-scale factory trawlers capable of remaining at sea for months and catching and processing vast quantities of fish, the need for national as well as international limits has become evident. Commercial fishing now often outpaces the ability of fish species to reproduce, leaving formerly fertile fishing grounds like the Grand Banks off the coast of Newfoundland severely depleted. To allow fish stocks to replenish themselves, Newfoundland declared a moratorium on cod fishing, with severe economic effects.

[B] License Requirements

Federal law has required licenses for certain types of commercial deep sea fishing for several decades. In 1977 the Supreme Court held that these federal statutes pre-empted a state from limiting such fishing to its residents.[9] In that same year Congress went further in the Magnuson-Stevens Act, which establishes a 200-mile offshore economic zone and limits catches to maximum numbers set by joint federal-state regional fishery advisory councils, through fishery management plans.[10] Federal licenses are required by the Act, which applies to, and limits, catches for both domestic and foreign vessels.

The Sustainable Fisheries Act, enacted in 1996, extends the reach of the Magnuson Act by explicitly requiring measures to prevent overfishing, rebuild depleted fish stocks, and minimize bycatch (the accidental taking of unsought species).[11]

[C] International Treaties

Since deep sea fishing is an activity performed by vessels of many nations, the need to balance economic viability against protecting fish stocks from depletion has assumed international dimensions. Treaties have been drafted, some under United

---

9. Douglas v. Seacoast Products, Inc., 431 U.S. 265 (1977).

10. 16 U.S.C. §§ 1811, 1852.

11. 16 U.S.C. §§ 1802(28, 29), 1853(a)(10), 1854(e); *see* Conservation Law Foundation v. Evans, 209 F. Supp. 2d 1 (D.D.C. 2001) (mandating compliance with Act by Secretary of Commerce).

Nations auspices, to restrict catches and particularly the bycatch or accidental catching of fish not sought by trawlers. To be effective, these agreements require internationally negotiated quotas on catches as well as boarding and inspection provisions. The international aspects of fish and wildlife protection and the impact of international agreements on the exploitation of whales and other endangered species are further discussed in § 10.05.

[D] Drift Nets

The use of drift nets, which cover prodigious amounts of the sea and often entrap turtles, dolphin and other species in need of protection, is also regulated by statute, and the barring from United States markets of fish caught by drift netting in violation of law has been upheld by the courts.[12] Federal legislation and regulations also protect sea turtles, many species of which are endangered, by requiring turtle excluder devices on shrimp trawlers to avoid these animals being enmeshed in nets intended for shrimp.[13] Here too, shrimp caught in violation of this statute may be barred from importation or sale in the United States.[14]

§ 10.03 Endangered Species Act and Related Statutes

[A] Background of Endangered Species Act

The need to preserve endangered species has become universally recognized in the past 30 years. Unfortunately, numerous species, as noted in § 10.01, had already become extinct, or on the verge of extinction, when Congress finally acted in 1973 with passage of the Endangered Species Act (ESA).[15] The ESA, built on the earlier but less effective Lacey Act, forbids the importation or sale of species that are listed as endangered by the Secretary of the Interior, or articles made from their hides or other parts.

In addition, the ESA protects the habitat of endangered species, which is now recognized to be at least as important as protecting such species from hunting. Specifically, the ESA bars federal government agencies from performing, funding, or permitting any activity that will jeopardize the critical habitat of a listed endangered species.[16]

---

12. Humane Society of U.S. v. Brown, 920 F. Supp. 178 (Ct. of Int'l Trade 1996).

13. 16 U.S.C. § 1538; 50 C.F.R. § 227.72(e)(2); *see* Louisiana ex rel. Guste v. Verity, 853 F.2d 322 (5th Cir. 1988).

14. Earth Island Inst. v. Christopher, 922 F. Supp. 616 (Ct. of Int'l Trade 1996).

15. 16 U.S.C. §§ 1531–1543. For an expanded discussion of the ESA, see Robinson, *Environmental Regulation of Real Property*, ch. 24.04(2) (Law Journal Press updated to 2022).

16. 16 U.S.C. § 1536.

[B] *Tennessee Valley Authority v. Hill* and the Creation of Endangered Species Committee

In the landmark *Tennessee Valley Authority v. Hill*,[17] the United States Supreme Court held that the ESA mandated the issuance of an injunction to block the construction of a federally-funded dam that imperiled the critical habitat of the snail darter, a fish listed as an endangered species. The Court ruled the Act's express mandate precluded a court from the customary balancing of the equities before determining whether to issue an injunction. The dam was halted even though it was largely completed and the snail darter had no commercial value.

Following this decision Congress amended the ESA to create an Endangered Species Committee, consisting of the Secretaries of Agriculture, the Army and the Interior, the heads of the EPA and National Oceanic and Atmospheric Administration, and the Chairman of the Council of Economic Advisors, as well as a resident of each affected state.[18] The committee has the authority to exempt a project from the critical habitat requirements where it finds no reasonable or prudent alternative exists and the project's benefits clearly outweigh the benefits of any alternative.

In the wake of the snail darter litigation, this committee met, but found an exemption for the dam unwarranted. The dam was nonetheless completed, however, under special legislation overriding the ESA's provisions.

The courts have strictly enforced the Act's mandate that the Interior Department designate critical habitats.[19]

[C] "Taking" of Endangered Species Is Prohibited

The ESA forbids the "taking" — that is, the hunting or killing — of species on the endangered list without a permit. The Supreme Court has held this provision bars construction of a real estate development that will destroy an endangered species' critical habitat, even though no federal agency action is involved.[20] This includes ordering a developer to remove a fence that interfered with the critical habitat of an endangered species.[21]

[D] Lesser Protection Exists for Threatened Species

In addition to its provision governing endangered species, the ESA also furnishes a lesser degree of protection to those species threatened with extinction, as opposed

---

17. 437 U.S. 153 (1978).

18. 16 U.S.C. § 1536(e).

19. Natural Resources Defense Council, Inc. v. United States Dep't of Interior, 113 F.3d 1121 (9th Cir. 1997).

20. Babbitt v. Sweet Home Chapter of Communities for a Great Oregon, 515 U.S. 687 (1995).

21. Rancho Viejo, LLC v. Norton, 323 F.3d 1062 (D.C. Cir. 2003).

to those actually endangered. Threatened species, which include the timber wolf, may be taken when necessary to protect people or livestock and where reasonable cause exists to believe the particular animal is responsible for the killing or danger involved.[22]

[E] Preemption Issues

The ESA for the most part does not preempt state law. Rather, it envisions cooperation with the states in the area of fish and wildlife conservation, traditionally within the states' jurisdiction, as is discussed in § 10.01. However, a federal permit to take an endangered species does preempt state laws forbidding the sale of articles made from that species.[23] This provision authorizes the sale of alligator skins and such under federal permit despite state laws that would otherwise bar the sale.

[F] Enforcement, Standing, and ESA's Citizen Suit Provision

Whether the ESA, and particularly its critical habitat provisions, apply to acts of the United States government beyond its borders is unclear at present. An Eighth Circuit ruling that those provisions apply extraterritorially was overturned (and vacated) when the Supreme Court ruled the plaintiffs lacked standing.[24] The ESA is enforceable both by the United States and through a citizen suit provision. However, in *Lujan v. Defenders of Wildlife*,[25] discussed in § 1.03, the Supreme Court held that despite that provision a conservation group and its members were without standing to challenge the failure of the United States Agency for International Development to consult with the Interior Department regarding the possible impact of projects outside the United States on the critical habitat of certain endangered species there. More recently, though, the Court gave a broader ruling to the ESA's citizen suit statute, holding it may be invoked by ranchers and other users of water from a reservoir from which withdrawals of water were restricted pursuant to the Act.[26] As the Court noted, the citizen suit provision is available to those asserting an economic as well as an environmental interest.

[G] Other Wildlife Protection Statutes

Federal law also protects the eagle,[27] and has been held not to amount to an unconstitutional de facto taking of property even though it prohibits the sale of eagle

---

22. Sierra Club v. Clark, 577 F. Supp. 783 (D. Minn. 1984), *aff'd in part, rev'd in part*, 755 F.2d 608 (8th Cir. 1985).

23. 16 U.S.C. § 1535(f); *see* Man Hing Ivory & Imports, Inc. v. Deukmejian, 702 F.2d 760 (9th Cir. 1983).

24. Defenders of Wildlife v. Hodel, 911 F.2d 117 (8th Cir. 1990), *rev'd on other grounds sub nom.*, Lujan v. Defenders of Wildlife, 504 U.S. 555 (1992).

25. 504 U.S. 555 (1992).

26. Bennett v. Spear, 520 U.S. 154 (1997).

27. 16 U.S.C. § 668.

feathers taken before the statute took effect.[28] The Supreme Court pointed out that possession of the articles was not unlawful, and that the provision barring sale of pre-existing items was designed to discourage violation of the statute. Additionally, federal law protects wild horses and burros on public lands.[29]

Another federal law, the Marine Mammal Protection Act,[30] bars the importing of seals and other marine mammals killed while young or nursing, or of their furs. In addition, the African Elephant Conservation Act[31] prohibits the import or sale of ivory from those animals, whose protection depends heavily on international treaties discussed at § 10.05. Finally, a federal statute, also dealt with in § 10.05, enables the United States to restrict imports of fish from countries that hunt whales in violation of the treaty protecting those animals.

§ 10.04 State Statutes

In addition to the federal Endangered Species Act, many states have enacted laws curtailing the sale of endangered wildlife and articles made from their hides and other body parts. New York, the first to do so, enacted its statute in 1970, three years before Congress passed the ESA. The New York law protects a greater number of species than does the federal Act, including all alligators, crocodiles, and tigers.[32] The state legislature explicitly listed these entire species as protected, instead of leaving it to the discretion of an agency to list a species (or subspecies), as does the federal Act. Thus, a far greater number of species are covered by the New York law.

New York's closing its markets to furs and leather from endangered species clearly helped spur Congress to enact the ESA. The courts have sustained state endangered species laws, rejecting claims of preemption by federal law as well as the argument that states lacked the power to protect non-native wildlife.[33] However, as noted in § 10.03[E], the ESA explicitly preempts state law where the seller has a valid federal permit to take the animal.

Other state laws restrict the sale of endangered wild birds, imported as pets.[34]

Unlike the ESA, however, most state statutes do not protect the habitat of endangered native wildlife from damage.

The Federal Lacey Act makes it a federal crime to violate any state law by engaging in various forms of wildlife commerce across state or national boundaries.[35] The

---

28. Andrus v. Allard, 444 U.S. 51 (1979).

29. 16 U.S.C. 1331 et seq.

30. 16 U.S.C. §§ 1361–1407.

31. 16 U.S.C. §§ 4201–4245.

32. N.Y. ENVTL. CONSERV. LAW § 11-0536.

33. A.E. Nettleton Co. v. Diamond, 264 N.E.2d 118 (N.Y. 1970), *app. dism. sub nom.*, Reptile Products Ass'n v. Diamond, 401 U.S. 969 (1971).

34. *See, e.g.*, N.Y. ENVTL. CONSERV. LAW § 11-1728 (upheld in *Cresenzi Bird Importers, Inc. v. New York*, 658 F. Supp. 1441 (S.D.N.Y. 1987), *aff'd*, 831 F.2d 410 (2d Cir. 1987)).

35. 16 U.S.C. 3372(a)(1).

Lacey Act also extends to falsifying records and other documentation, or failing to comply with state documentary requirements, in relation to state-protected wildlife.[36] The Lacey Act has also been extended to violations of the wildlife laws of federally recognized Native American tribes.[37] In 2008, the Lacey Act was amended to include the taking of, or illegal commerce in, plant species protected under federal, state, and international laws.[38] In addition to criminal prosecution, civil penalties up to $10,000 may be imposed.[39]

§ 10.05 International Controls

The safeguarding of endangered species requires, and receives, control at the international level. The Convention on International Trade in Endangered Species (CITES), adopted following the 1972 Stockholm United Nations sponsored conference on environmental protection (noted in § 13.01[A]), has largely curtailed the formerly extensive worldwide traffic in skins, furs, ivory, and the like from animals close to extinction. CITES, which virtually every trading nation has now signed, forbids such trade unless the habitat country's scientific authority certifies that the taking of the particular animal is not detrimental to its species' survival. The habitat nation's management authority must also certify that the animal was lawfully taken. Species are listed as endangered or threatened by an international body of wildlife biologists. Permits may be issued by the Secretary of the Interior for non-commercial use on the part of zoos, museums, and similar institutions.

CITES has greatly reduced the ability of game poachers to evade local laws by falsely describing the animal taken. Despite some resistance in east Asia, it has virtually ended the sale of elephant ivory. (A United States statute, described in § 10.03[G], bars the importation or sale of most ivory from African elephants.) However, a dispute continues over whether totally closing down the ivory market is in fact necessary. Zimbabwe, South Africa, and a few other habitat countries contend they have sufficient elephant populations to allow limited hunting under permits, with the profits from the ivory to be furnished to residents of the habitat area. They contend that by thus winning the allegiance of local inhabitants they can more effectively reduce poaching. The counter-argument, voiced by Kenya, Tanzania, and most other habitat nations, is that the most efficient way to end poaching is to halt the ivory trade entirely.

Although the African elephant remains under some risk, a far greater concern exists with regard to the rhinoceros, hunted to the verge of extinction chiefly because its horn is thought to have medicinal properties. While CITES renders rhinoceros

---

36. United States v. Kraft, 2006 U.S. App. LEXIS 1009 (8th Cir. 2006).

37. United States v. March, 2004 U.S. App. Lexis 20992 (9th Cir. 2004).

38. Food, Conservation and Energy Act of 2008, Pub. L. No. 110-246; http://www.aphis.usda.gov/newsroom.hot_issues/lacey_act/index.shtml; see also Asner and Pickering, "The Lacey Act and the World of Illegal Plant Products," 21 Environmental Law in New York 101–105 (Gerrard, ed., LexisNexis, June 2010). 16 U.S.C. 3371(f)(2).

39. U.S.C. 3373(a), (d).

hunting unlawful, poaching continues and doubtless will until education eliminates the medicinal market for the horn.

CITES, however, does not protect the habitat of endangered species from encroachment. This continues to increase as human populations expand in habitat countries and forests are cut down for agriculture, firewood, and development. These complex issues are further discussed in § 13.06 under biodiversity.

A separate treaty protects whales.[40] An International Whaling Commission has imposed a moratorium on commercial whaling since 1986, and has the authority to impose sanctions on violators, including restrictions on ocean fishing. Japan, and occasionally some other countries, have violated the treaty, but sanctions have generally not been enforced against them. Japan insists that its whaling is limited to the taking of whales for scientific research, although that claim has been disputed. The United States, although seemingly mandated by federal statute to curb imports of Japanese fish and seafood on proof of whaling violations, has not done so. In 1986, the Supreme Court ruled that the Government had discretion as to imposing such sanctions and declined to mandate their imposition.[41]

§ 10.06 Voluntary Creation of Wildlife Habitat

Biologists have turned in the past two decades to creating new habitat for endangered wildlife to offset the loss of existing habitat as well as losses inflicted by hunting. Species as varied as antelope, turtles, and alligators have benefited from created habitat. If animals can be commercially harvested, their survival is assured. Similarly, the development of ecotourism can safeguard species such as gorillas and elephants while shifting the attitudes of nearby residents away from poaching and toward protection and the economic benefits of furnishing services for visitors.

Two concerns have surfaced with regard to created habitat. The gene pool of isolated populations is limited, increasing the risk of mutations and susceptibility to disease. Likewise, ranchers have expressed fear that animals such as wild bovines and sheep kept in proximity to domesticated cattle and sheep can transmit their disease to domestic herds.

On balance, creating habitat surely seems likely to increase as natural habitats continue to shrink.

---

40. International Convention for the Regulation of Whaling, 161 U.N.T.S. 72 (1946).
41. Japan Whaling Ass'n v. American Cetacean Soc'y, 478 U.S. 221 (1986).

Chapter 11

Land Use

§ 11.01 Overview

Land use is a vital aspect of environmental law. It constitutes an important dimension of virtually every environmental topic. Issues of air and water quality, and waste disposal, turn as much on the location of the source as on the nature of the discharge. Wildlife protection is increasingly a function of safeguarding its habitat. In addition, science and the law recognize the need to preserve natural areas like wetlands, shorefronts, and forests, as well as historic landmarks and other significant parts of the built environment.

Land use decisions have traditionally been made at the local level under the American legal system. But it is clear that the state (and in certain instances the federal government) has the power and responsibility to protect environmentally valuable land, as this chapter will discuss.

Frequently, and understandably, local governments base their land use determinations in large measure on local concerns. A shopping center or other large-scale development may be welcomed as a means of increasing the town's assessed valuation, and thus avoiding the need to increase the real property tax rate. Other major developments may be viewed as providing employment. However, the environmental impacts of these projects may fall on other localities along with the one to benefit economically. These impacts may include traffic, noise, flooding, and concerns over water supply and waste disposal. This conflict between local and regional interests has led to the adoption of measures at the state government level to protect a variety of environmentally critical areas.

§ 11.02 Critical Areas:
Wetlands, Coastal Zones, Shorelands, and
Submerged Lands and Floodplains

[A] Wetlands

Wetlands, consisting of marshes, bogs, and similar areas, are recognized as being of the highest environmental importance. They are a breeding ground for commercially valuable fish and shellfish, and a habitat for migratory birds and other wildlife, and absorb vast quantities of storm water, thus reducing flood damage. In addition, wetlands process sewage from adjacent developed lands, obviating the need for costly sewage treatment plants. Finally, freshwater wetlands are a key source of potable water supply.

Unfortunately, these values were not translated into legal protection for wetlands for most of our history. About half the wetland areas existing in the United States when European colonization commenced have been lost. Many wetlands were drained or filled in for real estate development, mosquito control, and similar reasons. The

United States Army Corps of Engineers' stream channelization projects also destroyed numerous wetlands.

Starting in the late 1960s, the scientific community's awareness of the need to protect our remaining wetlands led to enactment of state and local statutes furthering that goal. These statutes generally require a permit, issued by a state or municipal environmental agency, to dredge, fill, drain, or otherwise alter a wetland. Wetlands are defined in terms of their vegetation and soil characteristics, and must be inventoried and mapped, so that owners are aware that their land is a designated wetland under the statute. Permits are issued on the basis of a balancing of wetland preservation with social and economic development needs. Some states, such as New York, have separate, although similar, statutes governing freshwater and tidal (saltwater) wetlands.[1] The statutes usually contain civil and criminal penalty provisions.

Wetlands are also subject to regulation under Clean Water Act § 404,[2] which requires a permit issued by the United States Army Corps of Engineers to discharge dredged or fill material into the waters of the United States. This statute is discussed in detail in § 6.07. The term "waters of the United States" is defined broadly enough in the Clean Water Act to encompass many wetland areas. In one noted case the Supreme Court held a wetland subject to the Act even though it had been inundated only five times in the past 80 years.[3]

However, the Supreme Court later, in *Rapanos* v. *United States*,[4] issued a fragmented decision regarding Clean Water Act jurisdiction over wetlands not directly connected to navigable waters. A four-justice plurality found there must be "a continuous flow of water in a permanent channel" linking the wetland to a navigable waterway. But Justice Kennedy, concurring, maintained "a significant nexus with navigable waters" suffices.

In addition, wetlands are protected from farming use by the "swampbuster" provisions of the federal agricultural statutes, described in § 11.08.

Landowners who are denied permits often contend that the state has deprived them of all reasonable value, and thus effected a taking of their property. This issue is dealt with in detail in § 1.05[C]. In the wetlands context, property frequently includes upland as well as regulated wetlands. The courts have held that, as long as the owner is free to develop the upland portion of the parcel, the state has not caused a taking, since the parcel, viewed as an entity, has not been deprived of all its reasonable value.[5]

In addition, since a taking requires a showing that the owner has been denied all reasonable investment-based expectations, courts will examine whether the owner obtained the property after the wetland regulation took effect. If so, the owner pre-

---

1. N.Y. ENVTL. CONSERV. LAW arts. 24 (freshwater wetlands), 25 (tidal wetlands).

2. 33 U.S.C. § 1344.

3. United States v. Riverside Bayview Homes, Inc., 474 U.S. 121 (1985).

4. 126 S. Ct. 2208 (2006).

5. *See, e.g.*, Gazza v. New York State Dept. of Envtl. Conserv., 679 N.E.2d 1035 (N.Y. 1997), *cert. denied*, 522 U.S. 813 (1997).

sumably paid a lower price, reflecting the possibility that a permit to develop the parcel might be denied. This likewise argues strongly against the validity of a taking claim.[6] The Supreme Court, however, has ruled that one who acquires the property after the regulatory statute's enactment is not necessarily barred from asserting a taking claim.[7] Some of the justices, though, sensibly noted that those facts would impose a greater burden on one claiming a taking since the owner's reasonable investment-based expectations would be lower.

[B] Coastal Zones, Shorelands, and Submerged Lands

[1] State and Local Statutes

Many states and localities strictly control development of their coastal zones and shorelines. Typical statutes require a permit for construction in these areas, recognizing that shorefront is subject to storms, hurricanes, and erosion. California's Constitution contains a provision which guarantees public access to its shoreline.[8] To implement that provision, the state created a Coastal Commission with permit jurisdiction over shorefront areas. In *Nollan v. California Coastal Commission*,[9] the state conditioned a permit to build a residence on the owners allowing the public to cross the property along the beach in order to walk from one state park to another. The United States Supreme Court overturned that condition as so unrelated to the purpose of the regulatory statute, and so invasive of the owners' right to exclude others from their property, as to amount to a taking.

Other states employ the public trust doctrine, described at § 3.06, to ensure access to beaches and shorefront.

Many states have enacted statutes protecting shorefront areas from development that can worsen erosion or endanger residents during storms. When development of a shorefront parcel is so restricted that the owner is denied all reasonable investment-based expectations, the owner may claim a de facto taking, as with the wetland laws dealt with in [A], *above*. Although it is often difficult to show a denial of all reasonable use, the Supreme Court ruled in *Lucas v. South Carolina Coastal Council*[10] that such proof supports a finding of a taking, requiring the state to pay for the property, unless the state can show that it could have prevented the construction at issue under common law principles such as nuisance or the public trust doctrine. In that situation the owner would be charged with knowledge that the state could enjoin development of the parcel, and thus would lack a reasonable investment-based expectation that he could build on the tract. In *Lucas*, the South Carolina courts, on remand,

---

6. Gazza v. New York State Dept. of Envtl. Conserv., 679 N.E.2d 1035 (N.Y. 1997), *cert. denied*, 522 U.S. 813 (1997).
7. Palazzolo v. Rhode Island, 533 U.S. 606 (2001).
8. CAL. CONST. art. 10, § 4.
9. 483 U.S. 825 (1987).
10. 505 U.S. 1003 (1992).

held that the state could not have enjoined the construction at common law, so that the state had to compensate the owner.[11]

[2] Coastal Zone Management Act

The federal government plays a major role in shorefront protection through the Coastal Zone Management Act.[12] Since Congressional power to regulate land use directly on other than federal lands is debatable, the Act uses the spending power to encourage states to adopt laws safeguarding their coastal areas. Coastal areas are quite broadly defined in the Act, and include the Great Lakes as well as shorelands, and extend outward to the outer limit of state ownership under federal law (see [3], *below*): three miles offshore on the Atlantic and Pacific coasts, 10.5 miles in the Gulf of Mexico with regard to Texas and Florida, and to the boundary with Canada in the Great Lakes.[13]

States may (though they need not) submit coastal zone management (CZM) plans to the Secretary of Commerce, who reviews them through the National Oceanic and Atmospheric Administration, an arm of the Department of Commerce. Plans approved by the Secretary render that state eligible for federal funds to implement coastal zone management. In addition, the Act offers a powerful further inducement through its consistency provision. Once a state CZM plan is approved by the Secretary of Commerce, federal activities affecting that state's coastal zone may be vetoed by the state unless they are consistent with that state's plan "to the maximum extent practicable."[14] This provision applies to activities performed or funded by the federal government. Activities licensed by the federal government, including offshore oil drilling, must be fully consistent with the state's CZM plan. This furnishes a strong weapon to states, although it is somewhat blunted by the President's power to exempt activities found to be in the paramount interest of the United States, or, in the case of offshore oil drilling, the power of the Secretary of the Interior to find the drilling "necessary in the interest of national security."

The states' ability to control activities through their approved CZM plans even encompasses federal lands, and empowers the state to preempt mining claims awarded by federal agencies such as the United States Forest Service.[15]

State CZM plans approved by the Secretary of Commerce range from comprehensive legislation requiring a state permit for coastal development, as in California (see the *Nollan* case, discussed in [1], *above*), to laws like New York's that leave regulatory jurisdiction to local governments, but subject to state guidelines.[16] Most of the states subject to the Act have submitted federally-approved plans.

---

11. 424 S.E.2d 484 (S.C. 1992).
12. 16 U.S.C. §§ 1451–1464.
13. 16 U.S.C. § 1453(1).
14. 16 U.S.C. § 1456.
15. California Coastal Comm'n v. Granite Rock Co., 480 U.S. 572 (1987).
16. N.Y. ENVTL. CONSERV. LAW § 34-0105.

[3] Underwater Lands

Submerged lands are governed by federal law beyond the traditional three-mile limit, except that in the Gulf of Mexico, a 10.5-mile limit applies to lands off Texas and Florida. Congress so provided in the Submerged Lands Act,[17] administered by the Secretary of the Interior. Under that Act, the Secretary must approve leases for offshore oil and gas, discussed in §6.06[D]. Within the limits delineated in the Act, the states have jurisdiction. The Coastal Zone Management Act, as noted in [2], *above*, enables the states to control offshore oil and gas drilling even in waters controlled by the federal government.

[C] Floodplains

All three levels of government play significant roles in limiting development in areas subject to periodic flooding. States and localities have legislation aimed at curbing construction of residences and other occupied structures in these areas. The federal flood insurance program provides great encouragement for state and municipal restrictions on floodplain development. Federally-subsidized flood insurance is essentially the only insurance available to reimburse owners damaged by flooding. Congress has limited the availability of this insurance to localities with "adequate land use and control measures (with effective enforcement provisions)."[18] This is a spur to the adoption of local floodplain legislation. The flood insurance program is supervised by the Federal Emergency Management Agency (FEMA), which has responsibility to evaluate the effectiveness of local floodplain legislation.

The extensive flooding in the Gulf Coast region caused by hurricane Katrina in 2005 has raised serious concerns about the sufficiency of levees along the Mississippi River built and maintained by the Army Corps of Engineers, as well as the effectiveness of FEMA.[19]

Laws curbing development in floodplains are subject to challenge as takings if they deprive the owner of all reasonable investment-based expectations. The courts will look at the nature of the uses permitted under the particular statute or ordinance. For example, if the land may be used for farming, recreation, parking or other activities enabling the owner to earn a reasonable return, there is no taking.[20]

However, the Supreme Court in *Dolan v. City of Tigard*[21] held that a floodplain restriction must be "roughly proportionate" to the goal of the ordinance. If not, it will be set aside as a taking, even though it may not in fact deny the owner all reasonable investment-based expectations. In *Dolan*, the city conditioned the granting

---

17. 43 U.S.C. §§ 1301–1315.

18. 42 U.S.C. § 4022.

19. *See* Douglas A. Kysar & Thomas D. McGarity, *Did NEPA Drown New Orleans? The Levees, the Blame Game, and the Hazards of Hindsight*, 56 DUKE L.J. 179 (2006); Stephen M. Griffin, *Stop Federalism Before It Kills Again: Reflections on Hurricane Katrina*, 21 ST. JOHN'S J.L. COMM. 527 (2007).

20. First English Evangelical Lutheran Church v. County of Los Angeles, 258 Cal. Rptr. 893 (1989), *cert. denied*, 493 U.S. 1056 (1990).

21. 512 U.S. 374 (1994).

of a permit to enlarge an existing store on the owner dedicating a portion of her parcel located in a floodplain as a public pathway. Although this clearly did not deprive her of all the reasonable value of the land, the Court nonetheless found that the disproportion between the exaction and its purpose amounted to a taking. The physical invasion aspect of the requirement that the owner dedicate a public path across her property surely influenced the Court in finding a taking.

§ 11.03 State Regional Planning

[A] Local Zoning and Its Environmental Implications

Traditionally, land use controls in the United States have been imposed through local zoning ordinances. The first, in the City of New York, was adopted in 1915. In the next decade, the Supreme Court, in the landmark *Euclid* case, sustained an Ohio zoning ordinance as against claims that it deprived a land-owner of property without due process, as well as the equal protection of the laws.[22] The Court found that the law had a rational basis, even though the owner contended that it reduced the value of the property by as much as 75 percent. It based its decision in large measure on an analogy to the law of public nuisance, holding that the village could legislate to ban nuisances that a court could have enjoined under common law principles. Zoning by local governments requires the state to delegate a portion of its police power to the municipal government. This is accomplished through enabling legislation authorizing localities to zone.

Zoning, dictating as it does how land may be used, has enormous environmental implications. Not only do zoning ordinances control future development within the particular locality, but they also greatly influence land use in surrounding areas. A large-scale residential, commercial, or industrial development impacts traffic, water supply, solid waste and sewage disposal, and other environmental concerns, often both within its own political entity and in adjacent towns. The host municipality receives the real property tax benefits to offset some of the environmental impacts. The neighboring localities do not.

An equally significant way in which local zoning may implicate environmental concerns relates to zoning measures designed to protect water supply and curtail sprawl and rapid expansion. These local laws, either part of or superimposed on zoning schemes, have been challenged as exclusionary—that is, aimed at fencing off localities from moderate-income home purchasers. These court challenges have usually been based on asserted denials of equal protection of the laws, or of the constitutionally protected right to travel. Courts have sustained local laws found to serve genuine environmental concerns.[23] However, other laws have been declared uncon-

---

22. Village of Euclid v. Ambler Realty Co., 272 U.S. 365 (1926).
23. *See* Construction Industry Ass'n v. City of Petaluma, 522 F.2d 897 (9th Cir. 1975), *cert. denied*, 424 U.S. 934 (1976).

stitutional, when the courts have found the professed environmental concerns to amount to a ruse to keep out affordable housing.[24]

[B] Need to Protect Environmentally Critical Areas

Some critical areas like wetlands, if destroyed, impose environmental effects far beyond the borders of the locality where they lie. Similarly, power plants and other such uses of land may inflict air and water pollution and other environmental impacts on other communities that do not benefit from the real property taxes those facilities pay. For these reasons, many states have reclaimed some of the police powers they had previously delegated to localities to control land use. Wetlands, shorefront areas, and coastal zones are frequently controlled by state as well as local law (see § 11.02). Power plants are generally subject to state siting provisions that supersede local zoning (see § 11.06). In addition, some states have enacted statewide land use measures to control large-scale development.

[C] State Planning and Land Use Statutes

States have adopted a variety of approaches to statewide land use control, ranging from statewide zoning, through state agency review of local zoning decisions, to imposing statewide standards for localities to use in their decision-making.

Hawaii has adopted zoning at the state level since 1961. Most land use decisions are made by a state Land Use Commission in this small state, heavily dependent on agriculture and tourism.[25] Planning is also performed by a state agency. The Land Use Commission divides the state into land use districts, and directly zones those districts devoted to conservation. Zoning in the other areas is administered by counties, but subject to state review of individual decisions, as well as the state Commission's power to classify and reclassify districts.

Vermont typifies the two-tiered approach, with state review of municipal zoning decisions involving large-scale residential, commercial, or industrial development.[26] Any construction involving 10 or more acres, or 10 or more residential units, requires both local and state approval. Vermont also has statewide planning.

In Florida, the legislature created regional planning agencies, which review all developments with regional impact. Here too, there is an effective State Land Development Plan.[27] However, municipalities with state-approved land use plans and zoning ordinances are exempt from state review.

These states have in common an economy largely driven by tourism and recreation. This surely eased the path of statewide land use legislation, and reduced the resistance

---

24. *See* Southern Burlington County NAACP v. Township of Mt. Laurel, 336 A.2d 713 (N.J. 1975), *cert. denied*, 423 U.S. 808 (1975).
25. HAW. REV. STAT. ANN. §§ 205-1 to 205-18.
26. VT. STAT. ANN., title 10, §§ 6001–6018.
27. FLA. STAT. ANN. §§ 163.3161–163.3215.

from developers and construction unions that has barred statewide measures in other states.

A number of states have adopted state standards for land use determinations, which municipalities are required to implement. Oregon,[28] Washington,[29] New Jersey,[30] and Maryland[31] have taken this road, and it was pursuant to the Oregon standards that the dedication of the public pathway in the *Dolan* case (see § 11.02[C]) was mandated.

Some other states have state agency review of local land use decisions in regions of the state found by the legislature to deserve special protection as environmentally critical areas. These include New York's Adirondacks[32] and New Jersey's Central Pine Barrens.[33] In a slightly different approach, the area surrounding Chesapeake Bay in Maryland and Virginia is protected by state land use development standards binding on local governments.[34]

Supplementing, or substituting for, state land use standards are the environmental quality review acts that exist in about half the states, discussed in § 4.02. These laws, which vary in their comprehensiveness and effectiveness from state to state, generally require state and municipal government agencies to prepare environmental impact statements and consider alternatives and mitigation measures when approving development projects with significant environmental effects.

Resistance to land use planning continues in many parts of the country. Even zoning by local governments is far from universal, and some large cities such as Houston, as well as many rural areas and towns, have no effective planning or municipal land use controls. In these areas, covenants by landowners — enforceable voluntary agreements, binding on future purchasers — sometimes provide a makeshift alternative by limiting land to residential use.

§ 11.04 Historic Preservation

[A] Municipal Controls Protecting Landmarks

One critical area in land use regulation is the protection of historic landmark structures. This is chiefly accomplished through municipal ordinances adopted, like local zoning laws, under state enabling legislation. Typically, a local historic landmark commission is empowered to declare buildings and other structures protected on the basis of their historic or architectural significance. A staff with expertise in these areas helps decide which structures are to be designated. Designation by the agency

---

28. OR. REV. STAT., Chs. 92, 215, 227.
29. WASH. REV. CODE ANN., Ch. 36.70.
30. N.J. STAT. ANN. § 52:18A-197, *et seq.*
31. MD. CODE ANN., Art. 66B.
32. N.Y. EXEC. L. § 801, *et seq.*
33. N.J. STAT. ANN. § 13:18A-1, *et seq.*
34. MD. CODE ANN., NAT. RES. § 8-302; VA. CODE ANN. § 62.1-69.5, *et seq.*

sometimes requires approval by a mayor, city council, or other political official or entity. It is also subject to judicial review.

Once a landmark is designated, any significant alteration requires a permit from the agency, in addition to meeting whatever requirements are contained in the local zoning ordinance. Whether the agency will issue a permit generally turns on the extent to which the alteration will affect the historic and architectural integrity of the structure. Some preservation laws safeguard the interior as well as the outside of buildings. Alteration without a permit may draw criminal or civil penalties, as well as injunctive relief.

Entire districts, as well as individual buildings, may be designated as historic, and subjected to permit requirements. This has occurred in the French Quarter (Vieux Carr´e) of New Orleans, as well as New York's Greenwich Village and Brooklyn Heights, and districts in Denver and Santa Fe.

[B] Landmarks and Taking Claims

Owners of landmark buildings have contended that denial of a permit amounts to a taking. To prevail, the owner must show a deprivation of all reasonable investment-based expectations, under the rules discussed in § 1.05[C]. This is a difficult burden to surmount, and especially so if the owner purchased after the building was designated a landmark. In such a case, the purchase price generally reflects the restriction on altering the structure imposed by the landmark law.

In *Penn Central Transportation Co. v. City of New York*,[35] the United States Supreme Court sustained historic preservation laws, resoundingly rejecting a taking claim. The case involved Grand Central Terminal, a monumental railroad station built in 1913, and a classic example of French beaux arts style. The city denied a permit to construct a 55-story office building above the terminal. The state courts had found this denial did not deprive the owner of all reasonable investment-based expectations, since it could still be used as a railway station and, together with its restaurants, newsstands, and other rental income, was not unprofitable. However, the owner argued in the Supreme Court that New York's preservation ordinance nevertheless constituted a taking of the air rights over the terminal, and was invalid as unequally applied to the property.

The Court rejected both of these contentions. It held that the air rights had not been taken, since the city had simply denied a permit for the particular high-rise structure, not for all construction atop the station. In any event, the Court found, air rights are not separate and distinct from the ownership of an entire parcel, which includes the land, the air rights above it (except as limited by law), and the ground beneath it. One may convey air rights, but if not conveyed, they remain as an integral part of the parcel. The Court further noted that in exchange for denying the permit,

---

35. 438 U.S. 104 (1978).

the city had given the owner transferable development rights (TDRs) — the right to transfer the owner's ability to develop to any contiguous property. These rights, which the owner may either use or sell, had sufficient value to offset any taking claim based on the air rights over the terminal.

The Court likewise rejected *Penn Central*'s alternative argument that the landmark law allowed the Commission to arbitrarily designate properties, and thus was tantamount to unconstitutional spot zoning. The owner conceded the validity of historic districts, in which both the benefits and burdens of landmark status are shared by all landowners, as in conventional zoning. But, it contended, designating a building in isolation was unconstitutional. In rejecting this claim, the Court found the landmark ordinance to be rational as applied to Grand Central, since the ordinance required the city to select properties for designation based on their architectural or historic significance, as determined by the Commission's staff. And, it pointed out, the owner had not sought judicial review of Grand Central's designation, but only challenged the later denial of permission to build above the station.

Penn Central was a Magna Carta for historic preservation laws. Under the rule of *Penn Central*, such laws are challengeable as takings *only* when the owner can show a denial of all reasonable investment-based expectations. A mere reduction in the value of property is not enough.

[C] Religious Buildings and Free Exercise Claims

As applied to religious structures, as they often are, landmark laws have been sustained as long as they do not deny the owner the ability to continue to use the building for religious purposes. When a house of worship is in such disrepair as to be no longer usable, and no likely source of funds for repair exists, a court may find that the denial of a permit to demolish or significantly alter the building constitutes a taking. However, if the building is still viable, protection under the landmark ordinance does not effect a taking.[36]

Churches have argued that preservation laws unconstitutionally interfere with the free exercise of religion. The courts have generally rejected such claims, holding that landmark ordinances, like zoning and other land use measures, are neutral laws of general applicability. As such they are to be sustained, as applied to a church, as long as they have a rational basis.[37]

This issue has been affected by the enactment of the Religious Land Use and Institutionalized Persons Act (RLUIPA), discussed at § 1.05[C][3][b], which limits land use restrictions on houses of worship that substantially burden the free exercise of religion.

---

36. Society for Ethical Culture v. Spatt, 415 N.E.2d 922 (N.Y. 1980).
37. Rector of St. Bartholomew's Church v. City of New York, 914 F.2d 348 (2d Cir. 1990), *cert. denied*, 499 U.S. 905 (1991).

[D] Maintenance and Rehabilitation

Landmark ordinances may, and generally do, require the owner to maintain the property in good repair. But they may not require the owner to rehabilitate the structure.[38] Nor may they dictate a particular form of ownership, such as converting a single-family residence to condominiums.[39]

Both federal and state law provide for tax deductions as incentives to rehabilitate landmark structures, although the 1986 federal income tax amendments reduced that deduction substantially.[40] These tax benefits are generally limited to property listed on the National Register of Historic Places, maintained by the Secretary of the Interior pursuant to the National Historic Preservation Act.[41]

[E] National Register of Historic Places

The National Register consists of "districts, sites, buildings, structures and objects significant in American history, architecture, archeology, engineering, and culture."[42] Listing on the National Register furnishes not only tax advantages, but also a measure of protection, though not as extensive as the protection afforded by local laws. The National Historic Preservation Act, however, requires all federal agencies to take into account, in advance of acting, the effect of any action performed, funded, or licensed by the federal government on any structure or site on the National Register.[43] The statute specifically requires agencies to give the Advisory Council on Historic Preservation reasonable opportunity to comment. This "§ 106 process," named for the section of the original 1966 Act, has protected many historic sites and buildings from destruction when federally aided highways, airports, housing developments, and similar projects are built.

Many states have enacted comparable laws limiting actions by state agencies affecting structures listed on state registers of historic places.[44]

§ 11.05 Wilderness Areas and Public Lands

Several important federal statutes govern the vast holdings of the United States, which are primarily located in the Western states and Alaska. In all, the federal gov-

---

38. FGL & L Property Co. v. City of Rye, 485 N.E.2d 986 (N.Y. 1985).

39. *Id.*

40. 26 U.S.C. § 47.

41. 16 U.S.C. § 470. For a more complete discussion of the NHPA and Historic Preservation in general, see Robinson, *Environmental Regulation of Real Property*, Ch.6 (Law Journal Press updated to 2022).

42. 16 U.S.C. § 470a(1)(A).

43. 16 U.S.C. § 470f.

44. *See, e.g.*, N.Y. PARKS, RECR. & HISTORIC PRESERV. LAW § 14.09; MASS. GEN. L. ch. 9, § 27c; CAL. PUB. RES. CODE § 5024(f).

ernment owns a prodigious 34 percent of the territory of the United States, including about half of Alaska. These lands are primarily administered by the National Forest Service, in the Department of Agriculture, and the Bureau of Land Management (BLM), in the Department of Interior. Other significant portions of these holdings are national parks and wildlife refuges, administered by the National Park Service and the Fish and Wildlife Service, respectively. Both these agencies are part of the Department of the Interior.

[A] National Forests

National Forests, originally created by the Forest Preserve Act of 1891,[45] are chiefly administered under the Multiple-Use Sustained-Yield Act.[46] Under this Act, the National Forest Service is to manage these areas for a variety of purposes so as to achieve "a high-level ... output of [their] renewable resources ... without impairment of the productivity of the land."[47] These uses include recreation, rangeland, timber, and mining. The latter two in particular have given rise to controversy. Timber companies have long removed much wood from Forest Service lands, and in recent decades have, with the advent of mechanization, turned to extensive clearcutting — the removal of all trees from a wide area. Though clearcutting has been severely criticized by environmental groups, it continues, and the courts have sustained the broad discretion of the Forest Service in permitting it.[48] The practice has also been criticized on economic grounds, since the timber companies pay the government far less than they earn from the lumber. Only when clearcutting interferes with the critical habitat of a species protected under the Endangered Species Act (see § 10.03), as with the spotted owl in the Pacific Northwest, has the Forest Service been obliged to curtail the practice. A Congressional compromise settling the spotted owl controversy was upheld by the Supreme Court in 1992, as against the claim that the statute interfered with the jurisdiction of the federal courts in violation of Article III of the Constitution by directing the courts as to how they must decide a pending case.[49]

Some environmental groups have urged that on both environmental and economic grounds, the removal of timber from federal lands should be halted altogether, and legislation has been introduced in Congress to accomplish this. It is certain to be resisted stoutly by the timber companies.

Mining, too has been criticized on Forest Service and other public lands. An 1872 statute, never significantly amended in this respect, enables hard rock miners to obtain a patent to extract minerals from federal lands for the remarkably generous fee of $5 an acre.[50] Attempts to increase the fee over the years have not succeeded.

---

45. 16 U.S.C. § 471(b).
46. 16 U.S.C. §§ 528–531.
47. 16 U.S.C. § 531(b).
48. Sierra Club v. Hardin, 325 F. Supp. 99 (D. Alaska 1971).
49. Robertson v. Seattle Audubon Soc'y, 503 U.S. 429 (1992).
50. 30 U.S.C. § 30.

Control of Forest Service as well as Bureau of Land Management lands is governed by the Federal Land Policy and Management Act.[51] Under this statute, the agencies may withdraw lands from private use such as mining, though this requires Congressional approval in certain cases.

[B] Bureau of Land Management Property

The Department of the Interior's Bureau of Land Management (BLM) administers the largest single portion of federal lands. These tracts, as noted in [A], *above*, are governed by the Federal Land Policy and Management Act. Much of this acreage is used for grazing. However, logging and mining, as described in [A], *above*, are also permitted.

[C] National Parks and Wildlife Refuges

Specific legislation governs national parks, administered by the National Park Service in the Department of the Interior, and wildlife refuges, operated by the Fish and Wildlife Service in that Department. Commercial logging and mining are off limits in national parks. Wildlife refuges are used chiefly for breeding grounds, but recreation, hunting, and fishing are generally allowed there, and mining is also authorized.[52]

The chief area of controversy with regard to national parks relates to funding for the National Park Service, which many judge to be so inadequate as to threaten the survival of the numerous structures in the parks. Many of these buildings are themselves historic and listed on the National Register (see § 11.04[E]). Hotels and restaurants within the parks are operated by concessionaires; and as with grazing, logging, and mining on other federal lands, concern has been expressed that the fees for these concessions are too low to compensate the Park Service adequately.

Another ongoing concern is the need to protect the entire ecosystems that encompass national parks. Efforts to protect bison, wolves, and similar threatened species within parks have been hampered by the killing of these animals beyond park borders. The patchwork nature of many parks also often hampers ecosystem preservation.

[D] Wilderness Protection

A specific statute, the Wilderness Act,[53] creates a national wilderness preservation system comprised of some lands from all four of the major categories of public lands: national forests, BLM lands, national parks, and wildlife refuges. In these areas, "where man himself is a visitor who does not remain,"[54] logging, mining, and other com-

---

51. 43 U.S.C. §§ 1701–1784.
52. 16 U.S.C. § 668dd.
53. 16 U.S.C. §§ 1131–1136.
54. 16 U.S.C. § 1131(c).

mercial exploitation are barred. Much dispute continues, however, as to timber removal in areas contiguous to wilderness.[55]

The states have comparable laws, governing wilderness areas controlled at the state level. The most dramatic, and oldest, is New York's constitutional provision, enacted in 1894, requiring all state-administered lands in the Adirondack and Catskill areas, denoted New York's "Forest Preserve," to remain "forever wild."[56]

§ 11.06 Power Plant Siting

[A] In General

Electric power plants are universally recognized as capable of causing significant environmental impacts. Coal and oil-fired generators create air pollution. Nuclear plants raise numerous serious issues with regard to radiation and disposal of nuclear waste, dealt with in § 12.02. Hydroelectric power plants impose concerns ranging from interference with navigation to the killing of fish. For these reasons, several statutory regimes have evolved governing the siting of various types of electric generating plants.

[B] Hydroelectric Power Plants

Federal statutes govern the location of hydroelectric plants. Enacted in 1920, the Federal Power Act[57] sets standards for those facilities. Applicants must obtain a license from the Federal Energy Regulatory Commission, which is required to weigh the need for the plant, as well as its impact on the navigability of the waterway on which the plant will be located, and ensure that the power plant conforms to a comprehensive plan for developing the waterway for a variety of uses, notably including recreation.[58] It was this provision that led to the landmark decision denying a license to the pumped-storage hydroelectric plant to be built at Storm King Mountain astride the Hudson River in New York's Hudson Highlands.[59] The Commission was found by the court to have failed to take into account the power plant's likely interference with fishing, hiking, and other recreational uses. (The decision is further discussed at § 4.01[A][2].) A 1986 amendment to the Act explicitly requires the Commission to consider a hydroelectric plant's impact on fish and wildlife, conservation, and environmental quality.[60]

---

55. Minnesota Pub. Interest Research Group v. Butz, 358 F. Supp. 584 (D. Minn. 1973), *aff'd*, 498 F.2d 1314 (8th Cir. 1974).

56. N.Y. CONST. art. XIV, § 1.

57. 16 U.S.C. §§ 791a-828c.

58. 16 U.S.C. § 803(a).

59. Scenic Hudson Preservation Conference v. Federal Power Comm'n, 354 F.2d 608 (2d Cir. 1965), *cert. denied*, 384 U.S. 941 (1966).

60. 16 U.S.C. § 797(e).

Hydroelectric plants may also be subject to state power plant siting laws. In addition, they must satisfy the requirements of Clean Water Act § 401[61] that they will not interfere with state water quality standards. *See* § 6.03[C][4]. The Supreme Court has ruled that a state may deny certification under § 401 to a hydroelectric plant likely to reduce the quantity of water in a fishing stream to a point that may impair the ability of fish to survive there.[62] The Court construed the term "water quality" in the statute broadly enough to encompass the quantity of water needed to support aquatic life.

[C] Nuclear Power Plants

Nuclear power plants, dealt with in greater detail at § 12.02, require licensing by the United States Nuclear Regulatory Commission, which has exclusive jurisdiction over radiation concerns. However, the need for, and siting of, nuclear plants are determined by state law, so that these facilities are also governed by state power plant siting laws.

[D] State Power Plant Siting Statutes

All other major electric generating plants, including those fired by coal, oil, or natural gas, are controlled by state siting laws. These statutes generally empower a state agency, usually either a public utility commission or an interagency siting board, to decide on the need for, and location of, power plants. These laws frequently apply to hydroelectric and nuclear power plants as well, although the states share jurisdiction with federal agencies over such plants.

Prior to the advent of state siting laws, localities could use their zoning power to exclude power plants, even when there existed strong environmental and economic reasons to place the plant in that locality. Other municipalities, anxious for the real property taxes a power plant would pay, might encourage the siting of an electric generating plant in an otherwise less suitable venue. For these reasons, both utilities and environmental advocates welcomed state power plant siting laws.

Under these statutes the state agency, after hearings, determines the site for power plants, often with the power to override local zoning. The municipality, local opponents of the facility, and of course the applicant itself may be parties to the proceeding. In some states the applicant is required to furnish funds for opponents to retain counsel and expert witnesses. The need for the power plant must also be shown, although in some states there also exist requirements for long-range planning of future electric power needs. If a power plant will emit air or water pollutants, it must obtain a permit under the Clean Air Act or Clean Water Act, which in some states may be issued by the siting agency instead of the environmental agency. Judicial review of siting decisions is available, and generally requires a challenger (whether challenging

---

61. 33 U.S.C. § 1341.

62. Public Utility Dist. No. 1 of Jefferson County v. Washington Dept. of Ecology, 511 U.S. 700 (1994).

the issuance or denial of a permit) to show a lack of substantial evidence in the record to support the determination.[63]

Similar procedures govern the federal hearings under which hydroelectric and nuclear power plants must secure licenses. Some specific features of nuclear plant licensing are discussed at § 12.02.

§ 11.07 Aesthetic Controls

A sizable number of localities have enacted land use regulations empowering a board of architectural review or similar body to ensure that new construction conforms to the area's existing architectural design. For example, in a town whose architecture is largely Victorian, or colonial, the board would have power to deny permission to build a modern structure.[64]

Courts are far more comfortable reviewing determinations of agencies with architectural expertise as to essentially aesthetic judgments than they are when obliged to render these sorts of judgments in the first instance. This is evidenced by the great reluctance of courts to hold that buildings or other structures are aesthetic nuisances or otherwise violative of general provisions of law. *See* the discussion at § 3.01[C].

Billboards are subject to controls both on aesthetic grounds and because they may distract motorists' attention. A few states, such as Vermont, and many municipalities, have banned commercial billboards entirely.

State and municipal statutes forbidding commercial billboards are valid exercises of the police power.[65] However, laws that bar billboards raise First Amendment free speech issues. For example, a local law barring all billboards but exempting on-site commercial signs was found by the Supreme Court to violate the First Amendment. As the Court pointed out, under this ordinance an on-site commercial billboard would be permitted, although an on-site billboard with a political or religious message would not. Thus, the statute improperly gave greater protection to commercial speech than to traditionally fully-protected speech.[66]

Billboard owners have also contended that a law requiring the signs' removal constitutes a taking, as is discussed in § 1.05[C]. The courts view a billboard like any non-conforming use in zoning: the owner is entitled to recoup its investment, but once that has occurred, the state or locality may constitutionally terminate the use.[67] In addition, some courts have held that when billboards are ordered removed for

---

63. Koch v. Dyson, 448 N.Y.S.2d 698 (App. Div. 1982).

64. Iodice v. Architectural Access Bd., 676 N.E.2d 1130 (Mass. 1997).

65. Metromedia, Inc. v. City of San Diego, 453 U.S. 490 (1981) (describing billboards as "visual pollution," *Id.* at 561 (Burger, C.J., dissenting)). For a more complete discussion of aesthetic controls, see Robinson, *Environmental Regulation of Real Property*, ch.7 (Law Journal Press updated to 2022). Billboards and signage are specifically addressed in subch. 7.04.

66. Metromedia, Inc. v. City of San Diego, 453 U.S. 537 (1981).

67. Modjeska Sign Studios, Inc. v. Berle, 373 N.E.2d 255 (N.Y. 1977).

reasons of safety (as opposed to aesthetics) the owner need not be compensated, even if its investment in the billboard has not been recovered.[68]

A federal statute, the Highway Beautification Act,[69] was enacted in 1965 to encourage states and local governments to remove commercial billboards within 660 feet of interstate and other federally-financed highways. States failing to remove such billboards forfeited a proportion of their federal funding for roads. Under a 1978 amendment to that statute, however, billboard owners must be compensated for removal, whether or not such payment would be constitutionally necessary to avoid a taking claim.[70] One court has lessened the severity of this provision by ruling that compensation need not be in money if the billboard owner's investment has already been recovered at the time removal is mandated.[71]

Automobile junkyards are covered by a related Highway Beautification Act provision that requires states to adopt laws to screen such areas from view along highways or lose some federal highway funding.[72] There is a compensation provision similar to that for billboards.[73]

§ 11.08 Agricultural Lands

Owners of farmlands, particularly those close to cities or in prime vacation regions, are under substantial inducement to sell off to developers. Land is traditionally taxed at its highest and best use, so that a farm will often be assessed on the basis of the value of its land if it were to be subdivided for residential construction. This creates a powerful incentive to sell the land. State and local governments have responded by creating agricultural districts within which real property taxes are lowered as long as the land is farmed. A related device is the purchase by local governments of the development rights to farms. Once the land may no longer be developed for residential or commercial use, it may be taxed only as farmland. Conservation easements, discussed in § 11.09, may also serve this purpose.

Several federal statutes are designed to foster soil conservation. Under the Soil and Water Conservation Act,[74] the United States Department of Agriculture offers a variety of incentives to farms and ranches that conserve land, including the purchase by the United States government of easements to protect environmentally critical farmlands.

Other federal statutes specifically safeguard wetlands on farms and farmlands particularly subject to erosion. Most important from an environmental perspective are

---

68. *Id.*
69. 23 U.S.C. § 131.
70. 23 U.S.C. § 131(g).
71. Suffolk Outdoor Advertising Co. v. Town of Southampton, 455 N.E.2d 1245 (N.Y. 1983).
72. 23 U.S.C. § 136.
73. 23 U.S.C. § 131(b).
74. 16 U.S.C. §§ 2001–2009.

the so-called "sodbuster" and "swampbuster" laws.[75] Under these provisions, farmers who use lands especially likely to erode, or wetland areas, become ineligible for federal payments in support of agricultural activity. These laws, controversial when first enacted, have been effective in safeguarding sensitive areas from environmental damage. The sodbuster provisions are specifically aimed at preventing the widespread soil erosion that led to the dust bowl of the 1930s.

Another major federal endeavor, the Conservation Reserve Program, enables farmers to receive government funds for environmentally critical lands that they exclude, or reserve, from agricultural use.[76] A similar Wetlands Reserve Program furnishes payments to farmers who protect wetlands.[77]

§ 11.09 Conservation Easements and Land Trusts

An important and chiefly private means of land use control, the conservation easement, has emerged in recent decades. A conservation easement enables a landowner to convey the rights to develop a parcel to a not-for-profit group or government body. In exchange, the owner often receives tax benefits, and open space is protected.

At common law, most easements only "ran with the land" — that is, bound future purchasers — if the easement was "appurtenant," that is, benefiting an adjacent landowner.[78] The typical easement of this sort furnished access to an otherwise landlocked parcel. Except for easements in favor of railroads and public utilities, other easements that were not appurtenant were considered "easements in gross" and did not run with the land.[79]

Since a conservation easement would be valueless if it did not bind future owners of the burdened property, it was necessary to enact statutes to authorize conservation easements running with the land. Most states have done so.

Because, as noted in § 11.08, land is generally taxed at its highest and best use, a conservation easement reducing that use by conveying the owners' right to develop often lowers real property taxes greatly. The holder of a conservation easement, whether a land trust or other not-for-profit entity or a government, must agree not to develop the parcel.

Federal income tax deductions are also available when a conservation easement is given in perpetuity to a not-for-profit or governmental entity.[80] These deductions

---

75. 16 U.S.C. §§ 3811–3815, 3821–3824.

76. 16 U.S.C. §§ 3831–3836.

77. 16 U.S.C. §§ 3837–3837f.

78. *See* Schnuck Markets, Inc. v. Soffer, 572 N.E.2d 1169 (Ill. App. 1991), *appeal denied*, 580 N.E.2d 134 (1991); Russakoff v. Scruggs, 400 S.E.2d 529 (Va. 1991).

79. An "easement in gross" is owned by one other than an adjacent owner benefited by the easement. *See* O'Neill v. Williams, 527 A.2d 322 (Me. 1987).

80. 26 U.S.C. § 170(f)(3)(B)(iii), (h).

are measured by the difference in the value of the property with and without the right to develop it. To be deductible, the easement must be for conservation purposes, such as open space preservation, public recreation, or wildlife habitat.[81]

Conservation easements may be terminated, but only perpetual easements are deductible for income tax purposes. They may be enforced by the not-for-profit or governmental holder. A federal program exists for the purchase of conservation easements on farmland.[82]

Land trusts are the not-for-profit private entities that hold most conservation easements. They range from national organizations with expert staffs to local and regional trusts staffed by volunteers.

81. 26 U.S.C. § 170(h)(4)(A)(i)–(iv).
82. 7 U.S.C. § 1997.

Chapter 12

Energy Production and Mineral Extraction

§ 12.01 Solar Energy and Wind Power

[A] Background

Each form of energy production produces some environmental effects. Power plants fired by coal and oil, and to a lesser extent natural gas, emit air pollutants, and contribute to global warming, an issue discussed in § 13.02. Hydroelectric power, while free of air and water pollution, raises issues involving stream disturbance and interference with fisheries. These are described in § 6.03[C][4]. Nuclear energy triggers concerns as to radiation as well as water quality, dealt with in § 12.02.

For these reasons, and because of the finite supply of oil, and the need to import large quantities of it, along with the emerging acknowledgement correlating the combustion of fossil fuels with the acceleration of climate change, both private industry and government have begun to turn in recent decades to solar and wind power as sources of energy.

[B] Solar Energy

The use of solar energy began to receive serious consideration during the 1970s with the OPEC oil shortage. While the sun is the ultimate source of all energy, tapping solar power directly to generate electricity or heat is a recent concept that had to await the development of technology such as solar-powered fuel cells. It is infinitely renewable and pollution free.

To encourage research into and marketing of solar energy, federal laws have been enacted to provide incentives for consumers to turn to this source. The Energy Conservation and Production Act offers federally guaranteed loans for energy conservation projects, including solar energy.[1] The federal Solar Investment Tax Credit provides tax benefits for residential solar systems placed in service by the homeowner (i.e., not those systems merely leased by homeowners), as well as for qualifying commercial properties which install photovoltaic systems. The program, however, will expire in 2024 unless it is renewed by Congress.[2] Several states have also enacted similar laws providing for loans and tax inducements. Solar energy had lagged as a viable alternative fuel for several years, largely because oil and natural gas prices have remained relatively constant since the increases of the 1970s. The availability of lower cost natural gas produced by hydrofracking and of shale oil from locations within the country has also eased anxieties about foreign sources of oil during the early part of the 21st century. However, the growing urgency about the consequences of climate

---

1. 42 U.S.C. § 6881.

2. 26 U.S.C. § 48; *see* U.S. Department of Energy Office of Energy Efficiency & Renewable Energy, https://www.energy.gov/sites/prod/files/2021/02/f82/Guide%20to%20Investment%20Tax%20Credit %20Commercial%20Solar%20PV%20-%202021.pdf.

change, readily apparent in increasingly unstable climate patterns, melting glaciers and ice caps, and extreme weather events, has encouraged renewed research and development into photovoltaic cells and other sources of renewable energy that do not rely on carbon-emitting fossil fuels.

As the federal administration periodically stalled its efforts under the pressure of political lobbying, many states and municipalities took up the challenge of reducing their reliance on fossil fuels in many respects, including the greater use of increasingly efficient solar cells, and many citizens have incorporated solar energy into the energy mix by installing solar panels. Some utilities have even provided financial incentives to residences and businesses in regions where the electrical grid is strained by excessive use or an inadequate energy supply during hot summer months. Properties using solar facilities can reduce the demands on utility systems during these time periods and also reverse the flow of energy by, in effect, selling the energy generated by domestic solar systems back to the utility. Parking lots, landfills, public spaces and other areas across the country are being covered by solar installations, which can double in some of those locations as sun shields for the properties underneath. Limitations on the more extensive use of solar energy arises from the practical fact that energy is not generated when the sun doesn't shine, northern and chronically cloudy regions necessarily have reduced sun exposure, and there are difficulties with transmission of the energy over substantial distances and with battery or cell storage. However, the escalating interest in energy efficiency and availability, as well as the stated goal of many states and to a lesser extent the federal government to aim for zero emissions energy generation by specified dates, has impressively driven research and development in these areas. Aside from solely local installations for residences and businesses, some areas of the country, such as the Southwest, are ideal for mass generation of solar energy.

An unresolved legal issue regarding solar energy is whether a landowner has an enforceable right to sunlight. Some states have protected this right by statute, but even these statutes mandate a balance between the right to solar access and an adjacent owner's right to build. Under the statutes, some courts have held that blocking access to sunlight constitutes a private nuisance.[3] Without such statutes, courts using common law principles usually find no cause of action for deprivation of solar access.[4] The sole exception is when light is maliciously blocked, through the building of a "spite fence."[5] Some localities have specifically guaranteed solar access for new construction in their zoning laws.[6] In addition, easements and covenants may furnish a guarantee of access.

---

3. Prah v. Maretti, 321 N.W.2d 182 (Wis. 1982).

4. Fontainebleau Hotel Corp. v. Forty-five Twenty-five, Inc., 114 So. 2d 357 (Fla. App. 1959).

5. Musumeci v. Leonardo, 75 A.2d 175 (R.I. 1950).

6. See the Boulder, Colorado law discussed in Adrian J. Bradbrook, *Future Directions in Solar Access Protection*, 19 ENVTL. L. 167 (1988).

[C] Wind Power

Wind power is an ancient source of energy, which has driven windmills and wells for centuries. It has gained a new lease on life as a means of generating electricity in recent decades. Like solar energy, it is an environmentally benign, renewable energy source. The Wind Energy Systems Act furnishes federal funding for research and development as well as for demonstration projects.[7] The statute, enacted in 1980 but still current in 2022, focused on the period's imbalance between supply and demand, with the supply disproportionately produced by foreign sources, rather than on the current concerns for climate change. Nevertheless, it provides a template for the development of wind power. As with solar energy, wind power is theoretically endless, except when the wind doesn't blow. As with solar energy, there are practical, although increasingly resolvable, challenges arising from efficient transmission and the storage of excess electrical energy generated by wind, which makes some locations less than ideal for wind generation. However, many locations are ideal. Offshore facilities operating with mammoth sized turbines are being built or planned along maritime coastlines from which electrical currents can be transmitted by cable to shoreside facilities for further transmission. Other areas in the high plains and mountain west can also provide reliable wind energy. Wind farms are rapidly being permitted by local authorities, and turbines are being installed in greater quantities throughout the country.

As with solar power, landowners lack a common law right of access to wind. Easements and covenants are traditional tools that can be repurposed under more current law to achieve such access.[8] Some states and municipalities have used zoning and other laws for this purpose.[9]

One significant environmental drawback to the use of wind power is that high-speed windmills can kill numerous birds, especially when located on hill summits to capture the maximum amount of wind. In addition, windmills in residential areas can generate noise and, to some people, can seem unsightly. The ostensible aesthetic drawbacks have been the source of objections by some coastal residents with reference to offshore facilities, although many other residents similarly situated are unperturbed, so that this can best be described as a NIMBY issue with subjective aspects. By the third decade of the 21st century, engineering solutions are being devised to reduce potential auditory impacts as well as avian mortality. One possible partial solution to the latter is to ascertain which bird species frequent a location and the expected heights of their flights, and reduce the height of the turbines accordingly.

---

7. 42 U.S.C. §§ 9201–9213.

8. *See, e.g.,* Town Board, Town of Richmond, New York, Wind Energy Facilities Law.

9. *See* OR. REV. STAT. §§ 105.905 (wind energy easement appurtenant), 105.910 (for the requirements to create a wind energy easement). *See also* Windustry, Wind Energy Easement and Lease Agreements (Sept. 2005), at https://rvs.umn.edu/Uploads/EducationalMaterials/b602d53b-67d2-4b90-80f7-5c4acd777715.pdf.

§ 12.02 Nuclear Energy

[A] Atomic Energy Act

Nuclear energy has been a significant source of electric power for the past half century. Its use has been subject to regulation under the Atomic Energy Act,[10] enacted in 1954. The Act preempts state and local laws with regard to all matters dealing with radiation.[11] The extent of this preemption is examined in [E], *below*.

The Atomic Energy Act was originally administered by the United States Atomic Energy Commission. In 1974, largely due to concern over the dual (and perhaps ambivalent) role of the Commission in both promoting and regulating nuclear power, Congress created the Nuclear Regulatory Commission (NRC). This agency's functions are, as its name indicates, solely regulatory in nature. The former promotional activities of the Atomic Energy Commission were transferred to the Department of Energy and are no longer of consequence.

The NRC's jurisdiction under the Atomic Energy Act does not, however, extend to radioactive waste. That is controlled under separate statutes, discussed in [D], *below*.

[B] Licensing Power Plants

Because of the serious safety and environmental risks associated with nuclear power plants, they were historically governed by a two-step licensing procedure pursuant to the Atomic Energy Act. Applicants had to first obtain a construction permit containing a date for the completion of the facility.[12] The applicant then was required to seek an operating license.[13] The Act's standards for an operating license are substantially more severe.[14] A 1992 amendment allows the Commission to issue a combined construction and operating license.[15] Operating licenses must be affirmed by an Atomic Safety and Licensing Board within the NRC before a plant may commence operation.[16] The Act provides for temporary operating licenses under which a plant may test its facilities.[17]

Judicial review of NRC licensing determinations is "extremely limited" since the Act "is hallmarked by the amount of discretion granted the Commission in working to achieve the statute's ends."[18]

---

10. 42 U.S.C. §§ 2011–2297g-4.

11. 42 U.S.C. § 2021; *see* Northern States Power Co. v. Minnesota, 447 F.2d 1143 (8th Cir. 1971), *aff'd*, 405 U.S. 1035 (1972).

12. 42 U.S.C. § 2235(a).

13. *Id.*

14. Power Reactor Development Co. v. International Union of Electrical Workers, 367 U.S. 396 (1961).

15. 42 U.S.C. § 2235(b).

16. 42 U.S.C. § 2241; *see* Union of Concerned Scientists v. Atomic Energy Comm'n, 499 F.2d 1069 (D.C. Cir. 1974).

17. 42 U.S.C. § 2242.

18. Commonwealth of Mass. v. United States Nuclear Regulatory Comm'n, 878 F.2d 1516, 1523 (1st Cir. 1989) (citing Siegel v. Atomic Energy Comm'n, 400 F.2d 778, 783 (D.C. Cir. 1968)).

Note that licensing requires compliance with the National Environmental Policy Act (NEPA) (see Chapter 4), and courts have ruled that issues of security against terrorism must be considered as part of that process.[19]

NRC licensing only deals with radiation concerns. The need for, and location of, nuclear power plants are issues of state law. State power plant siting agencies typically hold joint hearings with the NRC in order to dispose of radiation and other issues as efficiently as possible. Licensing of nuclear power plants requires an environmental impact statement pursuant to the National Environmental Policy Act (NEPA), as discussed in Chapter 4. Since these facilities often discharge heated water used in their reactors, they can cause thermal pollution of waterways, a danger to fish, and may require permits under the Clean Water Act as described in §6.03.

Whether the disposal of nuclear waste generated by a power plant must be dealt with in licensing proceedings is a topic that has generated much controversy. A rule adopted by the NRC provides that waste issues need not be decided at licensing hearings. This rule was twice challenged: first as violative of NEPA, and then as arbitrarily and capriciously adopted. The Supreme Court rejected both challenges. It held that NEPA did not require the Commission to hold evidentiary (trial-type) hearings before adopting the waste rule.[20] Addressing the substance of the rule, the Court later held it to be well within the agency's broad discretion.[21] Nuclear waste disposal is now governed by separate statutes, discussed at [D], *below*.

By the third decade of the 21st century, many of these structures and operations are aging, which adds an additional factor to this zero-emission mode of generating regional electricity. New York's Indian Point nuclear power plant, which had started operations in 1962, ended operations on April 30, 2021. From 2017 until the shutdown, New York's electric power generation resulted substantially from the combustion of natural gas, while nuclear power, initially stable, had been undergoing an incremental downturn after the second of three reactors was shut down on April 30, 2020, until the final reactor was deactivated a year later. Although the facility's owner had been seeking a 20-year renewal of the operating licenses for the two reactors still in operation after their 2013 and 2015 expirations, New York objected on environmental and public safety grounds. The facility was located 25 miles north of New York City's midtown, and the metropolitan region is densely populated, which added an element of risk which was a major consideration for denial of relicensing for the aging facility.[22] Similar licensing issues may arise with other aging nuclear facilities around the country. Meanwhile, the construction of new nuclear facilities or the significant retrofitting of older ones may meet political opposition in many locations on the basis of environmental

---

19. *See* San Luis Obispo Mothers for Peace v. Nuclear Regulatory Commission, 449 F.3d 1016 (9th Cir. 2006), *cert. denied*, 127 S. Ct. 1124 (2007).

20. Vermont Yankee Nuclear Power Corp. v. Natural Resources Defense Council, Inc., 435 U.S. 519 (1978).

21. Baltimore Gas & Elec. Co. v. Natural Resources Defense Council, Inc., 462 U.S. 87 (1983).

22. U.S. Energy Information Administration, at https://www.eia.gov/today.

considerations, safety concerns underscored by catastrophes involving nuclear re-actions in other parts of the world, and practical problems involving the disposal of nuclear wastes. Although the NRC's licensing decisions enjoy significant judicial deference as is noted above, that does not imply that NRC decision-making for aging or poorly located nuclear facilities is impervious to state and local concerns about emerging environmental and public safety risks.

[C] Evacuation Plans

The risk of a meltdown or other catastrophic accident at a nuclear power plant was initially viewed by the Atomic Energy Commission and its successor, the NRC, as minimal. A 1975 Reactor Safety Study by the Commission led to issuance of the Rasmussen Report,[23] discounting the likelihood of such an accident. Four years later, however, a near-meltdown occurred at the Three Mile Island nuclear facility in Pennsylvania. This led to the NRC's repudiation of the Rasmussen Report and imposition of important new safety requirements for both existing and future power plants.

Prime among these was the mandate for an approved emergency response plan, demonstrating how best to evacuate the area within 10 miles of each nuclear facility in the event of a significant incident threatening safety. Evacuation plans must be approved by the Federal Emergency Management Agency (FEMA) as well as the NRC.[24] FEMA was selected for this task because of its expertise in evacuating residents threatened by floods and hurricanes. In reviewing the adequacy of evacuation plans, the courts once again defer greatly to the expertise of the NRC, and have upheld an NRC decision to restart a nuclear plan despite FEMA's rejection of a plan.[25]

Evacuation plans ordinarily presuppose the cooperation of local police and other public safety personnel. If this cooperation is not forthcoming, a utility may submit its own evacuation plan,[26] although approval of such a plan is likely to prove more difficult.

[D] Radioactive Waste Disposal

[1] Nuclear Waste Policy Act

The serious safety and health issues posed by the need to properly dispose of nuclear waste were not originally given adequate recognition by government or the utilities constructing and operating power plants. As noted in [B], *above*, attempts to mandate consideration of waste disposal in licensing nuclear power plants were

---

23. U.S. Nuclear Regulatory Comm'n, Wash-1400, Nureg-75/014, Reactor Safety Study: An As-sessment of Accident Risks in U.S. Commercial Nuclear Power Plants, app. VI (1975).

24. 10 C.F.R. Part 50, App. E.

25. Commonwealth of Mass. v. United States Nuclear Regulatory Comm'n, 878 F.2d 1516 (1st Cir. 1989).

26. 10 C.F.R. § 50.47(c)(1)(iii).

rebuffed by the NRC and the courts. Although a few disposal facilities existed, there was no comprehensive regulatory scheme for ensuring the safe disposition of nuclear waste. The problem is magnified immeasurably by the prodigious length of time this waste remains hazardous — often for thousands of years.

In 1983 Congress acted, adopting the Nuclear Waste Policy Act.[27] High-level waste, defined to include spent nuclear fuel and other highly radioactive material, was to be deposited in sites to be recommended by the Secretary of Energy in consultation with the governors of the states containing those sites.[28] The President was to choose sites from this list, subject to the approval of the state's governor.[29] Congress was empowered to override a state's veto.[30]

Predictably, state governors early signaled their intention to disapprove sites within their borders. To break the impasse, Congress amended the Act in 1987 to effectively mandate selection of a site at Yucca Mountain, Nevada.[31] The gubernatorial veto provision was repealed. Selection does, however, require an environmental impact statement as well as a variety of tests and scientific findings.[32] The provision for Congressional overturning of a state's objection remains in the Act,[33] although, as noted, the state governor's power to veto a site was eliminated. It should also be noted, however, that the 1983 Supreme Court decision in *Immigration & Naturalization Service v. Chadha*[34] casts serious doubt on the power of Congress to override such a decision without Presidential approval. That decision set aside a similar provision that authorized either House of Congress to overturn a stay of deportation of an undocumented alien granted by the Attorney General. The Court held such provisions violated the Constitution's separation of powers by enabling Congress to, in effect, legislate while bypassing the required passage of a bill by both Houses and signature by the President.

As one might expect, Nevada has challenged the selection of Yucca Mountain. One court has ruled that the federal legislation did not deprive Nevada of rights of sovereignty under the Tenth Amendment or violate the Privileges and Immunities Clause.[35]

Other provisions of the Act establish an interim storage program at reactors themselves, where most high-level waste is currently being stored, or at storage facilities.[36]

---

27. 42 U.S.C. §§ 10101–10226.

28. 42 U.S.C. §§ 10101(12), 10132(b).

29. 42 U.S.C. § 10136.

30. 42 U.S.C. § 10135(c).

31. 42 U.S.C. § 10134; *see also* Pub. L. 107-200, 116 Stat. 735 (2002) (Joint Resolution Approving the Site at Yucca Mountain).

32. 42 U.S.C. § 10134.

33. 42 U.S.C. § 10135(c).

34. 462 U.S. 919 (1983).

35. State of Nevada v. Watkins, 914 F.2d 1545 (9th Cir. 1990), *cert. denied*, 499 U.S. 906 (1991). The Privileges and Immunities Clause is at U.S. Const. art. IV, § 2; *see also* Nuclear Energy Institute, Inc. v. Environmental Protection Agency, 373 F.3d 1251 (D.C. Cir. 2004).

36. 42 U.S.C. §§ 10152–10155.

Finally, the Act provides for "monitored retrievable storage": storage, under Department of Energy supervision, of spent fuel and other waste that can be retrieved for reprocessing into usable fuel.[37] The reprocessing of nuclear fuel is quite controversial, and the courts had earlier halted such a program for failure to comply with NEPA.[38] A major concern is that reprocessing spent fuel instead of storing it may render it available to terrorists.

[2] Low Level Radioactive Waste Policy Act

Low level nuclear waste, in contrast to high-level waste, is dealt with under a separate statute. This material, consisting of contaminated clothing, tools, and the like (as well as certain radioactive medical waste), is essentially left to state regulation. The Low Level Radioactive Waste Policy Act[39] encourages states to establish repositories for this material, or, with Congressional approval, to enter into interstate compacts to do so. Most states have joined such compacts. However, those that fail to either submit a disposal site for the NRC's approval or to enter a compact become subject to draconian provisions. By 1993, those states were required to take title to all low-level waste generated by any person in that state, and to assume legal liability for all damage caused by that waste.

That provision was successfully attacked as violative of the state sovereignty guarded by the Tenth Amendment to the Constitution, reserving to the states all powers not conferred on Congress (see discussion in § 1.05[D]). In *New York v. United States*,[40] the Supreme Court ruled the take-title provision invalid under the Tenth Amendment, since it "would 'commandeer' state governments into the service of federal regulatory purposes...."[41] Congress could, the Court held, regulate low-level waste directly, as it did high-level waste. Or it could leave it to the states. As a third option, Congress could induce states to regulate such waste by offering federal funds as an incentive, or by threatening to withhold them if states failed to act. But it could not force the states to control this waste on pain of thrusting legal liability on them.

[3] Transporting Radioactive Waste

Transporting radioactive waste is governed by the Hazardous Materials Transportation Act,[42] under which the United States Department of Transportation has adopted strict rules that preempt state law.[43]

---

37. 42 U.S.C. § 10161.
38. Natural Resources Defense Council, Inc. v. Nuclear Regulatory Comm'n, 539 F.2d 824 (2d Cir. 1976).
39. 42 U.S.C. §§ 2021b–2021j.
40. 505 U.S. 144 (1992).
41. *Id.*
42. 49 U.S.C. §§ 5101–5128.
43. Washington State Bldg. & Const. Trades Council v. Spellman, 518 F. Supp. 928 (E.D. Wash. 1981), *aff'd*, 684 F.2d 627 (9th Cir. 1982).

[E] State Controls and Preemption Issues

As noted in [A], *above*, the Atomic Energy Act preempts state and local laws relating to radioactivity. Thus, state statutes designed to control radiation emissions[44] or the shipment of nuclear materials[45] are invalid.

However, a California moratorium on constructing new nuclear power plants until the issue of radioactive waste disposal is resolved was upheld by the Supreme Court in *Pacific Gas & Electric Co. v. State Energy Resources Conservation and Development Commission.*[46] The Court ruled that the moratorium was not a preempted attempt to regulate nuclear waste, but rather a valid state decision addressed to the economic aspects of furnishing electric power to its citizens, a traditional state power. The Court reasoned that the increasing costs of nuclear waste storage and disposal thrust added expenses on California consumers, a subject the state had ample authority to regulate.

The Atomic Energy Act's preemption, however, bars a state from directing utilities to furnish a bond to cover their costs of decontaminating nuclear power plants before shutting them down.[47]

[F] Liability Issues

Tort liability for damage and injuries caused by a major nuclear incident is governed by the Price-Anderson Act.[48] That 1957 statute provides for strict liability up to a $560 million limit, but bars any recovery for greater amounts. The indemnification is to be furnished in part by the United States, and in part by private insurance. The statute does, however, explicitly authorize Congress to act to protect the public in excess of the Act's monetary limit — a power Congress would doubtless enjoy anyway.

The Act was challenged by a citizen group as a denial of property without due process of law, on the ground that it bars recovery for damages above its cap. This argument was rejected by the Supreme Court, which held that Congress could validly "remove the economic impediments in order to stimulate the private development of electric energy by nuclear power while simultaneously providing the public compensation in the event of a catastrophic nuclear incident."[49] Punitive damages are available in a suit under the Price-Anderson Act, one court has held.[50]

---

44. Northern States Power Co. v. Minnesota, 447 F.2d 1143 (8th Cir. 1971), *aff'd*, 405 U.S. 1035 (1972).

45. Washington State Bldg. & Const. Trades Council v. Spellman, 518 F. Supp. 928 (E.D. Wash. 1981).

46. 461 U.S. 190 (1983).

47. United Nuclear Corp. v. Cannon, 696 F.2d 141 (1st Cir. 1982).

48. 42 U.S.C. § 2210.

49. Duke Power Co. v. Carolina Envtl. Study Group, 438 U.S. 59, 83 (1978).

50. *In re* Three Mile Island Litigation, 605 F. Supp. 778 (M.D. Pa. 1985), *vacated on other grounds sub nom.* Kiick v. Metropolitan Edison Co., 784 F.2d 490 (3d Cir. 1986).

Damages for other than major nuclear incidents are governed by state law. The courts have rejected claims that state tort actions for compensatory damages are preempted by the Atomic Energy Act's provisions giving exclusive jurisdiction over the regulation of radiation to the NRC.[51] Suits for punitive damages arguably raise a closer question, but in a 5–4 decision in 1984, the Supreme Court held, in *Silkwood v. Kerr-McGee Corp.*,[52] that such actions were likewise not preempted by the Act. The Court ruled that punitive damages, although designed in part to deter future misconduct, were not sufficiently regulatory in nature to constitute an attempt to regulate radiation at the state level.

State-law nuisance actions seeking injunctions, however, have been found to be preempted by the Act, since the purpose of injunctive relief (as opposed to damages) is essentially regulatory.[53]

Actions against the United States under the Federal Tort Claims Act involving exposure to nuclear radiation have been unsuccessful, due to that Act's exemption from liability for discretionary acts of government officials. Thus, the failure of federal employees to warn of risks of exposure to radiation has been found to be discretionary, and therefore exempt from liability.[54]

However, suits against private defendants for damages due to leaks from storage of nuclear materials at governmental facilities have been successful.[55]

§ 12.03 Geothermal Energy

Geothermal energy, like solar and wind power (see § 12.01), has potential as a pollution-free and renewable source. Geothermal energy is steam from underground or underwater sites. The Ocean Thermal Energy Conversion Research, Development, and Demonstration Act[56] provides for federally-financed pilot projects. The related Ocean Thermal Energy Conversion Act[57] authorizes the National Oceanic and Atmospheric Administration, a division of the Department of Commerce, to license ocean thermal energy facilities in United States waters. Despite this legislation, geothermal power has hardly started to become a significant energy source.

---

51. McKay v. United States, 703 F.2d 464 (10th Cir. 1983).
52. 464 U.S. 238 (1984).
53. Brown v. Kerr-McGee Corp., 767 F.2d 1234 (7th Cir. 1985), *cert. denied*, 475 U.S. 1066 (1986).
54. Begay v. United States, 768 F.2d 1059 (9th Cir. 1985).
55. Cook v. Rockwell Intl. Corp., 273 F. Supp. 2d 1175 (D. Colo. 2006).
56. 42 U.S.C. §§ 9001–9009.
57. 42 U.S.C. §§ 9101–9168.

§ 12.04 Coal and Mineral Surface Mining

[A] Surface Mining Control and Reclamation Act

[1] Act Needed to Supplement State Controls

Surface mining, or strip mining, has largely replaced the traditional pit mining that prevailed for centuries. The advent of large-scale earth-moving equipment has made surface mining for coal and other minerals economically feasible. Although it avoids the hazards to health and safety that plagued pit mining, surface mining involves numerous serious environmental concerns. Removing huge quantities of soil, grass, and other vegetation, unless properly controlled, leads to erosion, landslides, the silting of rivers and streams, and the loss of valuable farmlands.

While state legislation has purported to regulate surface mining for decades, it was generally not effective and resulted in scant reduction in the environmental damage caused by the practice. For these reasons, Congress enacted the Surface Mining Control and Reclamation Act[58] in 1977. This statute empowers the Secretary of the Interior to regulate surface mining for coal, and particularly to ensure the reclamation of agricultural and other valuable land. Note that the Act only deals with coal mining. Surface mining for other minerals continues to be regulated by state law alone.

[2] Act Works in Tandem with State Regulation

Reflecting its goals, the Surface Mining Control and Reclamation Act's statement of purpose includes establishing "a nationwide program to protect society and the environment from the adverse effects of surface coal mining," assuring that land is reclaimed "as contemporaneously as possible" and that surface mining occur only where reclamation is feasible.[59]

The Act creates an Office of Surface Mining Reclamation and Enforcement within the Department of the Interior, headed by a director appointed by the President.[60] The Secretary of the Interior, "acting through the Office," may adopt regulations to control surface mining and approve or disapprove state programs.[61] States may control surface mining pursuant to a federally-approved plan. To be approved, a plan must contain sanctions for violations, proof of adequate state personnel, funding and enforcement, and a procedure for designating lands unsuitable for surface mining.[62] When a state has no federally-approved program, the Secretary of the Interior is to promulgate a regulatory program and enforce it.[63] However, state laws are not preempted unless they are inconsistent with the Act.[64]

---

58. 30 U.S.C. §§ 1201–1328.
59. 30 U.S.C. § 1202.
60. 30 U.S.C. § 1211(a), (b).
61. 30 U.S.C. § 1211(c).
62. 30 U.S.C. § 1253.
63. 30 U.S.C. § 1254.
64. 30 U.S.C. § 1255.

[3] Act Requires Reclamation and Restoring of Land

Permits are necessary for surface mining under either a federal or state program, and require a reclamation plan as well as liability insurance.[65] The Act sets forth detailed environmental performance standards governing restoration of land and topsoil in particular, including the contours to be restored and the disposal of spoil. Prime farmlands must be reclaimed under standards adopted by the Secretary of Agriculture.[66] Violations may result in the imposition of civil penalties by the Secretary of the Interior, cessation orders, and criminal punishment for willful violations.[67] In addition, the Act contains a citizen suit provision,[68] which may be used to enforce a state statute as well as the federal law.[69]

Under the Act, the Secretary of the Interior is to adopt standards for surface mining on federal lands.[70]

Suits have been brought to enjoin the practice of mountaintop mining, involving the removal of hilltops, causing spoil to pollute streams, as well as visual impacts. However, the courts have been reluctant to enjoin this activity thus far.[71] The Secretary may delegate authority over federal lands to a state.[72]

[4] Act Upheld as Valid Exercise of Congressional Power

The Surface Mining Control and Reclamation Act was challenged soon after its enactment as being beyond the federal government's commerce power, an interference with the states' reserved powers under the Tenth Amendment, and a de facto taking. See the discussion of these issues in §§ 1.04 and 1.05[C] and [D]. The Supreme Court upheld the Act in all respects, holding that the impacts of surface mining on agriculture, navigable rivers, and other aspects of the national economy justified Congressional legislation. It went on to rule that a de facto taking claim would have to await specific facts showing a deprivation of all reasonable use, and would not warrant a facial attack on the Act.[73]

---

65. 30 U.S.C. §§ 1257, 1258.

66. 30 U.S.C. § 1265(b)(7).

67. 30 U.S.C. §§ 1268, 1271.

68. 30 U.S.C. § 1270.

69. Molinary v. Powell Mountain Coal Co., 125 F.3d 231 (4th Cir. 1997), *cert. denied*, 522 U.S. 1118 (1998). *But see* Bragg v. Robertson, 248 F.3d 275 (4th Cir. 2001), *cert. denied*, 534 U.S. 1113 (2002) (citizen suit against state under Surface Mining Act barred by Eleventh Amendment).

70. 30 U.S.C. § 1273.

71. Kentuckians for the Commonwealth v. Rivenburgh, 317 F.3d 425 (4th Cir. 2003); Bragg v. Robertson, 248 F.3d 275 (4th Cir. 2001), *cert. denied*, 534 U.S.1113 (2002).

72. National Wildlife Federation v. Hodel, 839 F.2d 694 (D.C. Cir. 1988).

73. Hodel v. Virginia Surface Mining & Reclamation Ass'n, 452 U.S. 264 (1981); Hodel v. Indiana, 452 U.S. 314 (1981).

[B] Laws to Prevent Subsidence of Surface Lands

Traditional pit mining has long been the subject of state legislation to prevent subsidence — the caving-in of surface lands when the coal or other minerals have been removed from below. In 1922, a Pennsylvania statute prohibiting subsurface mining under a dwelling (unless the house was the property of the owner of the underground coal), in order to prevent subsidence, was set aside by the Supreme Court. In *Pennsylvania Coal Co. v. Mahon*,[74] a leading case in de facto taking law, the Court, by Justice Holmes, held that since this statute terminated the mining rights of the subsurface owner entirely, it deprived that owner of all reasonable use, and constituted a de facto taking. *See* § 1.05[C].

However, a 1987 Supreme Court decision, *Keystone Bituminous Coal Association v. DeBenedictis*,[75] sustained a statute designed to prevent subsidence that allowed subsurface owners to mine half the underground coal beneath a house. That fact made all the difference, for the statute did not deny the subsurface owner all reasonable use. In addition, the Court noted, the record contained far more public justification for the act, explicitly enacted "to protect the public interest in health, the environment, and the fiscal integrity of the area,"[76] than was present in *Pennsylvania Coal*.

§ 12.05 Synthetic Fuels

[A] Government Sponsorship of Alternative Fuel Research

Concern over climate change stemming from the use of fossil fuels derived from coal and oil (see § 13.02) has spurred interest in developing alternative fuels such as ethanol, which is produced from corn, sugar and similar substances that do not create carbon dioxide. Earlier, the oil importation crisis of the 1970s that fostered increased interest in solar energy and wind and geothermal power (see §§ 12.01, 12.03) also ignited proposals to develop synthetic fuels to replace oil.

Synthetic fuels were first used in Germany during World War I. The easy availability of petroleum products acted as a disincentive to further research in this area until the OPEC oil shortage of the early 1970s. The dramatic rise in prices and supply difficulties of that period, when Middle Eastern oil was largely withheld from the market for a time, generated new interest in synthetic fuels.

The late 1970s witnessed a dispute over whether government or private industry should develop synthetic fuels and whether this development ought to be exempt from environmental regulation. Some argued that research and development by the

---

74. 260 U.S. 393 (1922).
75. 480 U.S. 470 (1987).
76. *Id.*

United States government would eliminate the profit motive and lead to more efficient and cheaper synthetic fuels. Others objected to the use of public funds for this essentially private purpose and contended that private corporations would be both more appropriate and more efficient. Similarly, some contended the need to develop and market such fuels warranted exempting these projects from federal and state environmental control, while others stoutly resisted what they saw as a dangerous precedent for undermining environmental regulation.

In the end Congress compromised. In 1980, it created a United States Synthetic Fuels Corporation, which was to receive subsidies from the United States Department of Energy.[77] The Fuels Corporation was to be subject to environmental impact review under the National Environmental Policy Act (NEPA), discussed in Chapter 4, to the same extent as federally-financed private projects.[78] However, the energy crisis soon eased. Reception for the synthetic fuels program was unenthusiastic, and the program was terminated in 1986.[79]

[B] Federal Subsidies for Biomass Energy and Ethanol

A more enduring program than the Synthetic Fuels Program, also enacted in 1980, allocates a variety of federal subsidies for biomass energy and for alcohol-derived fuels, then known as "gasohol." The term "ethanol" has largely replaced gasohol in common parlance. Portions of the Energy Security Act govern these areas of energy research.[80] The Act provides for federally-insured loans, loan and price guarantees and federal purchases, along with direct financial aid.

Biomass fuel is defined as fuel produced by converting agricultural crops and wastes, wood, animal waste, or municipal waste into energy.[81] The Secretary of Agriculture and Secretary of Energy are to draw up plans to maximize biomass energy production. Ethanol, an alcohol product extracted from grain, is highlighted under the Act.[82] The statute provides for insured loans by the Secretary of Agriculture, and loan guarantees by both the Secretary of Agriculture, in the case of ethanol, and the Secretary of Energy, in the case of biomass using aquatic plants. Other forms of biomass, such as wood wastes, may be the subject of loan guarantees by either agency.[83]

Other provisions authorize the two secretaries to purchase biomass energy for use by federal agencies, and to furnish financial assistance to biomass energy producers.[84]

---

77. Former 42 U.S.C. §§ 8701–8795 (terminated by Pub. L. 99-272, Title VII, Subtitle E, Apr. 7, 1986, 100 Stat. 144).
78. Former 42 U.S.C. § 8743.
79. *See* Pub. L. 99-272, Title VII, Subtitle E, Apr. 7, 1986, 100 Stat. 144.
80. 42 U.S.C. §§ 8801–8871.
81. 42 U.S.C. § 8802(2), (3).
82. 42 U.S.C. § 8812.
83. 42 U.S.C. § 8812.
84. 42 U.S.C. §§ 8816, 8817.

In addition, federal loans are available to help construct municipal waste energy projects, along with price supports for such projects.[85]

Using municipal solid waste to generate energy through incineration has, however, raised serious environmental and public health concerns relating to hazardous air emissions and disposal of the ash (see § 7.03[B][4]). As a result, far fewer waste-burning incinerators have been built than were expected when this Act was passed in 1980.

The Act also encourages the use of ethanol by requiring a Presidential executive order mandating its use in federal motor vehicles "where available at reasonable prices and in reasonable quantities."[86] The executive order, issued by President Carter in 1981, called for ethanol as an "acceptable substitute motor fuel" but only "whenever feasible."[87] In fact, few if any government vehicles have been equipped for ethanol.

[C] Compressed Natural Gas, Electric, and Hydrogen Powered Vehicles

Pursuant to the Clean Air Act, as discussed in § 5.04, the automotive industry is obligated to develop a low-emission vehicle, and in some states, a zero-emission vehicle. These vehicles will almost certainly be powered by either compressed natural gas (CNG) or electricity. New Zealand and Brazil led the world in the use of CNG, and in the United States and abroad, many delivery trucks and metropolitan buses are already CNG-fueled.

Electric-powered vehicles increasingly are seen as a viable alternative to traditional gasoline powered vehicles, which have been long delayed by the lack of a battery powerful enough to operate for extended distances without being recharged. Under a 1976 statute, federal funds are available for research and development of electric vehicles[88] and the federal government has occasionally offered tax credits for their purchase. Interestingly, electric vehicles have been around for decades and initially competed with internal combustible engines in what was then a small market compared to today, but the limitations on battery life doomed the early industry. Nevertheless, by the third decade of the 21st century, electric vehicles are gaining market share, although the purchase prices can still be high. An important factor will be the widespread installation of charging stations around the country on par with the historic reliance on gasoline stations for traditional vehicles. The Biden Administration's Build Back Better proposed legislation, not enacted as of this writing, anticipates installing 550,000 charging stations around the country. This, of course, could be costly at the outset even if the transition to electric vehicles might promise significant economic advantages to drivers and to the nation on the back end, and the legislative outcome, which is manifesting significant resistance, cannot be ascertained at this time.

---

85. 42 U.S.C. §§ 8832, 8834.
86. 42 U.S.C. § 8871.
87. Exec. Order No. 12, 261, 46 Fed. Reg. 2023 (1981), reprinted in 42 U.S.C. § 8871.
88. 15 U.S.C. §§ 2501–2514.

One can expect that with the investment of greater resources in the industry, and the increased convenience of using electric vehicles, sales growth will drive down prices. However, the environmental benefits might reflect in part a mere shifting of some of the environmental costs. Electric vehicles, in addition to limitations on their range, have the drawback that the current they use must be generated at a power plant, so that the pollution may merely be transferred from the exhaust systems of gasoline powered vehicles to the power plant itself. This, then, circles back to improving the environmental performance of utilities. Hence, as with some other proposals for generating energy, there are some tradeoffs in terms of environmental impacts, although a net reduction of polluting emissions does provide environmental benefits along with benefits to public health as air pollution is ameliorated.

Hybrid vehicles, where energy alternates between gasoline combustion and electrical power generated by the vehicle itself as it drives on gas, have become a popular option in large part because of their impressive fuel economy.

Hydrogen-fueled vehicles, although not yet a market participant, appear to be totally pollution-free. In addition, hydrogen is in virtually limitless supply. In a hydrogen-fueled vehicle, water is first divided into its component elements, hydrogen and oxygen, using electricity derived from solar power. The energy released by the reaction between hydrogen and oxygen in turn powers a fuel cell, producing electric power to drive a motor. The federal statute furnishing funding for research into electric vehicles defines them broadly enough to encompass fuel cell-powered vehicles, including hydrogen-fueled cars as well.[89]

§ 12.06 Energy Conservation

[A] Automotive Fuel Efficiency

The 1970s oil shortage, now receding from the public's memory, nevertheless had an environmental benefit with the enactment of the Energy Policy and Conservation Act. The congressional motivation was that of national security, with the realization that our reliance on oil tethered the United States to unstable areas of the world. Yet, by empowering federal agencies to foster improved energy efficiency, the Act led the nation on a path towards reducing its use of oil and consequently emissions reductions, even if indirectly. Of course, those reductions were on a per unit basis, so that national emissions reductions could be adversely offset as Americans put more cars and other vehicles on the road. Nevertheless, the Act and related regulatory policies drove industry innovations which, with incrementally escalating emissions reductions, can achieve aggregate environmental benefits over time.

Automobiles, both domestic and imported, initially were subject to average fuel economy standards, set by statute at 27.5 miles per gallon for passenger cars manu-

89. 15 U.S.C. § 2502(4).

factured after 1984.[90] Since then, the fuel economy standards have undergone numerous revisions as applied to successive model years, as is discussed in §5.04[B].

The Corporate Average Fuel Economy (CAFE) standards impose average fuel economies for each automobile and truck fleet which vehicle manufacturers must achieve for specified model years.[91] EPA establishes the methodology for testing vehicle technologies and provides the fuel economy data that since 1984 has been used by the Department of Energy to publish its annual Fuel Economy Guide. The Department of Transportation, acting through its National Highway Traffic and Safety Administration (NHTSA), administers and enforces the CAFE program. As the CAFE standards are progressively raised, each fleet must become more fuel efficient. In 2012, CAFE standards for cars and light trucks (i.e., less than 8,500 pounds) for model years 2017 to 2021 required average fleet fuel economies ranging from 40.3 to 41 miles per gallon, rising to 46.7 miles per gallon for model year 2025. A reduction of the CAFE standards to 40.4 miles per gallon for model years 2021 to 2026 during the Trump Administration[92] was repealed on December 21, 2021 by the Biden Administration.[93] Further increases for model years 2027–2030 for cars and light trucks are presently under review.[94] An interesting result is that automobile manufacturers have realized competitive advantages to not only comply with enhanced efficiency standards but to acquiesce in even stricter standards, presumably because the particular company can better achieve those goals than national and international competitors. General Motors, in particular, has indicated that it will be carbon neutral by 2040.

"Non-passenger autos," including sport utility vehicles and the like, are outside of this provision. The Secretary of Transportation is empowered to set fuel economy standards for those vehicles, and has set considerably lower averages.[95]

The Act contains civil penalties for violation, which the Secretary of Transportation may impose.[96] State fuel economy standards are preempted unless identical to the federal standards.[97] Nevertheless, California has long benefited from a federal waiver that allowed that state to maintain stricter fuel efficiency and emission standards for cars manufactured or sold in the state. As a practical matter, considering California's

---

90. 49 U.S.C. §32902(b).

91. *See* U.S. Department of Transportation, "Corporate Average Fuel Economy (CAFE) Standards," at https://www.transportation.gov/mission/sustainability/corporate-average-fuel-economy-cafe-standards. For passenger vehicle standards, see 49 C.F.R. Part 531. For light truck standards, see 49 C.F.R. Part 533.

92. https://www.epa.gov/regulations-emissions-vehicles-and-engines/safer-affordable-fuel-efficient-safe-vehicles-final-rule.

93. Executive Order 13990. *See* NHTSA, "USDOT Proposes Improved Fuel Economy Standards for MY 2024–2026 Passenger Cars and Light Trucks," at https://www.nhtsa.gov/press-releases/fuel-economy-standards.

94. NHTSA, *id.*

95. 49 U.S.C. §32902(a); *see* 40 C.F.R. §600.002-85.

96. 49 U.S.C. §§32912, 32914.

97. 49 U.S.C. §32919.

considerable impact on the automobile industry and the unlikelihood that the industry will manufacture or sell cars with diverse emission standards, California's standards have effectively set national goals.

[B] Appliance Efficiency

Both electric and gas-powered consumer products, including refrigerators, air conditioners, furnaces, ranges and the like, are subject to labeling standards imposed by the Federal Trade Commission under the Energy Policy and Conservation Act.[98] This labeling is designed to enable consumers to choose appliances that are more energy-efficient than competing items. These products must also achieve substantive energy conservation standards spelled out in the Act. The Secretary of Energy is empowered to amend the standards.[99] These provisions generally preempt state regulations of products covered by the federal statute.[100] Violations may result in civil penalties imposed by the Federal Trade Commission or Secretary of Energy, as well as injunctions.[101] The Act also has a citizen suit provision.[102]

[C] Electricity Conservation

[1] Public Utility Regulatory Policies Act

In addition to the efficiency provisions for consumer appliances described in [B], *above,* Congress has legislated on a broader scale to encourage efficiency and conservation in electricity usage. The Public Utility Regulatory Policies Act (PURPA),[103] contains a variety of provisions aimed at fostering conservation.

Electric rates and service for many years favored greater use of electric power, rather than conservation. Rates per unit of electricity often declined with additional use — the "declining block" rate system. This led not only to increased use of oil and other fuels to operate power plants, but also to the construction of additional power plants with all their capital expense and environmental impacts (discussed in § 11.06).

Yet regulating the furnishing of electricity is a traditional state function. Rates and conditions of service are determined by state public utility commissions. How could Congress foster conservation-oriented controls at the state level without preempting the field completely, overturning decades of state jurisdiction? To order the states to legislate would likely run afoul of the Tenth Amendment, which reserves to the states powers not furnished to Congress by the Constitution. (See § 1.05[D], as well as the discussion of *New York v. United States* in § 12.02[D][2].)

---

98. 42 U.S.C. §§ 6292, 6294.
99. 42 U.S.C. § 6295.
100. 42 U.S.C. § 6297.
101. 42 U.S.C. §§ 6303, 6304.
102. 42 U.S.C. § 6305.
103. 16 U.S.C. §§ 824a-1 to -4, 2601–2645.

The approach Congress adopted in PURPA was to require state regulatory agencies to "consider" a series of standards designed to foster efficient use of electricity and conservation. The state agencies are then to determine "whether or not it is appropriate to implement [these standards] to carry out the purposes of" PURPA.[104] The Act makes clear that in the end, states need not adopt the standards. But they must provide public notice and hearings before deciding whether to adopt them, and must furnish to the Secretary of Energy and the public their reasons for failing to do so.[105] In practice, many states have adopted the standards and shifted to conservation-based rate structures.

These standards include requiring electric rates to reflect the actual costs of providing power, abandoning the use of declining block rates, and using rates varying with the time of day and season, to encourage off-peak use, and to reduce the need for new generating stations to supply power for peak usage.[106] In addition, states are to consider barring electric utilities from thrusting onto their consumers the costs of promotional advertising.[107]

The constitutionality of PURPA's approach was sustained by the Supreme Court in *Federal Energy Regulatory Commission v. Mississippi*.[108] The Court rejected claims that Congress had interfered with the states' reserved powers under the Tenth Amendment, and noted that Congress could have preempted the field entirely, had it chosen to do so.

[2] Fostering Small Power Producers

One major portion of PURPA in which Congress did directly mandate a significant shift in electricity policy deals with "cogeneration"—the generation of both electricity and steam heat or other forms of energy—and small power producers. Many electricity providers historically sought to prevent consumers from generating their own power by refusing to supply power to such small producers when needed, or imposing a heavy surcharge for that power. Since dams, windmills, and other small generators may not produce power every day, this created a major disincentive to small producers. Similarly, utilities often refused to purchase excess power produced by a small user, or paid only a pittance for it.

PURPA removes these disincentives to independent power producers by requiring utilities to sell electricity to them, and purchase electricity from them, at a "just and reasonable" rate.[109] This rate is defined as a rate that does not exceed the incremental cost—that is, the cost to the utility of producing that same amount of power. The Supreme Court ruled that the Federal Energy Regulatory Commission, which implements this provision, acted reasonably when it further defined the maximum rate

---

104. 16 U.S.C. § 2621.
105. 16 U.S.C. §§ 2621, 2626.
106. 16 U.S.C. § 2621(d).
107. 16 U.S.C. § 2623(b)(5).
108. 456 U.S. 742 (1982).
109. 16 U.S.C. §§ 824a-3(a)–(c).

to equal the utility's "full avoided costs" — that is, the costs of generating that power that the utility avoided.[110]

Unlike the earlier PURPA provisions, the provision relating to small producers is plainly within the power of Congress to mandate directly, since it directs the utilities, not the state agencies regulating them. Thus, as the Supreme Court ruled in *Federal Energy Regulatory Commission v. Mississippi*,[111] these requirements do not run afoul of the Tenth Amendment since they simply preempt any conflicting state rules in the traditional way.

---

110. American Paper Institute, Inc. v. American Electric Power Service Corp., 461 U.S. 402 (1983).
111. 456 U.S. 742, 759 (1982).

Chapter 13

International Aspects of Environmental Protection

Synopsis

§ 13.01 Basic Principles

[A] Treaties Governing Environmental Issues

Several noteworthy treaties and other international agreements govern major areas of environmental protection. However, unlike domestic, or national, environmental law, international environmental law offers far fewer sanctions for offenders and far fewer enforceable rules of conduct. Environmental agreements between nations commenced as early as a nineteenth-century treaty regarding navigation and fishing on the Rhine. In 1909, the United States and the United Kingdom entered into a Boundary Waters Treaty that barred either party from polluting waters on the border between the United States and Canada so as to injure health or property in the adjacent country.

A major step forward was the 1916 Migratory Bird Treaty, also between the United States and Britain, discussed at § 10.01. This treaty enabled the federal government to protect birds from indiscriminate hunting at a time when federal power to legislate under the Commerce Clause was circumscribed by Supreme Court decisions.

Additional treaties respecting animals and plants were entered into in later decades, including the London Convention on Preservation of Fauna and Flora in their Natural State, negotiated in 1933. These culminated in the Convention on International Trade in Endangered Species (CITES), described at § 10.05, a product of the vitally important 1972 Stockholm conference on the Human Environment.

Today, treaties address global warming, protection of the ozone layer of the upper atmosphere, biodiversity and other areas, dealt with in greater detail later in this chapter.

[B] Applicable Principles of International Law

In the absence of specific, enforceable treaty provisions, nations are sovereign within their jurisdictions. There are, however, certain significant principles of international law that have gained enough acceptance to be legally enforceable. These include the right of free navigation, which has led to liability for nations interfering with that right. In the 1949 *Corfu Channel* case,[1] the International Court of Justice found Albania liable to Britain for damage caused by its mining of the Adriatic Sea. This principle may well be applicable to a variety of environmental and related harms inflicted by one nation on another: oil spills, acid rain, and the like.

Another emerging doctrine in international environmental law, embodied in Stockholm Principle 21, is that while states have the sovereign right to exploit their own resources, they have a matching responsibility to ensure that no damage accrues to the environment of other states. This principle raises difficult issues. How far may a state destroy its rain forest, allow global warming by burning carbon-based fuels, or deplete the ozone layer? These thorny issues may be resolved by the language of specific international agreements, discussed in §§ 13.02–13.06.

The *Trail Smelter* Arbitration is illustrative.[2] In this pair of decisions in 1938 and 1941, the 1909 Boundary Waters Treaty was held to justify an injunction against continuing air pollution from a British Columbia smelter causing damage across the border in Washington. (The tribunal ultimately found the damage insufficient to warrant injunctive relief.)

Principles of liability for damages in the international arena are still developing. The *Trail Smelter* precedent, for example, was rejected by the former Soviet Union when claims were submitted to it after the nuclear meltdown at Chernobyl, which caused significant damage to agriculture in much of Europe due to radioactive exposure.

---

1. 1949 Int'l Ct. of Justice Rep. 4.
2. 3 R. Int'l Arb. Awards 1905 (1938, 1941).

The "precautionary principle" has also developed in recent decades, mandating that nations not cause serious or irreversible damage. This principle is embodied in the conventions on ozone layer protection and climate change. It raises issues as to the degree of proof necessary before remedial action is required, and whether the burden of proof is imposed on the source of the environmental injury or on those seeking to correct it.

[C] Sustainable Development and Population Increase

Another principle undergirding much of international environmental law is that of sustainable development. This concept refers to limiting development to actions that sustain, rather than deplete or destroy, resources such as forests, fisheries, and the like. Sustainable development might be likened to using the income, rather than depleting the capital, of natural resources. It recognizes that these resources are finite. This is a major concern since developing nations are using greater amounts of energy and fuel as they become more industrialized.

A related concern is that of population increase. Reducing environmental impacts from industry, transportation, and fuel use will be largely offset by the prodigious increases in population of recent decades. The world's population has doubled since the 1950s, now stands at over seven billion, and is expected to reach 10 billion by 2050. Increases are steeper in many developing countries where many families are larger, a substantial portion of the population is young, and pollution controls are minimal. If these nations continue to develop industrially, using greater amounts of energy and fuel per capita, the prospects for sustainable development will surely deteriorate unless alternative fuels are developed, as discussed in § 12.05.

[D] Conflicting Interests of Developed and Developing Countries

The conflict between the views and strategies of developed and developing countries pervades international environmental law. In general, developed countries tend to favor worldwide limits on activities with environmental impacts. Developing countries, in contrast, generally seek to impose stricter controls on nations that consume the most energy or resources, with exemptions or postponements for countries not yet fully industrialized or prosperous. Coupled with this is the frequent insistence of developing nations on financial aid and transfer of technology to enable them to meet environmental goals — demands that more technologically developed nations often resist. These conflicting goals are more fully discussed in connection with climate change in § 13.02 and biodiversity in § 13.06.

[E] War and the Environment

Finally, war has the potential for vast and severe impacts on the environment. Warring nations engage in scorched earth policies that destroy forests and agricultural lands, set fire to oil wells and refineries, and commit other environmental atrocities. During World War II, Allied aircraft bombed the dams that protected Germany's Rhine and Ruhr valleys from flooding, in an effort to destroy the German industrial base. The Germans had earlier devastated many of Poland's forests. Nuclear testing and bombing trigger environmental destruction of the first magnitude. Even when unused, nuclear weapons pose difficult problems of disposal.

A 1977 Convention on Military Use of Environmental Modification, amending the earlier Geneva Convention relating to the conduct of war, attempted to furnish some ground rules on this subject.[3] Nations that signed the Convention have agreed to avoid widespread, long-term and severe environmental damage stemming from war. However, the Convention allows conduct necessary for military operations — an exception that threatens to swallow the rule. Neither the United Nations nor the International Court of Justice have as yet come to grips with these issues.

§ 13.02 Global Climate Change

[A] Causes and Effects of Global Warming

Global warming is often conflated with the "greenhouse effect." Although the effects are related, the terms should be distinguished in the interest of clarity. The latter, the result of carbon dioxide, methane, and other gases naturally rising to the upper atmosphere, irrespective of human endeavors, protects the earth from excessive cold that would otherwise occur. These gases convert the atmosphere into a vast greenhouse, containing heat and infra-red energy radiated from the earth while letting in light and heat from the sun. Without them the earth would be about 60 degrees Fahrenheit colder on average. In contrast, global warming is caused by ever-increasing amounts of carbon dioxide, water vapor, methane, and similar gases, stemming from human activity, augmenting the natural greenhouse effect so as to warm the earth on a rising scale which is predicted to undermine current lifestyles and political and economic stability as the 21st century proceeds. Since the industrial revolution's novel and massive combustion of carbon-based fuels, accelerating during the latter part of the 20th century until the present, the release of "greenhouse gases," typically although not exclusively carbon based, has exacerbated the atmosphere's retention of heat. By 2020, greenhouse gas concentrations were at their highest levels in the past two million years.[4]

Evidence of accelerating global warming, widely accepted by the scientific community, has accumulated in recent decades. Scientists are now in agreement that this warming stems primarily from increased burning of coal, oil, and other fossil fuels,

---

3. Convention on the Prohibition of Military or any other Hostile Use of Environmental Modification Techniques, 1108 U.N.T.S. 151, 16 I.L.M. 88 (1977).

4. United Nations, Climate Action, at https://www.un.org/en/climatechange/what-is-climate-change. *See also* Intergovernmental Panel on Climate Change 2021: The Physical Science Basis, at https://www.ipcc.ch/report/ar6/wg1.

releasing great quantities of carbon dioxide into the earth's upper atmosphere. They also agree that global warming has likely begun to cause a rise in sea level and therefore coastal flooding, as well as loss of forests, increased and more volatile storms, and other severe effects. A predicted impact of great concern is that of increased desertification in tropical areas as water is lost through greater evaporation when the climate becomes warmer. There has also been a discernible increase in ocean temperatures which threaten marine ecosystems in many locations and maritime wildlife, which is acting as a multiplier effect on extreme weather events around the globe. Relatedly, as the glaciers in Greenland, the Antarctic icepack and traditionally frozen seas in arctic regions melt, those regions and their ecosystem not only are destabilized themselves, but because of the dynamic of ocean circulating currents, they pose global risks for coastal areas.

Scientists estimate a rise in the earth's average temperature of three to eight degrees Fahrenheit in the next century, caused by fossil-fuel consumption and related actions. This likely means a melting of the polar ice caps and a resulting in a two to eight-foot rise in the sea level. This will flood out many cities and coastal areas, destroying wetlands and causing salt water intrusion of aquifers, reducing potable water supplies. Low-lying countries like the Netherlands and Bangladesh could well be severely flooded, while island nations such as the Maldives and others in the Pacific Ocean and elsewhere likely will be submerged.

In addition, modeling indicates that the increased heat will likely cause greater evaporation, and the resulting water vapor will likely exacerbate the global warming process. The evaporation will cause deserts to expand and forests to dwindle. Crop yields will probably substantially decrease in many regions, leading to an overall food shortage in a world with an increasing population, which will create layers of social and political instability. The meteorological evidence has been accumulating that the numerous extreme weather events occurring in recent decades and accelerating during the 21st century can be causally related to the increased atmospheric and oceanic concentrations of heat energy. By an indirect route, climate change is also driving the acidification of the oceans, which in yet another manner has already been adversely impacting maritime ecosystems, especially coral reefs, which often are essential not only for wildlife but also as stabilizing structures for many coastal areas.[5]

Although global warming is primarily caused by fossil fuel burning, two other prime causes are deforestation and depletion of the ozone layer — each activity replete with environmental injury. Forests act as natural "sinks," absorbing carbon. Their destruction intensifies global warming. The interference with the ozone layer caused by chlorofluorocarbons (CFCs), discussed at § 13.03, likewise adds to warming since CFCs, like carbon and water vapor, reradiate heat back to the earth.

---

5. *See* Climate Science Special Report, Fourth National Climate Assessment, at https://science2017.globalchange.gov. This is the latest in assessments required by the Global Change Research Act of 1990. *See also* https://climate.nasa.gov/effects/.

Finally, methane contributes to global warming. This gas is produced by a variety of sources including wetlands, landfills, and cattle.

The skepticism that first greeted fears of global warming has largely dissipated as the scientific evidence mounts. Recognition that the burning of fossil fuels needs to be reduced has led to international as well as domestic measures. The same limits on coal and petroleum use benefit air quality and conserve energy as well. These perspectives are discussed in §§ 5.03, 5.04, and 12.06. As noted in § 5.04, the United States Supreme Court has directed EPA to consider carbon dioxide as an air pollutant.[6]

[B] The Climate Change Convention

The emerging international consensus on global warming resulted in the 1992 Climate Change Convention, a major product of the Rio de Janeiro Environmental Conference. The key provision of the Convention requires each signatory party to "adopt national policies and take corresponding measures on the mitigation of climate change, by limiting its ... emissions of greenhouse gases...."[7] Over 150 nations signed the agreement.

To implement the Convention, numerous countries proposed substantial reductions in greenhouse gas emissions. The European Union, Canada, Japan, and Australia, even before the Convention, had offered to freeze their emissions by 2000 and reduce them significantly thereafter. After some initial hesitation, the United States agreed to reduce emissions to its 1990 levels by 2012.[8]

In 1997, a conference at Kyoto, Japan to implement the Convention resulted in agreement among the major developed nations. The European Union agreed to reduce greenhouse gas emissions by 8 percent from its 1990 levels by 2010. The United States agreed to a 7 percent reduction and Japan to 6 percent within the same period.[9] The Kyoto agreement also permits emissions trading to help achieve these goals. The emission trading concept as a market-based incentive to reach compliance with environmental limits is described at § 2.03. A dispute over whether to include forests and other carbon sinks as a set-off against emissions, favored by the United States, Canada, and Brazil as major forested countries, was resolved in favor of that approach at Kyoto.

Since the Kyoto agreement constitutes a treaty, Senate ratification was necessary to make it binding law for the United States, which did not occur. However, with the ratification of Kyoto by Russia in 2004, the treaty, which takes effect when countries producing 55% of carbon emissions approve it, became effective as to the countries that signed on (excluding the United States).

---

6. Massachusetts v. Environmental Protection Agency, 127 S. Ct. 1438 (2007).

7. United Nations Framework Convention on Climate Change, 31 Int'l Legal Mats. (hereinafter I.L.M.) 849 (1992), art. 2(a).

8. Current Developments, 28 ENVT. RPTR. (BNA) 1237, Oct. 24, 1997.

9. Conference of the Parties to the Framework Convention on Climate Change: Kyoto Protocol adopted Dec. 10, 1997, in 37 I.L.M. 22, 24 (1998).

The conflict between developed and developing countries, described in § 13.01[D], has surfaced in regard to global warming. Developing countries contend that climate change mainly results from unduly great consumption, and particularly high energy use, in more developed nations. They argue that the developed countries should reduce their greenhouse gas emissions, share technology to accomplish this with developing countries, and assist them financially in reducing their emissions. The developed countries tend to the view that developing lands must curb population increases and reduce their emissions even if this slows economic expansion.

The 1992 Convention accepted the developing countries' arguments to the extent of requiring developed nations to furnish "financial resources to meet the agreed full costs incurred by developing country Parties in complying with their obligations," including technology transfers.[10]

The 1992 Convention, like many international agreements, continues to lack meaningful sanctions for nations in violation. It provides for negotiation between disputing parties, followed by non-binding mediation. There are further provisions for binding arbitration, and the submission of disputes to the International Court, but these require the consent of the parties in dispute.[11]

In 2015, 192 parties, which included 191 countries and the European Union acting as a unit, entered the Paris Agreement, which took legal effect on November 4, 2016. Although the United States withdrew under the Trump Administration, the Biden Administration immediately reentered it. The Paris Agreement had ambitious goals, but those were driven by the increasingly dire predictions of climate science. The Agreement acknowledged a climate tipping point, where the accumulating consequences of global climate change would be irreversible. Among its goals was to reduce greenhouse gas emissions to the extent necessary to restrain global temperature increases to a necessary maximum of 2 degrees Celsius during the 21st century, but to actually limit the global temperature rise to 1.5 degrees Celsius. To this end, the parties made national pledges with respect to their own reductions in emissions, their "Nationally Determined Contributions," which ostensibly have binding effect, and they agreed to review those commitments every five years. The wealthier parties also agreed to help poorer countries with financing to facilitate their efforts to reduce emissions and adapt to climate change. The Paris Agreement also provided a framework to monitor and report on the parties' efforts to achieve their climate goals. Operational details of the Paris Agreement were further discussed at the UN Climate Change Conference in Katowice, Poland, in December 2018, and in Glasgow, Scotland, in November 2021.[12]

---

10. United Nations Framework Convention on Climate Change, 31 I.L.M. 849 (1992), art. 3.

11. *Id.* at art. 14.

12. *See* United Nations Climate Action, the Paris Agreement, at https://www.un.org/en/climatechange/paris-agreement; United Nations Framework Convention on Climate Change, Climate Action Now: Summary for Policymakers 2018, at https://unfccc.int/resource/climateaction2020/spm/introduction/index.html.

Achieving the goals set forth in these agreements will plainly require a major strengthening of domestic law. In the United States, the Clean Air Act's controls on emissions, both from stationary sources and motor vehicles, are likely candidates, as are the energy conservation measures for vehicles, household appliances, and electric utilities adopted as far back as the 1970s (discussed at § 12.06). Finally, the prospect of alternative fuels like compressed natural gas and hydrogen (also described in § 12.06) offers enormous possibilities in curbing greenhouse gases. As earlier noted, the Supreme Court has directed EPA to consider listing carbon dioxide as an air pollutant (see § 5.04[B][1][6]) because of climate change concerns.

§ 13.03 Ozone Layer Protection

An issue distinct from, but similar in some ways to, climate change is that of depletion of the stratospheric ozone layer. This shield protects the earth from ultraviolet radiation from the sun. Its destruction would lead to a sizable increase in skin cancers and cataracts, as well as contributing to global warming (discussed in § 13.02).

In the 1970s it was discovered that this protective layer was being depleted by chlorofluorocarbons (CFCs) and related chemicals known as halons. These were in widespread use as propellants in aerosol spray cans, and in refrigeration and air conditioning equipment. Ironically, CFCs were chosen for these purposes because they were thought to be chemically inert. Chemically, when these substances reach the upper atmosphere, ultraviolet radiation from the sun breaks down the CFC and halon molecules, releasing chlorine atoms that attack ozone molecules. The ozone layer has already been damaged to a considerable degree, especially in the southern hemisphere.

Several countries, including the United States, enacted restrictions on the manufacture and use of CFCs. The 1990 Clean Air Act amendments so provide.[13] They mandate a phase-out of CFCs and halons by 2000, with some minor exceptions for medical and aviation safety uses. Existing products must be recycled to avoid their release into the atmosphere. Special provisions govern air-conditioners in motor vehicles.

Although these provisions are salutary, and a few other nations have adopted similar laws, international action clearly was needed to deal with the problem since virtually every country uses these substances and the effects of destroying the ozone layer are worldwide. Environmentally harmless alternatives to CFCs and halons now exist. They were first developed for spray cans, but are now available for refrigeration and airconditioners as well. The costs of these alternatives, originally significantly higher than those of CFCs and halons, have declined with their increased production and use.

A 1987 meeting led to the Montreal Protocol on Substances that Deplete the Ozone Layer, in which 47 signatory nations agreed to freeze production of these substances at 1986 levels and to reduce production and use by 50 percent by 1999.[14]

---

13. 42 U.S.C. §§ 7671–7671q.
14. Montreal Protocol on Substances that Deplete the Ozone Layer, 26 I.L.M. 1550 (1987).

With subsequent scientific data showing dramatic increases in ozone layer depletion, the Montreal agreement was soon amended. The 1990 London amendments
required a total phase-out of production and consumption by 2000.[15]

Scientists estimate that the damage already wrought to the ozone layer will take
about 75 years to dissipate. Nonetheless, the protocol is a landmark in worldwide
environmental protection and a success story in international cooperation.

§ 13.04 Basel Convention on Hazardous Waste Shipment

Since country after country began adopting laws to strictly control the disposal
of hazardous waste (see § 7.05 for a discussion of United States statutes on the subject),
both private industry and government agencies often responded by transporting such
wastes to developing nations for disposal. The nations so honored tended to be those
with rudimentary legal controls on waste disposal, or with controls that could be
easily circumvented.

Nations accepting hazardous waste shipments from other countries often impose
the environmental burdens of that disposal on others. Hazardous waste can pollute
coastal waters, rivers, and other watercourses that other countries share, or air that
crosses national boundaries. In such cases there is little law that the aggrieved nation
can use to restrain the disposal, mitigate its impacts, or even recover damages. *See*
the discussion in § 13.01[B].

An international consensus against dumping hazardous waste in less developed
countries was slow to develop, since the practice unfortunately was of economic
benefit to both the exporting and receiving countries. It finally resulted, however, in
the Basel Convention on the Control of Transboundary Movements of Hazardous
Wastes and their Disposal.[16] The process was aided by media reports of unlawful
dumping of hazardous waste in developing nations: the so-called "North-South problem." In keeping with this, many African and other developing countries urged a
total ban on transboundary hazardous waste shipment.

In the end, the Basel Convention provided that each party take measures to
ensure that international movement of hazardous wastes be "reduced to the minimum consistent with the environmentally sound and efficient management of such
wastes" and occur "in a manner which will protect human health and the environment against the adverse effects which may result from such movement."[17] Hazardous waste may not be shipped to countries that prohibit its importation, and

---

15. Montreal Protocol Parties: Protocol on Substances that Deplete the Ozone Layer (London
1990), 30 I.L.M. 537 (1991).
16. 28 I.L.M. 657 (1989).
17. Basel Convention, 28 I.L.M. 657 (1989), art. 4, § 2(d).

information about the effects of any such shipments must be furnished.[18] No such wastes may be shipped at all to Antarctica, a tempting destination but an environmentally fragile one.

As with many environmental treaties and international conventions, enforcement is a serious problem. Disputes are to be negotiated if possible, and if not, adjudicated by the International Court of Justice. However, there is no effective mechanism for penalizing offenders. Basel, at least, presents an international recognition of the scope of the problem and a means of dealing with it.

A follow-up agreement, the Bamako Convention on the Ban of the Import into Africa and the Control of Transboundary Movement and Management of Hazardous Wastes within Africa, was adopted in 1991.[19] The Bamako Convention bars the shipment of any hazardous wastes to Africa from other parts of the world.

§ 13.05 The Environment and Free Trade

The potential for conflict exists between environmental laws, both international and domestic, and agreements designed to further free trade. These laudable and seemingly unrelated goals can clash when environmental statutes are challenged as constituting discrimination against trade from nations with less strict standards.

The General Agreement on Tariffs and Trade (GATT) was adopted in 1947, long before environmental issues surfaced as a major legal concern. GATT, to which most important trading nations are signatories, bars domestic laws, such as tariffs, that restrict free trade among nations. Its underlying approach is that a free market will lead to greater worldwide economic benefits than will trade restrictions. However, when countries began adopting environmental regulations curtailing traffic in endangered species or foods exposed to pesticides in harmful amounts, these often were viewed as devices to restrict free trade that thereby violated GATT. GATT, and the system of international trade, do not require manufacturers or producers of goods to absorb the environmental costs of producing those goods.

While GATT specifically allows signatory countries to regulate health and the environment within their borders and to conserve local resources,[20] it does not provide for environmental laws aimed at protecting resources beyond a nation's borders. One view is that free trade benefits economic development that will foster both domestic and international environmental standards. The corollary view is that agreements like GATT are subverted by environmental statutes that restrict trade. Others maintain that environmental laws are justified, and are not intended to restrict free trade.

This issue came to a head in a decision by the tribunal administering the Uruguay Round of GATT, which ruled that a United States ban on importing tuna caught

---

18. *Id.* at art. 4, § 2(e), (f).
19. 30 I.L.M. 775 (1991).
20. General Agreement on Tariffs and Trade, art. 20 (b), (g).

with nets that trap dolphin violated GATT.[21] These statutes are discussed at § 10.02[D]. A subsequent ruling invalidated United States rules on gasoline emissions that imposed stricter requirements on foreign refiners than on domestic companies.[22] The rule was found to constitute both unjustifiable discrimination and less favorable treatment for imports, both violative of GATT.

Thereafter, the WTO ruled in 1998 that a United States law banning imports of shrimp from countries that failed to protect sea turtles by mandating the use of turtle excluder devices (TEDs) was a measure to conserve natural resources, authorized by GATT. But the WTO went on to rule the United States law discriminatory since it was only applied to four Asian countries.[23] The United States then modified its requirements, which were upheld by the WTO in 2001.[24]

GATT enables signatory counties to waive its provisions,[25] which furnishes a possible solution in limited circumstances. In addition, later treaties such as the Convention on International Trade in Endangered Species (CITES) (described in § 10.05) and the Montreal Convention relating to protection of the ozone layer (described in § 13.03) take precedence over GATT under the Vienna Convention on the Law of Treaties. Thus, the requirements of CITES and Montreal may not be challenged as violative of GATT, since those treaties are more recent than GATT.

§ 13.06 Biodiversity

[A] Importance of Maintaining Biodiversity

As described in § 10.05, international controls over traffic in the hides and other bodily parts of endangered species have been effectively implemented through the CITES treaty, one of the true successes in international environmental law. But curbing the trade in endangered wildlife is only the most dramatic part of the vastly more complex issue of preserving biodiversity — the extraordinary variety of life forms and the ecosystems that sustain them.

Biodiversity is usually analyzed in terms of three distinct concerns. Genetic diversity correlates with the diversity of members of a particular species. Ecological diversity relates to the number of species within a particular natural area or ecosystem. Ecosys-

---

21. General Agreement on Tariffs and Trade: Dispute Settlement Panel Report on United States Restrictions on Imports of Tuna, 30 I.L.M. 1594 (1991).

22. World Trade Org.: Report of Panel in *United States — Standards for Reformulated and Conventional Gasoline*, 35 I.L.M. 274 (1996). The World Trade Organization (WTO) administers GATT's provisions.

23. General Agreement on Tariffs and Trade: United States — Import Prohibition of Certain Shrimp and Shrimp Products, I.L.M. (1998).

24. General Agreement on Tariffs and Trade: United States — Import Prohibition of Certain Shrimp and Shrimp Products Recourse to Article 21.5, I.L.M. (2001).

25. *Id.*

tem diversity relates to the number of ecosystems within a geographic region.[26] It is recognized that to preserve biodiversity it is necessary to transcend the protection of individual species and safeguard entire ecosystems. Species are interconnected in numerous ways — for example, as predator and prey. Eliminating a prey species endangers its predators, while eliminating predators may enable prey species to reproduce to an extent that will cause overpopulation and damage crops, followed by population declines as food runs out. This has occurred with North American deer, where the elimination of wolves, bears, and other predators has resulted in overpopulation and the migration of deer into suburban areas where they are struck by vehicles and spread Lyme disease. Similarly, human encroachment on the territory of cougars and bears has led to unexpected encounters, in some cases leading to deaths.

Mankind has been enlarging its frontiers into the habitat of other species for thousands of years, but the process has accelerated enormously in the past century. Clearcutting forests, dredging and filling wetlands and coastal mangrove swamps, overfishing, and the like have greatly threatened biodiversity throughout the world. In particular, prodigious population increases put rain forests — the regions that support the largest variety of life — at risk. Agricultural technology has led to monocropping (farming a single crop) and the use of huge quantities of pesticides and herbicides. Monocropping leads to a loss of diversity in seeds and plants, greatly increasing the likelihood of blight. It was a prime cause of the Irish potato famine that killed hundreds of thousands in the mid-nineteenth century. As the genetic pool for farm crops shrinks, the remaining seeds and plants become far more vulnerable to disease and insects.

Safeguarding biodiversity requires, first, a recognition of the problem and a shift in attitude from the sheer exploitation of plant and animal life to an awareness of the need to protect ecosystems. Beyond this, specific steps include limiting forest clearcutting and slash-and-burn agriculture, more equitable and efficient use of farmland, especially in developing countries, restricting development that invades natural habitats, and preserving landraces (natural varieties of plants).

As in other areas of international environmental law, the perceived interests of developed and developing nations sometimes differ. Developing countries often take the view that these restrictions fall most heavily on impoverished countries seeking to expand their economies. They point out that most of the forests in Europe and eastern North America have long been clearcut, and that construction and monoculture farming in developing countries are desperately needed to provide hard currency. Developed countries are apt to respond that the world cannot afford the loss of additional biodiversity and that unrestrained development damages the entire planet.

---

26. *See* William M. Flevares, *Ecosystems, Economics, and Ethics: Protecting Biodiversity at Home and Abroad*, 65 S. CAL. L. REV. 2039 (1992).

[B] Convention on Biological Diversity

The 1992 Rio de Janeiro conference on the environment under United Nations auspices resulted in a Convention on Biological Diversity.[27] Its goals include finding ways to promote sustainable development, described in § 13.01[C], and to reduce the impacts of the types of economic expansion that endanger biodiversity. Over 165 nations have subscribed to it.

The Convention explicitly recognizes that states have both "the sovereign right to exploit their own resources" and "the responsibility to ensure that activities within their jurisdiction or control do not cause damage to the environment of other States or of areas beyond the limits of national jurisdiction."[28] It specifically calls for each signatory to protect "areas where special measures need to be taken to conserve biological diversity," restore degraded ecosystems, remove "alien species which threaten ecosystems, habitats or species," and respect the practices of indigenous communities with traditional lifestyles.[29] These practices are denominated "in situ" (on-site) conservation.

In addition, the Convention fosters "ex situ" (off-site) conservation by requiring signatories to conserve plants, seeds, and other components of biodiversity ex-situ, preferably in their country of origin. The collecting of these resources is to be done "so as not to threaten ecosystems and in-situ populations."[30] This clause recognizes the need to preserve plants and seeds away from their natural habitat on occasion, especially if the habitat should become threatened. Countries are also expressly mandated by the Convention to minimize impacts on biodiversity and to encourage traditional practices that are compatible with conservation and sustainable use.[31] These include the use of natural landraces or seeds.

[C] Use of Genetic Resources: Who Profits?

Much controversy surrounds the right to make use of genetic resources and how to share in the profits derived from that use. Many plants have important medicinal value. However, seeds, plants, and other natural resources cannot be patented. If a developed country produces a medicine or similar valuable substance from a native plant, the profits currently flow to the industrial producer, not to the habitat country. Many have urged that legal rights akin to intellectual property rights be established for native biota. One scholar has cited the example of the wild rosy periwinkle, a plant native to Madagascar, successfully used to treat Hodgkin's disease and other ailments. Madagascar receives no economic benefits from this discovery.[32]

---

27. 31 I.L.M. 818 (1992).
28. Convention on Biological Diversity, art. 3.
29. *Id.* at art. 8.
30. *Id.* at art. 9.
31. *Id.* at art. 10.
32. Shayana Kadidal, Note, *Plants, Poverty, and Pharmaceutical Patents*, 103 YALE L.J. 223 (1993).

In an effort to deal equitably with this difficult problem, the Convention provides that the "authority to determine access to genetic resources rests with the national governments" of their habitat countries. However, each signatory

> "shall endeavor to create conditions to facilitate access to genetic resources ... and not impose restrictions that run counter to the objectives of this Convention." Most important, signatory nations must legislate "with the aim of sharing in a fair and equitable way the results of research and development and the benefits arising from the commercial and other utilization of genetic resources."[33]

In addition, each signatory is to facilitate the transfer of technology relevant to sustainable use "under fair and most favorable terms."[34] This means developed countries must ensure that their corporations allow developing countries fair access to the technology that makes a plant valuable as a pharmaceutical. This provision, opposed by many pharmaceutical and related companies, essentially rejects the old view that plants and the like were the "common heritage of mankind" — a euphonious phrase that obviated any need to share profits with the habitat country.

The Convention, like so many environmental treaties, lacks an effective enforcement mechanism. It remains to be seen whether, and how, these provisions will be implemented, and what recourse exists if they are not.

[D] Debt-for-Nature Swaps

A final significant device in furthering biodiversity consists of debt-for-nature swaps. Both governments and not-for-profit conservation groups use this technique to absorb portions of the debt owed by developing countries to banks, governments, and other creditors by trading that debt for natural areas, such as rain forest. The natural areas thus remain protected. Under a variant, some pharmaceutical companies have agreed to lease, or purchase, natural regions, keeping them safeguarded from development in exchange for being able to profit from any medicinally useful plants found there.

---

33. Convention on Biological Diversity, art. 15.
34. *Id.* at art. 16.

Chapter 14

Innovations and Trends

§ 14.01 Introduction

Since the mid-1990s, EPA, reflecting political currents appearing elsewhere in the federal government, started to take a fresh look at its mission and how best to achieve it. Political opposition, joining that of industry, to increasingly intrusive environmental regulation and the sometimes harsh consequences of enforcement, including adverse impacts on businesses and under some circumstances local communities, was beginning to coalesce. In partial response, EPA added to its traditional enforcement task a cost efficiency role which mitigated some of the inflexibility of the existing enforcement regime. This shifting paradigm also reflected international currents that are increasingly incorporated into domestic policy making in the environmental field.

These varying approaches share the following key tenets:

- Regulatory flexibility, when warranted by beneficial environmental results;
- Reduced compliance costs;
- Various modes of "environmental management" by businesses;
- Encouraging industry to assume greater responsibility for self-discovery of environmental problems;
- Greater reductions in resource and energy consumption and generation of waste, and, to achieve all of the above, allowing industry, within certain parameters, to take the lead in devising more effective, user-friendly, and innovative policies and processes; and
- Greater collaboration with, and support of, local communities.

§ 14.02 The Long After-Lives of Chemical Products in Everyday Use

It would be hard to imagine modern life without the many economic and practical benefits of the chemical revolution that became ubiquitous during the last half of the 20th century. The early 21st century, though, has brought about a reckoning with the resilience in the environment, and also in our food and even our bodies, of many of those manufactured chemical products that seemed not only enormously helpful in so many areas of our lives and commerce but initially seemed relatively benign from a public health perspective and almost neutral with respect to pernicious effects on the environment.

Styrofoam provides an early example of a highly useful product that pervaded commerce but for which the environmental detriments became apparent over time. This polymer was originally devised in the 1940s as insulation for buildings. Since it is 98% air, it subsequently acquired maritime and recreational uses because of its buoyancy, value as packaging material because of its relative weightlessness and its ability to hold its shape either in forms or as the "peanuts" protecting the contents of packages being shipped, and eventually intruded itself into commerce and cuisine as the infamous "clamshells" insulating hot or cold fast food, grocery meats and disposable coffee cups. By the 1970s, medical evidence began to suggest that the styrene that was its major component might be carcinogenic, but the more tangible problem was that while it was fast filling landfills, it cannot be composted since it does not biodegrade. That, though, does not mean that Styrofoam does not break down. As is now also increasingly apparent with many plastic products as is noted below, Styrofoam crumbles into smaller units. This presented environmental impacts more drastic than overflowing landfills. Evidence was accumulating that Styrofoam beads released into nature as litter and, more dramatically into water bodies, were being ingested by wildlife. Being undigestible, these pellets could fill an animal's digestive system, impeding further feeding and leading to mortality and, by a different route, releasing harmful endocrine disruptors. Styrofoam eventually was restricted in its uses or even barred in many states as a result. It is anticipated that as of 2022, the Styrofoam packaging peanuts will be banned in New York.

Greater attention is now being paid, though, to other products that also impact the environment but which, it is increasingly apparent, also present risks to public health. These risks arise by stealth, since the very usefulness and pervasiveness of some products diverted attention away from potential long-term consequences of their use as well as their disposal. Two categories that are now on the environmental as well as medical radar screens are types of plastics, as well as perfluorinated alkyl substances and polyfluorinated alkyl substances (PFASs).

[A] Plastics That Won't Go Away

In an early attention getting scene of the iconic film *The Graduate*, an adult radiating self-perceptions of success and knowingness proselytizes to the young ingénue played by Dustin Hoffman, "plastics ... *plastics*," as the secret to future success. Our world is now awash with these derivatives of countless chemical permutations of petroleum that have lived a long life and in doing so have made our lives easier in countless ways. We now have the disturbing question, though: what to do about them after their useful life has ended? The problems are, at least, three-fold.

The more obvious problem is aesthetic as well as environmental: the worldwide accumulation of plastic trash, especially in the ocean. Landfill space is disproportionately consumed by plastic products of countless varieties. More visually, though, decades of maritime disposals of solid wastes have converted bands of ocean currents into giant floating trash heaps circulating with trans-oceanic currents. Once one moves beyond the aesthetics, though, the science is becoming increasingly urgent from a wildlife conservation perspective. It has long been observed that plastic products such as the joined loops that once held soda and beer sixpacks, and similar plastic products, trapped and often strangled waterfowl and marine mammals. Sea turtles, too, often mistake plastic bags for jellyfish, their common food source, which, when eaten, contribute to their demise. Plastics do not biodegrade, as food and paper wastes might. Rather, they break down into microplastics which can be consumed by wildlife, presenting problems similar to those of Styrofoam. Microplastics can work their way up the food chain, ultimately to humans. Moreover, the plastic wrap so common in all sectors of the food industry can also seed the food products with microplastics, with the long-term consequences for human consumption still being examined. Relatedly, testing has demonstrated that many hard plastic products such as food and beverage containers have been leaching dangerous chemicals, many of which pose carcinogenic risks and could be hormone disruptors. Here, too, the modern trend lines link environmental concerns with public health, and what were seen as unexceptional aspects of everyday commerce are coming under scrutiny.

[B] The Endemic Dangers of "Forever Chemicals"

Perfluorinated alkyl substances and polyfluorinated alkyl substances (PFASs) have been raising particular alarms in the environmental as well as the medical communities, the more so since they have been in such common use and they seem to easily find their way into our respiratory systems and the food chain as they circulate through our bodies in our blood, and they can even be passed on by mothers in breast milk. Over 9,000 of these chemicals, not found in nature, are used in food packaging, especially take-out containers; waterproofing on clothing, bedding, furniture and carpets; cosmetics, including the sunscreen that medical advice extols; non-stick pots and pans, notably Teflon and its derivative compounds; electronic equipment, including cell phones in regular use; foams used in fire-fighting activities; and numerous other everyday uses. Teflon and Scotchguard and "long chain" carbon compounds (i.e., a string of 12 carbon atoms) in this family of synthetic chemicals are no longer manufactured in this country as a result, although "short chain" compounds (a string of six carbon atoms) still are, which remains controversial. An evolving record indicates that industry had known of, and concealed, the dangers and covered up contaminated water supplies for decades. Claims are also made that when a particular PFAS either gets banned or is phased out under regulatory pressure, industry simply substitutes another, similar, one.

Growing medical evidence indicates that some of these chemicals are endocrine disruptors, and are associated with birth defects and with various organ cancers. They have been found in human and animal blood samples, and they present additional health concerns for which information is, as yet, still developing. Some estimates propose that PFASs can be found in 99% of Americans, and up to 110 million Americans may be drinking from water resources contaminated by PFASs. A study indicates that 49 states have PFAS-contaminated water supplies. PFASs are persistent in the environment, do not degrade, travel easily in liquid environments such as groundwater, and have achieved a global reach.

Regulatory steps with respect to future uses are being taken internationally, nationally, and by many states. This is an area of very active environmental and medical attention. Given the unlikelihood that the environment can be cleansed of them,

PFASs that already are extant will likely continue to present environmental and public health risks for the foreseeable future.[1]

§ 14.03 Community-Based Programs

Without abandoning its traditional regulatory and enforcement roles, the modern EPA has adopted a policy of cooperating with community-based programs, which often may be the most informative sources of information about local environmental conditions and potential solutions. As a practical matter, local residents and businesses are those most likely to be affected by pollution as well as strategies for reducing pollution, and often bear the costs in terms of inconveniences, expenses and quality of life imposed not only by pollution but also by the perception of heavy-handed federal enforcement. Hence, this approach presents benefits not only for community-based programs operating within the framework established by federal statutory and regulatory law, but also for EPA if, by partnering with credible local agencies and organizations, it can reduce its own operational responsibilities. This general partnership approach had already been seen with federal environmental statutes, notably but not only the Clean Air Act, which when enacted contemplated substantial delegation to state agencies acting within federal requirements. The modern initiatives, though, extend more of a resource focused approach rather than only a regulatory and enforcement approach towards local communities that, acting alone, may lack necessary resources for reducing pollution while also bolstering their local economies. Moreover, at a fundamental level, achieving the environmental objectives which are EPA's responsibility will often depend on local cooperation in contrast to local resistance.

The sea change in EPA policies started during the 1990s when EPA created the Compliance Incentives For Small Communities Initiative, which looked to accommodate small communities having difficulty complying with federal environmental regulations. The program contemplated setting priorities based on local conditions and needs, and correspondingly relaxing some regulatory requirements.[2] Coupled with this was the Community-Based Risk Assessment Project, which was intended to help communities engage in risk-based decision making, and to better educate them on the interaction between human health and ecological risks. EPA cooperated with communities to identify and evaluate risk management tools that are appropriate for the community, including training in risk assessment, comparative risk and risk assessment software and data bases, and technical assistance for the development of local pilot projects. The aim is to help communities set goals, prioritize, and achieve

---

1. *See, generally*, Environmental Working Group, *What are PFAS Chemicals?*, at https://www. ewg.org/pfaschemicals/what-are-forever-chemicals.html; Chem Trust, *PFAS — The "Forever Chemicals,"* at https://chemtrust.org/pfas; Harvard T.H. Chan School of Public Health, *Why more stringent regulation is needed for "forever chemicals,"* at https://www.hsph.harvard.edu/news/features/why-more-stringent-regulation-is-needed-for-forever-chemicals/.

2. 60 Fed. Reg. 55,569, 55,571 (Nov. 1995).

environmental results.[3] These and similar programs have expanded EPA's community outreach as a collaborative means of achieving environmental goals with an eye towards the growing data demonstrating the adverse public health consequences of regional contamination and, more recently, the shortcomings of some traditional land use planning in providing effective environmental strategies.

The modern EPA has acknowledged the intersection of environmental goals and local economic health, especially as demographics, industrial resources, the dynamic revolution in technology, commerce and land use have changed local economic and regulatory landscapes during the 21st century. Although environmental goals remain paramount, how to most efficiently achieve them requires sensitivity to these factors. In a 2015 report, EPA published case studies examining how a selection of cities and small towns successfully used local assets to rebuild their economies following the preceding Great Recession. The report noted that economic resilience often depended on flexible approaches that used local resources, even if other factors such as outside funding and large national employers also may have been beneficial. EPA acknowledged the beneficial role of cooperation on environmental goals with the federal government but also among community groups, especially fostering the beneficial redevelopment of polluted properties, other cleanups, reinvesting in existing infrastructure, protecting natural resources, and investing in modes of clean transportation.[4]

The intersection of land use, economics, civil engineering and environmental policies increasingly can be seen in the growing incorporation of "green infrastructure" into local community planning and building requirements as well as major cities.[5] Green infrastructure is the general term describing a wide array of land use and construction measures devised to achieve traditional and appropriate municipal goals but with a modern environmental sensibility — aesthetics, reducing erosion, containing and treating domestic sewage and other wastewater, diverting storm water, reducing summer heat, reducing traffic, expanding low-emission public transportation, and expanding green spaces and other open space, which are now increasingly associated with improvements in mental and physical health. Green infrastructure in these several manners also greatly helps to advance many of the environmental goals of the several statutes outlined in this book. However, while studies demonstrate that these multiple investments generate substantial savings over time, the upfront costs for some communities can be daunting and even prohibitive. Hence, EPA has provided grant programs to facilitate the growing trends towards innovative green infrastructure measures.[6] These include grants intended to help municipalities develop and implement strategies for neighborhoods to in-

---

3. *Id.*

4. *See* EPA, *How Small Towns and Cities Can Use Local Assets to Rebuild Their Economies: Lessons from Successful Places*, at https://www.epa.gov/sites/default/files/2015-05/documents/competitive_advantage_2015-508_final.pdf.

5. For a more comprehensive discussion of the subject, see ROBINSON, THE ENVIRONMENTAL REGULATION OF REAL PROPERTY § 7.07 (Law Journal Press).

6. *See* EPA, *Green Infrastructure Funding Opportunities*, at https://www.epa.gov/green-infrastructure/green-infrastructure-funding-opportunities.

corporate innovative green infrastructure appropriate for the particular communities, not only for environmental enhancement but also to support local economics and public health in ways that can provide examples for state and local leaders elsewhere. Among these several programs, EPA provides the funding for specialists who in several respects will design pilot projects in local neighborhoods as test cases for broader community involvement.[7]

EPA has also initiated a community public health project devised to interpret environmental health data for use by local planning and local risk management with the intention of promoting better public health as well as fostering research into multiple adverse health impacts in communities as well as from specific sources of pollution generated within communities. The program recognizes the growing scientific evidence about the cumulative health risks presented by rampant chemical proliferation in the environment as well as non-chemical health stressors. The goals include not only providing data but also providing models and other risk assessment tools, including those that are internet based, so as to facilitate better community environmental decision making, reduce health risks, and to evaluate sustainable solutions in these respects. The project contemplates collaboration among EPA regional and program officials, other federal organizations, and state, local and tribal organizations.[8]

§ 14.04 Locational Innovations for Generating Alternative Energy

With lagging congressional enthusiasm for restraining the extraction of, and commerce in, fossil fuels and the consequential generation of greenhouse gas emissions during recent history, coupled with the hostility of the Trump Administration towards many environmental policies, many states and local governments stepped up to act within their own bailiwicks. Moreover, investments in alternative energy facilities have drawn the interest of many businesses and even industrial actors. This trend accelerated when the Trump Administration pulled out of the Paris Climate Change Accord which the Obama Administration had been so effective in advancing. Hence, the growing public recognition of the acceleration of climate change and its consequences has spurred, and has benefited from, trends and innovation in these regards from the proverbial bottom-up rather than the traditional top-down focus of the federal government and EPA.

Solar panels, discussed in § 12.01, increasingly are being installed around the country not only on private residences and businesses, but also in public spaces and along streets and highways. Since solar energy started to emerge as a potential supplemental

---

7. *See* EPA, *Smart Growth: Greening America's Communities*, at https://www.epa.gov/smartgrowth/greening-americas-communities.

8. *See* EPA, *Science in Action: Innovative Research for a Sustainable Future: EPA's Community Public Health Project*, at https://epa/gov/sites/default/files/2013-12/documents/community-public-health-project.pdf.

energy source for residences and many commercial structures, as well as some state and local government buildings, the developing technology has greatly improved in efficiency and reduced the costs of solar panels. Meanwhile, investments are being made by utilities in solar farms located in sun-drenched and underpopulated regions of the country, particularly in the southwest. Wind turbines, also noted in § 12.01, are becoming more common for local businesses and communities. However, likely of greater consequence will be the giant turbines being installed along coastlines where they can perpetually capture ocean winds, and even on hilltops in many locations. Given the growing interest in this market, technology has been consistently improving to provide stronger, larger and more efficient turbines, although better engineering and siting decisions must be developed to reduce avian mortality, a regular consequence of wind turbines everywhere. The energy generated by the maritime turbines can be transmitted to shore facilities up and down coasts by a network of seabed cables.

The beneficial "brownfields" redevelopment of contaminated properties remediated up to an extent required by EPA or state or local agencies was discussed in § 7.07. However, other uses for contaminated properties and landfills are also being explored. These include the use of those properties, including mining sites, as locations to generate renewable energy. Solar panels can be roofed over acres of landfills as well as installed in abandoned industrial sites with no adverse environmental consequences but, to the contrary, the environmentally beneficial use of an otherwise useless airspace or industrial footprint. As an environmental benefit, the energy needs of local communities or businesses that otherwise would be generated by the combustion of fossil fuels can be offset to an extent, which helps to justify the investments. Funding and professional resources can be provided not only by EPA but also by the Economic Development Administration, Department of Agriculture, and Small Business Administration, as well as many state and local programs. Federal tax incentives are also available.[9]

Many municipal airports are also spread out over significant, often grass-covered, acreage. Proposals have been advanced to install solar and/or wind power facilities in carefully selected locations that will not interfere with flights and might minimize avian mortality, an outcome unfortunately associated with airports in many areas which might be complicated by wind turbines. By the strategic use of such underutilized space that would not otherwise be economically useful, airports have started to offset their own energy needs that otherwise would depend on fossil fuels.[10]

---

9. *See* Re-Powering America's Land Initiative: Financing Renewable Energy Projects on Contaminated Lands (May 2013), at https://epa.gov/sites/default/files/2015-06/documents/re-powering_financing_fact_sheet.pdf.

10. Travis L. DeVault, et al., *Airports Offer Unrealized Potential for Alternative Energy Production*, ENVIRONMENTAL MANAGEMENT (2012), at https://www.cavs.msstate.edu/publications/docs/2012/01/12576Devalut_et_al_2012_Airports_offer_unrealized_opportunity.pdf.

§ 14.05 Environmental Management Principles for Federal Agencies

[A] Code of Environmental Management Principles

Pursuant to a 1990s-era Executive Order, EPA developed a Code of Environmental Management Principles[11] to foster federal compliance with Right-To-Know Laws (see § 7.08) and pollution prevention requirements.[12] The Code underscores the view that federal agencies should assert leadership in environmental law and policy, but also reflects the public's demand that the federal government commit to a common environmental ethic, applicable to all of its many branches and agencies. Although EPA's focus has varied over time, especially under the direction of various presidential administrations, the Code provided a template for federal agencies which were expected to do the following:[13]

- Agree to a code of principles emphasizing pollution prevention, sustainable development, and state-of-the-art environmental management programs;

- Have EPA recognize qualifying federal facilities as "model installations"; and

- Encourage federal employees to demonstrate outstanding leadership in environmental practices, with special recognition accorded deserving individuals, departments and installations.

[B] Core Principles

Five broad principles are expected to be incorporated into management programs and objectives. Although implementation will vary with the functions of differing agencies, nevertheless all these goals, which incorporate performance objectives originally set forth in the Code, should be broadly incorporated into management policies. The goal is to make pollution reduction a key management objective, and to make all federal agencies act "cleaner." The principles require agencies to commit to the following:

- Developing and employing pollution prevention policies by the agency's top management;

- Implementing proactive programs that aggressively identify compliance problem areas and undertake pollution prevention measures;

- Enabling employees to perform their jobs in a manner consistent with environmental policies;

- Evaluating employees' environmental performance and requiring that employees be accountable for discharging environmental obligations; and

---

11. *See* 61 Fed. Reg. 54,062 (Oct. 1996).
12. *See* Exec. Order No. 12,856 (Aug. 3, 1993).
13. *Id.* at § 4-405.

- Regularly assessing their progress toward environmental goals and using the results to improve environmental performance. This involves "bench marking," by which agencies consistently evaluate themselves in comparison with other agencies.

One can track how diligently, or not, federal agencies achieved these goals over time and under top-down direction during some Administrations, yet these remain helpful principles going forward for achieving cohesive environmental policies among numerous federal agencies.

Since the promulgation of the Code, Environmental Management principles have been internationalized. EPA recognizes that the Environmental Management Systems model developed by the International Organization for Standardization for the ISO 14001 that was devised in 1996 has evolved into a successfully utilized template.[14] See the discussion in 14.09.

§ 14.06 Incentives for Self-Policing

EPA enforcement programs discussed elsewhere in this book demonstrate the draconian consequences of violating environmental standards or permits. Fear of enforcement has spawned a new trade in environmental auditing, which most facilities frankly admit reflects their concern that they, rather than EPA or state regulators, discover violations (see § 2.01). However, governmental resources are limited. EPA recognizes the fiscal and administrative limitations that interfere sometimes with its comprehensive compliance and enforcement efforts. The result is that EPA often relies on facilities to police themselves, as mandated by the many monitoring and reporting regulations discussed elsewhere in this book. EPA also promulgated a series of measures to encourage regulated entities to voluntarily discover, disclose, and correct environmental violations (see discussion of environmental audits in § 4.03). Repeated violators, or violations that result in imminent and substantial endangerment, are excluded from the program. EPA established a policy starting in the 1990s whereby it declined to recommend prosecution of a regulated entity that voluntarily disclosed violations discovered in an audit before an investigation was already being conducted.[15]

§ 14.07 Voluntary Partnerships between Businesses and EPA

EPA has created two related programs which are experimenting with a new model for achieving existing environmental goals as well as inducing businesses to exceed their minimal legal requirements at their own volition. These programs are the National Partnership for Environmental Priorities (NPEP) and the National Environ-

---

14. EPA, *Learn About Environmental Management Systems*, at https://www.epa.gov/ems/learn-about-environmental-management-systems.

15. 60 Fed. Reg. 66,706 (Dec. 1995).

mental Performance Track. In slightly different ways, businesses voluntarily participate as partners of EPA with the goal of reducing specified pollutants. The major goal of NPEP is to encourage industry as well as government to reduce the use, generation and release of specified "priority" chemicals. Priority chemicals persist in the environment, bioaccumulate and are toxic if released. EPA estimated that ninety percent of thirty-one priority chemicals are either used or generated when numerous household and industrial products are manufactured. The toxic chemicals end up in the environment by means of various waste streams and present health risks to humans and the environment. EPA's goal is to reduce these wastes by recycling, substituting other chemicals, or otherwise eliminating the chemicals from the waste stream.[16] The NPEP successfully removed in excess of 800,000 pounds of priority chemicals from the environment between the program's creation in 2002 and a study undertaken in 2007, and it received pledges for the removal of an additional two million pounds. In 2006, to augment NPEP, EPA established the National Challenge Commitment for Priority Chemicals with the goal of reducing by ten percent the use of thirty-one priority chemicals by industrial and governmental facilities within three years.[17] An "environmental priorities partner" can advance to becoming a "Performance Track member" by implementing a "challenge commitment." By 2016, participants had reduced or eliminated 3.6 million pounds of priority chemicals and an additional 6.8 million pounds of other hazardous chemicals.[18]

The Performance Track program, established in 2000, is managed by EPA's National Center for Environmental Innovation. Performance Track is a means to recognize businesses that implement effective environmental management programs, have a sustained record of compliance with environmental laws, demonstrate a commitment to quantifiable environmental goals, and allow for transparency to public review. However, the program is designed not only to recognize environmental compliance, but also to encourage environmental "excellence," by working with businesses that exceed the legal requirements burdening their operations. Performance Track requires as a minimum that environmental requirements be satisfied, but EPA also induces businesses to reduce costs and to invest in technological advances that promise further environmental benefits while at the same time enhancing a partner's competitive position. Members usually commit to four public, measurable, goals that will have beneficial environmental impacts. Hence, members might commit to, and implement, reducing the use of energy, materials and resources, reducing air emissions, and achieving other environmental goals. In addition to public recognition and a benevolent working relationship with EPA, members receive regulatory and administrative benefits from EPA and are assigned low priority for routine inspections.[19]

---

16. Patrick T. Peterson, *The National Partnership for Environmental Priorities Program*, ENVIRONMENTAL CLAIMS JOURNAL Vol. 21, No. 2 (May 13, 2009).

17. *See* www.epa.gov/epaoswer/osw/conserve/priorities.chemical.htm.

18. EPA, *Collaboration and Partnerships*, at https://archive.epa.gov/publicinvolvement/web/html/nationalpartnershipforenvironmentalpriorities.html.

19. *See* www.epa.gov/performancetrack; *see also* www.epa.gov/performancetrack/benefits/index.htm. For implementation, *see* www.epa.gov/performancetrack/implemen/index.htm. *See also* Tom

Members must report annually to EPA their success in implementing the goals to which they committed. EPA, itself, also issues annual progress reports. Between its founding in 2000 and 2007, the program was responsible for an aggregate reduction in water consumption in the amount of 1.9 billion gallons, the conservation of 9,000 acres of land, and the recycling of almost 120,000 tons of materials. As of 2007, there were about 450 members of the program, in 46 states and Puerto Rico, distributed among business and governmental units of all sizes.[20]

§ 14.08 Resource Conservation Challenges

EPA's Resource Conservation Challenge (RCC) was developed as a comprehensive series of inter-related initiatives in 2001. The RCC's goal is to reduce emissions of air pollution and the generation of waste to below legally allowable limits, and thus facilitate the "greening" of business as well as governmental operations. Additionally, the RCC encourages "green" purchases of equipment, supplies and other materials — and hence is an inducement to the manufacturing of "green" products and the installation of environmentally beneficial manufacturing processes.

The RCC focuses on certain areas which form the core of the program, although the list is non-exclusive and may expand in the future.[21] These include the reduction of municipal solid waste,[22] industrial waste,[23] and toxic chemicals,[24] as well as on changing the national focus on how electronic equipment is manufactured, used and discarded.[25] The RCC also incorporates a "Greening the Government" set of initiatives, applicable to federal agencies, that incorporates several of these goals, with respect to governmental procurement and operations.[26] EPA instituted the "WasteWise" program by which organizations help to reduce the aggregate municipal and industrial waste streams by designing their own waste reduction programs.

[A] Solid Waste

EPA has set a national goal of reducing municipal solid waste across the nation by 35 percent. Since the waste streams of our consumer society appear to be increasing, EPA's primary focus will be on tailoring particular strategies to particularly significant waste products. These include conventional recycling activities, such as encouraging

---

Petersen, *Beyond Compliance — EPA Performance Track Program, Environmental and Engineering Solutions, Inc.,* March 1, 2008.

20. *Id.* For information on members, and to review progress reports, *see* www.epa.gov/performance track/pubs.htm.

21. *See* www.epa.gov/epaoswer/osw/conserve/strat-plan.htm.

22. *See* www. epa.gov/epaoswer/osw/conserve/priorities/msw.htm.

23. *See* www.epa.gov/epaoswer/osw/conserve/priorities/bene-use.htm.

24. *See* www.epa.gov/epaoswer/osw/conserve/priorities/chemical.htm.

25. *See* www.epa.gov/epaoswer/osw/conserve/priorities/green.htm.

26. *See* www.epa.gov/epp>Purchasing(EPP); www.epa.gov/cpg>Guidelines(CPG).

the collection of paper for recycling, and cardboard, metal and plastic containers, also for recycling. However, the RCC also anticipates the collection of organic waste, such as food scraps and yard trimmings, which can be composted and beneficially re-used for environmentally friendly landscaping activities. The RCC program also encourages local communities to provide easy means by which people "on the go" can dispose of recyclable materials, such as food and beverage containers and paper waste, in public places.

[B] "Green" Electronics, Recycling and Safe Disposal

Electronic equipment has long been associated with some toxic materials, whether it be PCBs in transformers or various heavy metals, such as lead and mercury, in electronic components. The RCC, as an initial priority, is focused on the electronic equipment in most common use, such as personal computers, televisions and cell phones. The general goal is to reduce the toxicity of the components, by encouraging technological innovation and influencing how the products are designed and operated, but also by encouraging recycling, facilitating the creation of recycling markets for electronic equipment and ensuring eventual safe disposal. The RCC also included an implementation plan for the life cycle management of electronic equipment. Many of these initiatives contemplate that EPA will work with "plug-in partners" who will participate in the collection of used electronic products and devise means by which they can be reused.

Before electronic equipment can be reused, recycled or discarded, it must be purchased. The RCC provides an Electronic Product Environmental Assessment Tool (EPEAT) to help institutional purchasers of electronic equipment, such as computers, calculate the "environmental attributes" of the equipment being purchased. By applying the EPEAT criteria, a purchaser can calculate a score based on how environmentally friendly the product is in terms of its manufacture, operation, recycling potential and the environmental costs of disposal. The total number of points correlates with each product qualifying for a bronze, silver or gold rating. The eventual goal is to encourage the systematic purchase of greener electronic products, reduce environmental impacts during use and to manage in an environmentally beneficial manner the disposal of obsolete electronic products.

Many states and local governments have also initiated their own electronics collection, recycling and disposal programs. New York, for example, has a particularly robust program.[27]

[C] "Green" Buildings

If electronics are major aspects of modern American life, homes and offices understandably are more so. It should come as no surprise that the manner of their

---

27. *See* McKinney's Consolidated Laws of New York, *Environmental Conservation Law*, Title 26.

construction has as many environmental variables as does the location of the construction. Hence, the RCC also focuses on construction methods, with the goal of facilitating healthier and more resource efficient models of construction, renovation, operation, maintenance and demolition. These efforts include an enhanced focus on energy efficiency and the use of renewable energy, water conservation, the use of environmentally preferable building materials and specifications, the reduction of waste during construction and in subsequent operations, a healthier and more environmentally benign indoor environment, and coordinating construction activities with "Smart Growth" and sustainable development initiatives.[28] This trend, once viewed as marginally relevant to architecture and construction, by the 21st century was becoming very much mainstream, and the innovations are regularly supporting greener public policies and development.

EPA's Smart Growth policy overlaps considerably with the RCC green buildings initiative[29] and with green infrastructure discussed in 14.03, above. Generally, Smart Growth contemplates that construction patterns will accommodate the need to protect sensitive watersheds, reduce water use and minimize water pollution, incorporate cleaner transportation alternatives into planning, thereby also minimizing air pollution, and encourage the redevelopment of brownfields. Smart Growth is characterized by a common set of planning and construction principles. These include mixed land uses, compact building designs, a variety of housing types, walkable neighborhoods, and encouraging attractive communities that foster a strong sense of place. Additionally, Smart Growth contemplates the preservation of open space, including farm land and areas having natural beauty or those constituting critical environmental areas. Preferably, development should be directed towards existing communities, and community members should be involved in development planning and decision making.

§ 14.09 ISO 14001 and Environmental Management Systems

[A] International Organization for Standardization ("ISO")

[1] Background and Environmental Goals

The International Organization for Standardization ("ISO") is an international federation of some 130 member states that includes numerous bodies that have developed international standards. Since 1947, the ISO has established standards in manufacturing, trade, and the communications industries. In 1991, the ISO established

---

28. *See* www.epa.gov/opptintr.greenbuildings. For application of WasteWise principles to construction and design, see the EPA's newsletter, Update: Building for the Future (PDF), *available at* www.epa.gov/epaoswer/non-hw/reduce/wstewise/pubs/wwupda16.pdf.

29. *See* www.epa.gov/smartgrowth.

the Strategic Advisory Group on the Environment ("SAGE") to evaluate the need for uniform international environmental standards. SAGE established the ISO Technical Committee 207 in 1993 that devised the ISO 14000 series standards.[30]

The ISO 14000 series standards address environmental management systems, environmental auditing, labeling, and environmental performance evaluation. The most prominent aspects of the series to date are ISO 14001 and 14004, voluntary environmental management standards published in 1996. The goal is to have companies incorporate these principles into their operations. Environmental management, in particular, is offered as an alternative to traditional command-and-control regulatory enforcement, thus representing something of a philosophical approach, increasingly apparent in the EPA programs discussed elsewhere in this chapter. The ISO 14000 standards were revised in 2004 and again in 2015.[31] The ISO standards are voluntary.

[2] International Trade Aspects of ISO 14001

The ISO 14000 series has major international trade aspects, especially if the General Agreement on Tariffs and Trade (GATT) member states condition trade decisions on acceptance of the ISO 14000 standards.

[3] Industry Response to ISO Standards

The ISO standards, which ideally would result in regular disclosure to regulatory bodies — including the Securities and Exchange Commission — have been met with some caution by industry. There is concern that the comprehensive self-auditing system envisaged may trigger liability or adverse publicity at inopportune moments, and achievement of ambitious goals may only result in stricter permit conditions upon renewal. The concern also has been expressed that the widespread use of ISO 14001 as an industry standard might unduly escalate the common law duty of care for environmental injuries. Moreover, although the goal of many EPA-approved innovations has been to meet environmental goals while reducing compliance costs, integrating environmental management — and potentially increased auditing responsibilities — into everyday operations may herald novel and unanticipated costs.

[4] No Performance Standards for ISO 14001

ISO 14001 does not contain performance standards; it envisages a comprehensive framework for business operations and decision making that is intended to be integrated with national and local laws. International expertise has been tapped to devise how an environmental management system should look and operate. ISO 14001

---

30. For discussion of the early ISO 14000 standards, see generally Robert Clifford, *ISO 14000: The Work I Progress*, 3 ALBANY ENVTL. L. OUTLOOK 5 (1997), and Christopher Bell & Evan van Hook, *Practical Considerations in Implementing ISO 14001*, 3 ALBANY ENVTL. L. OUTLOOK 11 (1997).

31. *See What Is ISO 14001:2015 — Environmental Management Systems*, at https://asq.org/quality-resources/iso-14001.

likely will be the standard against which such systems will be evaluated as environmental management as a business philosophy takes hold.

[5] Features of ISO 14001

ISO 14001 has certain key ingredients. These include requiring all of the following:

- Adoption by the company or organization of policies specifically committed to pollution prevention and continual improvement in that regard;

- Implementation of procedures to identify significant "environmental aspects" of the operation or products (e.g., emissions, discharges, use of raw materials, energy, and water use);

- Identification of legal obligations;

- Setting objectively measurable environmental targets;

- Devising programs for reaching these targets within designated time frames;

- Provision by the company or organizational management of the resources for carrying out the program, identifying key personnel, and assigning them specific duties;

- Specific, documented procedures to control operations and activities associated with environmental aspects of the operation, and operating criteria to address situations not contemplated by these procedures;

- Procedures, revised as necessary, to identify and respond to emergencies;

- Training of employees to conform to the environmental management system in-place; ideally, every employee will be able to identify an environmental aspect of the operation, identify problems, and know how to respond. Given the complexity of many environmental statutes (e.g., hazardous waste), familiarizing employees with a comprehensive yet comprehensible set of rules may prove a significant challenge;

- Communication of environmental aspects of the operation and problems, with adequate feedback, to and from top management;

- Regular monitoring to uncover environmental lapses, but also to measure progress against the management system's standards and goals, as well as regular environmental audits;

- A document control system to protect and make available environmental, training and auditing records;

- Incorporation of corrective measures into operations, with individual employee responsibilities established;

- Top management review and accountability and, if necessary, modification of the system to accommodate deficiencies or changed circumstances; and

- Continual improvement, above and beyond mere legal compliance, as the core of the environmental management system, with all components of the system, noted above, reflecting a commitment to consistent improvement.

[B] Certification of Compliance with ISO Standards

Companies and organizations may not merely claim adherence to ISO 14001 principles; as the standards become part of the legal mainstream, compliance will have to be certified. In the United States, accreditation and certification is the responsibility of the American National Standards Institute.

[C] Environmental Management Systems

[1] Goal of an Environmental Management System

The overall goal of an environmental management system is for a company to commit to reducing or even preventing pollution, in a systematic, regularly accountable manner, resulting in continual improvement in this regard. But environmental management is contemplated as only an auxiliary to regulatory enforcement, rather than as a replacement for it. EPA characterizes an emergency management system as a methodical and cost effective manner of ensuring regulatory compliance while concurrently facilitating public health and the health of an organization's employees. Additionally, devising and implementing an effective environmental management system can also facilitate its goals, such as energy conservation, which may not fall within a regulatory ambit.[32]

[2] Stages of an Environmental Management System under ISO 14001

EPA has identified five main stages for organizations subscribing to ISO 14001:[33]

- *Commitment and policy*, wherein the organization's leadership commits to environmental improvements and establishes the environmental policy as its environmental policy;

- The *planning phase*, wherein the operation's environmental components, such as air pollution and hazardous waste that adversely affect people and the environment, are identified. Different organizations subscribing to the ISO 14001 standards may weigh different environmental factors differently, depending on their circumstances, which could lead to different environmental management planning. EPA illustrates this by noting that some organizations may elevate worker safety, environmental compliance, or costs of compliance over other criteria. Once the organization defines its environmental interests, it will establish its objectives and the relevant targets for achieving those goals. EPA describes objectives in terms of overall environmental goals, and targets as measurable results expected to be achieved by certain dates. Planning then progresses to crafting an action plan for achieving those targets which outlines steps and their scheduling in the progression towards the target and an allocation of responsibility.

---

32. https://www.epa.gov/ems/learn-about-environmental-management-systems.
33. https://www.epa.gov/ems/learn-about-environmental-management-systems.

- The next stage is *implementation* — moving from the drawing board to action. Employee training likely will be necessary, especially if the environmental management planning is unfamiliar. Employees, including outside contractors, should be impressed with the importance of executing the program. The implementation stage should ensure compliance with operating procedures, establishing effective lines of communication, and ensuring and preserving relevant documentation.

- During implementation, effective means of *evaluating* the organization's operations in terms of achieving the stated objectives and targets are established. If deficiencies are discovered, the organization's planning should account for corrective action.

- Finally, there should be a process by which upper management can *review* the evaluation to ascertain whether the environmental policies comport with the organization's values. If necessary, the environmental management system it employs can be revised to better achieve the stated goals. Evaluations and reviews should be an ongoing process to continually advance the organization's success in satisfying, and then elevating, its environmental goals.

§ 14.10 The Equator Principles

Commencing in 2002, the world's lending institutions entered the environmental management arena at the behest of the World Bank with the establishment of the "Equator Principles."[34] The most recent update, EP4 consisting of 10 Principles, was issued July 2020.[35] The Equator Principles, EP for short, is described as "[a] financial industry benchmark for determining, assessing and managing environmental and social risk in projects."[36] The participation of the World Bank, through its International Finance Corporation and private lenders, underscores the extent to which international financing for projects in developing countries, where environmental standards might be expected to be relaxed in favor of development needs, has replaced direct governmental contributions of capital. The Equator Principles provide a framework of environmental goals to guide lenders in making financing decisions. Lending institutions that voluntarily commit to the principles then promulgate policies and procedures to accommodate those goals in a manner best suited for each institution. The Equator Principles Financial Institutions (EPFIs) propose to incorporate into their lending decisions the goals of ensuring that the projects being financed are developed in a socially responsible manner "reflect[ing] sound environmental management practices."[37] Initially, twenty lending institutions adopted the Equator Principles, a group that now includes 127 financial institutions in 38 countries. Generally, participating lenders agree to review borrowers' proposals for project financing

---

34. *See* www.equator-principles.com.
35. https://equator-principles.com/app/uploads/The-Equator-Principles_EP$_July2020.pdf.
36. *Id.*
37. *Id.*, Preamble.

in the amount of $50 million or more to ensure the borrower's compliance with the lender's environmental principles, consonant with the Equator Principles. Lenders further agree not to extend financing for non-compliant projects.[38]

The guidelines that implement that Equator Principles operate by assigning projects for which financing is sought to categories of environmental risk, measured by standardized methodologies.[39] The 2020 update now incorporates climate change into an analysis by factoring in technologically and financially feasible alternatives to reduce greenhouse gas emissions during the design, construction and operation of a project, with further specificity provided in the Principles document.[40]

The most favorable risk score places an applicant in Category C, for which minimal or no environmental impacts are anticipated. Category B includes projects that pose moderate environmental risk. Projects that are likely to have significant environmental impacts "that are diverse, irreversible or unprecedented" are assigned to Category A. The borrower for category A projects must prepare an environmental assessment which targets issues of concern, and for Category A projects and some Category B projects, an environmental management plan that correlates with the environmental assessment. A Climate Change Risk Assessment is required for all Category A and some Category B projects, and for all projects for which emissions are expected to annually exceed 100,000 tons of carbon dioxide or the equivalent.

The environmental assessment must address local environmental and social factors, local or national laws and, if applicable, international agreements and treaties. The environmental assessment must also pay heed to the evolving ethos of sustainable development, and address the use of renewable natural resources. As might be expected, the environmental assessment also must analyze the project's anticipated effects on human health, including a range of environmental and non-environmental hazards, but also the anticipated impacts on cultural resources, and on biodiversity, particularly with regard to endangered species and threatened ecosystems. The impacts on indigenous or other local peoples, including potential resettlement, also must be set forth. The project's cumulative impacts, and means to mitigate the impacts, also must be available for public review. In effect, the Equator Principles graft onto international financing many of the routine disclosures that characterize environmental assessments in the United States (see discussion in Chapter 4).

The borrower must report regularly to the lender on its continuing compliance. If the elimination of a facility is contemplated, the borrower must do so in compliance with the management plan. The lender, for its part, commits, in furtherance of its

---

38. For the Equator Principles, *see* www.equator-principles.com. *See also* Stephen L. Kass & Jean M. McCarroll, *The Equator Principles: Lending with an Environmental Sting*, N.Y.L.J., April 23, 2004, at 3; Stephen L. Kass & Jean M. McCarroll, *The Revised Equator Principles*, N.Y.L.J., Sept. 1, 2006, at 3.

39. *See* www.equator-principles.com. For the guidelines, see exhibit I to the Equator Principles.

40. EP4, Annex A, at https://equator-principles.com/app/uploads/The-Equator-Principles_EP$_July2020.pdf.

own compliance with the Equator Principles, to independent monitoring of, and reporting on, the borrower's compliance with the lender's policies and procedures that implement the Equator Principles. For all Category A and Category B projects, the EPFI will require the client-borrower to develop and maintain an Environmental and Social Management System.

Reflecting modern sensitivities to the need to provide a role for local communities, especially those of indigenous peoples, the Equator Principles also require the borrower for Category A projects and significant Category B projects to consult with "affected groups," including indigenous peoples and NGOs, "in a structured and culturally appropriate way." To do so, the borrower must make available to the public the environmental assessment in the native language, and must incorporate into its planning the results of its consultations with local communities.[41] For all Category A and some Category B projects, the EPFI will require the client to establish effective grievance mechanisms by which affected communities as well as workers can state their concerns, for which resolution must be facilitated. The EP4 also requires an independent review by an Independent Environmental and Social Consultant for all Category A and many Category B projects.

The framework within which lenders and borrowers implement the goals of the Equator Principles suffers from being essentially voluntary on the part of the lenders, and the transparency required of borrowers may vary from place to place. EP4 requires clients to enter covenants to ensure compliance. The basic requirements of what the covenants would include is set forth in the document. If a client is non-compliant, the EPFI is directed to work with that client to remedy any default, but, if that fails, EP4 allows the EPFI to hold the client in default, if that is an appropriate remedy. The framework has proved useful as a starting point for incorporating clear and consistent environmental goals in the previously unbounded realm of international financing of projects in developing countries. Interestingly, lenders have thus stepped in to provide some environmental structure for these projects in many locations where local governmental controls are insufficient, lax or even entirely absent. As such, the Equator Principles may presage a useful paradigm for environmental policies applied internationally, and the related, and still-evolving, principle of sustainable development.

While the Equator Principles make due reference to compliance with all applicable laws, including developing international norms, the salient characteristic of the financing system and its dependent projects encompassed by the Equator Principles is contractual, in which the parties voluntarily enter mutually beneficial agreements. This manifests a carrot-and-stick approach to achieving environmental goals rather than the traditional command-and-control approach which, in any event, might have dubious value in the current international context. Hence, it is interesting that the underlying logic of the existing financing system parallels that which finds expression

---

41. *See* www.equator-principles.com.

in some of the EPA's recent initiatives discussed elsewhere in this Chapter. Environmental protection is kept front and foremost, including the related goal of consultation with local communities, but in a manner in which businesses perceive that they are receiving ascertainable benefits in exchange for incorporating environmentally responsible practices into their operations from the early planning stages of a project and as long as the lending institutions remain involved.

§ 14.11 Emerging Trends in Energy Production and Transmission

[A] Alternative Energy May Be Picking Up Steam, Fueled from Below

When the first three editions of this book were being written, environmental anxieties about climate change and national security anxieties about our national dependence on foreign oil supplies corresponded to the extent that the national discussion became increasingly focused on the benefits of developing and implementing so-called alternative energy technology—the use of solar, wind, geothermal, and other sources of energy and energy transmission that were not fossil fuels. One might observe that such an outcome, a steady shift away from fossil fuels and toward alternative energies as a manifestation of national policy, has been imperfect, often inefficient, only modestly economical, especially if coal remains inexpensive, and has certainly been influenced by political and economic headwinds. There have been some important events involving fuel during the current century. The technology of hydro-fracking, or "fracking" (see § 14.11[C], below) has advanced and has provided a steadier national supply of inexpensive natural gas, increasingly replacing fuel oil as an energy source, and effectively converting the United States from a net fuel importer to a net fuel exporter. International tension, although of a much different kind from that of the OPEC grip on international oil supplies during the last quarter of the 20th century, continues to factor into endeavors to scale down fossil fuel production, especially since European nations may increase their reliance of American gas exports as tensions with Russia, a more geographically convenient but geopolitically troublesome supplier, continue. The coal industry, though, has been in a continual state of decline. In effect, a moderately cleaner fossil fuel, natural gas, has been incrementally replacing dirtier oil and coal fuels, but environmental benefits may be illusory when one accounts for the various environmental detriments arising from natural gas extraction. Moreover, if carelessly released, as happens on a significant scale with leaks and so-called burnoffs at the gas wells, natural gas, being methane, is far more potent as a greenhouse gas than carbon dioxide. The result, thus far, is that the goal of energy independence as an alternative fuel motivator has been partially de-coupled from the evolution of policies to reduce the emissions of greenhouse gases, so that national security has not been markedly enhanced by the development of robust alternative energy industries, and Congress has been notably slow in encouraging domestic alternative energy innovation and development. With the advent of the Biden Administration, climate change policies, including support for alternative fuel innovation, development and even regulation, have been proposed, but, as of this writing, a badly divided Congress seems unable to take the initiative.

However, some interesting minor trends are incrementally gathering force that in different ways are likely to bring about some of the environmental benefits that increasingly are accepted as necessary responses to global warming. Among these is a slowly cohering market for several alternative energy technologies and production that is being supported from below — by private and commercial energy consumers, and local and state governments — in the absence of consistent and reliable national policy. To appreciate why a seemingly beneficial energy source, and with it the economic benefits to the industry that has the patents and the means of production, has not proceeded in anything like a straight line, one must take into account the economics of alternative energy production, where production prices, originally staggeringly high, are dropping, but competition from China, Denmark, Germany, and other countries that have supported technological developments is hurting the development of technological advances within the United States. Meanwhile, conservative political pundits have pilloried federal attempts to support the domestic industry, and Congress seems chronically disinterested in considering and then acting upon a long-range strategy of encouraging the domestic alternative energy industry.

Yet more and more people seem inclined to consider attaching solar panels to their roofs, and commercial properties in towns across the nation are adding solar panels and other forms of green energy self-generation in tandem with constructing new facilities or expanding existing ones. Local zoning ordinances are being amended to allow for solar panels, which even utilities are placing on telephone poles and elsewhere. For utilities in particular, breakdowns in the grid system by which electricity is transmitted have had drastic effects over the past few years, which provides utilities with inducements to diversify the generation and transmission of electricity. Major cities, such as New York City and Philadelphia, are enacting local laws and shaping public policy to encourage the incorporation of green energy devices into new construction and even for existing buildings, in recognition of the economic savings that can be achieved as the heat-island effects are reduced in warm months and sunlight is utilized to warm interior spaces in cold months. The desert southwest is especially well situated for solar panels spread over otherwise underutilized acreage, but, then, so are acres of the flat roofs crowding Manhattan and other densely populated urban areas. New York City, in particular, is modifying its building code, and entering public-private arrangements with developers and property owners, to gradually incorporate green energy into that energy-thirsty commercial behemoth. Even geothermal units are being explored for homes and businesses in areas around the country where the subsurface geology makes it economically feasible.

Wind energy, too, is increasingly moving from an aspirational notion to an economically rational means of energy production. As the technology improves, the costs are reduced, and profits can be reasonably anticipated. Wind turbines are literally popping up around the country. The desert southwest also provides a spacious, and windy, location for "wind farms" where gigantic turbines spin all day, every day, but so are many coastal areas. Substantial installations are either proposed or in development for locations on the continental shelf off of the coasts of Massachusetts, New Jersey, and New York's Long Island, as well as states further south, all potentially linked to each other and the coastal facilities by seabed transmission cables. Among the challenges still to be tackled are efficient means of transmitting the electrical energy over distances, reducing avian mortality and, in populated areas, reducing noise caused by turbines, securing transmission cables, and ensuring a ready market for the electricity being produced that will have to be competitive with electricity produced by conventional fossil fuels, notably coal. Economic uncertainties, initially following the Great Recession that was triggered in 2007–2008, and presently as the country and the world endure a devastating unanticipated pandemic, and the inevitable strains on state and corporate budgets, have slowed the process. However, the continuing interest by state governments as well as industry allows for optimism that wind energy installations will be a realistic and economically justifiable component of the regional and even the national energy mix before too long. In the absence of national leadership, the encouragement for alternative energy development from local governments and private energy consumers seems to be creating its own dynamic.

Alternative energy development ultimately depends on public support. As noted above, the economics of that kind of energy production is critically important for investments by families, businesses, and local governments. The near-term economic benefits, as also noted above, have been sometimes uneven, and longer-term investments have been adversely influenced by the unreliability of the market and reliance on intermittent tax breaks that may not be extended. Public policy should provide a greater impetus for the domestic development of these industries, but the conventional energy production sectors that are heavily invested in fossil fuels have not welcomed the competition, lip service aside, even if alternative energy will likely constitute only a modest portion of the national energy market for the near future. Push-back by the coal, oil, and gas industries has had well-publicized political results. Public perceptions of the need for alternative energy sources have been inconsistent, often swayed by so-called pocketbook considerations — again, the economics of the matter is important — and only intermittently engaged, as when a new outbreak of violence in the Middle East or outsized rhetoric from Venezuela either escalate the costs of gasoline or focus people on national security, itself rarely the subject of intense public focus.

Many companies and even states and municipalities are pledging to go carbon neutral by or before mid-century as the assessments of climate change from credible climate scientists and the United Nations are increasingly dire. The problem, of course, is that the hypothetical tipping point after which global warming and many of its consequences become irreversible has been slipping backwards towards the near future, so that lagging reductions in atmospheric carbon may make the mid-century mark too late.

Thus far, these promising developments lag behind the need for alternative energy sources, and the foreseeable future will not reduce the need for, and use of, fossil fuels. The challenge for environmental law and policy is to devise the means of encouraging innovations in alternative energy technology as well as technology for mitigating greenhouse emissions arising from the combustion of fossil fuels, without inviting a political backlash or seriously disrupting the flow of energy to businesses, consumers, and even government. While the need for a change in the national energy policy, to the extent there is an actual policy rather than a default reliance on fossil fuels, seems obvious, the politics and the economics of the current system have made it resistant to rapid change.

[B] Extreme Changes in Weather May Focus the Public on Climate Change and the Need to Modify Energy Policies

Another erstwhile minor trend that may become a major trend seems to be galvanizing public opinion, with an increasing acknowledgment by many people that global climate change seems real, that greenhouse gas emissions have at least some bearing on the meteorological dynamics, and thus our energy choices ultimately may be forced to fit a new set of problems. Recent history has visited so many extreme weather events, of such a variety, on so many regions of the country, with such severe and very expensive consequences, that the national conversation seems to be increasingly engaged, as of this writing, by the necessary adjustments that are taking place in everyday lives. Biblically scaled floods in the Midwest and in the Mississippi watershed, alternating with droughts in the West, and the seemingly annual violence visited upon coastal populations by hurricanes, have all moved to the center of the national radar screen. Although hurricanes in Florida and the Carolinas may seem historically unexceptional, and the flooding of low-lying New Orleans by Hurricane Katrina was devastating but explainable, New York City's inundation, along with the Jersey shore, coastal Connecticut, and other temperate zone regions by Superstorm Sandy accelerated the public's acknowledgment that the national climate was undergoing exceptional swings. Within the same time frame, tornados were leaping along with changes in the jet stream from the usual "tornado alley" in the lower Midwest to New Jersey, New York City, and the Southeast. Texas, with its historical connection to the oil industry and its conservative politics, traditionally has been holdout on climate mitigation policies. The state tends towards heat and aridity, not the seasonal frigidity of the northern Midwest. Yet, during the winter of 2021, with the increasingly unstable polar vortex that historically has sequestered arctic air in the arctic beginning to fragment, Texas went into a sudden and often deadly deep freeze. Unfortunately, that was coupled with a breakdown in the electric grid which, manifesting ostensible Texan self-reliance, has been unconnected to regional or national grids. Meanwhile, yet another hurricane soon slammed into New England, just edging past metropolitan New York, at summer's end.

The aggregation of these different, yet almost simultaneous, environmental cataclysms has caused an unprecedented scale of personal misery and economic destruction and will likely result in a review of environmental and land use policies around the country. The dramatic increase in extreme weather events is serving to dampen, so to speak, many of the unfounded political attacks on the evolving body of scientific information and the increasingly sophisticated weather modeling that paints a grim picture of how global climate change will increasingly stress individuals and societies.

As of the writing of the fourth edition of this book, national flood insurance policies are being revised, with correlating new requirements in construction methods and building designs, which will dramatically affect many families and businesses in newly enlarged flood zones. The result is that many people in areas seemingly distant from water bodies will find themselves in revised flood zones, and unable to obtain mortgages unless they procure flood insurance underwritten by FEMA. FEMA seems poised to require, for persons acquiring flood insurance, that the elevation of buildings' first floors be raised above a projected future flood level, and will likely not allow construction in particularly vulnerable areas to be insured under its program, which, in effect, eliminates many sources of financing. Local zoning may track the FEMA regulations; New York City has indicated that its building code will incorporate FEMA's proposed construction requirements, and other municipalities may adopt similar policies.

The coastal communities where such a predominance of the national population is located, where real estate values are generally high, and development has traditionally been particularly aggressive, will be especially affected by these and other new rules and policies. In addition to the proposed FEMA building restrictions, flood insurance premiums are set to increase substantially and thereby reduce the traditional congressionally ensured taxpayer subsidization of flood insurance and with it coastal development. As of this writing, with Superstorm Sandy's 13-foot surge still a recent memory, federal, state, and even municipal policies are still being developed, and thus cannot be described with certainty. The public, increasingly burdened with the historically significant expenses of responding to outsized storms, floods and droughts, incurred not only nationally but also by families and individuals, is beginning to connect extreme weather events and global climate change in a pragmatic way. These events may direct people and governmental actors down paths toward wiser energy choices that promise long-term benefits even if there are near-term investment costs, in the hope of avoiding the increasingly obvious costs of deferred decisions.

[C] Unconventional Means of Reaching Conventional Energy Supplies

During recent decades, many aspects of the extraction of oil and gas in the United States have undergone significant technological and economic changes, with the result that predictions are being made that we may actually experience an oil glut and in the near future will become a net exporter of oil.[42] Some commentary argues, with reference

---

42. See Charles C. Mann, What If We Never Run out of Oil? THE ATLANTIC, May 2013, p. 48; Clifford Krauss, *Expect the Unexpected*, NEW YORK TIMES, F1: April 25, 2013.

to global climate change, that rather than getting distracted into trying to end the use of fossil fuels, public policy should focus on carbon recapture in connection with fossil fuel combustion which, the argument goes, is becoming technologically more feasible and economical, and that the costs of electricity incurred by recapturing processes can be offset by the sale of the carbon products for commercial uses.[43] Investment and development interest has been directed towards carbon recapture and the like, and paper proposals may actually make it off of the drawing board in an economically feasible manner, but economic feasibility, thus far, seems to be elusive. In any event, while one may be circumspect about accepting such assumptions as solace that is dearly bought when the anticipated technological refinements and, just as important, the market remain unpromising, commentary does draw our attention to the significant advances in the energy industry and its market, many of them environmentally beneficial, since only the beginning of the new century.[44]

However, not all recent innovations in fuel extraction are environmentally beneficial, even if they may be an economic boon in some respects. In addition to the more conventional production of energy discussed in Chapter 12, *supra*, new methods of extracting natural gas from formerly inaccessible strata, and extracting oil from deposits that had been considered spent in the context of traditional engineering, have been dramatically reshaping the national energy picture. The technology, especially for "fracking," or fracturing deep geologic strata to release reserves of gas that were previously unreachable by any economically justifiable means, is especially new, while the proposed means of protecting subsurface water quality remains controversial as is noted below. Land use controls over wellhead locations and subsurface operations also raise jurisdictional issues, with some local communities trying to employ traditional land use authority to restrict or otherwise control fracking, while some states have been employing state mining and mineral extraction laws to exercise preemptive permitting authority. These land use battles have not yet been resolved in consistent manners. Moreover, many landowners do not fully realize that under the laws of some states, or perhaps because of real estate transactions by prior owners, they do not have subsurface property rights. When oil and gas companies acquire subsurface rights, and exploit them by drilling, they may be in conflict with the ostensible landowners. All of these issues will have environmental implications that will drive new perspectives and policies in environmental law, requiring new tools and perhaps sharpening some older ones.

Fracking in particular has rapidly become the new technology showing the greatest promise for ostensibly cheap energy. When geologists locate natural gas deposits in shale layers that previously could not be economically reached by conventional drilling, new drilling methods can be employed that reach the deposits by drilling horizontally, rather than only vertically. The mechanics of fracking employs massive quantities of pressurized fluids and chemicals that pulverize the shale — fracturing

---

43. See Daniel Sarewitza and Roger Plieke, Jr., *Learning to Live With Fossil Fuels*, The Atlantic, May 2013, p. 59.

44. Clifford Krauss, *Expect the Unexpected*, New York Times, F1, April 25, 2013.

it, thus "fracking" — and then push the gas deposits to the surface for extraction. The Marcellus shale formations that run through Pennsylvania and New York as well as other areas of the Northeast, seem to be especially promising, as also is the Bakken Shale formation in the Upper Midwest, but geological surveys suggest that shale gas deposits are liberally strewn elsewhere throughout the country.[45] Natural gas is a cleaner fuel than oil, and it certainly is more environmentally benign than coal in terms of combustion and also because of the damage often done to landscapes, streams, and ecosystems by coal mining. However, natural gas still results in the emissions of greenhouse gases. Natural gas is composed of methane, which is exponentially more damaging as a greenhouse gas than is carbon dioxide, although it lacks many of the contaminants found in the less gaseous fossil fuels. Fracking, in particular, has also been causing alarm over what many people fear may be permanent contamination of aquifers and other subsurface water reserves by the injection of chemicals and fluids. However, fracking is turning out to be extraordinarily productive, and gas prices fell dramatically (albeit intermittently), which undergirded the slow but ongoing recovery from the Great Recession. If one, in this moment in time, can overlook another unexpected interruption, the Covid pandemic, fracking seemed to promise an upward trend during which jobs relating to the extraction were plentiful, state tax revenues were boosted as were local taxes generated by increasing commerce where drilling occurs. Nevertheless, a lesson might be learned in that economic dynamics may be variable, but the environmental costs presently seem to be on a consistent upward trajectory.

The United States is still poised to become a major international exporter of natural gas, with correlating economic and political benefits.[46] From the perspective of environmental policy, this presents a conundrum. At a minimum, we will likely require the refinement of environmental regulations to address water quality and greenhouse gas emissions concerns, encourage a continuing shift from coal (which remains important for the generation of electricity in this country and especially in countries such as China and India) and oil towards natural gas without further marginalizing the emergence of alternative energy industries, while deflecting the charge that environmental regulation is puncturing the economic recovery, all the time being sensitive to the local and national political cross-currents. The challenge for environmental law and policy is to require that fracking be conducted in a manner that causes no contamination of subsurface water, because once the damage is done remediation may be unachievable, and that notwithstanding its widely perceived economic and political benefits, that its success does not sideline what seems to be the incrementally growing success in the development and implementation of alternative energy technology and the growth of an alternative energy market.

---

45. Edwin Dobb, *The New Oil Landscape*, NATIONAL GEOGRAPHIC, March 2012, 29.

46. Clifford Krauss, *Expect the Unexpected*, NEW YORK TIMES, F1, and Mark Scott, *Europe Struggles in Shale Gas Race*, NEW YORK TIMES, F7, April 25, 2013; Charles C. Mann, *What If We Never Run out of Oil?* THE ATLANTIC, May 2013, p. 48.

Excerpts from EPA Terms of Environment: Glossary, Abbreviations, and Acronyms

Introduction

"Terms Of Environment" defines in non-technical language the more commonly used environmental terms appearing in EPA publications, news releases, and other Agency documents available to the general public, students, the media, and Agency employees. The definitions do not constitute the Agency's official use of terms and phrases for regulatory purposes, and nothing in this document should be construed to alter or supplant any other federal document. Official terminology may be found in the laws and related regulations as published in such sources as the congressional Record, Federal Register, and elsewhere.

The terms selected for inclusion are derived from previously published lists, internal glossaries produced by various programs and specific suggestions made by personnel in many Agency offices. The chemicals and pesticides selected for inclusion ared-2 limited to those most frequently referred to in Agency publications or that are the subject of major regulatory or program activities.

Definitions or information about substances or program activities not included herein may be found in EPA libraries or scientific/technical reference documents, or may be obtained from various program offices. Those with suggestions for future editions should write to the Editorial Services Division, Office of Communications, Education, and Public Affairs, 1704, USEPA, Washington D.C. 20460.*

---

* *Authors' Note:* This file is identified as an EPA Record. To access the data associated with this Glossary follow this link http://www.epa.gov/OCEPATERMS.

EPA Terms

A

Abatement: Reducing the degree or intensity of, or eliminating, pollution.

Acid Deposition: A complex chemical and atmospheric phenomenon that occurs when emissions of sulfur and nitrogen compounds and other substances are transformed by chemical processes in the atmosphere, often far from the original sources, and then deposited on earth in either wet or dry form. The wet form, popularly called "acid rain," can fall as rain, snow, or fog. The dry forms are acidic gases or particulates.

Acid Rain: *See* acid deposition.

Aeration: A process which promotes biological degradation of organic matter in water. The process may be passive (as when waste is exposed to air), or active (as when a mixing or bubbling device introduces the air).

Aerobic Treatment: Process by which microbes decompose complex organic compounds in the presence of oxygen and use the liberated energy for reproduction and growth. (Such processes include extended aeration, trickling filtration, and rotating biological contractors.)

Agent Orange: A toxic herbicide and defoliant used in the Vietnam conflict, containing 2,4,5-trichlorophenoxyacetic acid (2,4,5-T) and 2-4 dichlorophenoxyacetic acid (2,4-D) with trace amounts of dioxin.

Air Pollutant: Any substance in air that could, in high enough concentration, harm man, other animals, vegetation, or material. Pollutants may include almost any natural or artificial composition of airborne matter capable of being airborne. They may be in the form of solid particles, liquid droplets, gases, or in combination thereof. Generally, they fall into two main groups: (1) those emitted directly from identifiable sources and (2) those produced in the air by interaction between two or more primary pollutants, or by reaction with normal atmospheric constituents, with or without photoactivation. Exclusive of pollen, fog, and dust, which are of natural origin, about 100 contaminants have been identified and fall into the following categories: solids, sulfur compounds, volatile organic chemicals, nitrogen compounds, oxygen compounds, halogen compounds, radioactive compounds, and odors.

Anaerobic Decomposition: Reduction of the net energy level and change in chemical composition of organic matter caused by microorganisms in an oxygen free environment.

Aquifer: An underground geological formation, or group of formations, containing usable amounts of groundwater that can supply wells and springs.

Attainment Area: An area considered to have air quality as good as or better than the national ambient air quality standards as defined in the Clean Air Act. An area may be an attainment area for one pollutant and a non-attainment area for others.

B

Biodegradable: Capable of decomposing rapidly under natural conditions.

Biodiversity: Refers to the variety and variability among living organisms and the ecological complexes in which they occur. Diversity can be defined as the number of different items and their relative frequencies. For biological diversity, these items are organized at many levels, ranging from complete ecosystems to the biochemical structures that are the molecular basis of heredity. Thus, the term encompasses different ecosystems, species, and genes.

Biological Oxygen Demand (BOD): An indirect measure of the concentration of biologically degradable material present in organic wastes. It usually reflects the amount of oxygen consumed in five days by biological processes breaking down organic waste.

Bubble: A system under which existing emissions sources can propose alternate means to comply with a set of emissions limitations; under the bubble concept, sources can control more than required at one emission point where control costs are relatively low in return for a comparable relaxation at a second emission point where costs are higher.

C

Catalytic Converter: An air pollution abatement device that removes pollutants from motor vehicle exhaust, either by oxidizing them into carbon dioxide and water or reducing them to nitrogen and oxygen.

Chlorofluorocarbons (CFCs): A family of inert, nontoxic, and easily liquefied chemicals used in refrigeration, air conditioning, packaging, insulation, or as solvents and aerosol propellants. Because CFCs are not destroyed in the lower atmosphere they drift into the upper atmosphere where their chlorine components destroy ozone.

Compressed Natural Gas (CNG): An alternative fuel for motor vehicles; considered one of the cleanest because of low hydrocarbon emissions and because its vapors are relatively non-ozone producing. However, it does emit a significant quantity of nitrogen oxides.

Cost/benefit Analysis: A quantitative evaluation of the costs which would be incurred versus the overall benefits to society of a proposed action such as the establishment of an acceptable dose of a toxic chemical.

Criteria Pollutants: The 1970 amendments to the Clean Air Act required EPA to set National Ambient Air Quality Standards for certain pollutants known to be hazardous to human health. EPA has identified and set standards to protect human health and welfare for six pollutants: ozone, carbon monoxide, total suspended particulates, sulfur dioxide, lead, and nitrogen oxide. The term "criteria pollutants" derives from the requirement that EPA must describe the characteristics and potential health and welfare effects of these pollutants. It is on the basis of these criteria that standards are set or revised.

D

DDT: The first chlorinated hydrocarbon insecticide (chemical name: Dichloro-Diphenyl-Trichloroethane). It has a half-life of 15 years and can collect in fatty tissues of certain animals. EPA banned registration and interstate sale of DDT for virtually all but emergency uses in the United States in 1972 because of its persistence in the environment and accumulation in the food chain.

Dioxin: Any of a family of compounds known chemically as dibenzo-p-dioxins. Concern about them arises from their potential toxicity and contaminants in commercial products. Tests on laboratory animals indicate that it is one of the more toxic man-made compounds.

Discharge: Flow of surface water in a stream or canal or the outflow of ground water from a flowing artesian well, ditch, or spring. Can also apply to discharge of liquid effluent from a facility or of chemical emissions into the air through designated venting mechanisms.

Dredging: Removal of mud from the bottom of water bodies. This can disturb the ecosystem and causes silting that kills aquatic life. Dredging of contaminated muds can expose biota to heavy metals and other toxics. Dredging activities may be subject to regulation under Section 404 of the Clean Water Act.

E

Effluent: Wastewater—treated or untreated—that flows out of a treatment plant, sewer, or industrial outfall. Generally refers to wastes discharged into surface waters.

Effluent Limitation: Restrictions established by a state or EPA on quantities, rates, and concentrations in wastewater discharges.

Emissions Trading: The creation of surplus emission reductions at certain stacks, vents, or similar emissions sources and the use of this surplus to meet or redefine pollution requirements applicable to other emission sources. This allows one source to increase emissions when another source reduces them, maintaining an overall constant emission level. Facilities that reduce emissions substantially may "bank" their "credits" or sell them to other industries.

Endangered Species: Animals, birds, fish, plants, or other living organisms threatened with extinction by man-made or natural changes in their environment. Requirements for declaring a species endangered are contained in the Endangered Species Act.

Environmental Assessment: An environmental analysis prepared pursuant to the National Environmental Policy Act to determine whether a federal action would significantly affect the environment and thus require a more detailed environmental impact statement.

Environmental Audit: An independent assessment of the current status of a party's compliance with applicable environmental requirements or of a party's environmental compliance policies, practices, and controls.

Environmental Impact Statement: A document required of federal agencies by the National Environmental Policy Act for major projects or legislative proposals significantly affecting the environment. A tool for decision-making, it describes the positive and negative effects of the undertaking and cites alternative actions.

Environmental Justice: The fair treatment of all races, cultures, incomes, and educational levels with respect to the development, implementation, and enforcement of environmental laws, regulations, and policies. Fair treatment implies that no population of people should be forced to shoulder a disproportionate share of the negative environmental impacts of pollution or environmental hazards due to a lack of political or economic strength levels.

F

Feasibility Study: (1) Analysis of the practicability of a proposal; e.g., a description and analysis of potential cleanup alternatives for a site such as one on the National Priorities List. The feasibility study usually recommends selection of a cost-effective alternative. It usually starts as soon as the remedial investigation is underway; together, they are commonly referred to as "RI/FS." (2) A small-scale investigation of a problem to ascertain whether a proposed research approach is likely to provide useful data.

Finding of No Significant Impact (FNSI): A document prepared by a federal agency showing why a proposed action would not have a significant impact on the environment and thus would not require preparation of an Environmental Impact Statement. An FNSI is based on the results of an environmental assessment.

Food Chain: A sequence of organisms, each of which uses the next, lower member of the sequence as a food source.

Fossil Fuel: Fuel derived from ancient organic remains, e.g., peat, coal, crude oil, and natural gas.

Fungi: (Singular: Fungus) Molds, mildews, yeasts, mushrooms, and puffballs, a group of organisms lacking in chlorophyll (i.e., are not photosynthetic) and which are usually non-mobile, filamentous, and multicellular. Some grow in soil, others attach themselves to decaying trees and other plants whence they obtain nutrients. Some are pathogens, others stabilize sewage and digest composted waste.

Fungicide: Pesticides which are used to control, deter, or destroy fungi.

G

Generator: (1) A facility or mobile source that emits pollutants into the air or releases hazardous waste into water or soil. (2) Any person, by site, whose act or process produces regulated medical waste or whose act first causes such waste to become subject to regulation. In a case where more than one person (e.g., doctors with separate medical practices) is located in the same building, each business entity is a separate generator.

Greenhouse Effect: The warming of the earth's atmosphere attributed to a build-up of carbon dioxide or other gases; some scientists think that this build-up allows the sun's rays to heat the earth, while infra-red radiation makes the atmosphere opaque to a counterbalancing loss of heat.

Ground Water: The supply of fresh water found beneath the earth's surface, usually in aquifers, which supply wells and springs. Because ground water is a major source of drinking water, there is a growing concern over contamination from leaching agricultural or industrial pollutants or leaking underground storage tanks.

H

Hazardous Air Pollutants: Air pollutants which are not covered by ambient air quality standards but which, as defined in the Clean Air Act, may reasonably be expected to cause or contribute to irreversible illness or death. Such pollutants include asbestos, beryllium, mercury, benzene, coke oven emissions, radionuclides, and vinyl chloride.

I

Indirect Source: Any facility or building, property, road or parking facility that attracts motor vehicle traffic and, indirectly, causes pollution.

Injection Well: A well into which fluids are injected for purposes such as waste disposal, improving the recovery of crude oil, or solution mining.

L

Landfills: (1) Sanitary landfills are disposal sites for non-hazardous solid-waste spread in layers, compacted to the smallest practical volume, and covered by material applied at the end of each operating day. (2) Secure chemical landfills are disposal sites for hazardous waste, selected and designed to minimize the chance of release of hazardous substances into the environment.

Leachate: Water that collects contaminants as it trickles through wastes, pesticides or fertilizers. Leaching may occur in farming areas, feedlots, and landfills, and may result in hazardous substances entering surface water, ground water, or soil.

M

Methane: A colorless, nonpoisonous, flammable gas created by anaerobic decomposition of organic compounds.

Mitigation: Measures taken to reduce adverse impacts on the environment.

N

National Pollutant Discharge Elimination System (NPDES): A provision of the Clean Water Act which prohibits discharge of pollutants into waters of the United States unless a special permit is issued by EPA, a state, or, where delegated, a tribal government on an Indian reservation.

National Priorities List (NPL): EPA's list of the most serious uncontrolled or abandoned hazardous waste sites identified for possible long-term remedial action under Superfund. The list is based primarily on the score a site receives from the Hazard Ranking System. EPA is required to update the NPL at least once a year. A site must be on the NPL to receive money from the Trust Fund for remedial action.

Navigable Waters: Traditionally, waters sufficiently deep and wide for navigation by all, or specified vessels; such waters in the United States come under federal jurisdiction and are protected by certain provisions of the Clean Water Act.

Non-Point Source: Diffuse pollution sources (i.e., without a single point of origin or not introduced into a receiving stream from a specific outlet). The pollutants are generally carried off the land by storm waters. Common non-point sources are agriculture, forestry, urban, mining, construction, dams, channels, land disposal, saltwater intrusion, and city streets.

O

Opacity: The amount of light obscured by particulate pollution in the air; clean window glass has zero opacity, a brick wall is 100 percent opaque. Opacity is an indicator of changes in performance of particulate control systems.

Ozone (O3): Found in two layers of the atmosphere, the stratosphere and the troposphere. In the stratosphere (the atmospheric layer 7 to 10 miles or more above the earth's surface), ozone is a natural form of oxygen that provides a protective layer shielding the earth from ultraviolet radiation. In the troposphere (the layer extending up 7 to 10 miles from the earth's surface), ozone is a chemical oxidant and major component of photochemical smog. It can seriously impair the respiratory system and is one of the most widespread of all the criteria pollutants for which the Clean Air Act required EPA to set standards. Ozone in the troposphere is produced through complex chemical reactions of nitrogen oxides, which are among the primary pollutants emitted by combustion sources; hydrocarbons, released into the atmosphere through the combustion, handling and processing of petroleum products; and sunlight.

Ozone Layer: The protective layer in the atmosphere, about 15 miles above the ground, that absorbs some of the sun's ultraviolet rays, thereby reducing the amount of potentially harmful radiation reaching the earth's surface.

P

Pesticide: Substances or mixture thereof intended for preventing, destroying, repelling, or mitigating any pest. Also, any substance or mixture intended for use as a plant regulator, defoliant, or desiccant.

Pesticide Tolerance: The amount of pesticide residue allowed by law to remain in or on a harvested crop. EPA sets these levels well below the point where the compounds might be harmful to consumers.

Photochemical Oxidants: Air pollutants formed by the action of sunlight on oxides of nitrogen and hydrocarbons.

Photochemical Smog: Air pollution caused by chemical reactions of various pollutants emitted from different sources.

Plume: (1) A visible or measurable discharge of a contaminant from a given point of origin. Can be visible or thermal in water as it extends downstream from the pollution sources, or visible in air as, for example, a plume of smoke. (2) The area of radiation leaking from a damaged reactor. (3) Area downwind within which a release could be dangerous for those exposed to leaking fumes.

Point Source: A stationary location or fixed facility from which pollutants are discharged; any single identifiable source of pollution, e.g., a pipe, ditch, ship, ore pit, factory smokestack.

Pollutant: Generally, any substance introduced into the environment that adversely affects the usefulness of a resource.

Potentially Responsible Party (PRP): Any individual or company — including owners, operators, transporters or generators — potentially responsible for, or contributing to a spill or other contamination at a Superfund site. Whenever possible, through administrative and legal actions, EPA requires PRPs to cleanup hazardous sites they have contaminated.

Prevention of Significant Deterioration (PSD): EPA program in which state and/ or federal permits are required in order to restrict emissions from new or modified sources in places where air quality already meets or exceeds primary and secondary ambient air quality standards.

Primary Waste Treatment: First steps in wastewater treatment; screens and sedimentation tanks are used to remove most materials that float or will settle. Primary treatment removes about 30 percent of carbonaceous biochemical oxygen demand from domestic sewage.

Publicly Owned Treatment Works (POTW): A waste-treatment works owned by a state, unit of local government, or Indian tribe, usually designed to treat domestic wastewaters.

R

Radionuclide: Radioactive particle, man-made or natural, with a distinct atomic weight number. Can have a long life as soil or water pollutant.

Remedial Investigation: An in-depth study designed to gather data needed to: determine the nature and extent of contamination at a Superfund site; establish site cleanup criteria; identify preliminary alternatives for remedial action; and support technical and cost analyses of alternatives. The remedial investigation is usually done with the feasibility study. Together they are usually referred to as the "RI/FS."

Remediation: (1) Cleanup or other methods used to remove or contain a toxic spill or hazardous materials from a Superfund site. (2) For the Asbestos Hazard Emergency Response program, abatement methods including evaluation, repair, enclosure, encapsulation, or removal of greater than three linear feet or square feet of asbestos-containing materials from a building.

S

Sanitary Sewers: Underground pipes that carry off only domestic or industrial waste, not stormwater.

Secondary Treatment: The second step in most publicly owned waste treatment systems in which bacteria consume the organic parts of the waste. It is accomplished by bringing together waste, bacteria, and oxygen in trickling filters or in the activated sludge process. This treatment removes floating and settleable solids and about 90 percent of the oxygen-demanding substances and suspended solids. Disinfection is the final state of secondary treatment. *See* primary waste treatment and tertiary treatment.

Smog: Air pollution associated with oxidants. *See* photochemical smog.

Source Reduction: Reducing the amount of materials entering the waste stream by redesigning products or patterns of production or consumption (e.g., using returnable beverage containers). Synonymous with waste reduction.

Source Separation: Segregating various wastes at the point of generation (e.g., separation of paper, metal, and glass from other wastes to make recycling simpler and more efficient).

Spoil: Dirt or rock removed from its original location — destroying the composition of the soil in the process — as in strip mining, dredging, or construction.

Strip-Mining: A process that uses machines to scrape soil or rock away from mineral deposits just under the earth's surface.

T

Tertiary Treatment: Advanced cleaning of wastewater that goes beyond the secondary or biological stage, removing nutrients such as phosphorus, nitrogen, and most BOD and suspended solids.

Tolerances: Permissible residue levels for pesticides in raw agricultural produce and processed foods. Whenever a pesticide is registered for use on a food or a feed crop, a tolerance (or exemption from the tolerance requirement) must be established. EPA establishes the tolerance levels, which are enforced by the Food and Drug Administration and the Department of Agriculture.

W

Wastewater: The spent or used water from a home, community, farm, or industry that contains dissolved or suspended matter.

Table of Cases

Table of Statutes

42 U.S.C. § 8743, 443
42 U.S.C. § 8802, 443
42 U.S.C. § 8812, 443
42 U.S.C. § 8871, 444
42 U.S.C. § 9601–9675, 31
42 U.S.C. § 9601, 190, 294, 296, 297, 299, 302, 300, 305, 306, 319, 320
42 U.S.C. § 9603, 298
42 U.S.C. § 9604, 292, 295, 297
42 U.S.C. § 9605, 295, 298
42 U.S.C. § 9606, 28, 292, 295
42 U.S.C. § 9607, 31, 298, 299, 300, 302, 306, 310, 311, 313, 316, 317, 318, 319, 320
42 U.S.C. § 9613, 315, 317, 320, 321, 322
42 U.S.C. § 9614, 248, 324
42 U.S.C. § 9620, 299, 302
42 U.S.C. § 9621, 249
42 U.S.C. § 9627, 310
42 U.S.C. § 9659, 12, 175
42 U.S.C. § 10134, 436
42 U.S.C. § 10135, 436
42 U.S.C. § 10136, 436
42 U.S.C. § 10161, 437
42 U.S.C. § 11001, 335, 336
42 U.S.C. § 11002, 337
42 U.S.C. § 11003, 336
42 U.S.C. § 11004, 335, 337
42 U.S.C. § 11021, 336, 337
42 U.S.C. § 11022, 337
42 U.S.C. § 11023, 337, 338, 339
42 U.S.C. § 11041, 335, 337
42 U.S.C. § 11042, 338
42 U.S.C. § 11043, 338
42 U.S.C. § 11045, 339
42 U.S.C. § 11046, 339, 340, 341
42 U.S.C. § 13257, 102
43 U.S.C. §§ 1301–1315, 414, 422
43 U.S.C. § 1301, 214, 275
43 U.S.C. § 1302, 214, 276
43 U.S.C. § 1311, 214, 276
43 U.S.C. § 1312, 214, 276
43 U.S.C. § 1313, 214, 276
43 U.S.C. § 1314, 214, 276
43 U.S.C. § 1331, 213, 214, 215, 276

43 U.S.C. § 1332, 213
43 U.S.C. § 1334, 213
43 U.S.C. § 1337, 214, 276
43 U.S.C. § 1340, 214, 276
43 U.S.C. § 1343, 215
43 U.S.C. § 1344, 214, 215, 276
43 U.S.C. § 1346, 215, 216
43 U.S.C. § 1347, 215
43 U.S.C. § 1348, 218
43 U.S.C. § 1349, 217, 218
43 U.S.C. § 1350, 218
43 U.S.C. § 1351, 215, 216, 217
43 U.S.C. § 1352, 217
43 U.S.C. § 1653, 212
43 U.S.C. § 6944, 254
46 U.S.C. § 215, 221
46 U.S.C. § 364, 221
46 U.S.C. § 3703, 219
46 U.S.C. § 3703a, 220
46 U.S.C. § 3714, 220
46 U.S.C. § 3718, 220
46 U.S.C. § 391a, 191
46 U.S.C. §§ 3701–3718, 218, 219, 220
49 U.S.C. § 1801, 280
49 U.S.C. §§ 5101–5128, 437, 446
49 U.S.C. § 32902, 446
49 U.S.C. § 32919, 446
49 U.S.C. § 44715, 395
49 U.S.C. § 47106, 395
49 U.S.C. §§ 47501–47510, 394, 395, 397
49 U.S.C. § 47506, 394
49 U.S.C. § 47506, 46
49 U.S.C. § 47528, 395

Other Federal Statutes

Comprehensive Environmental Response, Compensation, and Liability Act (CERCLA)
§ 101, 190
§ 103, 376
§ 104, 292
§ 106, 245, 292, 295, 298, 313, 314, 315
§ 107, 305, 306, 312, 313, 314, 315, 316, 317, 329

State Materials

Index